An Introduction to Statistics and Research Methods

Becoming a Psychological Detective

Stephen F. Davis
Emporia State University

Randolph A. Smith
Kennesaw State University

PEARSON

Prentice
Hall

Upper Saddle River, New Jersey 07458

To our students, who continue to show us how much fun and enjoyment psychological research and data analysis can provide.

Library of Congress Cataloging-in-Publication Data

Davis, Stephen F.
  An introduction to statistics and research methods : becoming a psychological detective /
Stephen F. Davis, Randolph A. Smith.—1st ed.
    p. cm.
  Includes bibliographical references and index.
  ISBN 0-13-150511-4 (casebound)
  1. Psychology—Research—Methodology—Textbooks. 2. Psychometrics—Textbooks.
I. Smith, Randolph A., 1951– II. Title.

BF76.5.D27 2004
150′.72—dc22   2004053359

Editorial Director: Leah Jewell
Executive Editor: Jessica Mosher
Director of Marketing: Beth Mejia
Managing Editor: Joanne Riker
Assist. Managing Editor (Production):
  Maureen Richardson
Permissions Specialist: Kathleen Karcher
Manufacturing Buyer: Tricia Kenny
Interior Design: GGS Book Services, Atlantic Highlands

Art Director: Jayne Conte
Cover Design: Karen Salzbach
Cover Illustration/Photo: Bob Commander/
  Images.com/CORBIS
Full-Service Project Management:
  GGS Book Services, Atlantic Highlands
Printer/Binder: R. R. Donnelley, Harrisonburg
Cover Printer: Lehigh Press

Credits and acknowledgments borrowed from other sources and reproduced, with permission, in this text-book appear on appropriate page within text.

Pearson Education, Ltd.
Pearson Education Australia PTY, Limited
Pearson Education Singapore, Pte., Ltd.
Pearson Education North Asia Ltd.

Pearson Education, Canada, Ltd.
Pearson Educación de Mexico, S.A. de C.V.
Pearson Education–Japan
Pearson Education Malaysia, Pte., Ltd.

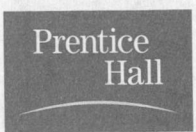

10 9 8 7 6 5

ISBN 0-13-150511-4

Contents

chapter 11

Inferential Tests of Significance I: *t* Tests   237

chapter 12

Designing and Conducting Experiments with More than Two Groups   265

chapter 13

Analyzing and Interpreting Experiments with More than Two Groups   280

chapter 14

Designing and Conducting Experiments with Multiple Independent Variables 311

chapter 15

Analyzing and Interpreting Experiments that Have Multiple Independent Variables 337

chapter 16

Alternative Research Designs 373

chapter 17

External Validity and Critiquing Experimental Research 408

chapter 18

Data Transformations and Nonparametric Tests of Significance 434

chapter 19

Nonexperimental Methods 460

chapter 20

Writing, Assembling, and Publishing an APA-Format Research Report 486

Preface

Note to the Instructor

From our vantage point, research in psychology is like a detective case—a problem presents itself, we discover clues, we evaluate bits of evidence that compete for our attention and accept or discard them, and then we prepare a report or summary of the case (research project) for consideration by our peers. When presented in this light, the research process in psychology will, we believe, be an interesting and stimulating endeavor for students. In short, our goal in this text is to attract students to psychological research and data analysis because of their inherent interest value.

To accomplish this goal, we have incorporated several pedagogical features in this text:

1. **Theme.** To provide a sense of relevance and continuity, the theme of the psychological researcher as detective runs throughout the text.

2. **Interactive Style of Writing.** Because we believe that the statistics–research methods text should be lively and engaging, we employ an interactive, conversational style of writing that we hope will help draw students into the material.

3. **The Psychological Detective Feature.** The questions or situations posed by these sections which appear throughout each chapter will encourage students to engage in critical thinking exercises. These sections also serve as excellent stimulants for productive class discussions.

4. **Marginal Definitions.** Key definitions appear in the margin, close to the introduction of the term in the text.

5. **Review Summaries.** To help students master smaller chunks of material, each chapter contains one or more review summaries.

6. **Check Your Progress.** A *Check Your Progress* feature follows each *Review Summary*. Students can use these sections to test their mastery of the material they have just completed. These sections should be especially helpful to students when preparing for quizzes and examinations.

7. **Statistical Exercises.** We have created fifteen exercises for each of the statistics chapters. These exercises will provide students with ample experience with the statistical formulas and calculations presented in each chapter.

8. **Student Research Examples.** To make the research process as relevant as possible to students, we have carefully selected student research projects to illustrate relevant concepts in each chapter.

We hope that these special features will provide students with a positive experience as they learn the fundamentals of psychological statistics and research methodology.

Note to the Student

Welcome to the world of psychological statistics and research. Throughout this text we have tried to make it clear that statistical analyses and psychological research are endeavors that you can (and should) become involved in. We hope that you will enjoy reading about the student projects that we use as research examples throughout this text. Student research projects are making valuable contributions to our field. We hope to see your name among those making such contributions!

At this point we encourage you to stop and review the list of pedagogical features highlighted in the *Note to the Instructor* section of this Preface.

Did you humor us by actually looking at that list? If not, please do so now. To make full use of this text you need to become actively involved. *These pedagogical features will help you*. Active involvement means that you need to stop and think about the *Psychological Detective* sections immediately when you encounter them, refer to figures and tables when directed to do so in the text, complete the *Check Your Progress* sections when they appear, and complete the *Exercises* which appear at the end of each statistics chapter. Becoming actively involved in this course helps the material come alive; your grade and your future involvement in psychology will thank you.

Acknowledgments

We express our appreciation to the consultants who suggested improvements for this text: David E. Anderson, Allegheny College; Jerome Lee, Albright College; Scott Bailey, Texas Lutheran University; Jason Kring, University of Central Florida; William Kelemen, California State University, Long Beach; Joe Hatcher, Ripon College; Cathy Grover, Emporia State University; Tony Juve, University of Missouri–Columbia; Kirsten Rewey, University of Minnesota (Twin Cities Campus); and Jo A. Meier, University of Houston–Clear Lake.

In many ways the final preparation of a text is only as good as the publisher. We extend our thanks to the hard-working people at Prentice Hall.

We also thank our families (Kathleen, SFD; Corliss and Tyler, RAS) for putting up with us during the preparation of this text. True friends and *real* supporters are few and far between!

Stephen F. Davis

Randolph A. Smith

1

The Science of Psychology

Welcome to the world of psychological research! Because the two of us have taught this course for over 50 years (combined!), we have seen the excitement that research can generate in student after student. Throughout this text we have tried to make it perfectly clear that research and data analysis are activities that you can (and should) become involved in. We hope you will enjoy reading about the student projects that we use as research examples throughout this text. Student research projects are making valuable contributions to our field, and we hope to see your name among those making such contributions!

To make full use of this text, you need to become actively involved. Active involvement means that you need to

1. Stop and think about **The Psychological Detective** sections immediately when you encounter them. Each of these sections asks you to think about a question concerning statistics or psychological research. Take full advantage of these sections; we designed them to help you think critically about statistics and psychological research. Critical thinking is vital to good detectives; we want you to become the best psychological detective possible.
2. Refer to figures and tables when directed to do so.
3. Complete the **Check Your Progress** features when they appear.
4. Complete the **Practice Problems** that appear at the end of each of the statistics chapters.

Becoming actively involved in this course helps the material come alive; your grade and your future involvement in psychology will thank you.

We purposely subtitled our text *Becoming a Psychological Detective* to convey the excitement and thrill that researchers have when they investigate questions that are at the core of what it means to be a psychologist. To make the text as lively as possible, we've included several quotes from the world's most famous detective, Sherlock Holmes. For example, Holmes reflected his passion for his work when he said, "I swear that another day shall not have passed before I have done all that man can do to reach the heart of the mystery" (Doyle, 1927, p. 732). Psychological researchers are just as passionate in their pursuit of the truth as Sherlock Holmes.

The parallels between conducting psychological research and working on a detective case are striking. The detective has to know the boundaries of the case (the experimenter develops a research question). The detective eliminates suspects (the researcher exercises control over unwanted factors), gathers evidence (the researcher conducts the experiment and makes observations), proposes a solution (the researcher uses statistical procedures to analyze research results and develop an interpretation), and offers a solution to the jury (researchers share their results and interpretations with their peers).

A Word About Statistics—we hope the bold-face type caught your attention. Because many students dread courses that have anything to do with mathematics, we want to let you know our views concerning statistics at the beginning of the book. We believe that statistics should be viewed as part of the psychologist's arsenal of research tools. They are not the major tools with which the researcher works, but they are very important ones. We will present our coverage in this context—tools that the psychological researcher uses. If you can appreciate the purpose and reason for using statistics, then you should be able to understand them with no difficulty. In short, statistics are to be used, not feared!

Our examination of psychological research begins by considering a research project that would intrigue even the best psychological detective:

> You have been receiving junk e-mails, inviting you to try out the many online dating services, for several months. Your typical response is to click the "delete" key; however, you finally start to wonder about online dating services. What characteristics do people look for in a potential date? Are there differences in the characteristics that men and women look for?

Such questions prompted Kim Driggers and Tasha Helms, students at Oklahoma State University, to conduct a research project that involved an evaluation of salary as a factor in dating. According to Driggers and Helms (2000), "Male and female college students viewed pictures of the opposite sex and rated the target's attractiveness and their own willingness to date the target" (p. 76). As you can see from Figure 1-1, they found that willingness to date increased as salary increased. Moreover, the female participants seemed to be more influenced than the male participants by the highest salary level.

For the time being we will not concern ourselves with exactly how Driggers and Helms gathered their information concerning willingness to date. Our concern at present is why they gathered this information. The answer really is quite straightforward—they had an interesting question that needed an answer. Asking and then attempting to

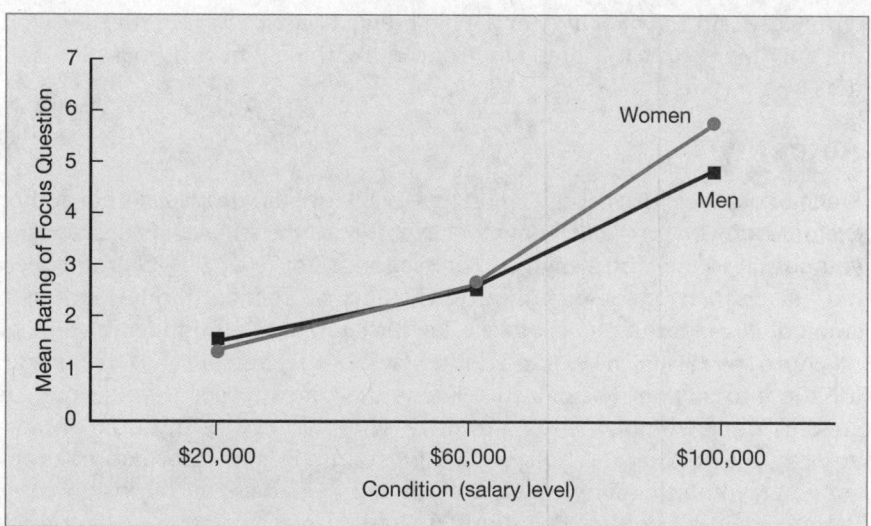

FIGURE 1-1   The mean rating of male and female participants for each condition ($20,000, $60,000, $100,000) on the focus question ("How willing would you be to go on a date with this person?").

Source: Figure 1 from Driggers, K. J., & Helms, T. (2000). The effects of salary on willingness to date. *Psi Chi Journal of Undergraduate Research, 5,* 76–80. Used with permission. Copyright © 2000 by Psi Chi, the National Honor Society in Psychology (www.psichi.org).

answer questions are at the heart of what psychologists do. In short, psychologists are in the business of acquiring new knowledge.

Ways to Acquire Knowledge

Although the task of acquiring new knowledge may sound simple, it is actually more difficult than it appears. The difficulty comes about because there is more than one way to acquire knowledge and because once knowledge is acquired, you need to ensure its *truthfulness*. Let's examine several methods that have been used to increase our store of knowledge. These techniques were suggested by the philosopher-scientist Charles S. Peirce, who helped to establish psychology in the United States in the 1880s. As you will see, the **validity** of the knowledge produced by some of these methods is doubtful.

> **Validity** The degree to which a knowledge claim is accurate.

Tenacity

> **Tenacity** Acceptance of knowledge or information simply because it has been presented repeatedly.

When we hear a statement repeated a sufficient number of times, we have a tendency to accept it as being true. Thus, **tenacity** refers to the continued presentation of a particular bit of information; no matter which way you turn, the same information seems to be present and you begin to believe it. According to the tenacity view of acquiring knowledge, you should begin to accept this repeated message as being true. For example, consider a young child whose older brother has repeatedly said "A witch lives in the old brown house on Maple Street." Because this is the only message that is presented concerning the old brown house on Maple Street, the child accepts it as fact.

Authority

Much of our daily behavior relies on the acceptance of knowledge from authorities. For example, do you *personally* know that exposure to the sun results in skin cancer, or do you put on lotion with a high sun protection factor (e.g., SPF 25) simply because you have taken the word of an authority? How many other authorities, such as ministers, automobile mechanics, stockbrokers, lawyers, and teachers, influence your daily life?

Authority also depends on another factor—the credibility of the person presenting the information. The detective knows that the knowledge you acquire is only as good as the credibility of the authority who presents it. Any time of day or night you can see "authorities" dispensing great amounts of information as they try to convince you to buy any number of different products on television commercials. What credentials do these "authorities" have? How accurate is the information they are providing?

From watching television commercials you should now be aware that tenacity and authority may not be completely independent of each other. Think of how many times (tenacity) you saw one specific commercial where Tiger Woods (authority) is selling a particular brand of automobile. The combination of these two factors may be stronger than either one alone.

Clearly, we are able to acquire new knowledge through tenacity and authority. However, this newly acquired knowledge may not be as valid as we would like. What problems can you identify with acquiring knowledge through tenacity and authority?

Tenacity and authority share two problems. First, you have no way of knowing if the knowledge you have gained is true. Merely because someone repeatedly told you the moon is made of green cheese does not make this statement true. The second problem concerns the inability (or unwillingness) of tenacity and authority to change in the face of contradictory evidence. When they hear conflicting evidence, individuals who have accepted knowledge based on tenacity or authority either ignore the evidence or find some way to discount it. For example, if you really believe the moon is made of green cheese, and an astronaut reports bringing back a rock from the moon, you might decide that the astronaut had never been to the moon and the claim that this rock came from the moon was an elaborate hoax.

Experience

Another way to gain knowledge is through direct experience. Surely if you experience something firsthand, there is no better or more accurate method for acquiring new information. Right? Unfortunately, this assumption is not always true. If you are color-blind or tone-deaf, your perception of the world is altered and your knowledge base may not be accurate. Likewise, a theory developed under the effects of a hallucinogenic drug may not conform to reality very well. Even normal individuals under normal conditions may see the world differently. Ask 10 people to describe a situation and you will likely get 10 different descriptions; we all see the world differently. Our past experiences and culture may make some events and behaviors seem more important than others. For example, a person from an Arab culture would expect interactions with other people, even casual acquaintances, to take place in very close proximity. Americans, on the other hand, are comfortable interacting with casual acquaintances at greater distances (e.g., 4 to 5 feet; Matsumoto, 1997). Hence, Americans would vividly recall close-proximity interactions because they are atypical occurrences.

Reason and Logic

This approach is based on the premise that we can apply reason and logic to a situation in order to gain knowledge and understanding. Typically, we start with an assumption and then logically deduce consequences based upon this assumption. This process is frequently called a **logical syllogism**. For example, we may start with the assumption that "beautiful people are good." Then when we meet Claudia, who is an attractive person, we would think, "Beautiful people are good (major premise). Claudia is a beautiful person (minor premise). Therefore Claudia is a good person (conclusion)." The fallacy of this deduction should be

Logical syllogism A scheme of formal logic or argument consisting of a major premise, a minor premise, and a conclusion.

apparent. We have no proof to support our original assumption that "beautiful people are good." Without such proof, we cannot trust our conclusion about Claudia. Before you say you are sure you would never fall prey to such faulty logic, we would like to point out that the "beautiful is good" stereotype is a thoroughly researched topic of social psychology (Dion, Berscheid, & Walster, 1972); it is a bias that many people fall prey to. For example, attractiveness affects first impressions when viewing photos on résumés (Mack & Rainey, 1990); attractive persons created more favorable first impressions.

Science

Each of the techniques for acquiring knowledge that we have discussed so far has had a major problem or problems associated with it. Hence, although psychologists may use these methods to generate hypotheses and stimulate research ideas, these methods will not likely add to our store of psychological knowledge. What method do psychologists prefer?

The year 1879 marks the beginning of modern psychological study. Although there are numerous other dates that could be used to mark the founding of psychology, most historians select 1879 because it marked the establishment of a research laboratory at the University of Leipzig (Germany) by Wilhelm Wundt. Wundt used the scientific method to gather new information. Over 100 years later psychologists continue to believe the scientific approach is best suited for adding to our knowledge of psychological processes.

The key elements in the scientific approach are

1. objective measurements of the phenomenon under consideration
2. the ability to verify or confirm the measurements made by other individuals
3. self-correction of errors and faulty reasoning
4. exercising control to rule out the influence of unwanted factors.

We will discuss each of these characteristics in the next section. For now, we will simply say the scientific method attempts to provide objective information that anyone who wishes to repeat the observation in question can verify.

 PSYCHOLOGICAL DETECTIVE Review the methods for acquiring knowledge that we presented. How does the scientific method avoid the problems associated with tenacity, authority, experience, and reason and logic?

When scientists use the scientific method they make observations and gather new information. However, we don't have to accept the scientists' knowledge claims on faith (authority) or merely because they are repeatedly discussed and presented (tenacity). The methods and procedures the scientist uses to acquire knowledge are open to public scrutiny, and should individuals decide to question the scientist's information, they are able to test the conclusions themselves. Thus, the possibility of individual experiences also can be ruled out. In short, researchers can verify the knowledge claims made by science; the other methods do not afford us this opportunity.

Components of the Scientific Method

In this section, we describe the features that characterize the scientific method. We will have much more to say about these characteristics in subsequent chapters.

Objectivity

In conducting a research project the psychologist, just as the good detective, strives to be as objective as possible. For example, psychologists select research participants in such a manner as to avoid biasing factors (e.g., age or sex). Researchers frequently make their measurements with instruments in order to be as objective as possible. We describe such measurements as being **empirical** because they are based on objectively quantifiable observations.

> **Empirical** Objectively quantifiable observations.

Confirmation of Findings

Because the procedures and measurements are objective, we should be able to repeat them and *confirm* the original results. Confirmation of findings is important for establishing the validity of research. Psychologists use the term **replication** to refer to a research study that is conducted in exactly the same manner as a previous study. By conducting a replication study, the scientist hopes to confirm previous findings. Other studies may constitute *replication with extension* whenever scientists generate new information at the same time that they confirm previous findings. For example, Matisha Montgomery, a student at the University of Central Oklahoma in Edmond, and her faculty advisor, Kathleen Donovan, replicated and extended the conditions reported to be responsible for the "Mozart effect" (the finding that participants' cognitive and spatial performance was better after listening to music by Mozart). Their results indicated that students actually performed worse on the cognitive and spatial performance tasks after listening to music by Mozart (Montgomery & Donovan, 2002).

> **Replication** An additional scientific study that is conducted in exactly the same manner as the original research project.

Self-Correction

Because scientific findings are open to public scrutiny and replication, errors and faulty reasoning that become apparent should lead to a change in the conclusions we reach. For example, some early American psychologists, such as James McKeen Cattell, once believed that intelligence was directly related to the quality of one's nervous system; the better the nervous system, the higher the intelligence (see Goodwin, 1999). To verify this predicted relation, Cattell attempted to demonstrate that college students who have faster reaction times (therefore, who have better nervous systems) earned higher grades in college (had higher levels of intelligence). However, his observations failed to support the predicted relation, and Cattell changed his view of intelligence and how to measure it.

> **Control** Two meanings: directly manipulating (1) a factor of interest in a research study to determine its effects or (2) other, unwanted variables that could influence the results of a research project.

Control

Probably no single term characterizes science better than **control**. Scientists go to great lengths to make sure their conclusions accurately reflect the way nature operates.

Imagine that an industrial psychologist wants to determine whether providing new, brighter lighting will increase worker productivity. The new lighting is installed and the industrial psychologist arrives at the plant to monitor production and determine if productivity increases.

 PSYCHOLOGICAL DETECTIVE   There is a problem with this research project that needs to be controlled. What is the nature of this problem and how can it be corrected?

The main problem with this research project concerns the presence of the psychologist to check on production after installation of the new lighting. If the researcher was not present to observe production before the lighting changes were made, then he should not be present following the implementation of these changes. If production increases following the lighting changes, is the increase due to the new lighting or to the presence of the researcher who is monitoring production? Unfortunately, there is no way of knowing. The psychologist must exercise control to make sure that the only factor that could influence productivity is the change in lighting; other factors should not be allowed to exert an influence by varying also.

Our example of the research on the effects of lighting on worker productivity (which is an actual research study) also illustrates another use of the term *control*. In addition to accounting for the effects of unwanted factors, *control* can also refer to the direct manipulation of the factor of major interest in the research project. Because the industrial psychologist was interested in the effects of lighting on productivity, a change in lighting was purposely created (control or direct manipulation of factors of major interest), whereas other, potentially influential but undesirable factors, such as the presence of the psychologist, were not allowed to change (control of unwanted factors).

When researchers implement control by directly manipulating the factor that is the central focus of their research, we say that an experiment has been performed. Because most psychologists believe that our most valid knowledge is produced by conducting an experiment, we will give this topic additional coverage in the next section. (Although the psychological experiment may produce the most valid data, there are numerous nonexperimental research methods that also can yield important research data; we will discuss them in Chapter 19.)

The Psychological Experiment

Experiment An attempt to determine the cause-and-effect relations that exist in nature. Involves the manipulation of an independent variable (IV), recording of changes in a dependent variable (DV), and control of extraneous variables.

In many respects you can view an **experiment** as an attempt to determine the cause-and-effect relations that exist in nature. Researchers are interested in determining those factors that result in or cause predictable events. In its most basic form, the psychological experiment consists of three related factors: the independent variable, the dependent variable, and extraneous variables.

Independent Variable

Independent variable (IV) A stimulus or aspect of the environment that the experimenter directly manipulates to determine its influences on behavior.

The factor that is the major focus of the research and that the researcher directly manipulates is known as the **independent variable (IV)**: *independent* because it can be directly manipulated by the investigator and *variable* because it is able to assume two or more values (often called *levels*). The IV is the causal part of the relation we seek to establish. Lighting was the IV in our previous example; it had two values: the original level and the new, brighter level. *Manipulation of the IV corresponds to one use of the term* control.

Dependent Variable

Dependent variable (DV) A response or behavior that the experimenter measures. Changes in the DV should be caused by manipulation of the IV.

The **dependent variable (DV)** consists of the recorded information or results (frequently called *data*; the singular is *datum*) of the experiment. The DV is the effect half of the cause-and-effect relation we are examining. In our example, level of productivity was the DV; the researcher measured it under the two conditions of the IV (original and brighter lighting). The term *dependent* is used because if the experiment is conducted properly, changes in DV scores will result from (depend on) the manipulation of the IV; the level of productivity will depend on the changes in lighting.

Extraneous Variables

Extraneous variable Undesired variables that may operate to influence the DV and, thus, invalidate an experiment.

Extraneous variables are those factors, other than the IV, that can influence the DV and change the results of your experiment. Suppose an experimenter has her participants complete several tasks. At the conclusion of the experiment, she compares performance on the tasks and finds that there is a large performance difference among the groups. Was the difference caused by the different tasks (the IV) or by the sequence of performing the tasks (an extraneous variable)? Unfortunately, when an extraneous variable is present we have no way of knowing whether the extraneous variable or the IV caused the effect we observe. Robyn Scali, a student at Catawba College in Salisbury, North Carolina, and her faculty advisor, Sheila Brownlow, were faced with just this problem; they had their participants complete three tasks. How did they deal with this potential extraneous variable? They indicated that "Because any given task may have influenced performance on subsequent tasks, we presented tasks in one of six different orders, with each task appearing first, second, and third, exactly two times" (Scali & Brownlow, 2001, p. 7). Obviously, *attention to extraneous variables is very important; it represents another use of the term* control.

Establishing Cause-and-Effect Relations

Why do psychologists hold experimental research in such high regard? The answer to this question involves the type of information that we gain. Although we might be very objective in making our observations and even though these observations are repeatable, unless we have directly manipulated an IV, we cannot really learn anything about cause and effect in our research project. Only when we manipulate an IV and control potential extraneous variables are we able to infer a cause-and-effect relation.

What is so important about establishing a cause-and-effect relation? Although objective, repeatable observations can tell you about an interesting phenomenon, these observations cannot tell you why that phenomenon occurred. Only when we can give a cause-and-effect explanation do we begin to answer the *why* question.

For example, Naomi Freeman, a student at Earlham College in Richmond, Indiana, and her faculty advisor, Diana Punzo, wondered if jurors were more persuaded by eyewitness testimony or DNA evidence. To answer this research question, they conducted an experiment (Freeman & Punzo, 2001) in which college students served as mock jurors. The student participants read one of two excerpts from a court transcript of a first-degree murder trial. In one excerpt the prosecution produced evidence from an eyewitness. In a second excerpt the prosecution presented DNA evidence. A practicing attorney assisted in the preparation of the excerpts. After the participants completed reading their particular excerpt they indicated whether they thought the defendant was guilty.

The IV (or *cause* in the cause-and-effect relation that they were examining) was the type of evidence the prosecution presented in the transcript: eyewitness testimony or DNA evidence. At the outset of the experiment, Freeman and Punzo (2001) hypothesized that the eyewitness testimony condition would result in more guilty verdicts than the DNA condition. Why? Based on previous research, they believed that "Although DNA evidence is extremely reliable, it is often ignored by jurors" (p. 110).

 PSYCHOLOGICAL DETECTIVE   Review the experiment we have just described. What extraneous variables did the researchers control? Should they have controlled any other extraneous variables? What was their DV?

Freeman and Punzo used several controls when they conducted this research. First, they randomly determined which transcript a participant read. Second, in order to create an equivalent sense of reality for the court transcript excerpts, an attorney assisted in their preparation. The type of evidence should be the only difference between the excerpts.

What other controls have you thought of? How about what happens to the excerpt when a participant finishes reading it? Should the participant be allowed to keep it? Unlike a real courtroom, if the excerpt is retained, then it could be referred to when the participant makes a decision of guilty or not guilty. In order to control for this potential problem, all participants returned their excerpts before answering any questions. Even though they tested the participants in small groups as they completed the experiment, the experimenters made sure that each participant answered all questions independently; collaboration with other participants would nullify our confidence in the cause-and-effect relation the researchers were trying to establish.

The participants' guilty or not guilty verdict was the DV. By comparing the number of guilty verdicts between the groups, Freeman and Punzo (2001) hoped to show that the type of evidence (cause) resulted in differences in guilty verdicts (effect); recall that they believed there would be more guilty verdicts from the participants who read the eyewitness excerpt.

Just like concluding a detective case, you now want to know what happened. Contrary to the initial predictions, the results showed that participants who read the DNA transcript produced significantly more guilty verdicts than did the participants who read the eyewitness transcript. By controlling extraneous variables, Freeman and Punzo (2001) established a cause-and-effect relation between type of evidence presented to mock jurors (IV) and number of guilty verdicts (DV). The greater our control of extraneous variables, the clearer our view of the cause-and-effect relation between the IV and the DV becomes. This arrangement of IV, DV, and extraneous variable control in Freeman and Punzo's experiment is diagrammed in Figure 1-2.

FIGURE 1-2   Diagram of the relation of the IV, DV, and extraneous variable controls in an experiment on the effect of DNA evidence and eyewitness testimony on jurors' verdicts.

REVIEW SUMMARY

1. Psychologists engage in the process of acquiring new knowledge. Although knowledge can be gained through **tenacity** (repetition) from an authority, from experience, or by reason and logic, science is the preferred method.

2. Three characteristics of the scientific method are that the use of (a) objective (**empirical**) findings that can be (b) confirmed by others and (c) corrected, if necessary, by subsequent research.

3. **Control** also is a distinguishing characteristic of science. Control can refer to (a) procedures for dealing with undesired factors in an experiment, and/or (b) manipulation of the factor of main interest in an experiment.

4. Experimenters seek to establish cause-and-effect relations between variables they manipulate (**independent variables** or **IVs**) and behavioral changes (**dependent variables** or **DVs**) that result from those manipulations. Control also is exercised over **extraneous variables** (unwanted factors) that can influence the DV.

CHECK YOUR PROGRESS

1. Radio announcers who repeat their messages over and over rely on the method of _____ to impart new knowledge to their listeners.

2. Because her astronomy teacher tells her Sirius is the brightest star in the sky, Eleanor believes that Sirius is brighter than other stars. Eleanor has acquired knowledge through

   a. authority   b. tenacity   c. experience   d. reason and logic

3. Why is personal experience not always a valid source of new knowledge?

4. Matching

   1. logical syllogism   A. conducting a research project over again

   2. empiricism   B. factor of central interest in an experiment

   3. replication   C. can contain a faulty assumption

   4. independent variable   D. objective measurements

   5. dependent variable   E. results of an experiment

5. Explain what is meant by the "self-correcting nature of science."

6. A researcher conducts a study to confirm the effects of a previously tested drug. This is an example of:

   a. objectivity   b. replication   c. control   d. repeated measures

7. Explain the nature of the cause-and-effect relations that psychological research attempts to establish.

8. Leo conducts a study that examines the effects of extracurricular involvement on levels of self-esteem. In this study, extracurricular involvement serves as the

   a. dependent variable   b. independent variable
   c. extraneous variable   d. intrinsic variable

The Research Process

Although conducting experiments is a crucial aspect of research, it is not the only activity that is involved. There are a number of interrelated activities that make up the research process. These activities appear in Table 1-1. As you can see, one activity leads to the next one until we share our research information with others and the process starts all over again. We will briefly describe each of these steps, but will cover them in greater detail in the following chapters.

Finding a Problem

Each research project begins as a problem or a question for which we are seeking an answer. Driggers and Helms (2000) wanted to know whether a person's salary affected the willingness of others to date that person; Freeman and Punzo (2001) wanted to know if the type of evidence presented in a trial affected the number of guilty verdicts.

TABLE 1-1   COMPONENTS OF THE RESEARCH PROCESS

Each component builds on the previous components until a new problem is developed and the process starts over again.

Problem	You detect a gap in the knowledge base or wonder about a relation.
Literature Review	Consulting previous reports determines what has been found in the research area of interest.
Theoretical Considerations	The literature review highlights theories that point to relevant research projects.
Hypothesis	The literature review also highlights hypotheses (statements of the relation between variables in more restricted domains of the research area). Such hypotheses will assist in the development of the experiment hypothesis—the predicted outcome of your research project.
Research Design	You develop the general plan for conducting the research project.
Conducting the Experiment	You conduct the research project according to the research design.
Data Analysis and Statistical Decisions	Based on the statistical analysis, you decide whether the IV exerted a significant effect on the DV.
Decisions in Terms of Past Research and Theory	The statistical results guide decisions concerning the relation of the present research project to past research and theoretical considerations.
Preparation of the Research Report	You write a research report describing the rationale, conduct, and results of the experiment according to accepted American Psychological Association (APA) format.
Sharing Your Results: Presentation and Publication	You share your research report with colleagues at a professional society meeting and/or by publication in a professional journal.
Finding a New Problem	Your research results highlight another gap in our knowledge base, and the research process begins again.

Reviewing the Literature

Once you have chosen the problem you plan to research, you must discover what psychologists already know about the problem. Thus, the next step is to find out what research studies already exist in this area. You may find that the exact experiment you have in mind has been conducted many times before. Hence, a modification of your idea, not a replication, may be more informative.

Theoretical Considerations

In the course of your literature review you will undoubtedly come across theories that researchers have developed in the area you have chosen to research. A **theory** is a formal statement of the relation among the relevant variables in a particular research area. Leon Festinger's (1957) cognitive dissonance theory is a good example of a psychological theory that has generated considerable research. Festinger proposed that tension is aroused when two beliefs, thoughts, or behaviors are psychologically inconsistent (dissonant). In turn, we are motivated to reduce this cognitive dissonance by altering our thoughts or behaviors to make them more compatible. For example, (1) believing that high cholesterol is bad for your health and (2) eating pizza (which raises cholesterol) almost every day are inconsistent. The dissonance created by having this incompatible belief and behavior might be reduced by deciding that the reports on the harmful effects of cholesterol really are not correct or by eating pizza less often. Many researchers have tested predictions from Festinger's theory over the years.

> **Theory** A formal statement of the relations among the IVs and DVs in a given area of research.

All good theories share two common properties. First, they represent an attempt to organize a given body of scientific data. If a theory has not been developed in a particular area of research, we are faced with the task of having to consider the results of many separate experiments and decide how these results are related to each other.

The second property shared by theories is their ability to point the way to new research. By illuminating the relations among relevant variables, a good (i.e., testable) theory also suggests what might logically happen if researchers manipulate these variables in certain ways. You can think of a theory as being like a road map of your home state. The roads organize and show the relations among the towns and cities. By using this map and a bit of logic, you should be able to get from point A to point B. Thus, theories that you encounter while conducting a literature review will help point you to a relevant research project.

Hypothesis

> **Hypothesis** An attempt to organize certain data and specific IV–DV relation within a specific portion of a larger, more comprehensive theory.

If a theory is like a road map of your home state, then you can think of a hypothesis as being like the map of a specific town in your state. The **hypothesis** attempts to state specific IV–DV relations within a selected portion of a larger, more comprehensive research area or theory. Within the general domain of cognitive dissonance theory, a number of studies have been concerned with just the finding that cognitive dissonance results in arousal. The hypothesized arousal occurs through increases in such physiological reactions as perspiration and heart rate (Losch & Cacioppo, 1990). Just as the map of your hometown may show you several ways to arrive at your destination, researchers may find that there is more than one route to their research objective. Hence, researchers may develop several hypotheses to answer the research question. For example, you might predict that a reduction in arousal would result in a decrease in cognitive dissonance. This prediction has been tested; one experiment showed that participants who consumed alcohol (arousal reduction) had reduced levels of cognitive dissonance (Steele, Southwick, & Critchlow, 1981).

As your research project takes shape, you will develop a specific hypothesis. This hypothesis, frequently called the **research** or **experimental hypothesis**, will be the predicted outcome of your research project. In stating this hypothesis you are stating a testable prediction about the relations between the IVs and DVs in your experiment. Based on the scientific literature you have reviewed, your experimental hypothesis will be influenced by other hypotheses and theories that researchers have proposed in your area of interest. For example, your hypothesis might be "If potential customers dress in old, worn-out clothes, then they will not be waited on as quickly as customers dressed in better clothing."

> **Research** or **experimental hypothesis** The experimenter's predicted outcome of a research project.

It is important that you be able to directly test the experimental hypothesis that you propose. This requirement means that you must be able to objectively define all the variables you will manipulate (IVs), record (DVs), and control (extraneous variables).

Research Design

> **Research design** The general plan for selecting participants, assigning participants to experimental conditions, controlling extraneous variables, and gathering data.

Once you have formulated your hypothesis, you need a general plan for conducting your research. This plan is called a **research design**; it specifies how you will select your participants and assign them to groups, the type of extraneous variable control(s) you will use, and how you will gather your data. (As you will see in Chapter 19, excellent research can use nonexperimental designs.)

Conducting the Experiment

The next step is to actually conduct the experiment. It is not a foregone conclusion that you will conduct your research in a laboratory. You may find yourself gathering research data in a shopping mall, an animal observation station, an archive, or hundreds of other possible locations. You will put all your preparations and controls to the test as you gather your research data.

Data Analysis and Statistical Decisions

Our experiment is not complete when we have gathered the data; the next step is to make sense of the data that we gathered. This is where statistics comes into play; statistics is the branch of mathematics that we will use to make sense of and analyze our data. Based on the results of our data analysis, we will decide whether manipulating the IV had an important (psychologists use the term *significant*) effect on the DV. In short, our statistical decisions will tell us whether we have found a cause-and-effect relation. If our statistical test indicates that a significant difference exists between the groups we tested, then we can infer that, if we have conducted a well-designed experiment, our IV manipulation was the cause of the DV effect we recorded. We will have much more to say about statistics and statistical significance later.

Decisions in Terms of Past Research and Theory

Once we make our statistical decisions, then we must interpret our results in light of past research and theory. Was our experimental hypothesis supported? Do our results agree with past research? How do they fit into the current theoretical structure in this research area? If our results do not fit perfectly, what changes need to be made in our interpretation or existing theory to accommodate them? Does lack of support for our hypothesis disconfirm the theory? We will have more to say about hypothesis testing and theories in subsequent chapters.

Experimenters want to be able to extend or generalize their experimental results as widely as they legitimately can. Would Driggers and Helms's (2000) experimental results on the effect of salary level and willingness to date generalize to other types of participants besides college students? Would Freeman and Punzo's (2001) data showing more guilty verdicts when college student mock jurors receive DNA evidence generalize to other types of participants and a real courtroom? These are the types of issues with which generalization deals.

Preparing the Research Report

Before you share the results of our research with the scientific community, you must prepare a written research report. You will prepare this research report according to the format prescribed by the American Psychological Association (APA). This format, often called APA format, is carefully detailed in the *Publication Manual of the American Psychological Association* (2001).

Although many specific details of APA format have evolved over the years, University of Wisconsin psychologist Joseph Jastrow originally proposed the basic structure of a research report in the early part of this century (Blumenthal, 1991). Jastrow's purpose in suggesting a standard format for all psychological papers was to make the communication of research results easier and more consistent. By using a standard form, researchers know exactly what to include in their papers and readers know where to look for specific experimental details, procedures, and results. We will discuss APA format in detail in Chapter 20. We encourage you to look at that chapter now and refer to it throughout the course; the more familiar you are with this format, the easier it will be for you to prepare your own report.

Sharing Your Results: Presentation and Publication

Once you have conducted the experiment, analyzed the data, and prepared the research report, it is time to share your results. The two most popular ways to accomplish this objective are to (1) present an oral paper or a poster at a psychological convention, and/or (2) publish an article in a professional journal.

TABLE **1-2** OPPORTUNITIES FOR UNDERGRADUATES TO PRESENT THEIR RESEARCH

STATE AND REGIONAL CONFERENCES

Southeastern Undergraduate Psychology Research Conference

Arkansas Symposium for Psychology Students

ILLOWA Undergraduate Psychology Conference

Mid-America Undergraduate Psychology Research Conference

Great Plains Students' Psychology Convention

Joint Meeting of the Association for Psychological and Educational Research in Kansas and the Nebraska Psychological Society

Michigan Undergraduate Psychology Paper Reading Conference

Minnesota Undergraduate Psychology Conference

Carolinas Psychology Conference

Delaware Valley Undergraduate Research Conference

Lehigh Valley Undergraduate Psychology Research Conference

University of Winnipeg Undergraduate Psychology Research Conference

The journal *Teaching of Psychology* also carries a listing of undergraduate student conferences. For additional information you also might want to try the Society for the Teaching of Psychology Web page, which features an excellent list (http://teachpsych.lemoyne.edu/teachpsych/div/converences undergraduate.html).

Even though many of you may be shaking your heads and saying, "I could never do that in a million years," we believe (and know, from experience) such accomplishments are within the grasp of most motivated undergraduate psychology students. In fact, such opportunities, especially for presenting papers and posters at psychological conventions, have increased dramatically in recent years. Paramount among these opportunities is a growing number of state and regional student psychology conventions. These events, summarized in Table 1-2, feature student presentations exclusively.

If there is not a student convention in your area, then you can consider presenting a paper in one of the Psi Chi (National Honor Society in Psychology) sessions at a regional convention. One of the six regional association meetings held each year (Eastern, Midwestern, Rocky Mountain, Southeastern, Southwestern, and Western Psychological Associations) should be close enough to offer a potential forum for your research (see Table 1-3). In addition to the sessions at these regional meetings, Psi Chi sponsors student paper sessions at the national meetings of the APA and the American Psychological Society. Finally, if none of these options is a viable opportunity for you to present your research, then you should consider starting a paper-reading or poster-presentation session on your own campus. Very successful annual events of this nature occur at many schools.

TABLE **1-3**   STUDENT SESSIONS SPONSORED BY PSI CHI
(NATIONAL HONOR SOCIETY IN PSYCHOLOGY)

Psi Chi routinely features paper and/or poster sessions at regional and national conferences.

Eastern Psychological Association	Rocky Mountain Psychological Association
Southeastern Psychological Association	Western Psychological Association
Midwestern Psychological Association	American Psychological Association
Southwestern Psychological Association	American Psychological Society

For information on Psi Chi and these sessions contact

Psi Chi National Office
P.O. Box 709
Chattanooga, TN 37043-0709
423-756-2044
psichi@psichi.org

The dates and locations of these conferences are routinely published in the *American Psychologist* (faculty members who belong to the APA receive copies of this journal).

Although the opportunities for students to publish a journal article may be a bit more difficult to find than opportunities to present a paper at a convention, such opportunities do exist. For example, *Modern Psychological Studies*, the *Journal of Psychological Inquiry* and the *Psi Chi Journal of Undergraduate Research* (see Table 1-4) are journals devoted to the publication of research conducted and reported only by undergraduate students. If your faculty advisor has made a significant contribution to the design and conduct of your project, then you can consider including him as a coauthor. The *Journal of Psychology and the Behavioral Sciences* is an annual journal that solicits manuscripts by students and faculty. Your faculty advisor also will be able to suggest other journals to which you can submit your paper. Although undergraduates typically do not publish by

TABLE **1-4**   PUBLICATION OPPORTUNITIES FOR STUDENTS

Several journals publish papers authored by students. Contact each journal to determine specific submission procedures.

1. *The Journal of Psychology and the Behavioral Sciences*
Professor John Brandi, Faculty Editor
Department of Psychology
Farleigh Dickinson University
Madison, NJ 07904

2. *Modern Psychological Studies*
Department of Psychology
University of Tennessee at Chattanooga
Chattanooga, TN 37043-2598

3. *Journal of Undergraduate Studies*
Department of Psychology
Pace University
861 Bedford Rd.
Pleasantville, NY 10570

4. *Psi Chi Journal of Undergraduate Research*
Psi Chi National Office
P.O. Box 709
Chattanooga, TN 37043-0709
423-756-2044

5. *Journal of Psychological Inquiry*
Dr. Mark E. Ware
Department of Psychology
Creighton University
Omaha, NE 68178
402-280-3193

"Well, you don't look like an experimental psychologist to me."

Attending a psychological convention will convince you that experimental psychologists are a most diverse group. Although you may not feel like an experimental psychologist now, completing a research project or two will change that situation.

themselves in the professional journals, collaborative papers featuring student and faculty authors are not uncommon.

The main point of this discussion is to encourage you to take advantage of the opportunities to share your research results with others. Much of the research you will read about in this book was conducted by students and then presented at conventions or published in journals such as the *Psi Chi Journal of Undergraduate Research* and *Journal of Psychological Inquiry*. If they can do it, so can you! Once you are involved in the research process, you will quickly find that it is a highly stimulating endeavor that never seems to end. There are always new problems to investigate.

Finding a New Problem

As you consider the relation of your experimental results to past research and theory and share your results with others who give you feedback, new research ideas will present themselves (see Horvat & Davis, 1998). Why didn't the results turn out exactly as predicted? Did you leave some extraneous variable uncontrolled? What would happen if you manipulated this or that variable in a different manner? The more deeply you immerse yourself in a research area, the more questions and problems you will find to research. As you can see from Table 1-1, we have now come full circle to the start of a new research project.

Why Is the Statistics-Research Methods Course Important?

When students are asked, "Why are you taking a course in statistics and research methods (or experimental psychology)?" typical response(s) might be these

"It's required for the major."
"I really don't know; I'll never calculate any statistics or conduct any research after this course."

As we go through this text, we hope to convince you that an understanding of statistics, research methods, and data analysis can give you some real advantages in the field of psychology. Here are a few of those advantages:

1. Assisting You in Other Psychology Classes. Because psychology's knowledge base rests on a foundation of research, statistical data, and data analysis, it makes sense that much of what you will cover in your other psychology classes will consist of research examples. The more completely you understand research methodology and the statistical procedures researchers use to arrive at their conclusions, the better you will be able to master the material in your other classes. Although this point might make sense to you for courses such as learning or perception, even courses such as personality and abnormal psychology are based on research, and research results are based on statistics.

2. Conducting an Original Research Project. Frequently, the statistics and research methods course includes or is followed by conducting an original student research project. If you have such an opportunity, take advantage of it and then plan to present and publish your research findings (refer to our earlier discussion of the research process).

3. Conducting a Research Project after Graduation. Your authors learned a long time ago that it is smart to "never say never." This caution also applies to you as students of psychology. Consider the following example: Several years ago, a very bright student took the research methods course with one of your authors. Although this student found the class sessions interesting and intellectually stimulating, she disliked the material and vowed that she would never have to think about research in psychology after the class was over. How wrong she was—her first job following graduation was conducting research for the Medical College of Virginia! If your career plans even remotely relate to the field of psychology, then the chances are quite good that you may have to conduct some type of research project as part of your job. Clearly, a course in research methods will provide a good understanding of what you will need to do in such instances. Even students who go into nonpsychological fields may use their training on the job to conduct research on nonpsychological topics.

4. Getting into Graduate School. There is no getting around the fact that psychology graduate admissions committees view a course in statistics and research methods very positively (Landrum & Davis, 2004; Keith-Spiegel & Wiederman, 2000; Lawson, 1995). Your having completed such a course tells the admissions committee that you have a good grasp of basic research methodology. Graduate programs in psychology value such knowledge. Having presented or published a research report is also rated very highly by graduate school admissions committees (Landrum & Davis 2004; Thomas, Rewey, & Davis, 2002).

5. Becoming a Knowledgeable Consumer of Research. Our society is flooded with knowledge claims. Many of these claims deal with psychological research and phenomena, such as the claims that a particular type of diet will improve your disposition, IQ tests are good (or bad), scientific tests have proven that this brand of cola tastes best of all, or that this toothpaste fights cavities better than the rest. How do you know which of these claims to believe?

If you understand the research on which these claims are based and the "facts" presented as supporting evidence (or that there is no supporting evidence), then you are in a position to make a more educated decision concerning such knowledge claims. The research methods course will give you the basic foundation from which you can make educated decisions concerning knowledge claims you encounter in your everyday life.

REVIEW SUMMARY

1. The research process consists of several interrelated, sequential steps: the problem, literature review, theoretical considerations, hypothesis, research design, conducting the experiment, data analysis and statistical decisions, decisions in terms of past research and theory, preparing the research report, sharing your results, and finding a new problem.

2. A **theory** is a formal statement of relations among variables in a particular research area, whereas a **hypothesis** attempts to state predicted relations among variables in a selected portion of a theory.

3. The **research or experimental hypothesis** is the experimenter's predicted outcome of a to-be-conducted experiment.

4. The **research design** specifies how the experimenter will (a) select participants, (b) form groups, (c) control extraneous variables, and (d) gather data.

5. We encourage students to submit their research reports for presentation at professional society meetings and for publication in journals.

6. The research methods course can (a) assist you in understanding research in other courses, (b) prepare you to conduct your own original research before you graduate, (c) increase your chances of being accepted to graduate school, and (d) make you a knowledgeable consumer of the results of psychological research.

CHECK YOUR PROGRESS

1. Briefly describe the steps involved in the research process.

2. "A formal statement of the relation among relevant variables in a research area" best describes:

   a. acquisition of knowledge by authority   b. a logical syllogism

   c. acquisition of knowledge by experience   d. a theory

3. You believe that giving rats a dose of vitamin C will improve their learning ability. This statement represents your

   a. theory   b. experimental design   c. problem   d. hypothesis

4. Which of the following is a method of sharing your results with the scientific community?

   a. presenting a paper at an undergraduate research conference

   b. presenting a paper or poster at a psychological convention

   c. publishing an article in a professional journal

   d. any of the above

5. Other than fulfilling a requirement, what are the reasons for taking a research methods or experimental psychology course? Describe them.

KEY TERMS

Validity, *4*	Independent variable (IV), *9*
Tenacity, *4*	Dependent variable (DV), *9*
Logical syllogism, *5*	Extraneous variable, *9*
Empirical, *7*	Theory, *14*
Replication, *7*	Hypothesis, *14*
Control, *8*	Research or experimental hypothesis, *15*
Experiment, *9*	Research design, *15*

LOOKING AHEAD

In this chapter we provided you a general introduction to how psychologists gather data. Subsequent chapters will build on and expand this general introduction. In Chapter 2 we will examine how you can find a researchable problem. Once we have identified the sources of research problems, then we will discuss the formulation of a good research hypothesis.

Research Ideas and Hypotheses

The Research Idea

The starting point for your project is a research idea or problem. You find a **research idea** when you identify a gap in the current knowledge base or an unanswered question that interests you. For example, in Chapter 1 we saw that Kim Driggers and Tasha Helms were interested in whether salary level was related to willingness to date. They found this information was not available and conducted research to correct this deficiency. In this section we will examine the characteristics of good research ideas and then explore several sources for research ideas.

> **Research idea**
> Identification of a gap in the knowledge base or an unanswered question in an area of interest.

Characteristics of Good Research Ideas

All possible solutions to a detective case are not equally likely. Likewise, not all research ideas are equally good. Good ideas have certain characteristics that set them apart from less acceptable ideas and problems.

Testable   The most important characteristic of a good research idea is that it is testable. Can you imagine trying to conduct research on a phenomenon or topic that you cannot measure or test? This situation would be like trying to answer the old question "How many angels can dance on the head of a pin?" For many years people have seen this question as unanswerable because we have no way to measure the behavior of an angel. Although you may be chuckling to yourself and saying, "I would never ask that kind of question," remember our caution in Chapter 1 about never saying never.

Suppose, for example, you became interested in cognitive processes in animals. Although humans can describe their thoughts, a research project designed to measure cognitive abilities in animals *directly* is doomed to failure before it starts. At present, the best one can do in this situation is to provide an indirect measure of animal cognition. Consider, for example, the research conducted by Irene Pepperberg on an African gray parrot named Alex. Pepperberg (1994) reported that Alex was able to acquire then concept of "blue key," and when asked "How many blue keys," Alex was able to examine a group of 10 to 14 items and answer how many blue keys were present. Certainly, Alex appears to have excellent cognitive abilities. The point we are making is that although some research problems, such as the number of angels dancing on the head of a pin, may never be testable, others such as animal cognition may lend themselves to evaluation through indirect tests. Moreover, just because a problem is not presently testable does not mean it will always remain in that category. You may have to wait for technology to catch up with your ideas. For example, scientists proposed synapses and neurotransmitters in the nervous system long before they were directly seen and verified.

Likelihood of Success   If you stop to think about it, each research project is a contest to unlock the secrets of nature. (If we already knew all of nature's secrets, there would be no need for research.) Given that our view of nature is not complete, we must try to arrange our research project to be as close to reality as possible (Medewar, 1979). The closer our project comes to approximating reality, the greater the likelihood of successfully unlocking some of the secrets of nature. Sometimes our view of nature is not very clear and our research does not work very well; consider the following example.

In the 1980s researchers claimed that a new chemical compound, denatonium saccharide, was the most bitter substance in existence. Because denatonium saccharide offered intriguing practical applications such as being an additive for plastic telephone and computer cable coverings and garbage bags to discourage destructive animal pests, one of your authors and several of his students began to conduct research on this noxious chemical. Our view of nature was that denatonium saccharide was incredibly bitter and that all creatures great and small would react to this substance in the same manner. To verify this prediction we began testing the aversiveness of denatonium saccharide with a variety of animals ranging from rats, grasshopper mice, and gerbils, to prairie dogs. Test after test yielded the same results: Our test animals did not behave toward denatonium saccharide as especially bitter or aversive (Davis, Grover, Erickson, Miller, & Bowman, 1987; Langley, Theis, Davis, Richard, & Grover, 1987). Following an experiment in which human participants rated denatonium saccharide as significantly more bitter than a comparable solution of quinine (Davis, Grover, & Erickson, 1987), our view changed. Denatonium saccharide is very bitter as far as humans are concerned; when testing animals, however, it does not have the same effect. Had we not changed our view of nature, we might still be conducting experiment after experiment wondering why our test animals were not behaving as they were "supposed" to.

Hence, in addition to testability, a second characteristic of the good research idea is that your chances for success are increased when your view of nature approximates reality as closely as possible.

PSYCHOLOGICAL DETECTIVE   Other than by direct trial-and-error investigation, how can we determine the relevant factors in our chosen research area?

Examining past research is your best bet. Those variables that were effective in previous studies are likely to be the ones that will work in your experiment. We will have more to say about that topic presently.

Sources of Research Ideas

There are two general sources of research ideas: nonsystematic and systematic. We will discuss each source in some detail.

Nonsystematic sources
Sources for research ideas that present themselves in an unpredictable manner; a concerted attempt to locate researchable ideas has not been made.

Nonsystematic Sources   **Nonsystematic sources** include those occurrences that give us the illusion that a research idea has dropped out of the sky. These sources are nonsystematic in that we have not made any concerted effort to locate researchable ideas; they present themselves to us in a somewhat unpredictable manner. Although we refer to these sources as nonsystematic, we are not implying that the researcher is unfamiliar with the research area. Good researchers are familiar with the published literature and previous research findings.

We do not seem to generate meaningful research ideas in areas with which we are not familiar.

Among the major nonsystematic sources of research ideas are inspiration, serendipity, and everyday occurrences.

Inspiration Some research ideas may appear to be the product of a blind flash of genius; in the twinkle of an eye an inspired research idea is born. Perhaps the most famous example of inspiration in science is Albert Einstein (Koestler, 1964). Ideas just seemed to pop into his mind, especially when he was sailing. Although such ideas just seem to appear, it is often the case that the researcher has been thinking about this research area for some time. We see only the end product, the idea, not the thinking that preceded its appearance.

> **Serendipity** Situations in which we look for one phenomenon but find something else.

Serendipity **Serendipity** refers to those situations where we look for one phenomenon but find another. Serendipity often serves as an excellent source for research ideas. According to B. F. Skinner (1961), "When you run onto something interesting, drop everything else and study it" (p. 81).

Consider the following scenario in which B. F. Skinner described his reaction to the malfunctioning of a pellet dispenser in an operant conditioning chamber (commonly called a Skinner box).

As you begin to complicate an apparatus, you necessarily invoke a fourth principle of scientific practice: Apparatuses sometimes break down. I had only to wait for the food magazine to jam to get an extinction curve. At first I treated this as a defect and hastened to remedy the difficulty. But eventually, of course, I deliberately disconnected the magazine. I can easily recall the excitement of that first complete extinction curve. I had made contact with Pavlov at last! . . . I am not saying that I would have not got around to extinction curves without a breakdown in the apparatus. . . . But it is no exaggeration to say that some of the most interesting and surprising results have turned up first because of similar accidents.

(Skinner, 1961, p. 86)

His initial reaction was predictable; he saw the malfunction as a nuisance and wanted to eliminate it. However, with the eyes of an insightful researcher, he saw beyond his temporary frustration with the broken equipment to a more important possibility. By disconnecting the pellet dispenser he could study extinction. All of the subsequent research conducted on extinction and the various schedules of reinforcement that were developed indicate that Skinner capitalized on this chance happening. It was truly a serendipitous occurrence.

Everyday Occurrences You do not have to be working in a laboratory to come in contact with good research ideas. Frequently, our daily encounters provide some of the best possibilities for research. Another incident from the life of B. F. Skinner provides an excellent example of this source for a research project.

When we decided to have another child, my wife and I decided that it was time to apply a little labor-saving invention and design to the problems of the nursery. We began by going over the disheartening schedule of the young mother, step by step. We

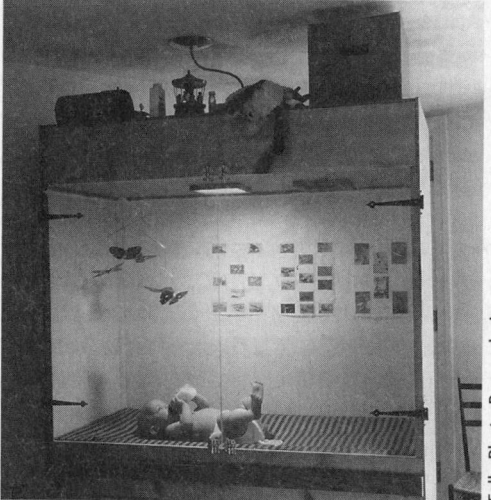

Falk. Photo Research, Inc.

FIGURE 2-1   Skinner's air crib.

asked only one question: Is this practice important for the physical and psychological health of the baby? When it was not, we marked it for elimination. Then the "gadgeteering" began. . . . We tackled first the problem of warmth. The usual solution is to wrap the baby in half-a-dozen layers of cloth—shirt, nightdress, sheet, blankets. This is never completely successful. Why not, we thought, dispense with clothing altogether—except for the diaper, which serves another purpose—and warm the space in which the baby lives? This should be a simple technical problem in the modern home. Our solution is a closed compartment about as spacious as a standard crib [see Figure 2-1]. The walls are insulated, and one side, which can be raised like a window, is a large pane of safety glass. . . . Our baby daughter has now been living [in this apparatus] for eleven months. Her remarkable good health and happiness and my wife's welcome leisure have exceeded our most optimistic predictions.

(Skinner, 1961, p. 420)

This description of the original Air Crib appeared in 1945. Subsequently, the Air Crib was commercially produced and several hundred infants were raised in them. Thus, an everyday problem led to an interesting, if not unusual, research project for B. F. Skinner.

It also is clear that your ability to see a potential research project as you go through your daily activities depends on some knowledge of your field of interest. Because B. F. Skinner was knowledgeable in the techniques of behavior control, he was able to conceptualize and develop the air crib. Because your authors are not well versed in archaeology, we do not see possible sites for excavations and discoveries. Conversely, an archaeologist would find it difficult to propose meaningful research problems in psychology.

Systematic sources
Thoroughly examined, carefully thought-out sources for research topics.

Systematic Sources   Study and knowledge of a specific topic form the foundation for **systematic sources** of research ideas. Research ideas developed from systematic sources tend to be carefully organized and logically thought out. The results of past research, theories, and classroom lectures are the most common examples of systematic sources for research ideas.

Past Research   As you read the results of past research, you gradually form a picture of the knowledge that has accumulated in a research area. Perhaps this picture will highlight our lack of knowledge, such as the influence of clothing on eyewitness credibility. On the other hand, you may find that there are contradictory reports in the literature; one research project supports the occurrence of a particular phenomenon, whereas other reports cast doubt on its validity. Perhaps your research project will be the one that isolates the variable(s) responsible for these discrepant findings! Your consideration of past research may also indicate that a particular experiment has been conducted only once and is in need of replication, or you may find that a particular project has been conducted numerous times and needs not replication but new research. In each of these instances our review of past research prompts a research project.

One specific type of past research that can serve as an excellent source of research ideas deserves special mention. The *failure to replicate* a previous finding creates an intriguing situation for the psychological detective. What features of the initial research resulted in the occurrence of the phenomenon under investigation? What was different about the replication that caused the results to turn out to be different?

THE FAR SIDE®   By GARY LARSON

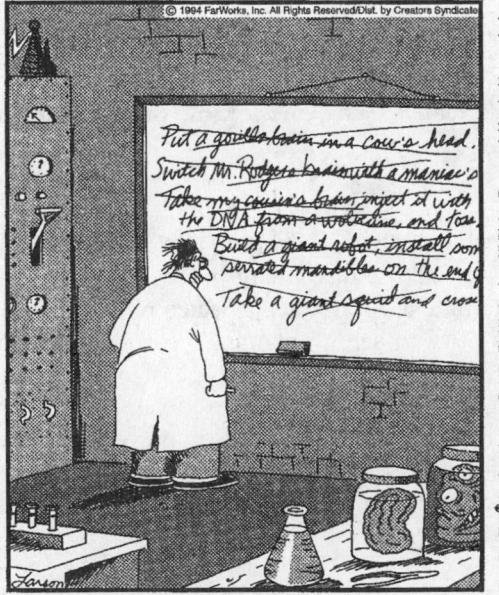

The curse of mad scientist's block

Unlike this poor fellow, psychologists find potential research ideas all around them.

Only continued research will answer these questions. As Sherlock Holmes would say, "Data! Data! Data! I can't make bricks without clay!" (Doyle, 1927, p. 318).

Theory   As we noted in Chapter 1, the two main functions of a theory are to organize data and guide further research. The guidance function of a theory provides an endless panorama of projects for researchers who take the time and trouble to master the theory and understand its implications.

Consider, for example, *social facilitation theory.* According to Robert Zajonc (1965), the presence of other people serves to arouse a person's performance. In turn, this increased arousal energizes the most dominant response. If you are a skilled pianist, then the presence of others at a recital will likely yield a stellar performance; playing well is the dominant response in this situation. If you are just learning to play the piano, mistakes may be your dominant response and the presence of others may result in an embarrassing performance. Based on this theory, researchers have conducted over 300 social facilitation studies involving thousands of participants (Guerin, 1986). Theory truly does guide research!

Classroom Lectures   Many excellent research projects are the results of classroom lectures. Your instructor describes research in an area that sparks your interest, and ultimately this interest leads you to develop and conduct a research project. Although lectures may not seem to be strictly nonsystematic or strictly systematic sources of research ideas, we chose to include them as systematic sources because they often include an organized review of relevant literature.

For example, after hearing a lecture on conditioned taste aversion, one of our students, Susan Nash, became interested in the topic. Subsequently, she did a term paper and conducted her senior research project in this area. Moreover, several of the research projects she conducted as a graduate student dealt with the process by which animals acquire taste aversions. Yes, one lecture can contain a wealth of potential research ideas; it will pay rich dividends to pay close attention to lectures and keep careful notes when you see potential topics for research.

Developing a Research Question

Regardless of the source of your research idea, your first goal should be to turn your idea into a question. Having a question in mind will guide you during the activities that we summarize in the remainder of the chapter. With little effort, you can probably recall instances in which a question has guided your research efforts in the past. For example, you may have had a chemistry set as a child. Like most children who have chemistry sets, you probably wondered to yourself "I wonder what will happen if I mix this chemical with that chemical?" Again, like most children, you probably proceeded to mix the chemicals and find out! In the examples we cited previously, don't you imagine that B. F. Skinner thought to himself "I wonder why the rat quit pressing the bar when the food magazine jammed?" or "I wonder if I can make taking care of a baby easier?" Those questions guided his research.

Likewise, we hope you remember times in classes when, after a particularly interesting point, you asked the professor "What would happen if they . . . ?" or "Has anyone ever tried to do that experiment this way?" Those are great examples of questions that could guide a research project for you. Once you have a question, all you need to do is find out how much psychologists already know about that question—you need to survey the literature.

Surveying the Psychological Literature

We have already mentioned the importance of being aware of past research several times in this chapter. However, simply telling someone to go look up the past research in an area may seem to be an insurmountable task. Michael Mahoney (1987) summarized the state of affairs as follows:

> The modern scientist sometimes feels overwhelmed by the size and growth rate of the technical literatures relevant to his or her work. It has been estimated, for example, that there are over 40,000 current scientific journals publishing 2 new articles per minute (2,880 per day and over one million per year). . . . These figures—which are, indeed, overwhelming—do not include books, newsletters, or technical monographs.
>
> Given the sizeable and growing number of active journals, one should not be surprised by the emergence and popularity of services that summarize, abstract, scan, and otherwise condense the literature into more feasible dimensions. No one would be able to "keep up" without the aid of such services.
>
> (p. 165)

Mahoney reflected the state of affairs in the later 1980s. There is no doubt that technological advances, such as online journals, have resulted in an even greater increase in the number of psychological publications currently being produced.

Given the vast amount of literature we may be dealing with, we need an organized strategy. Table 2-1 summarizes the procedures you should follow in reviewing the literature in a particular area. The steps are as follows:

1. Selection of Index Terms. The key to conducting a search of the literature is to begin with terms that will help you access the relevant articles in your chosen area. The terms you choose will be your guides. You need to find the psychological terms for the concepts you included in your research question. Psychologists may use different terms than the words you used in your question.

TABLE   2-1   STEPS IN CONDUCTING A SEARCH OF THE LITERATURE

1. **Selection of Index Terms.** Select relevant terms for your area of interest from the *Thesaurus of Psychological Index Terms*.

2. **Computerized Search of the Literature.** Use the selected index terms to access a computerized database, such as PsycINFO or PsycLIT.

3. **Obtaining Relevant Publications.** Use a combination of reading and notetaking, photocopying, interlibrary loan, and writing or e-mailing for reprints to obtain needed materials.

4. **Integrating the Results of the Literature Search.** Develop a plan that will facilitate the integration and usefulness of the results of the literature search.

An excellent starting place for selecting terms is the *Thesaurus of Psychological Index Terms* (APA, 2001). The first edition of the *Thesaurus* was based on the 800 terms used in *Psychological Abstracts* prior to 1973. These terms were expanded to include terms that described interrelationships and related categories, which is how you can find your question's concepts. Each edition of the *Thesaurus* is updated to include new terms.

Let's return to the investigation of salary as a factor in dating, which we introduced via the Driggers and Helms (2000) study in Chapter 1. Our research assistant, Casey Hadsall, a student at Emporia State University in Kansas, conducted the following search of the literature. She began her literature review with the *Thesaurus*. Figure 2-2 shows a page from the *Thesaurus* that contains relevant terms for the general topic of social dating. She selected "social dating" as her key term.

2. Computerized Searches of the Literature. Once she selected her key term, the next step was to use it to access a database. Currently, most colleges and universities turn to the APA's PsycINFO to search the published literature. Because the scope and nature of the database services that APA offers can vary widely, you should familiarize yourself with the services offered at your college or university. (You can learn more about APA's computerized data bases at www.apa.org.) For example, your school may not have online access to abstracts of all articles published from 1887 to the present. If your online database is not complete, you will need to consult *Psychological Abstracts* for abstracts of earlier journal articles. In short, you cannot be sure your search is complete unless you know what your database covers. It is important to make your review of the literature as thorough as possible in order to avoid repeating previous mistakes and needlessly replicating research that has already been conducted time and again. Your computer search provides the author(s), title, journal, volume, page numbers, and an abstract of each article. All you need to do is enter your index term(s) from the *Thesaurus* and let the computer do the rest. (An example of a PsycINFO printout that Casey Hadsall obtained appears in Figure 2-3 on p. 33.)

Once you have determined the number of publications in your chosen area, you can limit or expand your choices as you see fit. Because easy-to-follow instructions are provided, running the PsycINFO computer should pose no problems for you. If you are interested in just the most recent literature, you might also ask your librarian about PsycFIRST. PsycFIRST maintains only the last three years of entries and is handy for a quick scan of the most current literature.

What about the Internet? The amount of information that is available on the Internet staggers the imagination. Can this vast storehouse be tapped for the literature review? The answer is yes, but just as the good detective carefully evaluates the credibility of each witness and each piece of information, you must be very cautious. Let's see what the Internet can contribute on the topic of the effects of salary on dating. First, we selected a search engine, such as *Ask Jeeves* or *Google*, and asked it to search for "dating." This search yielded over 43 million hits! A quick perusal indicates that the vast majority of these entries is not appropriate to our task and can be disregarded. For example, sites such as *Amazing Love, Starmatch, Date-A-Doc,* and *Free Thinkers Match*, deal with dating *services* and are not in line with our goal of gathering information on the effects of salary on dating. Likewise, the three sites that deal with "radioactive dating" are not appropriate to our research topic. The Internet did not assist us in this instance. However, many reputable journals and scientific groups publish quality material on the Internet; it *can* be an excellent tool for the researcher.

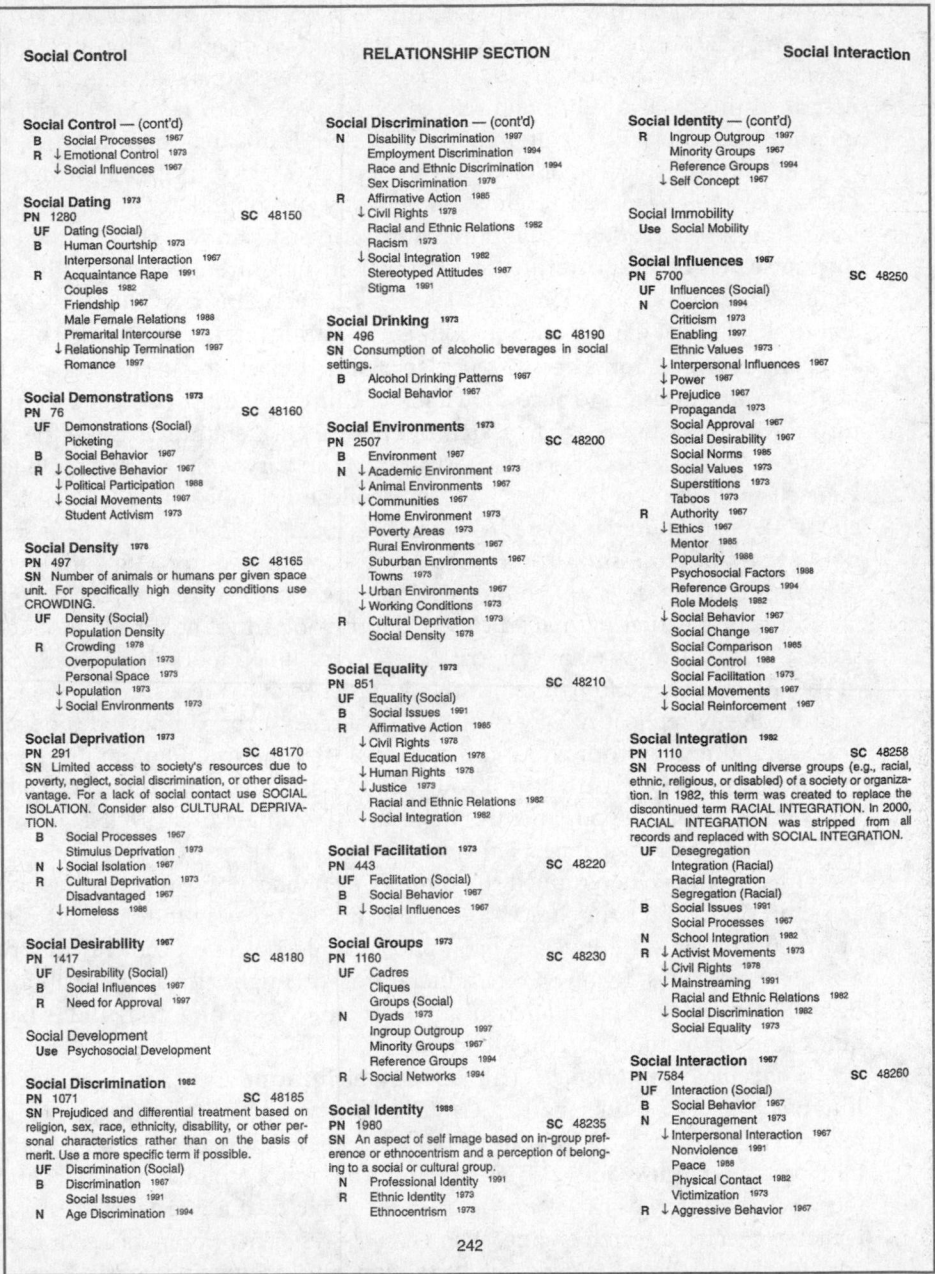

FIGURE 2-2 A Page from the *Thesaurus of Psychological Index Terms*.

However, you must be very careful when selecting information from the Internet to use in your literature review. What criteria should we use to evaluate sites? At present there are no universally accepted guidelines for evaluating Internet sites. However, we have found the following criteria to be useful (see Table 2-2 on p. 34).

PsycINFO

Journal of Youth & Adolescence, 1986 Dec Vol 15(6) 487-496

Characteristics of married and unmarried adolescent mothers and their partners.
Lamb, Michael E.; Elster, Arthur B.; Peters, Laura J.; Kahn, James S.; et al (U Utah, Salt Lake City, USA)

Summary: Studied a middle-class, urban-clinic sample of 275 mostly Caucasian adolescent mothers (aged 12-29 yrs) and their partners (aged 14-36 yrs). Couples married at the time of conception (n = 22) enjoyed more positive responses from prospective grandparents and earned more than couples not married at the time of conception, but they were more likely to be high-school dropouts, suggesting limits in their lifetime earning capacities and less likelihood in identifying one another as sources of emotional support. Couples who married between conception and delivery (n = 110) reported that prospective grandparents responded less favorably to the pregnancy, but while their current salaries were lower, they were more likely to be continuing with their education. Those married after conception had fewer antisocial and conduct disorders than Ss who chose to continue in a dating relationship. Overall, the couples who married after conception appeared to face less severe problems than either initially-married couples or steady daters. ((c) 1999 APA/PsycINFO, all rights reserved)

Key Phrase(s)	parental approval & salary level & educational status, 12-19 yr old unmarried vs married before conception vs delivery, mothers & their 14-36 yr old partners
Maj Subject(s)	Adolescent Fathers, Adolescent Mothers, Marital Status
Min Subject(s)	Adolescence, Adulthood, Childhood, Couples, Educational Background, Family Relations, Income Level, Parental Attitudes, Unwed Mothers
Class. Code	2840
Classification	Psychosocial & Personality Development
Population	Human, Male, Female
Age	Childhood (birth-12 yrs), Adolescence (13-17 yrs), Adulthood (18 yrs & older)
Language	English
ISSN	0047-2891
Document Type	Journal Article
Form/Content Type	Empirical Study

FIGURE 2-3 A printout from PsycINFO.

We hope these guidelines will be helpful as you surf the Web. Remember there are no quality controls on the Internet; anyone can create a Web site with any type of information.

3. Obtaining the Relevant Publications. Once you have assembled a listing of books and journal articles relevant to your area of interest, it is time to acquire copies. There are several techniques for going about this task; you will probably find that a combination of these strategies works best. First, find out what is available in your own library and plan to spend time reading this material and making photocopies for later use.

There are two options for obtaining items that are not available in your library. First, you can order them through the *interlibrary loan* department of your library. Most interlibrary loan services are reasonably fast and efficient. However, there may be a

TABLE 2-2   EVALUATING INTERNET RESOURCES

The WWW is a self-publishing medium in which anyone with the appropriate computer and software and an Internet connection can create and disperse information. Web pages should be evaluated carefully using some of the same criteria used to evaluate a print source. Be aware, however, that Web pages present additional evaluation challenges.

Authority	Who is the author? Is the author's name clearly visible? Is there a link to the author's e-mail address? What are the author's qualifications, education, and occupation? Has the author written articles or books other than Web pages? Check journal databases, such as Psyc INFO. Is there a link to additional information about the author? A personal home page? Is the source peer-reviewed or edited? If so, by whom? Does the author belong to an organization? If the page is authored by an organization, what additional information about that organization is available? Check the domain name of the URL (.gov, .edu, .com, .org, .net, .mil).
Accuracy	Are there clues to tell you that the information on the page is true? Does the author list sources? Is there a bibliography on the page? Can the information be verified elsewhere—perhaps in a print source? Are there obvious errors (spelling, grammar, etc.)?
Bias	Does the page reflect a particular bias or viewpoint? Does the author use inflammatory or provocative language? What is the purpose of the page? To inform? To sell or market a product or an idea? To entertain? To persuade? Why was this page written and for whom? (The Web can be a "soapbox" for organizations or people.) Is there advertising on the page? If there is advertising, can it be differentiated from the informational content?
Currency	When was the page first published and last updated? Are the facts on the page current? When was the information gathered? Are the links current?
Coverage	Is the page a complete document or an abstract/summary? Does the author adequately cover the topic? What time period is covered? Are there links to additional coverage? Does the page contain information that is pertinent to your research topic? How can you use this information?
Navigation/Design	Is the page easy to read? Does the background interfere with the page's content? Is the color "easy on the eyes"? Is the material presented in an orderly format? Do the graphics and images add to the presentation of the page? Are links appropriate to the topic of the page? Do they work? Is there a link at the bottom of the page to go back to the top? Is there a link on each supporting page to go back to the main page? Is there a comment link at the bottom of the main page? Do you need special software to view the information? Is there a fee to obtain the information?

Source: Binghamton University (http://library.lib.binghamton.edu/search/evaluation.html).

small fee for providing copies of journal articles. Second, for journal articles, you can write directly to the author to request a reprint (authors typically receive a supply of copies of each article they publish).

Writing for reprints has an added advantage; it allows you to request additional, related articles that the author may have published. With the advent of e-mail and the Internet, the task of communicating with researchers in your area of interest has become fast and convenient. Most authors are pleased to comply with such requests, and there is no charge for reprints. Your literature search is likely to uncover publications that are several years, even decades, old. Because authors receive a large number of reprints when they publish an article, the chances are good they will have copies of even their older articles; don't hesitate to ask. Concerned about addresses for authors? Your computer search lists the institutional affiliation of the author(s). Hence, you should be able to look up the institutional address in any number of the guidebooks to colleges and universities that are in your library. If you have only the author's name, then consult your faculty members to see if they have a membership directory for the APA or the American Psychological Society (APS). There is a good chance the author you are trying to locate will be a member of one or both of these associations. If so, you can get the institutional and e-mail addresses from a current membership directory. Another alternative is to do a *Google* search; you might be amazed how well this technique works.

4. Integrating the Results of the Literature Search. Once you have assembled the journal articles, book chapters, and books relevant to your research area, you will need to make sense of this material. This task can be formidable indeed; it will help if you have a plan.

Our students have found the following procedure to be quite effective. You also may find it useful in organizing the results of your literature search. As you read each article, keep good but succinct notes on each of the following aspects. Because most journal articles appear in the following sequence, your task will not be difficult. We will have more to say about how you actually write the results of your research in Chapter 20. For now, you need to master the task of summarizing what others have already written and published.

Reference Information. List the complete citation (in APA format; see Chapter 20) for the article you are abstracting. This information will facilitate completing the reference section of your research report.

Introduction. Why did the researchers conduct this experiment? What theory does this research seek to support?

Method. Use the following sections to describe how the project was conducted:

Participants. Describe the participants of the experiment. List such specifics as species, number, age, and sex.

Apparatus. Describe the equipment that the researcher used. Note any deviations from the standard apparatus, as well as any unusual features.

Procedure. Describe the conditions under which the participants were tested.

Results. Which statistical tests did the author use? What were the results of these statistical tests?

Discussion. What conclusions did the author(s) reach? How do these conclusions relate to theory and past research? Describe any criticisms of the research that occurred to you as you read the article (see the guidelines for critiquing research publications in Chapter 18).

Once you have completed taking notes on these sections, you should condense them so all this information will fit on one side of a sheet of paper. As you prepare these single sheets, be sure always to use the same sequence of headings that you followed in making your notes. An example of a completed sheet appears in Figure 2-4.

Once you have prepared all your relevant literature in this manner, it is an easy task to lay out the pages on a table and make comparisons and contrasts between research projects. Because you put the same type of information in the same location on each page, it is easy to make comparisons of the various aspects and details. Additionally, using a single sheet for each reference allows you to arrange and rearrange the references to suit your various needs: alphabetically to create a reference list, into separate stacks to represent positive and negative findings, and so forth.

As you have probably realized, the format we are suggesting is modeled after the accepted APA format for preparing papers (see Chapter 20). The experience you get in summarizing the results of your literature search will help you as you prepare a full-length APA-format paper. At this point, we are now ready to do something with the results of our literature survey.

Formulating the Research Hypothesis

Once you have completed your literature review, your own research begins to take shape. The next task is to develop a *research hypothesis*—a formal statement of your research question—taking into account what you learned from searching the literature.

Recall from Chapter 1 that the hypothesis is an attempt to organize data and IV–DV relations within a specific portion of a larger, more comprehensive research area or theory. Thus, hypotheses that have been supported by experimental research can make important contributions to our knowledge base.

Because you have yet to conduct your research project, the **research** or **experimental hypothesis** is our *prediction* about the relation that exists between the IV that you are going to manipulate and the DV that you will record. If the results of your experiment support your research hypothesis, then it has the potential to make a contribution to theory; you have some grounds on which to infer a cause-and-effect relation. In order to understand the nature of the research hypothesis, we will examine some of its general characteristics.

> **Research** or **experimental hypothesis** The experimenter's predicted outcome of a research project.

Characteristics of the Research Hypothesis

For the detective and the psychologist, all acceptable research hypotheses share certain characteristics—they are stated in a certain manner, they involve a certain type of reasoning, and they are presented in a certain format.

Wann, D. L., & Dolan, T. J. (1994). Spectators' evaluations of rival and fellow fans. *The Psychological Record, 44*, 351-358.

Introduction

Even though "sports fans are biased in their evaluations and attributions concerning their team" (p. 351), no research has examined the evaluations spectators make of other spectators. Hence the present experiment was conducted to examine spectators' evaluations of home team and rival fans.

Method

Participants - One hundred three undergraduate psychology students received extra credit for participation.

Instruments - A questionnaire packet consisting of an information sheet, Sports Spectator Identification Scale, a five-paragraph scenario describing the behavior of a home team or rival spectator at an important basketball game, and several questions concerning the general behavior of the spectator described in the scenario was given to each participant.

Procedure - The questionnaire packet was completed after an informed consent document was completed and returned. One-half of the participants read the home team fan scenario, while the remainder of the participants read the rival team fan scenario. The determination of which scenario was read was determined randomly.

Results

Analysis of variance was used to analyze the data. The results of these analyses indicated the home team fan was rated more positively than the rival team fan by participants who were highly identified with the home team. This pattern of results was not shown by lesser identified fans. Of particular note was the finding that the highly identified participants did not rate the rival team fan more negatively than did the lesser identified participants; they just rated the home team fan positively.

Discussion and Evaluation

These results support the authors' initial predictions that participants would give more positive evaluations of fans rooting for the same team and more negative evaluations of fans rooting for a different team. Wann and Dolan's prediction that such evaluations would be shown only by fans who were highly identified with their team also was supported. These predictions were seen to be in accord with social identity theory. The study appeared to be well conducted. The fact that the study was not conducted at a sporting event limits its applicability.

FIGURE 2-4 Sample of the summary of a journal article.

Source: Wann, D. L., Dolan, T. J. (1994). Spectators' evaluations of rival and fellow fans. *The Psychological Record*, 44, pp. 351–358.

Types of Statements

Because a research hypothesis is nothing more than a statement of what you believe will occur when you conduct an experiment, you must carefully consider the statements used in constructing it.

> **Synthetic statement**
> Statements that can be either true or false.

> **Analytic statement**
> Statements that are always true.

> **Contradictory statement** Statements that are always false.

Synthetic, Analytic, and Contradictory Statements A statement can be one of three types: synthetic, analytic, or contradictory.

Synthetic statements are those statements that can be *either true or false*. The statement "Abused children have lower self-esteem" is synthetic because although there is a chance that it is true, there also is a chance that it is false.

Analytic statements are those statements that are *always true*. For example, "I am making an *A* or I am not making an *A*" is an analytic statement; it is always true. You are either making an *A or* you are not making an *A*; no other possibilities exist.

Contradictory statements are those statements that are *always false*. For example, "I am making an *A and* I am not making an *A*" is a contradictory statement; it is always false. You cannot make an *A* and not make an *A* at the same time.

 Review the three types of statements that we just presented. Which one is best suited for use in our research hypothesis?

When you conduct an experiment, you are attempting to establish the existence of a cause-and-effect relation. At the outset of the experiment you do not know whether your prediction is correct or not. Therefore, synthetic statements, which can be true or false, must constitute your research hypothesis. If your research hypothesis is an analytic or contradictory statement, there is no need (or way) to conduct research on that topic. You already know what the outcome will be by merely reading the statements.

> **General implication form** Statement of the research hypothesis in an "if . . . then" form.

General Implication Form You must be able to state the research hypothesis in **general implication form** ("if . . . then" form). The "if" portion of such statements refers to the IV manipulation that we are going to make, whereas the "then" portion of the statement refers to the DV changes we expect to observe. An example of a general implication form statement would be the following:

If students in one group of third-graders receive an M&M each time they spell a word correctly, then their spelling performance will be better than that of a group of third-graders who do not receive an M&M for each correctly spelled word.

If you have read articles in the psychological journals, you are probably saying to yourself, "I don't recall seeing many statements in general implication form." You are probably correct; most researchers do not formally state their research hypothesis in strict general implication form. For example, the hypothesis about the third-graders and their spelling performance might have been stated thusly:

Third-graders who receive an M&M each time they spell a word correctly will spell better than third-graders who do not receive an M&M for each correctly spelled word.

Regardless of how the research hypothesis is stated, it must be restateable in general implication form. If it cannot be stated in this manner, then there is a problem with either your IV manipulation or the DV you have chosen to measure.

Starting with "If students in one group of third-graders . . . ," read the last general implication statement again. What IV is the researcher manipulating? What is the DV? In addition to being stated in general implication form, is this statement synthetic, analytic, or contradictory?

Whether the students receive an M&M after correctly spelling a word is the IV. The spelling performance of the two groups of third-graders is the DV. Because this statement has the potential to be true or false, it is synthetic.

The use of synthetic statements presented in general implication form highlights two additional, but related, characteristics of the research hypothesis. The **principle of falsifiability**, the first characteristic, means that when an experiment does not turn out as you predicted, then this result is seen as evidence that your hypothesis is false. If, after the experiment, the two groups of third-graders do not differ in spelling ability, then you must conclude you made a bad prediction; your research hypothesis was not an accurate portrayal of nature. Even though you do not want such results to occur, your research must be capable of producing results that do not support your experimental hypothesis.

Principle of falsifiability Results not in accord with the research hypothesis are taken as evidence that this hypothesis is false.

Because we use a synthetic statement for our research hypothesis, our results will never prove its truth absolutely; this is the second characteristic of the research hypothesis. Assume we did find that third-graders who received M&M's spelled better than third-graders who did not receive M&M's. Later we decide to replicate our experiment. Just because we obtained positive results the first time we conducted the experiment does not prove that our research hypothesis is unquestionably true and that we will always obtain positive results. When we conduct a replication, or any experiment for that matter, our hypothesis contains a synthetic statement that is either true or false. Thus, we can never absolutely prove a research hypothesis; we simply cannot yet disprove it. Certainly, as the number of experiments that support the research hypothesis increase, our confidence in the research hypothesis increases.

Types of Reasoning

In stating our research hypothesis, we also must be aware of the type of reasoning or logic we use. As we will see, inductive and deductive reasoning involve different processes.

> **Inductive logic**
> Reasoning that proceeds from specific cases to general conclusions or theories.

Inductive Logic   **Inductive logic** involves reasoning from specific cases to general principles. Inductive logic is the process that is involved in the construction of theories; the results of several independent experiments are considered simultaneously and general theoretical principles designed to account for the behavior in question are derived.

For example, John Darley and Bibb Latané (1968) were intrigued by a famous incident that occurred in 1964 in the Queens section of New York; a young woman named Kitty Genovese was stabbed to death. Given the number of murders that take place each year in any large city, this event may not seem especially noteworthy. However, an especially horrifying aspect of this murder was that the killer attacked the young woman on *3 separate occasions* in the course of half an hour and that 38 people saw the attacks or heard the young woman's screams. The killer was frightened off twice when people turned their lights on or called from their windows. However, on both occasions he resumed his attack. None of the people who witnessed the attack came to the victim's aid and no one called the police while she was being attacked. Why?

Darley and Latané (1968) reported the results of several experiments they conducted. On the basis of their results, they theorized that individuals who are alone are more likely to give assistance than when others are present. The finding that groups of bystanders are less likely than individuals to aid a person in trouble is known as the *bystander effect*. The development of this principle is an example of the use of inductive reasoning; several specific results were combined to formulate a more general principle.

> **Deductive logic**
> Reasoning that proceeds from general theories to specific cases.

Deductive Logic   **Deductive logic** is the converse of inductive logic; we reason from general principles to specific conclusions or predictions. Deductive logic is the reasoning process we use in formulating our research hypothesis. By conducting a search of the literature, we have assembled a large amount of data and considered several theories. From this *general* pool of information we seek to develop our research hypothesis, a statement about the relation between a *specific* IV and a *specific* DV. For example, based on previous research on the bystander effect, a social psychologist might make the following deductive statement:

If a person pretends to have a seizure on a subway, then that person will receive less assistance when there are more bystanders present.

 PSYCHOLOGICAL DETECTIVE   Read the preceding statement once again. Is this statement acceptable as a research hypothesis?

FIGURE 2-5   The relations between deductive and inductive reasoning.

Yes, this statement would appear to be acceptable as a research hypothesis. It is a synthetic statement (can be true or false) presented in general implication form (if . . . then). Moreover, deductive logic is involved: we have gone from a general body of knowledge (about the bystander effect) to make a specific prediction concerning a specific IV (number of bystanders present) and a specific DV (receiving assistance).

Certainly we are not maintaining that deductive and inductive reasoning are totally separate processes. They can, and do, interact with each other. As you can see from Figure 2-5, the results of several initial experiments in a particular research area may lead to the development of a theory in that area (inductive reasoning).

In turn, an examination of that theory and past research may suggest a specific research project (deductive reasoning) that needs to be conducted. The results of that project may result in modification of the theory (inductive reasoning), which prompts the idea for several additional research projects (deductive reasoning), and so forth. Clearly, the research process we described in Chapter 1 is based on the interplay between these two types of logical reasoning.

A New View of Hypothesis Testing

Robert Proctor and John Capaldi (2001), psychologists at Purdue University, have presented a new view of hypothesis testing that warrants considerable thought. They based their comments on the premise that research methodology is not a static, finished process; it is constantly in a state of change and flux. Principles may be rejected or modified. The data that researchers gather really determine the methods that are accepted and continue to be used.

They contended that hypothesis testing is not a simple affair; it "is a great deal more complicated than it seems on the surface" (Proctor & Capaldi, 2001, p. 179). Several factors can determine what the researcher does when an experimental hypothesis is confirmed (or disconfirmed). For example, the *importance* of the research problem may determine whether a researcher sticks with the problem, even if a specific hypothesis is disconfirmed. Likewise, the *promise* of the research program to answer theoretical questions may determine whether that research program flourishes.

Early in the developmental stages of a theory, hypothesis testing actually may be harmful. Because the researchers do not know all of the relevant variables (IVs, DVs, and especially extraneous variables), it may be very easy to disconfirm an experimental hypothesis and thereby disconfirm the theory. Proctor and Capaldi (2001) also argued that researchers are never really able to achieve a clear-cut test of a hypothesis. Why? No hypothesis is ever tested in complete isolation; we are always testing other things at the same time. For example, the adequacy of our research equipment is tested at the same time as we test a hypothesis. If the hypothesis was disconfirmed, was it due to an incorrect hypothesis or inadequate equipment? Likewise, we always make auxiliary assumptions, such as the effectiveness of randomization as a control technique, when we test a hypothesis. If these auxiliary assumptions are incorrect, we may reject a valid experimental hypothesis.

What should researchers do? Proctor and Capaldi (2001) suggested that researchers should use more inductive logic when a research area is new, because there is a high probability of disconfirming hypotheses when they might be true. Their suggestion would be to let the data be your guide. Sherlock Holmes made this point quite eloquently when he said, "I make a point of never having any prejudices, and of following docilely wherever fact may lead me" (Doyle, 1927, p. 407). The empirical results of your research will help reveal important relations. Hypothesis testing is important and valuable when it works. However, researchers must be sensitive to the drawbacks associated with it.

Directional versus Nondirectional Research Hypotheses

> **Directional research hypothesis** Prediction of the specific outcome of an experiment.

Finally, we must consider whether we are going to predict the direction of the outcome of our experiment in our research hypothesis. In a **directional research hypothesis** we specify the predicted outcome of the experiment. For example, if we test two groups, we could entertain *one* of the following directional hypotheses:

Group A will score significantly higher than group B.

or

Group B will score significantly higher than group A.

In either case, we are directly specifying the direction we predict for the outcome of our experiment. (Note that although we can entertain either of these directional hypotheses, we cannot consider both of them at the same time.)

> **Nondirectional research hypothesis** A specific prediction concerning the outcome of an experiment is not made.

On the other hand, a **nondirectional research hypothesis** does not predict the exact directional outcome of an experiment; it simply predicts that the groups we are testing will differ. Using our two-group example once again, a nondirectional hypothesis would indicate that

Group A's scores will differ significantly from group B's scores.

For this hypothesis to be supported, group A can score either significantly higher or significantly lower than group B.

Review the differences between directional and nondirectional hypotheses. How would you write a directional research hypothesis for the M&M's and third-grade spelling experiment we described earlier? How would you write a nondirectional hypothesis for this same experiment?

A directional hypothesis might read as follows:

> If students in one group of third-graders receive an M&M each time they spell a word correctly, then their spelling performance *will be better* than that of a group of third-graders who do not receive an M&M for each correctly spelled word.

Of course, you might predict that receiving M&M's would cause spelling performance to decrease and fall below that of the group that did not receive the M&M's. In either instance, you would be using a directional hypothesis.

A nondirectional hypothesis would read as follows:

> If students in one group of third-graders receive an M&M each time they spell a word correctly, then their spelling performance *will differ* from that of a group of third-graders who do not receive an M&M for each correctly spelled word.

In this instance, we are simply predicting the two groups will perform differently.

Which type of hypothesis, directional or nondirectional, should you choose? If the theory you are testing calls for it, and you are *relatively certain* of your prediction, then you may want to use a directional hypothesis. For reasons we will discuss later, your chances of finding a statistically significant result are increased when you use a directional hypothesis. However, if you adopt a directional hypothesis, there is no changing your mind. If the results turn out exactly opposite to your prediction, the only thing you can say is that you were wrong and that nature doesn't operate as you thought it did. Because nature has a way of playing cruel tricks on our predictions, most researchers take a more conservative approach and state a nondirectional research hypothesis. Even though it may be slightly more difficult to achieve statistical significance, there is less potential for disappointment with the outcome of the research project when you used a nondirectional hypothesis.

REVIEW SUMMARY

1. The starting point for the research project is the **research idea** or identification of a gap in our current knowledge base.
2. Good research ideas should be testable and have a high likelihood of success (closely approximate nature).

✗ 3. **Nonsystematic sources** of research ideas give the impression that the idea simply appeared with little or no forethought. Inspiration, **serendipity** (looking for one phenomenon, but finding another), and everyday occurrences are the major nonsystematic sources of research ideas.

4. Formal study and knowledge of a topic form the basis for **systematic sources** of research ideas. Past research and theories are the two main systematic sources of research ideas.

5. Developing a research question will help guide your research.

6. An organized approach is necessary to conduct a survey of the psychological literature. Such a search typically begins with the selection of index terms from the *Thesaurus of Psychological Index Terms*. Once you have selected these terms, you use them to access a computer database, such as PsycINFO, or the *Psychological Abstracts*. After you have identified and made copies of the relevant literature, you must integrate it in a meaningful manner.

7. Once the literature review is complete, the researcher is ready to develop a **research** or **experimental hypothesis**—the predicted outcome of the experiment.

8. The research hypothesis contains **synthetic statements** that can be either true or false and is stated in **general implication form** ("if . . . then").

9. The **principle of falsifiability** indicates that when an experiment does not turn out as predicted, the truthfulness of the research hypothesis is discredited. Because a research hypothesis is composed of synthetic statements, it can never be absolutely proved; it can only be disproved.

10. The development of the research hypothesis involves the use of **deductive logic** in which we reason from general principles to specific cases.

11. A **directional research hypothesis** is used when the *specific* direction or nature of the outcome of an experiment is predicted. When the experimenter does not predict the specific nature of the group differences, only that they *will differ*, a **nondirectional research hypothesis** is used.

CHECK YOUR PROGRESS

1. Matching
   1. research idea   A. look for one thing, find another
   2. serendipity   B. computer search of the literature
   3. PsycLIT/PsycINFO   C. identification of a gap in the knowledge base
   4. experimental hypothesis   D. always true
   5. synthetic statement   E. either true or false
   6. analytic statement   F. experimenter's predicted answer to research

2. Good research ideas must be _____ and have a high _____.

3. Distinguish between nonsystematic and systematic sources of research ideas. What are the specific ways each general source may be shown?

4. When we find something unexpected that is important in our research, what has occurred?

   a. inspiration   b. everyday occurrences   c. serendipity   d. theory

5. _Analytic_ are always true.

    a. Synthetic statements   b. Contradictory statements

    c. Statements presented in general implication form d. Analytic statements

6. Why are synthetic statements used in the experimental hypothesis? *no clear way its using logo*

7. Describe general implication form. Be thorough. *If... then*

8. Which of the following is *not* associated with the principle of falsifiability?

    a. synthetic statements   b. general implication form

    c. experimental hypothesis   d. analytic statements

9. The construction of theories involves *inductive* logic; the development of the exper-
    imental hypothesis involves *deductive* logic.

10. Concerning research hypotheses, most researchers

    a. state a directional research hypothesis

    b. state a nondirectional research hypothesis

    c. do not use a research hypothesis

    d. use a research hypothesis that makes no prediction

KEY TERMS

Research idea, *24*

Nonsystematic sources, *25*

Serendipity, *26*

Systematic sources, 27

Research or experimental
   hypothesis, *36*

Synthetic statement, *38*

Analytic statement, *38*

Contradictory statement, *38*

General implication form, *38*

Principle of falsifiability, *39*

Inductive logic, *40*

Deductive logic, *40*

Directional research hypothesis, *42*

Nondirectional research
   hypothesis, *42*

LOOKING AHEAD

In Chapters 1 and 2 we looked at the general nature of research, saw what constitutes
a good research question, and found out how to state a good research hypothesis.
However, you should be aware that research does not occur in a vacuum. Researchers
must take ethics into consideration when they conduct their projects. We examine the
topic of research ethics in Chapter 3.

Ethics in Psychological Research

The Need for Ethical Principles

Although it may appear that we are ready to begin our research project once we have developed our research hypothesis, this simply is not the case. We still have one major issue to deal with before we finalize our research design and start gathering data: We must consider the ethical nature of our research. The days of beating a confession out of a suspect with a rubber hose are gone for the detective. Likewise, psychologists must ask and answer such questions as "Are we putting our participants at risk?" "Is our experimental treatment harmful?" "Is the information we will gather from our experiment worth the potential risk and harm to participants?" Despite older views to the contrary, science does not operate in a moral vacuum (Kimmel, 1988).

Under the 1974 National Health Research Act, the United States government demands assurance that federally funded projects have been reviewed and approved by a group of the proposing scientist's peers and that human participants have given informed consent concerning research participation. Since that time, seeking approval for a project from a group such as a Human Subjects Review Panel, an Animal Care and Utilization Committee, or an Institutional Review Board has become standard practice.

What has prompted such concern with ethics? Although we could cite many unethical practices, we will describe four instances that created major concern: the medical atrocities of World War II, the Tuskegee syphilis project, the Willowbrook hepatitis project, and Stanley Milgram's obedience studies in the 1960s.

During World War II, Nazi doctors conducted a lengthy series of experiments on civilian prisoners of war to determine the effects of various viruses, toxic agents, and drugs. The prisoners had no choice concerning whether they participated. After World War II many of these doctors were tried in courts for the unethical practices they had inflicted on their unwilling participants. Many were found guilty and either hanged or given long prison sentences. The Nuremberg War Tribunal was responsible for developing a code of medical and research ethics (Sasson & Nelson, 1969). Among other things, the Nuremberg Code stressed consideration of the following ethical aspects of research:

1. Participants should consent to participate in research.
2. Participants should be fully informed of the nature of the research project.
3. Risks should be avoided whenever possible.
4. Participants should be protected against risks to the greatest extent possible.
5. Projects should be conducted by scientifically qualified personnel.
6. Participants have the right to discontinue participation at any time.

As we will see, the Nuremberg Code has had a major impact upon the APA code of ethics to which psychologists adhere.

In 1956 an outbreak of hepatitis at Willowbrook, a mental retardation facility, prompted doctors to begin *purposely* infecting newly-admitted patients in order to study the disease's development under controlled conditions. Approximately 10% of the new admissions were infected, placed in a separate ward, and not given treatment (Beauchamp & Childress, 1979). Even though the patients' parents agreed to this procedure, a number of parents felt they had agreed under pressure. Although considerable information that improved the future treatment of hepatitis was gained from this project, it involved a major ethical problem. The ethical problem involved the use of the patients for research purposes not related to mental disability. It is difficult to envision a relation between mental disability and the investigation of hepatitis.

The Tuskegee syphilis study (Jones, 1981) began in 1932 and continued into the early 1970s. The purpose of the study was to observe the course of the syphilis disease in untreated individuals. To accomplish this goal, 399 African-American men living in the area around Tuskegee, Alabama who were infected with syphilis were recruited as participants. Doctors told the men they were being treated for syphilis by the U.S. Public Health Service (USPHS). The men were not told the real purpose of the study, nor did they ever receive any treatment for syphilis. Moreover, local physicians were told not to treat these men for syphilis and the participants were told their USPHS treatment would be discontinued if they sought any sort of additional treatment for the disease. Although information about the course of syphilis may have been gained from this project, it was done at the physical expense of the unknowing participants, some of whom lost their lives.

 Review the points of research concern from the Nuremberg Code. Which of these principles did the Tuskegee syphilis study violate? How did the study violate these principles?

It would appear that, with the exception of the principle concerning the conduct of the project by a qualified scientist, all of the principles of the Nuremberg Code were violated. The men did not consent to participate, nor were they fully informed about the project. The participants were not protected against risks, and they certainly did not appear to have the right to decline to participate.

In Milgram's (1963) obedience-to-authority study, each participant was assigned the role of "teacher" in what was portrayed as a "learning experiment." Another "participant" (actually an accomplice of the experimenter) played the role of "learner." The teacher's task was to teach the learner a series of words. The teacher was told the purpose of the experiment was to determine the effects of punishment on memory. Every time the learner, who was in an adjacent room, made a mistake, the teacher was to correct the learner by administering an electric shock. Even though no shocks were actually administered, the teacher (true participant) did not know it, and the learner always acted as if shock had been administered.

Once the experimental session began, the learner purposely made mistakes so the teacher would have to administer shocks. With each mistake the experimenter instructed the teacher to increase the voltage level of the shock. As the mistakes (and voltage level) increased, the learner began to moan and complain and finally refused to answer any questions. The experimenter told the teacher to treat no response as a mistake and continue administering shocks. The session ended when the teacher (participant) reached the maximum level of shock or refused to administer any more shocks. Contrary to Milgram's initial prediction, the participants administered many shocks at what they assumed were *very high* voltage levels.

Although this research contributed to our understanding of obedience to authority, it was not without ethical problems. For example, rather than protecting the rights of the participants, the experimenter purposely made them feel discomfort and emotional distress by ordering them to continue administering the electrical shocks (Baumrind, 1964). Moreover, Milgram (1964) was not prepared for the amount of emotional upset his participants experienced. Even though this high level of discomfort was noted, Milgram made the decision to continue the research. To Milgram's credit, all participants received a debriefing session after they completed the experiment. During this session the researcher explained the purpose of the experiment and the "learner" talked with the real participant. Subsequently, all participants received a follow-up report describing the results of the experiment. Such debriefing and follow-up procedures were not mandatory in the early 1960s.

APA Principles in the Conduct of Research with Humans

Experiments such as the Tuskegee syphilis project and Milgram's study have led to the development of ethical guidelines by the APA. The APA adopted and published the original code of ethics in 1973; it was revised in 1982 and again in 2002.

The current ethical standards that pertain to Research and Publication appear in Table 3-1.

TABLE 3-1 APA ETHICAL STANDARD 8 FOR THE CONDUCT OF RESEARCH

8.01 Institutional Approval
When institutional approval is required, psychologists provide accurate information about their research proposals and obtain approval prior to conducting the research. They conduct the research in accordance with the approved research protocol.

8.02 Informed Consent to Research
(a) When obtaining informed consent as required in Standard 3.10, Informed Consent, psychologists inform participants about (1) the purpose of the research, expected duration, and procedures; (2) their right to decline to participate and to withdraw from the research once participation has begun; (3) the foreseeable consequences of declining or withdrawing; (4) reasonably foreseeable factors that may be expected to influence their willingness to participate such as potential risks, discomfort, or adverse effects; (5) any prospective research benefits; (6) limits of confidentiality; (7) incentives for participation; and (8) whom to contact for questions about the research and research participants' rights. They provide opportunity for the prospective participants to ask questions and receive answers.

(b) Psychologists conducting intervention research involving the use of experimental treatments clarify to participants at the outset of the research (1) the experimental nature of the treatment; (2) the services that will or will not be available to the control group(s) if appropriate; (3) the means by which assignment to treatment and control groups will be made; (4) available treatment alternatives if an individual does not wish to participate in the research or wishes to withdraw once a study has begun; and (5) compensation for or monetary costs of participating including, if appropriate, whether reimbursement from the participant or a third-party payor will be sought.

(Continued)

TABLE 3-1 (CONTINUED)

8.03 Informed Consent for Recording Voices and Images in Research
Psychologists obtain informed consent from research participants prior to recording their voices or images for data collection unless (1) the research consists solely of naturalistic observations in public places, and it is not anticipated that the recording will be used in a manner that could cause personal identification or harm, or (2) the research design includes deception, and consent for the use of the recording is obtained during debriefing.

8.04 Client/Patient, Student, and Subordinate Research Participants
(a) When psychologists conduct research with clients/patients, students, or subordinates as participants, psychologists take steps to protect the prospective participants from adverse consequences of declining or withdrawing from participation.

(b) When research participation is a course requirement or an opportunity for extra credit, the prospective participant is given the choice of equitable alternative activities.

8.05 Dispensing with Informed Consent for Research
Psychologists may dispense with informed consent only (1) where research would not reasonably be assumed to create distress or harm and involves (a) the study of normal educational practices, curricula, or classroom management methods conducted in educational settings; (b) only anonymous questionnaires, naturalistic observations, or archival research for which disclosure of responses would not place participants at risk of criminal or civil liability or damage their financial standing, employability, or reputation, and confidentiality is protected; or (c) the study of factors related to job or organization effectiveness conducted in organizational settings for which there is no risk to participants' employability, and confidentiality is protected or (2) where otherwise permitted by law or federal or institutional regulations.

8.06 Offering Inducements for Research Participation
(a) Psychologists make reasonable efforts to avoid offering excessive or inappropriate financial or other inducements for research participation when such inducements are likely to coerce participation.

(b) When offering professional services as an inducement for research participation, psychologists clarify the nature of the services, as well as the risks, obligations, and limitations.

8.07 Deception in Research
(a) Psychologists do not conduct a study involving deception unless they have determined that the use of deceptive techniques is justified by the study's significant prospective scientific, educational or applied value and that effective nondeceptive alternative procedures are not feasible.

(b) Psychologists do not deceive prospective participants about research that is reasonably expected to cause physical pain or severe emotional distress.

(c) Psychologists explain any deception that is an integral feature of the design and conduct of an experiment to participants as early as is feasible, preferably at the conclusion of their participation, but no later than at the conclusion of the data collection, and permit participants to withdraw their data. (See also Standard 8.08 Debriefing.)

8.08 Debriefing
(a) Psychologists provide a prompt opportunity for participants to obtain appropriate information about the nature, results, and conclusions of the research, and they take reasonable steps to correct any misconceptions that participants may have of which the psychologists are aware.

(b) If scientific or humane values justify delaying or withholding this information, psychologists take reasonable measures to reduce the risk of harm.

(c) When psychologists become aware that research procedures have harmed a participant, they take reasonable steps to minimize the harm.

Those standards dealing with (a) securing "informed consent" from the participants (Standard 8.02), and (b) using "deception" in research (Standard 8.07) have proved to be controversial.

PSYCHOLOGICAL DETECTIVE   Why do you think these principles have proved to be controversial in conducting psychological research?

Much psychological research, especially in the area of social psychology, has involved deception. Researchers believe that in many cases they can obtain honest and unbiased responses only when the participants are unaware of the true nature of the research. Hence, researchers find it difficult to give their participants a complete and accurate description of the experiment and to secure informed consent before the research is conducted.

Is Deception in Research Necessary?

Ideally, the researcher should be able to explain the purpose of a research project to the participants and enlist their cooperation. However, providing a *complete* explanation or description of the project may influence the participants' responses. Consider, for example, the research conducted by Kim Driggers and Tasha Helms (2000) on salary and willingness to date or by Naomi Freeman and Diana Punzo (2001) on the relative importance of DNA evidence and eyewitness testimony on juror's verdicts (see Chapter 1). Had the participants in these two studies known they were to evaluate the effect of salary on dating or the relative importance of DNA and eyewitness testimony, respectively, then their behavior could easily have been influenced by what they believed their responses were supposed to be. As we will see, it is very important in psychological research with human participants to try to ensure that the participants are not responding simply because (a) they have "figured out" the experiment and know how they are supposed to act or (b) they think the experimenter expects them to respond in a certain manner (see Rosenthal, 1966, 1985).

Hence, it is arguable that deception may be justified in some cases if our results are to be unbiased or uncontaminated by knowledge of the experiment and the expectancies that such knowledge may bring. If researchers use deception, how do they deal with obtaining informed consent for participation?

Informed Consent

Standard 8.02 indicates that the participants should give informed consent regarding their participation in a research project. This informed consent frequently takes the form of a statement concerning the research, which the participants sign before taking part in the research project. An example of an informed consent form appears in Figure 3-1. As you can see, this document gives the participants a general description of the project in which they are going to participate and informs them that no penalties will be invoked if they choose not to participate. Also, it clearly states that the participants have the right to withdraw their participation at any time they desire.

Informed Consent Document

Read this consent form. If you have any questions ask the experimenter and he/she will answer the question.

The Department of Psychology supports the practice of protection for human participants participating in research and related activities. The following information is provided so that you can decide whether you wish to participate in the present study. You should be aware that even if you agree to participate, you are free to withdraw at any time, and that if you do withdraw from the study, you will not be subjected to reprimand or any other form of reproach.

In order to help determine the relationship between numerous personality characteristics, you are being asked to complete several questionnaires. It should not take more than 30 minutes for you to complete these materials. These questionnaires will be completed anonymously.

"I have read the above statement and have been fully advised of the procedures to be used in this project. I have been given sufficient opportunity to ask any questions I had concerning the procedures and possible risks involved. I understand the potential risks involved and I assume them voluntarily. I likewise understand that I can withdraw from the study at any time without being subjected to reproach."

_____   _____
Participant and/or authorized representative   Date

FIGURE 3-1   An example of an informed consent document.

 Even though it may not be readily apparent, the process of informed consent has given researchers a new variable to evaluate. What is this variable?

The informed consent process itself and the information provided through this process have stimulated some interesting research. For example, Edward Burkley III, Shawn McFarland, Wendy Walker, and Jennifer Young (students at Southern Illinois University Edwardsville) evaluated the effect of having the "right to withdraw from the experiment" statement printed on the informed consent form. Two groups of students solved anagrams. One group of participants had the right to withdraw statement printed on their informed consent document, whereas the informed consent document for the second group did not contain this statement. Burkley et al. (2000) found that the students who had the statement printed on their form solved significantly *more* anagrams than students whose form did not contain this statement. Clearly, the informed consent process can have an impact on the results of an experiment. The influence of ethical procedures likely will offer researchers rich experimental opportunities for years to come.

Although the objectives of Standard 8.02 may not seem difficult to satisfy, there is one group of participants that creates special problems—children. For example, if you want to conduct a project using first-graders, your research proposal initially has to be approved by a college or university committee. (We will discuss Institutional Review Boards at the end of this chapter.) Once you secure this approval, then you need to contact the school system for approval. This approval may need to be granted at several levels—teacher, principal, superintendent, and school board. Each of these individuals will scrutinize your proposal thoroughly to safeguard the rights of the children. Once you have successfully cleared these hurdles, then you must secure permission from the parent or legal guardian of each child. The parent or legal guardian is the individual who will sign the informed consent form.

The more general the statement of the research project, the more room there is for the possible use of deception or for not completely explaining the project. For example, the informed consent document shown in Figure 3-1 does not explicitly tell the participants that they are taking part in a study that will examine the relation between interpersonal flexibility, self-esteem, and fear of death (Hayes, Miller, & Davis, 1993).

By deceiving participants about the true purpose of an experiment or not providing complete information about the experiment, the experimenter may take the chance of placing some participants "at risk." Who is to say that completing a particular survey or questionnaire will not provoke an intense emotional reaction in a given participant? Perhaps one of the participants in an investigation of child abuse was sexually molested as a preschooler and completing your questionnaire will reawaken those terrifying memories. You need to carefully consider all the possible reactions and evaluate their seriousness.

Participants at Risk and Participants at Minimal Risk

Participants at risk By participating in an experiment, the participants are placed under some type of physical or emotional risk.

Participants at minimal risk Participation in an experiment does not place the participants under physical or emotional risk.

Participants at risk are participants who, by virtue of their participation in the research project, are placed under some emotional or physical risk. Certainly, the participants in the Tuskegee syphilis study and Milgram's obedience studies were participants at risk. Securing informed consent from participants at risk is a mandatory condition.

Participants at minimal risk are participants who will experience no harmful effects through taking part in the research project. For example, Anastasia Gibson, Kristie Smith, and Aurora Torres (2000) observed the glancing behavior of customers at ATM machines (see Chapter 18). In this research the participants were at minimal risk; the recording of their glancing behaviors did not influence their physical or emotional well-being. Although desirable, it is not mandatory to secure informed consent from participants at minimal risk. In fact Gibson et al. (2000) indicated that "Because this study was a systematic naturalistic observation, participants did not complete a consent form" (p. 149).

But what about those participants at risk who are participating in a study involving deception? How do we satisfy the ethical guidelines in such a case?

First, the researcher should tell the participants about all aspects of the research that are potentially harmful. If the researcher uses deception, the participants should not be deceived about some potentially harmful aspect of the research. For example, it would not be acceptable to tell participants they will be taking a vitamin tablet when the drug they are to consume is a hallucinogen. When participants are informed about all potentially harmful aspects of a research project, then they are able to give valid informed consent about participating.

The second procedure used to satisfy the ethical guidelines when using deception is to thoroughly debrief the participants once the experiment is completed. We turn to that topic after considering the needs of certain special populations.

Vulnerable Populations

What the researcher considers to be a risky or potentially harmful situation may depend on the type of participants chosen for a project. For example, experiments involving physical exertion, such as testing the effects of exercise on subsequent memory tasks, which pose no risk to healthy participants, may constitute a significant risk for persons in poor health. Likewise, the age of the participant may be a relevant consideration in determining potential emotional harm or distress in studies involving the selection of liked and disliked peers.

Researchers must exercise special care when the research participants may not be capable of fully understanding what participation in a project may entail. Such participant groups might include children, patients with physical or mental disorders, or persons who have lower intelligence, low literacy, or speak English as a second language. In these instances the researcher must take special care to ensure that these individuals or their parents or legal guardians understand fully what is expected of them and any risks they may encounter in a research project. To understand the importance of taking these potentially vulnerable populations into account, imagine how you would feel if you were a college student in a foreign country where you didn't speak the language very well and you agreed to participate in a potentially hazardous research project without understanding the risks involved.

The Debriefing Session

Debriefing session The nature and purpose of an experiment are explained at its conclusion.

The **debriefing session**, usually the final step in conducting the research project, involves explaining to the participants the nature and purpose(s) of the project. Debriefing can be very important and should not be taken lightly by the researcher. Eliot Aronson and J. M. Carlsmith (1968) proposed several excellent guidelines for effective debriefing:

1. The researcher's integrity as a scientist must be conveyed to the participants. The researcher's personal belief in the scientific method is the foundation for explaining why deception was necessary and how it was employed in the research project.

2. If deception was used, the researcher should reassure the participants that it was not wrong or a reflection on their integrity or intelligence to feel that they have been tricked or fooled. Such feelings indicate that the deception used in the project was effective.

3. Because debriefing is usually the last step in the conduct of the research project, there may be a tendency to try to rush through it. This approach is not advisable. The participants have a lot of information to digest and try to understand; therefore, the debriefing session should progress slowly. The explanations should be clear and understandable.

4. The researcher should be sensitive to indications that the participants' discomfort is not being alleviated by the debriefing session and strive to correct this situation. The goal of the debriefing session is to return the participants to the same (or close to the same) mental and emotional state they were in at the beginning of the project.

5. The researcher should repeat all guarantees of confidentiality and anonymity that were made at the beginning of the project. For such assurances to be seen as believable, the researcher must have clearly established his or her integrity as a scientist.

6. Do not try to satisfy debriefing requirements by saying that you will send an explanation and the results of the project at a later date. For maximum effectiveness, you should conduct the debriefing session immediately following the experimental session; there are no "easier" ways to satisfy this obligation.

These guidelines define the ideal debriefing situation, and they should be followed as closely as possible. However, in most instances the debriefing session will not be overly time consuming. For example, Elvo Kuai-Long Sou, a student at Washington State University at Vancouver, and his faculty advisor, Lori Irving, surveyed the attitudes of U.S. and Macao college students toward mental illness (Sou & Irving, 2002). The researchers indicated that "Once the participants finished the survey, each of them received a debriefing sheet that explained the purpose of the study and provided basic information regarding mental illness and how to seek help for a mental health issue" (Sou & Irving, 2002, p. 18).

PSYCHOLOGICAL DETECTIVE   Review the discussion of debriefing. What is the main goal of the debriefing session?

The main purpose of the debriefing session is to explain the nature of the experiment, remove or alleviate any undesirable consequences the participants may be experiencing, and generally try to return them to the same state of mind they were in prior to the experiment. For example, Milgram was sensitive to the emotional state of his participants. After the research was complete, he sent the participants a five-page report that described the results and their meaning. The participants also completed a questionnaire; 84% indicated that they were glad they participated. In a one-year examination of 40 participants, a psychiatrist reported there was "no evidence . . . of any traumatic reactions" (Milgram, 1974, p. 197).

The debriefing session also can provide the experimenter with valuable feedback concerning the conduct of the experiment from the participants' viewpoint. Was the IV manipulation successful? If deception was used, was it successful? Were the instructions clear? The answers to these and other relevant questions can be obtained during the debriefing session.

The Ethical Use of Animals in Psychological Research

Up to this point our ethical considerations have dealt with research in which humans are the participants. Since Willard S. Small (1901) used the first rat maze at Clark University in 1900, considerable psychological research has involved the use of animals. The use of animals in psychological research has created considerable controversy, debate, and even violence in recent years. Supporters of animal research point to the numerous accomplishments and scientific breakthroughs that are based on the results of animal studies (e.g., Kalat, 1992; Miller, 1985). For example, such medical procedures as blood transfusions, anesthesia, painkillers, antibiotics, insulin, vaccines, chemotherapy, CPR, coronary bypass surgery, and reconstructive surgery are based on animal studies. For over 100 years psychologists have used animals in studies of learning, psychopathology, brain and nervous system functioning, and physiology. It is undeniable that animal research has yielded numerous important and beneficial results.

However, animal activists argue the price we have paid for such progress is too high. They point to problems with housing conditions, as well as the pain and suffering that research animals endure, and insist such treatment must stop (Miller & Williams, 1983; Reagan, 1983; Singer, 1975).

Although the debate between researchers and animal activists is likely to continue for some time, our present concern is with the ethical conduct of animal research. In addition to the concern over the ethics of human experiments, the 1960s also witnessed

TABLE 3-2	APA ETHICAL STANDARD 8.09—HUMANE CARE AND USE OF ANIMALS IN RESEARCH

(a) Psychologists acquire, care for, use, and dispose of animals in compliance with current federal, state, and local laws and regulations, and with professional standards.

(b) Psychologists trained in research methods and experienced in the care of laboratory animals supervise all procedures involving animals and are responsible for ensuring appropriate consideration of their comfort, health, and humane treatment.

(c) Psychologists ensure that all individuals under their supervision who are using animals have received instruction in research methods and in the care, maintenance, and handling of the species being used, to the extent appropriate to their role. (See also Standard 2.05, Delegation of Work to Others.)

(d) Psychologists make reasonable efforts to minimize the discomfort, infection, illness, and pain of animal subjects.

(e) Psychologists use a procedure subjecting animals to pain, stress, or privation only when an alternative procedure is unavailable and the goal is justified by its prospective scientific, educational, or applied value.

(f) Psychologists perform surgical procedures under appropriate anesthesia and follow techniques to avoid infection and minimize pain during and after surgery.

(g) When it is appropriate that an animal's life be terminated, psychologists proceed rapidly, with an effort to minimize pain and in accordance with accepted procedures.

an increase in the concern for the ethical treatment of animals. For example, the Animal Welfare Act of 1966 was national legislation specifically passed to protect research animals. The APA has also established ethical standards for the use of animals in psychological research (APA, 2002). Table 3-2 (see p. 56) presents these standards. These standards are designed to ensure humane treatment of animals used in research and for educational purposes. They have resulted in improved care and housing of animals.

Now that we have considered the ethical treatment of human and animal participants, let's examine the group that decides whether the proposed research should or should not be conducted. For the detective, the jury will make such decisions; in the case of the psychologist, our attention turns to the Institutional Review Board (IRB).

The Institutional Review Board

At some institutions the review panel for the use of human participants may be the Human Subjects Review Panel, whereas the Animal Care and Utilization Committee reviews proposals for animal research. At other institutions the **Institutional Review Board (IRB)** reviews both types of proposals. Although the exact name of the group may vary from institution to institution, its composition and functions are quite similar.

> **Institutional Review Board (IRB)** The university committee that is responsible for determining whether a proposed research project conforms to accepted ethical standards.

The typical IRB is composed of a cross-section of individuals. For example, if we examine a college or university IRB, we might find that it consists of faculty members from history, biology, education, psychology, and economics. Additionally, there will probably be one or two individuals from the community who are not associated with the institution. A veterinarian must be a member of the panel that reviews animal research proposals.

The task of this group is not to decide on the scientific merits of the proposed research; the scientist proposing the research is the expert in that area. The IRB's responsibility is to examine the proposed procedures, any psychological tests or questionnaires that will be used, the informed consent document, plans for debriefing the participants, the use of painful procedures in animal research, procedures for disposing of animals humanely, and so forth. If participants are at risk, will they be made aware of this risk before the experiment is conducted? Do participants have the ability to terminate participation at any time? Will debriefing counteract the effects of deception if it has been used? Is it possible that a particular questionnaire or survey may evoke a strong emotional reaction? In short, the IRB serves to ensure that the experimenter treats research participants, whether they are humans or animals, according to the established ethical guidelines. If the IRB determines that a proposed project does not meet ethical standards, the IRB can request that changes be made to bring the project in line with standards.

The Experimenter's Responsibility

Ultimately the experimenter is the single individual who is accountable for the ethical conduct of the research project. In accepting this responsibility, the researcher carefully weighs the *benefits* and *costs* of the project and then decides whether to conduct it. The new knowledge produced by the project represents the benefit. What about costs? Such factors as time and expense clearly are costs and must be considered. Whether the research will place the participants at risk is a major cost to deal with.

Students doing research as part of the requirements of a course also are responsible for conducting their projects in an ethical manner. Applications to use participants must be submitted to and approved by the appropriate IRB. In most cases the supervising faculty member signs such submissions.

The Participants' Responsibility

Clearly, research participants have numerous, important rights. Let's turn the situation around.

 Do participants also have ethical responsibilities? What should researchers be able to expect from their participants?

Korn (1988) indicated the research participant has the following responsibilities:

1. **Be on time for the research appointment.** The researcher and other participants are inconvenienced when participants are late for an appointment.

2. **Participants have the responsibility to listen carefully to the experimenter and ask questions in order to understand the research.** Such attention and questions are important for the participants to give informed consent and "receive the maximum education benefit from participation" (p. 77).

3. **Participants should take the research seriously and cooperate with the experimenter.** Regardless of the appearance of the research task, participants should take their role seriously and assume the researcher will provide an explanation later.

4. **When the study has been completed, participants share the responsibility for understanding what happened.** "Participants should ask questions that help to clarify the situation and enable them to learn more about the topic and method of research. Participants can be of great help by telling the researcher anything they think might be of interest" (p. 77).

5. **Participants have the responsibility for honoring the researcher's request that they not discuss the study with anyone else who might be a participant.** "Confidentiality works both ways" (p. 77). As part of the debriefing session, the researcher may ask the participants to not discuss the experiment with their friends. The participants are ethically responsible to honor this request; the disclosure of such information can invalidate the results of a research project (see Chapter 5).

Clearly, participants' responsibilities also must be factored into the ethical makeup of a research project. Unfortunately, participants' responsibilities usually receive the least amount of attention. Why? Many students become research participants because they are enrolled in introductory psychology and completion of the course carries some type of research participation requirement. The use of sign-up sheets posted on a "research participant" bulletin board or some other equally impersonal manner of contacting potential participants makes a discussion of participant responsibilities most difficult. The solution appears to rest with the class instructor's obligation to explain and discuss these responsibilities and benefits with his students.

Researchers' Ethical Obligations Once the Research Is Completed

The experimenter's ethical responsibilities do not end when the data are collected and the participants are debriefed. Experimenters are responsible for presenting the results of their research in an ethical manner. The two main problems encountered in this regard are plagiarism and fabrication of data.

Plagiarism

Plagiarism Using someone else's work without giving credit to the original source.

Plagiarism refers to using someone else's work without giving credit to the original author. Certainly, plagiarism is an obvious violation of the ethical standards of psychologists. Although it is difficult to believe that plagiarism occurs among established professionals, it does (Broad, 1980). Unfortunately, plagiarism is not an uncommon occurrence in colleges and universities. Although some students may view plagiarism as an easy way to complete an assignment or term paper, many students have told us that no one had ever explained plagiarism to them. The Department of Psychology at Bishop's University (1994) has clearly summarized what you need to do to avoid plagiarism. They suggested the following:

1. Any part of your paper that contains the exact words of an author must appear in quotation marks, with the author's name, and the date of publication and page number(s) of the source attached.
2. You should not adapt material with only minor changes, such as combining sentences, omitting phrases, changing a few words, or inverting sentence order.
3. If what you have to say is substantially your own words, but you took the facts or ideas from a particular author, then omit the quotation marks and reference with a parenthetical citation such as (Jones, 1949).
4. Always acknowledge secondary sources. (See p. 63)
5. You must reference every statement of fact and every idea or opinion not your own unless the item is part of common knowledge.
6. Do not hand in for credit a paper that is the same as or similar to one you have handed in elsewhere.
7. It is permissible to ask someone to criticize a completed paper before you submit it and to bring to your attention errors in logic, grammar, punctuation, spelling, and expression. However, it is not permissible to have another person rewrite any portion of your paper or to have another person translate into English for you a paper that you have written in another language.
8. Keep rough notes and drafts of your work and photocopies of material not available in your college or university library.

"These days, it's publish or perish."

©2004 Reprinted courtesy Bunny Hoest and Parade Magazine. William Hoest Enterprises, Inc.

In our experience, Guideline 2 is most problematic for students. If you reread this guideline, you will find that even paraphrasing an author's words is considered plagiarism. It is a good idea to read your sources thoroughly but to put them away when you write so you are not tempted to copy or paraphrase. For example, if you paraphrased the last sentence as "It is good to read your sources carefully but to put them away when you write so you will not be tempted to copy," you would be guilty of plagiarism.

Why would a scientist engage in plagiarism? Although the specific reason(s) will vary from individual to individual, the pressure to publish one's research findings probably represents the single greatest cause (Mahoney, 1987). Because one's job security (tenure) or salary increases are often directly tied to the publication record, research and publication may become the central focus in the professional career. In one's haste to prepare articles and build an impressive publication record, it may seem easier and quicker to "borrow" a paragraph here and a paragraph there, especially if writing is not an easy and enjoyable task.

Fabrication of Data

Fabrication of data
Those instances where the experimenter either deliberately alters or creates research data.

Fabrication of data refers to those instances where the experimenter either deliberately changes or alters data that were already gathered or simply makes up data to suit her needs. As with plagiarism, fabrication of data is an obvious ethical violation. Possibly the most famous instance of *apparent* data fabrication involved the famous British psychologist Cyril Burt (1883–1971). Burt's research on twins was influential in supporting the view that childrens' intelligence is largely inherited from their parents. His data went unchallenged for a number of years until researchers began to notice that he reported exactly the same results in different studies. Critics contended that it was very unlikely that exactly the same results would be produced in several different studies. Burt's supporters argued that Burt was elderly and likely forgot which data to present in which report. Unfortunately, scholars will not be able to resolve this debate because Burt's data were discarded shortly after his death. Researchers agree that Burt's publications have little scientific value.

PSYCHOLOGICAL DETECTIVE   What would cause a scientist to fabricate data?

Again, we can point to the pressure to "publish or perish." Remember, we use synthetic statements in our research hypothesis; hence, there is always a chance that a project will not turn out as we predicted. When the data do not turn out as we had hoped, there may be a temptation to "fix" the data in order to bring them in line with our predictions and theory. Certainly, it is much easier (and quicker) to change a few numbers here and there than it is to redo an entire experiment. It does not seem to be a very great step to go from changing a few numbers to eliminating the experiment altogether and fabricating all the data.

The consequences of having false information in the body of scientific knowledge should be obvious to you. By falsifying a research finding, the psychologist actually encourages other researchers to conduct projects on a topic that is doomed to failure! The expenditures in time, effort, participants, and money can be enormous. And because considerable research is supported by federal grants, the costs to the taxpayers can be substantial! Because data form the cornerstone of research reports, ethical conduct is of vital importance.

Lying with Statistics

In addition to the sanctions against plagiarism and the fabrication of data, researchers have a responsibility to present their results in an unbiased manner. On first glance, this responsibility may seem rather straightforward and inconsequential. After all, results are results, aren't they? The answer to that question is "yes and no." Yes, the basic results are not going to change; however, researchers exercise a great deal of individual choice and creativity in deciding what to present and how to present it. For example, a researcher could choose to selectively leave out important data and highlight other, possibly inconsequential, data. The researcher's choice of what to present and how to present it is so important in determining the conclusion your intended audience reaches, that Darrell Huff published a book entitled *How to Lie with Statistics* (Huff, 1954). In this book he described numerous "questionable" statistical practices designed to influence the consumer of this information. We will have more to say about the presentation of statistical results throughout the remainder of this book. For now, you should be aware that researchers have the responsibility to present their results in an unbiased manner. Like a good detective, you need to be sensitive to those instances in which evidence may be misleading or missing.

Citing Your References Correctly

When other people read your research report and note the references you used to support the research idea, the hypothesis you are testing, and your interpretation of the data, they assume that you have actually read each reference that you cite. This

TABLE 3-3	APA ETHICAL STANDARDS 8.10–8.15— REPORTING AND PUBLISHING YOUR RESEARCH

8.10 Reporting Research Results
(a) Psychologists do not fabricate data.

(b) If psychologists discover significant errors in their published data, they take reasonable steps to correct such errors in a correction, retraction, erratum, or other appropriate publication means.

8.11 Plagiarism
Psychologists do not present portions of another's work or data as their own, even if the other work or data source is cited occasionally.

8.12 Publication Credit
(a) Psychologists take responsibility and credit, including authorship credit, only for work they have actually performed or to which they have substantially contributed.

(b) Principal authorship and other publication credits accurately reflect the relative scientific or professional contributions of the individuals involved, regardless of their relative status. Mere possession of an institutional position, such as department chair, does not justify authorship credit. Minor contributions to the research or to the writing for publications are acknowledged appropriately, such as in footnotes or in an introductory statement.

(c) Except under exceptional circumstances, a student is listed as principal author on any multiple-authored article that is substantially based on the student's doctoral dissertation. Faculty advisors discuss publication credit with students as early as feasible and throughout the research and publication process as appropriate.

8.13 Duplicate Publication of Data
Psychologists do not publish, as original data, data that have been previously published. This does not preclude republishing data when they are accompanied by proper acknowledgment.

8.14 Sharing Research Data for Verification
(a) After research results are published, psychologists do not withhold the data on which their conclusions are based from other competent professionals who seek to verify the substantive claims through reanalysis and who intend to use such data only for that purpose, provided that the confidentiality of the participants can be protected and unless legal rights concerning proprietary data preclude their release. This does not preclude psychologists from requiring that such individuals or groups be responsible for costs associated with the provision of such information.

(b) Psychologists who request data from other psychologists to verify the substantive claims through reanalysis may use shared data only for the declared purpose. Requesting psychologists obtain prior written agreement for all other uses of the data.

8.15 Reviewers
Psychologists who review material submitted for presentation, publication, grant, or research proposal review respect the confidentiality of and the proprietary rights in such information of those who submitted it.

Source: American Psychological Association. (2002). Ethical principles of psychologists and code of conduct. *American Psychologist, 57*, 1060–1073. Reprinted with permission.

assumption makes good sense; if you designed a research project to test a theoretical prediction, then you should read about that theory firsthand.

On the other hand, there may be occasions when you *read about* an interesting and relevant piece of research and you simply cannot acquire a copy of the original report. Perhaps your library does not carry the journal in which this article was published, and you cannot obtain the paper on interlibrary loan. Lacking the author's address, you are at a standstill. Perhaps the research has not been published. What should you do when you cannot obtain a copy of the original report? If the paper is from a journal to which you do not have access, it may be tempting to cite and list this reference *as if* you had actually read the original. We caution you against adopting this practice; it is the researcher's ethical responsibility to cite and list *only* those works that have been read. In this instance you should cite the *secondary source* you are using.

Don't despair, there is a way you can include those unobtainable references in your research report. Here's how it works. Assume that you read a 1999 article by Smith and Davis that *described and referenced* a research project that Brown conducted in 1984. You would like to cite the paper by Brown, but you are unable to obtain it. In this instance you should cite the reference as follows:

Brown (as cited in Smith & Davis, 1999) found that . . .

In the reference section you would list only the Smith and Davis reference (the one you actually read). The appropriate way to cite and list references is covered in detail in Chapter 20. We encourage you to examine this material now. We agree that there are a lot of details to master when it comes to citing and listing references; please work hard on this skill. Sherlock Holmes's comment that "It has long been an axiom of mine that the little things are infinitely the most important" (Doyle, 1927, p. 194) is most appropriate in this context.

These, and other, APA ethical standards that are related to the presentation and publication of research data are shown in Table 3-3 (see p. 62).

Now, we do not want to leave you with the impression that plagiarism, fabrication of data, and misrepresentation of results and references characterize all or even many scientists; they do not. The vast majority of scientists enjoy designing and conducting their own research projects to see if they can unlock nature's secrets. However, it takes only a few unethical individuals to give science a bad name. We hope you will not be among the ranks of the unethical.

REVIEW SUMMARY

1. It is the experimenter's responsibility to ensure that a research project is conducted in an ethical manner.
2. The World War II atrocities perpetrated by Nazi doctors, the Willowbrook hepatitis project, the Tuskegee syphilis project, and psychological research such as Milgram's obedience studies have increased ethical concerns and awareness.
3. The APA has developed a set of Ethical Standards for the conduct of research with human participants.
4. Although the researcher should try to avoid it, using deception may be justified in order to yield unbiased responses.

5. Informed consent is a signed statement indicating that participants understand the nature of the experiment and agree to participate in it.
6. **Participants at risk** are individuals whose participation in an experiment places them under some emotional and/or physical risk. **Participants at minimal risk** are individuals whose participation in an experiment results in no harmful consequences.
7. The experimenter explains the nature and purpose of the experiment to the participants during the **debriefing session**. Although the debriefing session is designed to counteract any negative effects of research participation, it also can provide the experimenter with valuable information about the research procedures that were employed.
8. Ethical standards also exist for the conduct of research using animals.
9. The **Institutional Review Board** (**IRB**) is a group of the researcher's scientific and nonscientific peers who evaluate research proposals for adherence to ethical guidelines and procedures.
10. In addition to their rights and protection, participants also have several responsibilities.
11. Researchers have a responsibility to present their findings in an ethical manner. **Plagiarism** (the use of another's work without giving proper credit) and **fabrication of data** are the chief ethical infractions encountered in the presentation of research results.

CHECK YOUR PROGRESS

1. Describe the four projects that raised concern about the ethical conduct of research.
2. What aspects of the research endeavor did the Nuremberg Code stress?
3. In what types of research situations might the use of deception be justified? If deception is used, how can the need to provide "informed consent" be satisfied?
4. Participants in a research project who are placed under some emotional or physical risk are classified as:
   a. participants at risk
   b. participants at minimal risk
   c. volunteer participants
   d. participants at no risk
5. The main purpose of the _____ is to explain the nature of an experiment and remove any undesirable consequences.
   a. informed consent form
   b. Institutional Review Board
   c. Ethical Principles of Research with Human Participants
   d. debriefing session
6. Describe the guidelines for the ethical use of animals in psychological research.
7. What is an IRB? Describe the composition of the typical IRB. What responsibility does an IRB have?

8. With regard to the conduct of research, what is the ethical responsibility of the experimenter?
9. Distinguish between plagiarism and fabrication of data. What sets of pressures are responsible for these unethical actions?

KEY TERMS

Participants at risk, *53*

Participants at minimal risk, *53*

Debriefing session, *54*

Institutional Review Board (IRB), *57*

Plagiarism, *59*

Fabrication of data, *60*

LOOKING AHEAD

At this point you should have a good idea why psychologists value research so much, where they obtain their research ideas, and that ethical principles govern the conduct of research. In the next chapter we will begin our study of the various statistical procedures that psychologists use to make sense of and analyze their research data.

4

Basic Statistical Concepts, Frequency Tables, Graphs, Frequency Distributions, and Measures of Central Tendency

Just as detectives seek out clues and leads and gather data to help solve a case, psychologists also gather data to help answer research questions. Once they gather the evidence, detectives need to determine if it is real (meaningful). Likewise, in later chapters we will examine several statistical methods used to determine if the results of an experiment are meaningful (significant). The term *significant* is used to describe those instances where the statistical results are likely to have been caused by manipulation of the IV and not by other factors.

In this chapter we begin our examination of statistics. Keep in mind that we will be presenting statistics in the context of tools that psychologists use to help them with their research. This approach has allowed us to place the chapters on statistical procedures in close proximity to the appropriate research methods and topics. Thus, the statistics chapters are spread out, and you should not be overwhelmed by having to learn and digest a large number of mathematical concepts, terms, formulas, and applications all at once. We sincerely hope this approach will assist those of you who have convinced yourselves that you have a "math phobia." We are confident that you can master this material. Countless students have accomplished this feat in the past; if they can do it, so can you!

The Two Branches of Statistics

> **Statistics** Branch of mathematics that involves the collection, analysis, and interpretation of data.

Statistics is a branch of mathematics that involves the collection, analysis, and interpretation of data. The two main branches of statistics assist your decisions in different ways. We use **descriptive statistics** when we want to *summarize* a set or distribution of numbers in order to communicate their essential characteristics. One of these essential characteristics is a measure of the typical, or representative score, called a *measure of central tendency*. We discuss measures of central tendency at the end of this chapter. A second essential characteristic that we need to know about a distribution is how much variability or spread exists in the scores. We will have more to say about measures of variability in Chapter 6. **Inferential statistics** are used to analyze data after you have conducted an experiment to determine whether your independent variable had a significant effect. We will have much more to say about inferential statistics beginning in Chapter 9. However, before we start our discussion of how and why psychological researchers use statistics, we need to examine the measurements on which they are based.

> **Descriptive statistics** Procedures used to summarize a set of data.

> **Inferential statistics** Procedures used to analyze data after an experiment is completed. Used to determine if the independent variable has a significant effect.

Measurement

> **Measurement** The assignment of symbols to events according to a set of rules.

We can define **measurement** as the assignment of symbols to events according to a set of rules. Your grade on a test is a symbol that stands for your performance; the instructor assigned it according to a particular set of rules (grading standards).

Scales of Measurement

Scale of measurement
A set of measurement rules.

The *particular* set of rules used in assigning a symbol to the event in question is known as a **scale of measurement**. The four scales of measurement that are of interest to psychologists are nominal, ordinal, interval, and ratio scales. How you choose to measure the dependent variable (i.e., which scale of measurement you use) directly determines the type of statistical test you can use to evaluate your data once you complete your research project; hence, it is very important that you understand the scales of measurement.

Nominal scale A scale of measurement in which events are assigned to categories.

Nominal Scale The **nominal scale** is a simple classification system. For example, if you are categorizing the furniture in a classroom as tables or chairs, you are using a nominal scale of measurement. Likewise, recording responses to an item on a questionnaire as either *correct* or *incorrect* reflects the use of a nominal scale of measurement. The items being evaluated are assigned to mutually exclusive categories.

Ordinal scale A scale of measurement that permits events to be rank ordered.

Ordinal Scale When the events in question can be rank ordered, you are using an **ordinal scale** of measurement. Notice that we indicated *only* that the events under consideration could be rank ordered; we did not indicate that the intervals separating the units were comparable. Although we can rank the top four winners in a track meet (i.e., first, second, third, fourth), this rank ordering does not tell us anything concerning how far apart these athletes were. Perhaps it was almost a dead heat for first and second; maybe the first-place winner was far ahead of the second-place finisher.

Interval scale A scale of measurement that permits rank ordering of events with the assumption of equal intervals between adjacent events.

Interval Scale When the events in question can be rank ordered and equal intervals separate adjacent events, an **interval scale** should be used. For example, the temperatures on a Fahrenheit thermometer form an interval scale; rank ordering has been achieved *and* the difference between any two adjacent temperatures is the same: one degree. Notice that the interval scale does not have a true zero point, however. When you reach the "zero" point on a Fahrenheit thermometer, does temperature cease to exist? No, it is simply very cold. Likewise, scores on tests such as the SAT and ACT are interval scale measures.

Assume you are on a college admissions committee and you are reviewing applications. Each applicant's ACT score forms an integral part of your review. You have just come across an applicant who scored zero on the verbal subtest. What does this score tell you?

The score of zero should not be interpreted as meaning that this individual has absolutely no verbal ability. Because ACT scores are interval scale measurements, there is no true zero. Hence, a score of zero should be interpreted as meaning that the individual is very low in that ability. The same could be said for zero scores on the wide variety of tests, questionnaires, and personality inventories that psychologists routinely use in personality research. The presence of a true zero is characteristic only of the ratio scale of measurement.

> **Ratio scale** A scale of measurement that permits rank ordering of events with the assumptions of equal intervals between adjacent events and a true zero point.

Ratio Scale   The **ratio scale** of measurement takes the interval scale one step further. Just as the interval scale, the ratio scale permits the rank ordering of scores with the assumption of equal intervals between them. However, it also assumes the presence of a true zero point. Physical measurements, such as the amplitude or intensity of sound or light, are ratio measurements. These measurements can be rank ordered, and there are equal intervals between adjacent scores. However, when a sensitive measuring device reads zero, there is nothing there. Because of the true zero point, the ratio scale allows you to make ratio comparisons, such as twice as much or half as much. Figure 4-1 summarizes the four scales of measurement.

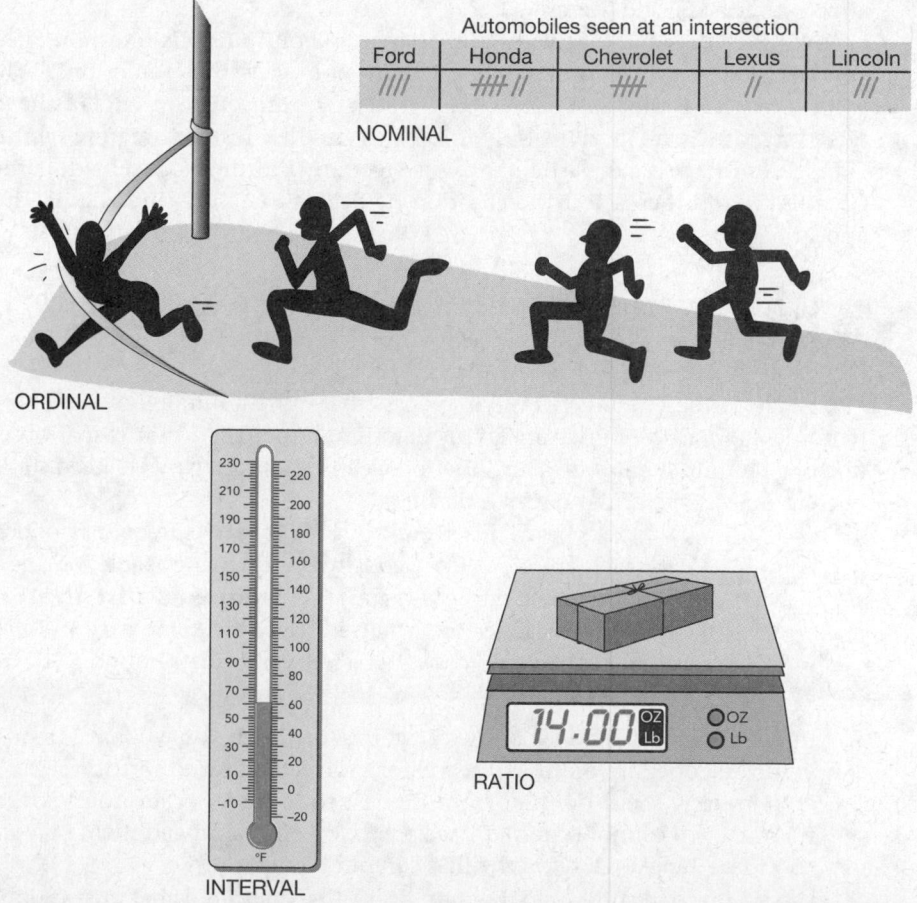

FIGURE 4-1   NOMINAL, ORDINAL, INTERVAL, AND RATIO SCALES OF MEASUREMENT.

Our discussion of scales of measurement has progressed from the nominal scale, which provides the least amount of information, to the ratio scale, which provides the greatest amount of information. When psychologists evaluate changes in the DV, they use a scale of measurement that will provide the most information; frequently, they select interval scales because they often do not use measurements that have a true zero. Scores on a personality test would be an example of an interval scale of measurement. Now that you know about the various scales of measurement, let's examine some of the things researchers may choose to do with the numbers (data) they collect.

Frequency Distributions

Jennifer Gonzales and Miriam Castillo, students at St. Edward's University (Austin, TX), and their faculty advisor, Alan Swinkles, studied *contagious emotions*—emotions that are transmitted from one person to another. For example, you may become happy simply because your friend is happy. Gonzales, Castillo, and Swinkles (2002) reported that the six most contagious emotions were happiness (H), excitement (E), sadness (S), anger (A), fear (F), and interest (I).

Now, let's assume that you have decided to continue this research. Specifically, you are interested in how students at your school view these emotions. Which one will they select as the most contagious? Thirty-five introductory students have volunteered to participate in your study in order to fulfill a research requirement for their course. You have each participant complete an informed consent document (see Chapter 3) and then select the emotion he believes is most contagious. The results appear below:

H, E, H, F, A, E, S, I, H, F, H, H, F, A, I, H, S, H, F, A, H, A, S, H, E, H, F, E, I, S, E, H, A, H, F

What do these results tell us? It appears that quite a number of students selected happiness (H) as the most contagious emotion. Other than that casual observation, nothing definite stands out. This situation clearly shows us why we need statistics; we need to make sense of our research results.

> **Frequency distribution**
> A table showing how often each score occurred.

Let's begin this process by looking at the frequency of occurrence for each emotion. If we construct a frequency table, our task will be simplified and our results clearer. A **frequency distribution** shows how often each score occurred. Here are some easy-to-follow steps that will help you construct a frequency distribution:

1. In one column make a list of the categories for which you will have frequencies. If your categories are ordinal, interval, or ratio (e.g., year of birth, weight, age, IQ, etc.) arrange them in order from highest to lowest. Because our categories are nominal and cannot be ranked (see p. 68), we have arranged them in alphabetical order (see Table 4-1). Label the first column "categories."
2. Create a second column to the right of the first column. Label this column "tally." Create a third column to the right of the second. Label this column "frequencies."

TABLE 4-1   CONSTRUCTING A FREQUENCY DISTRIBUTION

Original data: H, E, H, F, A; E, S, I, H, F, H, H,

F, A, I, H, S, H, F, A, H, A, H, S

E, H, F, E, I, S, E, H, A, H, F

FREQUENCY DISTRIBUTION

(1)	(2)	(3)	(4) PERCENTAGE (FREQUENCY/
CATEGORIES	TALLY	FREQUENCIES	TOTAL × 100)
Anger (A)	₦₦	5	14.29
Excitement (E)	₦₦	5	14.29
Fear (F)	₦₦ I	6	17.14
Happiness (H)	₦₦ ₦₦ II	12	34.29
Interest (I)	III	3	8.57
Sadness (S)	IIII	4	11.42
Total	35	35	100.00

STEPS:

1. Tally original data (Column 2).

2. Convert tallies to frequencies (Column 3).

3. Divide each frequency by total and multiply by 100 to determine percentage (Column 4).

3. As shown in Table 4-1, examine each score and make a tally for each score in the appropriate location in the tally column. Convert the tallies to frequencies and record them in the frequency column.

4. Calculate the percentage of occurrence for each category by dividing the frequency for each category by the total number of scores and then multiplying by 100. This figure appears in the final column.

5. You may want to add a fifth column that shows the cumulative percentages. The cumulative percentages are also known as *percentiles*.

PSYCHOLOGICAL DETECTIVE   What is the total number of scores in our example? What can we learn from this frequency table?

If you said that the total number of scores was 35 because 35 students participated in this research, then you are correct. The percentages tell us that the greatest number

(34.29%) of participants chose *happiness*, whereas only 8.57% selected *interest*. The remainder of the percentages fell between these two extremes.

Grouped Frequency Distributions

Grouped frequency distribution A table showing how often scores occurred in larger (combined) categories or intervals.

Once you have developed your frequency table, you may find there still are many scores to deal with and it is still difficult to get a clear picture of the data. By grouping frequencies and creating a **grouped frequency distribution**, you can reduce the number of categories and the meaning of your data becomes clearer. If you can order your categories numerically from lowest to highest, then you may want to group your frequencies into intervals. For example, whereas the original frequency distribution may list each score for the last psychology test, a grouped frequency distribution might list the scores in the intervals 90–100, 80–89, 70–79, 60–69, and below 60. Obviously we cannot group our contagious emotion data into intervals.

PSYCHOLOGICAL DETECTIVE Is it possible to create a grouped frequency table for the contagious emotion data we have been considering? If so, what categories might you group the six emotions into?

One possible approach would be to categorize the six emotions as either positive or negative. Using this system, we could assign happiness, excitement, and interest to the positive category and sadness, anger, and fear to the negative category. This grouped frequency table appears in Table 4-2. You can see that our participants believed the positive emotions (57.15%) were more contagious than the negative emotions (42.85%). So, the grouped frequency table does provide additional information concerning the data we have gathered; the students selected positive emotions more often than negative emotions. On the other hand, you should keep in mind that you pay a price for the increased clarity you gain with a grouped frequency distribution. For example, even though the grouped frequency distribution shows the percentage of participants who selected positive emotions, it no longer shows the percentages for each of the specific emotions. The nature of your research question and the type of data you need to answer that question will help you decide whether you need to use a grouped frequency distribution.

TABLE 4-2 GROUPED FREQUENCY DISTRIBUTION FOR CONTAGIOUS EMOTIONS DATA

CATEGORIES	FREQUENCY	PERCENTAGE
Positive emotions (excitement, happiness, and interest)	20	57.15%
Negative Emotions (anger, fear, and sadness)	15	42.85%

Keep in mind that we created our grouped frequency distribution strictly as an example. In reality, you probably would choose to use more than two grouped intervals, but how many intervals should you create? Researchers typically agree that the optimum number of grouped intervals is between 5 and 15. The next question you need to consider is how many categories should be grouped in each interval? In some instances, such as our contagious emotions data, the nature of the data may dictate the number of categories to be included in each interval. In those cases where the data do not provide clear guidelines, you should make sure that the number of categories in an interval is a whole number (e.g., 2, 3, 5, 6, 10).

REVIEW SUMMARY

1. **Statistics** involves the collection, analysis, and interpretation of data. **Descriptive statistics** are concerned with summarizing a set of data. Researchers use **inferential statistics** to analyze experimental data they have collected.
2. **Measurement** is the assignment of symbols to events according to a set of rules. A **scale of measurement** is a particular set of measurement rules.
3. A **nominal scale** is a simple classification system, whereas events can be rank ordered when an **ordinal scale** is used. Equal intervals separate rank-ordered events in an **interval scale**. The addition of a true zero to an interval scale results in a **ratio scale**.
4. **Descriptive statistics**, which summarize sets of numbers, include measures of central tendency and variability.
5. Researchers often create a **frequency distribution** to show how often each score occurred.
6. A **grouped frequency distribution** shows how often scores occur in larger (combined) categories or intervals.

CHECK YOUR PROGRESS

1. What kind of statistics summarize a set of numbers so we can understand and talk about them more intelligently?
   a. summary   b. normalized   c. inferential   d. descriptive
2. What kind of statistics are used to analyze data after an experiment is conducted?
   a. summary   b. normalized   c. inferential   d. descriptive
3. A simple classification system is best associated with a(n) _____ scale.
   a. ordinal   b. interval   c. nominal   d. ratio
4. Events are rank ordered and have equal spacing between them in a(n) _____ scale.
   a. ordinal   b. interval   c. nominal   d. ratio
5. Rank ordering, equal intervals, and a true zero are best associated with a(n) _____ scale.
   a. ordinal   b. interval   c. nominal   d. ratio

6. Researchers often create a _____ to show the distribution of each score.

   a. nominal scale
   b. inferential statistic
   c. frequency distribution
   d. descriptive statistic

7. A _____ shows how often scores occur in combined categories.

   a. ordinal scale
   b. inferential statistic
   c. descriptive statistic
   d. grouped frequency distribution

Graphing Your Results

Have you heard the old saying that "a picture is worth a thousand words"? That saying can be very true when you are trying to report statistical findings. If you have only one or two sets of scores, the task is simple: You can report the relevant values as part of the research paper or report you prepare.

What if you are dealing with several groups or sets of numbers? Now the task is complicated and the inclusion of several numbers in a paragraph of text might be confusing. In such cases you can use a graph or figure to your advantage. A picture may well be worth a thousand words. It is not uncommon to see a detective use a chart or graph to help make a point in the solution of a case. In preparing a research report, psychologists also use graphs effectively. There are several types of graphs for the researcher to choose from. Your choice of graphs will be determined by which one depicts your results most effectively *and* by the scale of measurement you used. For example, if you used a nominal scale of measurement, then you would likely use a pie chart or a histogram. We had nominal data with our contagious emotions research. Let's see how it would look if we graphed it.

> **Pie chart** Graphical representation of the percentage allocated to each alternative as a slice of a circular pie.

Pie Chart

If you are dealing with percentages that total 100%, then the familiar pie chart may be a good choice. The **pie chart** depicts the percentage represented by each alternative as a slice of a circular pie; the larger the slice, the greater the percentage. Figure 4-2 shows what our

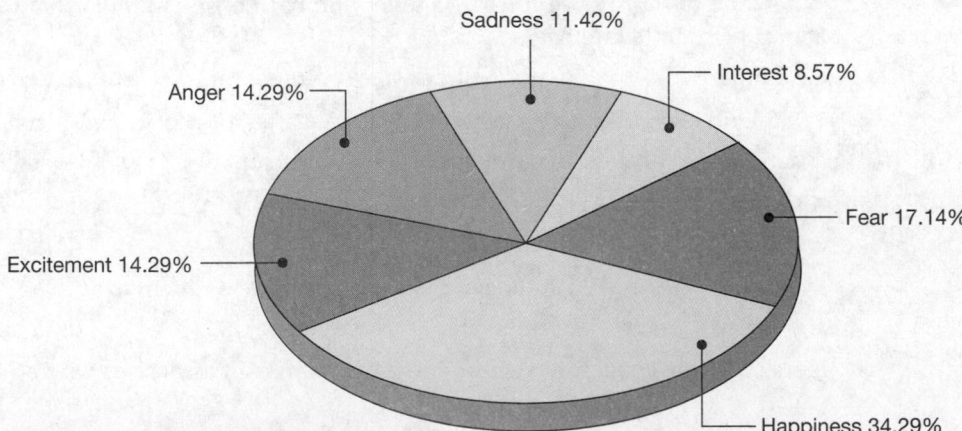

FIGURE 4-2 PIE CHART DEPICTING CONTAGIOUS EMOTIONS DATA.

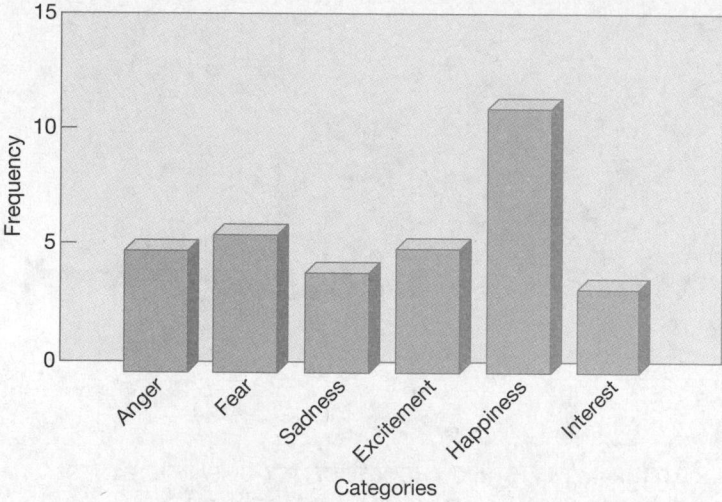

FIGURE 4-3 **BAR GRAPH OF CONTAGIOUS EMOTIONS DATA.**

original frequency table of contagious emotions looks like when it's plotted as a pie chart.

Bar Graph

The **bar graph** presents data in terms of frequencies per category. You will construct a bar graph when you are using nominal (or *qualitative*) categories. Qualitative categories are ones that *cannot* be numerically ordered from lowest to highest; only *quantitative* categories can be ordered in this manner. For example, the contagious emotions we studied are qualitative categories. There is no way to numerically order them.

Figure 4-3 shows a bar graph of our participants' preferences for the six contagious emotions. Placing a space between the bars lets the reader know that we are reporting qualitative categories (*nominal* data). You can see at a glance how many participants preferred each category. Think of how many words it would take to write about these results versus presenting them in a graph!

> **Bar graph** A graph in which the frequency for each category of a qualitative variable is represented as a vertical column or bar. The columns of a bar graph do not touch.

> **Histogram** A graph in which the frequency for each category of a quantitative variable is represented as a vertical column that touches the adjacent column.

Histogram

We also use the **histogram** to present our data in terms of frequencies per category. However, you must have *quantitative* categories in order to construct a histogram.

PSYCHOLOGICAL DETECTIVE Put your thinking cap on and see if you can describe what we mean by the term *quantitative categories*.

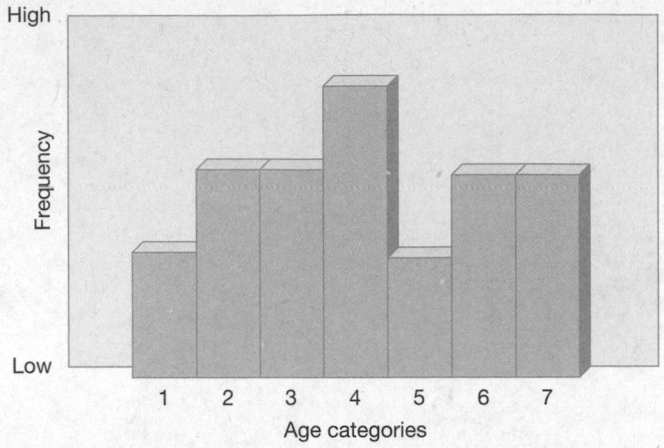

FIGURE 4-4   HISTOGRAM DEPICTING THE FREQUENCY OF PARTICIPANTS IN VARIOUS AGE CATEGORIES IN A DEVELOPMENTAL PSYCHOLOGY RESEARCH PROJECT.

If you went back and reread the section on bar graphs, you know that quantitative categories are categories that can be numerically ordered from lowest to highest. Because our contagious emotion research used qualitative categories, we depicted these data as a bar graph in Figure 4-3. However, because you can order ages from lowest to highest, they are quantitative categories and are perfect for the development of a histogram. Figure 4-4 shows a histogram for the age categories of participants in a developmental psychology research project. Because the histogram uses quantitative categories, the sides of the adjacent bars, unlike the bar graph, should touch each other (compare Figures 4-3 and 4-4).

Frequency polygon A graph that is constructed by placing a dot in the center of each bar of a histogram and then connecting the dots.

Frequency Polygon

If we mark the middle of the crosspiece of each bar in a histogram (see Figure 4-5A) with a dot, connect the dots, and remove the bars, we have constructed a **frequency polygon** (see Figure 4-5B).

The frequency polygon, like the histogram, displays the frequency of each number or score. The only differences between these two graphs are the use of bars in the histogram and the use of connected dots in the frequency polygon.

Line graph A graph that is frequently used to depict the results of an experiment.

Line Graph

Ordinate The vertical or Y axis of a graph.

Researchers often present the results of psychological experiments in a **line graph**. When constructing a line graph, start with two axes (or *dimensions*). The vertical, or Y, axis is known as the **ordinate**; the horizontal, or X, axis is known as the **abscissa** (see Figure 4-6). Our scores or data (the DV) are plotted on the ordinate. The values of the variable we manipulated (the IV) are plotted on the abscissa.

Abscissa The horizontal or X axis of a graph.

FIGURE 4-5   THE FREQUENCY POLYGON IS CONSTRUCTED BY PLACING A DOT IN THE CENTER OF EACH BAR OF A HISTOGRAM AND CONNECTING THE DOTS (PART A), REMOVING THE BARS AND EXTENDING EACH END TO THE BASE LINE (PART B).

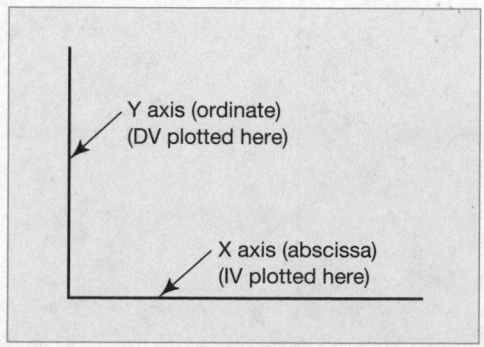

FIGURE 4-6   THE ORDINATE OR Y AXIS AND ABSCISSA OR X AXIS.

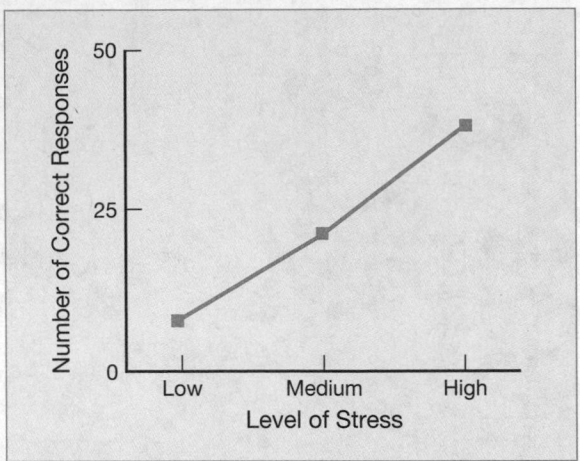

FIGURE 4-7 RESULTS OF A HYPOTHETICAL EXPERIMENT INVESTIGATING THE EFFECTS OF STRESS ON CORRECT RESPONDING IN AIR TRAFFIC CONTROLLERS.

How tall should the Y axis be? How long should the X axis be? A good rule of thumb is for the Y axis to be approximately *two-thirds* as tall as the X axis is long (see Figures 4-6 and 4-7). Other configurations will give a distorted picture of the data. For example, if the ordinate is considerably shorter, differences between groups or treatments will be obscured (see Figure 4-8A), whereas lengthening the ordinate tends to exaggerate differences (see Figure 4-8B).

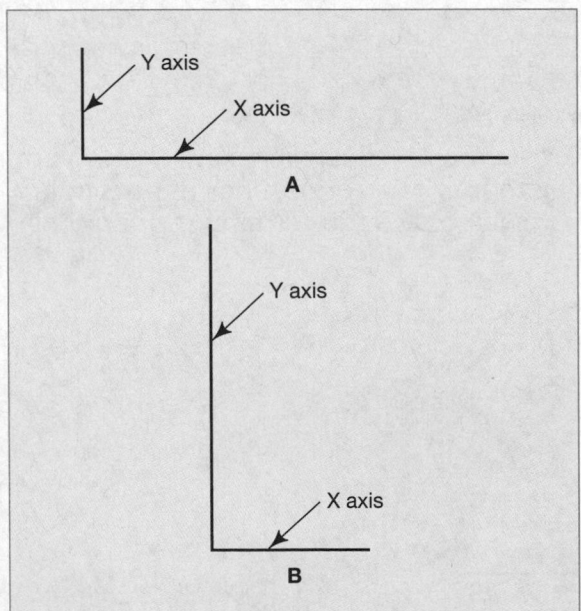

FIGURE 4-8 ALTERING THE X (ABSCISSA) OR Y (ORDINATE) AXIS CAN DISTORT THE RESULTS OF AN EXPERIMENT.

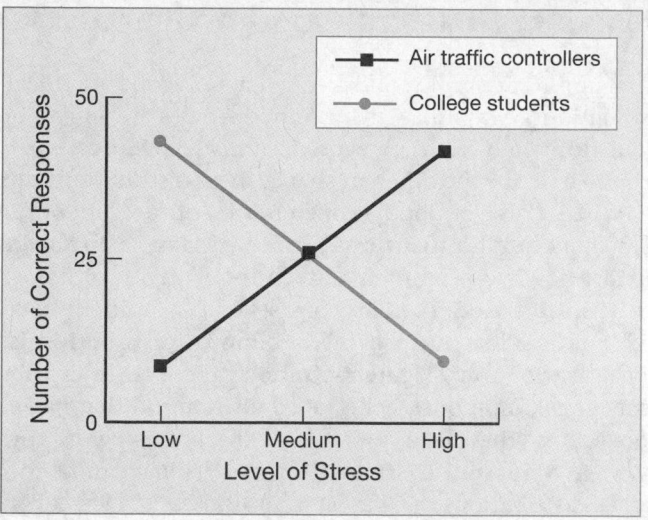

FIGURE 4-9   RESULTS OF A HYPOTHETICAL EXPERIMENT INVESTIGATING THE EFFECTS OF STRESS ON CORRECT RESPONDING IN AIR TRAFFIC CONTROLLERS AND COLLEGE STUDENTS.

In Figure 4-7 we plotted the results of a hypothetical experiment in which the effects of different levels of stress on making correct landing decisions by air traffic controllers were evaluated. As you can see, as stress increased, the number of correct responses increased. What if we had tested two different groups of participants: college students and air traffic controllers? How would we display the results of both groups on the same graph? All we need to do is add the data points for the second group and a legend or box that identifies the groups (see Figure 4-9).

Now we can see at a glance that the air traffic controllers, whose occupation is very stressful, made more correct responses as their stress level increased, whereas the converse was true for the college students.

When you graph the results of an experiment with more than one variable, how do you know which IV to plot on the abscissa? Although there is no fixed rule, a good guideline is to plot the variable that has the greatest number of levels on the abscissa. Thus, in Figure 4-9 three levels of stress were plotted on the abscissa rather than plotting the two levels of participants.

PSYCHOLOGICAL DETECTIVE   Why would you choose to plot the IV that has the greatest number of levels on the abscissa?

By plotting the IV that has the greater number of levels on the abscissa, you reduce the number of lines that will appear on your graph. The fewer lines there are, the less difficulty you will have when interpreting your graph. For example, had we plotted the type of participants in our stress experiment on the abscissa, then Figure 4-9 would have had three lines, one for each level of stress. We will discuss the accepted APA format for preparing graphs and tables in Chapter 20.

Frequency Distributions and Their Shapes

Unimodal distribution
A frequency distribution that has one high point or prominent category.

Bimodal distribution
A frequency distribution that has two high points or prominent categories.

Multimodal distribution A frequency distribution having several high points or prominent categories. (Technically, a bimodal distribution is a multimodal distribution.)

Normal distribution
A symmetrical, unimodal, bell-shaped distribution that has half of the scores above the mean and half of the scores below the mean.

Histograms, bar graphs, and frequency polygons graphically depict distributions—ways in which the frequencies are spread out or distributed in the various categories. Statisticians use several specific terms to describe the different shapes these distributions can assume.

When a distribution has one prominent category or high point, researchers call it a **unimodal distribution**. A **bimodal distribution** has two prominent categories or high points, whereas as **multimodal distribution** has several prominent categories or high points. (Strictly speaking, a bimodal distribution is a multimodal distribution.) Figure 4-10 shows these three distributions. A symmetrical, unimodal, bell-shaped distribution that has half of the scores above the mean and half of the scores below the mean is known as a **normal distribution**. We will have more to say about normal distributions in Chapter 6 (p. 133).

Technically, the frequencies in the two high points must be exactly the same for this distribution to be called a bimodal distribution. Likewise, technically, the frequencies in the high points of a multimodal distribution must be exactly the same. Despite these restrictions, researchers rarely demand exact equivalence of the high points in bimodal and multimodal distributions; a description of the general shape of the distribution appears to serve their purpose.

PSYCHOLOGICAL DETECTIVE   What would the distribution look like if the frequency in all categories was the same?

Rectangular distribution A frequency distribution in which each category contains the same number of scores.

If the frequency in all categories is the same, then there will be no prominent category or high point. As you can see in Figure 4-11, this distribution looks like a rectangle; hence, it is called a **rectangular distribution**.

Frequently, the data you plot on a graph, especially a line graph depicting the results of an experiment, will be the typical score, or measure of central tendency, from your data set. We will look at the various measures of central tendency next.

Measures of Central Tendency

Measures of central tendency tell us about the typical score in a distribution. The three measures of central tendency are the mode, the median, and the mean.

Unimodal distribution

Bimodal distribution

Multimodal distribution

FIGURE 4-10   UNIMODAL, BIMODAL, AND MULTIMODAL DISTRIBUTIONS.

Rectangular distribution

FIGURE 4-11   RECTANGULAR DISTRIBUTION.

Mode

> **Mode** The score in a distribution that occurs most often.

The **mode** is the number or event that occurs most frequently in a distribution. If students reported the following work hours per week:

12, 15, 20, 20, 20,

the mode would be 20.

Although you can calculate the mode for any scale of measurement, it is the only measure of central tendency that you can calculate if you have nominal data.

Median

> **Median** The number that divides a distribution in half.

The **median** is the number or score that divides the distribution into equal halves (i.e., the median is the 50th percentile). To be able to calculate the median, you must first rank order the scores. Thus, if you started with the following scores:

56, 15, 12, 20, 17,

you would need to rank order them as follows:

12, 15, 17, 20, 56.

Then it's an easy task to determine that 17 is the median (mdn).

What if you have an even number of scores, as in the following distribution?

1, 2, 3, 4, 5, 6

In this case the median lies halfway between the two middle scores (3 and 4). Thus, the median would be 3.5, halfway between 3 and 4. You can calculate the median for ordinal, interval, and ratio data.

Mean

> **Mean** The arithmetic average of a set of numbers. Found by adding all the scores in a set and then dividing by the number of scores.

The **mean** is defined as the arithmetic average. The traditional mathematical symbol for the mean is $\overline{X}$; however, more current usage and the publication format of the APA favors M as the symbol for the mean and we will use this symbol. (Your instructor may prefer that you use $\overline{X}$.) To find the mean we add all the scores in the distribution and then divide by the number of scores we added. For example, assume we start with the following:

12, 15, 18, 19, 16.

We use the Greek letter sigma, Σ, to indicate the sum. If X stands for the numbers in our distribution, then ΣX means to add the numbers in our distribution. If N

stands for the number of scores in the distribution, then the formula for the mean would be:

$$M = \Sigma X/N.$$

For the five numbers listed, $\Sigma X = 80$ and $N = 5$. Therefore,

$$M = \Sigma X/N = 80/5 = 16.$$

You can calculate the mean for interval and ratio data, but not for nominal and ordinal data.

Choosing a Measure of Central Tendency

Which measure of central tendency should you choose? The answer to that question depends on the type of information you are seeking and the scale of measurement you are using. If you want to know which score occurred most often, then the mode is the choice. However, the mode may not be very representative of the other scores in your distribution. Consider the following distribution:

1, 2, 3, 4, 5, 11, 11

In this case the mode is 11. Because *all* the other scores are considerably smaller, the mode does not accurately describe the typical score in this instance.

The median may be a better choice to serve as the representative score because it takes into account all the data in the distribution. However, there are drawbacks with this choice. The median treats all scores alike. Differences in magnitude are not taken into account. Thus, the median for *both* of the following distributions is 14:

Distribution 1: 11, 12, 13, **14**, 15, 16, 17   **mdn = 14**
Distribution 2: 7, 8, 9, **14**, 23, 24, 25   **mdn = 14**

When we calculate the mean, however, we take the *value* of each number into account. Although the medians for the two distributions above are the same, the means (M) are not:

Distribution 1: 11, 12, 13, 14, 15, 16, 17
$\Sigma X = 98$ $M = 98/7$ $M = 14.00$
Distribution 2: 7, 8, 9, 14, 23, 24, 25
$\Sigma X = 110$ $M = 110/7$ $M = 15.71$

The fact that the mean of Distribution 2 is larger than that of Distribution 1 indicates that the value of each individual score has been taken into account.

Because the mean takes the value of each score into account, it usually provides a more accurate picture of the typical score and is the measure of central tendency favored by psychologists. However, there are instances when the mean may be misleading. Consider the following distribution of charitable donations:

Charitable Donations: $1, 1, 1, 5, 10, 10, 100

mode = $1

mdn = $5

mean = $128/7   *M* = $18.29

If you wanted to report the "typical" gift, would it be the mode? Probably not. Even though $1.00 is the most frequent donation, this amount is *substantially* smaller than the other donations, and more people made contributions over $1.00 than made the $1.00 contribution. What about the median? Five dollars appears to be more representative of the typical donation; there are an equal number of higher and lower donations. Would the mean be better? In this example the mean is substantially inflated by *one* large donation ($100.00); the mean is $18.29 even though six of the seven donations are $10.00 or under. Although reporting the mean in this case may look good on a report of giving, it does not reflect the typical donation.

The lesson to be learned from this example is that when you have only a limited number of scores in your distribution, the mean may be inflated (or deflated) by extremely high (or extremely low) scores. When the scores in your distribution tend to cluster in one of the tails (i.e., a cluster of high scores or a cluster of low scores) the distribution is skewed. A **skewed distribution** is a nonsymmetrical distribution. Such distributions have one tail that is more spread out and long; this is the tail that has the fewer scores in it. The direction of this tail determines the nature of the skew of the distribution. When there is a cluster of lower scores, the smaller, more spread-out tail will be on the right (i.e., fewer high scores); this configuration is called a **positively skewed distribution** (see Figure 4-12A). When there is a cluster of higher scores, the smaller, more spread out tail will be on the left (i.e., fewer small scores); this configuration is called a **negatively skewed distribution** (see Figure 4-12B).

The median may be a better choice as your measure of central tendency when your distribution of scores is skewed. As the number of scores in your distribution increases, the influence of extremely large (or extremely small) scores on the mean decreases. Look what happens if we collect two additional $5.00 donations:

> **Skewed distribution**
> A nonsymmetrical distribution.

> **Positively skewed distribution** A nonsymmetrical distribution where there is a cluster of lower scores.

> **Negatively skewed distribution** A nonsymmetrical distribution where there is a cluster of higher scores.

Charitable Donations: $1, 1, 1, 5, 5, 5, 10, 10, 100

mode = $1 and $5

mdn = $5

mean = $138/9   *M* = $15.33

Note we now have two values ($1 and $5) for the mode (i.e., a *bimodal distribution*). The median stays the same ($5). However, the mean has decreased from $18.29 to

A

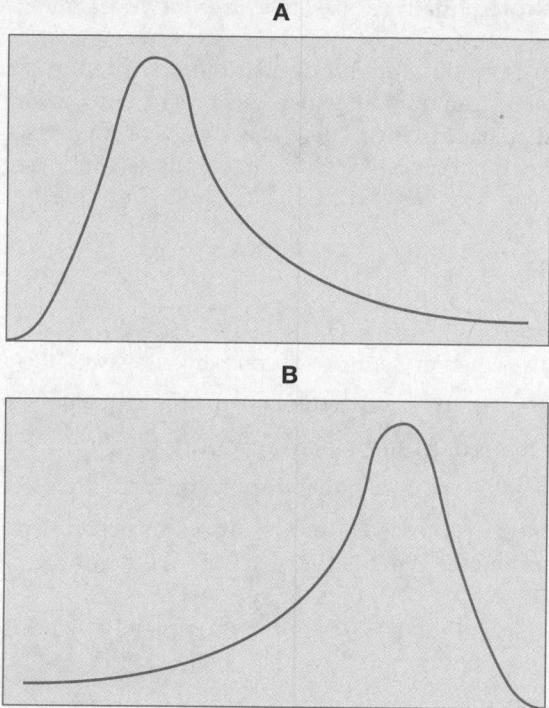

B

FIGURE 4-12   POSITIVELY SKEWED (PART A) AND NEGATIVELY SKEWED (PART B) DISTRIBUTIONS.

$15.33; the addition of only two additional low scores moved it closer to the median. Clearly, you need to give considerable thought to which measure of central tendency will best represent your data.

REVIEW SUMMARY

1. Researchers use graphs, such as the **pie chart, bar graph, histogram**, and **frequency polygon**, to depict frequencies or percentages.
2. Researchers use the **line graph** to depict experimental results. The DV is plotted on the vertical (Y, **ordinate**) axis, and the IV is plotted on the horizontal (X, **abscissa**) axis. A 2:3 relation of Y to X axes produces a representative figure.
3. Frequency distributions can assume one of several shapes. A **unimodal distribution** has one high point or prominent category. A **bimodal distribution** has two high points or prominent categories. A **multimodal distribution** has several high points or prominent categories, whereas each category contains the same number of scores in a **rectangular distribution**.
4. The **mode** is the most frequent score, whereas the **median** divides a distribution into two equal halves. The **mean** is the arithmetic average. Depending on the nature of the distribution, one or more of these measures of central tendency may

not reflect the typical score equally well. They are, however, identical in a **normal distribution**.

5. A **skewed distribution** is a nonsymmetrical distribution. There is a cluster of lower scores, and the more spread-out tail, which has fewer scores, is on the right in a **positively skewed distribution**. There is a cluster of higher scores, and the more spread-out tail, which has fewer scores is on the left in a **negatively skewed distribution**.

CHECK YOUR PROGRESS

1. What is a good graph to use when presenting several percentages that total 100%?
   a. pie chart   b. histogram   c. scatterplot   d. frequency polygon

2. A _____ presents data in terms of frequencies per category.
   a. pie chart   b. line graph   c. bimodal display d. histogram

3. You are constructing a line graph to depict the results of an experiment you just completed. What is the ordinate? What is the abscissa? What will be plotted on each of them?

4. What happens in a line graph, if the Y axis is not approximately two-thirds of the X axis?
   a. The data plot will be incorrect.
   b. The data plot will be misleading.
   c. We cannot plot the data on the graph.
   d. People will get the two axes confused.

5. A _____ has one high point or prominent category.
   a. unimodal distribution   b. bimodal distribution
   c. multimodal distribution   d. rectangular distribution

6. In a _____, all categories have the same number of frequencies.
   a. unimodal distribution   b. bimodal distribution
   c. multimodal distribution   d. rectangular distribution

7. The number that occurs most frequently is the _____.
   a. mean   b. median   c. mode   d. harmonic

EXERCISES

1. A researcher administers an altruism questionnaire to a random sample of 40 college students. The scores, which can range from 1 (low) to 10 (high), are as follows:

   4, 7, 7, 7, 8, 8, 7, 9, 4, 7, 3, 6, 9, 10, 5, 1, 4, 6, 6, 7, 5, 3, 2, 1, 8, 6, 6, 4, 8, 5, 10, 4, 8, 2, 7, 5, 9, 1, 4, 5

   Create a frequency distribution for these data.

2. Create a grouped frequency distribution from the frequency distribution in Exercise 1.

3. Create a pie chart based on the percentages in Exercise 2.

4. Create a histogram based on the frequencies in Exercise 2.

5. Convert the histogram in Exercise 4 to a frequency polygon.

6. A random sample of 15 students completes a perfectionism scale. The scores are:

    27, 11, 70, 17, 13, 27, 29, 12, 26, 18, 12, 27, 68, 12, 19.

    Calculate the mode, median, and mean for these data. Which one of these measures would you select as most representative of these data. Why?

7. Create a distribution of at least five numbers to meet the following requirements:

    a. The mean is greater than the mode.

    b. The median and the mean are equal.

    c. The median is greater than the mode.

8. Rebecca De Mayo (a student at Berry College, Mount Berry, Georgia) and her faculty supervisor, Dr. Kristen Diliberto, investigated false memories for pictures of men and women performing stereotypical and nonstereotypical household chores (De Mayo & Diliberto, 2003). The found that their 60 student participants had a total of 15 false memories when they viewed pictures of individuals performing stereotypical female chores. What was the mean number of false memories?

9. The mental health center on your campus has just conducted a survey to determine the most prevalent student complaints among eating disorders (ED), anxiety disorders (AD), depression (DE), and sleeping disorders (SD). The results are:

    ED, SD, SD, AD, SD, ED, DE, DE, DE, SD, SD, ED, SD, AD, AD, AD, DE, SD, AD, AD, ED, DE, AD, ED, DE, ED, AD, AD, DE, ED, ED, SD, DE.

    Create a frequency distribution for these data.

10. Create a bar graph based on the frequencies in Exercise 9.

11. Marianne Cipolletti (2003), a student at Georgian Court College, Lakewood, N.J., studied math anxiety in female college students as a function of exposure to math (defined as the number of math classes taken). She found that the mean math anxiety scores (higher score = higher math anxiety) were as follows:

    Low exposure (0–1 classes) = 3.02

    Moderate exposure (2–4 classes) = 3.15

    High exposure (4+ classes) = 3.20

    Create a line graph to depict these results.

12. A researcher collects the following data:

    1, 2, 3, 3, 3, 3, 4, 5, 6, 7, 7, 7, 7, 8, 9, 10.

    Draw the distribution that would best depict these data. What type of distribution is this? Why?

13. A researcher collects the following data:

    1, 2, 2, 2, 3, 3, 3, 4, 5, 6, 7, 7, 7, 8, 8, 8, 9, 10.

    Draw the distribution that would best depict these data. What type of distribution is this? Why?

14. A researcher administers a personal responsibility scale to a sample of students and records the following scores:

    27, 63, 49, 51, 59, 33, 66, 41, 61, 68, 23.

    What score appears at the 50th percentile?

15. Draw the distribution that best depicts the following data:

    1, 1, 1, 2, 2, 2, 2, 3, 3, 3, 3, 3, 4, 4, 4, 4, 4, 4, 5, 5, 5, 5, 5, 5, 5, 6, 6, 6, 6, 6, 7, 7, 7, 7, 8, 8, 8, 9, 9, 10, 10, 11.

    What type of distribution is this? Why?

16. Draw the distribution that best depicts the following data:

    1, 2, 3, 4, 5, 5, 6, 6, 7, 7, 7, 8, 8, 8, 9, 9, 9, 9, 9, 10, 10, 10, 10, 10, 10, 11, 11, 11, 11, 11, 11, 11.

    What type of distribution is this? Why?

KEY TERMS

LOOKING AHEAD

We hope you had no trouble with your first chapter on statistics. Although frequency distributions, graphs, and measures of central tendency convey considerable information, there is still more we can learn about the numbers we have gathered. We also need to know about the *variability* in our data; we will examine this topic and additional statistical methods in Chapter 6. However, in Chapter 5 we begin our in-depth consideration of experiments. First we carefully examine the variables involved in an experiment, then we consider procedures involved in the control of these variables.

chapter

The Basics of Experimentation I: Variables and Control

5

In this chapter we begin to examine methods and procedures that allow us to make cause-and-effect inferences. We begin by carefully examining the types of variables the researcher deals with: independent, extraneous, dependent, and nuisance variables. Recall from Chapter 2 that the experimenter directly manipulates *independent* variables, *dependent* variables change in response to the independent variable manipulation, and that *extraneous* variables can invalidate our experimental results. As we will see, *nuisance* variables cause our results to be less clear. Once we have discussed these variables and made their relation to the experiment clear, we will consider the procedures that researchers have developed to keep unwanted, extraneous variables from influencing the results of our experiment.

The Nature of Variables

> **Variable** An event or behavior that can assume two or more values.

Before jumping into a discussion of independent variables, let's look at the nature of variables in general. A **variable** is an event or behavior that can assume at least two values. For example, temperature is a variable; it can assume a wide range of values. The same could be said for height, weight, lighting conditions, the noise level in an urban area, anxiety, confidence, your responses to a test, as well as many other possibilities; each of these events can assume two or more values or levels.

So, when we discuss variables involved in a psychological experiment, we are talking about events or behaviors that have assumed *at least two values*. If the IV has only one level, we would have nothing to compare its effectiveness against. Assume you want to demonstrate that a new brand of toothpaste is the best on the market. You have a group of participants try the new toothpaste and then rate its effectiveness. Even though the entire group rates the toothpaste in question as "great," you still cannot claim that it is best; you do not have ratings from other groups using different brands.

Just as the IV must have at least two values, the DV also must be able to assume two or more values. Your toothpaste study would be meaningless if the *only* response the participants could make is "great"; more than one response alternative is needed.

The same logic applies in the case of extraneous variables. If two or more values are not present, then the event in question is not an extraneous variable. If all the participants in our toothpaste study are women, then we do not have to be concerned with sex differences between the groups that we test. (This point will be important later in the *Controlling Extraneous Variables* section of this chapter.) Notice that our concern about extraneous variables is quite different from our concern about IVs and DVs. Whereas we were concerned that the IV and DV have or are able to assume two or more values, we seek to avoid those instances where extraneous variables can assume two or more values.

Operationally Defining Variables

As you will recall from Chapter 2, we suggested that replication of past research can be a valuable source of research ideas. Let's assume you have located a piece of research that you want to replicate. You carefully read how the experiment was conducted and find that "each participant received a reward following every correct response." Assume this sentence is the only information you have concerning the *reward* and *response* involved in the experiment. If you asked 10 different researchers what reward they would use and what response they would record, how many different responses would you get? With this limited and vague information, chances are good that you would get as many different answers as people you asked. How valid will your replication be? If you use a totally different reward and a totally different response, have you even conducted a replication?

Problems and concerns such as these led a 1920s Harvard University physicist, Percy W. Bridgman, to propose a way to obtain clearer communication among researchers and thus achieve greater standardization and uniformity in experimental methodology (Goodwin, 1999). Bridgman's suggestion was simple: Researchers should define their variables in terms of the operations needed to produce them (Bridgman, 1927). If you define your variables in this manner, then other scientists can replicate your research by following the definitions you have given for the variables involved; such definitions are called **operational definitions**. Operational definitions have been a cornerstone of psychological research for nearly three quarters of a century because they allow researchers to communicate clearly and effectively with each other.

Operational definition
Defining the independent, dependent, and extraneous variables in terms of the operations needed to produce them.

To illustrate the use of operational definitions, let's return to the reward and response situation we described previously. If we define reward as "a 45-mg Noyes Formula A food pellet," then other animal researchers can use the same reinforcer by ordering a supply of 45-mg Formula A pellets from the P. J. Noyes Company. Likewise, if we define the response as "making a bar press in an operant conditioning chamber (Lafayette Model 81335)," then another researcher can replicate our research setup by purchasing the same piece of equipment from the Lafayette Instrument Company.

The experimenter must be able to clearly convey such information about all the variables involved in a research project. Hence, it is crucial to give operational definitions for independent, dependent, and extraneous variables, as well as for nuisance variables.

Independent Variables

Independent variable (IV) A stimulus or aspect of the environment that the experimenter directly manipulates to determine its influences on behavior.

As you saw in Chapter 1, **independent variables (IVs)** are those variables that the experimenter purposely manipulates. The IV constitutes the reason the research is being conducted; the experimenter is interested in determining what effect the IV has. The term *independent* is used because the IV does not depend on other variables; it stands alone. A few examples of IVs that experimenters have used in psychological research are sleep deprivation, temperature, noise level, drug type (or dosage level), removal of a portion of the brain, and psychological context. Rather than attempting to list all possible IVs, it is easier to indicate that they tend to cluster in several general categories.

Types of IVs

Physiological IV A physiological state of the participant that the experimenter manipulates.

Physiological   When the participants in an experiment are subjected to conditions that alter or change their normal biological state, a **physiological IV** is being used. For example, Susan Nash (1983), a student at Emporia State University in Emporia, Kansas, obtained several pregnant rats from an animal supplier. Upon their arrival at the laboratory, she randomly assigned half the rats to receive an alcohol-water mixture during gestation; the remainder received plain tap water. She switched the alcohol-exposed mothers to plain tap water when the pups were born. Thus, some rat pups were exposed to alcohol during gestation, whereas others were not. Nash tested all the pups for alcohol preference when they were adults and found that those animals that were exposed to alcohol (the physiological IV) during gestation drank more alcohol as adults. Nash received the 1983 J. P. Guilford-Psi Chi National Undergraduate Research Award for this experiment. Just as alcohol exposure was a physiological IV in Nash's experiment, administering a new drug to determine whether it is successful in alleviating schizophrenic symptoms also represents a physiological IV.

Experience IV Manipulation of the amount of training or learning.

Experience   When the effects of amount or type of previous training or learning are the central focus of the research, the researcher is using an **experience IV**. A study conducted by Monica Boice, a student at Saint Joseph's University in Philadelphia, and her faculty advisor, Gary Gargano, illustrates the use of experience as an IV. Boice and Gargano (2001) studied memory for items in a list as a function of the number of related cues that were presented at the time of recall. Some participants received zero cues, whereas other participants received eight cues. The number of cues is an experience IV. The results of this study indicated that, under some conditions, receiving eight related cues actually resulted in worse memory performance than did receiving no cues.

Stimulus   Some IVs fall into the category of **stimulus** or **environmental variables**. When researchers use this type of IV, they are manipulating some aspect of the environment. Kathy Walter, Sammi Ervin, and Nicole Williamson, students at Catawba College, Salisbury, North Carolina, conducted a study under the direction of Dr. Sheila Brownlow in which they used a stimulus IV (Walter, Brownlow, Ervin, & Williamson, 1998). They asked 144 college students to judge various traits of women who walked barefoot and in high heels. The stimulus variable was whether the person being judged was barefoot or wore heels. The results showed that when the women wore heels, student participants judged them as less sexy and more submissive than when they were barefooted.

Stimulus or **environmental IV** An aspect of the environment that the experimenter manipulates.

Participant characteristics Aspects of the participant, such as age, sex, or personality traits, that are treated as if they are IVs.

Participant   It is common to find **participant characteristics**, such as age, sex, personality traits, or academic major, being treated *as if* they are IVs.

PSYCHOLOGICAL DETECTIVE   Although many researchers may treat participant characteristics as if they are IVs, they really are not. Why?

To be considered an IV, the experimenter must directly manipulate the behavior or event in question. Although experimenters can manipulate physiological, experience, and stimulus IVs, they are not able to directly manipulate participant characteristics. Thus, experimenters do not consider them to be true IVs. The experimenter does not create the participants' sex or cause participants to be a certain age. Participant characteristics or variables are best viewed as classification, not manipulation, variables. The categories for participant variables are created before the experiment is conducted, and the experimenter simply assigns the participants to these categories on the basis of the characteristics they display.

Extraneous Variables (Confounders)

> **Extraneous variables** Uncontrolled variables that can cause unintended changes between groups.

As we saw in Chapter 1, **extraneous variables** are those factors that can have an *unintended* influence on the results of an experiment. Extraneous variables influence the difference *between* groups. Figure 5-1A, shows the relation of two groups without the influence of an extraneous variable; two possible effects of an extraneous variable are shown in Figures 5-1B and 5-1C. Thus, an extraneous variable can unintentionally cause groups to move closer together (Figure 5-1B) or farther apart (Figure 5-1C).

Review Figure 5-1 and the information we have presented about extraneous variables. The effect of an extraneous variable is similar to that of another major component of the experiment. What role does an extraneous variable appear to play in an experiment? How is the presence of an extraneous variable detrimental to the experiment?

The other component of an experiment that can influence the difference between groups is the IV. Thus, an extraneous variable can affect the outcome of an experiment. Just as other possible suspects can damage a detective's case beyond repair, the presence of an extraneous variable is devastating to research; it is not possible to attribute the results of the experiment to the IV. Why? There are two variables that may have caused the groups to differ: the IV you manipulated *and* the unwanted extraneous variable. You have no way to determine which of these two variables caused the differences you observed. In such instances, where we can attribute the results to an IV or to an extraneous variable, the experiment is **confounded**. (The terms *extraneous variable* and *confounder* are often used synonymously.) When an experiment is confounded, the best course of action is to discontinue the research and profit from your mistake. You can control the extraneous variable in the next experiment.

> **Confounding** A situation in which the results of an experiment can be attributed to either the operation of an IV or an extraneous variable.

To illustrate how confounding works, let's consider a reading comprehension study. We have first- and second-graders available to serve as participants. The

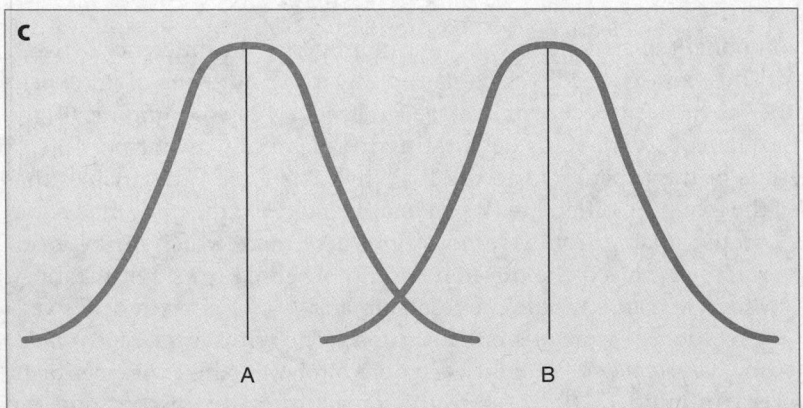

FIGURE 5-1   THE DIFFERENCE (A = STANDARD METHOD; B = NEW METHOD) BETWEEN TWO GROUPS WITH NO CONFOUNDER OPERATING (PART A). THE DIFFERENCE BETWEEN TWO GROUPS WHEN A CONFOUNDER IS PRESENT AND HAS MOVED THE GROUPS CLOSER TOGETHER (PART B). THE DIFFERENCE BETWEEN TWO GROUPS WHEN A CONFOUNDER IS PRESENT AND HAS MOVED THE GROUPS FARTHER APART (PART C).

researcher assigns all the first-graders to the standard method for teaching reading comprehension and all the second-graders to the new method. The researcher conducts the experiment and finds that the comprehension scores for students using the new method are substantially better than those of students using the standard method (see Figure 5-1C). What would have happened if the researcher assigned the second-graders to the standard method and the first-graders to the new method? We might have seen results like those in Figure 5-1B. Why did these two sets of results occur? In each instance it is arguable that a preexisting difference in reading comprehension created differences between the two groups (i.e., the preexisting difference acted *as if* it was an IV). Assuming the second-graders have superior reading comprehension, it seems reasonable to suggest that the new method seemed even more effective when the second-graders used it (i.e., the difference between the groups was exaggerated). However, when the second-graders used the standard method, the superior method used by the first-graders increased their scores and moved the groups closer together (i.e., group differences decreased). Certainly, all of this commentary is only speculation on our part. It is just as likely that the IV created the group differences that we observed. The main point is that we really do not know what caused the differences—the IV (type of method used) *or* the extraneous variable (grade level).

The presence of an extraneous variable is often very difficult to spot; it may take several knowledgeable individuals scrutinizing an experiment from every possible angle to determine whether one is present. If the experimenter detects an extraneous variable before conducting the experiment, then the experimenter can deal with the problem and can proceed with the experiment. We present techniques for controlling unwanted variables later in this chapter.

Dependent Variables

> **Dependent variable (DV)** A response or behavior that is measured. It is desired that changes in the DV are directly related to manipulation of the IV.

The **dependent variable (DV)** changes as a function of the level of the IV the participant experiences; thus, the value the DV assumes *truly depends* on the IV. The DV consists of the data or results of our experiment. As with all aspects of psychological research, experimenters must give the DV appropriate consideration when they formulate an experiment. The experimenter must deal with such considerations as selecting the appropriate DV, deciding exactly which measure of the DV to use, and whether to record more than one DV.

Selecting the DV

Because psychology often is defined as the science of behavior, the DV typically consists of some type of behavior or response. However, when the researcher administers the IV, it is likely that several responses will occur. Which one should the researcher select as the DV? One answer to this question is to look carefully at the experimental hypothesis. If you have stated your hypothesis in general implication form ("if . . . then"—see Chapter 2), the "then" portion of the hypothesis will give you an idea of the general nature of your DV. For the Boice and Gargano (2001) memory study the choice was easy; "The dependent measure was the number of words correctly recalled" (p. 119).

What if your hypothesis was more general and indicated only that you wanted to study "spatial abilities"? Where could you find information to help you choose a *specific* DV? We hope you are already a step ahead of us and have said that our literature review (see Chapter 2) can provide valuable guidelines. If researchers have used a particular response successfully as a DV in previous research, chances are good that it will be a good choice again. Another reason for using a DV that researchers have previously used is that you will have a comparison for your own results. Although totally different DVs may provide exciting new information, the ability to relate the results of experiments using different responses is more difficult.

Recording or Measuring the DV

Once you have selected the DV, you will have to decide exactly how you will measure or record it. Several possibilities exist.

Correctness   With this DV measure, the participant's response is either correct or incorrect. Because they counted the number of words their participants remembered correctly, Boice and Gargano (2001) used a correctness DV.

Rate or Frequency   If you are studying the lever-pressing performance of a rat or pigeon in an operant conditioning chamber (Skinner box), then your DV is likely to be the rate of responses that the animal shows. Rate of responding determines how rapidly participants make responses during a specified time period. You would plot your data in the form of a cumulative record with steeper slopes representing higher rates (i.e., large numbers of responses being made in shorter periods of time). Figure 5-2 shows some different rates of responding.

If you are studying the number of social interactions among children during free play at a kindergarten, you may want to record the frequency, rather than the rate, of responding. Hence, your DV would simply be the number of responses shown during a specified time period without any concern for how rapidly the participant makes them.

Degree or Amount   Often researchers record the DV in terms of degree or amount. In this instance, you do not record the number or frequency of the participant's responses, rather, you typically record a single number that indicates the degree or amount. Research conducted by Amie McKibban and Shawn Nelson, students at Emporia State University in Emporia, Kansas, studied satisfaction with life in college students (McKibban & Nelson, 2001). Scores on a Satisfaction With Life scale measured how satisfied (i.e., degree or amount) their participants were with life.

Latency or Duration   In many situations, such as studies of learning and memory, how quickly participants make a response (latency) or how long the response lasts (duration) are of particular interest. For example, Rachel Ball, Erica Kargl, J. Davis Kimpel, and Shana Siewert, students at Wheaton College in Wheaton, Illinois, were interested in the relation between a participant's mood and his or her reaction time measurement as a latency DV. They found that participants in sad and suspenseful moods

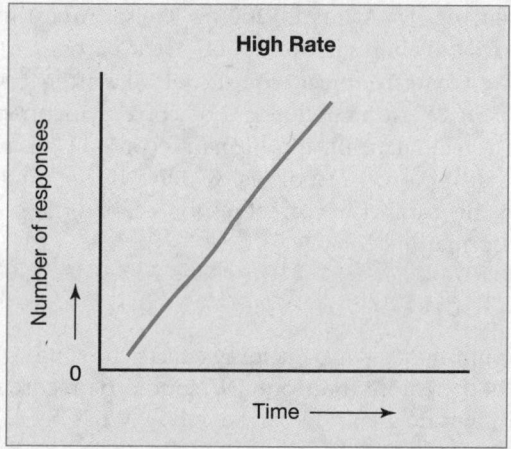

FIGURE 5-2   DIFFERENT RATES OF RESPONDING.

had slower reaction times than participants in a neutral mood (Ball, Kargl, Kimpel, & Siewert, 2001).

Should You Record More than One DV?

If you have the measurement capabilities, there is nothing to prohibit the recording of more than one DV. Possibly additional data will strengthen your knowledge claim in the same way it might strengthen a detective's case. Should you record additional DVs? The answer to this question really boils down to deciding whether recording additional DVs is going to add appreciably to your understanding of the phenomenon under study. If recording an additional DV makes a meaningful contribution, then you should give it serious consideration. If measuring and recording another DV does not make a substantive contribution, then it is probably not worth the added time and trouble. Often you can use previous research as a guide concerning whether you should consider recording more than one DV.

PSYCHOLOGICAL DETECTIVE — Consider a reversed eye–hand coordination (mirror tracing) experiment. The time taken to complete the tracing of a star pattern (a latency DV) while looking in a mirror is recorded. Is this DV sufficient to give you a good, complete picture of the performance of this task, or should you also record another DV?

You probably should record a second DV. The latency DV indicates only how long it took to trace the star pattern. Hence, the experimenter has no record of the number of errors (going beyond the boundaries of the figure) that participants made. The addition of a second DV that measures the number of errors (a frequency DV) will make a significant contribution to this experiment.

The need for more than one DV was seen in an experiment conducted by Janet Luehring, a student at Washburn University in Topeka, Kansas, and her faculty advisor, Joanne Altman (Luehring & Altman, 2000). These investigators studied male–female differences in spatial ability performance. Their participants performed a mental rotation (visualizing what an object would look like after it was rotated in space). Because the participant's performance could be correct, incorrect, or (because the task was timed) uncompleted, Luehring and Altman recorded *both correct and incorrect responses*. The number of incorrect responses, which was *not* equal to the total number of responses minus the number of correct responses, had the potential to provide additional, relevant information.

Characteristics of a Good DV

Although considerable thought may go into deciding exactly how the DV will be measured and recorded and whether more than one DV should be recorded, the experimenter still has no guarantee that a good DV has been selected. What constitutes a good DV? We want the DV to be *valid* and *reliable*.

The DV is **valid** when it measures what the experimental hypothesis says it should measure. For example, assume you are

Valid Measuring what is supposed to be measured

interested in studying intelligence as a function of differences in regional diet. You believe the basic diet consumed by people living in different regions of the United States results in differences in intelligence. You devise a new intelligence test and set off to test your hypothesis. As the results of your project start to take shape, you notice that the scores from the Northeast are higher than those from other sections of the country; your hypothesis appears to be supported. However, a closer inspection of the results indicates that participants not living in the Northeast miss only certain questions. Are all the questions fair and unbiased, or do some favor Northeasterners? You notice several questions about subways. How many individuals from Arizona are familiar with subways? Thus, your DV (scores on the intelligence test) may have a regional bias and may not measure the participants' intelligence consistently from region to region. A good DV must be directly related to the IV and measure the effects of the IV manipulation as the experimental hypothesis predicts it will.

> **Reliable** Producing consistent measurements

A good DV also is **reliable**. If the scores on an intelligence test are used as the DV, then we would expect to see similar scores when the test is again administered under the same IV conditions (a *test–retest procedure*). If the test gives the same individual different IQ scores at different times, it is not a reliable test.

Nuisance Variables

> **Nuisance variable** Unwanted variables that can cause the variability of scores within groups to increase

Nuisance variables are either characteristics of the participants or unintended influences of the experimental situation that make the effects of the IV more difficult to see or determine. It is important to understand that nuisance variables influence all groups in an experiment; their influence is not limited just to one specific group. When they are present, nuisance variables result in greater variability in the DV; the scores *within* each group spread out more. For example, assume you are interested in studying reading comprehension. Can you think of a participant characteristic that might be related to reading comprehension? How about intelligence or IQ?

Figure 5-3A shows the spread of the reading comprehension scores within a group when there are not wide differences in intelligence among the participants within the group. In this instance a nuisance variable is not operating.

You can see how the majority of the comprehension scores are similar and cluster in the middle of the distribution; there are relatively few extremely low and extremely high scores. Figure 5-3B shows the distribution of comprehension scores when there are wider differences in intelligence (i.e., a nuisance variable is present). Notice that the scores are more spread out; there are fewer scores in the middle of the distribution and more scores in the extremes.

How does a nuisance variable influence the results of an experiment? To answer that question, we need to add another group of participants to our example and conduct a simple experiment. Imagine we are evaluating two methods for teaching reading comprehension—the standard method and a new method. In Figure 5-4A we are comparing two groups that have not been influenced by the nuisance variable. The difference between these two groups is pronounced and clear; they overlap very little.

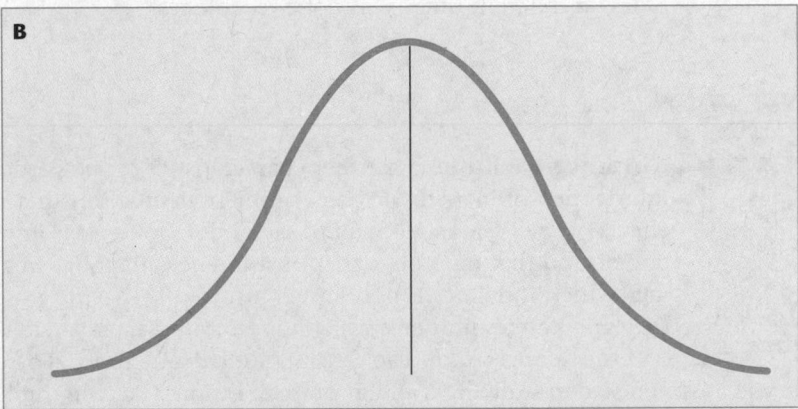

FIGURE 5-3 THE SPREAD OF SCORES WITHIN A GROUP WHEN A NUISANCE VARIABLE IS NOT OPERATING (PART A). THE SPREAD OF SCORES WITHIN A GROUP WHEN A NUISANCE VARIABLE IS OPERATING (PART B).

Let's add the effects of a nuisance variable, such as wide differences in verbal ability, to each group and then compare the groups. As you can see in Figure 5-4B, when the scores spread out more, there is greater overlap and the difference between the groups is not as distinct and clear as when the nuisance variable was not present. When a nuisance variable is present, our view of the experimental results is clouded; we are unable to see clearly the difference the IV may have created between the groups in our experiment. Notice that when the nuisance variable was added (Figure 5-4B), the *only* thing that happened was that the scores spread out in both extremes of each distribution—the relative location of the distributions did not change. *Nuisance*

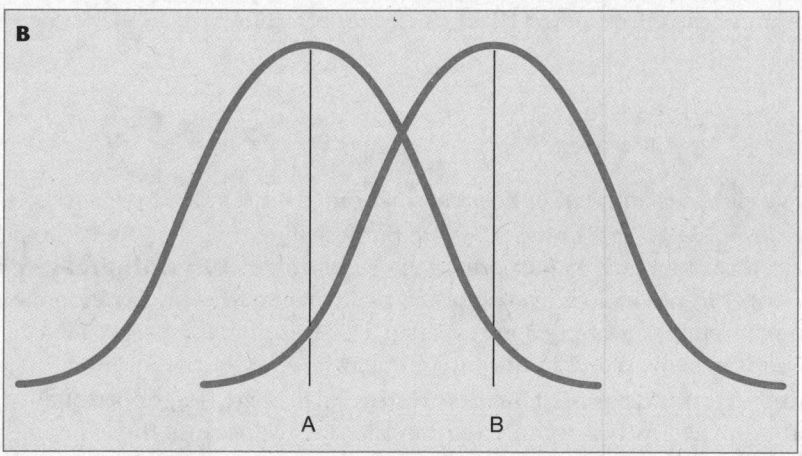

FIGURE 5-4   A COMPARISON OF TWO GROUPS WHEN A NUISANCE VARIABLE IS NOT OPERATING (PART A). A COMPARISON OF THE SAME TWO GROUPS WHEN A NUISANCE VARIABLE IS OPERATING (PART B).

variables increase the spread of scores within a distribution; they do not cause a distribution to change its location.

For each example indicate the nuisance variable and its effect.

1. An experimenter measures reaction time in participants ranging in age from 12 to 78 years.
2. The ability of participants to recall a list of words is being studied in a room that is located by a noisy elevator.
3. The laboratory where participants are tested for manual dexterity has frequent, unpredictable changes in temperature.

In the first situation, the wide age range is the nuisance variable. The younger participants should display faster reaction times than the older participants. Thus, the scores will spread into both ends of the distributions. The change in noise level due to the operation of the elevator is the nuisance variable in the second example, whereas the frequent, unpredictable temperature changes are the nuisance variable in the third example; in both examples the change in environmental conditions is likely to increase the spread of scores. Our goal as researchers is to keep nuisance variables to a minimum so the effects of the IV are as clear as possible.

REVIEW SUMMARY

1. A **variable** is an event or behavior that can assume at least two levels.
2. **Independent variables (IVs)** are purposely manipulated by the experimenter and form the core or purpose of the experiment. **Physiological IVs** refer to changes in the biological state of the participants, whereas **experience IVs** refer to manipulations of previous experience or learning. **Stimulus IVs** are manipulations in some aspect of the environment.
3. Although **participant characteristics** such as age, sex, or personality traits are often treated as IVs, technically they are not IVs because the experimenter does not directly manipulate them.
4. **Extraneous variables (confounders)** can have an unintended influence on the results of an experiment by changing the difference *between* the groups. When an extraneous variable is present, the experiment is confounded.
5. The **dependent variable (DV)** changes as a function of changes in the IV. The experimental hypothesis can provide possible guidelines concerning the selection of the DV. Past research also can assist the experimenter in selecting the DV.
6. The DV can be recorded in terms of correctness, rate or frequency, degree or amount, and latency or duration. If additional information will be gained, the

experimenter should consider recording more than one DV. A good DV is directly related to the IV (valid) and reliable.

7. **Nuisance variables** are variables that increase the variability of scores *within all groups*. The presence of nuisance variables makes the results of an experiment less clear.

CHECK YOUR PROGRESS

1. An event or behavior that can assume at least two values is a ~~variable~~

2. Matching

   1. DV   A. change in normal biological state
   2. extraneous variable   B. manipulation of environment
   3. physiological IV   C. can damage the experiment and its results
   4. experience IV   D. age
   5. stimulus IV   E. changes as a function of changes in IV
   6. participant variable   F. amount of previous learning

3. Your research involves determining the effects of persuasion on the strength of attitudes. You are using a ~~degree~~ measurement of the DV.

   a. correctness   b. rate   c. degree   d. duration

4. A good DV has two primary qualities; it is both ~~valid~~ and ~~reliable~~

   a. easy to identify; easy to measure

   b. dependent on the experimenter; identifiable

   c. valid; reliable

   d. positively correlated; negatively correlated

5. Under what conditions should you record more than one DV? ~~If additional info will be gained~~

6. Variables that result in greater within-group variability in the data are called _____.

   a. independent variables   b. confounders

   c. nuisance variables   d. uncontrolled variables

Controlling Extraneous Variables

Just as care and precision are crucial when a detective attempts to solve a case, control forms an integral component of psychological research. The experimenter must exercise control over both extraneous variables and nuisance variables so the results of the experiment are as meaningful (no extraneous variables present) and clear (minimal influence of nuisance variables) as possible. When you are dealing with a variable that can be clearly specified and quantified (e.g., sex, age, educational level, temperature, lighting intensity, noise level), then one of the five basic control techniques should be applicable. We describe these five basic control techniques—randomization, elimination, constancy, balancing, and counterbalancing—in the next section.

Basic Control Techniques

As we discuss the basic control techniques, it is important to keep in mind that their goals are to (1) produce groups that are equivalent prior to the introduction of the IV, thereby eliminating extraneous variables, and (2) reduce the effects of nuisance variables as much as possible.

Randomization A control technique that ensures that each participant has an equal chance of being assigned to any group in an experiment.

Randomization   We begin our discussion of control with randomization because it is the most widely used technique. **Randomization** guarantees that each participant has an equal chance of being assigned to any group in the experiment. For example, once the students had volunteered for the research on memory, Boice and Gargano (2001) indicated that "The participants were placed into one of the six experimental groups" (p. 120).

The logic behind using randomization is as follows: Because all participants have an equal likelihood of being selected for each group in an experiment, any unique characteristics associated with the participants should be equally distributed across all groups that are formed. Consider level of motivation, for example. Although it may not be feasible to measure each participant's level of motivation, this variable can still be controlled by randomly forming the groups in our experiment. Just by chance we would expect that *each* group would have some participants who are highly motivated, some participants who are moderately motivated, and some participants who are barely motivated. Thus, the groups should be equated with regard to the average level of motivation, as well as the myriad of other unknown and unsuspected extraneous variables that might be present.

PSYCHOLOGICAL DETECTIVE   Even though it is the most widely used control procedure, randomization has one major drawback. What is it?

Because we are never *fully* aware of the variables that randomization controls and thus do not know whether these variables are distributed evenly to all groups, we cannot be positive that this control technique is effective. It is possible that all the highly motivated participants will be randomly assigned to the same group. Also, you need to consider what is being controlled when randomization is employed. If you find yourself having some difficulty specifying exactly what is controlled by randomization, then you are on the right track. Randomization is used as a control technique for *all* variables that *might* be present that the experimenter is unaware of. If the experimenter is unaware of exactly which variables are being controlled and how effective the control is, then it should come as no surprise that the experimenter is never *completely* sure how effective randomization has been.

Elimination A control technique whereby extraneous variables are completely removed from an experiment

Elimination   When we know the extraneous variables or nuisance variables, our approach can be more direct. For example, we might choose to completely remove or **eliminate** the unwanted variable.

Sounds easy, but in practice you may find it quite difficult to *completely* remove a variable.

Shann Sagles, Sharon Coley, Germilina Espiritu, and Patricia Zahregian, students at Pace University in White Plains, New York, and their faculty advisor, Richard Velayo, used elimination as a control in their cross-cultural study of the identification of facial expressions. "The 35-mm photos of the target individuals, taken from the base of the chin to the top of the forhead, excluded their attire and body type. The rationale for this procedure was to *eliminate* [emphasis added] extraneous variables that may have influenced the participants' responses" (Sagles, Coley, Espiritu, Zahregian, & Velayo, 2002, p. 33). Thus, Sagles et al. guaranteed that clothing and weight did not affect their participants' responses.

When the variable in question consists of an entire category of events, such as noise, temperature, or lighting condition, it may be difficult—if not impossible—to eliminate. However, if the variable is a specific occurrence within one of these more general categories, such as temperatures above 80 degrees, then it may be possible to eliminate that *aspect* of the variable. In this situation, however, the experimenter is not just interested in eliminating a variable but also in producing and maintaining a constant condition under which the participants in the experiment are tested.

Constancy A control technique by which an extraneous variable is reduced to a single value that is experienced by all participants.

Constancy   When it is difficult or impossible to completely eliminate a variable, the experimenter may choose to exercise control by creating a uniform or constant condition that all participants experience. **Constancy** has become a standard control technique for many researchers. For example, experimental testing may take place in the same room, with the same lighting and temperature levels, and at the same time of day each day (if the experiment is conducted on more than one day). In this instance the location of the experiment, the temperature level, the lighting level, and the time of day have not been eliminated but, rather, have assumed a constant value.

Juan and Nancy are interested in determining which of two methods of teaching psychological statistics is best. Two statistics classes are available: Juan teaches one method to one class; Nancy teaches the second method to the other class. This experiment is confounded because Juan and Nancy each taught one of the classes, so it is impossible to tell whether differences between the classes are due to the method or the teacher. How would you use constancy to control this extraneous variable?

The easiest approach would be to have only one of the experimenters, Juan or Nancy, teach both classes. Thus, that extraneous variable, the teacher, is the same for both classes and the experiment is no longer confounded.

By making sure the experimental testing conditions do not vary unpredictably, constancy can also control for nuisance variables. When the testing conditions are the same from testing session to testing session, there is greater likelihood that the scores within the groups will not spread out as much because of the constancy. Constancy can also control nuisance variable effects produced by participant variables such as age, sex, and educational level. For example, in a study of the effects of massage and touch on body-dissatisfaction, Angela Larey, a student at Missouri Southern State College in Joplin, MO, "used only women [as participants] because they generally manifest greater body dissatisfaction than men" (Larey, 2001, p. 79). Recall that wide variations in such participant variables may result in greater spread of scores within the groups. If the technique of *stratified random sampling* (sampling only a certain type of participant, such as first-year college women between the ages of 18 and 19, see Chapter 9) is employed, then the variability among the participants' scores should be smaller because the participants are more homogeneous. Clearly, this procedure helps create constancy.

Although constancy can be an effective control technique, there are situations in which the unwanted variable(s) cannot be reduced to a single value that all partici- pants experienced in the experiment. What can be done in those instances where this variable assumes two or more values? The answer may lie in the control technique known as balancing.

> **Balancing** A control procedure that achieves group equality by distrib- uting extraneous variables equally to all groups.

Balancing   **Balancing** represents a logical extension of control through constancy. Thus, the groups in our experiment are balanced or equivalent when each group experiences *all* unwanted variables or *levels* of unwanted variables in the same manner or to the same degree.

In the simplest example of balancing we would test two groups; one group (the experimental group) would receive the IV, whereas the second group (the control or comparison group) would be treated identically but would not receive the IV. If the groups were balanced or equated with regard to extraneous variables, then we could tentatively conclude that differences between them were caused by the IV. This gen- eral situation is diagrammed in Table 5-1.

When the potential extraneous variables, such as various personality differences in human participants, are *unknown*, the experimenter uses randomization to form equiv- alent groups, and we assume that the respective extraneous variables are distributed equally to all groups. When the extraneous variables, such as sex of the experimenter,

TABLE 5-1 BALANCED EXTRANEOUS VARIABLES

When the extraneous variables are experienced in the same manner, the groups are said to be balanced

GROUP 1	GROUP 2
TREATMENT A	TREATMENT B
Ext. Var. 1	Ext. Var. 1
Ext. Var. 2	Ext. Var. 2
Ext. Var. 3	Ext. Var. 3
Ext. Var. 4	Ext. Var. 4

are known, then the experimenter can be more systematic in the use of the balancing technique to produce equivalent conditions.

PSYCHOLOGICAL DETECTIVE   Let's assume that one teacher cannot teach all the students included in Juan and Nancy's experiment; two are needed. How could balancing be used to remove the potential confounding due to a different teacher teaching each of the new methods?

As you can see in Table 5-2, an easy solution to their problem is to have Juan and Nancy each teach half the students under *each* method. Thus, the two teachers appear equally under each teaching method and the classes are balanced with regard to that potential confounding variable. This teaching example illustrates the simplest situation in which balancing is used to control one extraneous variable. Balancing can also be used with several extraneous variables (see Table 5-1); the only requirement is that each extraneous variable appear equally in each group.

TABLE 5-2	USING BALANCING TO ELIMINATE CONFOUNDING IN TEACHING TWO METHODS OF PSYCHOLOGICAL STATISTICS
JUAN	**NANCY**
25 students → Method 1	25 students → Method 1
25 students → Method 2	25 students → Method 2

Although elimination, constancy, and balancing offer the experimenter powerful control techniques, they are not able to deal with all control problems. In the next section we examine one of these problem situations, *sequencing* or *order*, and how to control it through counterbalancing.

Counterbalancing   In some experiments participants participate in more than one experimental condition. For example, you might want to conduct a cola taste test to determine which of two brands of cola is most preferred. As you set up your tasting booth at the local mall, you are sure you have taken all the right precautions: The tasting cups are all the same, the two colas will be poured from identical containers, the participants will consume the same amount of Cola A and then Cola B (in that order), and the participants will be blindfolded during the test so color differences will not influence their choice. Yes, your control seems to be perfect. Is it?

PSYCHOLOGICAL DETECTIVE   Review the experiment we have just described. What control procedures are being used? There is a problem that has been overlooked that needs to be controlled. What is this problem and how might it be controlled?

Constancy is achieved by ensuring that (a) the tasting cups are the same, (b) the colas are poured from identical containers, and (c) all participants consume the same amount of each cola. By blindfolding the participants, you have *eliminated* any problems that may be caused by differences in the visual appearance of the two colas. These are all relevant control procedures. The problem that is overlooked concerns the sequence or order for sampling the two colas. If Cola A is *always* sampled before Cola B and one cola is liked more, you cannot be sure if the preference is due to its great flavor *or* the fact that the colas were always sampled in the same order and this order may have influenced the participants' reactions. The technique used when a sequence or order effect must be controlled is known as **counterbalancing**. There are two types of counterbalancing: within-subject and within-group. **Within-subject counterbalancing** attempts to control the sequence effect within each participant, whereas **within-group counterbalancing** attempts to control this problem by presenting different sequences to different participants.

> **Counterbalancing**
> A procedure for controlling order effects by presenting different treatment sequences.

> **Within-subject counterbalancing**
> Presentation of different treatment sequences to the same participant.

> **Within-group counterbalancing**
> Presentation of different treatment sequences to different participants.

Within-Subject Counterbalancing   Returning to the problem of sequence in our cola challenge, we could deal with this problem by having each participant sample the two colas in the following sequence: ABBA. By using within-subject counterbalancing, each participant will taste Cola A once before and once after tasting Cola B. Thus, the experience of having tasted Cola A first is counterbalanced by tasting Cola A last.

Although it may seem to be relatively easy to implement within-subject counterbalancing, there is one major drawback to its use: Each participant must experience each condition more than once. In some situations the experimenter may not want or be able to present the treatments more than once to each participant. For example, you may not have sufficient time to conduct your cola challenge and allow each participant the opportunity to sample *each* brand of cola more than once. In such instances within-group counterbalancing may offer a better control alternative.

Within-Group Counterbalancing   Another way to deal with the cola challenge sequencing problem is to randomly assign half the participants to experience the two colas in the Cola A → Cola B sequence and the remaining half of the participants to receive the Cola B → Cola A sequence. The preference of participants who tasted Cola A before Cola B could be compared with the preference of the participants who tasted Cola B first.

Assuming that we tested six participants, the within-group counterbalanced presentation of the two colas would be diagrammed as shown in Table 5-3.

As you can see, three participants receive the A → B sequence, whereas three participants receive the B → A sequence. This basic diagram illustrates the three requirements of within-subject counterbalancing:

1. Each treatment must be presented to each participant an equal number of times. In this example each participant tastes Cola A once and Cola B once.
2. Each treatment must occur an equal number of times at each testing or practice session. Cola A is sampled three times at Tasting 1 and three times at Tasting 2.
3. Each treatment must precede and follow each of the other treatments an equal number of times. In this example Cola A is tasted first three times and is tasted second three times.

TABLE 5-3   WITHIN-GROUP COUNTERBALANCING FOR THE TWO-COLA CHALLENGE WHEN SIX PARTICIPANTS ARE TESTED

	TASTING 1	TASTING 2
Participant 1	A	B
Participant 2	A	B
Participant 3	A	B
Participant 4	B	A
Participant 5	B	A
Participant 6	B	A

Counterbalancing is not limited to two-treatment sequences. For example, let's assume that your cola challenge involves three colas instead of two. The within-group counterbalancing that will be needed in that situation is diagrammed in Table 5-4. Carefully examine this diagram. Does it satisfy the requirements for counterbalancing?

It appears that all the requirements have been met. Each cola is tasted an equal number of times (6), is tasted an equal number of times (2) at each tasting session, and precedes and follows each of the other colas an equal number of times (2). It is important to note that if we want to test more participants, they would have to be added in multiples of six. The addition of any other number of participants violates the rules of counterbalancing by creating a situation where one cola is tasted more than the others, appears more often at one tasting session than the others, and does not precede and follow the other colas an equal number of times. Try adding only one or two participants to Table 5-4 to see if you can satisfy the requirements for counterbalancing.

Table 5-4 also illustrates another consideration that must be taken into account when counterbalancing is used. When only a few treatments are used, the number of different sequences that will have to be administered remains relatively small and counterbalancing is manageable. When we tested two colas, only two sequences were involved (see Table 5-3); however, the addition of only one more cola resulted in the

TABLE 5-4   WITHIN-GROUP COUNTERBALANCING FOR THE THREE-COLA CHALLENGE WHEN SIX PARTICIPANTS ARE TESTED

	TASTING SESSION		
	1	2	3
Participant 1	A	B	C
Participant 2	A	C	B
Participant 3	B	A	C
Participant 4	B	C	A
Participant 5	C	A	B
Participant 6	C	B	A

addition of four sequences (see Table 5-4). If we added an additional cola to our challenge (Colas A, B, C, and D), we would now have to administer a total of 24 different sequences and our experiment would be much more complex to conduct! Our minimum number of participants would be 24 and if we wanted to test more than 1 participant per sequence, participants would have to be added in multiples of 24.

How do you know how many sequences will be required? Do you have to write down all the possible sequences to find out how many there are? No—you can calculate the total number of sequences by using the formula $n!$ (n factorial). All that is required is to take the number of treatments (n), factor or break that number down into its component parts, and then multiply these factors or components. Thus:

2! would be $2 \times 1 = 2$

3! would be $3 \times 2 \times 1 = 6$

4! would be $4 \times 3 \times 2 \times 1 = 24$

> **Complete counter-balancing** All possible treatment sequences are presented.

and so forth. When you can administer all possible sequences, you are using **complete counterbalancing**. Although complete counterbalancing offers the best control for sequence or order effects, often it cannot be attained when several treatments are included in the experiment. As we just saw, the use of 4 colas would require a minimum of 24 participants (4! = $4 \times 3 \times 2 \times 1 = 24$) for complete counterbalancing. Testing five colas would increase the number of sequences (and the minimum number of participants) to 120 (5! = $5 \times 4 \times 3 \times 2 \times 1 = 120$). In situations requiring a large number of participants to implement complete counterbalancing, either you can reduce the number of treatments until your time, financial, and participant resources allow complete counterbalancing, or you can complete the experiment without completely counterbalancing.

> **Incomplete counter-balancing** Only a portion of all possible sequences are presented.

Incomplete counterbalancing refers to the use of some, but not all, of the possible sequences. Which sequences are to be used and which ones are to be excluded? Some experimenters randomly select the sequences they will employ. Once the number of participants to be tested has been determined, the experimenter randomly selects an equal number of sequences. For example, Table 5-5 illustrates a possible random selection of sequences for conducting the cola challenge with 4 colas and only 12 participants.

Although random selection appears to be an easy approach to the use of incomplete counterbalancing, there is a problem. If you examine Table 5-5 carefully, you will see that although each participant receives each treatment an equal number of times, the other requirements for counterbalancing are not satisfied. Each treatment does not appear an equal number of times at each testing or practice session, and each treatment does not precede and follow each of the other treatments an equal number of times.

There are two approaches that can be adopted to resolve this problem, although neither one is completely satisfactory. We could randomly determine the treatment sequence for the *first* participant and then systematically rotate the sequence for the remaining participants. This approach is diagrammed in Table 5-6.

TABLE 5-5	RANDOMLY SELECTED TASTING SEQUENCES FOR THE FOUR-COLA CHALLENGE USING 12 PARTICIPANTS			
	TESTING SESSION			
	1	**2**	**3**	**4**
Participant 1	A	B	C	D
Participant 2	A	B	D	C
Participant 3	A	C	D	B
Participant 4	A	D	C	B
Participant 5	B	A	C	D
Participant 6	B	C	D	A
Participant 7	B	C	A	D
Participant 8	C	A	B	D
Participant 9	C	B	A	D
Participant 10	C	D	B	A
Participant 11	D	B	C	A
Participant 12	D	C	B	A

Thus, the first participant would taste the colas in the order B, D, A, C, whereas the second participant would experience them in the order D, A, C, B. We would continue systematically rotating the sequence until each cola appears once in each row and each column. To test a total of 12 participants, we would assign 3 participants to each of the four sequences. By ensuring that each treatment appears an equal number of times at each testing session, this approach comes close to satisfying the conditions for counterbalancing. It does not, however, ensure that the treatments precede and follow each other an equal number of times. A more complex procedure, the Latin square technique, is used to address this issue. Because of its complexity, this procedure is seldom

TABLE 5-6	AN INCOMPLETE COUNTERBALANCING APPROACH			

This approach involves randomly determining the sequence for the first participant and then systematically rotating the treatments for the following sequences.

	TASTING SEQUENCE			
	1	**2**	**3**	**4**
Participant 1	B	D	A	C
Participant 2	D	A	C	B
Participant 3	A	C	B	D
Participant 4	C	B	D	A

used. If you are interested in reading about its use, Rosenthal and Rosnow (1991) offer a nice presentation of its particulars.

Now that we have examined the mechanics involved in implementing complete and incomplete counterbalancing, let's see exactly what counterbalancing can and cannot control. To simply say that counterbalancing controls for sequence or order effects does not tell the entire story. Although counterbalancing controls for sequence or order effects, as you will see, it also controls for *carryover effects*. It cannot, however, control for *differential carryover*.

> **Sequence** or **order effects** The position of a treatment in a series determines, in part, the participants' response.

Sequence or Order Effects **Sequence** or **order effects** are produced by the participant's being exposed to the sequential presentation of the treatments. For example, assume we are testing reaction time to three types of dashboard warning lights: red (R), green (G), and flashing white (FW). As soon as the warning light comes on, the participant is to turn the engine off. To completely counterbalance this experiment would require 6 sequences and at least 6 participants (3! = 3 × 2 × 1 = 6). If we found the reaction time to the first warning light, regardless of type, was 10 seconds, and that improvements of 4 and 3 seconds were made to the second and third lights (regardless of type), respectively, we would be dealing with a sequence or order effect. This example is diagrammed in Table 5-7. As you can see, the sequence or order effect depends on *where* in the sequential presentation of treatments the participant's performance is evaluated, *not* which treatment is experienced.

TABLE 5-7 EXAMPLE OF SEQUENCE OR ORDER EFFECTS IN A COUNTERBALANCED EXPERIMENT

The performance increase shown in parentheses below each sequence indicates the effect of testing reaction time to red (R), green (G), and flashing white (FW) lights on an instrument panel at that particular point in the sequence. Thus, second and third testings result in increases of 4 and 3, respectively, regardless of the experimental task.

ORDER OF TASK PRESENTATION

R	G	FW
(0	4	3)
R	FW	G
(0	4	3)
G	R	FW
(0	4	3)
G	FW	R
(0	4	3)
FW	R	G
(0	4	3)
FW	G	R
(0	4	3)

Performance Increase →

Sequence or order effects will be experienced equally by all participants in counterbalanced situations because each treatment appears an equal number of times at each testing session. This consideration points to a major flaw in the use of randomized, incomplete counterbalancing: The treatments may not be presented an equal number of times at each testing session (see Table 5-5). Thus, sequence or order effects are not controlled in this situation.

> **Carryover effect** The effects of one treatment persist or carry over and influence responses to the next treatment.

Carryover Effects   When a **carryover effect** is present, the effects of one treatment persist to influence the participant's response to the next treatment. For example, let's assume that experiencing the green (G) warning light before the red (R) light always causes participants to *decrease* their reaction time by 2 seconds. Conversely, experiencing R before G causes participants to *increase* their reaction time by 2 seconds. Experiencing the flashing white (FW) warning light either before or after G has no effect on reaction time. However, experiencing R before FW increases reaction time by 3 seconds, and experiencing FW before R reduces reaction time by 3 seconds. In the R → G/G → R and R → FW/FW → R transitions, the previous treatment influences the participant's response to the subsequent treatment in a consistent and predictable manner. These effects are diagrammed in Table 5-8. Note that

---

TABLE 5-8 **EXAMPLE OF CARRYOVER EFFECTS IN A COUNTERBALANCED EXPERIMENT**

Carryover effects occur when a specific preceding treatment influences the performance in a subsequent treatment. In this example, experiencing Treatment G prior to Treatment R results in a decrease of 2 (i.e., −2), whereas experiencing Treatment R prior to Treatment G results in an increase of 2 (i.e., +2). Experiencing Treatment G prior to FW or Treatment FW prior to G does not produce a unique effect. However, experiencing Treatment R prior to FW results in an increase of 3, whereas experiencing Treatment FW prior to R results in a decrease of 3.

	SEQUENCE OF TREATMENTS		
	G	R	FW
Effect on Performance →	(0	−2	+3)
	G	FW	R
	(0	0	−3)
	R	G	FW
	(0	+2	0)
	R	FW	G
	(0	+3	0)
	FW	G	R
	(0	0	−2)
	FW	R	G
	(0	−3	+2)

counterbalancing includes an equal number of each type of transition (e.g., R → G, G → R, R → FW, etc.). Thus the opposing carryover effects cancel each other.

> **Differential carryover**
> The response to one treatment depends on which treatment was administered previously.

Differential Carryover Although counterbalancing can control many things, it offers no protection against differential carryover. **Differential carryover** occurs when the response to one treatment depends on *which* treatment is experienced previously. Consider an experiment investigating the effects of reward magnitude on reading comprehension in second-grade children. Each child reads three similar passages. After each passage is completed, a series of questions is asked. Each correct answer is rewarded by a certain number of M&M's (the IV). In the low-reward condition (A) children receive one M&M after each correct answer; three and five M&M's are received in the medium-reward (B) and high-reward (C) treatments, respectively.

Although this experiment might be viewed as another six-sequence example of counterbalancing (see Table 5-4), the effects may not be symmetrical as in the carryover example we just considered. The participant who receives the A → B → C sequence may be motivated to do well at all testing sessions because the reward progressively increases from session to session. What about the student who receives the B → C → A sequence? In this case the reward rises from three M&M's (Session 1) to five M&M's (Session 2), but then is reduced to one M&M (Session 3). Will the decrease from five M&M's to one M&M produce a unique effect, such as the student's refusing to participate, that the other transitions do not produce? If so, differential carryover has occurred, and

TABLE 5-9 EXAMPLE OF DIFFERENTIAL CARRYOVER IN A COUNTERBALANCED EXPERIMENT

Differential carryover occurs when performance depends on which specific sequence occurs. In the following example, experiencing Treatment A prior to Treatment B results in an increase of 6 (i.e., +6), whereas all other sequences result in an increase of 2 (i.e., +2).

	SEQUENCE OF TREATMENTS		
	A (1 M&M)	B (3 M&M'S)	C (5 M&M'S)
Effect on Performance →	(0	+6	+2)
	A	C	B
	(0	+2	+2)
	B	A	C
	(0	+2	+2)
	B	C	A
	(0	+2	+2)
	C	A	B
	(0	+2	+6)
	C	B	A
	(0	+2	+2)

counterbalancing is not an effective control procedure. Some possible effects of differential carryover in the M&M study are shown in Table 5-9. As you can see, the drastic decrease in performance produced by the C (five M&M's)-to-A (one M&M) transition is not canceled out by a comparable increase resulting from the A-to-C transition.

The potential for differential carryover exists whenever counterbalancing is employed. The experimenter must be sensitive to this possibility. A thorough review of the effects of the IV being used in your research can help sensitize you to the possibility of differential carryover. If this threat exists, it is advisable to employ a research procedure that does not involve presenting more than one treatment to each participant.

REVIEW SUMMARY

1. **Randomization** controls for extraneous variables by distributing them equally to all groups.

2. When experimenters use **elimination** as a control technique, they seek to completely remove the extraneous variable from the experiment.

3. **Constancy** controls an extraneous variable by creating a constant or uniform condition with regard to that variable.

4. **Balancing** achieves control of extraneous variables by ensuring that all groups receive the extraneous variables to the same extent.

5. **Counterbalancing** controls for sequence or order effects when participants receive more than one treatment. **Within-subject counterbalancing** involves the administration of more than one treatment sequence to each participant, whereas **within-group counterbalancing** involves the administration of a different treatment sequence to each participant.

6. The total number of treatment sequences can be determined by $n!$ When all sequences are administered, **complete counterbalancing** is being used. **Incomplete counterbalancing** involves the administration of fewer than the total number of possible sequences.

7. The random selection of treatment sequences, systematic rotation, or the Latin square approaches can be used when incomplete counterbalancing is implemented.

8. Counterbalancing can control for **sequence** or **order** and **carryover effects**. It cannot control for **differential carryover**, for which the response to one treatment depends on which treatment was experienced previously.

CHECK YOUR PROGRESS

1. Matching

    1. randomization   A. complete removal of the extraneous variable

    2. elimination   B. extraneous variable is reduced to a single value

    3. constancy   C. most widely used control procedure

    4. balancing   D. used to control for order effects

    5. counterbalancing   E. extraneous variable is distributed equally to all groups

2. The most widely used control technique is _____.

    a. randomization b. elimination c. constancy d. balancing e. counterbalancing

3. Balancing is a logical extension of _____.

    a. constancy   b. randomization   c. counterbalancing   d. elimination

4. Distinguish between within-subject and within-group counterbalancing.

5. What can $n!$ be used for? Calculate the value of $4!$

6. _____occurs when the response to one treatment depends on which treatment preceded it.

    a. Carryover   b. Differential carryover

    c. A sequence or order effect   d. Fault randomization

7. What is incomplete counterbalancing?

Internal Validity: Evaluating Your Experiment from the Inside

Internal validity A type of evaluation of your experiment; asks whether your IV is the only possible explanation of the results shown for your DV.

The concept of **internal validity** revolves around the question of whether your IV actually created any change that you observe in your DV. Researchers take many precautions aimed at increasing internal validity as they design and set up experiments. If you use adequate control techniques, your experiment should be free from confounding and you can, indeed, conclude that your IV caused the change in your DV.

Threats to Internal Validity

In this section we will alert you to several categories of factors that can cause problems with the internal validity of an experiment. These factors are details that you should attend to when planning and evaluating your experiment and when scrutinizing research done by other investigators. Sherlock Holmes stressed the importance of details when he said to his assistant, Dr. Watson, "Never trust to general impression, my boy, but concentrate yourself upon details" (Doyle, 1927, p. 196). The following list is drawn largely from the work of Donald T. Campbell (1957) and his associates (Campbell & Stanley, 1966; Cook & Campbell, 1979).

History A threat to internal validity; refers to events that occur between the DV measurements in a repeated measures design.

History We must beware of the possible extraneous variable of **history** when we test or measure experimental participants more than once. We might administer the IV between the DV measurements (pretest, posttest), or we may be interested in the time course of the IV effect—how participants react to the IV over time. In this case, history refers to any significant event, other than the IV, that occurs between DV measurements. Campbell and Stanley (1966) cited the example of a 1940 experiment concerning informational propaganda. Attitudes were measured and then students read some Nazi propaganda. However, before the posttest was given, France fell to the Nazis. The subsequent attitude measurement was probably much more influenced by the historical event than by the propaganda. Obviously, this is an extreme example; historical events of this impact are rare. However, Campbell and Stanley also used the term to refer to less significant events that might occur during a lengthy experimental session. Noise or laughter or other similar events could occur during a session that might distract participants and cause them to react differently from participants who did not experience the same events. The distraction would then serve as an extraneous variable and the experiment would be confounded. One of our goals is to control or eliminate such distractions.

Maturation   This label seems to refer to experimental participants growing older during the course of an experiment, but that is somewhat misleading. Although true maturation is possible during a longitudinal study, Campbell (1957) used the term with a slightly different meaning. He used **maturation** to refer to systematic time-related changes, but mostly of a shorter duration than we would typically expect. Campbell and Stanley (1966) gave examples of participants growing tired, hungry, or bored through the course of an experiment. As you can see, maturation would be possible in an experiment that extends over some amount of time. How much time must occur before maturational changes can take place could vary widely based on the experiment's demands on the participants, the topic of the experiment, or many participant variables (e.g., their motivation, how much sleep they got the night before, whether they have eaten recently, and so on). Maturational changes are more likely to occur in an experiment that uses repeated measurements of the DV because experimental participants are involved in the research for a longer period of time. You should attempt to safeguard against such changes if your experiment requires long sessions for your participants.

> **Maturation** A threat to internal validity; refers to changes in participants that occur over time during an experiment; could include actual physical maturation or tiredness, boredom, hunger, and so on.

Testing   **Testing** is a definite threat to internal validity if you test participants more than once. As Campbell (1957) noted, if you take the same test more than once, scores on the second test may vary systematically from the first scores simply because you took the test a second time. This type of effect is often known as a **practice effect**—your score does not change because of anything you have done other than repeating the test.

For example, the people who run the testing services for the two major college entrance exams (ACT and SAT) acknowledge the existence of testing effects when they recommend that you take their tests two or three times in order to achieve your maximum possible score. It appears that there is some "learning to take a college entrance exam" behavior that contributes to your score on such tests. This factor is separate from what the test is designed to measure (your potential for doing college work). Thus, those in charge are not surprised when your scores increase a little when you take the exam a second time; they actually expect an increase simply because you are familiar with the test and how it is given. However, two points about this specific testing effect are important to note. First, the effect is short-lived. You can expect to gain some points on a second (and perhaps third) attempt, but you will not continue

> **Testing** A threat to internal validity that occurs because measuring the DV causes a change in the DV.

> **Practice effect** A beneficial effect on a DV measurement caused by previous experience with the DV.

to gain points indefinitely just from the practice of taking the test. If improvement was constant, students could "max out" their scores merely by taking the test many times. Second, the expected improvement is small. Both the ACT and SAT administrators have a range of expected improvement that they consider normal. If you retake one of their tests and improve more than this normal range predicts, it is possible that your score will be questioned. You may be asked to provide documentation that accounts for your surprising improvement. If this documentation is not convincing, you may be asked to retake the test under their supervision. Unfortunately, the pressure to obtain scholarships (academic as well as athletic) has led some people to improve their scores through cheating or other unethical means.

In his discussion of testing effects, Campbell (1957) warned us against using **reactive measures** in our research. A measurement that is reactive changes the behavior in question simply by measuring it. Here's an example. One popular topic for social psychology research is attitude change. If you were going to conduct an experiment on attitudes and attitude change, how would you measure your participants' attitudes? If you are like most people, you probably responded "with an attitude questionnaire."

Reactive measures DV measurements that actually change the DV being measured.

Although questionnaires are commonly used to measure attitudes, they have a significant drawback. Can you figure out what this drawback is? Hint: This problem is particularly evident when you want to use an IV designed to change people's attitudes. Can you think of a means for overcoming this difficulty?

Many attitude questionnaires are reactive measures. If we ask you a number of questions about how you feel about people of different racial groups, or about women's rights, or about the President's job performance, you can probably figure out that your attitude is being measured. The problem with knowing that your attitude is being measured is that you can alter your answers on a questionnaire in any way you wish. For example, if a woman administers a questionnaire to you, you may give answers that make you appear more sympathetic to women's issues. If the questioner is of a different race than you, you may guard against giving answers that would make you look prejudiced. This type of problem is particularly acute if we use an experimental manipulation designed to change your attitude. If we give you a questionnaire about women's rights, then show you a pro–women's rights movie, then give you the questionnaire again, it doesn't take a rocket scientist to figure out that we're interested in finding out how the movie changed your attitude toward women's rights! What can you do to avoid this problem in your research?

Campbell (1957) advocated using **nonreactive measures** as much as possible. A nonreactive measure does not alter the participant's response by virtue of measuring it. Psychologists (and others) have devised many tools and techniques for nonreactive measures— one-way mirrors, hidden cameras and microphones, naturalistic

Nonreactive measures DV measurements that do not influence the DV being measured.

observation, deception, and so on. If we are interested in your attitude about women's rights, perhaps we should see whether you attend women's rights lectures or donate money to women's rights issues, ask you if you voted for a certain political candidate (who supported women's rights), or measure some other such behavior. In other words, if we can obtain some type of behavioral measure that is harder to fake than a questionnaire response, we may get a truer measure of your attitude. As a psychology student doing research, you should guard against using reactive measures, which are often appealing because they seem so easy to use.

Instrumentation (Instrument Decay)   As with maturation, Campbell's category of instrumentation has a broader meaning than is implied by its name. Part of Campbell's (1957) description of **instrumentation** referred to changes in measurement by various apparatuses, although his list now seems quite outdated (e.g., "the fatiguing of a spring scales, or the condensation of water vapor in a cloud chamber," p. 299). However, he also included human observers, judges, raters, and coders in this category. Thus, the broad definition of instrumentation refers to changes in measurement of the DV that are due to the measuring "device," whether that device is an actual piece of equipment or a human.

> **Instrumentation** A threat to internal validity that occurs if the equipment or human measuring the DV changes its measuring criterion over time.

This measurement problem related to equipment is probably less of an issue today than it was in "the good old days." (By the way, "the good old days" are probably defined as whenever your professor was in school.) We're sure your instructor has a horror story about the time the equipment broke down in the middle of an important day of data collection. The reality of the situation is that even today equipment can break down or can develop flaws in measurement. You should always check out your equipment before using it to collect data each day. One of the drawbacks of modern equipment, such as computers, is that it may break down, but that fact will not be obvious to you. Although you can certainly tell whether a computer is working, you may not be able to tell if it appears to be working but actually has a bug or a virus. A careful experimenter checks out the equipment each day.

The same principle should govern your use of humans as monitors or scorers in your experiment. Often, you may serve as both the experimenter and the monitor or scorer for your experiment. This dual role places an extra obligation on you to be fair, impartial, and consistent in your behavior. For example, if you are scoring responses from your participants, you should have a set answer key with any judgment calls you might face worked out beforehand. So that you will not unconsciously favor one group over the other, you should score the responses blind as to which group a participant belongs to. If you have other persons scoring or monitoring your experiment, you should check their performance regularly to ensure that they remain consistent. Researchers often calculate interrater reliability (how closely the observations of two raters or observers correspond with each other) to determine if instrumentation is a problem in a research project.

Statistical Regression   When you deal with extreme scores, it is likely that you will see *regression to the mean*. This concept merely means that if you remeasure participants who have extreme scores (either high or low), their subsequent scores are likely to regress or move toward the average or mean. The subsequent scores are still likely to be extreme in the same direction, but not as extreme. For example, if you made a very high *A* (or very low *F*) on the first exam, your second exam score will probably not be as high (or as low). If a 7'0" basketball player has a son, the son will probably be tall but will probably be shorter than 7'0". If a 4'6" jockey has a son, the son will probably be short, but taller than 4'6". When you have extreme scores, it is simply difficult to maintain that high degree of extremity over repeated measures.

How does **statistical regression** play a role in internal validity? It is fairly common to measure participants before an experiment in order to divide them into IV groups (based on whatever was measured). For example, imagine an experiment designed to test the effects of a study course for college entrance exams. As a preliminary measure, we give an ACT or SAT test to a large group of high school students. From this pool of students, we plan to select our experimental participants to take the study course. Which students are we likely to select? Why, of course, the ones who performed poorly on the test. After they take the study course, we have them retake the entrance exam. More than likely, we will find that their new scores are higher than the original scores. Why is this? Did the study course help the students improve their scores? It is certainly possible. However, isn't it also possible that regression to the mean is at work? When you score near the low end of a test's possible score, there's not room to do much except improve. Sometimes it is difficult for people to see this point—they are convinced that the study course must be responsible for the improvement. To help illustrate the power of statistical regression, imagine a similar experiment performed with students who made the highest scores on the entrance exams. We want them to take our study course also. After our study course, we find that their second test scores are actually lower than the first set! Did our study course lower their scores? We certainly hope not. Having made an extremely high score on the first test, it is difficult to improve on the second.

The advice concerning statistical regression should be clear. If you select participants on the basis of extreme scores, you should beware of regression to the mean as a possible explanation for higher or lower scores on a repeated (or similar) test.

> **Statistical regression**
> A threat to internal validity that occurs when low scorers improve or high scorers fall on a second administration of a test due solely to statistical reasons.

Selection   It should come as no surprise to you that **selection** can serve as a threat to internal validity. Before we conduct our experiment, it is imperative that we can assume that our selected groups are equivalent. Starting with equal groups, we treat them identically except for the IV. Then if the groups are no longer equal after the experiment, we can assume that the IV caused that difference.

Suppose, however, that when we select our participants, we do so in such a way that the groups are *not* equal before the experiment. In such a case, differences that we observe between our groups after the experiment may actually reflect differences that existed *before* the experiment began. On the other hand, differences after the experiment may reflect differences that existed *before* the experiment plus a treatment effect. Group differences that existed before the experiment are extraneous variables and the experiment is confounded.

Be careful not to confuse the selection problem with assignment of participants to groups. Selection typically refers to using participants who are already assigned to a

> **Selection** A threat to internal validity; if we choose participants in such a way that our groups are not equal before the experiment, we cannot be certain that our IV caused any difference we observe after the experiment.

particular group by virtue of their group membership. Campbell and Stanley (1966) cited the example of comparing people who watched a particular TV program to those who did not. People who choose to watch a program or not to watch a program probably differ in ways other than the knowledge of the program content. For example, it is likely that there are differences in people who watch and those who do not watch soap operas that are unrelated to the actual content of the soap operas. Thus, using soap opera viewers and non–soap opera viewers as groups to study the impact of a particular soap opera episode dealing with rape is probably not the best way to study the impact of that episode.

> **Mortality** A threat to internal validity that can occur if experimental participants from different groups drop out of the experiment at different rates.

Mortality   As you might guess, death is the original meaning of *mortality* in this context. In research that exposed animals to stress, chemicals, or other toxic agents, mortality could actually occur in significant numbers. Mortality could become a threat to internal validity if a treatment was so severe that significant numbers of animals in the treatment group died. Simply because they had survived, the remaining animals in the treatment group would probably be different in some way from the animals in the other groups. Although the other groups would still represent random samples, those in the particular treatment group would not.

In human research, **mortality** typically refers to experimental dropouts. Remember the ethical principle from Chapter 3 that gives participants the right to withdraw from an experiment at any point without penalty. A situation somewhat analogous to the animal example in the preceding paragraph could occur if many participants from one group withdraw from the experiment compared to small numbers from other groups. If such a differential dropout rate occurs, it is doubtful that the groups of participants would still be equal, as they were before the experiment began.

If your experiment contains a treatment condition that is unpleasant, demanding, or noxious in any way, you should pay careful attention to the dropout rate for the various groups. Differential dropout rates could also be a significant problem in research that spans a long time (weeks or months, for example). If one group shows a higher rate, your experiment may lack internal validity. One final word of caution: It is possible that groups in your experiment will not show different rates of dropping out but will have previously experienced different rates that helped compose the groups. Campbell (1957) cited the example of a very common experiment in educational settings, namely, making comparisons of different classes. Suppose we wish to determine whether our college's values-based education actually affects the values of the students. We choose a sample of freshmen and a sample of seniors and give them a questionnaire to measure their values in order to see whether their values are in line with our general education curriculum's values goals.

PSYCHOLOGICAL DETECTIVE   How might previous dropout rates damage the internal validity of this experiment?

Today is the final session of our lab on rats, and Willy, I don't think I have to remind you that this time if you eat yours, I'm not giving you another one.
We certainly hope that you never experience this type of mortality in your research!

In this experiment it should not surprise you to find that the seniors' values are more in line with our college's stated values. Although this effect *could* be a result of taking our values-based curriculum, it could also represent the effect of mortality through dropouts. Most colleges bring in large numbers of freshmen and graduate only some percentage of those students a few years later. What types of students are more likely to leave? Probably students whose values are not in line with the college's values are more likely to drop out than those who agree with the college's values. Thus, when we assess seniors' values, we are only measuring those students who did *not* drop out.

> **Interactions with selection** Threats to internal validity that can occur if there are systematic differences between or among selected treatment groups based on maturation, history, or instrumentation.

Interactions with Selection   **Interactions with selection** can occur when the groups we have selected show differences on another variable (i.e., maturation, history, or instrumentation) that vary systematically by groups. Let us give you an example for clarification. Suppose we are conducting a language development study in which we select our two groups from lower- and middle-class families. We wish to avoid selection as a threat to internal validity, so we pretest our children with a language test to ensure that our groups are equivalent beforehand. However, this pretesting could not account for the possibility that these two groups may show different maturation patterns, despite the fact that they are equal before the experiment begins. For example, if we look at children around the age of 1, we may find that the two classes of children show no language differences. However, by age 2, middle-class children might have larger vocabularies, talk more often, or have other linguistic advantages over lower class children. Then if we look at children who are 6, these linguistic advantages may disappear. If this were the case, comparing lower and middle-class children's language proficiency at age 2 would show a selection-maturation interaction that would pose a threat to internal validity. Although one group of children would show an advantage over another group, the difference would not be a reliable, lasting difference. Therefore, any conclusion we reached that implied the permanence of such an effect would be invalid because the difference would have been based on different maturation schedules of the two groups.

Similar interaction effects could occur between selection and history or between selection and instrumentation. A selection–history interaction that would jeopardize internal validity could occur if you chose your different groups from different settings—for example, different countries, states, cities, or even schools within a city. This problem is especially acute in cross-cultural research (see Chapter 7). These different settings allow for different local histories (Cook & Campbell, 1979) that might affect the outcome variable(s). The selection and history are confounded together because the groups were selected on a basis that allows different histories. An example of a selection–instrumentation interaction (based on human "instrumentation") would be using different interpreters or scorers for participants that come from two different countries, assuming the IV was related to the country of origin.

Diffusion or **imitation of treatment** A threat to internal validity that can occur if participants in one treatment group become familiar with the treatment of another group and copy that treatment.

Diffusion or Imitation of Treatments Diffusion or **imitation of treatments** creates a problem with internal validity by negating or minimizing the difference between the groups in your experiment. This problem can occur easily if your treatment involves providing some information to participants in one group but not to participants in another group. If the informed participants communicate the vital information to the supposedly uninformed participants, then the two groups may behave in identical manners.

 PSYCHOLOGICAL DETECTIVE If these two groups behave identically, what experimental conclusion would you draw? What would be wrong with this conclusion?

If the participants behave identically, the experimental outcome would indicate no difference between the groups based on the IV. The problem with this conclusion is that in truth, there would actually be no IV in the experiment because the IV was supposed to have been the difference in information between groups. It is typical for experimenters to request that participants not discuss details of the experiment until it is completed.

Experiments dealing with learning and memory are particularly susceptible to the imitation of treatments. For example, suppose we want to teach students in our classes a new, more effective study strategy. To simplify the experiment, we will use our 9:00 A.M. general psychology class as a control group and our 10:00 A.M. general psychology class as the experimental group. We teach the 9:00 A.M. class as usual, saying nothing to the students about how they should study for their quizzes and exams. In the 10:00 A.M. class, however, we teach our new study technique. After the first few quizzes and the first major exam, the students in the 10:00 A.M. class are so convinced of the effectiveness of their new study approach that they talk to their friends in the 9:00 A.M. class about it. Soon everyone in the 9:00 A.M. class knows about the new study technique and is also using it faithfully. At this point, we have the problem of treatment diffusion. Our participants in both groups are now using the same study strategy, which effectively no longer gives us an IV. It should be obvious that if you cannot guarantee control over the IV, the hope of having an experiment with internal validity is not strong.

Protecting Internal Validity

There are two approaches you could take to fight the various threats to internal validity. First, you can (and should) implement the various control procedures that we have discussed in this chapter. These controls were specifically developed to deal with such problems. The second approach involves the use of a standard procedure. Just as detectives use standard police procedures to help them protect their cases, experimenters use standard research procedures, called experimental designs, to help ensure internal validity. We will have more to say about several experimental designs in subsequent chapters.

How important is internal validity? It is only *the* most important property of any experiment. If you do not concern yourself with the internal validity of your experiment, you are wasting your time. Experiments are intended to derive cause-and-effect statements—to conclude that *X* causes *Y* to occur. You must take care to control any extraneous variables that might affect your dependent variable. You cannot count on your statistical tests to provide the necessary control functions for you. Statistical tests merely analyze the numbers you bring to the test—they do not have the ability to remove confounding effects (or even to discern that confounding has occurred) in the data you bring.

REVIEW SUMMARY

1. For your experiment to have **internal validity**, it must be free from confounding due to extraneous variables.
2. There are nine specific threats to internal validity that we must guard against.
3. The **history** threat can occur if meaningful events that would affect the DV occur between two measurements of the DV (repeated measures).
4. The **maturation** threat may occur if experimental participants show some change due to time passage during an experiment.
5. The **testing** threat results if participants respond differently on the second measure of a DV simply because they have previously responded to the DV.
6. An **instrumentation** threat can refer to equipment changes or malfunctions or to human observers whose criteria change over time.

7. **Statistical regression** is a threat that can occur when participants are selected because of their extreme scores on some variable. Extreme scores are likely to regress toward the mean on a second measurement.

8. The **selection** threat results if we select groups of participants in such a way that our groups are not equal before the experiment.

9. **Mortality** becomes a threat if participants drop out of the experiment in different rates for different conditions.

10. **Interactions with selection** can occur for history, maturation, or instrumentation. If we select participants in such a way that they vary on these dimensions, then internal validity is threatened.

11. **Diffusion** or **imitation of treatments** is a threat if participants learn about treatments of other groups and copy them.

CHECK YOUR PROGRESS

1. Changing the behavior simply by measuring it refers to _____.

   a. a reactive measure   b. a measured IV

   c. a manipulated IV   d. history

2. Comparing intact groups is likely to cause a problem because of _____.

   a. mortality   b. selection   c. maturation   d. history

3. Why is it important to evaluate your experiment for internal validity?

4. Match the internal validity threat with the appropriate situation.

   1. history   A. Your DV scorer gets sick and you recruit a new person to help you.

   2. maturation   B. You are conducting an experiment on racial prejudice and a race riot occurs between tests.

   3. testing   C. Your participants grow bored and disinterested during your experimental sessions.

   4. instrumentation   D. You use a before-and-after DV measurement and the participants remember some of their answers.

5. Match the threat to internal validity with the correct situation.

   1. statistical regression   A. Many participants find one treatment condition very boring and quit.

   2. mortality   B. You select boys from lower-class homes and girls from upper-class environments.

   3. selection   C. Students in your control group talk to students in the experimental group and imitate their treatment.

   4. diffusion of treatments   D. You select the worst students in the class and try a new tutoring strategy.

6. You want to compare the formal education of college students and senior citizens. You select a group of each type of participant and give each a written test of math, social studies, and grammatical information. What threat of internal validity appears likely in this situation? Why?

7. Experimental dropouts are a problem linked to _____.

   a. mortality   b. selection   c. maturation   d. history

KEY TERMS

Variable, *90*

Operational definition, *91*

Independent variable (IV), *91*

Physiological IV, *92*

Experience IV, *92*

Stimulus or environmental IV, *92*

Participant characteristics, *92*

Extraneous variables, *93*

Confounding, *93*

Dependent variable (DV), *95*

Valid, *98*

Reliable, *99*

Nuisance variable, *99*

Randomization, *104*

Elimination, *104*

Constancy, *105*

Balancing, *106*

Counterbalancing, *108*

Within-subject counterbalancing, *108*

Within-group counterbalancing, *108*

Complete counterbalancing, *110*

Incomplete counterbalancing, *110*

Sequence or order effects, *112*

Carryover effect, *113*

Differential carryover, *114*

Internal validity, *116*

History, *116*

Maturation, *117*

Testing, *117*

Practice effect, *117*

Reactive measures, *118*

Nonreactive measures, *118*

Instrumentation, *119*

Statistical regression, *120*

Selection, *120*

Mortality, *121*

Interactions with selection, *122*

Diffusion or imitation of treatment, *123*

LOOKING AHEAD

In this chapter we have explored the nature of variables in general and have seen the importance of selecting appropriate independent and dependent variables. The potentially damaging effects of nuisance variables and confounders have led to the development of procedures for their control. In the next chapter we continue our study of statistics; we examine the procedures that researchers use to summarize and describe their research findings.

Summarizing and Comparing Data: Measures of Variation, Distribution of Means and the Standard Error of the Mean, and z Scores

In our first discussion of using statistics in psychological research (Chapter 4), you learned that psychological researchers use *descriptive statistics* to make their data more clear and understandable. To accomplish this purpose, we saw that researchers can create frequency tables or prepare a graph to visually depict their data. They also can calculate measures of central tendency. In this chapter you will learn about other, more important, ways that researchers use statistics to describe their data. You will learn how to calculate statistical measures of the variability of the scores in your data. Additionally, we will examine the statistical procedure psychologists use to compare scores from different distributions.

Measures of Variability

You just got your last psychology test returned in class; your score is 64. What does that number tell you? By itself it may not mean very much. You ask your professor for additional information and find that the class mean was 56. You feel better because you were above the mean. However, after a few moments of reflection you realize you need still more information. How were the other scores grouped? Were they all clustered close to the mean or did they spread out considerably? The amount of **variability**, or spread, in the other scores will have a bearing on the standing of your score. If most of the other scores are very close to the mean, then your score will be among the highest in the class. If the other scores are spread out widely around the mean, then your score may not be one of the strongest. Obviously, you need a measure of variability to provide a complete picture of these data. The *range* and *standard deviation* are two measures of variability frequently reported by psychologists.

> **Variability** The extent to which scores spread out around the mean.

Range

> **Range** A measure of variability that is computed by subtracting the smallest score from the largest score.

The **range** is the easiest measure of variability to calculate; you rank order the scores in your distribution and then subtract the smallest score from the largest to find the range. Consider the following distribution:

1, 1, 1, 1, 5, 6, 6, 8, 25

When we subtract 1 (smallest score) from 25 (largest score), we find that the range is 24.

Range: highest score − lowest score = 25 − 1 = 24

However, other than telling us the difference between the largest and smallest scores, the range does not provide much information. Knowing the range is 24 does not tell us about the distribution of the scores we just considered. Consider Figure 6-1. The range is the same in 6-1A and 6-1B; however, the spread of the scores differs drastically between these two distributions. Most of the scores cluster in the center of the first distribution (Figure 6-1A), whereas the scores are spread out more evenly in the second distribution (Figure 6-1B). We must turn to another measure, the standard deviation, to provide additional information about how the scores are distributed.

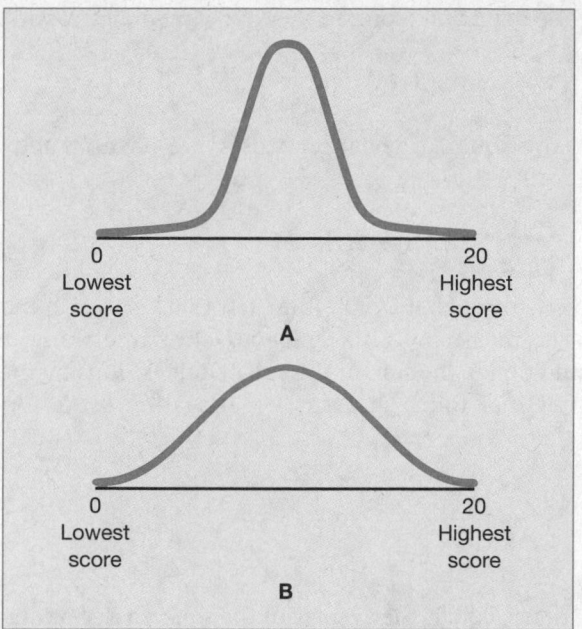

FIGURE 6-1   THE RANGE DOES NOT PROVIDE MUCH INFORMATION ABOUT THE DISTRIBUTION UNDER CONSIDERATION.

Variance

> **Variance** A single number that represents the total amount of variation in a distribution.

In order to obtain the standard deviation, we must first calculate the variance. You can think of the **variance** as a single number that represents the total amount of variability in the distribution. The variance of a sample is symbolized by S^2, whereas the variance of a population is symbolized by σ^2.

The larger the number, the greater the total spread of the scores. The variance and standard deviation are based on how much each score in the distribution deviates from the mean. The following formula shows this relation between a score (X) and the mean (M)

$$X - M$$

> **Deviation score** The difference between a score (X) and the mean (M).

This difference is called a **deviation score** and is symbolized by x. We can now define variance as the average of the sum of the squared deviation scores.

 Time to put your thinking cap on. Reread the discussion of *variance*. Now, see if you can write the formula for variance.

If you started by squaring the deviation scores in the following manner, good.

$$(X - M)^2$$

Because we need to sum the squared deviation scores, we have to add Σ to the formula.

$$\Sigma(X - M)^2$$

We almost have the complete formula; the only thing left to do is to find the average. If you remembered that the mean and an average are the same thing, then you probably said that we should divide the sum of the squared deviations by the number of scores (N). Adding that final touch gives us the deviation score formula for variance:

$$S^2 = \frac{\Sigma(X - M)^2}{N} \text{ or } S^2 = \frac{\Sigma x^2}{N}$$

To repeat in words: The variance equals the average of the squared deviation scores, or to put it another way, the variance equals the sum of the squared deviation scores divided by the number of scores. We hope the formula you came up with looks just like this one.

Let's put the deviation score formula to work to calculate the variance for the following set of numbers: 1, 1, 1, 2, 5, 6, 6, 8, and 25. The first thing we will do is calculate the mean:

$$M = \Sigma X/N = 55/9 = 6.1111$$

Table 6-1 shows the other components that are necessary to calculate the variance using the deviation score formula. Table 6-1 contains several bits of interesting information. First, if you look at the deviation score column, you will see that the sum of the deviation scores, Σx, is zero. In fact, this sum will always be zero because *the deviation scores are evenly distributed above and below the mean*. Because the mean is a balance point, the sum of the deviation scores above the mean will always equal the sum of the deviation scores below them. Because the values below the mean will always be negative, their sum will exactly cancel the positive values above the mean and the sum will be zero. If the sum isn't zero, then you know there is something wrong with your calculations.

From Table 6-1 we also know that $\Sigma x^2 = 456.8885$. Because we had 9 scores, $N = 9$. Plugging these values into our deviation score formula for variance we find that:

$$S^2 = \frac{\Sigma x^2}{N} = \frac{456.8885}{9} = 50.7654 = 50.77$$

Because it is tedious work (that may lead to calculation errors, *especially if decimals are involved*) to find all the deviation scores, square each one, and then sum all of these

| TABLE 6-1 | CALCULATING THE DEVIATION SCORES AND SQUARED DEVIATION SCORES | |

SCORE (X)	DEVIATION SCORE $(X - M) = x$	DEVIATION SCORE SQUARED $= x^2$
1	$1 - 6.1111 = -5.1111$	26.1233
1	$1 - 6.1111 = -5.1111$	26.1233
1	$1 - 6.1111 = -5.1111$	26.1233
2	$2 - 6.1111 = -4.1111$	16.9011
5	$5 - 6.1111 = -1.1111$	1.2345
6	$6 - 6.1111 = -0.1111$	.0123
6	$6 - 6.1111 = -0.1111$	.0123
8	$8 - 6.1111 = 1.8889$	3.5679
25	$25 - 6.1111 = 18.8889$	356.7905
$\Sigma X = 55$	$\Sigma x = 0$	$\Sigma(x)^2 = 456.8885$
$M = \Sigma X/N = 55/9 = 6.1111$		

squares, most researchers prefer to use the *raw score formula* to calculate the variance. This formula and the steps involved are as follows:

$$S^2 = \frac{\Sigma X^2 - (\Sigma X)^2 / N}{N}$$

Step 1 Square each raw score, then sum the squared scores.

Step 2 Sum the raw scores, then square this sum. Divide the squared sum by N.

Step 3 Subtract the product obtained in Step 2 from the total obtained in Step 1.

Step 4 Divide the product obtained in Step 3 by N.

Table 6-2 shows these sums, products, totals, and calculations. Plugging the values from Table 6-2 into the raw score formula, we see that:

$$S^2 = \frac{\Sigma X^2 - (\Sigma X)^2 / N}{N}$$
$$= \frac{793 - (3025)/9}{9} = \frac{793 - 336.1111}{9} = \frac{456.8889}{9} = 50.7654 = 50.77$$

Notice that we obtained exactly the same answer with the raw score formula as we did with the deviation score formula, and we had to contend with only one decimal. Regardless of which formula we use, once we have the variance we can use it to calculate the standard deviation. Also note that we do not round until the final steps of calculation.

TABLE	6-2	USING THE RAW SCORE FORMULA TO CALCULATE THE VARIANCE

SCORE (X)	X^2
1	1
1	1
1	1
2	4
5	25
6	36
6	36
8	64
25	625
$\Sigma X = 55$	$\Sigma X^2 = 793$

$(\Sigma X)^2 = 3025$

$$S^2 = \frac{\Sigma X^2 - (\Sigma X)^2 / N}{N} = \frac{793 - (3025/9)}{9} = 50.7654 = 50.77$$

Calculating and Interpreting the Standard Deviation

To calculate the **standard deviation (SD)** all we have to do is take the square root of the variance.

$$\text{standard deviation } (SD) = \sqrt{\text{variance}} = \sqrt{50.7654} = 7.1250 = 7.13$$

> **Standard deviation (SD)** A measure of variability equal to the square root of the variance; has important relations to the normal curve.

As with the variance, the larger the standard deviation, the greater the variability or spread of scores.

Rather than providing printouts from a specific statistics software package, we are using generic printouts in the text. Because computer statistics packages provide slightly different information, we show you information you might reasonably expect to find on your printout. As you can see, the computer informs us that we entered nine numbers. A sample computer printout listing the mean, variance, and standard deviation for the nine scores we just used to calculate the variance and standard deviation appears in Table 6-3.

TABLE	6-3	COMPUTER PRINTOUT SHOWING MEAN, STANDARD DEVIATION, AND VARIANCE

M	*SD*	VARIANCE	RANGE	*N*
6.11	7.13	50.77	24.00	9

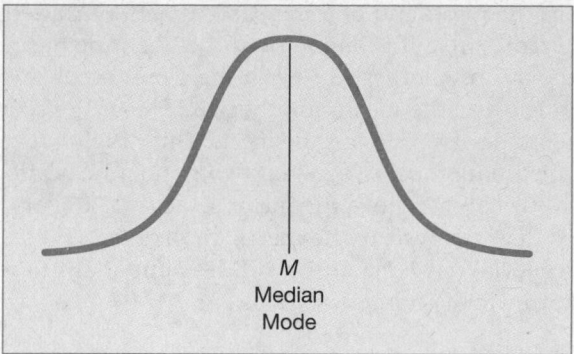

FIGURE 6-2   A SYMMETRICAL OR BELL-SHAPED NORMAL DISTRIBUTION.

> **Normal distribution** A symmetrical, bell-shaped distribution having half of the scores above the mean and half of the scores below the mean.

Now that we have found the standard deviation, what does it tell us? To answer that question we must consider the normal distribution (also called the *normal curve* or the *bell curve*). The concept of the **normal distribution** is based on the finding that as we increase the number of scores in our sample, many distributions of interest to psychologists become symmetrical or bell-shaped.

In the normal curve, the majority of the scores cluster around the measure of central tendency with fewer and fewer scores occurring as we move away from it. As you can see in Figure 6-2, the mean, median, and mode of a normal distribution all have the same value.

Normal distributions and standard deviations are related in interesting ways. For example, distances from the mean of a normal distribution can be measured in standard deviation units. Consider a distribution with an *M* of 56 and *SD* of 4; a score of 60 falls one *SD* above the mean (+1 *SD*), whereas a score of 48 is two *SD*s below the mean (−2 *SD*), and so on. As you can see in Figure 6-3, 34.13% of all the scores in *all* normal

FIGURE 6-3   THE RELATION OF STANDARD DEVIATIONS AND THE NORMAL DISTRIBUTION.

distributions occur between the mean and one standard deviation *above* the mean. Likewise, 34.13% of all the scores in a distribution occur between the mean and one standard deviation *below* the mean. Another 13.59% of the scores occur between one and two standard deviations *above* the mean; another 13.59% of the scores occur between one and two standard deviations *below* the mean. Thus, slightly over 95% of all the scores in a normal distribution occur between two standard deviations below the mean and two standard deviations above the mean. Exactly 2.28% of the scores occur beyond two standard deviations *above* the mean; another 2.28% of the scores occur beyond two standard deviations *below* the mean. It is important to remember that these percentages hold true for *all* normal distributions.

Review Figure 6-3 for a moment. Why isn't the percentage of scores from 0 to 1 SD above (or below) the mean the same as the percentage of scores from 1 to 2 SD above (or below) the mean?

As we move away from the mean (either above or below), the scores become progressively different from the mean. Because larger scores occur less frequently and the scores between 1 and 2 *SD*s are larger than those from 0 to 1 *SD*, the percentage of scores from 1 to 2 *SD*s will be lower than the percentage of scores from 0 to 1 *SD*.

Now, let's return to your test score of 64 that we mentioned at the beginning of the section on variability. You know the mean of the class is 56. If the instructor also tells you that the standard deviation is 4, what would your reaction be? Your score of 64 would be two standard deviations above the mean. You should feel pretty good. Your score of 64 puts you in the top 2.28% of the class (50% of the scores below the mean + 34.13% from the mean to one standard deviation above the mean + 13.59% that occur between one and two standard deviations above the mean)! See Figure 6-4A.

What if your instructor told you the standard deviation was 20? Now your score of 64 does not stand up as well as it did when the standard deviation was 4 (see Figure 6-4B). You are above the mean but a long way from being even one standard deviation above the mean (see Figure 6-4B).

When we describe the shape of a normal distribution, how flat or peaked it is, we are dealing with **kurtosis**. There are three types of kurtosis— *leptokurtic, mesokurtic*, and *platykurtic*. Figure 6-5 depicts these three types of distributions. As you can see, the **leptokurtic** distribution is tall and peaked. Because the scores are definitely clustered around the mean, the standard deviation will be smaller in a leptokurtic distribution. Most researchers believe the **mesokurtic** (*meso* means middle) distribution is the ideal example of a normal distribution. As you can see, the mesokurtic distribution is between

Kurtosis Term pertaining to the shape (how peaked or flat) of a distribution.

Leptokurtic A tall, peaked distribution.

Mesokurtic A middle-shaped distribution as compared to a leptokurtic and a platykurtic distribution.

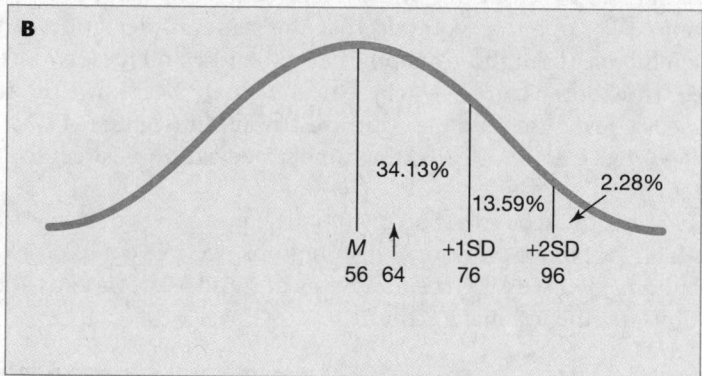

FIGURE 6-4   THE SHAPE OF THE NORMAL DISTRIBUTION CAN INFLUENCE THE MEANINGFULNESS OF A SCORE.

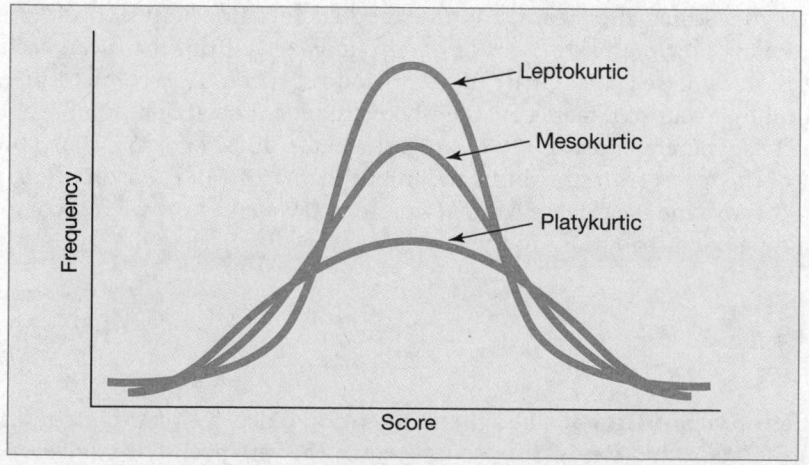

FIGURE 6-5   LEPTOKURTIC, MESOKURTIC, AND PLATYKURTIC DISTRIBUTIONS.

> **Platykurtic** A broad, flat distribution.

the tall, skinny leptokurtic distribution and the **platykurtic** distribution, which is broad and flat.

 PSYCHOLOGICAL DETECTIVE   How would you describe the nature of the standard deviation in the mesokurtic and platykurtic distributions? Hint: part of the answer can be found in Figures 6-4 and 6-5.

If you said that the standard deviation in the mesokurtic distribution is larger than that of the leptokurtic distribution, you are correct! Now, what about the platykurtic distribution? We hope that you said that the standard deviation of the platykurtic distribution is larger than those of both the leptokurtic and mesokurtic distributions (Figure 6-5). How does Figure 6-4 help with the answer? It shows the relation between the standard deviation for a mesokurtic distribution (Figure 6-4A) and a platykurtic distribution (Figure 6-4B). Clearly, the standard deviation is larger for the platykurtic distribution.

Because the *percentage* of the scores that occurs from the mean to the various standard deviation units is the same for *all* normal distributions, we can compare scores from different distributions by discussing them in terms of standard deviations above or below the mean. Consider the following scores:

TEST #	YOUR SCORE	M	SD	RELATION OF YOUR SCORE TO THE M
1	46	41	5	1 SD above
2	72	63	4	Over 2 SDs above
3	93	71	15	Over 1 SD above

Even though your scores, the means, and the standard deviations differ considerably, we can determine how many standard deviation units away from the mean each of your scores is. In turn, we can compare these differences. When these comparisons are made, we find that your scores are consistently one standard deviation or more above the mean. Thus, you are consistently in at least the top 15.87% of the class (100% minus 50% of the scores *below* the mean and minus the 34.13% of the scores from the mean to 1 SD above the mean). We will have more to say about how we can compare scores from different distributions in the next section.

REVIEW SUMMARY

1. Measures of **variability** include the **range** (difference between high and low scores) and **standard deviation** (square root of the variance). The **variance** is a single number that represents the total amount of variability that is present.

2. The standard deviation conveys considerable information about the **normal distribution** that is under consideration.

3. **Kurtosis** refers to the shape of the normal distribution. A **leptokurtic** distribution is tall and peaked, whereas a **platykurtic** distribution is broad and flat. A **mesokurtic** distribution is viewed as the ideal normal distribution and falls in between these two extremes.

CHECK YOUR PROGRESS

1. Why does the range not convey much information about variability?

2. The _____ is a single number that represents the total amount of variability in a distribution.

   a. variance   b. standard deviation   c. range   d. mean

3. How does the standard deviation relate to the normal curve?

4. Kurtosis refers to _____.
   a. the shape of a distribution
   b. the percentage of scores in the final standard deviation
   c. the percentage of scores in the standard deviation closest to the mean
   d. the number of standard deviation units above the mean

5. A leptokurtic distribution _____.
   a. is broad and flat
   b. is the ideal normal distribution
   c. is tall and peaked
   d. does not have any standard deviations

Distribution of Means and the Standard Error of the Mean

So far we have determined the variance and standard deviation for samples and populations. Statisticians and researchers frequently deal with another set of numbers for which they calculate these two measures. Let's set the stage with the following scenario: You are interested in the IQ scores of the 2,000 sixth-grade boys in your community.

You begin your examination of IQ scores by selecting 30 random samples; each sample contains the IQ scores for 10 students ($N = 10$). You calculate the mean IQ for each sample you select.

PSYCHOLOGICAL DETECTIVE Can you think of another, more accurate and descriptive, name for the data set you have collected?

> **Distribution of means**
> A distribution in which the separate scores are sample means.

We hope you looked at the heading for this section and put two and two together and said that you have a distribution of means. A **distribution of means** (also known as a sampling distribution) is exactly what the term implies: The "scores" in the distribution are means, not scores from individual participants. A distribution of means has several interesting characteristics. Keep in mind that these characteristics assume that you have selected a large number of samples from which you have calculated the means.

1. The distribution of means will approximate a normal distribution (bell curve) if the population is a normal distribution or if each sample you randomly select contains at least 30 scores. If the distribution of means is a normal distribution, then we already have considerable information concerning the percentage of scores falling in the respective standard deviations.

2. The mean of a distribution of means will be the same as the mean of the population. Using the Greek letter mu, μ, to symbolize the mean of a population, and μ_M to symbolize the mean of a distribution of means, we can say that $\mu_M = \mu$.

3. You can calculate the variance for a distribution of means; you simply treat each mean as a raw score and proceed as you would in calculating any variance. Once you have calculated the variance of a distribution of means, it is interesting to note that this variance is equal to the population variance divided by the number in each of your samples. The relevant formula for this relation is:

$$\sigma_M^2 = \frac{\sigma^2}{n}$$

4. As with any other variance, the standard deviation of a distribution of means is the square root of the variance of the distribution of means. The relevant formula is:

$$\sigma_M = \sqrt{\sigma_M^2}$$

You are likely to see this formula written as:

$$\sigma_M = \frac{\sigma}{\sqrt{n}}$$

> **Standard error of the mean (SEM)** The square root of the variance of a distribution of means

The standard deviation of a distribution of means has a special name—the **standard error of the mean (SEM)**. Some researchers simply call it the *standard error* (*SE*). The SEM tells you how much variability you can expect to find in the population from which you drew the sample(s) in your research.

Why is it important to know about the variability of means in the population? The answer to this question introduces you to a topic that we will have much more to say about in later chapters—using samples as estimates of populations. The larger the SEM, the greater the variability among the means that make up that data set and therefore, the greater the likelihood that the mean(s) in question may have come from some other population. When the SEMs are large and the two distributions overlap considerably, it is not clear which population the sample mean came from. However, when the SEMs are much smaller and the two populations do not overlap greatly, it is clear where the sample means came from. We saw this same principle at work in Chapter 5 when we examined nuisance variables (see Figure 5-4, p. 101).

We will have much more to say about using samples to estimate population characteristics in later chapters. Let's conclude this chapter by considering an issue that we proposed earlier—wouldn't it be helpful to be able to compare scores from different distributions?

z Scores

By calculating the mean, variance, and standard deviation, you are able to see exactly where a particular score stands in relation to other scores *in that distribution*. Wouldn't it be nice to be able to compare scores across different distributions? For example, let's assume that your scores on your first three psychology tests are 62, 67, and 76. Are these scores good or bad? Unless you have some additional information, it is difficult to answer these questions.

What sort of information would you need to answer that question? We hope you recognized that query as a review question and were able to answer it easily by saying that you would like to know the mean and standard deviation. Here are the relevant data:

Test 1: your score 62, $M = 57.11$, $SD = 2.47$

Test 2: your score 67, $M = 62.46$, $SD = 3.21$

Test 3: your score 76, $M = 68.93$, $SD = 4.06$

Clearly, this additional information assists you greatly in answering the original question. You know that all of your test scores are at least one standard deviation above the mean; so, you are *at least* in the top 15.87% of the class on each test.

 PSYCHOLOGICAL DETECTIVE   How did we arrive at 15.87%?

We hope that you took a quick look back at Figure 6-3. Here you can see that the total percentage (keep in mind that percentage equals amount of area accounted for) that appears above (or below, for that matter) 1 SD is 15.87% (13.59% + 2.15% +.13%).

> **z score** A measure, in standard deviations, of the distance of a raw score above or below the mean. They typically range from +3 to −3.

Can we be a bit more precise? Yes, and this is where z scores come in. z scores are based on the standard deviation concept. Verbally, we can define a **z score** as the distance, in standard deviations, of a raw score above or below the mean. They typically range from +3 to −3. Let's see how to calculate z scores and then we will look at their uses and advantages. The formula for a z score is as follows:

$$z = \frac{X - M}{SD}$$

So, for example, your z score for Test 1 would be:

$$z = \frac{X - M}{SD} = \frac{62 - 57.11}{2.47} = \frac{4.897}{2.47} = 1.98$$

Now it's your turn to do a little work. *Before you read further,* try your hand at calculating the z scores for Tests 2 and 3.

We hope your figures look like the following:

$$z \text{ Test 2} = \frac{X - M}{SD} = \frac{67 - 62.46}{3.21} = \frac{4.54}{3.21} = 1.41$$

$$z \text{ Test 3} = \frac{X - M}{SD} = \frac{76 - 68.93}{4.06} = \frac{7.07}{4.06} = 1.74$$

Now let's examine the data we have just calculated and see what we can learn from it. We know that:

z Test 1 = 1.98

z Test 2 = 1.41

z Test 3 = 1.74

Look at these numbers and recall our definition of the z score. You can see that the z score does tell you, in standard deviations, how far a raw score is above or below the mean. z scores have a mean of zero and a SD of 1. So, these three z scores tell you, in standard deviation units, how far above the mean you scored on each of the three tests. Have you considered this type of information previously? Yes, remember when we indicated that each score was *at least in the top 15.87% of the class*? Now you know exactly how many SDs each score is above the mean. You can use Table A-1 in Appendix A (pp. 539–542) to determine *exactly* what percentage of the class scored below (and above) you on each test. Let's see how this works with Test 1.

1. Locate your z score of 1.98.
2. The column next to the z of 1.98 indicates that 47.61% of the scores occur from the M to that z score.

3. If 50% of the scores occur above the *M* and 50% of the scores occur below the *M*, then 97.61% of the scores occur below your *z* of 1.98 (50% below the *M* + the 47.61% that occur above the *M*).

4. Subtracting 97.61% from 100% gives you the percent of scores *above* you on Test 1: 2.39%.

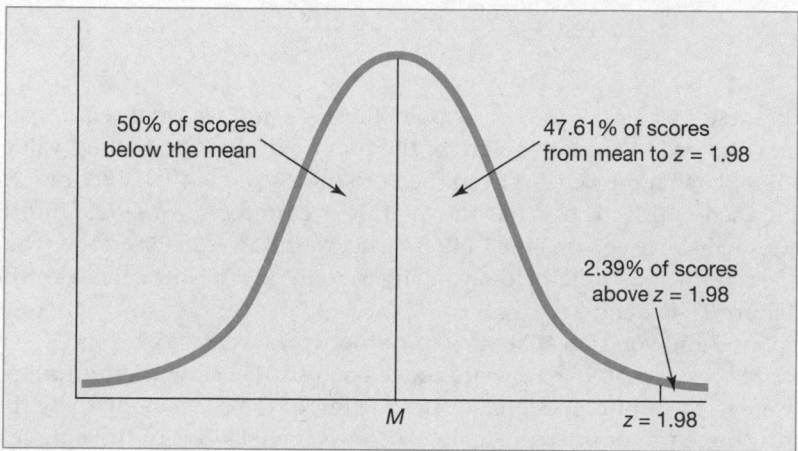

FIGURE 6-6   THE LOCATION OF A POSITIVE z SCORE.

What about Tests 2 and 3? Table A-1 shows that 42.07% of the scores occur from the X to the *z* score of 1.25 for Test 2, whereas 45.91% of the scores occur from the X to the *z* score of 1.74 for Test 3. These results indicate that you were above 92.07% of the scores on Test 2 and 95.91% of the scores on Test 3. Subtracting these two percentages from 100%, lets you know that 7.93% and 4.09% of the scores were *above* you on Tests 2 and 3, respectively. In short you did quite well, relative to your classmates, on all three tests. Of course, we can't guarantee that your instructor will see things exactly this way. The important point is that the *z* scores have allowed us to compare the scores for three different tests that have different *M*s and *SD*s.

   So far we have considered *z* scores that have a positive value. Can *z* scores have negative values? If so, under what circumstances would they occur?

Yes, negative *z* scores occur. The score in question is *below* the *M*. For example, if the *M*s and *SD*s were the same, what would the *z* scores be on Tests 1, 2, and 3

if you had scored 51 (Test 1), 56 (Test 2), and 62 (Test 3)? Here are the relevant calculations:

$$z \text{ Test } 1 = \frac{51 - 57.11}{2.47} = \frac{-6.11}{2.47} = -2.47$$

$$z \text{ Test } 2 = \frac{56 - 62.96}{3.21} = \frac{-6.96}{3.21} = -2.17$$

$$z \text{ Test } 3 = \frac{62 - 68.93}{4.06} = \frac{-6.93}{4.06} = -1.71$$

What do these z scores tell us? Let's look at Table A-1 and see what sense we can make of them. Disregard the negative sign for the time being and locate the z value of 2.47. You will notice that the percent from the M to the z score is 49.32. Because we have a negative z score, this means that the 49.32% occurred *below the M*. Unfortunately, 99.32% scored above you on Test 1 (49.32% below the M + 50.00% above the M); that means that only .68% were below you (100% − 99.32%). Now calculate where your scores fell for Tests 2 and 3.

For Test 2 did you find that 98.50% of the scores were above you (1.50% below) and that for Test 3 that 95.64% were above you (4.36% below)? Unfortunately, these scores were not nearly as good, relative to the rest of the class taking these three tests, as the first three we considered. Figure 6-7 shows the relations of these three negative z scores.

To conclude this section, we would like to show you how to convert a z score back to a raw score. The procedure really is quite simple. Here's the formula:

$$X = (z)(SD) + M$$

FIGURE 6-7   THE LOCATION OF NEGATIVE Z SCORES.

For example, if we knew that $z = -1.71$, $SD = 4.06$, and $M = 68.95$, then

$$X = (-1.71)(4.06) + 68.95$$
$$X = 62.01$$

Check the last example for negative z scores and you will see that 62.00 is the score we started with.

Confidence Intervals

Interval estimate An estimated range that is likely to include the population parameter of interest.

Statisticians have combined their knowledge of the normal curve and an interest in distributions of sample means to produce another important concept: confidence intervals. As we have already indicated, researchers often use sample characteristics, such as the mean or variance, as an estimate of a population characteristics, such as the mean or variance. Researchers also make **interval estimates**; that is, they estimate the range or interval that is likely to include the population characteristic (called a **parameter**), such as the mean or variance. An interval estimate that has a specific percentage, such as 68%, 95%, or 99%, associated with it is called a **confidence interval**.

Parameter Characteristic of a population.

For example, assume that we have a distribution of sample means that has the following characteristics:

$M = 75$

$SD = 10$

Confidence interval An interval that has a specific percentage associated with it.

You already know that 34.13% of the scores occur from the mean to -1 SD and that another 34.13% of the scores occur from the mean to $+1$ SD. Applying this logic to our data, we can say that 68.26% of the scores will occur between 65 and 85:

$10(-1\ SD)$	M	$10(+1\ SD)$
-10		$+10$
65	75	85

We have just established the 68% (technically the 68.26%) confidence interval. You can be 68% confident that the population mean will be between the end points or *confidence limits* of 65 and 85.

Although 68% confidence is pretty good, we usually want to be more accurate than 68%. We typically are satisfied only with 95% or 99% confidence intervals.

PSYCHOLOGICAL DETECTIVE
Generally speaking, how would you go about calculating the 95% and 99% confidence intervals?

This is one of the most difficult psychological detective questions we have asked so far; we hope that you spent some time thinking about it. If you considered how we established the 68% confidence interval and then reasoned that if you knew the exact number of standard deviation units that form the confidence limits for the 95% and 99% confidence intervals, respectively, we applaud your logic! If you know these confidence limits in terms of standard deviation units, then it will be a simple procedure to multiply them by your calculated standard deviation, do a bit of subtracting and adding, and *voila*! You have the confidence intervals you are seeking. Now, where can we find the requisite confidence limit values? You are still on the right track if you turned to Table A-1 and looked for a *z* score that occurs 47.50% above (and below) the mean and a *z* score that occurs 49.50% above (and below) the mean.

PSYCHOLOGICAL DETECTIVE   Why did we select these particular percentages?

The specific confidence intervals we want to establish form the basis of the answer to that question. For the 95% confidence interval we are seeking confidence limits that will encompass a total of 95% (47.50% above the mean and 47.50% below the mean). Likewise, for the 99% confidence interval we are seeking confidence limits that will encompass a total of 99% (49.50% above the mean and 49.50% below the mean). In checking Table A-1, you will see that 47.50% of a normal distribution occurs from the mean to a *z* score of 1.96. Unfortunately, the *z* score for *exactly* 49.50% is not listed; hence, we selected 49.49%. We find from Table A-1 that 49.49% of a normal distribution occurs from the mean to a *z* score of 2.57. Keep in mind that you will use these *z* scores any time you want to calculate a 95% or 99% confidence interval. All you have to do is multiply the standard deviation you have calculated from your data by the appropriate *z* score. Here are the calculations for the two confidence intervals for our sample data:

95% Confidence Interval

1. Multiply *SD* by −*z* score and +*z* score

$$SD \times -z \text{ score (below mean)} \qquad SD \times +z \text{ score (above mean)}$$
$$10 \times -1.96 = -19.60 \qquad\qquad 10 \times 1.96 = 19.60$$

2. Subtract the first product from the mean to establish the lower confidence limit.

$$75 - 19.60 = 55.40$$

3. Add the second product to the mean to establish the upper confidence limit.

$$75 + 19.60 = 94.60$$

4. The 95% confidence interval is 55.40–94.60. We can be 95% sure that the population mean falls between these two extremes.

99% Confidence Interval

1. $SD \times -z$ score: $10 \times -2.57 = -25.70$ (lower limit)

   $SD \times +z$ score: $10 \times 2.57 = 25.70$ (upper limit)

2. $75 - 25.70 = 49.30$ (lower confidence limit)
3. $75 + 25.70 = 100.70$ (upper confidence limit)
4. The 99% confidence interval is 49.30–100.70. We can be 99% sure that the population mean falls between these two extremes.

REVIEW SUMMARY

1. The means of a set of samples comprise the separate scores in a **distribution of means.**
2. The square root of the variance of a distribution of means is the **standard error of the mean** (**SEM**). Knowing the SEM is helpful by assisting researchers to estimate population characteristics based on sample statistics.
3. A **z score** is defined as the distance, measured in standard deviations, above or below the mean. Mathematically, a z score is equal to the raw score minus the mean divided by the standard deviation.
4. z scores allow researchers to compare scores from difference distributions.
5. Because raw scores can occur above and below them mean, z scores can assume positive and negative values.
6. Researchers construct **interval estimates** to identify the range or interval that is likely to include a population characteristic (know as a population **parameter**).
7. An interval estimate that has a percentage associated with it is called a **confidence interval**.

CHECK YOUR PROGRESS

1. The square root of the variance of a distribution of means is the _____.
   a. mean deviation
   b. inverse estimator
   c. standard error of the mean (SEM)
   d. mean variability estimator
2. Describe the usefulness of the SEM.
3. A _____ is the distance, measured in standard deviations, above or below the mean.
   a. raw score
   b. valid measurement
   c. reliable measurement
   d. z score

4. Positive z scores are based on raw scores that are _____.

    a. below the mean   b. above the mean

    c. from different distributions   d. from the same distribution

5. Negative z scores are based on raw scores that are _____.

    a. below the mean   b. above the mean

    c. from different distributions   d. from the same distribution

6. z scores are useful because _____.

    a. they allow researchers to make accurate predictions

    b. they allow researchers to compare scores from the same distribution

    c. they allow researchers to compare scores from different distributions

    d. they come exclusively from bimodal distributions

7. Researchers hope that an interval estimate will include a _____.

    a. a unimodal distribution

    b. a bimodal distribution

    c. a population parameter

    d. an independent variable

8. When compared to a 95% confidence interval, a 99% confidence interval is _____ likely to include the population characteristic of interest.

    a. less   b. more   c. equally   d. These two intervals cannot be compared.

EXERCISES

1. A researcher recorded the following scores:

    17, 26, 11, 82, 16, 23, 39, 42, 8, 28, 33, 38, 19, 14

    Calculate the range.

2. Calculate the variance for the data in Exercise 1.

3. A researcher selects 25 samples from a population. The means of these samples are:

    17, 24, 27, 22, 19, 28, 16, 14, 16, 27, 31, 26, 16, 19, 30, 15, 28, 18, 17, 25, 17, 20, 21, 15, 18

    What is your best estimate of the population mean?
    What is the variance of this distribution of means?
    What is the SEM?

4. Establish the 95% and 99% confidence intervals for Exercise 3.

5. You had a grade of 83 on your last psychology test. Other relevant information: $M = 76.80$, $SD = 3.10$

    Convert your grade to a z score and interpret this z score.

6. Calculate the range, variance, and SD for the following distributions:

    a. 0.10, 0.22, 0.33, 0.44, 0.55, 0.66, 0.77

    b. 10, 22, 33, 44, 55, 66, 77

    c. 100, 220, 330, 440, 550, 660, 770

7. On a measure of self-esteem the mean is 60 and the *SD* is 10. Convert each of the following scores to a *z* score.

    67, 52, 78, 81

8. Calculate the deviation score for each of the following scores:

    1, 2, 3, 4, 5, 6, 7, 8,

    Calculate the variance using the deviation score formula. Calculate the *SD*.

9. A year after their parents divorced, the female and male children completed an adjustment scale. The female child scored 68 (*M* for females = 60, *SD* = 4.75), whereas the male child scored 71 (*M* for males = 63, *SD* = 5.47). Which of these children has made the best adjustment? Explain your answer (be sure to include the results of your calculations in your explanation).

10. Present the results from Exercise 9 as a graph.

11. Find the mean, median, sum of squared deviations, variance, and *SD* for the following data:

    2.0, 1.6, 4.1, 3.4, 2.8

12. Five people have the following *z* scores on Test 1 (*M* = 50, *SD* = 5). What are their raw scores?

    Person 1, $z = 2.00$ Person 2, $z = 1.50$ Person 3, $z = 3.00$ Person 4, $z = 1.26$

    Person 5, $z = -1.86$

13. Assume that a population has a *SD* of 15. Calculate the SEM (i.e., *SD*) of the distribution of means for the following samples:

    $n = 4, n = 9, n = 16$

14. Calculate the 95% and 99% confidence intervals for each of the following data sets:

	Population *M*	Population *SD*	Sample size	Sample *M*
Set 1	20	4	20	18
Set 2	100	10	100	107
Set 3	50	6	50	42

15. Calculate the raw score for each of the following:

    a. $z = 2.08$, *SD* = 6.31, *M* = 27.14

    b. $z = 0.73$, *SD* = 21.42, *M* = 111.06

    c. $z = -1.47$, *SD* = 4.78, *M* = 12.68

    d. $z = 3.81$, *SD* = 12.49, *M* = 38.17

KEY TERMS

Variability, *128*

Range, *128*

Variance, *129*

Deviation score, *129*

Standard deviation (*SD*), *132*

Normal distribution, *133*

Kurtosis, *134*

Leptokurtic, *134*

LOOKING AHEAD

Following our second excursion into the realm of statistics, we continue our examination of the basics of experimentation in Chapter 7. There we will discuss the selection of appropriate types and numbers of participants and the actual collection of research data.

The Basics of Experimentation II: Final Considerations, Unanticipated Influences, and Cross-Cultural Issues

7

In this chapter we continue our discussion of research basics by considering the type and number of participants who will take part in the research, the type of apparatus or testing equipment that will be used, whether the experimenter or participants may be extraneous variables, and the cross-cultural implications of research.

Participants

Both the type and the number of participants who take part in a research project are important considerations in the formulation of an experiment. We discuss these aspects in this section.

Types of Participants

A moment's reflection will indicate there is a wealth of potential organisms that can serve as participants in a psychological experiment. For example, animal researchers might choose from bumblebees, flies, dolphins, chimpanzees, elephants, rats, and so on. Likewise, researchers dealing with humans might choose as their participants infants, young adults, the aged, the gifted, the handicapped, or the maladjusted, among many others. The range of participants for your research project may be overwhelming. Which one represents the best choice? There are three guidelines that can help you answer this question: *precedent*, *availability*, and the *nature of the problem*.

Precedent   If your literature review indicates that researchers have worked with a particular type of participant successfully in prior research projects in your area of interest, then you may want to consider using this type of participant. For example, when Willard S. Small (1901) conducted the first rat study in the United States, he began a **precedent**, or established pattern, that continues to this day. Likewise, the precedent for using college students (especially those enrolled in introductory psychology) has a venerable history. For example, research in the area of human memory and cognitive processes relies heavily on projects conducted with college students. How strong is this reliance? We selected a copy of the *Journal of Experimental Psychology: Learning, Memory and Cognition* (Vol. 24, No. 4, July 1998) at random and examined it. There were 15 articles published in this issue, with 12 reporting results from experiments that used college students exclusively as participants, whereas 3 reported using paid volunteers/participants who may have been college students. It is noteworthy that in many of the articles about experiments that used college students, the participants were drawn from a subject pool or participated in order to receive partial course credit.

> **Precedent** An established pattern

PSYCHOLOGICAL DETECTIVE   Such precedents for the selection of participants have their advantages and disadvantages. What are they?

The fact that a particular type of participant has been used repeatedly in psychological research ensures that a body of knowledge exists about that type of participant. Researchers can take advantage of this wealth of knowledge as they plan their research. They can implement already validated procedures without expending hours of exploratory testing and designing new equipment. Being able to draw on this body of already proven techniques means the *likelihood of success* (see Chapter 2) is increased.

However, the continual use of one type or species of participant can limit the generalizability of the information gathered in the experiment (see the discussion of external validity in Chapter 17). For example, although the study of self-esteem in college students may tell us about this trait in that group, it may not tell us much about self-esteem in the general population. Likewise, although the choice to use white rats in an experiment may be prompted by the extensive literature that already exists on this animal, additional rat studies may not provide any useful information about other species.

Availability   The continued use of white rats and college students also stems from another source, their availability. White rats are relatively inexpensive, at least compared to many other animals, and are easy to maintain. Likewise, college students, especially those students enrolled in introductory psychology classes, constitute an easily accessible population from which to draw participants. For example, in his study of male and female differences in altruism (unselfishly helping another person), Nicholas Schroeppel, a student at the University of Nebraska in Lincoln, and his faculty advisor, Gustavo Carlo, administered questionnaires to college students (Schroeppel & Carlo, 2001). Likewise, college students served as participants in the study by Burkley et al. (2000) on the effect of the wording of the informed consent document (see Chapter 3). The researchers could have selected participants from the general population for both of these experiments; however, they used college students because they were available. In addition to their availability, college students are inexpensive participants because researchers do not usually pay them for their participation. At some institutions, participation in a research project(s) may be a course requirement, thus ensuring the ready availability of research participants. However, availability does not guarantee that the researcher selected the best or most appropriate participants.

Clearly, availability of one type of participant may preclude the use of others. In turn, we have seen that developing a large body of knowledge about a particular type of participant can result in pressures to use that participant in future research projects. Obviously, the problem can easily become circular. The precedent for using one type of participant is established and leads to the development of an extensive literature concerning that type of participant, which further encourages the use of that type of participant.

Type of Research Project   Often the nature of your research project will determine the type of participant you decide to use. For example, if you are interested in studying the visual ability of birds of prey, you are limited to studying birds such as eagles, vultures, hawks, and owls; ducks, geese, and songbirds are not predators. Likewise, if you want to study hallucinations and delusions, then you have limited your choice of potential participants to humans who are able to communicate and who experience those phenomena.

Consider the research project conducted by Molly Claus, a student at Nebraska Wesleyan University in Lincoln, Nebraska. She was interested in studying the relation between toy preferences and assertiveness. The nature of this research question dictated that she use children as participants; she studied preschoolers. Her research indicated that children who played with masculine toys (e.g., trucks and blocks) were more assertive than children who chose to play with feminine toys (e.g., a tea set).

Number of Participants

Once you have decided what type of participant to use in your research project, you must then determine how many participants you are going to test. In making this decision, there are numerous factors that you must take into account. Some of these factors include:

1. **Finances.** How much will it cost to test each participant? Animals must be purchased and cared for. It may be necessary to pay humans for their participation. Does the person who actually conducts the experiment need to be paid? If so, this cost also must be considered; it will rise as you test additional participants.
2. **Time.** As you test additional participants, time requirements will increase, especially if you test participants individually.
3. **Availability.** The sheer number of participants that are available may influence how many you choose to use in your experiment.

In addition to these more practical considerations, there is another factor that enters into our determination of the number of participants we will use. This factor is the amount of variability we expect to be present within each group. The less *within-group* variability (i.e., the more homogeneous the participants), the fewer participants we will need. Conversely, the greater the *within-group* variability (i.e., the more heterogeneous the participants), the greater the number of participants we will need.

What is the reasoning behind these statements about variability and the number of participants to be tested in an experiment? In thinking about this question, you may want to review the material on nuisance variables (see Chapter 5).

When a nuisance variable, in this case the heterogeneous nature of the participants, is present, the scores within each group spread out considerably and the amount of group overlap is increased. The variability of the scores makes it more difficult to see absolute differences between the groups. One way to deemphasize these extreme scores is to test more participants. By increasing the number of scores (i.e., participants), we should increase the number of scores that cluster in the center of the distribution and, therefore, decrease the impact of the extreme scores. When nuisance variables are not present (i.e., the groups are more homogeneous), there are fewer extreme scores and the differences between the groups can be seen more clearly.

> **Power** The probability that the statistical test will be significant (i.e., the experimental hypothesis is accepted when it is true).

The number of participants tested is related to the power of our statistical test. **Power** is the likelihood (probability) that the statistical test will be significant (i.e., the experimental hypothesis is accepted when it is true). Generally speaking, the greater the number of participants, the higher the power of your statistical test. So, it is to your advantage to use as many participants as possible under the specific constraints of your research. Upper level statistics books routinely discuss power and present formulas and tables that will aid you in determining the number of participants you will need to test in order to achieve significance.

You should also use your literature review as a guideline concerning the number of participants you need to use in your experiment. If previous studies in your area have successfully employed a certain number of participants, then you can assume you will need to test a comparable number. For example, based on precedent, Kimberly Kiker (2001), a student at the University of Florida in Gainesville, chose to use 20 first-grade school children and 20 third-grade school children in her research on measurement errors in young children. However, if you are conducting a project in an area that has not received much research attention, then you will want to test as many participants as possible given your financial, time, and availability constraints.

Apparatus

While you are deciding on the number and type of participants to be used in your research, you also need to consider the type of apparatus, if any, you will be using. It is possible to use apparatus for both presenting the IV and recording the DV.

IV Presentation

Often the nature of the IV will influence the type of apparatus one chooses to use. For example, Michael Jones (2001), a student at Lincoln Memorial University in Harrogate, Tennessee, was interested in studying the effects of noise and sex of participant on recall and spatial task (completing a block design) performance of children between 9 and 11 years old. He presented unstructured white noise (static), a popular song, or no noise, respectively, to three groups of children. His experiment dictated that he use audio equipment. He recorded the popular song on a continuous-loop tape that played the same song over and over. He presented the song and the white noise at exactly 74 dB, as measured by a digital sound meter. The results of this study indicated that participants in the white noise condition performed better on both tasks than did the group of children who heard the popular song.

The possible ways you can present the IV are limited by the type of IV you are manipulating, by finances, and by your own ingenuity. Clearly, the presentation of certain types of IVs requires specialized equipment. For example, the administration of a particular type of light wave will require a specialized projector. On the other hand, presenting food to a hungry rat that has learned to press a lever does not have to involve the purchase of an expensive Skinner box or food-pellet dispenser. We have seen very effective, handmade Skinner boxes and food-delivery systems! For example, a sturdy cardboard box works just fine in place of a commercial Skinner box. What about the

First published in the APA Monitor. Reprinted by permission of Warren Street.

"Besides operant equipment, Professor, have the federal cutbacks hurt you?"

Although large research laboratories may require extensive funds and elaborate equipment, you can conduct meaningful research on a limited budget with little or no fancy equipment.

lever? No problem. Anything that protrudes into the box that the rat can learn to press or touch will work fine. In fact, some students have simply drawn a circle on one wall and required that the rat touch it with its nose before food is delivered. A piece of plastic tubing can serve as the food-delivery system. Simply fasten the tubing to the outside of the box so that one end is at the top and the other end enters the box near the bottom and is situated over a small dish. Dropping a piece of food down the tube results in a reinforcer being delivered into the food dish in the box. Some creative thought at this stage of planning can often save you substantial amounts of money.

DV Recording

Although recording evidence at the scene of a crime in great detail may be a major concern to the detective, recording the DV is such a fundamental task that it sometimes is taken for granted or overlooked by the psychologist. However, there are problems and options to be addressed. For example, you do not want the researcher's presence to interfere with or modify the participant's behavior. Sometimes being inconspicuous may mean that the researcher will need to use a simple paper-and-pencil data sheet instead of elaborate electronic equipment. In short, it is important for the observers to be inconspicuous while recording the data.

PSYCHOLOGICAL DETECTIVE — Although technologically sophisticated equipment can be beneficial in conducting research, there are potential drawbacks associated with its use. What are some of these drawbacks?

Whether presenting the IV or recording the DV, the experimenter should not become a slave to the equipment that is available. Just because you have access to a certain piece of equipment does not mean that you must use it. If a handheld stopwatch provides better (or equivalent) data than an elaborate computer setup, then the experimenter should prefer the less elaborate equipment. If researchers begin to rely too heavily on their equipment, then the choice of research problems may start to be dictated by the equipment, not by the researchers' creativity. In such situations there is more concern for the IV that can be presented by the equipment than there is for the problem that is being investigated. Also, the presence of elaborate pieces of equipment assumes that the researcher has sufficient funds to provide appropriate maintenance for such equipment. Consider the problems you would face with your research if it depended on a particular piece of equipment that was broken and you had no funds to pay for its repair.

In some instances a good pair of eyes may be your best equipment. Consider the following exchange between Sherlock Holmes and Dr. Watson:

> "What can you learn from this battered old felt?" Watson asks Holmes. "Here is my lens. You know the methods."
> "I can see nothing."
> "On the contrary, Watson, you can see everything."

> (Doyle, 1927, p. 246)

REVIEW SUMMARY

1. **Precedent**, availability, and the nature of the problem are factors that influence the choice of participants to use in psychological research.
2. The number of participants used in a research project will be determined by financial considerations, time constraints, and participant availability.
3. The use of homogeneous groups of participants allows the experimenter to use smaller groups, whereas heterogeneous groups dictate using more participants.
4. Automated equipment can be used for IV presentation and DV recording, but often quality data can be recorded with less sophisticated equipment.

CHECK YOUR PROGRESS

1. Explain the relation between precedent and the type of participant used in a research project.
2. Why are white rats and college students the favorite participants in psychological research?
3. Group homogeneity is best associated with _____.

   a. testing a larger number of participants

   b. testing a smaller number of participants

   c. multiple-strata sampling

   d. nonrandom sampling

4. One of the best guidelines for the number of participants to use in a successful research project is _____.

   a. cost   b. availability   c. past research   d. type of IV presentation

5. You would like to assess the effects of trauma in people's lives but have ethical problems with causing traumatic events to occur to people. You have a problem with _____.

   a. IV presentation   b. IV recording   c. DV presentation   d. DV recording

6. Describe the concern the experimenter must be aware of when using automated equipment to present the IV or the DV.

Although you may believe that you are ready to move forward with your research project, we still have some preliminary issues to deal with. Just as the good detective is careful, precise, and thorough, researchers cannot exercise too much care in developing their experiments. In the following sections we highlight two potential extraneous variables that often go overlooked: the experimenter and the participant. As the science of psychology has matured, researchers have paid increasing attention to these factors.

The Experimenter as an Extraneous Variable

Just as the characteristics of the detective can influence the responses of the suspects who are questioned, several aspects of the experimenter can influence the responses of the participant (Rosenthal, 1976). First we explore experimenter characteristics; then we will consider experimenter expectancies.

Experimenter Characteristics

Both physiological and psychological attributes of the experimenter can influence the outcome of your research. Physiological characteristics include such variables as age, sex, and race. Research has shown that each of these variables can have an influence on participants' responses. For example, Robert Rosenthal (1977) has shown that male experimenters are more friendly to their participants than female experimenters are.

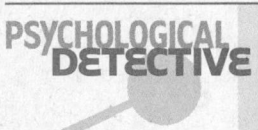 If all participants in an experiment are tested by the same experimenter, then constancy (see Chapter 5) is established and this extraneous variable is controlled. If such control is exercised, why are experimenter characteristics, such as age, sex, and race, of potential concern?

Even though constancy is achieved by having one experimenter conduct the research project, it is possible the experimenter will influence the participants in a unique manner. Perhaps the friendliness of a male experimenter will encourage all participants to perform at a very high level, thus making the differences between the treatment groups less evident. Hence, problems can arise when one attempts to compare the results of similar research projects conducted by different experimenters. If these projects yield different results, you cannot be sure if the differences are attributable to differences in the IV or to effects created by the different experimenters.

Psychological attributes of the experimenter that can influence the results of an experiment include personality characteristics such as hostility, anxiety, and introversion or extraversion. An experiment conducted by an experimenter who is highly anxious is likely to yield different results than an experiment conducted by a confident, self-assured experimenter. The same is true for other personality characteristics.

Experimenter Expectancies

In addition to physiological and psychological characteristics, the experimenter's expectations concerning the participants' behavior can, and do, affect performance. The experimenter's expectations cause him or her to behave toward the participants in such a manner that the expected response is, indeed, more likely shown. The experimenter is literally a cause of the desired or expected response.

Are experimenter expectancies best categorized as extraneous variables that can confound the experiment, or are they simply nuisance variables that serve to obscure the effects of the IV?

If experimenter expectancy is operating in your experiment, you cannot tell whether your results are due to the influence of the IV or experimenter expectancy; hence they are best labeled as confounders.

Such effects have been demonstrated in both human and animal experiments. One of the most widely cited studies of the effects of human experimenter expectancy involved the IQ scores of grade-school children (Rosenthal & Jacobson, 1968). At the start of the school year all children in the classes that were studied took an IQ test. Then, several children in each class were randomly selected and the respective teachers were told that these children were "intellectual bloomers." Several months later when all the children retook the IQ test, the IQ scores of the intellectual bloomers had increased more than those of the other children. Because the intellectual bloomers were randomly selected, it is doubtful that they were intellectually superior. However, they were perceived in this manner and were treated differently by the teachers. In turn, these students responded in accordance with the teachers' expectations.

Experimenter expectancy is not limited just to studies of humans; even rats will perform in accordance with what the experimenter anticipates. Rosenthal and Fode (1963) told half the students in a class that the rats they were going to train were "maze bright"; they told the remainder of the students that their rats were "maze dull." In actuality, there were no differences among the rats at the start of the project. However, the results were consistent with the students' expectations: The "bright" rats learned the maze better and more quickly than did the "dull" rats. Because the rats did not differ at the start of training, this study clearly highlights the strong effects that experimenter expectancies can have on participants' performance. Because Rosenthal and his colleagues were among the first to systematically study experimenter expectations, the results of such expectations are often called **Rosenthal effects**.

> **Rosenthal effect** The experimenter's preconceived idea of appropriate responding influences the treatment of participants and their behavior.

Controlling Experimenter Effects

Physiological and Psychological Effects   The reason that experimenters have traditionally paid little attention to these variables may be clear by now: They are difficult to control. For example, to achieve constancy, *all* these characteristics would have to be measured in *all* potential experimenters and then the choice of experimenters would be determined by the level of each factor that was desired—a difficult, if not impossible, task. Likewise, we saw in Chapter 6 that balancing can be used to avoid confounding due to the sex of the experimenter. Although this control technique equates the groups for experimenter sex, it does not simultaneously control for other physiological and psychological characteristics. At present the most common procedures for controlling general experimenter characteristics are to (1) use standardized methods; (2) use careful training to a set standard when the experimenter administers procedures; and (3) standardize appearance, attitude, and so forth as much as possible. Replicating your research also provides a good check on possible experimenter effects; if you replicate the findings with a different experimenter, then experimenter effects are less likely to be a factor. A thorough literature review will help make you aware of any relevant experimenter variables in your area of research interest.

Experimenter Expectancies   There are several things that can be done to reduce, or possibly eliminate, experimenter expectancies. First, the instructions that the experimenter gives to the participants should be carefully prepared so their manner of presentation will not influence the participants' responses. Likewise, any instructions concerning scoring the participants' responses should be as objective and concrete as possible and should be established before beginning the experiment. If these instructions are subjective, then there is room for experimenter expectancies to dictate how they will be scored.

A second method for controlling experimenter expectancies involves the use of instrumentation and automation. For example, instructions to participants may be tape-recorded prior to experimental testing in order to reduce any influences the experimenter might have. In many instances, potential influences of the experimenter are eliminated through the use of printed instructions or computer displays. Also, automated equipment can ensure the accurate recording and storage of response data. In some instances the participants' responses are entered directly at a computer terminal and thus are stored and ready for analysis at any time.

> **Single-blind experiment** An experiment in which the experimenter (or participants) is unaware of the treatment the participants are receiving.

A third method for minimizing experimenter expectancies is to conduct a single-blind experiment. The **single-blind experiment** keeps the experimenter in the dark regarding which participants receive which treatment(s). (As we will see, this procedure can be used to control participant effects as well.) For example, suppose you are conducting an experiment that tests the effects of different descriptions of an individual's degree of altruism on the amount of warmth that individual is perceived to possess. Quite likely the different written descriptions will be printed in such a way that they all have the same appearance (constancy). If these different descriptions have the same demographic cover sheet, then all materials will appear to be identical. If another experimenter is in charge of determining which participants read which descriptions and arranging the order in which to distribute the testing materials to the participants, then the experimenter who actually conducts the research sessions will not know which participants are reading which descriptions at any session and therefore experimenter expectancies cannot influence the participants' responses. The single-blind procedure can also be used effectively when the IV consists of some type of chemical compound, whether it be in tablet or injection form. If all tablets or injections have the same physical appearance, the experimenter will be unaware of which participants are receiving the active compound and which participants are receiving a placebo. The experimenter truly does not know what treatment condition is being administered in single-blind experiments of this nature.

Participant Perceptions as Extraneous Variables

Just as the experimenter can unintentionally influence the results of an experiment, so can the participants. As you will see, there are numerous aspects of the participants' perception of the research project that can operate as extraneous variables and nuisance variables.

Demand Characteristics and Good Participants

If you have ever served as a participant in a psychological experiment, you know that most participants believe they are supposed to behave in a certain manner. As we have seen, the cues that participants use to guide their behavior may come from the experimenter; they may also be part of the experimental context or IV manipulation. When participants use these cues to determine what the experimenter's hypothesis is and how they are supposed to act, the cues are referred to as the **demand characteristics** of the experiment (Orne, 1962). In short, participants in psychological research may attempt to figure out how they are supposed to respond and then behave in this manner. The desire to cooperate and act as the participants believe the experimenter wants them to is called the **good participant effect** (Rosenthal & Rosnow, 1991).

Allison Dickson, James Morris, and Keri Cass, students at Southwestern University in Georgetown, Texas, and their faculty advisor, Traci Giuliano, investigated race, stereotypes, and college student perceptions of rap and country music performers. The "participants made judgments about either a black or a white musician who performed either rap or country music" (Dickson, Giuliano,

Demand characteristics Features of the experiment that inadvertently lead participants to respond in a particular manner.

Good participant effect The tendency of participants to behave as they perceive the experimenter wants them to behave.

Reprinted from *The Chronicle of Higher Education*. By permission of Mischa Richter and Harold Bakken.

"Haven't we met in a previous experiment?"

It is important that participants not communicate about the nature of a psychological experiment.

Morris, & Cass, 2001, p. 175). Rather than tell the participants that they were studying the effects of race and stereotypes, the researchers simply "asked them to contribute to an investigation exploring 'people's perceptions of music'" (Dickson et al., 2001, p. 177). Had they divulged the exact nature of their hypothesis, then the demand characteristics would have been quite strong and the participants might have tried to decide which group they were in and how they were expected to respond. Dickson et al. (2001) found that the participants rated the black rap performer more favorably than the black country performer. The participants also rated the white country performer more favorably than the white rap performer.

PSYCHOLOGICAL DETECTIVE   Although experimenters have an ethical responsibility (see Chapter 3) to inform the participants about the general nature of the experiment, we have just seen that they usually do not want to reveal the exact nature of their experimental hypothesis. To do so can introduce strong demand characteristics that could influence the participants' behavior. Do demand characteristics operate as extraneous variables or nuisance variables?

Depending on how participants perceive the demand characteristics, they can operate either as an extraneous variable or as nuisance variables. If it is very clear to the participants which group they are in and how that group is expected to act, then the demand characteristics are functioning as extraneous variables and the experiment is confounded. When the experiment is completed, the experimenter will not be able to tell if the differences between the groups were due to the effects of the IV or the demand characteristics. If, however, the participants perceive the demand characteristics *but* are not sure which group they are in, then the demand characteristics may function as a nuisance variable. In this situation we would expect the demand characteristics to produce both increases and decreases in responding within all groups. Thus, the scores of *all* groups would spread out more.

Response Bias

Several factors can produce a response bias on the part of research participants. Here we examine such influences as yea-saying and response set.

Yea-Saying   You most likely know individuals who seem to agree with everything, even if agreeing sometimes means that they contradict themselves. We may never know whether these individuals agree because they truly believe what they are saying or they are simply making a socially desirable response at the moment. Clearly, these individuals, known as **yea-sayers**, who say yes to all questions, pose a threat to psychological research. (Individuals who typically respond negatively to all questions are known as **nay-sayers**. Individuals who always pick the average also pose a threat.) Contradicting one's own statements by answering yes (or no) to all items on a psychological inventory or test seriously threatens the validity of that participant's score.

> **Yea-sayers** Participants who tend to answer "yes" to all questions.

> **Nay-sayers** Participants who tend to answer "no" to all questions.

> **Response set** The experimental context or testing situation influences the participants' responses.

Response Set   Sometimes the experimental context or situation in which the research is being conducted can cause participants to respond in a certain manner or have a **response set**. The effects of a response set can be likened to going for a job interview: You take your cues from the interviewer and the surroundings. In some cases you will need to be highly professional, whereas in other interview situations you can be a bit more relaxed.

Consider the two following descriptions of an experimenter and the testing room in which the research is being conducted. In the first instance the experimenter is wearing a tie and a white laboratory coat. The experiment is being conducted in a nicely carpeted room that has pleasing furnishings, several bookcases, and attractive plants; it looks more like an office than a research room. The second experimenter is dressed in jeans, a sweatshirt, and tennis shoes. In this case the research is being conducted in a classroom in a less-than-well-kept building. Have you already developed a response set for each of these situations? Will you be more formal and perhaps give more in-depth or scientific answers in the first situation? Even though the second situation may help put you at ease, does it seem less than scientific? Notice that our descriptions of these two situations did not make reference to the physiological or psychological characteristics of the experimenters or to the type of experiment being conducted. Hence, we are dealing with an effect that occurs in addition to experimenter and demand effects.

Likewise, the nature of the questions themselves may create a response set. For example, how questions are worded or their placement in the sequence of items may prompt a certain type of response; it may seem that a socially desirable answer is being called for.

Also, it may seem that a particular alternative is called for. In such cases a response bias is developed. Clearly, response set can be a major influence on the participant's response.

Controlling Participant Effects

As we have seen, there are aspects of the participant that can affect the results of our research. Although such factors are rather difficult to control, several techniques have been developed.

Demand Characteristics   You will recall that one technique used to control for experimenter expectancies is to keep the experimenter in the dark by conducting a single-blind experiment. This same approach can be applied to the control of demand characteristics, only this time the participants will be unaware of such features as the experimental hypothesis, the true nature of the experiment, or which group they happen to be in.

It takes only a moment's thought to reach the conclusion that these two approaches can be combined; we can conduct an experiment in which both the experimenter and the participants are unaware of which treatment is being administered to which participants. Such experiments are known as **double-blind experiments**.

Double-blind experiment An experiment in which both the experimenter and the participants are unaware of which treatment the participants are receiving.

Regardless of whether a single- or a double-blind experiment is conducted, it is likely that the participants will attempt to guess what the purpose of the experiment is and how they should respond. It is difficult to conceal the fact that they are participating in an experiment, and the information provided to them prior to signing the informed consent document (see Chapter 3) may give the participants a general idea concerning the nature of the experiment.

Let's assume that you conduct a single- or double-blind experiment and leave your participants to their own devices to guess what the experiment is about. In this case you may be introducing an unwanted variable into your research project. Is this factor an extraneous variable or a nuisance variable? What effect(s) might it have?

It is almost certain that all participants will not correctly guess the true nature of the experiment and which group they are in. Those participants who make correct guesses may show improved performance; those participants who make incorrect guesses may have inferior performance. If the ability to correctly guess the nature of the experiment and which group one is in is comparable in all groups, then the scores within *all* groups will spread out. You have introduced a *nuisance variable* that will make it more difficult to see the differences that develop between the groups. Is there any way to avoid this problem? The answer is yes.

Another technique that can be used to control for demand characteristics is to give all participants incorrect information concerning the nature of the experiment. In short, the experimenter purposely deceives *all* the participants, thus disguising the true nature of the experiment and keeping the participants from guessing how they are supposed to respond. Although this procedure can be effective, it suffers from two drawbacks. First, we have already seen that the use of deception raises ethical problems with regard to the conduct of research. If deception is employed, a good IRB (see Chapter 3) will be careful to make sure it is a justifiable and necessary procedure. The second problem is that the information used to deceive the participants may result in erroneous guesses about the nature of the experiment; the participants are then responding to the demand characteristics created by the deception. Clearly, demand characteristics may be very difficult to control.

Yea-Saying   The most typical control for yea-saying (and nay-saying) is to rewrite some of the items so that a negative response represents agreement (control for yea-saying) or a positive response represents disagreement (control for nay-saying). Once some of the items have been rewritten, the experimenter needs to make a decision concerning the order for their presentation. All the rewritten items should not be presented as a group. One presentation strategy is to randomize the complete list, thereby presenting the original and rewritten items in an undetermined sequence. This approach works quite well with longer lists. If the list is shorter, within-subject counterbalancing can be used. Table 7-1 illustrates these two presentation styles and the use of within-subject counterbalancing.

Response Set   The best safeguard against response set is to review all questions that are asked or items to be completed to see if a socially desired response is implied in any manner. The answer given or response made should reflect the participant's actual feelings, attitudes, or motives rather than an attempt to appear intelligent, well-adjusted, or otherwise "normal." Checking for response set offers excellent opportunities for pilot testing and interviewing of participants to determine if the questions or behavioral tasks create a particular outlook. Additionally, you should carefully examine the nature of the experimental situation or context to avoid the presence of undesired cues.

TABLE   7-1   CONTROLLING FOR YEA-SAYING

The following yes-no items are based on the Type A scale developed by Friedman and Rosenman (1974). In Part A a "yes" answer is associated with the Type A personality. Yea-sayers, even though they are not Type A persons, would likely be assigned to this category with such questions. In Part B half of the items are rewritten so that a "no" answer is associated with Type A characteristics. Within-subject counterbalancing is also used with the items in Part B.

A. "Yes" answers are associated with Type A characteristics.
   1. Do you play games like Monopoly to win?
   2. Do you eat, speak, and walk rapidly?
   3. Do you constantly schedule more activities than time allows?
   4. Do you feel a sense of guilt if you try to relax?

B. Yes answers (Items 1 and 4) *and* "no" answers (Items 2 and 3) are associated with Type A characteristics. The 1(yes)–2(no)–3(no)–4(yes) sequence illustrates within-subject counterbalancing.
   1. Do you play games like Monopoly to win?
   2. Do you eat, speak, and walk slowly?
   3. Do you constantly schedule just enough activities to fill the time available?
   4. Do you feel a sense of guilt if you try to relax?

REVIEW SUMMARY

1. Experimenter characteristics can affect the results of an experiment. Physiological experimenter characteristics include such aspects as age, sex, and race. Psychological experimenter attributes include such personality characteristics as hostility, anxiety, and introversion or extraversion.

2. Experimenter expectancies can produce behaviors in the experimenter that influence participants to make the desired response. Such experimenter expectancy effects are often called **Rosenthal effects**.

3. Because of their potential abundance, experimenter characteristics are difficult to control.

4. Experimenter expectancies can be controlled through the use of objective instructions and response-scoring procedures, as well as instrumentation and automation. A **single-blind experiment**, in which the experimenter does not know which participants are receiving which treatments, also can be used to control experimenter expectancies.

5. **Demand characteristics** refer to those aspects of the experiment that may provide the participants with cues concerning the experimenter's hypothesis and how they are supposed to act. Demand characteristics can be controlled through the use of single-blind and **double-blind experiments** (where both the experimenter and the participants do not know which treatment the participants receive).

6. The desire to cooperate and act in accordance with the experimenter's expectation is called the **good participant effect**.

7. Response bias is caused by several factors. **Yea-saying** refers to the tendency to answer "yes" to all questions; **nay-saying** refers to the tendency to answer "no" to all questions. Yea- and nay-saying are controlled by writing some items in such a way that a negative response represents agreement (control for yea-saying) and a positive response represents disagreement (control for nay-saying).

8. When the experimental situation or context prompts a certain response, a **response set** has been created. The best safeguards against response set are careful scrutiny of the experimental situation, thorough review of all questions, pilot testing, and interviewing the participants.

CHECK YOUR PROGRESS

1. Explain how the experimenter can be an extraneous variable.

2. Matching

1. age, sex, race	A. psychological experimenter effects
2. hostility or anxiety	B. experimenter expectancies
3. Rosenthal effects	C. physiological experimenter effects
4. single-blind experiment	D. control for demand characteristics and experimenter expectancies
5. double-blind experiment	E. control for experimenter expectancies

3. An experiment in which the researcher doesn't know which treatment the participants are receiving _____.

   a. is a blind experiment   b. is a confounded experiment

   c. cannot be replicated   d. is unable to employ randomization

4. Explain how instrumentation and automation can control experimenter expectancies.

5. Demand characteristics refer to _____.

   a. demands the experimenter places on the participants

   b. cues that tell the participants how to act

   c. IRB requirements for conducting research

   d. the need to publish research in order to receive tenure and promotion

6. Which of the following is an example of response bias?

   a. demand characteristics   b. single-blind experiment

   c. nay-saying   d. balancing

The Interface Between Research and Culture

The recent and continuing explosion in information technology, coupled with the availability of inexpensive air travel, highlights the diverse, multicultured nature of our planet. For example, it is common to see live reports on the television evening news from countries on the other side of the world. In our own country the "information super-highway" instantly links diverse peoples in the farthest reaches of the United States.

As we complete the material on the basics of experimentation, it is important to keep such cultural differences in mind; they may influence how research is conceptualized, conducted, analyzed, and interpreted. To this end, cross-cultural psychology has grown dramatically in recent years. The goal of **cross-cultural psychology** is to determine whether research results and psychological phenomena are universal (found in individuals from different cultures) or specific to the culture in which they were reported. Before we examine cross-cultural research, we need a definition of culture.

> **Cross-cultural psychology** Branch of psychology whose goal is to determine the universality of research results.

PSYCHOLOGICAL DETECTIVE   Rather than simply giving you a definition of culture, we would like you to spend a few minutes on this topic. Before reading further, decide which aspects or features should be included in a definition of culture.

You probably began thinking about culture with the word *similar*. After all, it's the similarities that help define our culture and distinguish it from other cultures. If you then started listing the important aspects that serve to distinguish cultures, you're on the right track. Among the important features that differentiate one culture from another are attitudes, values, and behaviors. Moreover, these culture-defining atti-tudes, values, and behaviors must be long-lasting or enduring. This enduring quality indicates that these attitudes, values, and behaviors are communi-cated or transmitted from one generation to the next. Putting these considerations together, we can tentatively define **culture** as the lasting values, attitudes, and behaviors that a group of people share and transmit to subsequent generations. It is important to note that our definition does not imply that race and nationality are synony-mous with culture. Individuals can be of the same race or nationality and not share the same culture. Carrying this thought one step further, we can see that several cultures may exist within the same country or even in the same large city. Now, let's see how culture is related to what we consider to be truth.

> **Culture** Lasting values, attitudes, and behaviors that are shared by a group and transmitted to subsequent generations.

Culture, Knowledge, and Truth

> **Etic** A finding that is the same in different cultures.

> **Emic** A culture-specific finding.

A finding that occurs across cultures is called an **etic**. You can think of an etic as a universal truth or principle. The finding that reinforce-ment increases the probability of the response it follows appears to be an etic; people of all cultures respond to reinforcement similarly. In contrast, an **emic** is a finding that is linked to a specific culture. The value placed on independence and individuality is an emic; it varies from culture to culture. Some cultures (e.g., the United States) are individualistic and place a pre-mium on individual accomplishments. Other cultures (e.g., China) are collectivist and stress contributions to the welfare of the group. Emics represent truths that are relative to different cultures, whereas etics represent absolute truths. Given the great diversity of cultures, it should not surprise you to find that the number of emics is considerably greater than the number of etics.

At this point you may be wondering how this discussion relates to a course in research methods or experimental psychology. Consider this issue before reading further.

If the goal of your research project is to discover the effects of IV manipulations only within a certain culture, then this discussion may have little relevance. However, few researchers purposely set their research sights on only a single culture (also see Chapter 17). In fact, the question of culture may never enter the researcher's mind as a study is taking shape. Similarly, when the data are analyzed and conclusions are reached, cultural considerations may not be addressed. The result is a project that one *assumes* is not culture dependent. In short, researchers often become very **ethnocentric**—they view other cultures as an extension of their own. Hence, they interpret research results in accord with the values, attitudes, and behaviors that define their culture and assume that these findings are applicable in other cultures as well. For

> **Ethnocentric** Other cul-tures are viewed as an extension of one's own culture.

THE BASICS OF EXPERIMENTATION II

example, many researchers likely consider the *fundamental attribution error* (Ross, 1977) in which actions are attributed to the individual, even in the face of compelling situational cues, to be a universal finding. Although the fundamental attribution error is shown in individualistic, Western societies (Gilbert & Malone, 1995), situational cues are taken into account in collectivist societies and this effect is appreciably smaller (Miller, 1984). Chapter 17 will have more to say about the generalizability of research findings when we consider the external validity of our research.

The Effect of Culture on Research

If you step back from your culture and try to put research in a more international perspective, it is clear that culture influences all aspects of the research process. We will consider cultural effects on the choice of the research problem, the nature of the experimental hypothesis, and the selection of the IV and the recording of the DV. In order to solve their respective problems, the detective and the research psychologist need a broad base of information that includes cultural information.

Choice of the Research Problem   In some cases there may be no doubt that the choice of your research problem is culture dependent. For example, let's assume you are interested in studying the nature of crowd interactions at a rock concert. Whereas this topic may represent a meaningful project in the United States, it has much less relevance to a psychologist conducting research in the bush country of Australia. In this example, culture clearly dictates the nature of the research project; some problems are important in one culture but not in another. Likewise, whereas the study of individual achievement motivation is a topic of considerable interest and importance in an individualistic society like the United States, it would be a less important research topic in a collectivist society like China (Yang, 1982).

Nature of the Experimental Hypothesis   Once you have selected a problem that is relevant beyond your own culture, then you must deal with the experimental hypothesis. For example, even though the study of factors that determine one's personal space is relevant in a number of cultures, the creation of an experimental hypothesis that applies to all cultures will be most difficult. In some cultures very little personal space is the norm, whereas considerable personal space is expected in other cultures. For example, Italians typically interact within a smaller personal space (i.e., they prefer closer proximity) than either Germans or Americans (Shuter, 1977). Such cultural differences may lead to very different hypotheses.

Selection of the IV and the DV   Culture also can influence the selection of the IV and the DV. In technologically advanced cultures such as the United States, Japan, or Great Britain, IV presentation may be accomplished via a computer. Likewise, DV measurement and recording also may be done by computer. Because such technology is not available in all cultures, the choice of the IV and the procedure for recording the DV may differ considerably. For example, handheld stopwatches, not digital electronic timers, may be used to record the time required to complete an experimental task. Similarly, the participants may read the stimulus items in booklet form, rather than having them presented at set intervals on a video screen by a computer. In fact, stimuli that have high (or low) meaning in one culture may not have the same meaning in another culture.

Methodology and Analysis Issues

In either conducting or evaluating cross-cultural research, a number of methodological issues will necessitate careful and thorough consideration. Among these issues are the participants and sampling procedures used, the survey or questionnaire employed, and the effects of cultural response set on data analysis.

Participants and Sampling Procedures   The basic question here is whether the sample of participants is representative of the culture from which they were drawn. Do sophomore college students represent the culture of the United States? What steps has the researcher taken to ensure that the sample is representative of the culture in question? For example, extreme differences may exist between samples drawn from large urban centers and those drawn from rural areas.

Assuming you can satisfy the requirement that a sample is representative of its culture, you are likely to be faced with an equally difficult task: being able to ensure that samples from two or more cultures are equivalent before conducting the research. We have stressed, and will continue to stress, the importance of establishing group equivalence before an IV is administered. Only when group equivalence is demonstrated can we have confidence in saying that our IV has had an effect in producing any differences we observe.

Let's assume you are reading research reports from three different cultures. All three investigations used freshman-level college students as participants. Can you assume that the requirements of group equivalence among these studies has been satisfied through the use of this common type of participant?

Even though the same *type* of participant—freshman college students—was used, you cannot assume the groups were equivalent before the research was conducted. Before you can make this assumption, you must be able to demonstrate that the same type of student attends college in all three cultures and that the "freshman" designation is equivalent across all three cultures. Perhaps the collegiate experience in one culture is quite different from the collegiate experience in another culture and therefore attracts students who differ from those in the culture with which it is being compared. For example, economics may dictate that only the wealthy attend college in some cultures. In short, assessing group equivalence will not be an easy task for cross-cultural research.

Type of Survey or Questionnaire Used   Although an existing survey or questionnaire may work in a few instances, most likely the researcher will not be able to use it for research in a different culture. The chances are good that the questionnaire or survey will have to be translated into a different language. Assuming the translation has been completed, how do you know that it is accurate and the correct meanings have been retained? The same word can have different meanings in different cultures. One technique for evaluating the accuracy of the translation is to have a *back translation* done. This procedure involves having another person translate the translated questionnaire back into its original language. If the back translation and the original version match, then the original translation was successful. The importance of the back translation is clearly reflected by Sou and Irving (2002) in their comments on the limitations of their research on student attitudes toward mental health in the United States and Macao (see Chapter 3). These researchers said, "the survey items created for this study did not receive a backward translation to ensure reliability between the Chinese and English versions; therefore, group differences may be due to inherent differences in the meaning of the survey items after translation" (Sou & Irving, 2002, p. 21).

Aside from these problems that are faced in translating the instrument into another language, there is the very real problem of whether the other cultures to be tested value the concept that is to be measured or evaluated. If they do not, then the survey or questionnaire is worthless.

Even if you determine that the concept or trait in question is valued in other cultures, there remains the problem of making sure that the *specific items* are equivalent when the survey or questionnaire is prepared for use in other cultures. Just translating the items into another language may not be sufficient. For example, a question about riding the subway that is appropriate for an industrialized society may have no meaning in less-developed cultures or in some parts of the industrialized society. Clearly, the same comment can be made for questions dealing with customs, values, and beliefs.

Cultural Response Set   Earlier in this chapter you learned that research participants may begin an experiment with a preexisting response set; some participants may be yea-sayers and others are nay-sayers. We have the same general concern, only on a larger scale, when conducting cross-cultural research.

> **Cultural response set**
> Tendency of a particular culture to respond in a certain manner.

In this instance it is the response of the entire culture, not individual participants, that concerns us. A **cultural response set**, or tendency of a particular culture to respond in a certain manner, may be operative. How often have individuals in another culture answered questions on a Likert-type rating scale like those commonly used in the United States? What reaction(s) will they have to being tested by such a scale? Just because you use such scales effectively in your research does not mean participants in other cultures will find them easy to understand and answer. The same comments can be made about any survey or questionnaire that is used. Both the type of questionnaire (Likert-type scale, true-false, multiple choice, etc.) and the nature of the items themselves may intensify an already existing cultural response set.

How do you know if a cultural response set is present? If differences exist among the groups tested in various cultures, a cultural response set may be operating.

PSYCHOLOGICAL DETECTIVE   The presence of a cultural response set is one possible cause for the differences among groups from various cultures. What other factor might cause such differences? What problem is created if you cannot distinguish between these two causes?

If you indicated that the influence of a manipulated IV or differences in the specific trait being measured could also be responsible for the differences among groups, you are absolutely correct. If you then indicated that an extraneous variable is present and the research would be confounded (see Chapter 5) if the researcher could not distinguish whether the scores on a questionnaire were caused by the trait or IV or the cultural response set, then you are correct again. Remember that our research results are worthless when a confounder is present. Hence, it is vitally important that cultural response set be accounted for whenever you are conducting or evaluating cross-cultural research.

The purpose of this section was not to teach all the fine points of cross-cultural research; it would take an entire book to accomplish that goal. Rather, we wanted to make you aware of these issues and problems before we began our discussion of statistics and research designs. Being acquainted with the issues involved in cross-cultural research will make you a better consumer of psychological research, regardless of where it is conducted.

REVIEW SUMMARY

1. The goal of **cross-cultural psychology** is to determine whether research findings are culture specific (i.e., **emics**) or universal (i.e., **etics**).
2. **Culture** can influence the choice of a research problem, the nature of the experimental hypothesis, and the selection of the IV and the DV.
3. In conducting or comparing cross-cultural research, the cultural representativeness of the participants and the sampling procedures used to acquire the participants must be carefully evaluated.
4. The appropriateness of a survey or questionnaire for cross-cultural research must be evaluated. Once the general trait or concept has been accepted, then the specific items must be examined and deemed acceptable for cross-cultural use.
5. The presence of a **cultural response set** must be considered when conducting cross-cultural research.

CHECK YOUR PROGRESS

1. The goal of cross-cultural psychology is best described as _____.
   a. determining if psychological findings are universal
   b. testing a variety of participants
   c. using a variety of test equipment
   d. conducting tests in a variety of locations
2. A finding linked to a specific culture best describes _____.
   a. ethnocentrism   b. an ertic   c. an emic   d. an etic
3. Why is the goal of cross-cultural research incompatible with ethnocentrism?
4. In what ways can culture affect the conduct of psychological research?

5. The tendency of a culture to behave in a certain way best describes _____.

    a. an etic   b. cultural response set

    c. ethnocentrism   d. the just world stereotype

KEY TERMS

Precedent, *150*

Power, *153*

Rosenthal effect, *158*

Single-blind experiment, *158*

Demand characteristics, *159*

Good participant effect, *159*

Yea-sayers, *161*

Nay-sayers, *161*

Response set, *161*

Double-blind experiment, *162*

Cross-cultural psychology, *165*

Culture, *166*

Etic, *166*

Emic, *166*

Ethnocentric, *166*

Cultural response set, *169*

LOOKING AHEAD

In the next chapter we return to our consideration of statistical principles. We will consider the topic of correlation, or the degree to which two variables relate to each other. Then we will see how psychologists use this relation, or correlation, between two variables to make predictions.

Correlation and Prediction

Correlation

In this chapter we examine another statistical technique that psychologists use extensively—*correlation*. **Correlation** is the extent to which two variables are related. If the two variables are highly related, then knowing the value of one of them will allow you to predict the other variable with considerable accuracy. The less highly related the variables, the less accurate your ability to predict one when you know the other.

> **Correlation** The extent or degree to which two variables are related.

The Nature of Correlation

Just as in the successful completion of a detective case, prediction plays an important role in psychology. Nowhere is this aspect of psychology more apparent than when moving from high school to college. You probably took a college entrance examination (such as the SAT or ACT) while you were in high school. Based on the results of this exam, you and your admissions counselor were able to make a prediction about your grades in college. Similarly, should you plan to go on for graduate training after you complete your undergraduate degree you probably will take another entrance examination. Depending on your area of interest, you might take the Graduate Record Examination (GRE), the Law School Admission Test (LSAT), the Medical College Admission Test (MCAT), or some similar test. The underlying belief is that these admissions tests are related to success in college or graduate school. In other words, the scores on the admissions tests and grades are correlated—students who score high on the admissions tests are the students who will earn top grades; the more highly related the two variables, the better our prediction becomes. However, even though two variables may be highly correlated, you should not assume that one variable caused the other variable. There is an old saying that our teachers drilled into our heads, and we would like to repeat their wisdom for you: *Correlation does not imply causation.* It is possible that a third variable is involved. A rather far-fetched example illustrates this point quite well. In an introductory statistics class, a student told one of your authors about a correlational study that investigated the relation between the number of telephone poles erected in Australia each year for the 10 years following World War II and the yearly birth rate in the United States during the same time period. The result was a very high, positive correlation. The point of the example was to illustrate that correlation does not imply causation. It also illustrates the likely presence of a third variable. It is arguable that the increasingly better worldwide economic conditions that followed World War II encouraged both industrial development (the increase in telephone poles in Australia) and the desire to have a family (the higher birth rate in the United States).

The Scatterplot: Graphing Correlations

We use a **scatterplot** (also called a *scatter diagram*) to depict a correlation. Here's how to construct a scatterplot. First, you list the values that one of the two variables can assume on the ordinate (see Chapter 4). Then, you list the values the second variable can assume on the abscissa (see Chapter 4). Although you can list either variable on either axis, most researchers prefer to list the variable they will predict with on the abscissa (X axis). For our admissions

> **Scatterplot** A graphical depiction of a correlation.

(Courtesy of Warren Street)

"There's a significant NEGATIVE correlation between the number of mules and the number of academics in a state, but remember, correlation is not causation."

test scores–grades example, we would use scores on the admissions test to predict grades; therefore, we would list admissions test scores on the abscissa (X axis) and grades on the ordinate (Y axis).

Now, you are ready to plot your data. Remember, you are interested in the relation between two variables (designated as the X and Y variables, respectively); hence, you will consider a pair of scores for each participant. We created the following data to serve as a correlation example. Let's assume that your college has the following SAT and grade point average (GPA) data for several students who graduated last year:

	SAT SCORE (X)	CUMULATIVE GPA (Y)
Student 1	980	2.02
Student 2	1070	2.45
Student 3	1020	2.63
Student 4	1240	3.11
Student 5	880	2.09
Student 6	1110	2.75
Student 7	1350	3.72
Student 8	1080	2.38
Student 9	1230	3.06
Student 10	1470	3.48

Let's create a scatterplot for these data. Because we want to use SAT scores to predict success in college (as measured by cumulative GPA), we will list GPAs (Y variable) on the vertical axis (ordinate or Y axis) and SAT scores (X variable) on the horizontal axis (abscissa or X axis). We've plotted the data for Students 1 and 2 in Figure 8-1A.

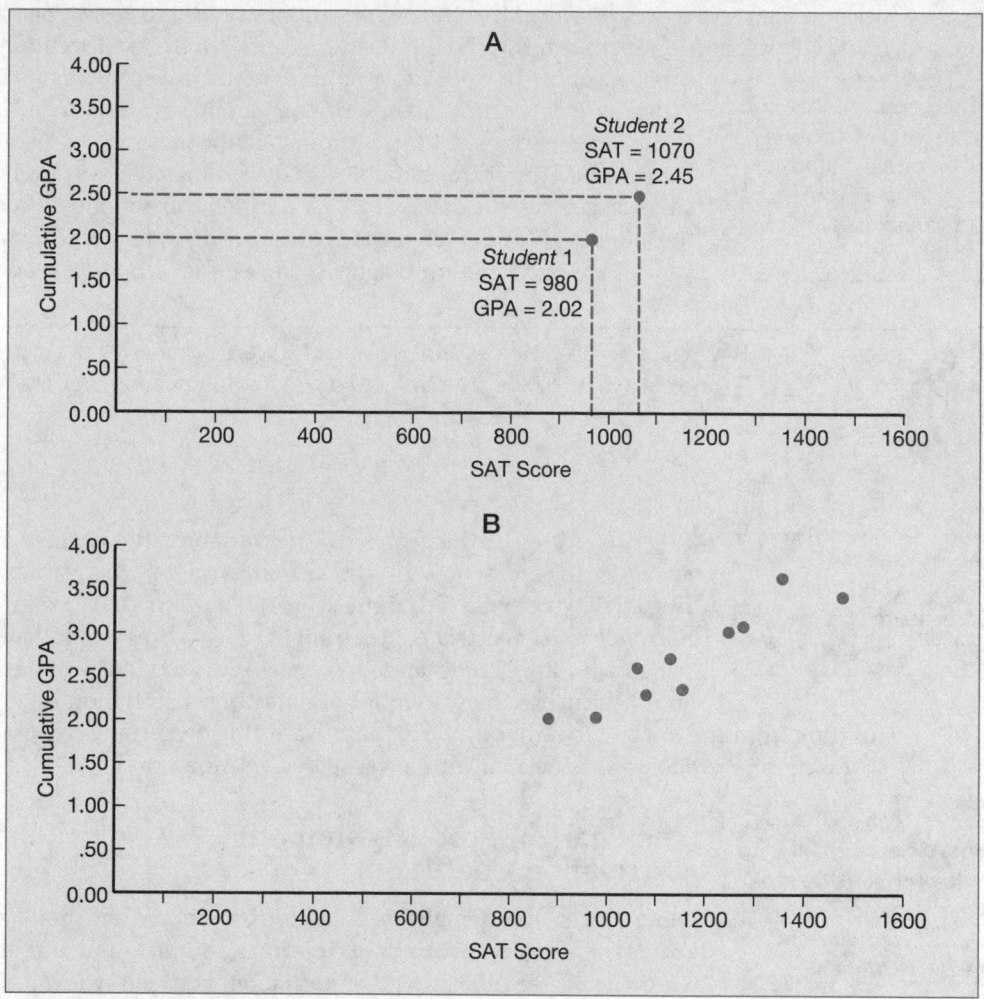

FIGURE 8-1 DEVELOPMENT OF A CORRELATION SCATTERPLOT FOR SAT SCORES AND GPAS. Plotting students 1 and 2 (part A). Complete scatterplot depicting the correlation between SAT scores and GPAs (part B).

Notice that each student's point on the graph is located where that student's SAT score and GPA intersect. In Figure 8-1B you can see what the data for all 10 students look like. You will see a lot of white space on the left of Figures 8-1A and 8-1B because few students have cumulative GPAs lower than 2.00 or SAT scores lower than 800.

PSYCHOLOGICAL DETECTIVE   Based on this scatterplot, do you think SAT scores are good predictors of success in college?

Because high SAT scores are paired with high GPAs and lower SAT scores are paired with lower GPAs, it appears that the answer to this question is yes. (In the next section we will show you how to calculate a more precise answer to this question.) When an *increase* in the scores of one variable is accompanied by an *increase* in the scores of the other variable, the variables are **positively correlated**. The scores in our SAT–GPA example are positively correlated. In general, the scatterplot of a positive correlation will run from the lower left of the graph toward the upper right; higher scores on one variable are associated with higher scores on the second variable.

> **Positive correlation** As scores on one variable increase, scores on the second variable also increase.

What situation would exist if our variables were *negatively correlated*? In general, what will the scatterplot of a negative correlation look like?

> **Negative correlation** As scores on one variable increase, scores on the second variable decrease.

When *increases* in the scores of one variable are accompanied by *decreases* in the scores of the other variable, the variables are **negatively correlated**. If the scores in our SAT–GPA example had been negatively correlated, then higher SAT scores would have been paired with lower GPAs and vice versa. We hope that you have been able to visualize the scatterplot of a negative correlation as generally running from the upper left corner of the graph toward the lower right corner; higher scores on one variable are associated with lower scores on the second variable.

> **Correlation coefficient** A single number that represents the degree of relation (i.e., "co-relation") between two variables.

The Pearson Product–Moment Correlation Coefficient

More precise mathematical predictions are based on the *correlation coefficient*. A **correlation coefficient** is a single number that represents the degree of relation (i.e., *corelation*) between two variables.

Sir Francis Galton (1822–1911) developed the basic ideas of correlation. Galton, who was independently wealthy, devoted his time to studying and investigating those things that interested him. According to E. G. Boring (1950), the eminent historian of psychology, Galton

> "was a free-lance and a gentleman scientist. He was forever seeing new relationships and working them out, either on paper or in practice. No field was beyond his possible interest, no domain was marked off in advance as being out of his province"
>
> (p. 461).

For example, Galton studied such varied topics as the weather and fingerprints. He also proposed that a person's intelligence was directly related to the quality of the nervous system: The better the nervous system, the higher the intelligence. To be able to measure the predictive relation between these two variables, Galton's assistant, Karl Pearson (1857–1936), developed the Pearson product–moment correlation coefficient.

Statisticians have developed several correlational measures. For example, *Kendall's coefficient of rank correlation* measures correlation when both variables are ordinal. The *phi coefficient* yields a measure of correlation for nominal data arrayed in 2 × 2 contingency tables (see Chapter 19), and the *contingency coefficient* measures correlation for larger tables. The *point biserial correlation* provides a measure of relation between a nominal variable and an interval variable.

Pearson product–moment correlation coefficient
The correlation coefficient researchers calculate when both variables are interval or ratio scale measurements. Symbolized by *r*.

The **Pearson product–moment correlation coefficient** (symbolized by *r*) is the most common measure; researchers calculate it when both the X variable and the Y variable are interval or ratio scale measurements and the scatterplot appears linear. Mathematically, we can define *r* as the average of the cross-products of *z* scores. Stated as a formula:

$$r = \frac{z_X z_Y}{N}$$

Using this formula to calculate *r* means that you would have to convert all scores on both the X and Y variables to *z* scores (see Chapter 6). Then, you would multiply the two *z* scores for each pair of scores and sum these products. Finally, you would divide this total by the number of paired scores (*N*). Obviously, converting each raw score to a *z* score is going to involve considerable time and effort, and, if fractions are involved, invite calculation errors. Is there a quicker way to get to the same goal?

Yes, there is a raw-score formula for calculating *r*, and we think you will find it easier to work with. The raw score formula for *r* is:

$$r = \frac{N\Sigma XY - (\Sigma X)(\Sigma Y)}{\sqrt{[N\Sigma X^2 - (\Sigma X)^2][N\Sigma Y^2 - (\Sigma Y)^2]}}$$

Where *N* = number of pairs of scores

Now, let's actually calculate the correlation coefficient for the SAT–GPA data we plotted in Figure 8-1. In Table 8-1, we've added several appropriate columns to our original set. These columns will help us keep our calculations organized appropriately. You will find everything you need to calculate *r* in Table 8-1. Plugging the appropriate numbers into the formula, we find that *r* = .93. Clearly, our fictitious SAT scores and cumulative GPAs are highly and positively related. However, what exactly does an *r* = .93 mean? We will answer that question after we consider the range of values that *r* can assume.

The Range of *r* Values

Perfect negative correlation Exists when an increase of one unit in one variable is always accompanied by the same proportional decrease in the other variable.

A correlation coefficient can range in value from −1.00 to +1.00. A correlation coefficient of −1.00 indicates that there is a **perfect negative correlation** (see Figure 8-2) between the two variables of interest. That is, whenever we see an increase of one unit in one variable, there is *always* the same proportional decrease in the other variable.

| TABLE | 8-1 | CALCULATING A PEARSON PRODUCT–MOMENT CORRELATION COEFFICIENT USING THE RAW-SCORE FORMULA |

	SAT (X)	X²	GPA (Y)	Y²	XY
Student 1	980	960,400	2.02	4.0804	1979.60
Student 2	1070	1,144,900	2.45	6.0025	2621.50
Student 3	1020	1,040,400	2.63	6.9169	2682.60
Student 4	1240	1,537,600	3.11	9.6721	3856.40
Student 5	880	774,400	2.09	4.3681	1839.20
Student 6	1110	1,232,100	2.75	7.5625	3052.50
Student 7	1350	1,822,500	3.72	13.8384	5022.00
Student 8	1080	1,166,400	2.38	5.6644	2570.40
Student 9	1230	1,512,900	3.06	9.3636	3763.80
Student 10	1470	2,160,900	3.48	12.1104	5115.60
	$\Sigma = 11{,}430$	13,352,500	27.69	79.5793	32503.60
	$M = 1143$		$M = 2.769$		

$$(\Sigma X)(\Sigma Y) = (11{,}430)(27.69) = 316{,}496.70$$

$$r = \frac{N\Sigma XY - (\Sigma X)(\Sigma Y)}{\sqrt{[N\Sigma X^2 - (\Sigma X)^2][N\Sigma Y^2 - (\Sigma Y)^2]}}$$

$$= \frac{(10)(32{,}503.60) - 316{,}496.70}{\sqrt{[10(13{,}352{,}500.00) - (11{,}430)(11{,}430)][10(79.5793) - (27.69)(27.69)}}$$

$$= \frac{8539.30}{\sqrt{(2{,}880{,}100)(29.0569)}} = \frac{8539.30}{\sqrt{83686777.69}} = \frac{8539.30}{9148.0478} = .93$$

Consider the following scores on Tests X and Y:

	TEST X	TEST Y
Student 1	49	63
Student 2	50	61
Student 3	51	59
Student 4	52	57
Student 5	53	55

For each unit of increase in a score on Test X, there is a corresponding *decrease* of two units in the score on Test Y. Given this information, you are able to predict that if Student 6 scores 54 on Test X, that student's score on Test Y will be 53.

In reality very few negative correlations are perfect; however, the closer we come to −1.00, the better our predictive power. Just because a correlation is negative doesn't

FIGURE 8-2 A SCATTERPLOT SHOWING A PERFECT NEGATIVE CORRELATION.

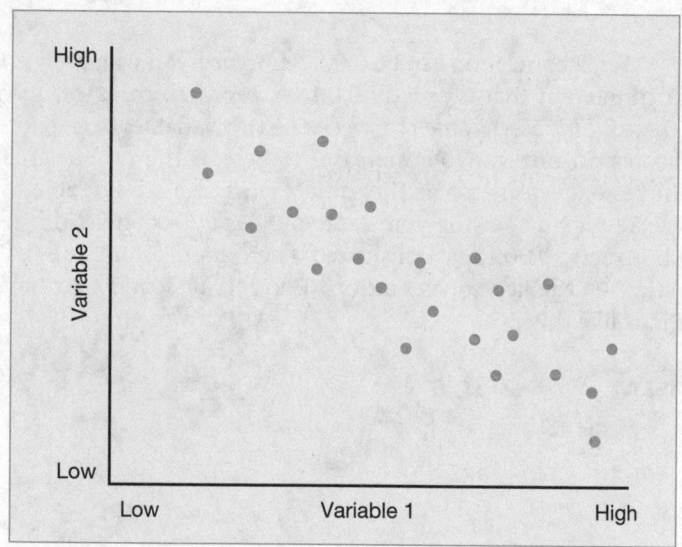

FIGURE 8-3 A SCATTERPLOT SHOWING A NONPERFECT NEGATIVE CORRELATION.

mean that we lose any predictive power. Figure 8-3 shows a negative correlation that isn't perfect; notice how the scores do not fall exactly in a straight line. They do, as we said earlier, run from the upper left of the graph to the lower right.

PSYCHOLOGICAL DETECTIVE   We indicated that correlations range from −1.00 to +1.00. Is there such a thing as a 0.00 (zero) correlation? If so, what does it mean?

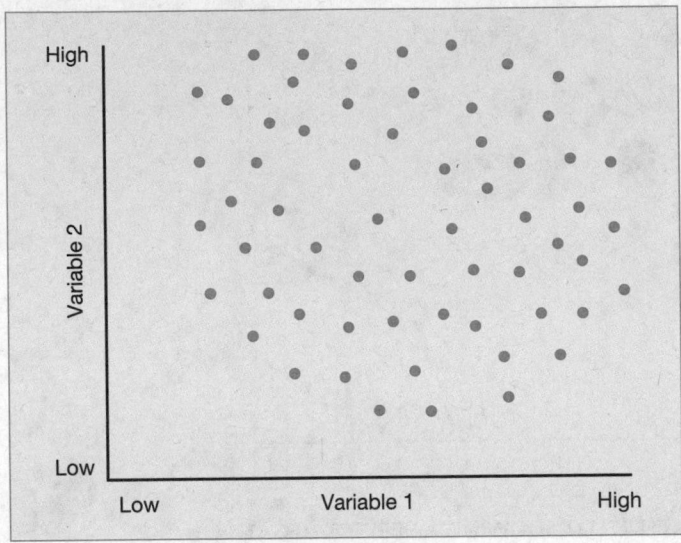

FIGURE 8-4 A SCATTERPLOT SHOWING A ZERO CORRELATION.

> **Zero correlation** Two variables under consideration are not related.

Yes, a correlation can be 0.00. (However, you will rarely encounter a correlation that is exactly 0.00.) A **zero correlation** means that there is *little or no relation* between the two variables (see Figure 8-4). As scores on one variable increase, scores on the other variable may increase, decrease, or be the same. Hence, we are not able to predict how you will do on Test Y by knowing your score on Test X. A correlation coefficient does not have to be exactly 0.00 to be considered a zero correlation. The inability to make good predictions is the key consideration. Two sets of scores that have a zero correlation might look like this:

	TEST X	**TEST Y**
Student 1	58	28
Student 2	59	97
Student 3	60	63
Student 4	61	60
Student 5	62	50

> **Perfect positive correlation** Exists when an increase of one unit in one variable is always accompanied by the same proportional increase in the other variable.

In this case the correlation between Test X and Test Y is 0.04. A correlation that small indicates that you will not be able to predict Test Y scores by knowing Test X scores; you are dealing with a zero correlation or no relation.

A correlation coefficient of +1.00 indicates that there is a **perfect positive correlation** between the two sets of scores (see Figure 8-5). That is, when we see an *increase* of one unit in one variable, we *always* see a proportional *increase* in the other variable.

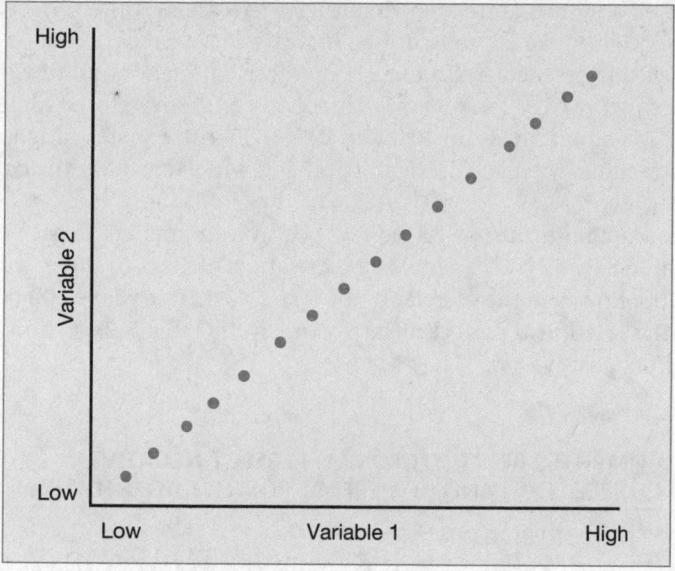

FIGURE 8-5 A SCATTERPLOT SHOWING A PERFECT POSITIVE CORRELATION.

Notice that when we have a perfect positive correlation, the scores fall in a straight line from lower left to upper right. (As you saw in Figure 8-1B. When the correlation is not perfect the scores will not be exactly in a straight line.) Consider the following scores on Tests X and Y:

	TEST X	TEST Y
Student 1	25	40
Student 2	26	43
Student 3	27	46
Student 4	28	49
Student 5	29	52

In this example there is an *increase* of three units in the score on Test Y for every unit increase on Test X. The perfect positive correlation leads you to predict that if Student 6 scores 30 on Test X, then her score on Test Y will be 55.

 Now that we have reviewed the basics of correlation, we would like you to think about the following question. Why don't perfect (either positive or negative) correlations occur frequently in the real world?

The existence of a perfect correlation indicates there are no other factors present that influence the relation we are measuring. This situation rarely occurs in real life. Think about correlating test scores. To obtain a perfect correlation, all of the participants would have to score high (or low) on the second test if they scored high (or low) on the first test. This situation is not likely to occur. Such factors as fatigue, illness, boredom, and distractions will likely have an effect and will likely make the correlation less than perfect.

Examples of computer printouts for perfect positive and perfect negative correlations appear in Table 8-2. As you can see, the correlation of Tests X and Y with themselves is always 1.00; however, the correlation of Test X with Test Y is −1.00 (Table 8-2, section A) when the relation is perfect negative and 1.00 (Table 8-2, section B) when the relation is perfect positive.

TABLE 8-2 COMPUTER PRINTOUT FOR (A) PERFECT NEGATIVE CORRELATION AND (B) PERFECT POSITIVE CORRELATION

A. PERFECT NEGATIVE CORRELATION

PEARSON CORRELATION MATRIX

	TEST X	TEST Y
TEST X	1.00	
TEST Y	−1.00	1.00

NUMBER OF OBSERVATIONS: 5

B. PERFECT POSITIVE CORRELATION

PEARSON CORRELATION MATRIX

	TEST X	TEST Y
TEST X	1.00	
TEST Y	1.00	1.00

NUMBER OF OBSERVATIONS: 5

REVIEW SUMMARY

1. A **correlation coefficient** is a single number that represents the degree of relation between two variables. Many predictions are based on correlations.
2. Researchers calculate the **Pearson product–moment correlation coefficient** when both variables are interval or ratio scale measurements.
3. A **perfect negative correlation** (−1.00) exists when an increase of one unit in one variable is always accompanied by a proportional decrease in the other variable. A **perfect positive correlation** (+1.00) exists when an increase of one unit is always accompanied by a proportional increase in the other variable.

A **zero correlation** (0.00) indicates that there is no relation between the variables under consideration.

CHECK YOUR PROGRESS

1. The degree of relation between two variables is represented by a _____.
   a. bimodal distribution
   b. median
   c. standard deviation
   d. correlation coefficient

2. Explain the difference between a positive correlation and a perfect positive correlation.

3. What does a correlation coefficient of 0.00 indicate about the relation between two variables?

   a. no relation

   b. weak positive relation

   c. perfect positive relation

   d. perfect negative relation

4. Which correlation coefficient below would offer the best predictions of scores on Test X from scores on Test A?

   a. +0.73   b. −0.87   c. 0.00   d. +0.42

Interpreting Correlation Coefficients

Let's return to the question that we asked earlier: What exactly does our $r = 0.93$ between SAT scores and GPAs mean? One way to answer that question is to determine if our correlation is significant. However, before we make that determination, you need to understand what the statisticians and psychological researchers mean by *significant*. When they are referring to research results, **statistically significant** means that a research result occurred *rarely by chance*. In other words, some other factor, such as the IV in an experiment, was effective and likely produced the results under consideration. We will have much more to say about the concept of statistical significance in subsequent chapters.

> **Statistically significant** A research result that occurred rarely by chance.

 How does this use of the term *significant* relate to correlation?

To answer this question, you need to keep in mind that your data represent only a sample of the population of all instances of the two variables you are examining. If you had the population of scores for both variables, you could calculate the correlation and see *exactly* how these two variables are related. However, you have only sample data and you are using these data to give you some idea about how these two variables are related in the population. If the correlation you calculate is sufficiently large that it would occur rarely by chance, then you have reason to believe that these two variables are related.

How do psychological researchers and statisticians define *rarely by chance*? We hope that your other psychology classes and the psychology journal articles you have read enabled you to answer this question. According to Lehmann (1993), Sir Ronald Fisher (1890–1962) was responsible for setting the standard for statistical significance at the *.05 level*. This standard means that researchers consider that a statistical result is significant when it occurs *by chance* 5 times out of 100. Researchers who want to be more cautious with their decisions might adopt a .01 level of significance.

 How does a researcher who uses the .01 level define significance?

This researcher has defined significance as a statistical result that would occur by chance 1 time in 100 replications of the research.

So, is our $r = .93$ significant? We can answer that question by looking at Table A-2 (pp. 542–543).

Step 1   Enter the *df* column (the far left column). Here we find that $df = N - 2$. Keep in mind that when you are dealing with correlations N equals the number of *pairs* of scores. For our SAT–GPA example, we had 10 pairs of scores. Because $N - 2 = 10 - 2 = 8$, we know that we should be looking at numbers on row 8.

Step 2   Find which column you will enter on row 8. At the top of Table A-2, you can see that the columns are labeled as either "levels two-tailed test" or "levels one-tailed test." We will discuss one- and two-tailed tests later. For right now let's use the "two-tailed test" columns. Assuming that we have set our significance level, then we would use the .05 column.

Step 3   Determine the *critical value* (the value from the table that *our calculated r* must equal or exceed to be significant). Moving down the .05 column to the row for 8 *df* brings us to the value .6319.

Step 4   Compare your calculated *r* with the table value to determine significance. Because .93 is greater than .6319, we can conclude that our correlation is significantly different from 0 at the .05 level.

Effect Size

Even though statistical significance is an important component of psychological research, it may not tell us very much about the magnitude or importance of our results. Keep in mind that we are still discussing the statistical importance of your research results.

Effect size The size or magnitude of the effect caused by an IV or the size or magnitude of a correlation.

The statistical view of importance takes into account the magnitude of size of your significant effect; statistical significance does not tell us anything about effect size. **Effect size** refers to the size or magnitude of the effect an IV produced in an experiment or the size or magnitude of a correlation.

Unfortunately, a research result can be significant and, yet, the effect size may be quite small. We hope you are wondering how this seemingly incompatible state of affairs can occur. Let's begin our explanation by indicating that, generally speaking, as our sample size gets larger, the critical value needed to achieve significance becomes smaller. You can see this inverse relation in Table A-2. As df (which are based on sample size) become larger, all the table values become smaller. Let's use our SAT–GPA correlation as an example. With $df = 8$, your correlation had to be equal to or greater than .6319 to be significant at the .05 level.

 PSYCHOLOGICAL DETECTIVE What would the critical value for significance at the .05 level be if you had 47 pairs of scores?

We hope you remembered that $df = N - 2 = 47 - 2 = 45$. So, if you enter the .05 column for a two-tailed test at the row for $df = 45$, you see that the critical value to achieve significance is .2875. There is quite a difference between .6319 and .2875.

Coefficient of determination The squared Pearson product moment correlation coefficient (r^2). When multiplied by 100, the coefficient of determination indicates the percentage of variance accounted for.

Let's see how this difference created by sample size relates to effect size. It's easy to calculate the effect size for a Pearson product–moment correlation; all you have to do is square the correlation efficient. Statisticians and psychological researchers refer to the squared correlation coefficient, r^2, as the **coefficient of determination**. When we are considering a correlation, the coefficient of determination multiplied by 100 tells us what percentage of the variance is accounted for by the correlation (Rosenthal & Rosnow, 1984).

$$r^2 \times 100 = \text{percentage of the variance accounted for by the correlation}$$

The higher r^2 becomes, the more variance is accounted for by the relation between the two variable under study. Lower r^2 values indicate that factors, *other than* the two variables of interest, are influencing the relation we are interested in.

Returning to our SAT–GPA data. We find that

$$r^2 = .93^2 = .8649$$
$$.8649 \times 100 = 86.49\% \text{ of the variance accounted for by the correlation of SAT scores and GPAs}$$

The coefficient of determination indicates that the relation between SAT scores and GPAs accounts for a large percentage (86.49%) of the variance; there appear to be few other factors that influence this relation. Hence, the ability to predict a student's GPA based on his SAT score should be good.

What if we had 52 pairs of scores and our $r = .32$? First, let's see if this correlation is significantly different from 0. First, we need to determine the df.

$$df = N - 2 = 52 - 2 = 50$$

Entering the row for $df = 50$, we see that the critical value for significance at the .05 level is .2732. Because our correlation ($r = .32$) is larger than .2732, we conclude that it is significant. However, when we calculate the coefficient of determination, we find that

$$r^2 = .32^2 = .1024$$
$$.1024 \times 100 = 10.24\% \text{ of the variance accounted for by}$$
$$\text{the correlation of SAT scores and GPAs}$$

Even though this correlation is significantly different from 0, the relation between the two variables accounts for only slightly over 10% of the variance. Nearly 90% of the variance is accounted for by other, unknown factors. Viewed in this light, the relation measured by our correlation, even though it is significant, is not that large or meaningful. There are numerous other factors that we are unaware of that influence this relation. Our predictive power is far from perfect in this instance.

We will have more to say about other measures of effect size in later chapters. For right now, keep in mind that determination of effect size is a topic that is rapidly growing in importance among psychological researchers and statisticians. In fact, some statisticians (e.g., Kirk, 1996, 2003) can envision a time when the reporting of effect size will be more common than significance testing. Indeed, the latest edition of the *Publication Manual of the American Psychological Association* (2001) says, "You are encouraged to provide effect-size information" (p. 18) when you prepare your research report.

Prediction

Regression The prediction of one variable from knowledge of another variable.

Criterion variable The variable that is being predicted.

Predictor variable The variable that is being predicted from.

In this chapter we have seen how researchers can use correlations to assist them in making predictions. In this section we look more closely at the process of prediction or, as some statisticians call it, *regression*. Generally speaking, **regression** refers to the prediction of one variable from our knowledge of another variable.

Although it is not necessary to specify which variable is being used to predict and which variable is being predicted when we calculate correlation coefficients, it is necessary to specify these variables when we are dealing with regression. We label the variable that is *being predicted* as the Y variable and refer to it as the **criterion variable**. We label the variable that we are *predicting from* as the X variable and refer to it as the **predictor variable**. In other words, we use X to predict Y. We next examine the z-score model for making predictions.

The Regression Equation

> **Regression equation**
> The basic statistical equation that is the basis for prediction.

The **regression equation** is the statistical basis of prediction. The regression equation states:

$$\hat{Y} = a + bX$$

The "hat" indicates that we are making a prediction of a score on the Y variable (criterion variable)

The predictor variable

The slope of the regression line (the regression coefficient)

The point at which the regression line intersects the Y axis, known as the Y intercept

> **Regression line**
> Graphical display of the relation between values on the predictor variable and predicted values on the criterion variable.

Now, before we work with the regression equation, the definitions for a and b in the regression equation indicate that we need to discuss the regression line. The **regression line** is a graphical display of the relation between values on the predictor variable and predicted values on the criterion variable; it is similar to the scatterplot that we have used to display correlations. We will show you how to construct a regression line shortly.

Obviously, we need to determine the values of a and b before we can use the regression equation to make predictions. Let's start with b. There are two ways you can calculate b. First, if you already know r and the SDs for the X and Y variables, then:

$$b = r \, \frac{SD_{Y}}{SD_{X}}$$

SD of Y variable

SD of X variable

XY Correlation coefficient

The second way to calculate b involves the following formula:

$$b = \frac{N\Sigma XY - (\Sigma X)(\Sigma Y)}{N\Sigma X^2 - (\Sigma X)^2}$$

If you have calculated the XY correlation, then calculating b with the second formula will be simple. If you find your b value is negative, don't worry, b will be negative when r is negative. It will be positive when r is positive.

Once you have calculated b, then:

$$a = M_{Y} - b\,M_{X}$$

Mean of X

Regression coefficient

Mean of Y

Now let's return to our SAT–GPA example and see how this formula works. Recall that Table 8-1 detailed the calculations for the SAT–GPA correlation. We will use some of those calculations to determine b. More specifically:

$$b = \frac{N\Sigma XY - (\Sigma X)(\Sigma Y)}{N\Sigma X^2 - (\Sigma X)^2} = \frac{\overset{\text{From Table 8-1}}{8539.30}}{\underset{\text{From Table 8-1}}{2,880,100}} = .003$$

Once we have determined b, it's easy to calculate a:

$$a = M_Y - bM_X$$
$$= 2.769 - (.003)1143$$
$$= 2.769 - 3.429$$
$$= -.66$$

Now, let's make some predictions. We'll start with our basic formula:

$$\hat{Y} = a + bX$$
$$= -.66 + .003X$$

An applicant has an SAT = 1120. What do you predict as a GPA for this applicant?

$$= -.66 + .003(1120)$$
$$= -.66 + 3.36$$
$$\hat{Y} = 2.70$$

What is your prediction for an applicant with SAT = 600?

$$= -.66 + .003(600)$$
$$= -.66 + 1.80$$
$$\hat{Y} = 1.14$$

Let's return to our consideration of the regression line.

Constructing the Regression Line

There are two ways to construct the regression line. First, you could calculate several predicted values, plot these values, connect these points, and then extend the line to the Y intercept. This procedure works fine; however, it carries with it the potential for calculation errors and inaccurate points.

A second procedure that is less likely to have calculation errors involves the following steps:

Step 1   Locate the Y intercept (a).

Step 2   Plot M_Y and M_X.

Step 3   The line that passes through these points is the regression line.

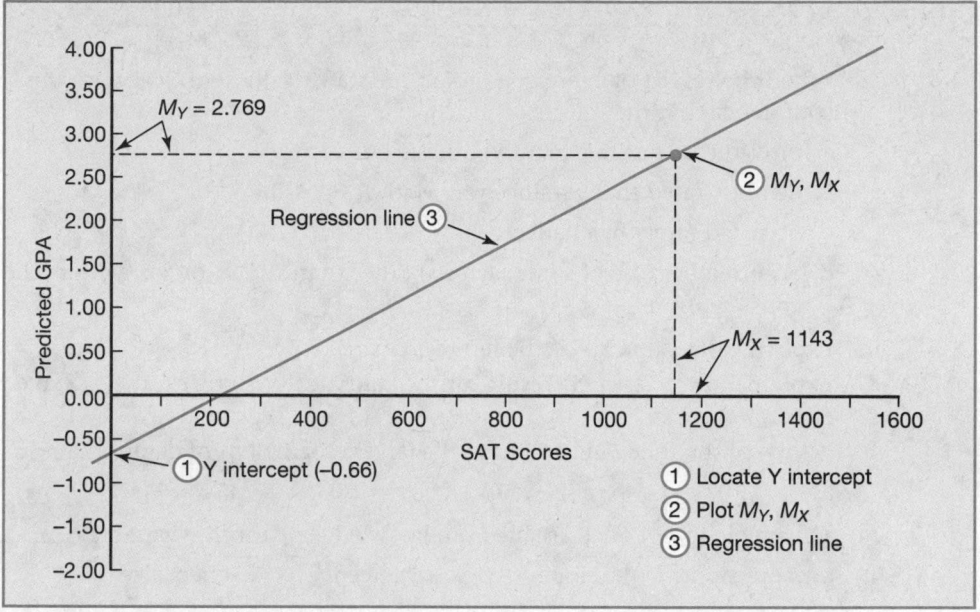

FIGURE 8-6 CONSTRUCTING A REGRESSION LINE.

Slope The steepness of the regression line.

Y intercept The point at which the regression line crosses the vertical (Y) axis.

Figure 8-6 shows the construction of the regression line for the SAT–GPA data we have been considering. Remember, the steepness of the regression line is known as the **slope**, whereas the point at which this line crosses the vertical axis is the **Y intercept**.

REVIEW SUMMARY

1. A research result is **statistically significant** when it occurs rarely by chance.
2. Researchers have selected the .05 level (occurs 5 times in 100 by chance) as the standard for statistical significance.
3. **Effect size** refers to the size or magnitude of the effect an IV caused or the size or magnitude of a correlation.
4. A research result can be statistically significant but have a small effect size.
5. The **coefficient of determination**, r^2, when multiplied by 100, indicates the percentage of the variance accounted for by a Pearson product–moment correlation.
6. **Regression** is the prediction of scores on one variable (the **criterion variable**) from a knowledge of another variable (the **predictor variable**).
7. The **regression line** is a graphical display of the relation between values on the predictor variable and predicted values on the criterion variable.
8. The steepness of the regression line is known as **slope**, whereas the point at which the regression line crosses the ordinate (Y axis) is the **Y intercept**.

CHECK YOUR PROGRESS

1. When the results of a research project are statistically significant, we can say with confidence that they _____.

   a. proved that our research hypothesis was correct

   b. demonstrated that variance was as low as possible

   c. occurred rarely by chance

   d. occurred because of some factor(s) other than the IV or correlation under consideration

2. Explain what is meant by the term *effect size*.

3. Explain how a research result can be statistically significant, yet have a small effect size.

4. Which of the following will have the largest coefficient of determination?

   a. $r = .30$ b. $r = -.40$ c. $r = .50$ d. $r = -.60$

5. The prediction of one variable from knowledge of another variable is _____.

   a. regression   b. slope   c. Y intercept   d. effect size

6. Describe the regression equation.

7. The _____ is a graphical display of the relation between values on the predictor variable and predicted values on the criterion variable.

   a. slope   b. steepness   c. regression line   d. Y intercept

EXERCISES

1. Your psychology teacher has repeatedly told your class that the more you study, the better you will do on the tests. You decide to verify this statement. You randomly select 12 classmates and ask them how long they studied for the last test and what grade they made. Here are the data:

Student	Hours studied	Grade
1	17	91
2	12	73
3	8	70
4	14	86
5	10	71
6	3	62
7	20	87
8	11	76
9	7	68
10	16	84
11	9	66
12	15	83

Calculate the correlation between these two variables and test it for significance. Which variable is the predictor variable? Which variable is the criterion variable?

2. Calculate the coefficient of determination for Exercise 1. Interpret this coefficient.
3. Create a scatterplot for Exercise 1.
4. Another classmate told you that she studied 25 hours. What would you predict she scored on the test? Use both methods to solve this problem.
5. Construct the regression line for Exercise 4.
6. Create a scatterplot that has 15 dots for each of the following situations:

   a. perfect positive correlation

   b. positive, but not perfect, correlation

   c. near zero correlation

   d. perfect negative correlation

   e. negative, but not perfect, correlation

7. Calculate the correlation between the following two sets of data:

Participant	Measure 1	Measure 2
1	27	16
2	15	19
3	24	17
4	17	18
5	21	14
6	19	15

   Describe the nature of this correlation. Is it significant?

8. Calculate the correlation between the following two sets of data:

Participant	Measure 1	Measure 2
1	14	67
2	22	43
3	24	11
4	17	26
5	6	41
6	11	17
7	2	3

   Describe the nature of this correlation. Is it significant?

9. Calculate and interpret the effect size for Exercises 7 and 8.
10. Using the results from Exercise 7, assume that Participant 7 scored 29 on Measure 1. What would you predict that Participant 7 would score on Measure 2? Construct the regression line for Exercise 7.
11. Below are three data sets. Calculate the correlation coefficient between the two tests for each set. Test each correlation for significance at the .01 level.

Participant	Set 1		Set 2		Set 3	
	Test 1	Test 2	Test 1	Test 2	Test 1	Test 2
1	68	67	63	91	57	93
2	73	68	64	73	61	26
3	75	66	67	88	66	67
4	81	83	68	81	71	18
5	86	79	72	79	75	91

6	88	91	76	71	83	73
7	90	86	81	67	89	52
8	94	88	87	65	94	28

12. Calculate the effect size for each data set in Exercise 11. Which set shows the strongest effect? Why? (Be thorough.)

13. With regard to Exercise 11, Participant 9 has the following scores for Test 1:

Set 1	Set 2	Set 3
Test 1 = 83	Test 1 = 75	Test 1 = 67

What do you predict Participant 9 will score on Test 2 in each of these three sets?

14. Repeat Exercise 13, but use the Test 2 scores you just calculated to predict Test 1 scores.

15. An industrial psychologist has developed a productivity scale that predicts job satisfaction. The prediction formula is:

$$\text{Job satisfaction score} = 1.54 + (.63)(\text{productivity score})$$

Calculate the predicted job satisfaction score for the following workers:

Worker	Productivity score
1	74
2	37
3	81
4	68
5	55

KEY TERMS

Correlation, *173*

Scatterplot, *173*

Positive correlation, *176*

Negative correlation, *176*

Correlation coefficient, *176*

Pearson product-moment correlation coefficient, *177*

Perfect negative correlation, *177*

Zero correlation, *180*

Perfect positive correlation, *180*

Statistically significant, *183*

Effect size, *185*

Coefficient of determination, *185*

Regression, *186*

Criterion variable, *186*

Predictor variable, *186*

Regression equation, *187*

Regression line, *187*

Slope, *189*

Y intercept, *189*

LOOKING AHEAD

In the next chapter we will continue exploring the use of statistics in psychological research. There we will have more to say about the normal curve. Also, we will introduce the important topics of probability and sampling.

Probability, the Normal Curve, and Sampling

Descriptive statistics
Procedures used to summarize a set of data.

In Chapters 4 and 6, we introduced you to **descriptive statistics**, so you now know how to summarize a set of data from an experiment. The next step is to analyze those data to determine whether our IV had a significant effect on our DV. To make such decisions, we use **inferential statistics**. Before we introduce inferential statistics, however, we must first consider the topic of probability.

Inferential statistics
Procedures used to analyze data after an experiment is completed; used to determine whether the IV has a significant effect.

The Nature and Logic of Probability

Probability
Determination of the likelihood that a given event will occur.

Probability is at the heart of inferential statistics. We will use probability to determine the likelihood that a given outcome from our experiment was either probable or not. Any time we work with a sample rather than the entire population, we must use statistics and probability to draw conclusions. If we could measure the entire population, then we would have no uncertainty about our results and would not need to use probability. For some reason, probability is a topic that often gives students some difficulty. However, you have been using probability for most of your life, so pay close attention and you should do well. Paying attention is important because it is critical that you understand probability so that you will understand how to make decisions from your inferential statistics. Thus, let's examine how we use probability all the time in everyday life, although we might not always realize that we are using it.

Suppose your friend asks you, a week in advance, to go on a trip to a large city 50 miles away in order to see a concert because he has an extra ticket. Your friend expects to get back from the concert by 1:00 A.M. You know that you have an exam the day after the concert.

 How might you use probability to help you make your decision?

Subjective probability
Your estimate of the probability of a given event's likelihood.

Whether you realize it or not, you will probably use **subjective probability** to help you make this decision. You may first think about the likelihood that you can study enough for your exam during the next week so that you can feel prepared for the exam before you leave for the concert. If you believe (a prediction of sorts) that you can study enough between now and then, you may then think about your friend's reliability. Does the arrival home of 1:00 A.M. sound accurate? Is your friend reliable enough that you can expect him to be willing to leave immediately after the concert to drive home, or is he likely to want to stop somewhere and use extra time on the way home? Finally, you will probably think about whether getting home at 1:00 A.M. will allow you to be well rested for the exam. If your class is at 8:00 A.M., your assessment of your readiness after a few hours of sleep will be quite important. If your exam is at 1:00 P.M., then you will not worry so much about getting enough sleep.

When assessing subjective probabilities, notice that we did not mention numbers anywhere. Typically, when you see probabilities, you are likely to see numbers.

PSYCHOLOGICAL DETECTIVE   How many different ways can you think of numbers being used for probability?

If you came up with three different ways that numbers can denote probability, give yourself a pat on the back! When you hear about the odds of something taking place, you will often hear numbers used: The odds of the Tigers winning the championship game are 1 in 3. From this sentence, you would know that the Tigers have a chance to win the game, but they are the underdog because the odds of the other team winning are 2 in 3.

Percentage A standard method of designating a portion of a total; ranges from 0% (none of the total) to 100% (all of the total).

Percentages are an extremely common way to use numbers to denote probability: The Tigers have a 33% chance of winning the championship game. Because of our familiarity with common percentages such as this one, we know that the Tigers have 1 chance in 3 of winning the game. Finally, **proportions** also use numbers to designate probability: The Tigers have a .33 chance of winning the championship game. Again, we know that the Tigers have a 1/3 probability of winning the game.

Proportion A standard method of designating a portion of a total; ranges from .00 (none of the total) to 1.00 (all of the total); particularly used in statistics rather than percentages.

If you are like many students, you may feel more comfortable with percents than you do proportions. However, you need to get over that feeling because probability in statistics is almost always based on proportions. Perhaps a quick refresher is in order. Proportions and percentages show exactly the same information, but on different scales. Whereas percentages range from 0% to 100%, proportions range from .00 to 1.00. Thus, to translate from a percentage to a proportion, you simply divide by 100 or move the decimal two places to the left. Similarly, to change a proportion to a percentage, you would multiply by 100 or move the decimal two places to the right. Thus, 50% is equal to a proportion of .50. Keep these translation rules in mind; they will come in handy.

Null hypothesis A hypothesis that says that all differences between groups are due to chance (i.e., not the operation of the IV).

The reason that probability is so important for researchers is that inferential statistics tests allow us to determine the probability that our results came about by chance. The basic premise behind inferential statistics is that we assume that there is no difference between the groups in our experiment. This assumption is referred to as the **null hypothesis**. If we have only two groups in our experiment, we would write the null hypothesis as:

$$M_1 = M_2$$

This equation says that the mean of Group 1 is equal to the mean of Group 2.

Does anything about that claim strike you as a bit odd?

Alternative (or **experimental) hypothesis** A hypothesis that says that all differences between groups are not due to chance (i.e., the effect of the IV).

We hope that you thought it would be odd to assume *no* difference between our means—after all, our goal is to show differences between our means, isn't it? If this was your thought, you're on target. When we conduct a statistical test, we actually have two assumptions we are testing simultaneously; the test helps us choose between the two. The second hypothesis is known as the **alternative** (or **experimental) hypothesis**. We would write the alternative hypothesis as

$$M_1 \neq M_2$$

The alternative hypothesis is typically the one that the experimenter hopes to support in the experiment. As a safeguard against bias, we start off assuming the null hypothesis and let the data and statistical test demonstrate otherwise. This process is somewhat akin to the United States court system, which assumes that an individual is innocent until "proven" guilty.

Why did we use quote marks around *proven* in the previous sentence?

Actually, courts of law are quite similar to our statistical process. Rarely, if ever, is a defendant truly *proven* guilty if you assume that proven means 100% certainty. Even courts use a probabilistic procedure. Jurors and judges find defendants guilty when they have a high degree of certainty of guilt, and they withhold judgment (declare the defendant not guilty) when they have a high degree of uncertainty about guilt. Although DNA testing may yield extremely small chances of the guilty party being someone other than the defendant, even DNA tests cannot give us 100% certainty. In a similar fashion, our statistics cannot give us a 100% certain answer either. Thus, we have to make our decisions based on a high degree of certainty or uncertainty, which is why we rely on probability to help us draw conclusions. This point is crucial; we will return to it later in the chapter *and* throughout the remainder of the book.

The results of an inferential statistical test can tell us whether the results of an experiment would occur frequently or rarely by chance. If the difference between our groups is zero or small, our inferential statistic would also be small. Inferential statistics with *small* values occur *frequently by chance*. If the result occurs often by chance, we say that the difference between our groups is not significant and conclude that our IV *did not* affect the DV. In this case we would accept the null hypothesis. On the other hand, if the difference between our groups is large, our inferential test would yield a large value. Inferential statistics with *large* values occur *rarely by chance*. When our results occur infrequently by chance, we say that the difference between our groups is significant and conclude that some factor other than chance is at work. If we have conducted our experiment properly and exercised good control (see Chapters 5 and 7), then our significant statistical result gives us reason to assume that the IV we manipulated was effective (i.e., that the IV *did* affect the DV).

When do we consider that an event has occurred rarely by chance? Traditionally, psychologists say that any event that occurs by chance 5 times or fewer in 100 occasions is a rare event. Thus, you will see frequent mention of the ".05 level of significance" in journal articles. This statement means that a result is considered significant if it would occur 5 or fewer times by chance in 100 replications of the experiment when the null hypothesis is actually true.

PSYCHOLOGICAL DETECTIVE   How can a result be significant (i.e., we conclude the means are different) when the null hypothesis is actually true?

We hope that this question occurred to you—if it did, you are doing a great job at understanding what's going on. Technically, we should not find different means if the null hypothesis is actually true. Think about this idea in the context of a situation that may be familiar to you: Did you take the SAT or ACT more than once? The null hypothesis would predict no difference (or only small differences) between your two (or more) test scores. After all, you are the same person being measured twice. Thus, any two scores of yours should be quite similar. That's the same thing we would expect in an experiment when the IV has no effect. In that case, we would have two equal groups being treated equally except for an IV. But if the IV has no effect, we would essentially have two equal groups being treated equally. Thus, their mean scores should be relatively equal. Any large difference between the two groups would be due just to chance, not to the IV. That large difference should, however, be a rare occurrence—something that would not happen very frequently at all. Therefore, if a large difference could happen 5 or fewer times out of 100 just by chance, we will assume it is unlikely that chance is the proper explanation.

Let's return to the ACT/SAT example. A small difference in scores would not surprise us. However, would you be surprised if there's a large difference? If your score increased (or decreased) dramatically, it might be an indication that something other than chance is "going on." In an experimental context, suppose you took a course designed to raise your ACT/SAT score. Afterward, you scored considerably higher. If the difference is larger than you would expect to occur by chance, you have found a significant increase in your test score. If you have held all other factors constant, then you have evidence that the course did raise your score.

Notice how all of these examples have referred to the probability of chance. You should be able to see why it is important to talk about probability before moving on to inferential statistics.

A Conceptual Statistical Note

In our discussion of null and alternative hypotheses, we used the symbol *M* to designate the group means and showed you that the comparisons were between the means for the two groups. This is the type of comparison you will make with your data. Conceptually, however, statisticians and researchers wish to compare the two populations represented by the two groups so that they can draw a conclusion about the effects of the IV in the populations of interest. Thus, the conceptual null hypothesis is $\mu_1 = \mu_2$, and the conceptual alternative hypothesis is $\mu_1 \neq \mu_2$. However, it is usually impossible to measure an entire population to determine μ, so we resort to sampling and end up comparing sample means (*M*) in our statistical tests. So, although we used *M*s in our formulas for null and alternative hypotheses for your understanding, the statistical null and alternative hypotheses would use the population means.

> **Normal distribution** A symmetrical, bell-shaped distribution that has half of the scores above the mean and half of the scores below the mean.

> **Standard deviation** A measure of variability equal to the square root of the variance; has important relations to the normal curve.

> **z score** A measure, in *SD* of the distance of a raw score above or below the mean.

Probability and the Normal Curve

In Chapter 6 we introduced you to the **normal distribution** and showed you the relation of the **standard deviation** to that distribution. Figure 9-1 will refresh your memory about how the standard deviation divides the normal curve into various percentages. Because we can easily transform percentages to proportions, we can work from the normal distribution and make probabilistic statements. However, unlike our earlier examples from real life, these probabilities are not subjective, but are true and accurate. The shape and spread of the normal distribution never changes, so the probability associated with a **z score** of a certain size will never change. This concept is true for statistical tests in general. We use probabilities

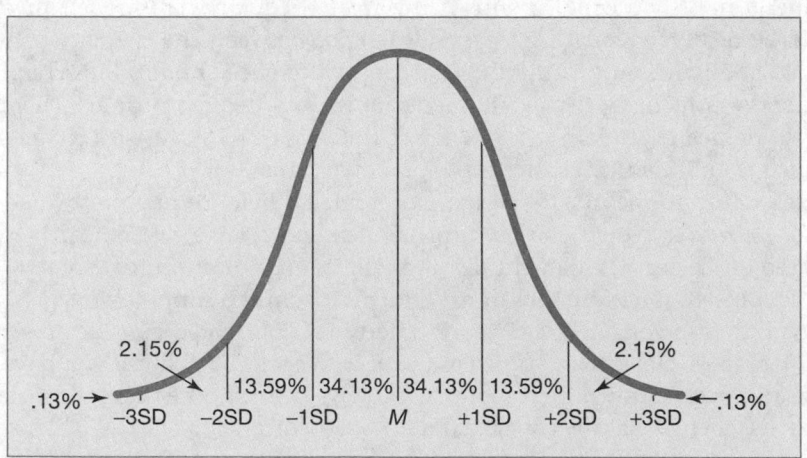

FIGURE 9-1 THE RELATION OF STANDARD DEVIATIONS AND THE NORMAL DISTRIBUTION.

from statistical tests because they are objective, which allows us to avoid making subjective guesses about the outcomes of our research.

Let's see how we can use the normal distribution to find probabilities and make decisions. Suppose you know that a particular college requires an SAT score of 1250 for entrance. You wonder just how exclusive this college is. We can determine the probability that a randomly selected person will score 1250 on the SAT by finding a z score for the score of 1250. Recall the z score formula from Chapter 6:

$$z = (X - M) / SD$$

Parameter A statistical value for an entire population.

We learn from the Educational Testing Service (the company that developed the SAT) that the population mean for the SAT is 1000 with a standard deviation of 100. A statistical value of an entire population is called a **parameter**. Although it may be unusual, sometimes we do know such values. Using our formula for z, the z score for 1250 is:

$$z = (1250 - 1000) / 100 = 250/100 = 2.50$$

Turning to Table A-1, we find that a z score of 2.50 has .4938 of the scores from the mean to that z score. We remember from Chapter 6 that the normal curve has .5000 of all scores above the mean, which leaves only .0062 (.5000 − .4938) for the probability of a z score above 2.50. Thus, the probability of a randomly selected person having an SAT above 1250 is only .0062. Another way of conceptualizing this result is that only .0062 of the population would be expected to have SAT scores above 1250. Thus, the college is pretty exclusive.

Probability and Decisions

At this point, you may be wondering how we use probability to make decisions about experimental findings. It is actually a fairly simple, straightforward process. We will use a statistical test to find the probability of a given event occurring by chance. We will then compare that probability to the critical probability for making our decision—the .05 level of significance that we mentioned earlier. If the probability of our statistic occurring by chance is above .05, then we decide that chance is still a possible explanation for our finding. Therefore, we are uncertain about our outcome and we conclude that it is possible that our finding is due to chance. In other words, we accept the null hypothesis and we have found a result that is not significant.

PSYCHOLOGICAL DETECTIVE   Can you figure out what we will do if the probability of chance is less than .05?

If our statistical test yields a probability of chance of less than .05, we believe that chance is *not* a likely explanation for our finding. Thus, we reject the null hypothesis

Reprinted from *The Chronicle of Higher Education*. By permission of Mischa Richter and Harald Bakken.

"On the other hand, if you're not interested in good and evil, this one would give you a good understanding of statistical probability."

A good background in statistics should keep you from becoming this desperate.

and accept the alternative hypothesis. In this case, our statistical result is significant—we believe that the IV is responsible for the difference in the DV.

Comparing a Sample to a Population: The One-Sample *t* Test

It is often the case that we would like to compare a sample mean to a population mean. We could make such a comparison for an experimental question (e.g., Did a study course help to raise the students' SAT scores?) or a nonexperimental question (e.g., Are there really two scoops of raisins in each box of Raisin Bran?). To answer such a question, we need to obtain a sample and compare its mean to the mean of the population. For the sample experimental question, we would need to have a group of students take the study course and then take the SAT so that we would have a sample of SAT scores. For the sample nonexperimental question, we would need to buy boxes of Raisin Bran and measure the quantity of raisins in each box so that we would have a sample of raisin "scores." We showed you a similar problem a few paragraphs ago when we asked about the probability of a randomly selected person having an SAT of 1250. This type of problem that we're introducing, however, asks the question about a *sample* mean rather than an individual mean.

To work on such a problem, rather than using the normal distribution as we did for *z* scores we need to introduce a new statistical distribution. The **t distribution** is similar to the normal distribution in shape. However, the *t* distribution is used for smaller samples than we would usually have for using the normal distribution.

> **t distribution** A distribution used in place of the normal distribution for small samples; it resembles a normal distribution but is less peaked.

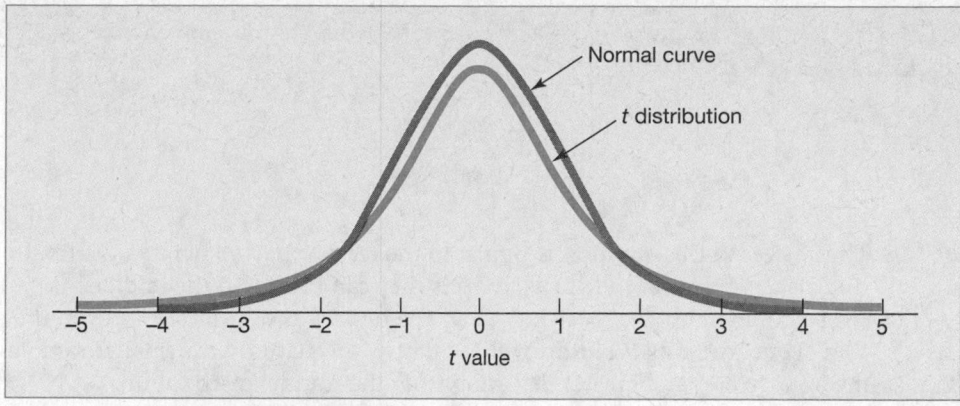

FIGURE 9-2 **TWO DIFFERENT DISTRIBUTIONS.**

Statisticians assume that large samples of 30 or more will typically fit the normal distribution well. When we have a large number of scores, they will usually cluster in the middle, and a nice normal curve will take shape. But if we have a small number of scores, the normal curve could not have as high a peak because there wouldn't be enough scores to build up in the middle. As you can see in Figure 9-2, the *t* distribution is flatter in the middle and higher on the tails compared to the normal distribution.

Critical region The region in a distribution that signifies research significance; usually the extreme .05 of a distribution.

Being higher on the tails concerns us because the **critical region** for a statistical test (the .05 region) is located in the tails of the curves (see Figure 9-3). Using a normal distribution for small samples will give us misleading probabilities and, therefore, misleading conclusions. One other interesting concept regarding the *t* distribution is that, unlike the normal curve, it does not retain a constant shape. Instead the *t* distribution changes shape somewhat based on the size of the sample.

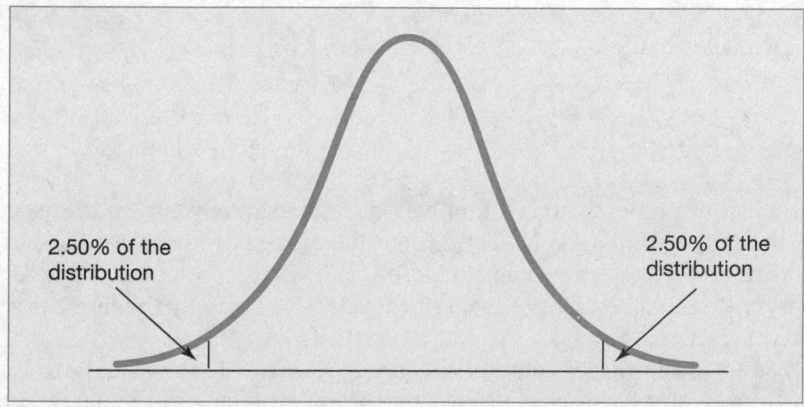

FIGURE 9-3 **CRITICAL REGION FOR THE *t* DISTRIBUTION.**

The answer to this question is similar to the reason that we have a *t* distribution in the first place: The fewer the scores, the less they can pile up in the middle. Also, the fewer the scores in a distribution, the greater the impact one score can have on the distribution. Thus, the *t* distribution will get flatter and flatter with smaller samples, which means a greater and greater deviation from the normal distribution.

Although we have talked about the *t* distribution changing shape with sample size, we need to introduce a new statistical concept at this point. The *t* distribution technically changes shape based on its number of degrees of freedom. By **degrees of freedom** we mean the ability of a number in a given set to assume any value. This ability is influenced by the restrictions imposed on the set of numbers. For every restriction, one number is determined and must assume a fixed or specified value. For example, assume we have a set of 10 numbers, and we know the sum of these numbers to be 100. Knowing that the sum is 100 is a restriction; hence, one of the numbers will be determined or fixed. In Example 1 below, the last number *must* be 15 because the total of the first 9 numbers (which can assume any value) is 85.

> **Degrees of freedom**
> The ability of a number in a specified set to assume any value.

Numbers	1	2	3	4	5	6	7	8	9	10	sum
Example 1	6	12	11	4	9	9	14	3	17	15	100
Example 2	21	2	9	7	3	18	6	4	5	?	100

As in the first example, the first 9 numbers can assume any value. In this example the sum of the first 9 numbers is 75. Thus, the value of the last number is fixed at 25. The importance of degrees of freedom should be clear when you look at Table A-3, which shows us critical *t* values. Notice that critical values of *t* vary by the number of degrees of freedom (first column).

If you examine the *df* column in Table A-3, you will see that the values for *df* are continuous until you reach 30. At that point, the *df* jump by larger and larger increments.

As you can see from the table, the likelihood of this problem arising is quite high if you have large samples. The rule of thumb is that you should *never* give yourself degrees of freedom that you don't actually have. Instead, always use the value that is lower than your actual *df*. For example, if you have 53 participants, which would give you 52 *df*, you should use the row for 40 *df*. If you used the row for 60 *df*, you would be giving your statistical test more **power** (see Chapter 7) than it actually has. You would also increase your chances of making a statistical error, which we will discuss later in the chapter.

> **Power** The probability that a statistical test will be significant (i.e., the experimental hypothesis will be accepted when it is true).

> **One-sample *t* test** An inferential test to compare a sample mean to a population mean.

Let's look at an example of a **one-sample *t* test**. Suppose a company that markets an SAT study course has called you in as a statistical consultant. The company has taken a random sample of 25 students who are currently taking the SAT study course. Although you wish the company had measured the students before they took the course, the fact that they are a random sample means that they should not differ from the larger population of students. Thus, you can assume that these students are neither more nor less bright than the general student population. This assumption allows you to compare the mean SAT score of the students after taking the course to the general population parameter. The formula for a one-sample *t* test is:

$$t = (M - \mu) / \text{SEM}$$
$$\text{SEM} = SD / \sqrt{N}$$

Notice the similarity of this *t* formula to the *z* score formula from Chapter 6. Instead of using a single score (X) we use a sample mean (*M*), and instead of a *SD*, we use a standard error. We use a standard error because samples are much less variable than individual scores.

At the end of the course, the 25 students have a mean SAT score of 1060. The company wants you to help them decide if the course was effective. The null hypothesis in this case is:

$$M = \mu$$

In other words, if the study course has no effect, we would expect the students to have a mean approximately equal to the mean of the general population (1000). The alternative (or experimental) hypothesis is:

$$M \neq \mu$$

Notice that we adapted our general null and alternative hypotheses from earlier in the chapter to fit our specific case of comparing a sample mean to a population mean. Now we are ready to make our calculations.

$$t = (1060 - 1000) / (100 / \sqrt{25}) = 60 / (100 / 5) = 60 / 20 = 3.00$$

Before we can check this result with our t table, we need to know the number of degrees of freedom. In this case, $df = N - 1 = 25 - 1 = 24$. Using Table A-3, we move down the leftmost column until we find 24 df. Reading across from that number, we find the critical values of t at various levels of significance.

 Earlier you learned about the .05 level of significance. Why do you think there are additional values in the t table?

Although the .05 level is the most commonly used level for significance, it is not universal. Thus, most statistics tables provide other significance levels for researchers who wish to use them. Also, as you will see in just a moment, having additional levels in the tables allows us to get a better idea of the probability of chance of our results. For now, we read across on the 24 df row until we find the .05 column (two-tailed test). You should find the value of 2.064. This value is your critical t value. If your calculated t is equal to or exceeds this critical value, then the probability of chance is *less* than the column value of .05.

 Is the calculated t larger or smaller than the critical t? Based on that answer, what is the proper conclusion regarding the null and alternative hypotheses? Based on that answer, what is the proper conclusion regarding the SAT study course?

Our calculated t (3.00) is indeed larger than the critical table value (2.064). Thus, the probability of chance being responsible for the mean score of 1060 is less than .05. Because $p < .05$, we reject the null hypothesis and accept the alternative hypothesis. Assuming that the researchers have run a well-controlled study, we will conclude that students who took the SAT study course scored higher (1060) on the SAT than the national average (1000):

$$t(24) = 3.00, p < .05.$$

The end of that sentence shows you the standard way for us to communicate our findings, according to the APA's *Publication Manual* (2001). You need to communicate all the statistical information as well as your conclusion so an informed reader can see what you found. We will present in-depth information on APA style in Chapter 20.

If you return to the *t* table and continue across the column from left to right, you will see that our calculated *t* of 3.00 is also larger than two more critical values of *t* at different significance levels. Because 3.00 is larger than the tabled value of 2.797, you can also conclude that the probability of chance is less than .01.

 Is the probability of chance for this finding also less than .001?

This question tests your ability to use the *t* table. At .001 with 24 *df*, the critical *t* value is 3.745, which is larger than our calculated *t* of 3.00. Thus, the probability of chance is *not* less than .001. However, we now know that the probability of our result being due to chance is somewhere between .01 and .001 ($.001 < p < .01$, which means that the probability of chance is less than .01 but greater than .001), which gives us a better idea about the likelihood of chance being responsible for our result. Researchers typically report their results at the lowest possible level of chance, so we can amend our statistical conclusion from earlier as follows: $t(24) = 3.00, p < .01$.

Marginal Significance   You may have heard the old saying that "Close only counts in horseshoes and hand grenades." Well, statistics is a little like horseshoes and hand grenades. Imagine how you would feel if you ran your statistical test and the computer printout showed .06 as the probability of chance. You might groan and think, "I missed significant findings by only .01! Why couldn't it have been .05 instead of .06?" Researchers are just like you—they would have the same thought. Thus, many researchers will label the area between .05 and .10 as **marginal significance**. This conclusion essentially means that your result was almost significant, but not quite. Typically, researchers will go ahead and discuss results that are marginally significant in their articles. However, they will likely use "hedge words" in those discussions—you will be likely to see the words "may" and "might" more often in their discussions (e.g., "These results may indicate that . . .").

> **Marginal significance**
> Refers to statistical findings that have a probability of chance between .05 and .10; essentially means "almost significant."

One-Tailed versus Two-Tailed Tests of Significance

> **Two-tailed test**
> A nondirectional test of significance.

You probably noticed that Table A-3 had two rows across the top—one for a **two-tailed test** and one for a **one-tailed test**. Recall from Chapter 2 that you can state your experimental (or alternative) hypothesis in either a directional or a nondirectional manner. Earlier in this chapter, we showed you the nondirectional form: $M_1 \neq M_2$. If you use the directional form, then you are specifying exactly how (i.e., the direction) the results will turn out. For the example we have been considering, an experimental hypothesis stated in general implication form (see Chapter 2) might be as follows:

> **One-tailed test**   A directional test of significance.

If students take an SAT study course, then they will score higher than the national average on the SAT.

Written in the format we saw earlier in the chapter, this experimental hypothesis would be $M_1 > M_2$ (or $M_1 > M_2$, depending on which direction you were predicting).

Because we predict that the students' scores will be *higher* than the national average, we have a directional hypothesis. If we simply indicate that we expect a difference between the students and the national average and do not specify the exact nature of that difference, then we are using a nondirectional hypothesis.

 PSYCHOLOGICAL DETECTIVE   What outcome(s) would be possible with a two-tailed test of our hypothesis?

A two-tailed test allows three possible outcomes: The students could score higher than the national average, lower than the national average, or not differently from the national average.

Now, how do directional and nondirectional hypotheses relate to the *t* test? A one-tailed *t* test evaluates the probability an outcome in only one direction (greater than *or* less than), whereas the two-tailed *t* test evaluates the outcome in both possible directions (greater than *and* less than). If you've associated directional hypotheses with one-tailed tests and nondirectional hypotheses with two-tailed tests, you're correct.

Figure 9-4 depicts the relation between the type of experimental hypothesis, directional versus nondirectional, and the type of *t* test, one-tailed versus two-tailed, used. As you can see, the region of rejection is larger and only in one tail of the distribution when you conduct a one-tailed test (Figure 9-4A). The probability of the result occurring by chance alone is *split in half and distributed equally to the two tails* of the distribution when you use a two-tailed test (Figure 9-4B).

Although the calculations for a one-tailed test of significance and a two-tailed test of significance are the same, you would consult different columns in the *t* table. For the SAT study course example we conducted a two-tailed test of significance; 2.064 was our critical value at the .05 level of significance. Hence, a *t* value equal to or greater than 2.064 is significant (see Table A-3 in the Appendix). Had we used a one-tailed test, our critical value at the .05 level of significance would have been 1.711 (see Table A-3).

Because a lower value is required for significance with a one-tailed test of significance, it is somewhat easier to find a significant result. If this is the case, why don't experimenters always state directional experimental hypotheses? The main reason is that researchers don't always know exactly how an experiment will turn out. If we could predict the outcome of each experiment before it was conducted, there would be no need to do the experiment. If you state a directional hypothesis and then obtain the opposite result, you must reject your hypothesis. Had you stated a nondirectional hypothesis, your experiment would have confirmed your prediction that there would be a difference between the groups. When we conduct a *t* test, we are usually interested in either outcome; imagine how disappointed the company would be if students actually scored lower on the SAT test after taking the course!

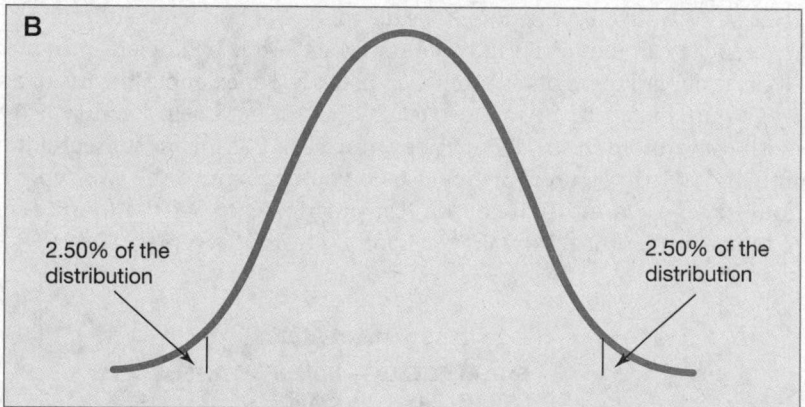

FIGURE 9-4 REGIONS OF REJECTION FOR (A) A ONE-TAIL TEST AND (B) A TWO-TAIL TEST. A. With a one-tailed test the region of rejection of the null hypothesis is located in one tail of the distribution. Directional hypotheses, such as A > B, are associated with one-tail tests. **B.** With a two-tailed test the region of rejection of the null hypothesis is distributed evenly to both tails of the distribution. Nondirectional hypotheses, such as A ≠ B (A does not equal B), are associated with two-tailed tests.

When Statistics Go Astray: Type I and Type II Errors

Type I error Accepting the alternative (experimental) hypothesis when the null hypothesis is true.

Unfortunately, not all our inferences will be correct. Recall that we have determined that an experimental result is significant only when it occurs rarely by chance (i.e., 5 times or less in 100). There always is the chance that your experiment represents one of those 5 times in 100 when the results did occur *by chance*. Hence, the null hypothesis is true and you will make an error in accepting your experimental hypothesis. We call this faulty decision a **Type I error** (alpha, α).

You would increase your probability of making a Type I error if you accepted your experimental hypothesis, although it had a high probability of chance, or if you use more degrees of freedom than you actually have. The experimenter directly controls the probability of making a Type I error by setting the significance level.

PSYCHOLOGICAL DETECTIVE   How could you reduce the probability of making a Type I error?

> **Type II error** Accepting the null hypothesis when the alternative (experimental) hypothesis is true.

You are less likely to make a Type I error with a significance level of .01 than with a significance level of .05. However, the more extreme or critical you make the significance level (e.g., going from .05 to .01) to avoid a Type I error, the more likely you are to make a Type II or beta (B) error. A **Type II error** involves rejecting a *true* experimental hypothesis. Unlike Type I errors, Type II errors are not under the direct control of the experimenter. We can indirectly cut down on Type II errors by implementing techniques that will cause our groups to differ as much as possible. For example, the use of a strong IV and larger groups of participants are two techniques that will help avoid Type II errors.

We will have more to say about Type I and Type II errors in subsequent chapters. The summary table in Figure 9-5 should help you distinguish the two types of errors: You should keep in mind that the typical practice is to set the alpha level at .05 because it places the probability of Type I and II errors at acceptable levels.

| | | **True State of Affairs** | |
		EXPERIMENTAL HYPOTHESIS IS TRUE	**NULL HYPOTHESIS IS TRUE**
Your Decision	**Experimental Hypothesis Is True**	Correct Decision	Type I (α) Error
	Null Hypothesis Is True	Type II (β) Error	Correct Decision

FIGURE 9-5 DECISION MATRIX FOR STATISTICAL DECISIONS.

REVIEW SUMMARY

1. Researchers use **probability** to help determine whether experimental results are significant.
2. Probability can take the form of odds, **percentages**, or **proportions**. Statistical tests typically use proportions.

3. The **null hypothesis** assumes no difference in an experiment. The **alternative** (or **experimental**) **hypothesis** assumes that there is a difference.

4. The most commonly used guideline for significant findings is the **.05 level of significance**.

5. A **normal distribution** of scores is a bell-shaped, symmetrical distribution. A *t* **distribution** is similar to the normal, but flatter in the middle and higher on the tails.

6. The *t* distribution changes shapes as the degrees of freedom change. The larger the sample, the more closely the *t* distribution approximates the normal distribution.

7. Researchers use a **one-sample *t* test** to compare a sample mean to a population mean.

8. A **one-tailed test** of significance allows a researcher to predict a difference in a specific direction. A **two-tailed test** of significance allows a researcher to test a difference in either direction.

9. Even though lower critical values are associated with one-tailed tests, which makes it easier to attain significance, most experimental hypotheses are nondirectional because the researchers do not know exactly how the research will turn out.

10. Sometimes the results of an inferential statistical test produce an incorrect decision. An experimental hypothesis may be incorrectly accepted (**Type I error**) or incorrectly rejected (**Type II error**).

CHECK YOUR PROGRESS

1. Why is it necessary for experimenters to use probability when stating their conclusions rather than drawing definite conclusions?

2. If you were conducting an experiment to determine the effect of caffeine on performance, what would your null hypothesis, nondirectional alternative hypothesis, and directional hypothesis be?

3. Could you analyze data from the experiment in Question #2 with a one-sample *t* test? What would be necessary to use that test?

4. What does "level of significance" mean? How do you determine level of significance?

5. If it is easier to obtain a significant result with a one-tailed test, why would an experimenter ever state a nondirectional experimental hypothesis and be forced to use a two-tailed test?

6. A one-tailed test of significance is associated with a _____.

   a. directional hypothesis   b. nondirectional hypothesis

   c. positive correlation   d. negative correlation

7. The Type I error _____.

   a. is under the direct control of the experimenter

   b. always occurs 5% of the time

   c. is specified by the experimental hypothesis

   d. all of the above

   e. none of the above

8. If you could compare all men and women in the world, you would find that men are significantly more aggressive. You conduct an experiment and find no difference in aggression between men and women. You have made a _____.

a. correct decision

b. Type I error

c. Type II error

d. Type III error

Sampling Considerations and Basic Research Strategies

Having completed our coverage of basic experimental and statistical strategies, we conclude this chapter with a consideration of two issues that the researcher must consider whether conducting experimental or nonexperimental research: sampling and basic research strategies. Sampling deals with the question of who will participate in our research project and whether they are a representative group. Once we have dealt with sampling issues, then we must decide on our main research strategy. The main strategies used by researchers are the single-strata, cross-sectional, and longitudinal approaches.

Sampling

Assume that you want to determine which of two new titles for the college newspaper—*The Wilderbeast* (named after your school mascot) or *The Observer*—appeals most to the student body. You ask the 36 students in your senior-level biopsychology course and find that 24 prefer *The Observer* and 12 prefer *The Wilderbeast*. You report your findings to the publications advisory board and recommend that they choose *The Observer* as the new title.

PSYCHOLOGICAL DETECTIVE — Should the publications advisory board accept your recommendation? Are there some reasons to question your findings?

The publications advisory board should not accept your recommendation. Unlike Sherlock Holmes who said, "I presume nothing," (Doyle, 1927, p. 745), you seem to have made some assumptions. The main problem with your data concerns the students you surveyed. Is your senior-level biopsychology class representative of the entire campus? The answer to this question must be a resounding "no"; only senior-level psychology majors take this class. Moreover, a quick check of the class roster indicates that the majority (67%) of the students in your class are women. Clearly, you should have selected a group of students more representative of the general student body at your college.

Population The complete set of individuals or events.

Sample A group that is selected to represent the population.

Random sample A sample in which every member of the population has an equal likelihood of being included.

Random sampling without replacement Once chosen, a score, event, or participant cannot be returned to the population to be selected again.

Random sampling with replacement Once chosen, a score, event, or participant can be returned to the population to be selected again.

We shall designate the general student body as the **population** or complete set of individuals or events that we want to represent. The group that we select to represent the population is called the **sample**. When every member of the population has an equal likelihood of being selected for inclusion in the sample, we have created a **random sample**. Random sampling is important because it should create a sample that is representative of the population.

How would you obtain a random sample of students on your campus to take the newspaper title survey? Computer technology has made this task quite simple; you simply indicate the size of the sample you desire and a computer program can randomly select a sample of that size from the names of all currently enrolled students. Because a name is not eligible to be chosen again once you have selected it, this technique is called **random sampling without replacement**. If you can return the chosen name to the population and have it eligible for selection again, the procedure is termed **random sampling with replacement**. Because psychologists do not want the same participant to appear more than once in a group, random sampling without replacement is the preferred technique for creating a random research sample.

Suppose a computer has randomly selected a sample of 80 students from the entire student body and you are examining the printout. Even though you selected this sample randomly, it also has some apparent problems. Just by chance the majority of the students selected are freshmen and sophomores. Moreover, men make up the majority of this sample. The views on the two newspaper titles held by this group of randomly selected students may not be much better than our original sample. What can we do to produce an even more representative sample?

There are two techniques that we can use to increase the representativeness of our sample. The first procedure is quite simple: We can select a larger sample. Generally speaking, the larger the sample, the more representative it will be of the population. If we randomly selected 240 students, this larger sample would quite likely be more representative of the general student body than our original sample of 80 students. Although larger samples may be more like the population from which they are drawn, there is a potential drawback. Larger samples mean that we will need to test more participants. In our project dealing with the two newspaper titles, the testing of additional participants may not present any major problems. However, if we were administering a lengthy questionnaire or paying participants for their participation, increasing the number of participants may create unmanageable time or financial obstacles.

Stratified random sampling Random samples are drawn from specific subpopulations or strata of the general population.

If simply increasing the sample size does not offer a good solution to the problem of achieving a representative sample, the researcher may want to use the technique of stratified random sampling. **Stratified random sampling** involves dividing the population into subpopulations or strata and then drawing a random sample from one or more of these strata. For example, one logical subdivision of a college student body would be by classes: freshmen, sophomores, juniors, and seniors. You could then draw a random sample from each class. How many students should you include in each stratum? One option would be for each stratum to contain an equal number of participants. Thus, in our newspaper title project we might include 20 participants from each academic classification. A second option would be to sample each stratum in proportion to its representation in the population. If freshmen comprise 30% of the student body, then our random sample would contain 30% freshmen. What about the number of men and women sampled in each stratum? We could have equal numbers or we could sample in proportion to the percent of men and women in each stratum. As you have probably surmised, the use of stratified random sampling indicates that you have considerable knowledge of the population in which you are interested. Once you have this knowledge, you can create a sample that is quite representative of the population of interest. A word of caution is in order, however. Although it may be tempting to specify a number of characteristics that your sample must possess, you can carry this process too far. If your sample becomes too highly specified, then you will be able to generalize or extend your results only to a population that has those very specific characteristics.

One stratum that frequently appears in research reports is the subject or participant pool that many colleges and universities use. In these instances students, typically enrolled in introductory psychology, have the option (among others) of participating in psychological research in order to fulfill a course requirement. Once students have volunteered to participate in a research project, the researcher can randomly assign them to specific groups or treatment conditions. For example, in the research on the wording of the informed consent document by Burkley, McFarland, Walker, and Young (2000) that we considered in Chapter 3, the authors indicated that

> Twenty-five undergraduate university psychology students (2 men, 23 women) volunteered to participate. Participants were randomly assigned to either the control or experimental group. Participants received class credit for their involvement in the study
>
> (Burkley et al., 2000, p. 44).

Basic Research Strategies

Even though you have chosen your sample, you cannot simply rush out to start testing participants. You need to give some thought to the research question and how you can best conduct your project in order to answer that question. There are three basic approaches you can adopt: single-strata, cross-sectional, and longitudinal.

The **single-strata approach** seeks to acquire data from a single, specified segment of the population. For example, a particular Gallup Poll may be interested only in the voting preferences of blue-collar workers. Hence, a sample composed only of individuals from this stratum would be administered a voter-preference survey. This approach typically seeks to answer a rather specific research question.

When the single-strata approach is broadened to include samples from more than one stratum, a cross-sectional approach is being

Single-strata approach Gathering data from a single stratum of the population of interest.

Cross-sectional research Comparison of two or more groups during the same, rather limited, time period.

employed. **Cross-sectional research** involves the comparison of two or more groups of participants during the same, rather limited, time span. For example, a researcher may want to compare voter preferences of different age groups. To acquire this information, the researcher obtains random samples of voters aged 21, 31, 41, 51, 61, and 71 and compares their responses to a voter preference survey.

Perhaps the researcher wants to obtain information from a group of participants over an extended period of time. In this instance, the researcher would conduct a **longitudinal research project**. First, the researcher would obtain a random sample from the population of interest; then this sample would complete an initial survey or test. The same participants would then be contacted periodically to determine what, if any, changes had occurred during the ensuing time in the behavior of interest. This group of individuals, born in the same time period and repeatedly tested or surveyed, is called a **cohort**. For example, a researcher might be interested in the changes in the degree of support for environmental conservation that occur as individuals grow older. To evaluate such changes, the researcher randomly selects a group of grade-school children. Every five years, the researcher contacts all members of this cohort and administers an environmental conservation survey. Table 9-1 allows you to compare these three different research strategies.

Longitudinal research project Obtaining research data from the same group of participants over an extended period of time.

Cohort A group of individuals born during the same time period.

TABLE **9-1** SINGLE-STRATA, CROSS-SECTIONAL, AND LONGITUDINAL RESEARCH STRATEGIES

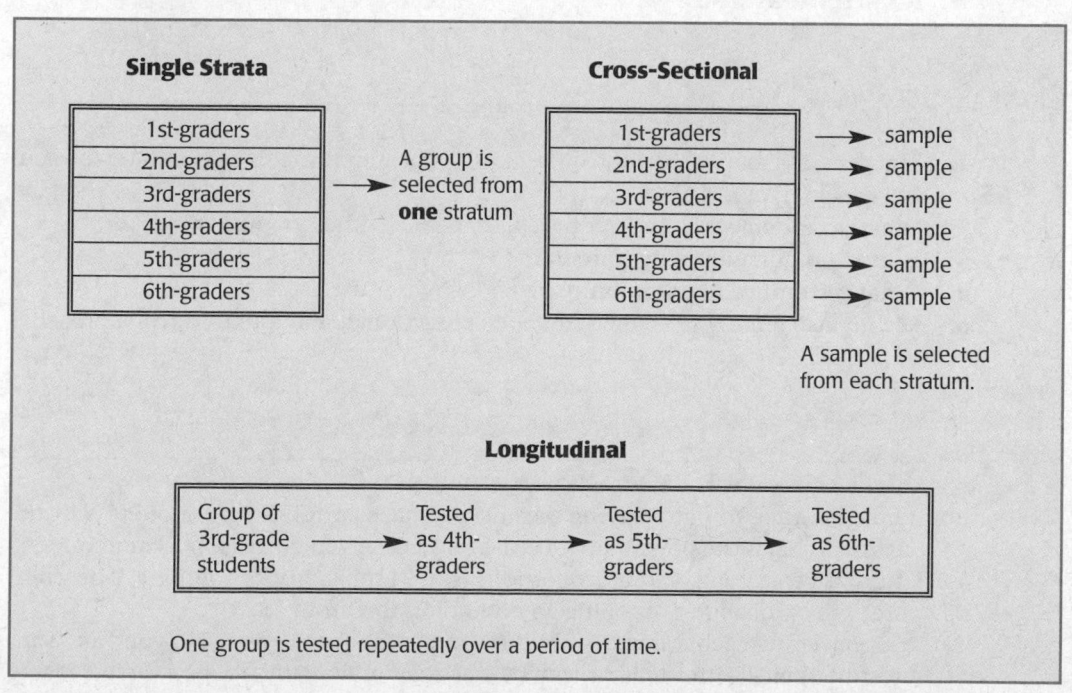

It is important that you remember that sampling concerns and decisions about your basic research strategy apply to both nonexperimental and experimental research projects. Moreover, our concerns with sampling and research strategy do not end at this point. For example, we had a great deal to say about the importance of randomization when we discussed experimental control in Chapter 5. Likewise, once we have decided on our basic research strategy, we will have to consider such details as how many groups of participants need to be tested to answer our research question. The topics fall under the general heading of experimental design; we begin our discussion of this topic in Chapter 10.

REVIEW SUMMARY

1. The **sample** of individuals who complete a research project should be representative of the **population** from which it is drawn.
2. When a **random sample** is selected, every member of the population has an equal likelihood of being selected. When **random sampling without replacement** is used, a person or item cannot be returned to the population once it has been selected. When **random sampling with replacement** is used, selected persons or items can be returned to the population to be selected again.
3. **Stratified random sampling** involves dividing the population into subpopulations or strata and then drawing random samples from these strata.
4. Basic research strategies include investigating (a) a **single stratum** of a specified population, (b) samples from more than one stratum in a **cross-sectional project**, or (c) a single group of participants over an extended time period in a **longitudinal study**.

CHECK YOUR PROGRESS

1. The general group of interest is the _____. The group that is selected to represent the general group is a _____.
2. What is random sampling? With replacement? Without replacement?
3. Why is random sampling important?
4. What is stratified random sampling and why is it used?
5. Distinguish among the single-strata, cross-sectional, and longitudinal approaches to research.

EXERCISES

1. Imagine that you are playing a game and need to roll a 1 on a die to win the game. What is the probability of rolling a 1? Give your answer as a common fraction, a percentage, and a proportion. Is the probability of rolling a 1 different from the probability of rolling any other number from 2 to 6?
2. Suppose you teach a group of children who seem above average to you. You want to test their IQs to determine whether they're actually above average. Using

numbers, write your null hypothesis. Write your alternative hypotheses for both a one-tailed *and* a two-tailed test.

3. Suppose you have calculated a z score in Exercise 2. The z score you found is 2.68. What is the probability of this z score? On the basis of this probability, do you think the children are truly above average or not? Why?

4. Suppose you have calculated a z score in Exercise 2. The z score you found is 1.04. What is the probability of this z score? On the basis of this probability, do you think the children are truly above average or not? Why?

5. Suppose you have calculated a z score in Exercise 2. The z score you found is 1.38. What is the probability of this z score? On the basis of this probability, do you think the children are truly above average or not? Why?

6. If you plan to conduct a one-sample *t* test with 20 participants (one-tailed test), how many degrees of freedom will you have? What will your critical *t* value be?

7. If you plan to conduct a one-sample *t* test with 10 participants (one-tailed test), how many degrees of freedom will you have? What will your critical *t* value be? Why are your critical *t* values different for Exercises 6 and 7?

8. Suppose the Higher Score Company advertises that their study course can raise your GRE score. You are skeptical, so you find a random sample of 10 people who are willing to take the course. At the end of the course, they obtain a mean score of 1038 on the GRE (1000 is considered average), with a *SD* of 57 points. Using a two-tailed test, can you conclude that the Higher Score course achieved its goal?

9. For Exercise 8, what would your conclusion be if you ran a one-tailed test? What potential problem might you create by using a one-tailed test?

10. Suppose the Higher Score Company advertises that their study course can raise your GRE score. You are skeptical, so you find a random sample of 20 people who are willing to take the course. At the end of the course, they obtain a mean score of 1038 on the GRE (1000 is considered average), with a standard deviation of 57 points. Using a two-tailed test, can you conclude that the Higher Score course achieved its goal?

11. Suppose the Higher Score Company advertises that their study course can raise your GRE score. You are skeptical, so you find a random sample of 100 people who are willing to take the course. At the end of the course, they obtain a mean score of 1008 on the GRE (1000 is considered average), with a standard deviation of 57 points. Using a two-tailed test, can you conclude that the Higher Score course achieved its goal?

12. Seniors in the psychology department take a departmental exam each year in their capstone course. Over past years, seniors have accumulated the following statistics:

$$M = 41.3 \qquad SD = 5.8$$

This year's seniors made the scores below. Are they any better or worse than the typical students from the department?

40 45 38 49 37 41 47 44 37 43 44 40 35 39 44

13. Seniors in the psychology department take a departmental exam each year in their capstone course. Over past years, seniors have accumulated the following statistics:

$$M = 41.3 \qquad SD = 3.8$$

This year's seniors made the scores below. Are they any better or worse than the typical students from the department?

44 46 39 49 39 45 48 44 38 44 48 42 38 39 45

14. Seniors in the psychology department take a departmental exam each year in their capstone course. Over past years, seniors have accumulated the following statistics:

$$M = 41.3 \qquad SD = 2.8$$

This year's seniors made the scores below. Are they any better or worse than the typical students from the department?

40 35 38 41 33 40 37 42 37 34 40 38 35 39 44

15. Considering your answers to Exercises 12–14, in which case would you be *most likely* to make a Type I error? Why?

KEY TERMS

Descriptive statistics, *194*

Inferential statistics, *194*

Probability, *194*

Subjective probability, *194*

Percentage, *195*

Proportion, *195*

Null hypothesis, *195*

Alternative (or experimental) hypothesis, *196*

Normal distribution, *198*

Standard deviation, *198*

z score, *198*

Parameter, *199*

t distribution, *200*

Critical region, *201*

Degrees of freedom, *202*

Power, *203*

Marginal significance, *205*

Two-tailed test, *205*

One-tailed test, *205*

Type I error, *207*

Type II error, *208*

Population, *211*

Sample, *211*

Random sample, *211*

Random sampling without replacement, *211*

Random sampling with replacement, *211*

Stratified random sampling, *211*

Single-strata approach, *212*

Cross-sectional research, *213*

Longitudinal research project, *213*

Cohort, *213*

LOOKING AHEAD

So far, we have considered sources of researchable problems (Chapter 1), developed an experimental hypothesis (Chapter 2), considered the ethics involved in conducting research (Chapter 3), scrutinized our experiment for possible extraneous variables and nuisance variables (Chapter 5), and implemented control procedures to deal with these extraneous variables (Chapters 5 and 7). In addition, we have covered the basics of statistics and statistical reasoning (Chapters 4, 6, 8, and 9). Now we are ready to combine all of these elements in an experimental design. In Chapter 10 we consider experimental designs involving the use of two groups of participants. We will consider more complex designs in subsequent chapters.

chapter

10

Designing and Conducting Experiments with Two Groups

Experimental Design: The Basic Building Blocks

We are now ready to begin an experiment. Or are we? Although we have chosen a problem, read the relevant literature, developed a hypothesis, selected our variables, instituted control procedures, considered the participants, and examined several selected statistics, we are still not ready to start the experiment. Before we can actually begin, we must select a blueprint. If you were about to design a house, you would be faced with an overwhelming variety of potential plans—you would have many choices and selections ahead of you. Fortunately, selecting a blueprint for your experiment is simpler than designing a house because there are a relatively small number of standard choices that experimenters are likely to use in designing experiments.

Selecting a blueprint for your experiment is just as important as doing so for a house. Can you imagine what a house would look like if you began building it without any plans? The result would be a disaster. The same is true of "building" an experiment. We refer to the research blueprint as our **experimental design**. In Chapter 1 you learned that an experimental design is the general plan for selecting participants, assigning those participants to experimental conditions, controlling extraneous variables, and gathering data. If you begin your experiment without a proper design, your experiment may "collapse" just as a house built without a blueprint might. How can an experiment collapse? We have seen students begin experiments without any direction only to end up with data that fit no known procedure for statistical analysis. We

> **Experimental design**
> The general plan for selecting participants, assigning participants to experimental conditions, controlling extraneous variables, and gathering data.

also have seen students collect data that have no bearing on their original question. Thus, we hope not only that you will use this text during your current course but also that you will keep the book and consult it as you design research projects in the future.

In this chapter we will begin developing a series of questions in a flowchart to help you select the correct design for your experiment. As Charles Brewer, distinguished professor of psychology at Furman University, is fond of saying, "If you do not know where you are going, the likelihood that you will get there borders on randomness." If you don't design your experiment properly, the probability that it will answer your research question is slim. Sherlock Holmes knew this lesson well: "No, no: I never guess. It is a shocking habit—destructive to the logical faculty" (Doyle, 1927, p. 93).

When you were a child and played with Legos or Tinkertoys, you probably got a beginner's set first. This set was small and simple, but with it you learned the basics of building. As you got older, you could use larger sets that allowed you to build and create more complicated objects. The parallel between children's building sets and experimental design is striking. In both cases the beginner's set helps us learn about the processes involved so that we can use the advanced set later; the basic set forms the backbone of the more advanced set. In both cases combining simple models increases the possibilities for building, although more complex models must still conform to the basic rules of building.

> **Principle of parsimony**
> The belief that explanations of phenomena and events should remain simple until the simple explanations are no longer valid.

The Two-Group Design

In this chapter we examine the most basic experimental design, the two-group design, and its variations. This design is the simplest possible one that can yield a valid experiment. In research situations, we typically follow the **principle of parsimony**, also known as Ockham's (or Occam's) razor. William of Ockham, a fourteenth-century philosopher, became famous for his dictum "Let us never introduce more than is required for an explanation" (McInerny, 1970, p. 370). In research, we apply the principle of parsimony to research questions, just as detectives apply the principle of parsimony to their investigations: Don't needlessly complicate the question that you are asking. The two-group design is the most parsimonious design available.

> **Independent variable (IV)** A stimulus or aspect of the environment that the experimenter directly manipulates to determine its influences on behavior.

> **Dependent variable (DV)** A response or behavior that is measured. It is desired that changes in the DV be directly related to manipulation of the IV.

How Many IVs? Figure 10-1 shows the first question we must ask ourselves in order to select the appropriate design for our experiment: "How many **independent variables (IVs)** will our experiment have?" In this chapter and Chapter 12, we will deal with experimental designs that have one IV. You will remember (see Chapter 5) that an IV is a stimulus or aspect of the environment that the experimenter directly manipulates to determine its influences on behavior, which is the **dependent variable (DV)**. If you want to determine how anxiety affects test performance, for example, anxiety would be your IV. If you wish to study the effects of different therapies on depression, the different therapies would be your IV. The

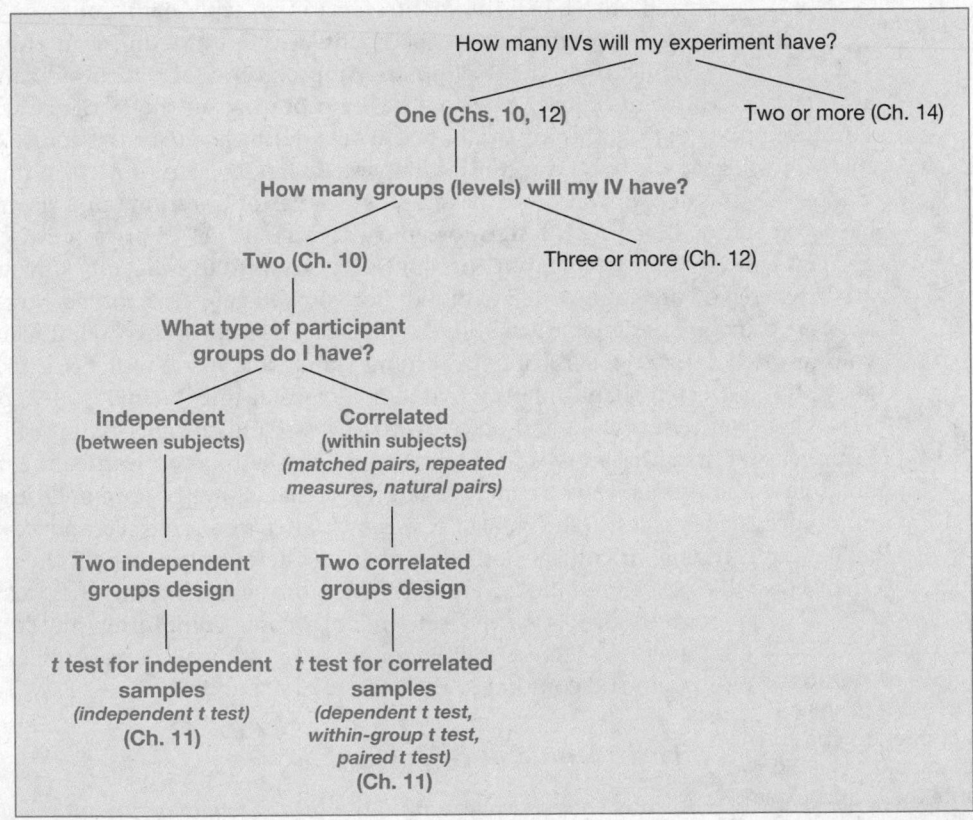

FIGURE 10-1 EXPERIMENTAL DESIGN QUESTIONS.

simplest experimental design has only one IV. We will look at research designs with more than one IV in Chapter 14.

A minority of the published research studies uses one IV. Does that mean that experiments with one IV are somehow poor or deficient? No, there is nothing wrong with a one-IV design; however, such a design is simple and may not yield all the answers an experimenter desires. However, simple is not necessarily bad! Inexperienced researchers or researchers who are beginning to investigate new areas often prefer single-IV designs because they are easier to conduct than multiple-IV designs and it is simpler to institute the proper control procedures. Also, the results of several one-IV experiments, when combined in one report, can describe complex phenomena.

How Many Groups? Assuming we have chosen to use a single-IV design, we then come to our second question (see Figure 10-1) in determining the proper experimental design: "How many groups will I use to test my IV?" In this chapter, the answer is two. Although an experiment can have a single IV, it must have at least two groups.

Why must we have two groups but only one IV?

Extraneous variables Undesired variables that may operate to influence the DV and, thus, invalidate an experiment.

The simplest way to find out whether our IV caused a change in behavior is to compare some research participants who have received our IV to some others who have not received the IV. If those two groups differ, and we are assured that we controlled potential **extraneous variables** (see Chapter 5), then we conclude that the IV caused the participants to differ. So, the way that we have two groups with only one IV is to make the two groups differ in the amount or the type of the IV that they receive. Note carefully that the last statement is *not* the same as saying that the groups have different IVs.

The most common manner of creating two groups with one IV is to present some amount or type of IV to one group and to withhold that IV from the second group. Thus, the *presence* of the IV is contrasted with the *absence* of the IV. These differing amounts of the IV are referred to as the **levels** (also known as *treatment conditions*) of the IV. Thus, in the common two-group design, one level of the IV is none (its absence) and the other is some amount (its presence). Notice that the presence and absence of an IV is conceptualized as two differing levels of the same IV rather than as two different IVs. Now let's return to our earlier examples.

Levels Differing amounts or types of an IV used in an experiment (also known as *treatment conditions*).

If you were interested in the effects of anxiety on test performance or the effects of therapy on depression, how would you implement an experimental design so that you could compare the presence of the IV to the absence of the IV?

In the first example, you would need to compare anxious test-takers (first level) to nonanxious test-takers (second level). In the second, you would compare depressed people receiving therapy (first level) to depressed people who were not receiving therapy (second level).

Experimental group In a two-group design, the group of participants that receives the IV.

Control group In a two-group design, the group of participants that does not receive the IV.

In this presence-absence situation, the group of participants receiving the IV is typically referred to as the **experimental group**. It is as if we were conducting the experiment on them. The group that does not receive the IV is known as the **control group**. The members of this group serve a control function because they give us an indication of how people or animals behave under "normal" conditions—that is, without being exposed to our IV. They also serve as a comparison group for the experimental group. We will use statistics to compare performance scores on the DV for the two groups to determine whether the IV has had an effect. When our two groups differ significantly, we assume that the difference is due to the IV. If the groups do not differ significantly, we conclude that our IV had no effect.

Let's look at a research example using the two-group design. Kristen McClellan, a student at Madonna University in Livonia, Michigan, and her faculty advisor, Edie Woods, studied interactions between salesclerks and customers. They chose a mall that attracts a wide variety of customers (e.g., age, culture, socioeconomic class); then they randomly selected 27 stores from the 175 in the mall. They were particularly interested in how salesclerks would react to customers who have a disability. Their IV was the disability of hearing loss. Thus, their experimental group of salesclerks encountered pairs of customers who were deaf (easily identifiable because they entered the store conversing in sign language), and the control group of clerks had the chance to wait on hearing pairs of customers. McClellan and Wood (2001) randomly assigned 77 salesclerks to either the experimental or control group and had the confederates (customers) enter the store. The confederates unobtrusively timed how long it took a salesperson to approach and offer assistance after initial eye contact. (They did not obtain informed consent from the clerks because the clerks were participants at minimal risk; see Chapter 3.) McClellan and Woods found that the clerks in the experimental group

CONTROL GROUP   OUT OF CONTROL GROUP.

Fortunately, we deal with control groups and experimental groups in psychological research!

INDEPENDENT VARIABLE (CUSTOMER HEARING)
EXPERIMENTAL GROUP   **CONTROL GROUP**

Customers were deaf	Customers were not deaf

FIGURE 10-2 THE BASIC TWO-GROUP DESIGN.

took significantly longer on average (3.9 minutes) to wait on the deaf customers than the clerks in the control group, who took 1.3 minutes to wait on the hearing customers. This basic two-group design is depicted in Figure 10-2. Researchers frequently use block diagrams such as the one in Figure 10-2 to graphically portray the design of an experiment. Note that the IV (customer hearing) heads the entire block, with the two levels of the IV comprising the two subdivisions of the block. We will use this building block notation throughout the three chapters concerning experimental design so that you can conceptualize the various designs more easily.

Assigning Participants to Groups   We have yet another question to face before we can select our experimental design: We must decide how we plan to assign our research participants to groups. (Before the 1994 edition, the *Publication Manual of the American Psychological Association* referred to research participants as "subjects." You are likely to read this term in older research studies; you may also hear the term for some time before the psychological language becomes standardized—it's hard to teach old psychologists new tricks!) We can assign our participants either randomly or in some nonrandom fashion. We will examine random assignment first.

Random Assignment to Groups   As you saw in Chapter 5, an often-used approach for assigning participants to groups is **random assignment**. Given that we are dealing with only two groups, we could flip a coin and assign participants to one group or the other on the basis of heads or tails. As long as we flip a fair coin, our participants would have a 50–50 chance of ending up in either group. Remember that random assignment is *not* the same as **random selection**, which we also learned about in Chapter 5. Random selection deals with choosing your research participants, whereas random assignment refers to putting those participants into their groups. Random assignment is concerned with control procedures in the experiment, whereas random selection influences the generality of the results. We will examine the generality issue more closely in Chapter 17.

When we randomly assign our participants to groups, we have created what are known as **independent groups**. The participants in one group have *absolutely no* ties or links to the participants in the other group; they are independent of each other. If you tried to relate or pair a participant in one group to one in the other group, there would be no logical way to do so. When we wish to compare the performance of participants in these two groups, we are making what is known as a **between-subjects comparison**. We are interested in the difference *between* these two groups of participants who have no ties or links to each other.

Random assignment A method of assigning research participants to groups so that each participant has an equal chance of being in any group.

Random selection A control technique that ensures that each member of the population has an equal chance of being chosen for an experiment.

Independent groups Groups of participants that are formed by random assignment.

Between-subjects comparison Refers to a contrast between groups of participants who were randomly assigned to groups.

Terminology in experimental design can sometimes be confusing—for some reason, it has never been standardized. So, you may hear different people refer to *independent groups designs, randomized groups designs*, or *between-subjects designs*. All these names refer to the same basic strategy of randomly assigning participants to groups. The key to avoiding confusion is to understand the principle behind the strategy of random assignment. When you understand the basic ideas the names will make sense. As you can see in Figure 10-1, when we have one IV with two levels and participants who are assigned to groups randomly, our experiment fits the two-independent-groups design.

Random assignment is important in experimental design as a control factor. When we randomly assign our research participants to groups, we can usually assume that our two groups will now be equal on a variety of variables (Spatz, 2001). Many of these variables could be extraneous variables that might confound our experiment if left uncontrolled (see Chapter 5). Random assignment is one of those statistical procedures that is *supposed* to work—in the long run. However, there are no guarantees that it will create the expected outcome if we select a small sample. For example, we would not be surprised to flip a coin 10 times and get 7 or 8 heads. On the other hand, if we flipped a coin 100 times, we would be quite surprised if we obtained 70 or 80 heads.

Thus, when we randomly assign participants to groups, we expect the two groups to be equal on a variety of variables that could affect the experiment's outcome. Think back to McClellan and Woods's (2001) experiment dealing with customers with and without hearing disability and salesclerks' response times. When we described their experiment, we were careful to point out that the researchers *randomly* assigned some clerks to wait on deaf customers and *randomly* assigned some clerks to wait on hearing customers. What if they had picked the most polite clerks to wait on the hearing customers (control group)? Putting the polite clerks in the control group would cause the clerks' politeness to vary systematically with levels of the IV (that is, polite clerks would wait on hearing customers, but less-polite clerks would not). Such assignment to groups would result in a **confounded experiment** (see Chapter 5). If the results showed that the control group clerks waited on the hearing customers faster than the experimental group clerks waited on deaf customers, we could not draw a definite conclusion about why that happened. They might have responded more quickly because they were more polite, because they were waiting on hearing customers, or because of the combination of these two factors. Unfortunately, with a confounded experiment, there is no way to determine which conclusion is appropriate. If McClellan and Woods had conducted their experiment in this manner, they would have wasted their time.

Confounded experiment An experiment in which an extraneous variable varies systematically with the IV; makes drawing a cause-and-effect relationship impossible.

Let us remind you of one more benefit of random assignment. In Chapter 5 you learned that random assignment is the only technique we have that will help us control unknown extraneous variables. For example, in McClellan and Woods's (2001) experiment, what extraneous variables might affect students' performance? We have already identified the clerks' politeness as a possibility. However, the researchers did not have access to any politeness measure for the clerks. Other variables that we do not even consider could also play a role in the clerks' performance; hence McClellan and Woods were careful to randomly assign their clerks to experimental and control groups. Random assignment should equate any differences between the two groups.

Can you think of a flaw in McClellan and Woods's reasoning behind random assignment?

Random assignment is a technique that should work in the long run. Because McClellan and Woods assigned 77 clerks to the two groups, there is a good chance that random assignment made the groups perfectly equal. However, if they had measured only a few salesclerks, random assignment might not have created equal groups. If you thought of this potential problem, congratulations! What can we do when we conduct an experiment with small numbers of participants?

Nonrandom Assignment to Groups   In the previous section, we saw a potential pitfall of random assignment—the groups may not turn out equal after all. If we begin our experiment with unequal groups, we have a problem. Remember that random assignment should create equal groups in the long run. In other words, as our groups get larger, we can place more confidence in random assignment achieving what we want it to.

> **Correlated assignment** A method of assigning research participants to groups so that there is a relationship between small numbers of participants; these small groups are then randomly assigned to treatment conditions (also known as *paired* or *matched assignment*).

Suppose we are faced with a situation in which we have few potential research participants and we are worried that random assignment may not create equal groups. What can we do? In this type of situation, we can use a nonrandom method of assigning participants to groups. What we will do is either capitalize on an existing relationship between participants or create a relationship between them. In this manner, we know something important about our participants before the experiment and will use **correlated assignment** (also known as *matched, nonrandom,* or *paired assignment*) to create equal groups. Thus, we use correlated assignment whenever there is a relationship between the participants in the groups. (Be careful—correlated assignment has *nothing* to do with computing a correlation coefficient.) There are three common ways to use correlated assignment.

> **Matched pairs** Research participants in a two-group design who are measured and equated on some variable before the experiment.

1. Matched Pairs. To create **matched pairs**, we must measure our participants on a variable (other than our IV) that could affect performance on our experiment's DV. Typically we measure a variable that could result in confounding if not controlled. After we have measured this variable, we create pairs of participants that are equal on this variable. After we have created our matched pairs, we then randomly assign participants from these pairs to the different treatment conditions.

If this description seems confusing, an example should help clarify matters. Imagine that we wanted to replicate McClellan and Woods's salesclerk study because we were worried that random assignment may not have created equal groups. Suppose we suspect that female salesclerks tend to wait on customers faster than male clerks (probably a totally fictitious supposition, but it makes a good example). In this situation, we would be concerned if the ratio of female to male clerks differed between the groups. If we flip a coin to assign clerks to groups, the sex ratio of the groups might be higher in one group. Therefore, we decide to use matched assignment to groups. First, we create our matched pairs. The first pair consists of two clerks of the same sex; the second pair is another two clerks of the same sex. (We pair all the other clerks by sex also.) For each pair, we flip a coin to determine which clerk to assign to the experimental group and which clerk to assign to the control group. Then we repeat the procedure for our second pair, and so on. After we complete this matched assignment, we have an experimental group and a control group that are perfectly balanced in terms of sex. We have used matched assignment to create equal groups before our experiment begins. (Note: In this hypothetical example, if there were an odd number of clerks, one clerk would not have a match, and we could not use that clerk in the experiment.)

In what way is matched assignment guaranteed to create equal groups when random assignment is not?

The beauty of matched assignment is that we have measured our participants on a specific variable that could affect their performance in our experiment and we have equated them on that variable. When we use random assignment, we are leaving this equating process to chance. Remember, we must match on a variable that could affect the outcome of our experiment. In the fictitious example we just used, you would need to be certain that sex was linked to salesclerks' performance. If you cannot measure your participants on a variable that is relevant to their performance in your experiment, then you should not use matched assignment. If you match your participants on a variable that is not relevant to their performance, then you have actually hurt your chances of finding a significant difference in your experiment (see *Statistical Issues* in the *Advantages of Correlated Group Designs* section later in this chapter).

Repeated measures An experimental procedure in which research participants are tested or measured more than once.

2. Repeated Measures. In **repeated measures**, we use the ultimate in matched pairs—we simply measure the same participants in both treatment conditions of our experiment. The matched pairs here are perfectly equal because they consist of the same people or animals tested across the entire experiment. No extraneous variables should be able to confound this situation because any difference between the participants' performance in the two treatment conditions is due to the IV. In this type of experiment, participants serve as their own controls.

Why is it not possible to use repeated measures in all experiments? Try to think of two reasons.

Thinking about using repeated measures for our groups forces us to consider some practical factors:

a. Can we remove the effects of the IV? McClellan and Woods (2001) did not do anything to the salesclerks that had lasting effects—waiting on deaf customers should not affect how clerks respond to other customers in the future. However, in the study cited in Chapter 3, Burkley et al. (2000) could not use repeated measures in their experiment because they could not remove the effects of reading a particular consent form on the students in their experiment. Think about it carefully—even though they could have allowed students to read the second form, they could not have removed the effects of reading the other form first. If the students remembered the previous form, giving them a new form would not remove its effects. Sometimes when researchers cannot remove the effects of an IV, they attempt to deal with this problem by using counterbalancing (see Chapter 5). By balancing the effects across groups, researchers hope that the effects end up equal across those groups.

b. Can we measure our DV more than once? To this point, we have not focused on the DV in this chapter because it has little to do with the choice of an experimental design. However, when you consider using repeated measures, the DV is highly important. When you use repeated measures, the DV is measured multiple times (at least twice). McClellan and Woods could have used repeated measures by having each clerk wait on both a deaf and a hearing customer. However, in some cases, it is simply not possible to use the same DV more than once. In Burkley et al.'s (2000) experiment, once the students had solved the anagrams, solving the anagrams could not be used again as a DV. In other cases, we may be able to use a similar DV but we must be cautious. To use repeated measures on solving anagrams in Burkley et al.'s experiment, we would need two different sets of anagrams, one for testing students with each type of consent form. If we use two different forms of our DV, we must ensure that they are comparable. Although we could use two sets of anagrams, they would have to be equally difficult, which might be hard to determine. The same would be true of many different DVs such as mazes, tests, puzzles, and computer programs. If we cannot assure comparability of two measures of the same DV, then we should not use repeated-measures designs.

c. Can our participants cope with repeated testing? This question relates at least to some degree to the ethics of research, which we covered in Chapter 3. Although no specific ethical principles speak to the use of repeated measures, we should realize that requiring extended participation in our experiment might affect participants' willingness to take part in the research. Also, in extreme cases, extended time in a strenuous or taxing experiment could raise concerns for physical or emotional well-being. Another of our worries in this area is whether human participants will agree to devote the amount of time that we request of them in a repeated-measures design.

It is important that we think about these practical considerations when weighing the possibility of a repeated-measures design. Although repeated-measures designs are one of our better control techniques, there are some experimental questions that simply do not allow the use of such a design.

Natural pairs Research participants in a two-group design who are naturally related in some way (e.g., a biological or social relationship).

3. Natural Pairs. Natural pairs is essentially a combination of matched pairs and repeated measures. In this technique, we create pairs of participants from naturally occurring pairs (e.g., biologically or socially related). For example, psychologists who study intelligence often use twins (natural pairs) as their research participants. This approach is similar to using the same participant more than once (repeated measures) but allows you to compose your pairs more easily than through matching. Thus, when you see an experiment that uses siblings, parents and children, husbands and wives, littermates, or some biological relationship between its participants, that experiment has used natural pairs.

In summary, whenever there is a relationship between participants in different groups, we are using a correlated-groups design. By looking at Figure 10-1, you can see that planning an experiment with (a) one IV that has (b) two levels, in which you plan to use (c) correlated assignment of participants to groups, results in the *two-correlated-groups design*. Participants who have been matched on some variable or who share some relationship would have scores that are related. When we wish to compare the performance of such participants, we are making what has traditionally been known as a **within-subjects comparison**. We are essentially comparing scores within the same participants (subjects). Although this direct comparison is literally true only for repeated-measures designs, participants in matched or natural pairs are the same with regard to the matching variable.

Within-subjects comparison Refers to a contrast between groups of participants who were assigned to groups through matched pairs, natural pairs, or repeated measures.

Let's look at a student example of a two-correlated-groups design. A major area of study in psychology is the effect of stress on the body and the body's reactions. Rachel Wells (2001), a student from Nebraska Wesleyan University, in Lincoln, Nebraska, found that previous researchers had used a mental arithmetic test to induce stress in participants. She wanted to determine the effects of such a test on college students' bodily reactions. She had students count backward from 715 by 13, telling them that most students could complete the task in 4 minutes. Immediately after counting for 4 minutes, she measured the participants' heart rate and blood pressure. Students then spent 10 minutes completing questionnaires as a nonstressful rest period. After the 10-minute period, Wells measured the participants' heart rate and blood pressure again. The students showed a decrease in both heart rate and blood pressure, demonstrating that the mental arithmetic was, indeed, stress provoking.

Because she used repeated measures, Wells's experiment is a good example of a correlated-groups design. She measured the students' body signs after a stressful event and then again after a rest period. The measurement after the stressor was a posttest; the measurement after rest served as the comparison period. Often in such research, the experimenter might measure the body reactions *before* inducing the stressor; this measurement would be a pretest. In Wells's experiment, the IV was the stress induced and the DVs were the students' physiological reactions to the stress. Some of the particularly important participant (subject) variables that Wells controlled by the use of repeated measures were participants' ages (perhaps younger or older people have different reactions to stress), time of day (perhaps physiological indicators vary by the time of day), and students' intelligence (perhaps brighter students would find the task less stressful). All these extraneous variables (and others) were controlled because the *same* students took both the pretest and posttest.

What if Wells had wanted to use matched pairs rather than repeated measures? Remember that matching should occur on a relevant variable—one that could be an extraneous variable if left unchecked. Suppose that these students varied widely in their math ability. Wells might have wanted to create matched pairs based on that ability, thinking that math ability would likely affect performance on the counting task, which could determine the level of stress each student felt. Wells could have used other variables for matching as long as she felt certain that the variables were related to the students' physiological indicators.

Could Wells have run this experiment using natural pairs? Based on the information given to you, there is no indication that natural pairs of students existed. If the students were sets of twins, then the experiment would be ideally suited for natural pairs. It seems unlikely that there was any factor that made these students natural pairs, so if pairing was important to Wells, she would have needed to create pairs by matching on some variable.

REVIEW SUMMARY

1. Psychologists plan their experiments beforehand using an **experimental design**, which serves as a blueprint for the experiment.
2. The **two-group design** applies to experimental situations in which you have one IV that has two levels or conditions.
3. Two-group designs often use an **experimental group**, which receives the IV, and a **control group**, which does not receive the IV.
4. **Randomly assigning** research participants to groups results in **independent groups** of participants.
5. **Correlated groups** of research participants are formed by creating **matched pairs**, using **natural pairs**, or by measuring the participants more than once (**repeated measures**).

CHECK YOUR PROGRESS

1. Why can't we conduct a valid experiment with only one group?
2. The differing amounts of your IV are known as the _____ of the IV.
3. How are independent groups and correlated groups different? Why is this difference important to experimental design questions?
4. Matching

   1. random assignment   A. brother and sister

   2. natural pairs   B. take the same test each month

   3. repeated measures   C. two people with the same IQ

   4. matched pairs   D. flipping a coin

5. In what type of situation do we need to be most careful about using random assignment as a control technique?

6. You are planning an experiment that could use either independent groups or correlated groups. Under what conditions should you use a correlated-groups design? When is it acceptable to use random assignment?

7. Random assignment is more likely to create equal groups when _____.

   a. small samples are involved

   b. large samples are involved

   c. a directional hypothesis is being tested

   d. a nondirectional hypothesis is being tested

Deciding on a Basic Design

Because there are two different two-group designs, researchers must choose whether they want to design their experiment with independent or correlated groups. You may be wondering how researchers make such a choice. In the next sections, we will cover some issues that psychologists must consider as they plan their research studies. Read carefully—you may be facing this choice yourself in the future!

Comparing Two-Group Designs

Looking at Figure 10-1 again, you can see that the two-independent-groups design and the two-correlated-groups, design are quite similar. Both designs describe experimental situations in which you use one IV with two groups. The only difference comes in how you assign your participants to groups. If you simply assign on a random basis, you use the two-independent-groups design. On the other hand, if you match your participants on some variable, if you test your participants twice, or if your participants share some relationship, you use the two-correlated-groups design.

Choosing a Two-Group Design   Now that you have two experimental designs that can handle very similar experimental situations, how can you choose between them? Should you use independent groups, or should you use correlated groups of some sort?

You may remember we said that random assignment is supposed to "work" (i.e., create equal groups) in the long run. Therefore, if you are using large groups of participants, random assignment should equate your groups adequately. The next question, of course, is how large is large? Unfortunately, there is no specific answer to this question—the answer may vary from researcher to researcher. If you are using 20 or more participants per group, you can feel fairly safe that randomization will create equal groups. On the other hand, if you are using five or fewer participants in a group, randomization may not work. Part of the answer to the question of numbers boils down to what you feel comfortable with, what your research director feels comfortable with, or what you think you could defend to someone. In McClellan and Woods's (2001) study, there were 77 salesclerks to divide into two groups. Given our guidelines, this number is quite adequate to use random assignment to create independent groups. On the other hand, although Wells (2001) had 41 students to participate in the experiment, she may have decided to use repeated measures because she was worried about individual levels of stress that could have created a great deal of variability. Whatever you decide, it is critical to remember that the larger your samples, the more likely random assignment is to create equal groups.

Advantages of Correlated-Groups Designs   There are two primary advantages correlated-groups designs provide for researchers: control and statistical issues. Both advantages are important to you as an experimenter.

Control Issues   One basic assumption that we make before beginning our experiment is that the participants in our groups are equal with respect to the DV. When our groups are equal before the experiment begins and we observe differences between our groups on the DV after the experiment, then we can attribute those differences to the IV. Although randomization is designed to equate our groups, the three methods for creating correlated-groups designs give us greater certainty of equality. We have exerted control to create equal groups. Thus, in correlated designs, we have some "proof" that our participants are equated beforehand. This equality helps us reduce some of the error variation in our experiment, which brings us to the statistical issues.

Between-groups variability Variability in DV scores due to the effects of the IV.

Statistical Issues   Correlated-groups designs can actually benefit us statistically because they can help reduce error variation. You might be wondering, "What is error variation, anyhow?" In an experiment that involves one IV, you essentially have two sources of variability in your data. One source of variation in your data should occur as a result of your IV—scores on the DV should vary due to the two different treatment groups you have in your experiment. This source of variation, referred to as **between-groups variability**, is what you are attempting to measure in the experiment. There are other factors that can cause variation in the DV, such as individual differences, measurement errors, and extraneous variation—collectively known as **error variability**. As you might guess, our goal in an experiment is to *maximize* the between-groups variability and *minimize* the error or within-groups variability.

Error variability Variability in DV scores due to factors other than the IV, such as individual differences, measurement error, and extraneous variation (also known as *within-groups variability*).

Why is it important to reduce error variability? Although formulas for different statistical tests vary widely, they all reduce to the following general formula:

$$\text{statistic} = \frac{\text{between-groups variability}}{\text{error variability}}$$

Remember that the probability of a result occurring by chance goes down as the value of your statistic increases. Thus, larger statistical values are more likely to show significant differences in your experiment. Your knowledge of math tells you that there are two ways to increase the value of your statistic: *increase* the between-groups variability or *decrease* the error variability. (Increasing between-groups variability is a function of your IV [see Chapter 5]; we will not discuss that option here.)

Can you figure out why using a correlated-groups design can help reduce error variability?

Earlier in this section we listed individual differences as one source of error variability. Correlated-groups designs help reduce this source of error. If in our treatment groups we use the same participants or participants who share some important characteristic, either naturally or through matching, those participants will exhibit smaller individual differences between the groups than will randomly chosen participants. Imagine how dissimilar to you another participant would be if we chose that person at random. Imagine how similar to you another participant would be if that person was related to you, had the same intelligence as you, or (in the most obvious situation) was you! So, if we use a correlated design, error variability due to individual differences should decrease, our statistic should increase, and we should have a greater chance of finding a significant difference due to our IV.

Why did we use the hedge word "should" three times in the preceding sentence? Remember, when we discussed matched pairs earlier, we said that matching on an irrelevant variable could actually hurt your chances of finding a significant difference. If you match on an irrelevant variable, then the between-groups differences do not decrease. If the between-groups differences do not decrease, your error variability is the same as if you had used an independent-groups design, which results in identical statistical test results. When we use a statistical test for a correlated-groups design, we must use a larger critical t value than we would have if we conducted the same experiment with an independent-groups design. (The statistical reason for this difference is that we give up some **degrees of freedom** in the correlated-groups design relative to an independent-groups design. We discussed the issue of degrees of freedom in Chapter 9. Remember that the df for the independent-groups design is equal to the total number of participants minus 2, whereas it is the number of *pairs* of participants minus 1 in the correlated case.)

> **Degrees of freedom**
> The ability of a number in a specified set to assume any value.

A smaller critical t value makes it seem that it would be easier to reject the null hypothesis in an independent-samples situation than in a correlated-groups situation. Yet we said earlier that the correlated-groups situation could benefit us statistically. What's going on? You must remember that a correlated-groups design should reduce the error variability and result in a larger statistic. Typically, the statistic is increased more than enough to make up for the lost degrees of freedom. Remember that this reasoning is based on the assumption that you have matched on a relevant variable. Matching on an irrelevant variable does not reduce the error variability and will not increase the statistic—in which case the lost degrees of freedom actually hurt your chances of finding significance. We will show you an actual statistical example of this point at the end of the statistical interpretation section in Chapter 11.

Advantages of Independent-Groups Designs   The chief advantage of independent-groups designs is their simplicity. Once you have planned your experiment, choosing your participants is quite easy—you merely get a large number of participants and randomly assign them to groups. You don't need to worry about measuring your participants on some variable and then matching them; you don't need to worry about whether each participant can serve in all conditions of your experiment; you don't need to worry about establishing or determining a relationship between your participants—these concerns are relevant only to correlated-groups designs.

Does the statistical advantage of correlated-groups designs render independent-groups designs useless? We cannot argue about the statistical advantage—it is real. However, the difference in critical t values mentioned earlier may not be overwhelming. As the number of experimental participants increases, the difference becomes smaller and smaller. If you expect your IV to have a powerful effect, then the statistical advantage of a correlated-groups design will be lessened.

One final point should be made in favor of independent-groups designs. Remember that in some situations it is simply impossible to use a correlated-groups design. Some circumstances do not allow repeated measures (as we pointed out earlier in the chapter), some participant variables cannot be matched, and some participants cannot be related in any way to other participants.

So what is the elusive conclusion? As you might guess, there is no simple, all-purpose answer. A correlated-groups design provides you with additional control and a greater chance of finding statistical significance. On the other hand, independent-groups designs are simpler to set up and conduct and can overcome the statistical advantages of correlated-groups designs if you use large samples. So, if you have large numbers of participants and expect your IV to have a large effect, you are quite safe with an independent-groups design. Alternatively, if you have only a small number of experimental participants and you expect your IV to have a small effect, the advantages of a correlated-groups design would be important to you. For all those in-between cases, you need to weigh the alternatives and choose the type of design that seems to have the greatest advantage.

Variations on the Two-Group Design

To this point, we have described the two-group design as if all two-group designs were identical. This is not the case. Let's look at two variations on this design.

Comparing Different Amounts of an IV   Earlier we said that the most common use of two-group designs was to compare a group of participants receiving the IV (experimental group) to a group that does not receive the IV (control group). Although this is the most common type of two-group design, it is not the only type. The presence-absence manipulation of an IV allows you to determine whether or not the IV has an effect. For example, McClellan and Woods (2001) were able to determine that customers who have a hearing disability received help from salesclerks slower than customers who do not have such a disability; Wells (2001) found that her students did react to a mental arithmetic task in a stressful manner. An analogous situation to using the presence-absence manipulation in detective work is trying to sort out the clues that relate to the guilt or innocence of a single suspect.

However, a presence-absence IV manipulation does not allow you to determine the precise effects of the IV. McClellan and Woods did *not* discover whether having salesclerks wait on deaf customers caused a large or small delay in offering help, only that the clerks responded more slowly. Wells did not determine how stressful mental arithmetic was compared to other tasks, only that it did increase stress.

Typically, after we determine that a particular IV has an effect, we would like to have more specific information about that effect. Can we produce the effect with more (or less) of the IV? Will a different IV produce a stronger (or weaker) effect? What is the optimum amount (or type) of the IV? These are just a few of the possible questions that remain after determining that the IV had an effect. Thus, we can follow up on our IV presence-absence experiment with a new two-group experiment that compares different *amounts* or *types* of the IV to determine their effectiveness. Similarly, a detective may have two suspects and be faced with the task of sorting the evidence to decide which suspect is more likely the guilty party.

Some IVs simply cannot be contrasted through presence-absence manipulations. For example, Erin Vaughn (2002) of Ouachita Baptist University in Arkadelphia, Arkansas, was interested in the effects of stereotyping on "person perception." In her experiment, Vaughn wanted to assess the effects of the tendency to stereotype people on the basis of physical attractiveness (IV) on pairing pictures of men and women into dating couples (DV). This question would make little sense in an IV presence-absence situation—people could show more or less of a tendency to stereotype, but not zero or total tendency. Therefore, Vaughn compared differing amounts of this IV. Based on participants' answers to a survey, she formed "high tendency to stereotype" and "low tendency to stereotype" groups. When she compared these two groups' pairings of men and women, she found that people who have a high tendency to stereotype created more pairings in which men and women were similar in physical attractiveness. Thus, the tendency to stereotype affected the way that participants believed that dating couples "paired up" in Vaughn's experiment.

The key point to notice when we conduct an experiment contrasting different amounts of our IV is that we no longer have a true control group. In other words, there is no group that receives a zero amount of the IV. Again, we are not trying to determine whether the IV has an effect—we already know that it does. We are merely attempting to find a difference between differing types or amounts of our IV.

Dealing with Measured IVs   To this point, every time we have mentioned IVs in this text, we have emphasized that they are factors that the experimenter *directly manipulates*. Technically, this statement is correct only for a **true experiment**. In a true experiment, the experimenter has total control over the IV and can assign participants to IV conditions. In other words, the experimenter can manipulate the IV. McClellan and Woods (2001) were able to assign their clerks to either the deaf-customer group or the hearing-customer group. If you wish to assess the effects of two different reading programs on teaching children to read, you can assign nonreading children to either program.

> **True experiment** An experiment in which the experimenter directly manipulates the IV.

As you saw in Chapter 5, there are many IVs (participant IVs) that psychologists wish to study but cannot directly manipulate; we measure them instead. For example, Nicholas Schroeppel, a student at the University of Nebraska in Lincoln, Nebraska, and Gustavo Carlo, his faculty sponsor, examined sex differences in altruistic (helping) behaviors (2001). Because they were not able to directly manipulate the sex of their participants

> **Ex post facto research**
> A research approach in which the experimenter cannot directly manipulate the IV but can only classify, categorize, or measure the IV because it is predetermined in the participants (e.g., IV = sex).

(of course!), Schroeppel and Carlo conducted **ex post facto research** (see Chapter 8). In the context of the present chapter, they used a two-group design. The participants completed scales to measure sympathy, perspective taking, and social desirability; they also received $2 in payment for participation and had the chance to donate any amount of that money to one of four charities. Schroeppel and Carlo found that women scored higher on the sympathy scale and on average donated more money than men ($1.59 compared to $1.16). The men and women did not differ on the perspective taking or social desirability scales. Based on what we know about sex differences in empathy, Schroeppel and Carlo's finding may not be surprising. We can even develop hypotheses about why women tend to be more empathetic. However, we must be cautious in our interpretation. Perhaps women are biologically predisposed to be more nurturing, or maybe society reinforces women more for behaving empathetically. In any case, although we do know from Schroeppel and Carlo's research that women scored higher than men on sympathy and donated more money than men, we are not certain why they scored higher.

The drawback of ex post facto research is certainly a serious one. Conducting an experiment without being able to draw a cause-and-effect conclusion is limiting. Why would we want to conduct ex post facto research if we cannot draw definitive conclusions from it? As we mentioned earlier, some of the most interesting psychological variables do not lend themselves to any type of research other than ex post facto. If you wish to study the genesis of female-male differences, you have no option other than doing ex post facto studies. Also, as psychologists continue to conduct ex post facto research, they do make progress. Attempting to specify the determinants of intelligence involves ex post facto research—surely you remember the famous heredity-versus-environment debate over IQ. What we *think* we know today is that both factors affect IQ: Psychologists believe that heredity sets the limits of your possible IQ (i.e., your possible minimum and maximum IQs) and that your environment determines where you fall within that range (Weinberg, 1989). Thus, it seems clear that we should not abandon ex post facto research despite its major drawback. We do, however, need to remember to be extremely cautious in drawing conclusions from ex post facto studies. Detectives, of course, are always faced with ex post facto evidence—it is impossible to manipulate the variables *after* a crime has been committed.

REVIEW SUMMARY

1. **Correlated-groups designs** provide more control because they guarantee equality of the two groups.
2. Correlated-groups designs generally reduce **error variability** and are more likely to achieve statistically significant results.
3. An advantage of **independent-groups designs** is that they are simple to conduct. With large numbers of research participants, they are also strong designs.
4. Researchers often use two-group designs to compare different amounts (or types) of IVs.
5. We cannot manipulate some IVs, so we must resort to measuring them and conducting **ex post facto research**, which cannot demonstrate cause-and-effect relations.

CHECK YOUR PROGRESS

1. Why is it important that our two groups be equal before the experiment begins?
2. The variability in DV scores that can be attributed to our experimental treatments is called _____ _____; variability from other sources is labeled _____ _____.
3. Which three factors cause variation in DV scores (error variability)?
   a. nonrandom assignment, random assignment, and mixed assignment
   b. individual differences, measurement errors, and extraneous variables
   c. placebo effects, measurement errors, and the IV
   d. variance, *SD*, and the mean
4. Compare and contrast the advantages and disadvantages of independent- and correlated-groups designs.
5. Other than the consent form and mental arithmetic IV examples given in the chapter, give two examples of IVs for which you might wish to compare differing amounts.
6. List three examples of IVs not in the text that you would have to study with ex post facto experiments.

KEY TERMS

Experimental design, *219*

Principle of parsimony, *219*

Independent variable (IV), *220*

Dependent variable (DV), *220*

Extraneous variables, *221*

Levels, *221*

Experimental group, *222*

Control group, *222*

Random assignment, *223*

Random selection, *223*

Independent groups, *223*

Between-subjects comparison, *223*

Confounded experiment, *224*

Correlated assignment, *225*

Matched pairs, *225*

Repeated measures, *226*

Natural pairs, *228*

Within-subjects comparison, *228*

Between-groups variability, *231*

Error variability, *231*

Degrees of freedom, *232*

True experiment, *234*

Ex post facto research, *235*

LOOKING AHEAD

In this chapter we examined the notion of planning an experiment by selecting a research design. In particular, we examined the basic building-block designs with one IV and two groups. In the next chapter we will find out how to analyze data from this type of design.

Inferential Tests of Significance I: *t* Tests

Inferential Statistics

Once you have conducted a two-group experiment, you need to perform a statistical test on the data that you gathered. The results of this test will help you decide if the IV was effective or not. In other words, inferential statistical tests allow you to make an inference about your results—you will decide if your results are *significant*. Before we look at specific statistical tests, let's pause for a moment to see how your experimental design and statistical tests are integrated and to examine the logic of inferential statistics.

The Relation Between Experimental Design and Statistics

At the beginning of Chapter 10 we compared experimental design to a blueprint and said that you needed a design to know where you were headed. When you carefully plan your experiment and choose the correct experimental design, you also accomplish another big step. Selecting the appropriate experimental design determines the particular statistical test you will use to analyze your data. Because experimental design and statistics are intimately linked, you should determine your experimental design *before* you begin collecting data to ensure there will be an appropriate statistical test you can use to analyze your data. Remember, you don't want to be a professor's classroom example of a student who collected data only to find out there was no way to analyze the data!

Courtesy of Sidney Harris.

Unlike the warning on this truck, psychologists view data and statistical procedures as tools to help answer research questions.

The Logic of Significance Testing

Significant A statistical result that is not likely to have occurred by chance ($p < .05$).

You may remember from Chapter 9 that we consider the result of an experiment to be statistically **significant** when it occurs rarely by chance. In such instances we assume that our IV produced the results. Although Sherlock Holmes wasn't speaking of a psychological experiment, he captured the intent of significance testing when he said, "How often have I said to you that when you have eliminated the impossible, whatever remains, *however improbable*, must be the truth?" (Doyle, 1927, p. 111).

What Is Significant? The results of an inferential statistical test tell us whether the results of an experiment would occur frequently or rarely *by chance*. Inferential statistics with small values occur *frequently by chance*, whereas inferential statistics with large values occur *rarely by chance*. If the difference between groups is small, then that result could occur often by chance, so we say that it is not significant and conclude that our IV did not affect the DV. In that case we would accept the **null hypothesis**, which says that the differences between groups are due to chance (i.e., not due to the operation of the IV). However, if the difference between our groups is large, that result of our inferential statistical test could occur rarely by chance (i.e., it is significant), so we conclude that some factor other than chance is operative. If we have conducted our experiment properly and exercised good control (see Chapters 5 and 7), then our significant statistical result gives us reason to believe the IV we manipulated was effective (i.e., did cause the difference in the DV scores).

Null hypothesis A hypothesis that says that all differences between groups are due to chance (i.e., not the operation of the IV).

PSYCHOLOGICAL DETECTIVE Why is *good control* necessary to conclude that our IV caused the difference in the DV scores?

You should remember that one meaning of exerting control is to remove the effects of potential extraneous variables. If we have removed the extraneous variables from the scene, the IV should be the only factor affecting the DV.

When do we consider that an event occurs rarely by chance? Traditionally psychologists say that any event that occurs by chance alone 5 times or fewer in 100 occasions is a rare event. Thus, you will see frequent mention of the ".05 level of significance" in journal articles. This statement means that a result is considered significant (not due to chance) if it would occur 5 or fewer times by chance in 100 replications of the experiment when the null hypothesis is true. As the experimenter, you decide on the level of significance before the experiment is conducted.

Samples and Populations Typically our ultimate interest is not in the samples we have tested in an experiment but in what these samples tell us about the population from which we drew them. In short, we want to generalize, or *infer*, from our samples to the larger population.

"I'm sorry, but you've been rejected at the .05 level."

Reprinted by permission of Warren Street.

Random selection A control technique that ensures that each member of the population has an equal chance of being chosen for an experiment.

Random assignment A control technique that ensures that each participant has an equal chance of being assigned to any group in an experiment.

We have diagrammed this logic in Figure 11-1. First, researchers **randomly select** a sample from a specified population (Figure 11-1A) and then **randomly assign** participants in the sample to different groups (see Chapter 9). We assume that random selection and assignment will produce two equivalent groups: Any differences between the groups are due solely to chance factors. In Figure 11-1B we see the results of our experiment; the manipulation of the IV caused the groups to be significantly different. At this point generalization begins. Based on the significant difference that exists between the groups, we *infer* what would happen if our treatments were administered to all individuals in the population. In Figure 11-1C we have generalized from the results of our research using the two samples to the entire population (see Chapter 17 for more on generalization). We are inferring that two separate groups would be created in the population due to the administration of our IV.

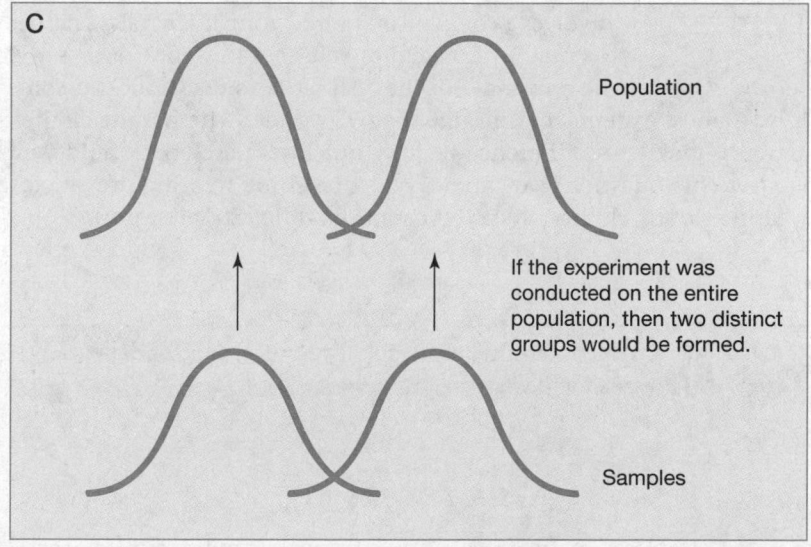

FIGURE 11-1 RANDOM SAMPLES ARE DRAWN FROM A POPULATION (PART A). THE ADMINISTRATION OF THE IV CAUSES THE SAMPLES TO DIFFER SIGNIFICANTLY (PART B). THE EXPERIMENTER GENERALIZES THE RESULTS OF THE EXPERIMENT TO THE GENERAL POPULATION (PART C).

Analyzing Two-Group Designs

t test An inferential statistical test used to evaluate the difference between two means.

Interval-level data Measurement that permits rank ordering of events with the assumption of equal intervals between adjacent events.

Ratio-level data Measurement that permits rank ordering of events with the assumptions of equal intervals between adjacent events and a true zero point.

Independent groups Groups of participants that are formed by random assignment.

In Chapter 10 we looked at one-IV, two-group designs. Referring to the flowchart in Chapter 10 (see p. 220), you will see that this type of experimental design requires a **t test** to analyze the resulting data (assuming you have **interval-level data** or **ratio-level data**). You can also see that there are two different types of t tests for two-group designs. For a two-**independent-groups** design, you would use a t test for independent samples (also known as an independent t test) to analyze your data. For a two-correlated-groups design, you would analyze your data with a t test for correlated samples (also called a dependent t test, a within-groups t test, or a paired t test).

Let's make certain that the relation between experimental design and statistics is clear. A t test is indicated as the appropriate statistical test because you conducted an experiment with one IV that has two levels (treatment conditions). The decision of *which* t test to use is based on how you assigned your participants to their groups. If you used random assignment, then you will use the t test for independent samples. If you used repeated measures, matched pairs, or natural pairs, then you would use the t test for correlated samples.

In this chapter, we will develop a research example to illustrate the use of t tests. For years you have heard the old saying that "clothes make the person." You decide to experimentally test this old adage by determining whether type of clothing influences the time it takes a salesperson to wait on customers. The specific research study involves a comparison of how long it will take salespeople to wait on customers who are dressed either in sloppy or dressy clothes. To help set the stage for the remainder of the chapter, let's take a look at some details of our hypothetical experiment. Imagine that we wonder whether the clothes students wore actually make any difference in how quickly salesclerks would wait on them. To answer this question, we choose students (some wearing dressy clothes and some wearing sloppy clothes) to collect data from different salesclerks.

 PSYCHOLOGICAL DETECTIVE   Which statistical test would you use to analyze data from this experiment and why?

The simplest way to answer these questions is to use our flowchart in Figure 10-1. There is only one IV: the type of clothing worn. That IV has two levels: dressy and sloppy. The next question to answer is how we assigned the participants to their groups. That information was not present in our brief description, so we can't tell precisely which statistical test to use. We can tell, however, that we will use a *t* test to analyze the data because of having one IV with two groups.

The *t* Test for Independent Samples

To set up the study, imagine that you randomly select 16 salesclerks from a store at the mall and then randomly assign these clerks to one of two groups of 8 clerks. Group A will wait on customers in dressy clothes; Group B will wait on customers in sloppy clothes. Because you formed the groups randomly at the start of the experiment, you assume they are comparable before they are exposed to the IV.

PSYCHOLOGICAL DETECTIVE Now is it clear which *t* test you would use to analyze data from this experiment? Why?

Because the clerks in Group A have no relation to, or effect on, the clerks in Group B, these groups are *independent* of each other. Thus, you should use the *t* test for independent samples.

You recruit some students to go shopping at a mall. The students for the Group A clerks wear dressy clothes to the shopping mall, whereas the students for the Group B clerks wear sloppy clothes to the mall. Each student enters a store in the mall and uses a silent, inconspicuous stopwatch to measure the time (in seconds) it takes a salesperson to offer service. (Keep in mind that student shoppers only recorded these data; the salespersons actually produced the data.) The "latency-to-service" scores (this is a latency DV, see Chapter 5) for the two groups appear in Table 11-1.

PSYCHOLOGICAL DETECTIVE Do you think the salesclerks waited on the students in dressy clothes more quickly?

Just looking at the difference between the groups suggests this might be the case; the mean score of Group B is almost 15 seconds higher than that of Group A. On the other hand, there is considerable overlap between the two groups; several of the latency-to-serve scores were similar for students dressed in sloppy clothes and the students in the dressy clothes. Is the difference you obtained large enough to be genuine, or is it just a chance happening? Merely looking at the results will not answer that question. Instead, we will use a statistical test to determine whether the results are significant.

Remember, the *t* test is an inferential statistical test used to evaluate the difference between the means of *two groups* (see Chapter 10 for research designs using two groups). Because the two groups in our latency-to-service experiment were independent, we will

TABLE 11-1	TIME FOR SALESCLERKS TO WAIT ON CUSTOMERS (IN SECONDS)
GROUP A (DRESSY CLOTHES)	**GROUP B (SLOPPY CLOTHES)**
37	50
38	46
44	62
47	52
49	74
49	69
54	77
69	76
$\Sigma X = 387$	$\Sigma Y = 506$
$M = 48.38$	$M = 63.25$

use an independent-groups t test. (We will discuss the correlated-groups t test later in this chapter.)

Calculating t by Hand

The formula for an independent samples t test appears below:

$$t = \frac{M_1 - M_2}{\text{SE}_{\text{diff}}}$$

The formula that we will actually use to calculate the t test is somewhat more complicated, but it is equivalent to the simpler formula and can still be reduced to a simple recipe: a difference between two means divided by an estimate of variability. In fact we will return to this idea again and again as we cover other statistical tests. If you examine the formula carefully, you will see that it requires you to make some preliminary calculations before actually using the formula. Calculating the means is simple; you've been doing that since elementary school. Calculating the variability index (in this case, the **standard error (SE)** of the difference between means) takes several steps and, as you can see below, requires different formulas depending on whether the two groups are equal or different in size. We must calculate the standard error of the difference because we have two groups that contribute to overall variability rather than only one as when we previously encountered the SEM.

> **Standard error (SE)**
> The standard deviation of a sampling distribution.

If $N_1 \neq N_2$:

$$\text{SE}_{\text{diff}} = \sqrt{\left(\frac{\Sigma X_1^2 - \frac{(\Sigma X_1)^2}{N_1} + \Sigma X_2^2 - \frac{(\Sigma X_2)^2}{N_2}}{N_1 + N_2 - 2} \right) \left(\frac{1}{N_1} + \frac{1}{N_2} \right)}$$

If $N_1 = N_2$:

$$\text{SE}_{\text{diff}} = \sqrt{\frac{\Sigma X_1^2 - \frac{(\Sigma X_1)^2}{N_1} + \Sigma X_2^2 - \frac{(\Sigma X_2)^2}{N_2}}{N_1(N_2 - 1)}}$$

TABLE 11-2 CALCULATING t TEST FOR INDEPENDENT GROUPS

GROUP A DRESSY CLOTHES	X_1^2	GROUP B SLOPPY CLOTHES	X_2^2
37	1369	50	2500
38	1444	46	2116
44	1936	62	3844
47	2209	52	2704
49	2401	74	5476
49	2401	69	4761
54	2916	77	5929
69	4761	76	5776
$\Sigma = 387$	$\Sigma = 19437$	$\Sigma = 506$	$\Sigma = 33106$
$M_1 = 48.38$		$M_2 = 63.25$	

First, we will calculate the SE_{diff} because that takes several steps. Our sample sizes are equal, so we will use the formula for equal Ns.

$$SE_{diff} = \sqrt{[\Sigma X_1^2 - ((\Sigma X_1)^2/N_1) + \Sigma X_2^2 - ((\Sigma X_2)^2/N_2)]/N_1(N_2 - 1)}$$
$$= \sqrt{[19437 - ((387)^2/8) + 33106 - ((506)^2/8)]/8(8-1)}$$
$$= \sqrt{[19437 - 18721.125 + 33106 - 32004.5]/56}$$
$$= \sqrt{(715.875 + 1101.5)/56}$$
$$= \sqrt{1817.375/56}$$
$$= \sqrt{32.453} = 5.697$$

Now that we have our SE_{diff}, we can now calculate our t statistic.

$$t = M_1 - M_2 / SE_{diff}$$
$$= 48.38 - 63.25 / 5.697$$
$$= -14.87 / 5.697$$
$$t = -2.61 \text{ (remember that the sign is inconsequential if you are using a two-tailed test)}$$

Standard deviation (SD) A measure of variability equal to the square root of the variance; has important relations to the normal curve.

The calculations are not terribly difficult; however, they are similar to the calculations you would use to calculate a **standard deviation (SD)**. Step-by-step calculation of our t appears in Table 11-2. As you can see, our calculated t value is 2.61. (In most cases, we use the absolute value of t. We'll address this issue later in the chapter.)

You can use an alternative formula for SEM that will be simpler *if* you have already calculated *SD*s for both groups. That formula is:

$$SEM = \sqrt{\left(s_1 / \sqrt{N_1}\right)^2 + \left(s_2 / \sqrt{N_2}\right)^2}$$

However, this formula will *not* be simpler if you have to compute the *SD*s first.

Once we have calculated our *t* value, we must follow several steps in order to interpret its meaning:

> **Degrees of freedom (*df*)** The ability of a number in a specified set to assume any value.

Step 1 Determine the **degrees of freedom (*df*)** involved. For our clothing problem:

$$df = (N_A - 1) + (N_B - 1)$$
$$= (8 - 1) + (8 - 1)$$
$$= 14$$

Step 2 We use the degrees of freedom to enter a *t* table (see Table A-3 in the Appendix). This table contains *t* values that occur by chance. We will compare our *t* value to these chance values. To be significant, the calculated *t* must be equal to or larger than the one in Table A-3.

Step 3 We enter the *t* table on the row for 14 degrees of freedom. Reading across this row, we find that a value of 2.145 occurs by chance 5% of the time (.05 level of significance). Because our value of 2.61 is larger than 2.145 (the .05 value in the table for 14 *df*), we can conclude that our result is significant (has a probability of occurring by chance less than .05). Thus, the type of clothing had a significant effect on latency to service. This result is one that occurs fewer than 5 times in 100 by chance. Had we chosen a different level of significance, such as once in 100 occurrences (.01), the table value is 2.977 and we would conclude that our result is *not* significant.

Statistical Issues Remember that in Chapter 10 we contrasted the advantages of independent-groups and matched-groups tests. We noted that matched-groups tests tend to reduce error variability, thus providing a statistical advantage. However, this advantage occurs only if you have matched your participants on a relevant variable. If you match on an irrelevant variable, your error variability does not decrease but your degrees of freedom do. In the two-correlated-groups situation, the degrees of freedom are equal to $N - 1$, where N represents the number of *pairs* of participants. In the two-independent-groups situation, the degrees of freedom are $N - 2$, where N represents the *total* number of participants.

In our example in the previous section, we had 8 participants in each group, so our *df* for the independent-groups test were $8 + 8 - 2 = 14$. However, if we used the same participants in a correlated-groups format, our *df* would be $8 - 1 = 7$. Referring to Table A-3, we find that the critical *t* value (.05 level) with 14 *df* is 2.145, whereas it is 2.365 with 7 *df*. Based on these numbers, it would seem to be easier to achieve significance in the independent-groups situation because the critical *t* value is smaller. Although the critical *t* for the correlated-groups situation is larger, remember that correlated groups should reduce the error variation, thus resulting in a larger calculated *t* value. The loss of *df* is usually more than offset by a larger calculated *t*. Therefore, correlated-groups experiments are often more likely to detect a difference that actually exists.

Computer Analysis of *t* Test for Independent Samples

Most psychologists do not calculate *t* tests by hand, but use a computer program instead. (When doing homework problems, you may wish to do your work by hand and then use a computer program to check your work.) The computer printout for our *t* test appears in Table 11-3. Rather than providing printouts from a specific statistics software package, we are using generic printouts in the text. Statistics packages provide slightly different information; we will show you information you might reasonably expect to find on your printouts. Although it takes some searching through the printout, again we find that our *t* value is 2.61. Thus, our hand calculations and computer output are in agreement.

 PSYCHOLOGICAL DETECTIVE What should you do if your hand calculations and computer output do not agree?

The answer to this detective question is the same as you have heard in math courses: Recheck your work! If you are like most students, you will want to blame the computer, but the odds are low that the computer made an error.

TABLE 11-3 COMPUTER OUTPUT FOR *t* TEST FOR INDEPENDENT GROUPS

GROUP 1 = DRESSY CLOTHING

GROUP 2 = SLOPPY CLOTHING

VARIABLE = SALESCLERKS' RESPONSE TIME

GROUP	*N*	MEAN	*SD*	SE
GROUP 1	8	48.38	10.113	3.575
GROUP 2	8	63.25	12.544	4.435

F_{MAX} TEST   *F* = 1.634   *P* = 0.222

EQUAL VARIANCES ASSUMED

T = 2.61   *DF* = 14   *P* = 0.021   COHEN'S *D* = 0.92

EQUAL VARIANCES NOT ASSUMED

T = 2.61   *DF* = 13.4   *P* = 0.021   COHEN'S *D* = 0.92

Descriptive statistics Procedures used to summarize a set of data.

In looking at the full computer output, we usually examine the **descriptive statistics** first. The descriptive statistics are at the top of the printout. We see that Group 1 (defined at the top of the printout as "Dressy clothing") had 8 cases, a mean salesperson response time of 48.38 seconds, a *SD* of 10.11 seconds, and a SE of 3.58 seconds. Group 2 (the "Sloppy clothing" group) had 8 cases, a mean salesperson response time of 63.25 seconds, a *SD* of 12.54 seconds, and a SE of 4.44 seconds. Be cautious at this point—an old saying we learned regarding computers is "Garbage in, garbage out (GIGO)." This saying simply means that if you enter incorrect numbers into a computer, you will get incorrect numbers out of the computer. You should always verify any numbers you enter and, as much as possible, double check the output. "Wait a minute," you may be saying; "what's the use of using a computer if I have to check its work?" We're not suggesting that you check up on the computer but that you check up on yourself! For example, suppose the computer information for Group 1 or Group 2 showed the number of cases to be seven. You would know that the computer didn't read one number—perhaps you entered only seven scores or perhaps you mislabeled one score. With only eight scores, it is simple enough to calculate the mean for each group yourself. Why should you do that? If you find the same mean that the computer displays, you can be reasonably certain that you entered the data correctly and, therefore, can go on to interpret your statistics. Remember that we previously verified both our means and our *t* value by comparing our hand calculations and computer output.

The second set of statistics provided contains only two statistical values: *F* and *p*. These values represent the results of a test known as F_{max}, a statistic used to test the assumption of **homogeneity of variance** for the two groups (Kirk, 1968). Homogeneity of variance simply means that the variability of the scores of the two groups is similar. To use a *t* test we must assume that the variances are similar. In this particular example, our assumption is justified because the probability of chance for the *F* value is .22; well above the standard .05 cutoff. Because we have homogeneity of variance, we will use the third block of information ("Equal Variances Assumed") to interpret our test.

In the second set of information, if our *p* value was less than .05, we would have found **heterogeneity of variance**, meaning that the variability of the scores of the two groups was *not* comparable. Thus, we would be violating a mathematical assumption for using the *t* test. Fortunately, statisticians have developed a procedure that allows us to interpret our statistics despite heterogeneity. In such a case, we would use the fourth block of information ("Equal variances not assumed") rather than the third block. If the variances of the two groups are equivalent, we can pool or combine those estimates. However, if the variances are not equivalent, we must keep them separate. Again, in our current example, because the F_{max} statistic is not significant ($p = .22$), we will use the statistical results under the "Equal variances assumed" heading.

Generally speaking, *t* tests are **robust** with regard to the assumption of homogeneity (Kirk, 1968). A robust test is one that can tolerate violations of its assumptions and still provide accurate answers.

Homogeneity of variance The assumption that the variances are equal for two (or more) groups you plan to compare statistically.

Heterogeneity of variance Occurs when we do not have homogeneity of variance; this means that our two (or more) groups' variances are not equivalent.

Robust Refers to a statistical test that can tolerate violations of its assumptions (e.g., homogeneity of variance) and still yield results that are valid.

Kirk noted that the t test is so robust that the homogeneity assumption is often not even tested. Therefore, the statistics package you use may not provide information about the F_{max} statistic (and thus probably will not give you equal and unequal variance estimates).

Looking at the third set of information, we again find that our t value (calculated by the computer) is 2.61. The computer tells us that we have 14 degrees of freedom ($N_1 + N_2 - 2$). Rather than having to locate these values in a t table to determine significance, we can use the significance level provided by the computer: The probability is .021. Thus, the probability that two means as different as these could have come from the same population by chance is less than 3 in 100. This probability is less than the magical .05 cutoff, so we conclude that these two means are significantly different (i.e., the difference between them is *not* due to chance).

Some statistical packages may not automatically print the degrees of freedom for you, so it is important to remember how to calculate df. Also, some programs may not provide the probability of your result as part of the printout; then you would have to make this determination yourself. In such a case, you would merely use the t table (Appendix Table A-3) just as we showed you after calculating our t by hand. In this case, you would find that the probability of the t we found is less than .05. (Computer output typically provides exact p values [.021 in this case], whereas statistical tables simply allow you to compare your result to standard p values such as .05 or .01.)

In addition, the computer output shows that Cohen's d is 0.92. Table 11-4 shows you the formula for d and the steps involved in calculating the effect size index by hand. We learned in Chapter 8 that a d of 0.8 or larger is considered a large effect size. This information helps to confirm that customers' attire plays a major role in determining salesclerks' speed of helping. This decision completes the process of interpreting the computer output. Our next task is describing our statistical information in terms of the experiment we conducted.

TABLE 11-4   CALCULATING d AFTER t TEST FOR INDEPENDENT GROUPS

The formula for d (with equal sample sizes) is:

$$d = M_1 - M_2/s$$

Not surprisingly, we have multiple steps to find d. First, we'll find s using the formula below:

$$s = SE_{diff} \sqrt{N_1}$$
$$= 5.697(\sqrt{8}) = 5.697(2.828) = 16.11$$

Now that we have calculated s, we can find d.

$$d = 48.38 - 63.25 / 16.11$$
$$d = -14.87/16.11$$
$$d = .92 \text{ (Remember that .80 is a large effect size, so this difference is substantial.)}$$

Translating Statistics into Words

Think back to the logic of an experiment: We start an experiment with two equal groups and treat them identically (for control purposes) with one exception (our IV—type of dress); we measure the two groups (on our DV—time to provide service) in order to compare them. At this point, based on our statistical analyses, we know that we have a significant difference (i.e., not due to chance) between our two means because the probability of the difference occurring by chance was less than .05. If two equal groups began the experiment and they are now *unequal*, to what can we attribute that difference? If our controls have been adequate, our only choice is to assume that the difference between the groups is due to the IV.

Looking at our example, we have decided that the groups of students dressed in two different types of clothing received help from clerks in different amounts of time. Many students stop at this point, thinking that they have drawn a complete conclusion from their experiment.

Why would this conclusion be incomplete? Can you develop a complete conclusion before proceeding?

Saying that students who are dressed differently get waited on in different amounts of time is an incomplete conclusion because it specifies only a difference, not the *direction* of that difference. Whenever we compare treatments and find a difference, we want to know which group has performed at a better or higher level. In a two-group experiment, this interpretation is quite simple. Because we have only two groups and we have concluded that they differed significantly, we can further conclude that the group with the higher mean score has outscored the group with the lower mean score (remember that high scores do not always indicate superior performance, as in this case).

To fully interpret the results from this experiment, we examine our descriptive statistics and find that the salespeople waiting on students dressed in sloppy clothes had a mean response time of 63.25 seconds, whereas the salespeople waiting on well-dressed students averaged 48.38 seconds. Thus, we can conclude that salesclerks waiting on nicely dressed customers responded more quickly than those waiting on sloppily dressed customers. Notice that this statement includes both the notion of a difference *and* the direction of that difference.

When we draw conclusions from our research, we want to communicate those results clearly and concisely in our experimental report. To accomplish these two objectives, we use both words and numbers in our communication. This communication pattern is part of the **APA style** for preparing research reports that we will consider in Chapter 20 (APA, 2001). We will introduce the form for statistical results here. Bear in mind that you are trying to communicate—to tell what you found in words and provide statistical information to support those words. For example,

APA style Accepted APA form for preparing reports of psychological research.

if you were writing an interpretation of the results from our sample experiment, you might write something like the following:

> Salesclerks who waited on well-dressed customers ($M = 48.38$, $SD = 10.11$) took significantly less time, $t(14) = 2.61$, $p = .021$, to respond to customers than salespeople who waited on customers dressed in sloppy clothing ($M = 63.25$, $SD = 12.54$). The effect size, estimated with Cohen's *d*, was .92.

Notice that the words alone give a clear account of the findings—a person who has never taken a statistics course could understand this conclusion. The inferential statistics regarding the test findings support the conclusion. The descriptive statistics (M = mean, SD = standard deviation) given for each group allow the reader to see how the groups actually performed and to see how variable the data were. This standard format allows us to communicate our statistical results clearly and concisely.

REVIEW SUMMARY

1. **Inferential statistics** help the experimenter decide whether the IV was effective. A **significant** inferential statistic is one that occurs rarely by chance.
2. The statistical test you use for analyzing your experimental data is related to the experimental design you choose.
3. The ***t* test** is an inferential statistic that is used to test the differences between two groups.
4. When you have one IV with two groups and use randomly assigned research participants, the appropriate statistical test is the *t* test for **independent samples**.
5. Computer printouts of statistics typically give descriptive statistics (including means and *SD*s) and inferential statistics.
6. To communicate statistical results of an experiment, we use APA format for clarity and conciseness.

CHECK YOUR PROGRESS

1. Matching

   1. significant   A. nondirectional hypothesis
   2. inferential statistics   B. result occurs infrequently by chance
   3. Type I error   C. rejecting a true null hypothesis
   4. Type II error   D. tests conducted to determine if the IV had an effect
   5. one-tailed test   E. directional hypothesis
   6. two-tailed test   F. rejecting a true experimental hypothesis

2. What is meant by "level of significance"? How is the level of significance determined?
3. Explain the logic involved when an independent-groups *t* test is conducted.
4. What information do we look for first on a computer printout? Why?

5. If the variability of our two groups is similar, we have _____; if the variability of the groups is dissimilar, we have _____.

6. When we write a report of our experimental results, we explain the results in _____ and _____.

7. Interpret the following statistics: Group A ($M = 75$); Group B ($M = 70$); $t(14) = 2.53$, $p < .05$

The *t* Test for Correlated Samples

> **Correlated groups**
> Groups of research participants that are related in some way—through matching, repeated measures, or natural sets.

Remember that we covered two different two-group designs in Chapter 10. Now we discuss analyzing the two-correlated-groups design. Our experiment concerning the salespeople was an example of the two-independent-groups design, which would *not* require a *t* test for correlated samples.

 How could you modify this experiment so that it used correlated groups rather than independent groups?

> **Matched pairs** Research participants in a two-group design who are measured and equated on some variable before the experiment.

> **Repeated measures** An experimental procedure in which research participants are tested or measured more than once.

> **Natural pairs** Research participants in a two-group design who are naturally related in some way (e.g., a biological or social relationship).

You should remember that there are three methods for creating **correlated groups**: **matched pairs**, **repeated measures**, or **natural pairs**. If your modified experiment used one of these techniques, you made a correct change. As an example, let's assume that we were worried about the difference between salesclerks confounding our experiment. To better equate the clerks in our two groups, we decided to use the repeated-measures approach. We decide to measure each salesclerk's time to respond to two customers—once for a dressed-up customer and once for a sloppily dressed customer. Before beginning our experiment, we know that the salespeople are identical for the two groups, thus removing individual differences as a potential **confounding** variable.

Next, we conduct our experiment. We measure the response time of each of the eight clerks waiting on both types of customers (based on different types of dress). Given this hypothetical example, the scores from Table 11-1 would now represent repeated-measures time scores rather than independent scores, so the *t* test for correlated samples is the appropriate test.

Calculating *t* by Hand

As you might guess, the correlated *t* test uses a different formula than the independent *t* test, as you can see below:

$$t = \frac{M_1 - M_2}{s_{\overline{D}}} = \frac{M_1 - M_2}{s_D / \sqrt{N}}$$

> **Confounding** A situation in which the results of an experiment can be attributed to either the operation of an IV or an extraneous variable; caused by an uncontrolled variable that varies systematically with the IV.

Although the formula is different, it still follows the general rule for statistical tests that we noted earlier: a difference between groups divided by a measure of variability. For the correlated *t* test, the measure of variability is the standard error of the **deviation scores** (standard error of the deviation scores because we are subtracting each pair of scores). Unlike the independent *t* test, a correlated samples *t* test cannot have different samples sizes—the scores *must* occur in pairs. Thus, there is only one formula for the standard error this time (see below):

> **Deviation scores**
> The difference between any single score and the mean of the distribution $(X - M)$.

$$s_D = \sqrt{\dfrac{\Sigma D^2 - \dfrac{(\Sigma D)^2}{N}}{N - 1}}$$

$$D = M_1 - M_2$$

where N = number of pairs of scores

Again, calculating the SE is quite similar to computing a *SD*. Given that both SEs and *SD*s measure variability, the similarity in the formulas should not be surprising. The figures for the hand calculation of the correlated *t* appear in Table 11-5. This time, our *t* value is equal to 5.46. (Again, we typically can ignore the negative sign; more on this topic later.)

Computer Analysis of *t* Test for Correlated Samples

After analyzing the data with our computer package, we find the output in Table 11-6. (Please note that it is *not* legitimate to analyze the same data with two different statistical tests. We are doing so in this chapter merely for example's sake. If you tested real-world data multiple times, you would increase the probability of making an error. We will address such errors at the end of the chapter.)

Look at Table 11-6. Again, we first look for the descriptive statistics and find them at the top of the printout. Of course, because we used the same data, we have the same descriptive statistics as for the independent-samples test. Salesclerks waiting on the students wearing sloppy clothing responded in an average of 63.25 seconds with a *SD* of 12.54 and a SE of 4.44. The students who wore dressy clothes received help in 48.38 seconds with a *SD* of 10.11 and a SE of 3.58. Remember that there are 8 *pairs* of scores (representing the 8 clerks) rather than 16 individual scores. This difference between the two *t* tests will be important when we consider the degrees of freedom.

The second block of information shows us the size of the difference between the two means as well as its *SD* and SE. (Researchers rarely use this information, so it may not appear in your computer output.) The third block gives you some information about the relation between the pairs of participants (or the same participant for repeated measures). Here you can determine whether the paired scores were correlated. Remember from Chapter 10 that we want them to be correlated so that we will gain the additional statistical control available by using the correlated-groups design.

TABLE **11-5**   CALCULATING *t* TEST FOR CORRELATED GROUPS

Although we have the same data that we used for our independent *t* test, we do not square the scores. Instead, we calculate the difference between each pair of scores and square those differences.

DRESSY CLOTHES	SLOPPY CLOTHES	D	D²
37	50	−13	169
38	46	−8	64
44	62	−18	324
47	52	−5	25
49	74	−25	625
49	69	−20	400
54	77	−23	529
69	76	−7	49
$\Sigma = 387$	$\Sigma = 506$	$\Sigma = -119$	$\Sigma = 2185$
$M_1 = 48.38$	$M_2 = 63.25$		

First, we will calculate s_D

$$s_D = \sqrt{[\Sigma D^2 - (\Sigma D)^2 / N] / N - 1}$$
$$= \sqrt{[2185 - (-119)^2 / 8] / 8 - 1}$$
$$= \sqrt{[2185 - 1770.125] / 7}$$
$$= \sqrt{414.875 / 7} = \sqrt{59.268} = 7.699$$

Now we can use s_D to calculate $s_{\overline{D}}$

$$s_{\overline{D}} = s_D / \sqrt{N}$$
$$= 7.699 / \sqrt{8} = 7.699 / 2.828 = 2.722$$

Now we are ready to calculate our *t* statistic:

$$t = M_1 - M_2 / s_{\overline{D}}$$
$$t = 48.38 - 63.25 / 2.722 = -14.87 / 2.722$$
$$t = -5.46 \text{ (Again, the sign is not important because we ran a two-tailed test.)}$$

Positive correlation As scores on one variable increase, scores on the second variable also increase.

As you can see in this example, the scores were highly **positively correlated** (see Chapter 8). In our example, this result implies that if a salesclerk waited on one student quickly, he or she tended to also wait on the other student quickly.

In the fourth block we find the results of our inferential test. We obtained a *t* value of 5.46 with 7 degrees of freedom.

TABLE **11-6**   **COMPUTER OUTPUT FOR *t* TEST FOR CORRELATED GROUPS**

GROUP 1 = DRESSY CLOTHING

GROUP 2 = SLOPPY CLOTHING

VARIABLE = SALESCLERKS' RESPONSE TIME

	N	MEAN	SD	SE
GROUP 1	8	48.38	10.113	3.575
GROUP 2	8	63.25	12.544	4.435
MEAN DIFFERENCE = 14.875			SD = 7.699	SE = 2.722
CORR. = 0.790	p = 0.020			
t = 5.463	df = 7	p = 0.001	COHEN'S d = 1.93	

PSYCHOLOGICAL DETECTIVE   We have 16 data points (8 clerks measured twice each) in our experiment but only 7 degrees of freedom. In our earlier example, we had 16 participants and 14 degrees of freedom. What is the difference in this case?

You should remember that our degrees of freedom for correlated samples cases are equal to the number of pairs of participants minus 1. If this is fuzzy in your memory, refer back to the *Statistical Issues* section earlier in this chapter.

The computer tells us that the probability of a *t* of 5.46 with 7 *df* is .001. With such a low probability of chance for our results, we would conclude that there is a significant difference between the clerks' response times to differently dressed students. In other words, we believe that it is highly unlikely that the difference between our groups could have occurred by chance and that, instead, the difference must be due to our IV. The effect size information, Cohen's *d*, provides ample support for our conclusion as *d* is 1.93. Remember that 0.8 represents a large effect size, so the effect of the IV is quite substantial in this analysis. (See Table 11-7 for the formula and computational steps for *d*.)

Translating Statistics into Words

Our experimental logic is exactly the same for this experiment as it was for the independent samples case. The only difference is that with our matched participants, we are more certain that the two groups are equal before the experiment begins. We still treat our groups equally (control) with the one exception (our IV) and measure their performance (our DV) so that we can compare them statistically.

To translate our statistics into words, it is important to say more than the fact that we found a significant difference. We must know what form or direction that significant

TABLE 11-7   CALCULATING *d* AFTER *t* TEST FOR CORRELATED GROUPS

The formula for *d* (with correlated samples) is:

$$d = M_1 - M_2/s$$

Again, we have multiple steps to find *d*. First, we'll find *s* using the formula below:

$$s = (s_{\overline{D}})\sqrt{N_1}$$
$$= 2.722(\sqrt{8}) = 2.722(2.828) = 7.698$$

Now that we have calculated *s*, we can find *d*.

$$d = 48.38 - 63.25 / 7.698$$
$$d = -14.87 / 7.698$$
$$d = 1.93$$

(Remember that .80 is a large effect size, so this difference is extremely large. Also, the *d* for the independent samples test was .92—this difference in *d*s shows the added power of the correlated samples test.)

difference takes. With the *t* test for correlated samples, we are again comparing two groups, so it is a simple matter of looking at the group means to determine which group outperformed the other. Of course, because we are using the same data, our means are identical: The sloppily dressed students received help in a mean of 63.25 seconds compared to 48.38 seconds for the well-dressed students.

 PSYCHOLOGICAL DETECTIVE How would you write the results of this experiment in words and numbers for your experimental report?

Did you find yourself flipping back in the book to page 251 to look at our earlier conclusion? If so, that's a good strategy because this conclusion should be quite similar to the earlier conclusion. In fact, you could almost copy the earlier conclusion as long as you made several important changes. Did you catch those changes? Here's an adaptation of our earlier conclusion:

> Salespeople who waited on well-dressed customers (*M* = 48.38, *SD* = 10.11) took significantly less time, *t*(7) = 5.46, *p* = .001, to respond to the customers than when they waited on customers dressed in sloppy clothes (*M* = 63.25, *SD* = 12.54). The effect size, estimated with Cohen's *d*, was 1.93.

As you can see, four numbers in the sentences changed: We had fewer degrees of freedom, our *t* value was larger, our probability of chance was lower, and our effect size was much larger. In this *purely hypothetical* example in which we analyzed the same data twice (a clear violation of assumptions if you were to do this in the real world), you can see the advantage of correlated-groups designs. Although we lost degrees of freedom compared to the independent-samples case earlier in the chapter, the probability that our results were due to chance actually decreased and our effect size increased dramatically. Again, we gained these advantages because our matching of the participants helped to decrease the variability in the data.

You can see a vivid illustration of what we gained through matching by examining Table 11-8. In this example, we have used the same data from this chapter, but shuffled the scores for the second group before we ran a *t* test for correlated samples. Such a situation would occur if you matched your participants on an irrelevant variable (remember that we mentioned this possibility earlier in the chapter). As you can see by comparing Tables 11-8 and 11-6, the descriptive statistics remained the same because the scores in each group did not change. However, in Table 11-8, the correlation between the two sets of scores is now −.88. Because there is a **negative correlation** between our scores, the *t* value is 1.91, even lower than it was in our *t* test for independent groups (see Table 11-3). The marked change comes when we compare the inferential statistics in Tables 11-6 and 11-8. The original analysis showed a *t* of 5.46 with $p = .001$. In contrast, with a negative correlation between the pairs of scores, the new analysis shows a *t* of 1.91 with $p = .097$ and an effect size of 0.68 (the smallest of our three analyses). Thus, these results did not remain significant when the positive correlation between the participants reversed. Again, the key point to remember is that when using a correlated-groups design, the groups should actually be positively correlated.

> **Negative correlation**
> As scores on one variable increase, scores on the second variable decrease.

TABLE 11-8 COMPUTER OUTPUT FOR *t* TEST FOR CORRELATED GROUPS (SHUFFLED DATA)

GROUP 1 = DRESSY CLOTHING

GROUP 2 = SLOPPY CLOTHING

VARIABLE = SALESCLERKS' RESPONSE TIME

GROUP	*N*	MEAN	*SD*	SE
GROUP 1	8	48.38	10.113	3.575
GROUP 2	8	63.25	12.544	4.435
MEAN DIFFERENCE = 14.88			SD = 21.977	SE = 7.770
CORR. = −0.880	*p* = 0.004			
t = 1.91	*df* = 7	*p* = 0.097	COHEN'S *d* = 0.68	

Important Reminders

Before we end this chapter, we need to remind you of two more important factors that we must consider when using inferential statistics. These considerations are *not* specific to *t* tests, so be sure to file these away for future reference.

One-Tailed and Two-Tailed Significance Tests

Recall from Chapter 9 that you state your experimental hypothesis in either a directional or a nondirectional manner. If you use the directional form, then you are specifying exactly how (i.e., the direction) the results will turn out. For the example we have been considering, an experimental hypothesis, stated in general implication form (see Chapter 2), might be as follows:

> If students wear dressy clothes to the shopping mall, then the time it takes a salesperson to offer to serve them will be different than the latency to service for students dressed in sloppy clothes.

Nondirectional hypothesis A specific prediction concerning the outcome of an experiment is not made.

Directional hypothesis Prediction of the specific outcome of an experiment.

Because we predict that the latency to service for the students wearing dressy clothes will differ from that of the students wearing sloppy clothes, we have a **nondirectional hypothesis**. If we indicate that we expect a difference between the two groups *and* we specify the exact nature of that difference, then we are using a **directional hypothesis**.

Now, how do directional and nondirectional hypotheses relate to the *t* test? A one-tailed *t* test evaluates the probability of only one type of outcome, whereas the two-tailed *t* test evaluates the probability of both possible outcomes. You may remember earlier in the chapter that when we calculated *t* tests by hand we found negative *t* values. In both cases, we told you to ignore the negative sign. The reason we could ignore the sign was that we ran two-tailed tests, so it did not matter whether the *t* value was positive or negative. However, in a one-tailed test, you would be predicting a difference in only one direction, so the sign would be crucial. Remember from Chapter 9 that researchers typically use two-tailed tests of significance.

 Can you think of a situation in which a one-tailed test would be appropriate?

This question is a challenging one. First, consider that there are three possible outcomes in a two-group experiment: Group A could score higher than Group B, Group A could score lower than Group B, or there could be no difference. Our rule of thumb for selecting a one-tailed test is that if two of the possible outcomes would lead you to the same decision, a one-tailed test may be appropriate. For example, imagine that a computer salesman shows up to try to sell you a computer. Being a research-minded person, you suggest an experiment to compare the computer to the computer you already own. Although there are three possible outcomes of this experiment (the other computer is better, your computer is better, or there is no difference), two of those outcomes will result in the same behavior on your part. If your computer is better or there is no difference, you will not buy the new computer. Only if the other

> **Type I error** Accepting the experimental hypothesis when the null hypothesis is true.

computer is better will you consider buying it. Thus, you could conduct a one-tailed test to decide only if the new computer is better than yours.

Type I and Type II Errors

Remember from Chapter 9 that we can make two different types of errors when drawing conclusions from our research. For example, if the null hypothesis is true but you accept the experimental hypothesis, you have made a **Type I error** (alpha, α). However, if you reject a *true* experimental hypothesis, you have made a **Type II error**. Consult Figure 9-5 (p. 208) if you need to refresh your memory.

> **Type II error** Accepting the null hypothesis when the experimental hypothesis is true.

 In our hypothetical experiment, we concluded that salesclerks took longer to wait on customers dressed in sloppy clothes. Given the alternatives in Figure 9-5, which outcomes from the grid are possible in this example?

First, we could have made a correct decision—we rejected the null hypothesis that clerks' wait times would be equal for the two clothing groups, and that should be the true situation. However, there is also a chance ($p = .021$ in this case) that we made a Type I error in rejecting the null hypothesis of no difference when it was actually true. Remember that experimenters typically set the alpha level at .05 because it places the probability of Type I and Type II errors at acceptable levels.

The Continuing Research Problem

Research is a cyclical, ongoing process. It would be rare for a psychologist to conduct a single research project and stop at that point because that one project had answered all the questions about the particular topic. Instead, one experiment usually answers some of your questions, does not answer others, and also raises new ones for your consideration. As you have studied the work of famous psychologists, you may have noticed that many of them established a research area early in their careers and continued working in that area for the duration of their professional lives. We're not trying to say that the research area you choose as an undergraduate will shape your future as a psychologist—although it could! Rather, we are merely pointing out that one good experiment often leads to another.

We want to show you how research is an ongoing process as we move through the next four chapters with our continuing research problem. We sketched out a research problem in Chapter 10 (comparing how customers' style of dress affects salespeople's performance) and asked you to help us solve the problem through experimentation.

We will continue to examine this problem throughout the next four chapters so that you can see how different questions we ask about the same problem may require different research designs. This research problem is purely hypothetical, but it has an applied slant to it. We hope the continuing research problem helps you see how a single question can be asked in many different ways *and* that a single question often leads to many new questions.

To make certain you understood the logical series of steps we took when choosing a design, let's review those steps, paying particular attention to our experimental design questions shown in Figure 10-1:

Step 1   After reviewing relevant research literature, we chose our IV (style of dress) and our DV (salesclerk response time).

Step 2   Because we were conducting a preliminary investigation into the effects of clothing on salesclerks' reactions, we decided to test only one IV (the style of dress).

Step 3   Because we wanted to determine only whether clothing style can affect the performance of salespeople, we chose to use only two levels of the IV (dressy clothing versus sloppy clothing).

Step 4a   If we have a large number of participants available, then we can use random assignment, which yields independent groups. In this case, we would use the two-independent-groups design and analyze the data with a *t* test for independent groups.

Step 4b   If we expect to have a small number of participants and need to exert the maximum degree of control, we choose to use a design with repeated measures or matched groups, thus resulting in correlated groups. Therefore, we would use a two-correlated-groups design for the experiment and analyze the data with a *t* test for correlated groups.

Step 5   We concluded that salespeople responded more quickly to customers in dressy clothes than to customers dressed in sloppy clothes.

REVIEW SUMMARY

1. When you have one IV with two groups and use matched pairs, natural pairs, or repeated measures with your participants, the appropriate statistical test is the *t* test for **correlated samples**.

2. The *t* test for correlated samples is advantageous statistically (compared to the *t* test for independent samples) if the scores are positively correlated.

3. A **one-tailed** *t* test is appropriate when a directional hypothesis is made, whereas a **two-tailed** *t* test is conducted when the research states a nondirectional hypothesis.

4. Even though lower critical values are associated with one-tailed tests, making it easier to achieve significance, most experimental hypotheses are nondirectional because the researchers do not know exactly how the result will turn out.

5. Sometimes the results of an inferential statistical test produce an incorrect decision. An experimental hypothesis may be incorrectly accepted (**Type I error**) or incorrectly rejected (**Type II error**).

CHECK YOUR PROGRESS

1. Which statistical test would you use if you compared the stereotyping of a group of male executives before and after an antidiscrimination bill passed through Congress? Explain your reasoning.

2. Compared to the *t* test for independent groups, the *t* test for correlated samples has _____ degrees of freedom.

   a. fewer

   b. more

   c. exactly the same number

   d. none of these; it is impossible to compare degrees of freedom between statistical tests

3. A one-tailed test of significance is associated with a _____.

   a. directional hypothesis

   b. nondirectional hypothesis

   c. positive correlation

   d. negative correlation

4. The Type I error _____.

   a. is under the direct control of the experimenter

   b. always occurs 5% of the time

   c. is specified by the experimental hypothesis

   d. all of the above

   e. none of the above

5. If you could compare all men and women in the world, you would find that men are significantly more aggressive. You conduct an experiment and find no difference in aggression between men and women. You have made a _____.

   a. correct decision

   b. Type I error

   c. Type II error

   d. Type III error

6. Why do we describe research as a cyclical, ongoing process? Give an example of how this cycling might take place.

EXERCISES

1. Suppose a friend approaches you and tells you that she wants to use age as her IV and that she wants to use a *t* test to analyze her data. She wants to know if this experimental design is possible and how to set up her experiment. What do you say in response to her questions?

2. You have conducted an experiment in which you had men and women rate their attitude toward a movie before and after they viewed it. Which type of *t* test should you use to analyze your data? Why?

3. You have conducted an experiment in which you compared sex differences on reaction time to different types of images presented for very short times. Which type of *t* test should you use to analyze your data? Why?

4. You are curious as to whether male or female dogs have a better sense of smell. To ensure the groups' equality, you choose a male and a female dog from each of 10 litters and test their sense of smell by sex. Which type of *t* test should you use to analyze your data? Why?

5. You want to compare two GRE study methods—a study course versus a study book. To make sure the groups are equal, you pair students based on their GPAs and then randomly assign one of each pair to the course or study group. Which type of *t* test should you use to analyze your data? Why?

6. You set up an experiment in which you randomly assign students to groups. One group of students has parents help them with their homework and the other group has no parental help. The students take a quiz over the material with the results below. What should you conclude about the role of parental help?

Help:	10	9	6	8	10	9	8	7	9	8
No help:	9	7	7	6	8	7	7	7	8	7

7. You set up an experiment in which you randomly assign students to groups. One group of students has parents help them with their homework and the other group has no parental help. The students take a quiz over the material with the results below. What should you conclude about the role of parental help?

Help:	10	9	6	8	10	9	8	7	9	8
No help:	9	8	7	7	9	8	7	9	10	7

8. You set up an experiment in which you randomly assign students to groups. One group of students has parents help them with their homework and the other group has no parental help. The students take a quiz over the material with the results below. What should you conclude about the role of parental help?

Help:	10	9	6	8	10	9	8	7	9	8
No help:	9	7	8	6	8	7	8	7	8	7

9. You set up an experiment in which you have parents help their students with homework during one unit but give their students no help during a second unit. The students take a quiz over both units with the results below. What should you conclude about the role of parental help?

Help:	10	9	6	8	10	9	8	7	9	8
No help:	9	8	7	6	8	8	7	7	9	7

10. You set up an experiment in which you have parents help their students with homework during one unit but give their students no help during a second unit. The students take a quiz over both units with the results below. What should you conclude about the role of parental help?

Help:	10	9	6	8	10	9	8	7	9	8
No help:	9	8	7	8	9	8	7	7	9	8

11. You set up an experiment in which you have parents help their students with homework during one unit but give their students no help during a second unit. The students take a quiz over both units with the results below. What should you conclude about the role of parental help?

Help:	10	9	6	8	10	9	8	7	9	8
No help:	9	8	7	9	8	8	7	7	9	7

12. Write an APA-style conclusion for one of your findings in Exercises 6–8.
13. Write an APA-style conclusion for one of your findings in Exercises 9–11.
14 Suppose a friend brought you the computer data shown below and said that he could not interpret it. He asks for you to use your statistical knowledge to help him out. What can you tell him?

Group	N	M	SD
Group 1	21	53.9	13.4
Group 2	21	45.8	11.7
t = 3.32	df = 40		p = .002

15 Suppose a friend brought you the computer data shown below and said that she could not interpret it. She asks for you to use your statistical knowledge to help her out. What can you tell her?

Group	N	M	SD
Group 1	21	53.9	8.4
Group 2	21	54.8	9.7
t = 1.33	df = 40		p = .19

KEY TERMS

Significant, *239*
Null hypothesis, *239*
Random selection, *240*
Random assignment, *240*
t test, *242*
Interval-level data, *242*
Ratio-level data, *242*
Independent groups, *242*
Standard error (SE), *244*
Standard deviation (SD), *245*
Degrees of freedom (*df*), *246*
Descriptive statistics, *248*
Homogeneity of variance, *248*
Heterogeneity of variance, *248*

Robust, *248*
APA style, *250*
Correlated groups, *252*
Matched pairs, *252*
Repeated measures, *252*
Natural pairs, *252*
Confounding, *253*
Deviation scores, *253*
Positive correlation, *254*
Negative correlation, *257*
Nondirectional hypothesis, *258*
Directional hypothesis, *258*
Type I error, *259*
Type II error, *259*

LOOKING AHEAD

In this chapter we have seen how experimental design and statistical analysis are intricately linked. In particular, we examined the most basic experiment with one IV and two groups and have learned how to analyze data from such an experiment. In the following chapter we will enlarge this basic design by adding more groups to our one IV. This enlarged design will give us the capability to ask more penetrating questions about the effects of our IV and to obtain more specific information about those effects.

Designing and Conducting Experiments with More than Two Groups

Experimental Design: Adding to the Basic Building Block

Experimental design
The general plan for selecting participants, assigning participants to experimental conditions, controlling extraneous variables, and gathering data.

In Chapter 10 we learned many concepts and principles about **experimental design** that are basic to planning *any* experiment, not merely the basic two-group experiment. When we come to one of those topics in this chapter, we will briefly review it and refer you back to Chapter 10 for the original discussion.

In this chapter we will add to our basic building-block design. Consider our previous analogy: As a child you quickly mastered the beginner's set of Legos or Tinkertoys. You learned to build everything there was to build with that small set and wanted to go beyond those simple objects to build larger, more exciting creations. To satisfy this desire, you got a larger set of building materials that you could combine with the starter set in order to build more complicated objects. Despite the fact you were using a larger set of materials, the basic principles you learned with your starter set still applied.

Experimental design works in much the same way. Researchers typically want to move beyond two-group designs so they can ask more complicated and interesting questions. Fortunately, they don't have to start from scratch—that's why we referred to the two-group design as the basic building-block design in Chapter 10. Every experimental design is based on the two-group design. Although the questions you ask may become more complicated or sophisticated, your experimental design principles will remain constant. In the same way, when detectives are faced with a more difficult case, they continue to use the basic investigative procedures they have learned.

It is still appropriate to think of your experimental design as the blueprint of your experiment. We hope the following analogy convinces you of the need for having an experimental design. Although you *might* be able to get by without a blueprint if you're building a dog house, it is unlikely you would want to build *your* house without a blueprint. Think of building a small house as being equivalent to using the two-group design from Chapter 10. If you need a blueprint to build a house, imagine how much more you would need a blueprint to build an apartment building or a skyscraper. We will work toward the skyscrapers of experimental design in Chapter 14.

The Multiple-Group Design

Here, we will consider an extension of the two-group design. Turn back to Figure 10-2 (p. 223) for just a moment. What would be the next logical step to add to this design so that we could ask (and answer) slightly more complex questions?

Independent variable (IV) A stimulus or aspect of the environment that the experimenter directly manipulates to determine its influence on behavior.

How Many IVs?   The first question that we ask when considering any experimental design is the same: "How many **independent variables (IVs)** will I use in my experiment?" (see Figure 12-1). In this chapter, we will continue to consider experiments that use only one IV. We should remember that although one-IV experiments may be simpler than experiments that use multiple IVs (Chapter 14), they are not inferior in any way. Many students who are designing their

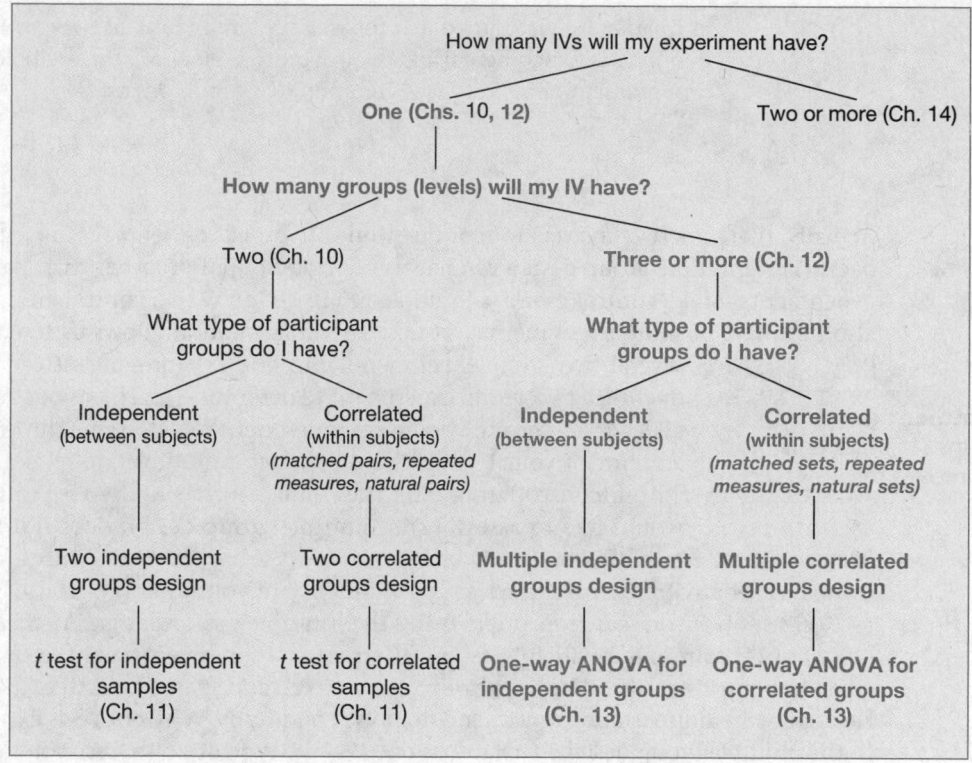

FIGURE 12-1 EXPERIMENTAL DESIGN QUESTIONS.

Principle of parsimony
The belief that explanations of phenomena and events should remain simple until the simple explanations are no longer valid.

Levels Differing amounts or types of an IV used in an experiment (also known as *treatment conditions*).

first research study decide to throw in everything except the kitchen sink as an IV. A well-designed experiment with one IV is vastly preferable to a sloppy experiment with many variables thrown together. Remember the **principle of parsimony** from Chapter 10—if a one-IV experiment can answer your questions, use it and don't complicate things needlessly.

How Many Groups?   Once we have chosen to conduct a one-IV experiment, our second question (see Figure 12-1) revolves around how many groups we will use to test the IV. This question marks the difference between the multiple-group design and the two-group design. As their names imply, a two-group design compares two **levels** of an IV, whereas a multiple-group design compares three or more levels of a single IV. Thus, we could compare three, four, five, or even more differing levels of amounts of an IV. This experimental situation is similar to that experienced by a detective faced with multiple suspects. Instead of merely investigating two people, the detective must conduct simultaneous investigations of several individuals.

In Chapter 10 we learned that the most common type of two-group design uses experimental and control groups. How will the multiple-group design differ from that common two-group design?

Actually, there are two answers to that question—if you got either, pat yourself on the back. (1) A multiple-group design *can* have a control group. But rather than having an experimental and a control group, a multiple-group design with a control group would also have two or more experimental groups. This combination allows us to condense several two-group experiments into one experiment. Instead of conducting a two-group experiment to determine whether your IV has an effect and a second two-group experiment to determine the optimum amount of your IV, you could conduct a multiple-group experiment with a control group and the number of **treatment groups** you would like to assess. (2) A multiple-group design does not have to have a control group. If you already know that your IV has an effect, you can simply compare as many treatment groups as you would like in your multiple-group design.

> **Treatment groups**
> Groups of participants that receive the IV.

Let's look at a research example using the multiple-group design. Michael Jones (2001) of Lincoln Memorial University in Harrogate, Tennessee, wanted to determine whether noise affected children's performance on recall and spatial tasks (see Chapter 7). He used white noise (static), music, and no noise conditions. Why does this experiment fit the multiple-group design? First, it has one IV—the type of noise. Second, the IV has more than two levels—it has three, based on the three different noise conditions. Thus, as you can see in Figure 12-1, with one IV and three levels, this experiment requires a multiple-group design. We can draw the block diagram depicted in Figure 12-2 to portray this experimental design. If you compare Figures 10-2 and 12-2, you can easily see how the multiple-group design is an extension of the two-group design.

Two of the groups in Figure 12-2 are experimental groups. Does this experiment use a control group? Yes, the no noise condition served as a control group. In this experiment, Jones was interested in the various differences among the three groups based on their differing types of noise. He found that children in the white noise condition performed better than children in the music condition; children in the no noise condition scored between the two noise conditions but were not significantly different from either group. In statistical terminology, then, Jones found results that supported the experimental hypothesis (i.e., that there was a difference between the performance of the groups as a function of noise condition). However, support for the experimental hypothesis is not the same as *proving* the experimental hypothesis. Did Jones *prove* that noise

INDEPENDENT VARIABLE (Type of Noise)

EXPERIMENTAL GROUP 1	EXPERIMENTAL GROUP 2	EXPERIMENTAL GROUP 3
White noise	Music	No Noise

FIGURE 12-2 THE MULTIPLE-GROUP DESIGN USED BY JONES (2001).

affects children's performance on recall and spatial performance? No, he merely demonstrated that there was a difference that was unlikely to have occurred by chance for the noise conditions he used and for his groups of participants. What about using different sounds? What about using different research participants—musicians or adults, for example? File away this clue for future exploration. In Chapter 18 we will talk about how to generalize our results beyond the specific participants in our experiment.

Suppose you wished to test more than three noise conditions. Could you use a multiple-group design in such a case? Why or why not? If so, what would happen to the block design in Figure 12-2?

Independent groups
Groups of participants that are formed by random assignment.

Yes, you could use the multiple-group design if you had four or five noises to assess. In fact, it could be used if there were 10, 20, or 100 sounds. The only requirement for using the multiple-group design is an experiment with one IV and more than two groups (see Figure 12-1). Practically speaking, it is rare that researchers use multiple-group designs with more than four or five groups. If we did use such a design with more than three groups, we would merely extend our block diagram, as shown in Figure 12-3.

INDEPENDENT VARIABLE (Type of Noise)

EXPL GROUP 1	EXPL GROUP 2	EXPL GROUP 3	EXPL GROUP 4	EXPL GROUP 5
Noise 1	Noise 2	Noise 3	Noise 4	Noise 5

FIGURE 12-3 HYPOTHETICAL MULTIPLE-GROUP DESIGN WITH FIVE GROUPS.

Correlated groups
Groups of research participants that are related in some way—through matching, repeated measures, or natural sets.

Assigning Participants to Groups   After we decide to conduct a multiple-group experiment, we must decide about assignment of research participants to groups (see Figure 12-1). Just as in Chapter 10, we choose between using **independent groups** or **correlated groups**.

Independent Samples (Random Assignment to Groups)   Remember that with **random assignment** each participant has an equal chance of being assigned to any group. In his experiment on the effects of noise on performance, Jones (2001) used random assignment when he assigned children to groups—all 60 children had a 1 in 3 chance of being in the no noise, white noise, or music group. When we use large groups of participants, random assignment should create groups that are equal on potential extraneous variables such as personality, age, and sex. Recall from Chapter 10 that random assignment allows us to control extraneous variables about which we are unaware. Thus, random

Random assignment
A method of assigning research participants to groups so that each participant has an equal chance of being in any group.

Control procedure One of several steps experimenters take to ensure that potential extraneous variables are controlled. Examples include random assignment, matching, and so on.

Confounded experiment An experiment in which an extraneous variable varies systematically with the IV; makes drawing a cause-and-effect relation impossible.

assignment serves as an important **control procedure**. For example, we would not want to use music with only boys or girls. We want to spread the different levels of the IV across all types of participants in order to avoid a **confounded experiment**. Suppose we put all girls in the music condition and all boys in the white noise condition. When we tabulated our results, we would not be able to draw a clear conclusion about the effects of noise because noise was confounded with participant sex. In other words, we couldn't be sure whether a significant difference between groups was caused by the noise difference between the groups *or* the sex difference between the groups.

Random assignment results in participants who have no relation to participants in other groups; in other words, the groups are independent of each other. We are interested in comparing differences between the various independent groups. As shown in Figure 12-1, when we use random assignment in this design, we end up with a multiple-independent-groups design.

Correlated Samples (Nonrandom Assignment to Groups) In the multiple-group design, we have the same concern about random assignment that we did with the two-group design: What if the random assignment does not work and we begin our experiment with unequal groups? We know that random assignment *should* create equal groups, but that it is most likely to work in the long run—that is, when we have many participants. If we have few participants or if we expect only small differences due to our IV, we may want more control than random assignment affords us. In such situations, we often resort to using nonrandom methods of assigning participants to groups and thus end up with correlated groups. Let's examine our three ways of creating correlated groups and see how they differ from the strategies discussed in Chapter 10.

cathy®   **by Cathy Guisewite**

Because she is tasting chocolate Santas in a nonsystematic way (rather than assigning Santas to groups), Cathy's gluttony illustrates random selection.

Is Cathy using random assignment or random selection in this cartoon? You may want to look back at Chapter 9.

1. Matched Sets. Matched *pairs* are not appropriate for the multiple-group design because we have at least three groups, so we must use matched *sets*. The principle for forming matched sets is the same as that for forming matched pairs. Before our experiment, we measure our participants on some variable that will affect their performance on the DV. Then we create sets of participants who are essentially the same on this measured variable, often known as the **matching variable**. The size of the sets will, of course, depend on how many levels our IV has. If our IV has five levels, for example, then each set would have five participants equated on the matching variable. After we create our matched sets, we then randomly assign the participants within each set to the different groups (treatments).

> **Matching variable** A potential extraneous variable on which we measure our research participants and from which we form sets of participants who are equal on the variable.

Returning to Jones's experiment, suppose we believed that participant sex would be an extraneous variable because we were playing Britney Spears's music (which Jones did). To ensure equality of his groups on sex, Jones could have used sets of three participants who were matched on sex, with each participant then randomly assigned to one of the three groups. In this manner, he would have assured that the distribution of participant sex was uniform across all three groups. If all three of his groups had the same sex composition (regardless of whether it was 50–50), then participant sex could not be an extraneous variable.

One final caution is in order. We should remember that the potential extraneous variable must actually affect performance on the DV or else we have hurt our chances of finding a significant difference.

2. Repeated Measures. Other than the fact that participants perform in three or more conditions rather than only two, repeated measures in the multiple-group design are identical to repeated measures in the two-group design. When you use repeated measures in the multiple-group design, each participant must take part in *all* the various treatment conditions. Thus, for Jones to have used repeated measures, each child would have participated in the no noise, white noise, and music conditions.

PSYCHOLOGICAL DETECTIVE   Can you see any possible flaws in conducting Jones's experiment using a repeated-measures design? (Hint: Consider some of the practical issues from Chapter 10 about using repeated measures.)

Several problems could occur if we attempted the noise experiment with a repeated-measures design. Would you have one child perform the same task three different times? This approach would not seem to make any sense. The children might become suspicious about the differing noises; they would probably be able to figure out what the IV was. Or they might get tired from performing the task three times and not try hard on the third attempt. Conversely, they might get better with repeated trials and perform best on the third attempt. What about using three different tasks? Again, this approach could be problematic. Could we logically assume that children performed differently because of the noise? Not necessarily, because different tasks would have to cover different skills or knowledge. Students would be more likely to perform well on a task that dealt with a skill they enjoyed or had previously learned. Thus, we might be measuring the response rate to different tasks rather than to different types of noises! It seems that this experiment simply would not work well as a repeated-measures design. Remember that we mentioned this possible problem in Chapter 10—it is not possible to conduct all experiments using repeated measures.

3. Natural Sets. Using natural sets is analogous to using natural pairs except that our sets must include more than two research participants. Using multiple groups takes away our ability to use some interesting natural pairs such as twins or husbands and wives, but other possibilities for using natural sets do exist. For example, many animal researchers use littermates as natural sets, assuming that their shared heredity makes them more similar than randomly selected animals. In a similar fashion, if your research participants were siblings from families with three (or more) children, natural sets would be a possibility. Most natural pairs or sets involve biological relationships.

We create multiple-correlated-groups designs when we use matched sets, repeated measures, or natural sets. The critical distinction is that the participants in these types of groups are related to each other in some way—we are comparing differences *within* groups (or within subjects, to use the old terminology). On the other hand, in independent-groups designs, the participants have no common relationship. Thus, we compare differences *between* differing groups of subjects.

Kimberly Walker and her faculty advisors James Arruda and Keegan Greenier (1999) of Mercer University in Macon, Georgia, conducted an experiment that used a multiple-correlated-groups design. They were interested in measuring how accurately people respond on the Visual Analogue Scale (VAS). The VAS is a self-report scale used for people to indicate internal states such as mood, hunger, or pain. Participants respond on the VAS by making a mark somewhere along a line, typically 100 millimeters (mm) in length, that has marks at the ends designating extreme low and high values of the internal state. Walker et al. asked participants to make marks at distances of 10, 20, 30, 40, 50, 60, 70, 80, and 90 mm along the line. They calculated participants' errors by subtracting the difference between the actual distance and the marked distance. By measuring the errors over nine distances, Walker et al. could compare data to determine whether errors were more likely at different points along the line.

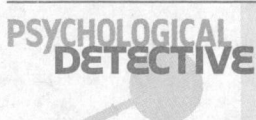 Why does the Walker, Arruda, and Greenier experiment illustrate a correlated-groups design? Which particular correlated-groups technique did they use? Why do you think they used a correlated-groups design?

In this experiment, the IV was actual distance, measured in mm. Thus, there were nine levels of the IV. They measured each participant on each different distance, so the correlated groups were a result of using repeated measures. Walker et al. probably used a repeated-measures design because it would take an enormous number of participants if they had each participant serve in only one distance group (nine groups of people needed). Also, it would have been an inefficient use of participants to use nine different groups. Finally, by having people participate in all levels of the IV, Walker et al. did not have to worry about the assumption that the groups were equivalent before the experiment began. By using each person as his or her own control across the nine measurements, the question of group equality was answered. The use of repeated measures helped control many subject variables that *might* have affected participants' performance on the VAS—factors such as motivation, spatial ability, and sex.

Walker et al. (1999) found that the participants were more accurate in making marks at the beginning and end of the VAS line than in the middle of the line. They explained their results as being due to a perceptual phenomenon—the law of visual angle. Further, they recommended adding depth cues to the VAS to increase accuracy on the task.

REVIEW SUMMARY

1. 1. Psychologists plan their experiments beforehand using an **experimental design**, which serves as a blueprint for the experiment.
2. You use the **multiple-group design** for experimental situations in which you have one **independent variable** (**IV**) that has three or more levels or conditions.
3. A multiple-group design may or may not use a **control group**. If there is a control group, there are at least two experimental groups in addition.
4. You form **independent groups** of research participants by **randomly assigning** them to treatment groups.
5. You form **correlated groups** of research participants by creating matched sets, using natural sets, or measuring each participant more than once (repeated measures).

CHECK YOUR PROGRESS

1. Why is the two-group design the building block for the multiple-group design?
2. The simplest possible multiple-group design would have _____ IV(s) and _____ treatment group(s).
3. What advantage(s) can you see in using a multiple-group design rather than a two-group design?
4. Devise an experimental question that could be answered with a multiple-group design that you could not answer with a two-group design.
5. Why are matched sets, repeated measures, and natural sets all considered *correlated-groups* designs?

Deciding on an Experimental Design

As in Chapter 10, we have to make a decision about how to design our potential experiment. Just as in Chapter 10, there are two multiple-group designs to choose from. However, researchers who want to design an experiment with one IV also need to choose between multiple-group designs and the two-group designs. In the next sections, we will examine the various advantages and disadvantages of these experimental designs. As we warned you in Chapter 10: Read carefully—you may be facing this choice yourself in the future!

Comparing the Multiple-Group and Two-Group Designs

The multiple-group design is highly similar to the two-group design. As a matter of fact, all you have to do to change your two-group design into a multiple-group design is add another level (or more) to your IV. Given this high degree of similarity, how would we compare these two designs?

In choosing a design for your experiment, your paramount concern is your experimental question. Does your question require only two groups to find an answer, or does it necessitate three or more groups? This question almost seems like a "no-brainer," but you should not take it for granted. Following the principle of parsimony from Chapter 10, we want to select the simplest design possible that will answer our question.

In Chapter 10 we provided you with an ideal situation for a two-group design: an experiment in which we merely wish to determine whether or not our IV has an effect. Often such an experiment is not necessary because that information already exists in the literature. You should never conduct an experiment to determine whether a particular IV has an effect without first conducting a thorough literature search (see Chapter 2). If you find no answer in a library search, then you should consider conducting a two-group (presence–absence) study. If, however, you find the answer to that basic question and wish to go further, then a multiple-group design might be appropriate.

After these considerations, what do you do when you face a situation in which either a two-group design or a multiple-group design is appropriate? Although this answer may sound odd, you should think about your (future) results. What will they look like? What will they mean? Most critically, what will the addition of any group(s) beyond the basic two tell you? If the information that you expect to find by adding a group or groups is important and meaningful, then by all means add the groups. If, however, you're not really certain what you might learn by adding to the two groups, then you may be complicating your life needlessly to do so.

Think back to the two student examples cited in this chapter. Did the researchers learn important information by adding an extra group to their two groups? Jones (2001) found that task performance differed with three different types of noise (no noise, white noise, and music). Some people would probably wish for more levels in this experiment rather than for fewer. In fact, one of your first thoughts when you read about Jones's experiment earlier may have been, "I wonder how students would respond to _____?" (Fill in the blank with a sound that bothers you or that you enjoy). You may believe that his experiment was not a fair test of the question about performance based on noise level, especially if you disagree with his noise choices. So it appears that Jones made a wise decision in using a multiple-group design rather than a two-group design. In fact, it might have been more informative had he used an even larger multiple-group design.

Walker et al. (1999) measured peoples' responses on the VAS to nine different distances. They clearly benefited by using a multiple-group design. If they had simply measured the responses on short or long distances, they would have found little error in the responses.

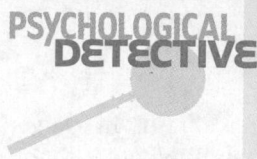

Suppose Walker et al. (1999) wanted to use a smaller or larger multiple-group design—say measuring people's responses over 5 or 15 distances rather than 9. Would it be possible to use such a small or large multiple-group design?

Could you use a multiple-group design with 5 or 15 groups or measurements? Sure you could. The only limitation would be a practical consideration—could you secure enough participants to take part (for matched sets or natural sets), or can the participants cope with being measured so many times (for repeated measures)? The Walker et al. experiment used repeated measures, so our concern would be for the experimental participants. In this case, all that would happen to the participants is that they would be measured either fewer or more times. So this experiment would be no problem to run over 5 measurement distances; participants would have fewer responses to make. The question is whether 5 distances would give the experimenters all the information they needed. On the other hand, using 15 measurements might make the task extremely difficult for the participants to discriminate; it would require more of the experimenters' time. Using 9 levels of an IV for repeated measures is quite unusual, so it is much more likely that other experimenters would use smaller, rather than larger, experimental designs.

In summary, the multiple-group and two-group designs are quite similar. However, there are important differences between them that you should consider when choosing an experimental design for your research project.

Comparing Multiple-Group Designs

As you might guess, our comparison of the multiple-independent-groups design to the multiple-correlated-groups design is going to be fairly similar to our comparison of the two-group designs in Chapter 10. However, practical considerations become somewhat more important in the multiple-group designs, so our conclusions will be somewhat different.

Choosing a Multiple-Group Design   Again, your first consideration in choosing an experimental design should always be your experimental question. Once you have decided on an experiment with one IV and three or more groups, you must determine whether you should use independent or correlated groups. If only one of those choices is viable, you have no further considerations to make. If, however, you could use either independent or correlated groups, you must make that decision before proceeding.

Control Issues   As with the two-group designs discussed in Chapter 10, your decision to use the multiple-independent-groups design versus the multiple-correlated-groups design revolves around control issues. The multiple-independent-groups design uses the control technique of randomly assigning participants to groups. If you have a substantial number of research participants (at least 10 per group), you can be fairly confident that random assignment will create equal groups.

Multiple-correlated-groups designs use the control techniques of matching, repeated measures, or natural pairs to assure equality of groups and to reduce error variability. Recall the equation that represents the general formula for a statistical test:

$$\text{statistic} = \frac{\text{between-groups variability}}{\text{error variability}}$$

Reducing the error variability in the denominator of the equation will result in a larger computed statistical value, thereby making it easier to reject the null hypothesis. You may remember from Chapter 11 that using a correlated-groups design reduces your degrees of freedom, which makes it somewhat more difficult to achieve statistical significance and reject the null hypothesis. However, the reduced error variability typically more than offsets the loss of *df*. Therefore, correlated designs often produce stronger tests for finding statistical significance.

Practical Considerations   Matters of practicality become quite important when we contemplate using a multiple-correlated-groups design. Let's think about each type of correlated design in turn. If we intend to use *matched sets*, we must consider the potential difficulty of finding three (or more) participants to match on the extraneous variable we choose. Suppose we conduct a learning experiment and thus wish to match our participants on IQ. How difficult will it be to find three, four, five, or more participants (depending on the number of levels we use) with the same IQ? If we cannot find enough to make a complete set of matches, then we cannot use those participants in our experiment. Therefore, we may lose potential research participants through the requirement of large matched sets. We may be limited in our use of *natural sets* by set size also. How much chance would you have of running an experiment on triplets, quadruplets, or quintuplets? Using animal littermates is probably the most common use of natural sets in multiple-group designs. When we use *repeated measures* in a multiple-group design, we are requiring each participant to be measured at least three times. This requirement necessitates more time for each participant or multiple trips to the laboratory, conditions the participants may not be willing to meet. We hope this message is clear: If you intend to use a multiple-correlated-groups design, plan it very carefully so that these basic practical considerations do not sabotage your experiment.

What about practical considerations in multiple-independent-groups designs? The multiple-independent-groups design is simpler than the correlated version. The practical factor you must take into account is the large number of research participants you will need to make random assignment feasible *and* to fill the multiple groups. If participants are not available in large numbers, you need to consider using a correlated design.

Drawing a definite conclusion about running independent versus correlated multiple-group designs is not simple. The correlated designs have some statistical advantages, but they also require you to take into account several practical matters that may make using such a design difficult. Independent designs are simple to implement, but they force you to recruit or obtain many research participants to assure equality of your groups. The best advice we can provide is to remind you that each experiment presents you with unique problems, opportunities, and questions. You need to be aware of the factors we have presented and to weigh them carefully in conjunction with your experimental question when you choose a specific research design for your experiment.

Variations on the Multiple-Group Design

In Chapter 10 we discussed two variations on the two-group design. Those same two variations are also possible with the multiple-group design.

Comparing Different Amounts of an IV This "variation" on the multiple-group design is not actually a variation at all—it is part of the basic design. Because the smallest possible multiple-group design would consist of three treatment groups, every multiple-group design must compare different amounts (or types) of an IV. Even if a multiple-group design has a control group, there are at least two different treatment groups in addition.

> **Placebo effect** An experimental effect that is due to expectation or suggestion rather than the IV.

If we already know that a particular IV has an effect, then we can use a multiple-group design to help us define the limits of that effect. In this type of experiment, we often add an important control in order to account for a possible **placebo effect**. For example, is it possible that some of the effects of coffee on our alertness are due to what we *expect* the coffee to do? If so, a proper control group would consist of people who drink decaffeinated coffee. These participants would be blind to the fact that their coffee does not contain caffeine. This group, without any caffeine, would show us whether there are any placebo effects of coffee.

> **Ex post facto research** A research approach in which the experimenter cannot directly manipulate the IV but can only classify, categorize, or measure the IV because it is predetermined in the participants (e.g., IV = sex).

Dealing with Measured IVs All the research examples we have cited in this chapter deal with manipulated IVs. It is also possible to use measured IVs in a multiple-group design. In Chapter 10 you learned that research we conduct with a measured rather than manipulated IV is termed **ex post facto research**. Remember that we cannot randomly assign participants to groups in such research because they already belong to certain groups. Thus, the groups may be different at the beginning of the research. We cannot draw cause-and-effect explanations from such an experiment because we do not directly control and manipulate the IV ourselves. Still, an ex post facto design can yield interesting information and, because the design does use some controls, we may be able to rule out some alternative explanations. Let's look at a student example of an ex post facto design with a measured IV.

Amanda Gray and her advisor Jennifer Lucas (2001) at Agnes Scott College in Decatur, Georgia, used an ex post facto approach in their study of commuters' perceptions of travel impedance and driver stress (see Chapter 19). They used Novaco, Kliewer, and Broquet's (1990) Subjective Impedance Scale to classify their participants' perceptions of travel impedance as high, average, or low. Why does this experimental design fit the multiple-group format? Does it have one IV? Yes, perception of travel impedance. Does it have three or more levels of that one IV? Yes, the high, average, or low perception. These perceptions were their measured IV—the researchers could not assign commuters to one of the different perception groups; they could only measure which level of perception each commuter exhibited.

Gray and Lucas (2001) found that the high-perceived-impedance group reported the highest level of driver stress, and the average group reported more driver stress than the low-perceived-impedance group. Notice that the multiple-group design allowed Gray and Lucas to detect a difference between one group versus the two other groups *and* a difference that occurred among all three groups. These types of findings show the advantage of the multiple-group design over the two-group design. Remember these various types of differences because we will return to them in Chapter 13 when we cover statistical analysis of multiple-group designs.

REVIEW SUMMARY

1. Experimenters often have to choose between multiple-group and two-group designs. Multiple-group designs are useful because they can add important information beyond a two-group design.
2. **Multiple-correlated-groups designs** provide extra advantages for experimental control relative to **multiple-independent-groups designs**.
3. Practical considerations in dealing with research participants make the multiple-correlated-groups designs considerably more complicated than multiple-independent-groups designs.
4. Multiple-group designs exist primarily to allow comparisons of different amounts (or types) of IVs.
5. Researchers can use measured IVs in multiple-group designs, which results in **ex post facto studies**.

CHECK YOUR PROGRESS

1. What is the real limit on the number of groups that can be included in a multiple-group design? What is the practical limit?
2. Make a list of the factors you would consider when choosing between a multiple-group design and a two-group design.
3. Correlated-groups designs are often advantageous to use because they _____.
4. Why are practical considerations of using a multiple-correlated-groups design more demanding than for using a two-correlated-groups design or a multiple-independent-groups design?
5. If we wished to compare personality traits of firstborn, lastborn, and only children, what type of design would we use? Would this represent a true experiment or an ex post facto study? Why?

KEY TERMS

Experimental design, *266*

Independent variable (IV), *266*

Principle of parsimony, *267*

Levels, *267*

Treatment groups, *268*

Independent groups, *269*

Correlated groups, *269*

Random assignment, *269*

LOOKING AHEAD

In this chapter, we furthered our knowledge about research design and how it fits with particular experimental questions. Specifically, we looked at an extension of the basic building-block design by using one IV and three or more groups. In the next chapter, we will look at the statistical analysis process for the multiple-group design.

Analyzing and Interpreting Experiments with More Than Two Groups

Before Your Statistical Analysis

We will remind you that in Chapter 11 you learned that experimental design and statistical analysis are intimately linked. You *must* go through the decision-making process we have outlined before you begin your experiment in order to avoid the possibility that you will run your experiment and collect your data only to find out that there is no statistical test that you can use to analyze your data.

One-way ANOVA A statistical test used to analyze data from an experimental design with one independent variable that has three or more groups (levels).

One-way ANOVA for independent groups A one-way ANOVA that uses independent groups of participants (also known as *completely randomized ANOVA*).

One-way ANOVA for correlated groups A one-way ANOVA that uses correlated groups of participants (also known as *repeated-measures ANOVA*).

Analyzing Multiple-Group Designs

In Chapter 12 we looked at designs that have one IV with three (or more) groups. The appropriate analysis for these multiple-group designs is the *analysis of variance* (ANOVA) statistical procedure. As you will see, we will also use ANOVA to analyze our designs that include more than one IV (see Chapter 15); hence there are different types of ANOVAs and we will need some way to distinguish between them. In this chapter, we are looking at an ANOVA for one IV; researchers typically refer to this procedure as a **one-way ANOVA**.

You remember that we have looked at both multiple-independent-groups and multiple-correlated-groups designs in Chapter 12. So, we need two different types of one-way ANOVA to analyze these two types of designs, just as we needed different *t* tests in Chapter 11. As you can see from Figure 12-1 (p. 267), when we assign our participants to multiple groups randomly, we will analyze our data with a **one-way ANOVA for independent groups**. On the other hand, if we use matched sets, natural sets, or repeated measures, we will use a **one-way ANOVA for correlated groups** to evaluate our data.

Planning Your Experiment

In Chapter 11 we featured the statistical analysis of data from an experiment designed to compare the response time of salesclerks as a function of their customers' clothing. That example, of course, cannot serve as a data analysis example for this chapter because it represented a two-group design.

PSYCHOLOGICAL DETECTIVE   Suppose we have already conducted the sample experiment covered in Chapter 11. How could we conduct a follow-up experiment using a multiple-groups design?

The *most* similar experiment would be one in which clerks at the mall waited on students dressed in three different types of clothing rather than just two. Suppose that we decide to investigate further because we found (in Chapter 11) that salespeople responded more quickly to customers in dressy clothes than to those dressed in sloppy clothes. We decide to add an intermediate clothing group—we choose to add casual clothing as our third group. Again, we need to consider the **operational definition** of our new IV group. We define casual clothing as slacks and shirts (e.g., khakis and polo shirts) for both male and female customers. We have 24 students in the class, so we have 8 students as "stimuli" in each of the three groups (one group for each type of clothing). We have the students go to the same store on the same day and randomly choose a department in which to browse. The store is large and employs many clerks, so there is no problem with finding a different clerk for each student. This random choice of clerks allows the salesclerks to be randomly assigned to the three groups (a requirement to create independent groups). An observer goes with the students to unobtrusively time the salesclerks' response time to each student, which is the DV. You can see the clerks' response times in Table 13-1. Let's discuss the basis behind the ANOVA procedure before we look at our statistical analyses.

Rationale of ANOVA

We introduced a concept closely related to ANOVA in the *Control Issues* section in Chapter 10; you may wish to refer back to that section. You will remember that variability in your data can be divided into two sources—**between-groups variability** and **error variability** (also known as **within-groups variability**). The between-groups variability represents the variation in the DV that is due to the IV, whereas the error variability is due to factors such as individual differences, errors in measurement, and extraneous variation. In other words, error variability refers to *any* variability in the data that is not a product of the IV. Look at Table 13-2, which is a slightly altered version of Table 13-1.

TABLE 13-1 SALESCLERKS' RESPONSE TIMES FOR HYPOTHETICAL CLOTHING STYLE EXPERIMENT

CLOTHING STYLES		
DRESSY	**SLOPPY**	**CASUAL**
37	50	39
38	46	38
44	62	47
47	52	44
49	74	50
49	69	48
54	77	70
69	76	55
Mean = 48.38	Mean = 63.25	Mean = 48.88

TABLE **13-2**   **SALESCLERKS' RESPONSE TIMES FOR HYPOTHETICAL CLOTHING STYLE EXPERIMENT**

PSYCHOLOGICAL DETECTIVE   What type of variability do you think is represented by the arrows in Table 13-2? What type of variability do you think is shown in the circled columns? If you have trouble with these questions, reread the previous paragraph.

The variability *between* the groups' response times represents the variability caused by the IV (the different types of clothing). Therefore, the arrows represent the between-groups variability. If the times differ among the three groups of clerks, the clothes should be responsible for the difference (assuming we have controlled extraneous variables). On the other hand, error variability should occur among the participants *within* each particular group (thus its name, *within-groups variability*); this is the variability represented by the circled columns. One major source of within-groups variability is the differences within all the participants in a group—what we have labeled individual differences. Different people (or nonhuman animals) will score differently on the DV simply because they are different organisms.

"Wait a minute," you may say. "What we have just described as within-groups variability—individual differences, measurement errors, and extraneous variation—can occur between the groups just as easily as within the groups." This thought represents very good thinking on your part. Your point is correct and is well taken. Thus, when we are calculating an ANOVA, we must change the formula that we reviewed in Chapter 12:

$$\text{statistic} = \frac{\text{between-groups variability}}{\text{error variability}}$$

The fact that we can find error between our groups as well as within our groups forces us to alter this formula to the general formula shown below for ANOVA. The F symbol is used for ANOVA in honor of Sir Ronald A. Fisher (1890–1962), who developed the ANOVA (Spatz, 2001).

$$F = \frac{\text{variability due to IV} + \text{error variability}}{\text{error variability}}$$

If our IV has a strong treatment effect and creates much more variability than all the error variability, we should find that the numerator of this equation is considerably larger than the denominator (see Figure 13-1A). The result, then, would be a large F ratio. If, on the other hand, the IV has absolutely no effect, there would be no variability due to the IV, meaning we would add 0 for that factor in the equation. In such a case, our F ratio should be close to 1 because the error variability between groups should approximately equal the error variability within groups. This situation is depicted in Figure 13-1B.

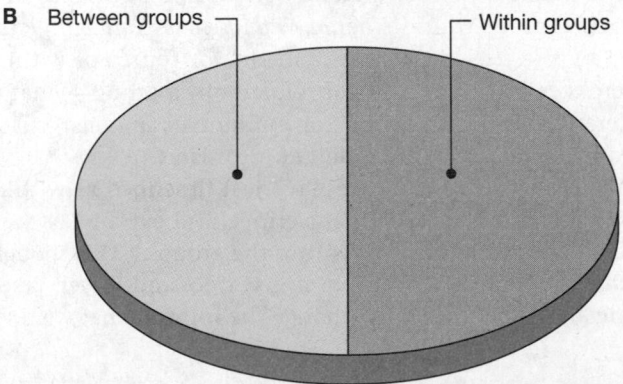

FIGURE 13-1 POSSIBLE DISTRIBUTIONS OF VARIABILITY IN AN EXPERIMENT.

The notion that has evolved for the ANOVA is that we are comparing the ratio of between-groups variability (variability due to the IV) to within-groups variability. Thus, the F ratio is conceptualized (and computed) with the following formula:

$$F = \frac{\text{between-groups variability}}{\text{within-groups variability}}$$

A simple way to think of ANOVA is that you are dividing the treatment effect plus error by error. When the IV has a significant effect on the DV, the F ratio will be large; when the IV has no effect or only a small effect, the F ratio will be small (near 1). You may wish to place a bookmark at this page—we will refer back to it shortly.

One-Way ANOVA for Independent Groups

With the addition of a third group, our experimental design has become slightly more complicated than the two-group design of Chapter 10. As you will see, adding a third group (or more) creates an interesting statistical problem for us so that we often need to compute an extra statistical test to explore significant findings. (Just in case you ever see such an analysis, one-way ANOVA can also be used for experiments with only two groups. We presented only the t test for such designs to minimize overlap and possible confusion.)

Calculating ANOVA by Hand

Let's begin with a quick review of our experimental design. We have three different groups of salesclerks waiting on customers dressed in dressy, casual, or sloppy clothing.

PSYCHOLOGICAL DETECTIVE   Why does this experimental design require a one-way ANOVA for independent groups?

Three important aspects of the design dictate a one-way ANOVA for independent groups. First, there is one IV (clothing). Second, there are three levels of the IV (dressy, casual, sloppy). Third, the salesclerks are in independent groups—the groups were formed randomly and there is no matching, repeated measures, or natural sets.

The ANOVA is complicated enough that we cannot give you one simple formula for it as we could with a t test. Instead, we must calculate the variability in the DV scores that is attributable to various sources. From our formula for F that we saw just a few paragraphs ago, you can see that we need to find the variability associated with the IV (between groups) and error (within groups). Just as with our SD formula, we need to find the sum of the squared deviation scores (the difference between each score and the overall mean, squared and summed; see Chapter 6). In ANOVA terminology, we refer to

Sum of squares The amount of variability in the DV attributable to each source.

this sum as the **sum of squares**. Again, just as with the *SD* calculation, we will use a simpler, more accurate formula for calculating the sum of squares by hand. In a one-way ANOVA for independent samples, we need to calculate the sum of squares for three sources: total, between groups (due to the IV), and error (all variability *not* due to the IV). Our calculations appear in Table 13-3. By now, you should be familiar with our initial steps from Chapter 6; we calculate the sum for each group's scores, we square all the scores, and we calculate the sum of the squared scores for each group (see Table 13-3a).

Total sum of squares The total amount of variability in the data from an experiment.

Total Sum of Squares   The formula for calculating the **total sum of squares** appears in Table 13-3b; it is similar to the formula that we have been using since first encountering standard deviations. Thus, although we are using it in a slightly different context, it should not cause you any difficulty. Notice that we are working with total scores for the three groups and overall. After we find the total sum of squares (3688), we will partition (divide) it into its two components (IV and error).

Treatment sum of squares The amount of variability in the data due to the IV.

Treatment Sum of Squares   The **treatment sum of squares** is the variability that is due to the three different types of clothing (IV) in this particular experiment. Again, you should notice a basic similarity in this formula and those we have used previously (see Table 13-3c). Notice that each of the three groups contributes variability in this formula. This process should make sense to you because we are finding the amount of variability *between* the groups.

Error sum of squares The amount of variability in the data due to sources other than the IV.

Error Sum of Squares   The **error sum of squares** is the variability that is due to all sources other than clothing (IV) in this experiment (factors such as individual differences, errors in measurement, and extraneous variation). The basics of the formula again are similar to what we've seen and used before (see Table 13-3d). Notice that these computations work with each group individually before summing. We hope this process makes sense because we are computing the amount of variability *within* the groups.

When we have computed all three sources of variability, we can double-check our calculations. The sum of the treatment sum of squares (1141.75) and the error sum of squares (2546.25) should equal our total sum of squares (3688). If they do not match, you have made a calculation error somewhere.

Mean Square   Based on our generic formula for *F*, you might expect to simply divide the treatment sum of squares by the error sum of squares to find your *F* ratio. However, there is an intermediate step: We must first compute our **mean square** for each of these sums of squares. As you might guess from the word "mean," mean square is similar to the average amount of variability attributable to each source. Let us explain and clarify: If we simply divide the treatment sum of squares by the error sum of squares, that is an unfair comparison that would favor the error term. What we mean by "favoring the error term" is

Mean square The "averaged" variability for each source; computed by dividing each source's sum of squares by its *df*.

TABLE 13-3 CALCULATIONS FOR ONE-WAY ANOVA FOR INDEPENDENT SAMPLES

Salesclerks' Time to Respond to Customers Based on Customer Clothing

a. Find the sum of scores for each group. Square each score and sum those squares by group. Find the sum across conditions for each clerk (or matched clerks).

Dressy	D^2	Sloppy	S^2	Casual	C^2	Σ All Scores	Σ All Squared Scores
37	1,369	50	2,500	39	1,521		
38	1,444	46	2,116	38	1,444		
44	1,936	62	3,844	47	2,209		
47	2,209	52	2,704	44	1,936		
49	2,401	74	5,476	50	2,500		
49	2,401	69	4,761	48	2,304		
54	2,916	77	5,929	70	4,900		
69	4,761	76	5,776	55	3,025		
Σ 387	19,437	506	33,106	391	19,839	1,284	72,382

b. Calculate the total sum of squares with a formula that should remind you of calculating a *SD*:

$$SS_{tot} = \Sigma X^2 - (\Sigma X)^2/N = 72,382 - (1,284)^2/24 = 72,382 - 68,694 = 3,688$$

c. Calculate the clothing sum of squares (again, this step should seem familiar):

$$SS_{clo} = \Sigma[(\Sigma X)^2/n] - (\Sigma X)^2/N = 387^2/8 + 506^2/8 + 391^2/8 - (1284)^2/24$$

$$= 18,721.125 + 32,004.5 + 19,110.125 - 68,694 = 1141.75$$

d. Now we calculate the error sum of squares:

$$SS_{error} = \Sigma\,[\Sigma X^2 - (\Sigma X)^2/N] = (19,437 - 387^2/8) + (33,106 - 506^2/8) + (19,839 - 391^2/8)$$

$$= 715.875 + 1,101.5 + 728.875 = 2,546.25$$

e. We must calculate the *df* for each of the sums of squares:

$$df_{tot} = N - 1 = 24 - 1 = 23$$

$$df_{clo} = n_{clo} - 1 = 3 - 1 = 2$$

$$df_{error} = N - n_{groups} = 24 - 3 = 21$$

f. To find our mean squares, we divide the sums of squares for our IV and error by their respective *df*:

$$MS_{clo} = SS_{clo}/df_{clo} = 1,141.75/2 = 570.88$$

$$MS_{error} = SS_{error}/df_{error} = 2,546.25/21 = 121.25$$

g. Now, to find our *F* ratio, we divide the MS of the IV by the MS for the error term:

$$F = MS_{clo}/MS_{error} = 570.88/121.25 = 4.71$$

h. To find the effect size, η^2 (eta = squared), use the following formula:

$$\eta^2 = (F)(df_{clo})/(F)(df_{clo}) + df_{error}$$

$$= 4.71(2)/4.71(2) + 21$$

$$= 9.42/30.42 = .31$$

that there are many more potential sources for error variation than for treatment variation. In this experiment, there are only three treatment groups, but there are 24 different salesclerks. Thus, each sum of squares is based on a different number of deviations from the mean (Keppel, Saufley, & Tokunaga, 1992). In this case, if you divided the treatment sum of squares by the error mean square, you would find a very small ratio, which would be misleading.

Degrees of freedom
The ability of a number in a specified set to assume any value.

In order to directly compare the error and treatment effects, we must calculate a mean square for each. However, rather than dividing the treatment sum of squares by the number of treatment groups and the error sum of squares by the number of participants, we instead divide them by their respective **degrees of freedom (*df*)**. The *df* (see Table 13-3e) for the treatment effect is equal to the number of groups minus one (i.e., $3 - 1 = 2$ in this case). The *df* for the error term equals the number of participants minus the number of groups (i.e., $24 - 3 = 21$ in this case). The total *df* equals the number of participants minus one (i.e., $24 - 1 = 23$ in this experiment). Just as with the mean squares, the total *df* is equal to the sum of the *df* for the treatment and error effects ($21 + 2 = 23$).

Variance A single number that represents the total amount of variation in a distribution; also, the square of the standard deviation; σ^2.

Now we are ready to compute our mean squares. As you can see in Table 13-3f, the mean square for both the treatment and error terms is equal to that term's sum of squares divided by its *df* (treatment = $1,141.75/2 = 570.88$; error = $2,546.25/21 = 121.25$).

We should note at this point that a mean square is analogous to an estimate of the **variance**, which you should remember (see Chapter 6) as being equal to the square of the *SD* (σ^2). Once we have the mean squares, we can then create our ratio of variation. Rather than drawing pie charts like those in Figure 13-1, we compute an *F* ratio to compare the two sources of variation.

F Ratio Referring to the bookmark we advised you to use a few pages back, we find that the *F* ratio is equal to the between-groups variability (due to the IV) divided by the within-groups variability (due to error). Because we are using mean squares as our estimates of variability, the equation for our *F* ratio becomes

$$F = \frac{\text{mean square between groups}}{\text{mean square within groups}}$$

Thus, we calculated our *F* ratio of 4.71 as shown in Table 13-3g by dividing 570.88 by 121.25.

PSYCHOLOGICAL DETECTIVE Look back at Figure 13-1. Can you draw a comparable figure for this *F* ratio?

Our *F* ratio of 4.71 means that the variability due to the IV (clothing) is almost 5 times as large as the variability due to other sources (error). Thus, your drawing should have

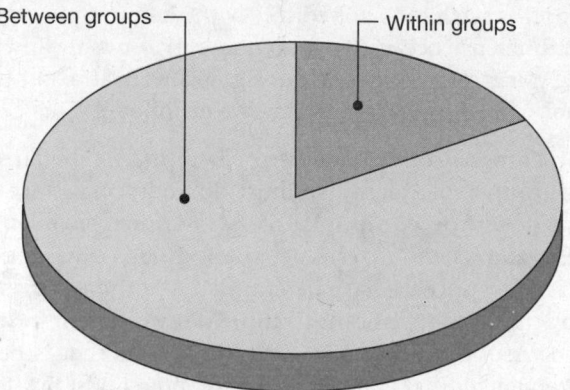

Between groups ─┐   ┌─ Within groups

FIGURE 13-2 DISTRIBUTION OF VARIABILITY FOR DIFFERENT CLOTHING EXPERIMENT.

had the within-groups variability "pie wedge" as even a smaller piece than that shown in Figure 13-1a. Your drawing should look something like Figure 13-2. The larger the F ratio, the larger the between-groups pie wedge would be in comparison to the within-groups wedge.

Now that we have our F ratio, we need to find the probability of it occurring by chance. Remember in Chapter 11, we used our t ratio and df to find the probability of chance from the t table. For ANOVA, this activity is somewhat different than using a printed t table because in ANOVA we have two values for df. Remember that our degrees of freedom are 2 (between groups, in the numerator) and 21 (within groups, in the denominator). When we look in the F table (see Table A-4), the column shows the numerator df and the row shows the denominator df. In this case, you must find 2 in the numerator column and 21 on the denominator line and locate the intersection of those two numbers. At that point you will see 3.47 as the .05 cutoff and 5.78 as the .01 cutoff. Because our F value of 4.71 is between these two numbers, the probability that it could have occurred by chance is less than .05 but greater than .01. Thus, you should write $p < .05$ *or* $.01 < p < .05$ (to be as specific as possible). Sherlock Holmes stated, "I could only say what was the balance of probability" (Doyle, 1927, p. 93).

PSYCHOLOGICAL DETECTIVE Given that $p < .05$ (or $.01 < p < .05$), what conclusion is appropriate about the effects of clothing on salesclerks' responses?

Part of the answer to this question is old, and part is new. The old part is that $p < .05$ tells us that there is a significant difference (i.e., not due to chance). Thus, we know that the different types of customers' clothes affected the clerks' responses. With the two-group design, we would be finished with our calculations at this point and could go on to interpreting our statistics in words. With significant findings in a two-group design, we merely note the higher mean and conclude that it is significantly higher than the other mean. However, this decision procedure is not correct with the multiple-group design when we find a significant difference because we have more than two means. We know there is significance among our means because of our significant F ratio, but which one is different from which one? From a significant F ratio, we cannot tell.

> **Post hoc comparisons**
> Statistical comparisons made between group means after finding a significant F ratio.

Post hoc Comparisons   To discern where the significance lies in a multiple-group experiment, we must do additional statistical tests known as **post hoc comparisons** (also known as *follow-up tests*). These tests allow us to determine which groups differ significantly from each other once we have determined that there is overall significance (by finding a significant F ratio). Many different post hoc tests exist, and there is much debate over these tests that is beyond the scope of this text. Simply remember that you will need to conduct post hoc tests if you find overall significance in a one-way ANOVA.

In Table 13-4, you see the calculations for a post hoc test known as the Tukey HSD (an abbreviation for *honestly significant difference*). The formula for the Tukey HSD is fairly simple; we divide the differences between pairs of means by our SE. After calculating your value, you must use Table A-5 to find its probability. As with most statistical tests, finding that $p < .05$ is sufficient to detect a difference between two groups.

TABLE 13-4   CALCULATIONS FOR TUKEY HSD

$HSD = (M_1 - M_2) / s_{\bar{X}}$ where $s_{\bar{X}} = \sqrt{MS_{error}/n}$

Because all our groups have 8 clerks in them, $s_{\bar{X}}$ will remain a constant, so we can calculate it first:

$s_{\bar{X}} = \sqrt{MS_{error}/n} = \sqrt{121.25/8} = \sqrt{15.156} = 3.893$

Comparing clerks waiting on customers in dressy clothing to those waiting on customers in sloppy clothes:

$HSD = (M_1 - M_2)/s_{\bar{X}} = (48.38 - 63.25)/3.893 = -14.87/3.893 = -3.82$

Comparing clerks waiting on customers in sloppy clothing to those waiting on customers in casual clothes:

$HSD = (M_1 - M_2)/s_{\bar{X}} = (63.25 - 48.88)/3.893 = 14.37/3.893 = 3.69$

Finally, comparing clerks waiting on customers in dressy clothes to those waiting on customers in casual clothes:

$HSD = (M_1 - M_2)/s_{\bar{X}} = (48.38 - 48.88)/3.893 = -0.50/3.893 = -0.13$

Using Table A-5, we find that the critical HSD with 20 df_{error} (21 is not listed) for an IV with 3 levels is 3.58 at the .05 level and 4.64 at the .01 level. We can ignore the sign of our calculated HSDs because the difference between means could be in either direction (two-tailed).

Thus, we determine that there is a difference in two of the three comparisons: dressy versus sloppy and sloppy versus casual (both differences at $p < .05$). By checking the means, we find that the clerks were slower in waiting on customers in sloppy clothing than customers in either dressy *or* casual clothing. There was no difference in the time clerks took to wait on customers in dressy and casual clothing.

The Tukey test allows you to test all pairwise comparisons, meaning that you can test the difference between all sets of two means (Keppel, Saufley, & Tokunaga, 1992). In looking at Table 13-4, we see that Group 2 is significantly different at the .05 level from both Group 1 and Group 3 according to the Tukey test. This result means that the clerks took significantly longer to wait on sloppily-dressed students (63.25 seconds) than either those in casual (48.88 seconds) or those in dressy clothes (48.38 seconds). No other groups differed significantly from each other, meaning that there was no statistical difference in the time it took clerks to wait on students dressed well or casually.

We have now finished with our calculations of our one-way ANOVA for independent groups. First, from our ANOVA, we found that the type of clothing customers wore did affect salesclerks' response times. Because we had three groups and, thus, three means, we turned to post hoc comparisons to discover where the differences were significant. Using the Tukey HSD test, we found that salesclerks waited on customers in dressy or casual clothing more quickly than they waited on sloppily dressed customers.

> **Source table** A table that contains the results of ANOVA. *Source* refers to the source of the different types of variation.

Source Table   As with all statistical results, there is a standardized way of reporting the results. The output from ANOVA is typically referred to as a **source table**. In Table 13-5, you see "Source" printed on the left side of the page. Source tables get their name because they isolate and highlight the different sources of variation in the data. In the one-way ANOVA table, you see two sources of variation: between groups and within groups.

 PSYCHOLOGICAL DETECTIVE   Do you remember what the terms "between groups" and "within groups" refer to?

Between groups is synonymous with our treatment (IV) effect, and *within groups* is our error variance. The sum of squares, the sum of the squared deviations around the mean, is used to represent the total variability of the DV in the experiment (Kirk, 1968). In Table 13-5, you see that the total sum of squares (variability in the entire

TABLE 13-5   SOURCE TABLE FOR ONE-WAY ANOVA FOR INDEPENDENT GROUPS

Source	Sum of squares	df	Mean square	F	p
Between groups (clothing)	1,141.75	2	570.88	4.71	.02
Within groups (error)	2,546.25	21	121.25		
Total	3,688.00	23			

experiment) is 3,688, which we partitioned into between-groups sum of squares (1,141.75) and within-groups sum of squares (2,546.25). Remember that the between-groups sum of squares added to the within-group sum of squares should always be equal to the total sum of squares (1,141.75 + 2,546.25 = 3,688).

In the next column, we report the *df* for each source of variation. Again, as with the sums of squares, the between-groups *df* added to the within-group *df* must equal the total *df* (2 + 21 = 23). The next column shows the mean squares for the two sources of variability (each sum of squares divided by its *df*).

After reporting the mean squares, we have a column for our *F* ratio. Because it represents the effect of the IV, we write the *F* ratio on the line for the between groups source. Finally, we report the probability of chance for our *F* ratio. Interestingly, there is no standard way to report the results from our post hoc comparisons in a source table. Later we will show you that there *is* a standard way to report those results in text. If you wanted, you could list the post hoc findings under the source table.

Computer Analysis of ANOVA for Independent Groups

It is even more common for psychologists to use a computer program to analyze a one-way ANOVA than the *t* tests we covered in Chapter 11. Once again we will look at generic computer output to give you experience with typical output so that you can better generalize your knowledge to the particular statistical package that is available to you. The results appear in Table 13-6. A quick glance at the source table shows you that the *F* ratio, as calculated by the computer, is 4.71; thus, our hand and computer calculations are in agreement.

Interpreting Computer Statistical Output We examine results from a one-way ANOVA because we have one IV with three groups. We used the ANOVA for independent samples because we randomly assigned salesclerks to the three different clothing conditions. The DV scores represent the clerks' response times to differently attired customers.

As usual, we first look for information about descriptive statistics. You will find the descriptive statistics in the top portion of Table 13-6. Before going on, remember that we recommended that you make sure you have entered your data correctly in the computer by checking the means using a calculator. It will take only a few minutes but will spare you from using an incorrect set of results if you somehow goofed when you put the numbers in the computer. We can see that Group 1 (clerks responding to customers in dressy clothes) had a mean response time of 48.38 seconds, Group 2 (sloppy clothing) had a mean of 63.25 seconds, and Group 3 (casual clothes) responded in 48.88 seconds on the average. So, we do see numerical differences among these means, but we do not know if the differences are large enough to be significant until we examine the inferential statistics. We also see the *SD* and SE (*SD* divided by $\sqrt{n}$) for each group (the times for Group 2 are more variable than those of the other two groups), as well as 95% confidence intervals (see Chapter 6). You may remember that confidence intervals provide a range of scores between which μ (the true population mean) should fall. Thus, we are 95% confident that the interval of 40.34 to 57.41 seconds contains the population mean for all clerks responding to customers in casual clothing.

The inferential statistics appear immediately below the descriptive statistics. We see the heading "One-way ANOVA," which lets us know that we have actually computed a

TABLE 13-6 COMPUTER OUTPUT FOR ONE-WAY ANOVA FOR INDEPENDENT SAMPLES

GROUP	N	MEAN	SD	SE	95% CONF. INT.
1 (DRESSY)	8	48.38	10.11	3.57	39.92–56.83
2 (SLOPPY)	8	63.25	12.54	4.44	52.76–73.74
3 (CASUAL)	8	48.88	10.20	3.61	40.34–57.41

ONE-WAY ANOVA: RESP. TIME BY CLOTHING

SOURCE	SUM OF SQUARES	df	MEAN SQUARES	F RATIO	PROB.
BETWEEN GROUPS	1,141.75	2	570.88	4.71	.02
WITHIN GROUPS	2,546.25	21	121.25		
TOTAL	3,688.00	23			

POST HOC TEST: TUKEY HSD WITH SIGNIFICANCE LEVEL .05

* INDICATES SIGNIFICANT DIFFERENCES SHOWN FOR PAIRINGS

		G r p 1	G r p 2	G r p 3
MEAN	CLOTHING			
48.38	GROUP 1			
63.25	GROUP 2	*	*	
48.88	GROUP 3			

one-way ANOVA. The subheading shows us that we have analyzed the variable "Resp. time" in relation to the "Clothing" variable. This label simply means that we have analyzed our DV (Resp. time, the clerks' response times) by our IV (Clothing, the three styles of dress). Did the different clothing styles have an effect? From Table 13-6, you find that the "F ratio" is 4.71, which matches what we calculated by hand. The next entry you see is the "Prob." value, .02. This probability of chance for these data (if the null hypothesis is true) is certainly lower than .05, so the difference is significant. Although the computer printed the probability for you, you could also determine the significance level from the F table (see Table A-3). Of course, you would get the same significance level we found after our hand calculations: $p < .05$ or $.01 < p < .05$. Remember that although we would be through with our computer output if we were using a two-group design, there is still the step of post hoc tests because we ran a multiple-groups design.

At the bottom of Table 13-6, you see the results of the Tukey post hoc tests. We see that Group 2 is significantly different at the .05 level from both Group 1 and Group 3 according to the Tukey test. This result means that the clerks took significantly longer to wait on sloppily-dressed students (63.25 seconds) than either those in casual (48.88 seconds) or those in dressy clothes (48.38 seconds). No other groups differed significantly from each other, meaning that there was no statistical difference in the time it took clerks to wait on students dressed well or casually.

As in Chapter 11, we hope that you are learning general principles about computer printouts rather than specific words or terms for which you will blindly search. If you understand the general principles, interchanging *between groups* with *clothing* (or the name of some other IV) should not be problematical for you—different statistical programs may simply use different ways of getting at the same thing (much like having slightly different names for the same test). For example, don't be surprised to see the label *error* rather than *within groups*—both terms mean the same thing. The important conclusion is that, given the same data, any two programs should find the same results.

Translating Statistics into Words   Let us remind you, as we did in Chapter 11, that the results of any statistical test are only as good as your experimental procedures. In other words, if you have conducted a sloppy experiment, your statistical results will be meaningless. When we draw the conclusion that our IV has caused a difference in the DV scores, we are assuming that we conducted a well-controlled experiment and that we removed extraneous variables from the scene. If you find that extraneous variables have confounded your experiment, you should not interpret your statistics because they are now meaningless. This is the same reason detectives must learn specific ways to collect evidence in the field. If they collect contaminated evidence, all the lab tests in the world cannot yield a definitive conclusion.

Based on our inferential statistics, we can conclude that the clothing customers wear is important because clerks took differing amounts of time to wait on customers depending on how they were dressed.

PSYCHOLOGICAL DETECTIVE   Although this conclusion is technically correct, it is a poor conclusion. Why? How would you revise this conclusion to make it better?

This conclusion is poor because it is incomplete. Reread the sentence and decide what you learn from it. All you know is that salesclerks waited on students who wore some type of clothing more quickly than students who wore some other clothing. Thus, you know that clothes can make a difference but you don't know which type of clothing led to faster responses. To write a good conclusion, we must go back to our inferential statistics, particularly the post hoc tests. In Table 13-6, we find that students wearing dressy clothes were waited on in 48.38 seconds, students wearing sloppy clothes received attention in 63.25 seconds, and students wearing casual clothes got help in 48.88 seconds. The significant F ratio lets us know that there is significance *somewhere* among those means. The Tukey post hoc comparison tests informed us that the differences between Group 2 and both Groups 1 and 3 were significant. To interpret this difference, we must examine our descriptive statistics. When we examine the means, we are able to conclude that students in shabby clothes got help significantly more slowly than the students in dressy or casual clothes. *No other mean differences were significant.*

We must determine how to communicate our statistical findings in APA format. We will use a combination of words and numbers. There are many different ways to write this set of findings in an experimental report. Here is one example:

> The effect of different clothing on salespersons' response time was significant, $F(2, 21) = 4.71$, $p = .02$. The proportion of variance accounted for by the clothing effect (η^2) was .31. Tukey tests indicated ($p < .05$) that clerks waiting on customers dressed in sloppy clothes ($M = 63.25$, $SD = 11.73$) responded more slowly than clerks waiting on customers in dressy ($M = 48.38$, $SD = 9.46$) or casual clothes ($M = 48.88$, $SD = 9.55$). The response times of clerks waiting on customers in dressy and casual clothes did not differ from each other.

The words alone should convey the meaning of our results. Could someone with no statistical background read and understand these sentences if we removed the numbers? We think so. The inferential test results explain our finding to readers who have a statistical background. The descriptive statistics allow the reader to observe exactly how the groups performed and how variable that performance was. We used a new effect size measure so that you can see there is more than one type available. The effect size information reported here, η^2, tells you the proportion of variance in the DV (response times) accounted for by the IV (clothing). (An easy way to calculate η^2 simply uses the F ratio and the between-groups and within-group df; see Table 13-3h.) The reader has an expectation about what information to look for because we write our results in this standard APA format. You will find this type of communication in results sections in experimental articles. As you read more results sections, this type of communication will become familiar to you.

REVIEW SUMMARY

1. When your experimental design consists of one IV with three or more groups, and you have randomly assigned participants to groups, the proper statistical analysis is a one-way ANOVA for independent groups (**completely randomized ANOVA**).

2. ANOVA partitions the variability in your DV into **between-groups variability** (due to the IV) and **within-group variability** (due to sources of error). We then compute a ratio between these two sources of variation known as the F ratio.

3. ANOVA results are typically shown in a **source table**, which lists each source of variance and displays the F ratio for the effect of the IV.

4. A significant *F* ratio merely indicates that there is a significant difference some-
    where among your various groups. **Post hoc comparisons** are necessary to
    determine which groups differ from each other.
5. An effect size index, η^2, indicates the proportion of variance in the DV accounted
    for by the IV.
6. Using APA format for our statistical results allows us to convey our findings in
    both words and numbers in a clear and concise manner.

CHECK YOUR PROGRESS

1. Suppose you wish to compare the ACT or SAT scores of the freshman, sophomore,
    junior, and senior classes at your school to determine whether differences exist
    among those students. Draw a block diagram of this design. What design and sta-
    tistical test would you use for this research?
2. When we look at our *F* ratio and its probability in a multiple-group design, why
    can't we examine the descriptive statistics directly to reach a conclusion about our
    experiment?
3. The variability that is due to our IV is termed the _____ _____ variance, whereas
    the variability due to individual differences and error is the _____ _____ variance.
4. Suppose you conducted the experiment summarized in Question 2 and found the
    following statistics: $F(3, 24) = 4.07$, $p < .05$. On the basis of this information, what
    could you conclude?
5. What additional information do you need in Question 4 to draw a full and com-
    plete conclusion?
6. You decide to test how people's moods vary by the four seasons. Can you use the
    experimental design you have read about in this chapter for this research project?
    How would you design the project?
7. You choose to test people's preferences for fast-food hamburgers, and you have
    McDonald's, Burger King, Wendy's, and White Castle franchises in your town.
    How could you use a between-groups design for this project?

One-Way ANOVA for Correlated Groups

Now we will look at the one-way ANOVA for correlated samples. The sample experiment about clothing and clerks' response times we have used so far in the chapter fits
the multiple-group design for independent samples and thus is not appropriate to analyze with the one-way ANOVA for correlated samples.

 PSYCHOLOGICAL DETECTIVE

How could the experiment concerning salesclerks' reactions to customers' style of dress be modified so that it used correlated groups
rather than independent groups?

To be correct, you should have proposed the use of matched sets, natural sets, or repeated measures in your modified experiment. The best choices would involve matched sets or repeated measures; we don't think that using natural sets is feasible in this situation—you're not using littermates, and finding sets of triplets who are all salesclerks is most unlikely! If you chose matched sets, you must decide on a matching variable. It is difficult to know what variable on which you should match salesclerks that would be related to their reactions to different clothing styles. Matched sets would not be a good choice for forming correlated groups.

Imagine that you conduct your experiment at a small store that employs only a few salesclerks. In order to have enough data points, you decide to have each salesclerk respond to a customer in each of the three clothing groups. Because you would measure each clerk's response times to all three styles of dress, you would control possible individual differences between the clerks. (Another scenario that might lead you to use repeated measures would occur if you decided that it is likely that some variable in salesclerks, such as attitude, might affect their response times to customers in different types of clothing. Using repeated measures would allow you to essentially cancel out differences between different clerks, because each clerk would wait on a customer in each clothing group.)

You are now ready to begin the experiment. The students each dress in one of the three styles and enter the store. Because we are using repeated measures, we know for certain that the clerks in the three groups are equated (because they are the same clerks in each group). Given this hypothetical example, the scores in Table 13-1 would now represent sets of response times from eight salesclerks. (Remember that in the real world, it is not legitimate to analyze the same data with two different statistical tests. This is a textbook, certainly not the real world, and we are doing this as an example only.)

Calculating ANOVA by Hand

Again, the correlated-groups ANOVA is complicated enough that we cannot give you one simple formula because we must calculate the variability in the DV scores that is attributable to various sources. Once again, we need to find the variability associated with the IV (between groups) and error (within groups). In a one-way ANOVA for independent samples, we calculated the sum of squares for three sources: total, between groups (due to the IV), and error (all variability *not* due to the IV). However, in this case, we must also calculate the sum of squares for our participants. Because we expect our participants' scores to be correlated, we are going to be able to take that variability out of the error variability. Our calculations appear in Table 13-7. Our initial steps are familiar; we calculate the sum for each group's scores, square all the scores, and calculate the sum of the squared scores for each group (see Table 13-7a). In addition, note that we perform the same type of calculation across participants that we do for each group.

Total Sum of Squares   The formula for calculating the total sum of squares appears in Table 13-7b; it is again similar to the *SD* formula that we have been using. We are working with total scores for the three groups and overall. After we find the total sum of squares (3,688), we will partition (divide) it into its three components (IV, participants, and error).

TABLE 13-7 CALCULATIONS FOR ONE-WAY ANOVA FOR CORRELATED SAMPLES

Salesclerks' Time to Respond to Customers Based on Customer Clothing

a. Find the sum of scores for each group. Square each score and sum those squares by group. Find the sum across conditions for each clerk (or matched clerks).

Dressy	D^2	Sloppy	S^2	Casual	C^2	Sum by Clerk	Σ All Squared Scores
37	1,369	50	2,500	39	1,521	126	
38	1,444	46	2,116	38	1,444	122	
44	1,936	62	3,844	47	2,209	153	
47	2,209	52	2,704	44	1,936	143	
49	2,401	74	5,476	50	2,500	173	
49	2,401	69	4,761	48	2,304	166	
54	2,916	77	5,929	70	4,900	201	
69	4,761	76	5,776	55	3,025	200	
Σ 387	19,437	506	33,106	391	19,839	1,284	72,382

b. Calculate the total sum of squares with a formula that should look familiar:

$$SS_{tot} = \Sigma X^2 - (\Sigma X)^2/N = 72{,}382 - (1{,}284)^2/24 = 72{,}382 - 68{,}694 = 3{,}688$$

c. Calculate the clothing sum of squares (again, this step should seem familiar):

$$SS_{clo} = \Sigma\,[(\Sigma X)^2/n] - (\Sigma X)^2/N = 387^2/8 + 506^2/8 + 391^2/8 - (1{,}284)^2/24$$

$$= 18{,}721.125 + 32{,}004.5 + 19{,}110.125 - 68{,}694 = 1{,}141.75$$

d. Calculate the participant sum of squares (this step is new, but uses the same general principle you have probably noticed by now) by summing across each clerk (participant):

$$SS_{part} = \Sigma\,[(\Sigma P)^2/n] - (\Sigma X)^2/N$$

$$= 126^2/3 + 122^2/3 + 153^2/3 + 143^2/3 + 173^2/3 + 166^2/3 + 201^2/3 + 200^2/3 - (1{,}284)^2/24$$

$$= 5{,}292 + 4{,}961.33 + 7{,}803 + 6{,}816.33 + 9{,}976.33 + 9{,}185.33 + 13{,}467 + 13{,}333.33 - 68{,}694$$

$$= 2{,}140.65$$

e. Now we calculate the error sum of squares by subtraction:

$$SS_{error} = SS_{tot} - SS_{clo} - SS_{part} = 3{,}688 - 1{,}141.75 - 2{,}140.65 = 405.60$$

f. We must calculate the *df* for each of the sums of squares:

$$df_{tot} = N - 1 = 24 - 1 = 23$$

$$df_{part} = n_{part} - 1 = 8 - 1 = 7$$

$$df_{clo} = n_{clo} - 1 = 3 - 1 = 2$$

$$df_{error} = (n_{part} - 1)(n_{clo} - 1) = (7)(2) = 14$$

g. To find our mean squares, we divide the sums of squares for our IV and error by their respective *df*:

$$MS_{clo} = SS_{clo}/df_{clo} = 1{,}141.75/2 = 570.88$$

$$MS_{error} = SS_{error}/df_{error} = 405.60/14 = 28.97$$

h. Now, to find our *F* ratio, we divide the MS of the IV by the MS for the error term:

$$F = MS_{clo}/MS_{error} = 570.88/28.97 = 19.71$$

Treatment Sum of Squares   The treatment sum of squares is the variability that is due to the three different types of clothing (IV) in this particular experiment. There is a basic similarity in this formula and those we have used previously (see Table 13-7c). Each treatment group contributes variability in this formula; we continue to find the amount of variability between the groups. However, because the participants can be the same (repeated measures) or somewhat the same (matched groups), you may hear this variability referred to as within group variability.

> **Participant sum of squares**   In an ANOVA for correlated groups, the variability that is due to individual differences among the participants.

Participant Sum of Squares   The **participant sum of squares** is the variability that is due to differences between participants (based on the old terminology, you may hear this referred to as *subjects* sum of squares). Because we have a variety of different participants in any experiment, we would expect individual differences to create some variability in the data (see Table 13-7d).

Error Sum of Squares   The error sum of squares is the variability that is due to all sources other than clothing (IV) and participants in this experiment (in the between-groups ANOVA, error sum of squares included individual differences, but in this analysis, it includes only errors in measurement and extraneous variation). The formula is simple because we obtain the error (what is left over) by subtraction (see Table 13-7e).

Mean Square   As we did earlier in this chapter, in order to directly compare the error and treatment effects, we must calculate a mean square for each. You should remember that we divide them by their respective *df* (see Table 13-7f). The *df* for the treatment effect is equal to the number of groups minus one (i.e., 3 − 1 = 2 in this case). The *df* for participants is the number of participants in a group minus one (i.e., 8 − 1 = 7). The *df* for the error term equals the *df* for treatment multiplied by the *df* for participants (i.e., 2 × 7 = 14). The total *df* equals the total number of observations (data points) minus one (i.e., 24 − 1 = 23 in this case). The total *df* is equal to the sum of the *df* for the treatment, participant, and error effects (2 + 7 + 14 = 23).

Now we are ready to compute our mean squares. As you can see in Table 13-7g, the mean square for the treatment, participant, and error terms is equal to that term's sum of squares divided by its degrees of freedom (treatment = 1,141.75/2 = 570.88; participant = 2,140.65/7 = 305.81; error = 405.59/14 = 28.97).

Let us remind you that a mean square is analogous to an estimate of the variance, which you remember (see Chapter 6) as the square of the *SD* (σ^2). Once we have the mean squares, we can then create our distribution of variation. Rather than drawing pie charts like those in Figure 13-1, we compute an *F* ratio to compare the two sources of variation.

***F* Ratio**   We hope that you remember that the *F* ratio is equal to the between-groups variability (due to the IV) divided by the within-groups variability (due to error). Because we are using mean squares as our estimates of variability, the equation for our *F* ratio becomes:

$$F = \frac{\text{mean square between groups}}{\text{mean square within groups}}$$

Thus, our *F* ratio of 19.71, as shown in Table 13-7h, was derived by dividing 570.88 by 28.97.

Look back at Figure 13-1. Can you draw a comparable figure for this *F* ratio?

Our *F* ratio of 19.71 means that the variability due to the IV (clothing) is almost 20 times as large as the error variability. Thus, your drawing should have had the within groups variability "pie wedge" as a tiny piece.

Now that we have our *F* ratio, we need to find the probability of it occurring by chance. Remember that we must use two values for our *df* to find the probability of chance from the *F* table (Table A-3). Our *df* are 2 (between groups) and 14 (within groups), so you must find 2 in the numerator column and 14 on the denominator line and locate the intersection of those two numbers. At that point you will see 3.74 as the .05 cutoff and 6.51 as the .01 cutoff. Because our *F* value of 19.71 is larger than these two numbers, the probability that it could have occurred by chance is less than .01.

Given that $p < .01$, what conclusion is appropriate about the effects of clothing on salesclerks' responses?

Because $p < .01$, we know that there is a significant difference (i.e., not due to chance). Thus, we know that the different types of customers' clothes affected the clerks' responses. Just as with the between-groups ANOVA, we know there is significance among our means because of our significant *F* ratio, but which one is different from which one? From a significant *F* ratio, we cannot tell.

Post hoc Comparisons   Again we must use post hoc comparisons to determine which groups differ significantly from each other once we know there is overall significance (by finding a significant *F* ratio). In Table 13-8, you see the calculations for the Tukey HSD. Remember that we use Tukey's HSD to test all pairwise comparisons, so we can compare all three groups to each other. After computing HSD, we use Table A-5 to find its probability. From Table 13-8, we see that Group 2 is significantly different at the .05 level from both Group 1 and Group 3 according to the Tukey test. This result means that the clerks took significantly longer to wait on sloppily dressed students (63.25 seconds) than either those in casual (48.88 seconds) or those in dressy clothes

TABLE 13-8 CALCULATIONS FOR THE TUKEY HSD

Fortunately, the formula for HSD does not change for the correlated samples one-way ANOVA:

$$HSD = (M_1 - M_2)/s_{\bar{X}} \quad \text{where } s_{\bar{X}} = \sqrt{MS_{error}/n}$$

Because all our groups have eight clerks in them, $s_{\bar{X}}$ will remain a constant, so we can calculate it first:

$$s_{\bar{X}} = \sqrt{MS_{error}/n} = \sqrt{28.97/8} = \sqrt{3.621} = 1.903$$

Comparing clerks waiting on customers in dressy clothing to those waiting on customers in sloppy clothes:

$$HSD = (M_1 - M_2)/s_{\bar{X}} = (48.38 - 63.25)/1.903 = -14.87/1.903 = -7.81$$

Comparing clerks waiting on customers in sloppy clothing to those waiting on customers in casual clothes:

$$HSD = (M_1 - M_2)/s_{\bar{X}} = (63.25 - 48.88)/1.903 = 14.37/1.903 = 7.55$$

Finally, comparing clerks waiting on customers in dressy clothes to those waiting on customers in casual clothes:

$$HSD = (M_1 - M_2)/s_{\bar{X}} = (48.38 - 48.88)/1.903 = -0.50/1.903 = -0.26$$

Using Table A-5, we find that the critical HSD with 14 df_{error} for an IV with 3 levels is 3.70 at the .05 level and 4.90 at the .01 level. We can ignore the sign of our calculated HSDs because the difference between means could be in either direction (two-tailed).

Thus, we determine that there is a difference in two of the three comparisons: dressy versus sloppy and sloppy versus casual. By checking the means, we find that the clerks were slower when waiting on customers in sloppy clothing than customers in either dressy *or* casual clothing. There was no significant difference in the time clerks took to wait on customers in dressy and casual clothing.

Notice that the differences are significant at the .01 level for the correlated samples test rather than .05 as with the independent samples test. This difference illustrates the greater power of the correlated samples test despite "losing" *df* in the error term.

(48.38 seconds). No other groups differed significantly from each other, meaning that there was no statistical difference in the time it took clerks to wait on students dressed well or casually.

We have now finished with our calculations of our one-way ANOVA for correlated groups. First, from our ANOVA, we found that the type of clothing customers wore did affect salesclerks' response times. Because we had three groups and, thus, three means, we turned to post hoc comparisons to discover where the differences were significant. Using the Tukey HSD test, we found that salesclerks waited on customers in dressy or casual clothing more quickly than they waited on sloppily dressed customers.

Source Table As we did with our results earlier in the chapter, we compile a source table to show our statistical results. In the one-way ANOVA table for correlated groups, you see three sources of variation.

PSYCHOLOGICAL DETECTIVE   Do you remember why there are three sources of variation instead of just two as in the independent-groups analysis?

Although we still have the treatment (IV) effect and error, we added the variability due to our participants to our source table. In Table 13-9, you see that the total sum of squares (variability in the entire experiment) is 3,688, which we partitioned into the clothing (IV) sum of squares (1,141.75), participants sum of squares (2,140.65), and within-groups sum of squares (405.59). All three of these sums of squares added together should always be equal to the total sum of squares (1,141.75 + 1,141.75 + 405.59 = 3,688).

In the next column, we see the *df* for each source of variation. Again, as with the sums of squares, the sum of degrees of freedom must equal the total degrees of freedom (2 + 7 + 14 = 23). The next column shows the mean squares for the three sources of variability (each sum of squares divided by its *df*).

After reporting the mean squares, we have a column for our *F* ratios. Finally, we report the probability of chance for our *F* ratios and, if necessary, the results from our post hoc comparisons in a source table. It is fairly common to ignore the results dealing with the participants. As you might guess, this finding is almost always significant, but it tells us only that the individual participants performed differently. Such a finding is rarely of interest. The main purpose of measuring the variability due to the participants is to extract it from the error variability.

Computer Analysis of ANOVA for Correlated Groups

You can see the computer results for the one-way ANOVA for correlated samples in Table 13-10.

Interpreting Computer Statistical Output   The descriptive statistics appear at the top of Table 13-10. As you can see, we obtain the sample size, mean, *SD*, SE, and 95% confidence interval for each group. The descriptive statistics for the three groups match what we previously saw in Table 13-6, which is certainly logical. Although we are now using a correlated-samples analysis, nothing has changed about the samples

TABLE 13-9   SOURCE TABLE FOR ONE-WAY ANOVA FOR CORRELATED SAMPLES

Source	Sum of squares	df	Mean square	F	p
Between groups (clothing)	1,141.75	2	570.88	19.71	<.001
Participants	2,140.65	7	305.81	10.56	<.001
Within cells (error)	405.59	14	28.97		
Total	3,688.00	23			

TABLE 13-10 COMPUTER OUTPUT FOR ONE-WAY ANOVA FOR CORRELATED SAMPLES

GROUP	N	MEAN	SD	SE	95% CONF. INT.
1 (DRESSY)	8	48.38	10.11	3.57	39.92–56.83
2 (SLOPPY)	8	63.25	12.54	4.44	52.76–73.74
3 (CASUAL)	8	48.88	10.20	3.61	40.34–57.41

ONE-WAY ANOVA: RESP. TIME BY CLOTHING (CORR. SAMP.)

SOURCE	SUM OF SQUARES	df	MEAN SQUARES	F RATIO	PROB.
CLOTHING	1141.75	2	570.88	19.71	.000
SUBJECTS	2140.65	7	305.81	10.56	.000
WITHIN CELLS	405.59	14	28.97		
TOTAL	3688.00	23			

POST HOC TEST: TUKEY HSD WITH SIGNIFICANCE LEVEL .01

* INDICATES SIGNIFICANT DIFFERENCES SHOWN FOR PAIRINGS

		Grp 1	Grp 2	Grp 3
MEAN	CLOTHING			
48.38	GRP 1			
63.25	GRP 2	*		*
48.88	GRP 3			

themselves. So, we see the same means, SDs, and confidence intervals that we have seen before.

The other information that we see in Table 13-10 is our source table. The entries in this particular source table vary slightly from the tables we looked at earlier. Although you may begin to believe that this is some sinister plot hatched just to confuse you, you need to focus on the basic information, remembering that terms are used slightly differently in different situations. Here, our three sources of variance are labeled

"Clothing," "Subjects, and "Within cells." Because you know that we are comparing different types of clothing as our IV, it should be clear that "Clothing" represents the effect of our IV and "Within cells" represents our source of error variation (refer back to Table 13-2 to see our within-cell variation pictorially represented by the circles). "Subjects," of course, represents the variability between different sales clerks. When we examine the source table, we find that the F ratio for the clerks' response times for different clothing styles is 19.71, with 2 (numerator) and 14 (denominator) df, which results in a probability of chance of .000, according to the computer.

> **Asymptotic** Refers to tails of distributions that approach the baseline but never touch the baseline.

This situation illustrates one of our pet peeves with computerized statistical programs. You may have previously learned that the tails of distributions are **asymptotic**—that is, the tails extend into infinity and never touch the baseline. This fact means that the probability of a statistic is *never* .000. No matter how large the statistic gets there is always some small amount of probability under the tails of the distribution. Unfortunately, people who design statistics software either have a limited number of columns to work with *or* they don't think about this issue, so they have the computer print a probability of .000, implying that there is no uncertainty. In light of this problem, we advise you to list $p < .001$ if you ever find such a result on your computer printout.

Pardon the digression, but you know how pet peeves are! Back to the statistics. The overall effect of the clothing is significant, which leads us to wonder which clothing styles differ from each other. This source table looks different from the one in Table 13-6 because it shows the effects of two IVs—Clothing and Subjects. Although the Subjects effect is significant, remember that it does not tell us anything very important: We simply learn that there were significant differences between the eight salesclerks' response times. In other words, we found individual differences between the salesclerks. This effect is an expected one and is not profound. Typically, you would ignore this effect. However, the Subjects effect *is* important statistically. If you compare Tables 13-6 and 13-10, you will see that the correlated samples ANOVA has taken the Subjects variability (mean square) out of the Within cells (or error) variability compared to the Within groups (or error) term in the independent-samples ANOVA. This difference demonstrates the power of the correlated-samples analysis to reduce variability in the error term and create a larger F ratio.

We used a Tukey test for post hoc comparisons. Again, we found that Group 2 (sloppy clothing) was significantly different ($p < .01$) from both Group 1 (dressy clothes) and Group 3 (casual clothes). However, Groups 1 and 3 did not perform significantly differently. Notice that our significant differences are at the .01 level rather than .05 as with the independent samples case. This change is another indication of the increased power of the correlated-samples analysis.

Translating Statistics into Words   Our experimental logic is no different from that for the independent-samples ANOVA. The only difference is that we used a somewhat more stringent control procedure in this design—we used repeated measures with our participants rather than assigning them to groups randomly.

Our conclusions should combine our numbers with words to give the reader a clear indication of what we found. Remember to include information both about any difference that was found as well as the directionality of such a difference.

How would you write the results of this experiment in words and numbers for an experimental report?

Although the conclusion for the correlated-samples test is similar to that for the independent-groups test, it is different in some important ways. We hope you figured out those important differences. Here's a sample conclusion:

The effect of three different clothing styles on clerks' response times was significant, $F(2, 14) = 19.71$, $p < .001$. The proportion of variance accounted for by the clothing effect (η^2) was .74. Tukey tests showed ($p < .01$) that clerks took longer to respond to customers dressed in sloppy clothes ($M = 63.25$, $SD = 11.73$) than to either customers in dressy clothes ($M = 48.38$, $SD = 9.46$) or customers in casual clothes ($M = 48.88$, $SD = 9.55$). Response times did not differ between the clerks waiting on customers in dressy or casual clothing.

Did your conclusion look something like this? Remember, the exact wording may not necessarily match—the important thing is that you have all the critical details covered.

 There are five important differences between this conclusion and the conclusion for the independent groups ANOVA. Can you find them?

The *first* difference comes in the *df*. There are fewer *df* for the error term in the correlated-groups ANOVA (within cells) than for the independent-samples case (within groups). *Second*, the *F* value for the correlated groups test is larger than for the independent situation. The larger *F* value is a result of reducing the variability in the denominator of the *F* equation. This difference in *F* values leads to the *third* difference, which is the probability of chance. Despite the fact that there are fewer *df* for the correlated-samples case, its probability of being due to chance is lower (smaller). *Fourth*, the proportion of variance accounted for by the clothing effect (η^2) was considerably larger (for computational steps, see Table 13-3h). *Fifth*, the post hoc tests show a lower (smaller) probability of being due to chance in the correlated-groups situation.

These last three differences most clearly show the advantage of a correlated-groups design. Because using repeated measures reduced some of the error variability, the probability of the difference coming about by chance is smaller than in the independent-samples case. Thus, the conclusion from the correlated-groups design yields the clearer finding (reducing the chance of a Type I error). We cannot promise that correlated-groups designs will always allow you to find a clearer difference than independent-groups designs. However, we can tell you that correlated-groups designs do increase your odds of detecting smaller significant differences because such designs reduce error variance.

The Continuing Research Problem

In Chapters 10 and 11 we began our continuing research project by looking at clerks' response times as a function of how customers were dressed. Clerks' times were significantly higher when they waited on customers in sloppy clothing than when they waited on well-dressed customers. Because of this result, we decided to pursue this research further and, in this chapter, compared the effects of three different styles of clothing to each other. On the basis of our results, we can state that salespeople wait on customers in dressy or casual clothing more quickly than they wait on customers in sloppy clothing.

Is our research project complete at this point? As you might have realized, we could compare an endless number of styles of dress. This research problem could go on forever! In all seriousness, you might have wondered about the effects of other possible IVs on salesclerks' response times. As we begin to ask more complicated questions, we must move to more complex designs to handle those questions. As we move to Chapter 14, we will be able to continue our research problem with an experiment using more than one IV at a time.

Let's review the logical steps we took in conducting this experiment. Refer back to Figure 13-1 to take note of our experimental design questions.

Step 1   After conducting a preliminary experiment (Chapter 11) and determining that salesclerks wait on well-dressed customers more quickly, we decided to further test the effects of different clothing (IV) on clerks' response times (DV).

Step 2   We chose to test only one IV (clothing) because our research is still preliminary.

Step 3   We tested three different styles of dress because they seemed to be likely ways that customers might dress.

Step 4a   With access to many salesclerks, we used random assignment to the three groups and, thus, a multiple-independent-groups design. We used a one-way ANOVA for independent groups and found that clerks responded more quickly to customers in dressy or casual clothes than to customers in sloppy clothes.

Step 4b   With smaller numbers of clerks, we chose to use repeated measures. Thus, we used a multiple-within-group design and a one-way ANOVA for correlated groups. Clerks responded to sloppily dressed customers more slowly than to well-dressed or casually dressed customers.

Step 5   We concluded (hypothetically) that customers should not dress in sloppy clothes if they desire quick help in a store.

REVIEW SUMMARY

1. When your experimental design has one IV with more than two groups and you have used matched sets, natural sets, or repeated measures, you should analyze your data with a one-way ANOVA for correlated groups (**repeated-measures ANOVA**).

2. ANOVA partitions the variability in your DV into **between-groups variance** (due to the IV and participants) and **within-groups variance** (due to sources of error). We then compute a ratio, between these three sources of variation, known as the F ratio.

3. The variance due to participants simply reflects individual differences and is typically ignored.

4. ANOVA results are typically shown in a **source table**, which lists each source of variance and displays the F ratio for the effect of the IV.

5. A significant F ratio merely indicates that there is a significant difference somewhere among your various groups. **Post hoc comparisons** are necessary to determine which groups differ from each other.

6. An effect size index, η^2, indicates the proportion of variance in the DV accounted for by the IV.

7. Using APA format for our statistical results allows us to convey our findings in both words and numbers in a clear and concise manner.

8. Previous experiments often lead to further questions and new experiments. The multiple-group design is an ideal design to follow up on the results from a two-group experiment.

CHECK YOUR PROGRESS

1. You wonder whether students who take the ACT or SAT three times are able to significantly improve their scores. You select a sample of such students and obtain their three scores. What type of experimental design does this question represent? Draw a block diagram of it. What statistical test would you use to analyze the data?

2. What are the three sources of variability in a correlated-groups design?

3. Suppose you conducted the experiment summarized in Question 1 and found the following statistics: $F(2, 24) = 4.07$, $p < .05$. On the basis of this information, what could you conclude?

4. What additional information do you need in Question 3 to draw a full and complete conclusion?

5. In the continuing research problem from this chapter, why was it important to have the (hypothetical) knowledge from the similar study in Chapter 11?

6. You decide to test how people's moods vary by the four seasons. How would you plan the project to use a correlated-groups design?

7. You choose to test people's preferences for fast-food hamburgers, and you have McDonald's, Burger King, Wendy's, and White Castle franchises in your town. How can you tackle this question with a correlated-groups experimental design?

EXERCISES

1. Suppose a friend approaches you and tells you that she wants to use age as her independent variable and that she wants to use a one-way ANOVA to analyze her data. She wants to know if this experimental design is possible and how to set up her experiment. What do you say in response to her questions?

2. Suppose a friend approaches you and tells you that he wants to use age and sex as his independent variables and that he wants to use a one-way ANOVA to analyze his data. He wants to know if this experimental design is possible and how to set up his experiment. What do you say in response to his questions?

3. You have conducted an experiment in which you had freshmen, sophomores, juniors, and seniors rate their attitudes toward a course before and after they took it. Which type of ANOVA should you use to analyze your data? Why?

4. You have conducted an experiment in which you compared married, single, and divorced people's reactions to different types of TV commercials. Which type of ANOVA should you use to analyze your data? Why?

5. You are curious as to whether dogs have a better sense of smell, vision, or touch. To ensure the groups' equality, you choose three dogs from each of 10 litters and test their ability to learn a maze with odor, visual, or tactile cues. Which type of ANOVA should you use to analyze your data? Why?

6. You want to compare three GRE study methods—a study course versus a study book versus no preparation (control). To make sure the groups are equal, you make sets of three students based on their GPAs and then randomly assign one of each set to the course, study group, or control group. Which type of ANOVA should you use to analyze your data? Why?

7. You set up an experiment in which you randomly assign students to one of three groups based on how they study for a quiz. Group 1 simply reads the chapter, Group 2 reads and takes notes, and Group 3 reads, takes notes, and uses a study guide. Analyze the quiz scores and draw a conclusion about the different study techniques.

Group 1:	7	8	4	6	7	4	9	6	8	7
Group 2:	9	4	6	7	8	6	7	4	8	8
Group 3:	7	6	5	6	8	7	6	7	8	8

8. You set up an experiment in which you randomly assign students to one of three groups based on how they study for a quiz. Group 1 simply reads the chapter, Group 2 reads and takes notes, and Group 3 reads, takes notes, and uses a study guide. Analyze the quiz scores and draw a conclusion about the different study techniques.

Group 1:	7	6	4	6	7	4	7	6	8	7
Group 2:	7	4	6	7	8	6	7	4	6	8
Group 3:	7	7	7	7	8	7	7	7	8	8

9. You set up an experiment in which you randomly assign students to one of three groups based on how they study for a quiz. Group 1 simply reads the chapter,

Group 2 reads and takes notes, and Group 3 reads, takes notes, and uses a study guide. Analyze the quiz scores and draw a conclusion about the different study techniques.

Group 1:	7	6	4	6	7	4	7	6	8	7
Group 2:	7	4	6	7	8	6	7	4	6	8
Group 3:	9	7	8	7	8	7	7	7	8	8

10. You design an experiment in which students take a quiz under one of three study conditions. Group 1 simply reads the chapter, Group 2 reads and takes notes, and Group 3 reads, takes notes, and uses a study guide. To ensure equality of groups, you match sets of three students on their prior quiz grades and then assign one from each set to each group. Analyze the quiz scores and draw a conclusion about the different study techniques.

Group 1:	7	8	4	6	7	4	9	6	8	7
Group 2:	9	4	6	7	8	6	7	4	8	8
Group 3:	7	6	5	6	8	7	6	7	8	8

11. You design an experiment in which students take a quiz under one of three study conditions. Group 1 simply reads the chapter, Group 2 reads and takes notes, and Group 3 reads, takes notes, and uses a study guide. To ensure equality of groups, you match sets of three students on their prior quiz grades and then assign one from each set to each group. Analyze the quiz scores and draw a conclusion about the different study techniques.

Group 1:	7	6	4	6	7	4	7	6	8	7
Group 2:	7	4	6	7	8	6	7	4	6	8
Group 3:	7	7	7	7	8	7	7	7	8	8

12. You design an experiment in which students take a quiz under one of three study conditions. Group 1 simply reads the chapter, Group 2 reads and takes notes, and Group 3 reads, takes notes, and uses a study guide. To ensure equality of groups, you match sets of three students on their prior quiz grades and then assign one from each set to each group. Analyze the quiz scores and draw a conclusion about the different study techniques.

Group 1:	7	6	4	6	7	4	7	6	8	7
Group 2:	7	4	6	7	8	6	7	4	6	8
Group 3:	7	6	6	7	8	7	7	7	8	8

13. Write an APA-style conclusion for any of the results from Exercises 7–9.

14. Write an APA-style conclusion for any of the results from Exercises 10–12.

15. Suppose a friend brought you the computer data shown below and said that she could not interpret it. She asks for you to use your statistical knowledge to help her out. What can you tell her?

Group	N	M	SD
Group 1	55	89.14	12.72
Group 2	55	88.95	15.02
Group 3	55	96.69	12.98

$F(2, 168) = 4.78$ $p = .009$

KEY TERMS

One-way ANOVA, *281*

One-way ANOVA for independent groups, *281*

One-way ANOVA for correlated groups, *281*

Operational definition, *282*

Between-groups variability, *282*

Error variability, *282*

Within-groups variability, *282*

Sum of squares, *286*

Total sum of squares, *286*

Treatment sum of squares, *286*

Error sum of squares, *286*

Mean square, *286*

Degrees of freedom, *288*

Variance, *288*

Post hoc comparisons, *290*

Source table, *291*

Participant sum of squares, *299*

Asymptotic, *304*

LOOKING AHEAD

In the next chapter, we will make a significant alteration in our basic design by adding a second IV. This expanded design will give us the ability to ask much more sophisticated questions about behavior because most behaviors are affected by more than one variable at a time.

14

Designing and Conducting Experiments with Multiple Independent Variables

Experimental Design: Doubling the Basic Building Block

This chapter will continue building on the experimental design material that we first encountered in Chapter 10. We will see many familiar concepts from the two previous experimental design chapters (Chapters 10 and 12), as well as from earlier in the text (e.g., IVs, DVs, extraneous variables, control, and so on). So you can expect some of this chapter to be a review of familiar concepts. However, we will apply those concepts in a new and different framework—the factorial experimental design.

Let's return to our analogy for experimental design that we first saw in Chapter 10—that of building objects with Legos or Tinkertoys. Chapters 10 and 12 presented the beginner's set and a slightly larger version of that beginner's set, respectively. Now, with the factorial design, we encounter the top-of-the-line, advanced set that has all the possible options. When you bought the largest set of building materials, you could build anything from very simple objects to extremely complicated structures; the same is true of experimental design. Using a factorial design gives us the power we need to devise an investigation of several **factors** or **independent variables (IVs)** in a single experiment. Factorial designs are the lifeblood of experimental psychology because they allow us to look at *combinations* of IVs at the same time, a situation that is quite similar to the real world. A factorial design is more like the real world because there are probably few, if any, situations in which your behavior is affected by only a single factor at a time. Imagine trying to isolate only one factor that affected your ACT or SAT scores! What about intelligence, motivation, courses you had taken, a test time of 8:00 on Saturday morning, health, and so on?

> **Factors** Synonymous with IVs.

> **Independent variables** Stimuli or aspects of the environment that are directly manipulated by the experimenter to determine their influences on behavior.

In Chapter 12 we used another analogy for our experimental designs—we compared the two-group design to a house, the multiple-group design to an apartment building, and the factorial design to a skyscraper. The idea behind this analogy was not to frighten you into worrying about how complex factorial designs are, but instead to make two points. First, as we have already mentioned, even complex designs are based on principles that you encountered previously with simple designs. As you move from building a house to a skyscraper, most of the principles of building remain the same. They are merely used on a larger scale. This formula is true also for experimental design: Although we will be dealing with more complex designs in this chapter, you already have the majority of the background you need from Chapters 10 and 12. Second, just as building larger buildings gives you more decisions and options, designing larger experiments gives you more decisions and options. Decisions, of course, imply responsibility. You will have to take on additional responsibility with a factorial design. Rather than planning an experiment that has only one IV, you will be planning for two or three (or possibly even more) IVs. Additional IVs mean that you have more factors to choose and control. By taking on additional responsibilities, you also gain additional information. By moving from a one-IV experiment to a two-IV experiment, you will gain information about a second IV *and* the interaction between the two IVs. We will soon discuss interactions in depth. Let's examine the factorial design first.

The Factorial Design

In this chapter, we will expand the basic two-group design by doubling it. Look back at Figure 10-2 and imagine what would happen if you doubled it. Of course, one possible result of doubling Figure 10-2 would be a design that we have already covered in Chapter 12—a multiple-group design with four levels. That design would result in an experiment similar to the continuing research problem of Chapter 12 if we planned an experiment contrasting the effects of four different styles of clothing rather than three. However, this type of doubling would be an extension rather than an expansion. We would take one IV with two levels (dressy clothes and shabby clothes) in Chapter 10 and extend it from two to four levels.

 What would an *expansion* (rather than an extension) of Figure 10-2 look like? You may wish to draw a sketch of your answer.

Does your drawing resemble Figure 14-1? Contrast Figure 14-1 with Figures 10-2 and 12-2. Do you see the difference? To what can you attribute this difference? You'll find the answer in the next section.

How Many IVs?   In Chapters 10 and 12, the first question we faced when considering the choice of experimental designs dealt with how many IVs our experiment will have. Nothing has changed in Chapter 14—we still begin with "How many independent variables will I use in my experiment?" (see Figure 14-2). For the first time, though, we have a different answer. We are moving into more complex designs that use at least two IVs. We refer to any design that uses at least two IVs as a **factorial design**. The factorial

> **Factorial design** An experimental design that has more than one IV.

FIGURE 14-1 SIMPLEST POSSIBLE FACTORIAL DESIGN (2×2).

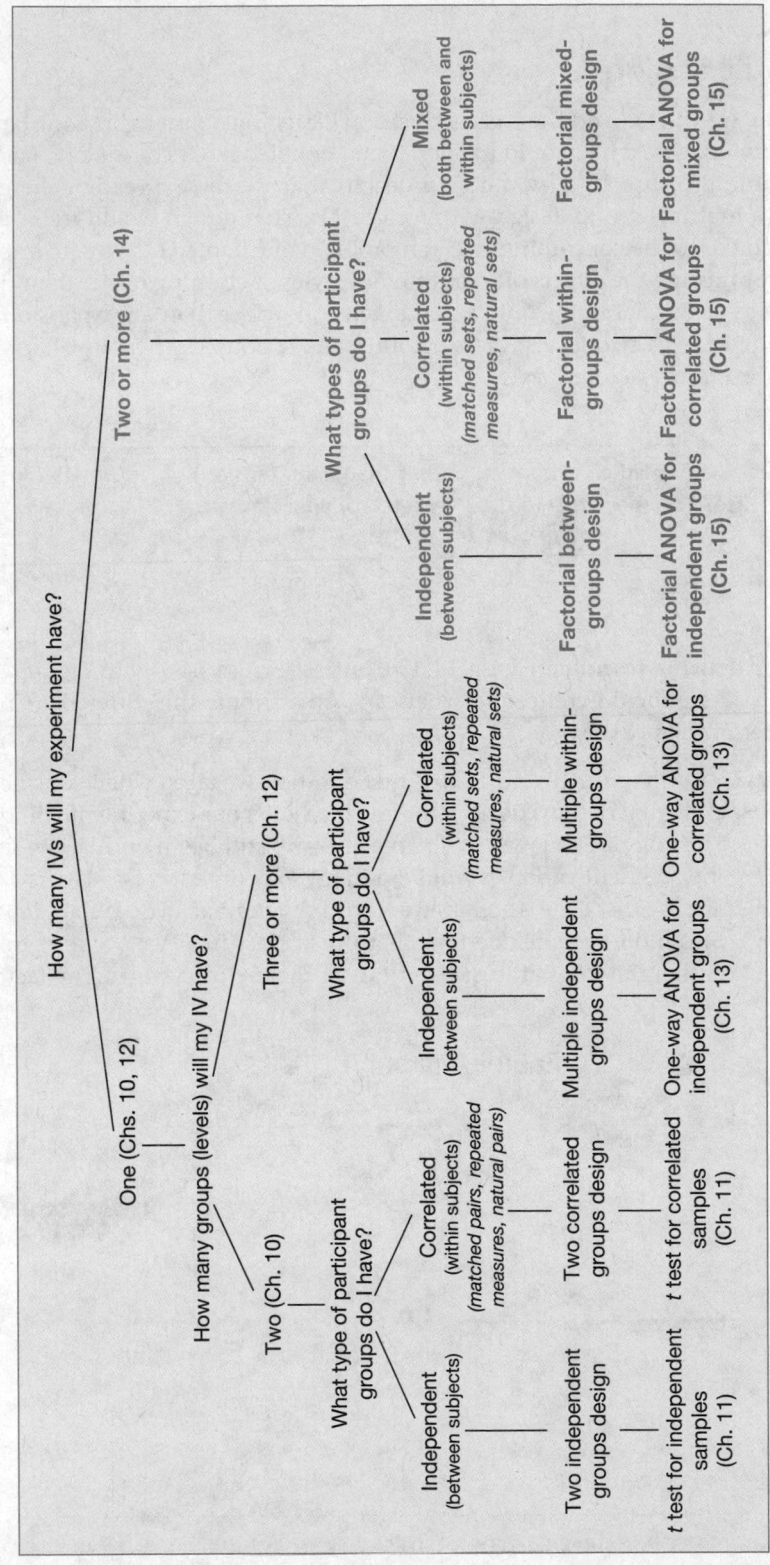

FIGURE 14-2 EXPERIMENTAL DESIGN QUESTIONS.

design gets its name because we refer to each IV as a factor; multiple IVs, then, yield a factorial design. Theoretically, there is no limit to the number of IVs that can be used in an experiment. Practically speaking, however, it is unlikely that you would want to design an experiment that has more than two or three IVs. After that point, the increased complexity is such that it would tax your ability to conduct the experiment and your skill to interpret the results. Real-life detectives often face complex cases that are similar to factorial designs. Imagine that you are a detective confronted with several suspects and that you are faced with evaluating the means, motive, and opportunity for each suspect. Can you see how such a situation is analogous to a factorial design?

How Many Groups or Levels?   When looking at Figure 14-2 you will notice that this question, which we asked in both Chapters 10 and 11, does not appear on the relevant portion of the flowchart. The reason for its absence is simple: Once you have two (or more) IVs, you will use a factorial design. The number of levels for each factor is unimportant at this point.

Let's return to Figure 14-1 for a moment. Do you see how it represents 2 two-group designs stacked on top of each other? That is what we meant earlier by doubling or expanding the two-group design. If we take 2 two-group designs and combine them, we end up with the design pictured in Figure 14-1, which has two IVs that each have two levels. This figure represents the simplest possible factorial design, which is known as a *2 × 2 design*. This 2 × 2 shorthand notation tells us that we are dealing with a design that has two factors, (IVs) because there are two digits given, and that each of the two factors has two levels because each digit shown is a 2. In other words, the *number* of numbers tells us how many IVs there are; the *value* of each number tells us how many levels each IV has. Finally, when we complete the implied multiplication, this notation also tells us how many unique treatment combinations (or groups) our experiment requires. A 2 × 2 design requires four treatment combinations (two times two), whereas a 3 × 3 design would require nine treatment combinations, and a 2 × 4 design would have eight treatment combinations.

PSYCHOLOGICAL DETECTIVE   Suppose you had an experiment that had one IV with two levels, one IV with three levels, and another IV with four levels. What would the shorthand notation for this design be?

Because there are three IVs, there will be three digits in the answer. Each digit represents the number of levels of one of the IVs. Thus, your answer should have been "a 2 × 3 × 4 design."

Figure 14-1 shows an additional design notation. Various factors are often designated by letters, so the first factor is labeled Factor *A*, the second as Factor *B*, and so on. The levels within a factor are often designated by the letter that corresponds to the factor and with a number to differentiate the different levels. Thus, the two levels within the first factor would be labeled A_1 and A_2. If the factor has more than two levels, we continue numbering them in similar fashion until we reach the last level (e.g., A_1, A_2, $A_3 \ldots A_n$), where n represents the number of levels of the factor.

What might such a 2×2 design look like in real life? To begin answering this question, refer to Figure 10-2, where we diagrammed the two-group experiment of McClellan and Woods (2001), in which they compared the response times of salesclerks to deaf and hearing customers.

 PSYCHOLOGICAL DETECTIVE How could you expand McClellan and Woods's (2001) experiment so it becomes a 2×2 factorial? Draw a diagram.

First, we hope you drew a design like that shown in Figure 14-3. The first IV (A) should be customer hearing, with the two levels representing the experimental group (customers who were deaf) and the control group (customers who were not deaf). The second IV (B) could be any possible variable, as long as the two groups differ on that IV. For example, let's say that you are interested in determining whether the effects of the customers' hearing status vary due to the salesclerks' sex (as we mentioned in Chapter 10). Therefore, your second IV (a measured rather than manipulated IV) would be the sex of the clerks, with your two groups composed of women versus men. This particular experimental design appears in Figure 14-3. Four treatment groups are required, one for each possible combination of the two levels of the two treatments. Thus, we would have a group of female salesclerks who wait on deaf customers, a group of female salesclerks who wait on hearing customers, a group of male salesclerks who wait on deaf customers, and a group of male salesclerks who wait on hearing customers.

We hope it is clear to you that this 2×2 design is composed of 2 two-group designs. One two-group design contrasts the effects of customers' hearing, and the second two-group design contrasts the effects of salesclerks' sex. At this point, you might ask, "Wouldn't it be simpler to run two separate experiments rather than combining them both into one experiment?" Although it might be somewhat easier to run two

Factor A (customer hearing)

	Deaf Customers	Hearing Customers
Women	deaf customers waited on by female clerks	hearing customers waited on by female clerks
Men	deaf customers waited on by male clerks	hearing customers waited on by male clerks

Factor B (salesclerk sex)

FIGURE 14-3 EXPANSION OF MCCLELLAN AND WOODS'S (2001) HEARING DISABILITY STUDY.

experiments, there are two disadvantages of conducting separate experiments. First, it is not as time efficient as running one experiment. Even if you used the same number of participants in the experiment(s), two experiments will simply take longer to complete than one; there are fewer details to deal with in one experiment than in two. Imagine how inefficient it would be for a detective to complete an investigation of one suspect before even beginning the investigation of a second suspect! Second, by running two experiments, you would lose the advantage that you gain by conducting a factorial experiment—the interaction.

Main effect Refers to the sole effect of one IV in a factorial design.

Interaction The joint, simultaneous effect on the DV of more than one IV.

When we jointly combine two IVs in one experiment, we get all the information we would get from two experiments plus a bonus. In the example using McClellan and Woods's (2001) experiment, we will still determine the solitary effect of customer hearing *and* the solitary effect of salesclerk sex. In a factorial experiment, these outcomes from the IVs are termed the **main effects**. The bonus that we get from a factorial experiment is the **interaction** of the two IVs. We will discuss interactions at length later in Chapter 15, but let us provide you a preview at this point. Suppose we ran the customer hearing/salesclerk sex study and found the results shown in Figure 14-4.

PSYCHOLOGICAL **DETECTIVE**   Can you interpret the main effects in Figure 14-4? Did customer hearing have any effect? Did salesclerk sex have any effect? Study the graph carefully to answer these questions.

It does appear that the customer hearing factor had an effect on clerks' response times. Both groups of clerks (men and women) seemed to respond more slowly when the customer was deaf; notice how the lines for both groups go down as they move from left (deaf customers) to right (hearing customers). On the other hand, sex of the salesclerks seems to have made no difference in their time to help. It appears that both

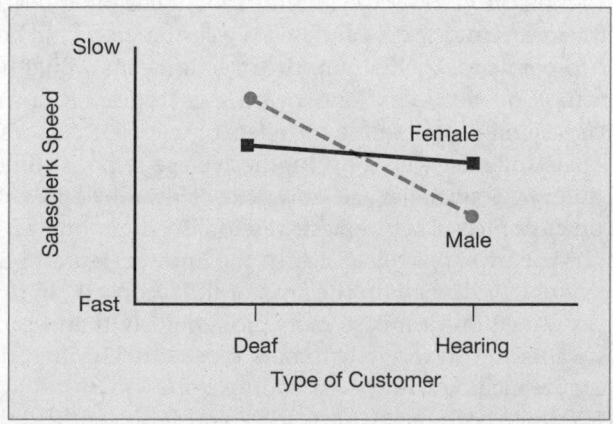

FIGURE 14-4 HYPOTHETICAL RESULTS OF CUSTOMER HEARING/SALESCLERK SEX EXPERIMENT.

men and women waited on customers in approximately the same amount of time. If you average the two points on the women's line and average the two points on the men's line, the two means are virtually identical.

The crossing pattern you see graphically portrayed in Figure 14-4 illustrates an interaction effect. We find significant interactions when the effects of one IV change as the level(s) of the other IV changes. Another common way of describing interactions is that *the effects of one IV depend on the particular level of another IV*. If these descriptions are difficult for you to understand, look at Figure 14-4 and ask yourself whether the effects of the customer's hearing are the same for both groups of salesclerks. Although the response times of both sexes increased when they waited on customers who were deaf, it is clear that this effect was much more pronounced for the male clerks, who were much slower waiting on deaf customers than hearing customers. On the other hand, the female clerks responded similarly to both deaf and hearing customers, although they were slightly slower when waiting on customers who were deaf. This difference for female clerks might not even be significant. If you were describing these results to someone, would it be correct to say merely that salesclerks were slower when they waited on deaf customers? Or should you note that the effect of customer hearing seemed to vary as a function of the sex of the clerks—that the customer's hearing greatly affected the response time in men but had only a small or nonexistent effect for women? It is apparent that the second conclusion, although more complex, paints a much clearer and more accurate picture of the results. Thus, it seems that the effects of customer hearing depend on the sex of the salesclerks; the effect of one IV depends on the specific level of the other IV.

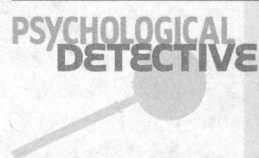 Can you interpret the main effects *and* interactions in Figures 14-5 and 14-6? Did the customer hearing have any effect? Did salesclerk sex have any effect? Was there an interaction? Study the graphs carefully to answer these questions.

Let's look at Figure 14-5 first. To answer the question about customer hearing, you have to figure out what the means for the deaf and hearing customers would be. Notice that if you average the two points for each group, the overall means would be nearly equal—the salesclerks waited on both deaf and hearing customers in a moderate amount of time. In similar fashion, to determine the effect of salesclerk sex, we have to find the means for the female and male clerks. Again, the average response time for the clerks does not seem to differ by gender—female and male clerks took about the same amount of time to wait on customers. The simplest way to discern an interaction is to look for lines on the graph that are *not* parallel. Clearly, the lines in Figure 14-5 are not parallel. Thus, the effects of one IV depend on the level of the second IV. In this hypothetical case, female clerks waited on deaf customers more quickly than hearing customers, but male clerks waited on hearing customers more quickly than deaf customers. Note that you have to include both IVs in your explanation of the significant interaction. So, Figure 14-5 shows both main effects to be nonsignificant and the interaction to be significant. How did you do at deciphering those results?

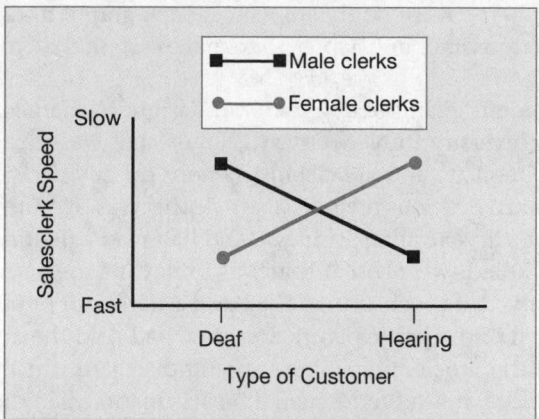

FIGURE 14-5 HYPOTHETICAL RESULTS OF CUSTOMER HEARING/SALESCLERK SEX EXPERIMENT.

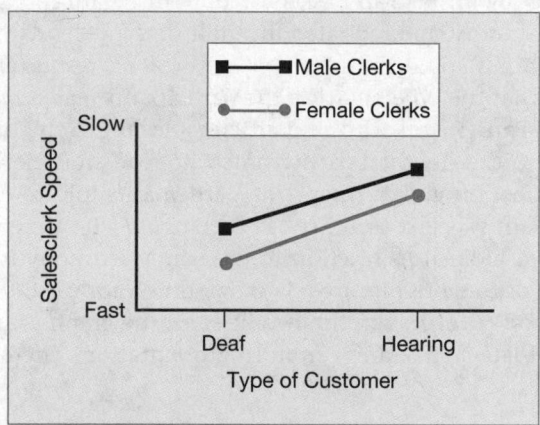

FIGURE 14-6 HYPOTHETICAL RESULTS OF CUSTOMER HEARING/SALESCLERK SEX EXPERIMENT.

Now we turn to Figure 14-6. We will go through the same set of questions. If we examine the means based on the type of customer, we find that deaf customers received help more quickly than hearing customers. Also, we see that female clerks tended to give help more quickly than male clerks. Thus, both main effects show significance. How about the interaction? The lines look roughly parallel, don't they? Notice that we can explain each main effect without having to refer to the second IV: Deaf customers received help more quickly (regardless of sex of the salesclerk). Female clerks were faster than male clerks (regardless of the customers' hearing). Therefore, the interaction is not significant in Figure 14-6.

We have not covered all the possible outcomes of a two variable experiment. With two main effects and an interaction, any possible combination of significant and non-significant effects can occur. All three can be significant, all three can be nonsignificant, or any combination in between. You must be able to look at such graphs and interpret them. We will return to interactions later in Chapter 15 to make certain that you understand them fully.

Let's look at an actual student example of a factorial design. Vania Gauthreaux (2000), a student at Tulane University in New Orleans, Louisiana, was interested in studying the effects of pretrial publicity and judicial instructions on jury decisions. Half of Gauthreaux's participants read a fictitious prejudicial article that was relevant to a particular crime (armed robbery of a dry-cleaning business), and half read a fictitious article about a crime (an arson that killed two people) that was irrelevant to the particular crime. The participants then served as mock jurors—they read a transcript of the armed-robbery trial. Gauthreaux told half the participants, after they had read the article and transcript, that they had read the article in error and should disregard it (similar to a judge's admonition to ignore illegal testimony). Then, the participants rated the guilt of the defendant. This combination of treatments is shown in Figure 14-7. As you can see, there are two IVs (type of article read and "judicial" instructions), each with two levels.

Participants began the experiment by completing forms and reading the article (relevant or irrelevant). Afterward, the experimenter told half the participants that the article had been in their packet by mistake and asked them to disregard it. Then, participants read the fictitious trial transcript and rated the guilt of the defendant as well as the strength of the prosecution's and defense's case. Gauthreaux's results appear in Figure 14-8. The graph shows that the type of article the participants read affected the guilt ratings of the defendant. Participants who read articles relevant to the trial story rated the defendant as being more guilty than participants who read an irrelevant article. The instruction had no effect on guilt ratings—the participants told to disregard the article thought the defendant was just as guilty as participants who were not told to disregard the article. Thus, a judicial instruction to disregard testimony in a legal case may have no effect. Both of these results are relatively straightforward; there was no interaction between the two IVs. Although the two lines on the graph are not perfectly parallel, they do not deviate significantly from that orientation. Therefore, we

Pretrial Article Read

	Relevant	Irrelevant
"Judicial" Instruction — Disregard Article		
"Judicial" Instruction — No Instruction		

FIGURE 14-7 DIAGRAM OF GAUTHREAUX'S (2000) EXPERIMENT.

Source: Adapted from V. M. Gauthreaux, 2000. Relating pretrial publicity, judicial instruction, and thought suppression with guilt ratings, *Psi Chi Journal of Undergraduate Research*, 5, 21–28.

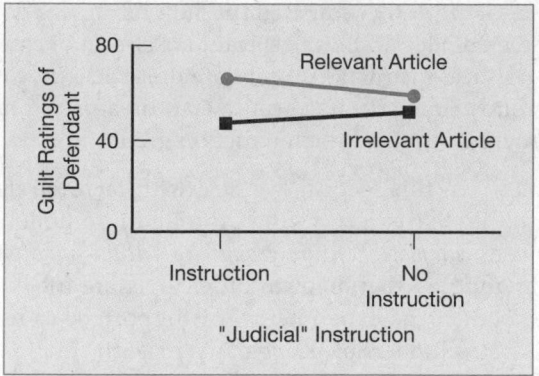

FIGURE 14-8 RESULTS FROM GAUTHREAUX'S (2000) EXPERIMENT.

Source: Adapted from V. M. Gauthreaux, 2000. Relating pretrial publicity, judicial instruction, and thought suppression with guilt ratings, *Psi Chi Journal of Undergraduate Research*, 5, 21–28 (Table 1).

can conclude that reading a relevant article before judging guilt caused higher ratings of guilt, regardless of "judicial" instructions.

Independent groups
Groups of participants that are formed by random assignment.

Correlated groups
Groups of participants formed by matching, natural pairs, or repeated measures.

Mixed assignment
A factorial design that has a mixture of independent groups for one IV and correlated groups for another IV. In larger factorial designs, at least one IV has independent groups and at least one has correlated groups (also known as *mixed groups*).

Assigning Participants to Groups As in Chapters 10 and 12, the matter of how we assign our research participants to groups is important. Again, we have two options for this assignment—**independent groups** or **correlated groups**. However, this question is not answered in such a simple manner as in the two-group and multiple-group designs, each of which had only one IV. Matters can become more complicated in a factorial design because we have two (or more) IVs to deal with. All IVs could have participants assigned randomly or in a correlated fashion, or we could have one IV with independent groups and one IV with correlated groups. We refer to this last possibility as **mixed assignment** (or *mixed groups*).

Random Assignment to Groups Factorial designs in which *both* IVs involve random assignment may be called *between-subjects factorial designs* or *completely randomized designs* (see Figure 14-2). These labels should make sense from our discussion of between- and within-groups variance in Chapter 10. Between-groups variance refers to variability between independent groups of participants, which results from random assignment.

Gauthreaux (2000) used a completely randomized design for her experiment dealing with judgments of guilt as a function of type of article and "judicial" instructions. She randomly assigned participants to one of the four possible treatment groups based on type of article (relevant/irrelevant) and instruction (presence/absence). Thus, her experiment required the use of four independent groups of participants; she used four groups ranging from 18 to 22 participants. Each group was independent of the others in the experiment.

After she collected the data, Gauthreaux compared the guilt ratings for defendants *between* those participants who read relevant and irrelevant articles and *between* those participants who did and did not hear instructions to ignore the article they read. The comparisons were between-groups comparisons because Gauthreaux had randomly assigned the participants to article groups and the instruction groups.

Nonrandom Assignment to Groups   In this section, we deal with factorial designs in which participant groups for *all* IVs have been formed through nonrandom assignment. We refer to such designs as *completely within-groups* (or *within-subjects*) *designs*. We may want to resort to nonrandom assignment in order to assure the equality of participant groups before we conduct the experiment. It is important to remember, particularly in research with small numbers of participants or with small IV effects, that random assignment cannot guarantee equality of groups. Let's take a brief look at the three methods of creating correlated groups.

1. Matched Pairs or Sets. Matching can take place in either pairs or sets because factorial designs can use IVs with two or more levels. The more levels an IV has, the more work matching for that variable takes simply because of having to form larger sets of participants that are equated on the matching variable. Also, the more precise the match that is necessary, the more difficult matching becomes. For example, matching on sex or educational level may be fairly simple. However, matching on college major or family background may be more difficult. Likewise, when more than one IV uses matching, the demand for a large number of a specific type of research participant may become overwhelming. For instance, using matched participants for both IVs in a 2×2 experiment requires four matched groups, a 2×3 requires six such groups, and a 3×3 design would necessitate nine matched groups. Imagine what would happen in an experiment with three IVs! For this reason, factorial designs that use matching for all IVs are relatively rare.

2. Repeated Measures. You will remember that a repeated-measures design is one in which participants take part in all levels of an IV. In a completely within-groups experiment using repeated measures, participants would take part fully and completely; that is, they would participate in every possible treatment combination. As you might imagine, this requirement often makes it difficult or impossible to conduct an experiment with repeated measures on multiple IVs.

Would it have been possible to conduct Gauthreaux's (2000) experiment with repeated measures on both IVs? If it were possible, would it be wise to do so? Why or why not?

To answer the first question, you have to understand its implication. Look at Figure 14-7. To conduct this experiment using repeated measures on both IVs, each participant would experience each of the four possible conditions. Could a single participant read both relevant and irrelevant articles? Certainly yes, but not at the same time. Could a single participant get and not get instructions to ignore the article read? Yes, *if* the participant read two different articles. Thus, it would be possible to have repeated measures on both IVs.

Given that it is *possible* to use repeated measures on both variables, would it be wise to do so? "Being wise" is a little harder question to answer than "being possible," because it involves a value judgment. However, if you can think of a problem that has a design, then it is probably *not* wise to use that design. There is a fairly obvious problem in using repeated measures on both factors in Gauthreaux's design. Isn't it logical to assume that participating in all four conditions would alert participants to the two independent variables in the experiment? If the participants can figure out what an experiment is about, then you have to worry about their expectancies and demand characteristics (see Chapter 7) affecting their responses in the experiment. So, although it would be possible to use repeated measures for the independent variables, it probably would not be wise to do so.

Of course, not all factorial experiments have these types of problems with using repeated measures. It is possible to design an experiment with multiple IVs in which you expose participants to all treatment combinations. As you have probably guessed by now, the smaller the design, the more feasible it is to include the same participants in all conditions of the experiment. Thus, a 2×2 design would be the most likely candidate for a totally repeated measures design.

3. Natural Pairs or Sets. Using natural groups in a totally within-subjects design has the same difficulties as the matched pairs or sets variation of this design, but it would be even harder. If it would be difficult to form matched pairs or sets to participate in a factorial design, imagine how much harder it would be to find an adequate number of naturally linked participants. At least when we match participants, we usually have a large number to measure in our attempt to make matches. To use natural sets, we would have to find substantial numbers of natural groups. As we noted in Chapter 10, experimenters rarely use this approach other than for animal littermates. We will not consider natural sets in this chapter because of their infrequent use.

Let's examine a student research project that used a factorial design with a totally within subjects approach. Paula Selvidge (2000), a student at Wichita State University in Wichita, Kansas, was interested in the effects of type of recall task and serial position on location memory for visual stimuli. Selvidge used a computer to show her participants a 5×5 grid (i.e., 25 squares) that had a small triangle located in one square of the grid. She used serial position (where the triangle was located on which trial) as one IV because she showed participants five consecutive displays, so she could determine the level of memory for each of the five trials. She varied the recall task in one of three ways: free recall (participants could recall the five triangles' positions in any order), serial recall (participants had to recall the five triangles' positions in order of the trials), or probe recall (participants viewed a 5×5 grid with a circle in one position and had to tell whether they had seen a triangle in that position). Thus, Selvidge's design was a 3 (recall task) $\times$ 5 (serial position) design.

 Draw a block diagram of Selvidge's experiment. Be sure to label it completely.

Serial Position

FIGURE 14-9 BLOCK DIAGRAM OF SELVIDGE'S (2000) EXPERIMENT.

We hope you drew a diagram like that in Figure 14-9. If so, good job! If not, review the material earlier in this chapter concerning number of IVs and levels of IVs.

Participants in Selvidge's experiment saw 15 grids, 5 (for each of the 5 serial positions) in each of the 3 recall conditions (free, serial, probe). The fact that participants saw grids from all 15 possible treatment conditions means that repeated measures were used for both IVs; the participants used each recall strategy for all the serial positions. Selvidge found a significant interaction between recall task and serial position such that recall went down across serial position for free and serial recall but showed a *V*-shaped pattern (higher recall at beginning and end of the list) for probe recall. Had Selvidge conducted this experiment as two separate two-variable designs, she would never have gained the information about the interaction between recall task and serial position.

Mixed Assignment to Groups   Because factorial designs have at least two IVs, we have the opportunity for a new type of group assignment that we have not yet encountered in the single-IV designs. As we mentioned previously, mixed assignment designs involve a combination of random and nonrandom assignment, with at least one IV using each type of assignment to groups. In a two-IV factorial design, mixed assignment involves one IV with random assignment and one IV with nonrandom assignment. In such designs, the use of repeated measures is probably more likely than other types of nonrandom assignment. What we often end up with in a *mixed factorial design* is two independent groups that are measured more than once (repeated measures). Such an experimental plan allows us to measure a difference between our groups and then determine whether that difference remains constant over time or across different types of stimuli. Mixed designs combine the advantages of the two types of designs. The conservation of participants through the use of repeated measures for a between-subjects variable makes for a popular and powerful design.

Let's consider a student research example using a mixed design. Jennifer Bonds-Raacke, Kendra Wright, and Jessica Lewin, students from Christian Brothers University in Memphis, Tennessee, and Elizabeth Nelson, their faculty advisor, conducted a study to examine students' attitudes toward animal behavior as a function of source and time. They had 85 undergraduates (41 men, 44 women) read an article about animal cognition from one of two sources (*Journal of Experimental Psychology* or *National Enquirer*); a control group read an article about gambling with no source cited. Bonds-Raacke et al. (2001) measured students' attitudes toward the locus of animals' behavior (instinctive versus cognitive) immediately after reading the article and again a week later.

What are the two IVs in this experiment, and what are their respective levels? Which is the between-groups variable and which is the within-groups variable? How would you describe this experimental design in shorthand notation? What is the DV in this experiment?

One IV is type of article, with three levels. The second IV is time of attitude measurement, with two levels. Type of article is the between-groups variable because participants read only one article. The three groups were independent—there was no relationship or pairing between participants who read the different articles. Time was the within-groups variable—students participated in all conditions of this variable, as they gave attitude judgments immediately after reading the article and a week later. Because this experiment had two IVs, one (type of article) with three levels and one (time) with two levels, it was a 3×2 design (traditionally, in a mixed design, the between-subjects variable is listed first and the within-subjects variable listed second). Finally, the DV was the students' ratings of the animal behaviors. The experimenters compared students' ratings for the three types of articles and for the two different times of measurement.

In their experiment, Bonds-Raacke et al. (2001) found a significant main effect of article type, with no main effect of time and no interaction between the two variables. Students who read the article from *Journal of Experimental Psychology* rated animal behavior as more cognitive than students who read the article from *The National Enquirer* or an unrelated article on gambling. Interestingly, the researchers found no effect for time, which they expected, based on attitudinal research on the sleeper effect. The *sleeper effect* shows that attitudes often show greater effect of a message after passage of time (Myers, 2002). Perhaps students found cognitive explanations for animal behavior to be unlikely, so that attitudes were unlikely to change over time. However, other potential hypotheses also exist, as Bonds-Raacke et al. (2001) noted: "There are many possible reasons why the sleeper effect was not replicated" (p. 35). They raised possible explanations of insufficient time for the sleeper effect to occur, difficulty in comprehending the articles, and apathy. The possible explanations for Bonds-Raacke et al.'s results should remind you to seek alternative explanations for your experimental results. Perhaps a follow-up experiment would help you find the correct explanation.

REVIEW SUMMARY

1. The plan by which psychologists guide their experiments is known as the **experimental design**.
2. If you have an experiment that consists of two (or more) IVs, you will use a **factorial design**.

3. The number of levels of each IV is not important in choosing the particular factorial design you will use.

4. Combining two IVs in an experiment allows you to test for **interactions**—that is, situations in which the effect of one IV depends on the specific level of another IV.

5. When you randomly assign research participants to their groups, you have **independent groups**. If all the IVs in your factorial design use independent groups, you are employing a between-subjects factorial design.

6. When you use matched pairs or sets, repeated measures, or natural pairs or sets, you have **correlated groups**. If all IVs in your experiment use correlated groups, you are using a within-subjects factorial design.

7. Mixed factorial designs result from using both independent groups and correlated groups in a factorial design. At least one IV must use independent groups and at least one must use correlated groups.

CHECK YOUR PROGRESS

1. How is the two-group design related to the factorial design? Draw a picture as part of your answer.

2. Why is there a practical limit to the number of IVs you could use in an experiment?

3. You have conducted a 2×2 experiment; what information will you obtain from the analysis?

   a. The effects of IV A

   b. The effects of IV B

   c. The effects of $A \times B$

   d. All of the above

4. Matching

   1. mixed factorial design   A. fraternity members versus nonmembers; men versus women

   2. totally between-groups design   B. fraternity members matched for family income measured twice

   3. totally within-groups design   C. fraternity members versus nonmembers measured twice

5. The simplest possible factorial design would have _____ IV(s) and _____ total treatment group(s).

6. Devise an original example of a factorial design that uses mixed assignment to groups.

Choosing an Experimental Design

At this point, you have discovered that there are three major types of experimental designs—two-group, multiple-group, and multiple IV. Each of these three types of experimental designs has at least two subtypes, based on participant assignment variables (independent versus correlated groups, plus mixed assignment for multiple IV designs). As a beginning researcher, you may find this array of experimental designs almost overwhelming as you plan your first experiment. Now we will cover some basic issues that researchers must face as they plan their studies. We hope this information will be helpful to you as you plan your research.

Comparing the Factorial Design to Two-Group and Multiple-Group Designs

As we mentioned earlier, factorial designs are based on the basic building-block designs we encountered in Chapters 10 and 12. We create factorial designs by combining two of our basic building-block designs into a single design. Detectives use basic investigative principles as their building blocks even in complex cases.

You may remember that we described two-group designs as being ideal for a preliminary investigation of a particular IV in a presence–absence format (refer back to Figure 10-2). In a similar fashion, 2 × 2 factorial designs may be used for preliminary investigations of two IVs. If you look at Figure 14-3, where we created a hypothetical expansion of McClellan and Woods's (2001) hearing study, you can see we used that design to make a preliminary investigation of salesclerks' responses based on customer hearing (deaf versus hearing) and sex of the clerks (female versus male). When we completed this experiment, we would have information about whether customer hearing and clerks' sex have any effects on clerks' response times. Suppose we wished to go further: What if we wanted to delve deeper into the effects of customer impairment or sex?

In Chapter 12 we found that the multiple-group design could be used to conduct more in-depth investigations of an IV that interests us. We took our basic two-group design and extended it to include more levels of our IV. We can make the same type of extension with factorial designs. Figure 14-10 shows an extension of Figure 14-3 to include three levels of one IV, thus creating a 3 × 2 factorial design (of course, there is no way to add a third level to salesclerks' sex!). Notice that Figure 14-10 is simply a three-level, multiple-group experiment and a two-group experiment combined into one design. From this hypothetical design, we get much more specific information about the effects of customer disability because we used three different types of customers with

FIGURE 14-10 COMBINATION OF TWO MULTIPLE-GROUP DESIGNS.

two types of disabilities rather than just the presence versus absence of disability, as shown in Figure 14-3. Just as with the multiple-group design, there is no limit to the number of levels for any IV in a factorial design. Also, the number of levels of the IVs can be unequal (as in this case) or equal. Thus, we could create 2×5 factorial designs, 3×3 factorial designs, 3×6 factorial designs, and so on.

To this point, our discussion of Figure 14-10 has not added anything that we couldn't obtain by conducting two separate experiments. Whether we conduct one factorial experiment or two single-IV experiments, we will uncover information about the effects of our main effects or IVs. However, as we have already seen, the true advantage of factorial designs is that they measure interaction effects. We have mentioned several times that interaction effects enable us to better understand the complexities of the world in which we live.

Unfortunately, we frequently come across students who are not interested in learning about complex relations as characterized by interaction effects. Instead, they would prefer to conduct single-IV experiments because the results from such experiments are simpler to understand. We are not against simple research designs—they contribute a great deal to our ability to understand the world—but we are against the attitude that says, "I want to use simple research designs because they are easier." If your sole reason for choosing a research design is that it is simpler, we believe that you are making a choice for the wrong reason. Remember that we have cautioned you to choose the simplest research design that will *adequately test your hypothesis*. It is possible that the simplest research design available will *not* adequately test your hypothesis. For example, if we already have a great deal of information about a particular IV, then a presence-versus-absence manipulation of that IV is probably too simple. By the same token, if we already know that changes in a particular DV are caused by complex factors, then a simple design may not advance our knowledge any further. Let us provide you with an example in the following paragraph to illustrate what we're talking about.

Let's suppose that a friend, Joe, wishes to conduct research on why college students make the grades that they do. In this research grades will be the DV, and Joe wants to isolate the IV that causes those grades. One logical choice for a factor that causes grades is intelligence because it stands to reason that more intelligent students will make higher grades and less intelligent students will make lower grades. Joe knows that he cannot give intelligence tests to a large number of college students, so he decides to use ACT or SAT scores as a rough measure of intelligence. Joe chooses a group of students who have high ACT or SAT scores and a group of students who have low ACT or SAT scores and compares their respective grades. Sure enough, Joe finds that the students in the high group have higher GPAs than those in the low group. Joe is excited because his hypothesis has been confirmed. He writes a report about his results and goes on his merry way, telling everyone he meets that intelligence causes differences in college students' grades.

 Is there anything wrong with the scenario we have just sketched for you? Do you see any specific flaws in the research itself? Do you see any flaws in the reasoning or in the original design?

Is this research flawed? Not really—there are neither obvious violations of experimental guidelines nor obvious extraneous variables. A better answer is that the original reasoning is flawed, or at least too simplistic.

Think about the original question for a moment. Do you believe that ACT or SAT scores can be used to explain *everything* there is to know about college students' grades? If you are like most students, your answer will be a resounding no. We all know students who entered college with low test scores, perhaps even on probation, but who have gone on to make good grades. On the other hand, we know students who entered with academic scholarships yet flunked out. Clearly, there must be more to grades than intelligence or whatever entrance exams measure. What about factors such as motivation and study skills? What about living in a dorm versus an apartment? What about being married versus being single? What about belonging to a sorority or fraternity versus being an independent? All these factors could contribute to some of the variability in GPA that we observe among college students. Thus, if we decide to "put all our eggs in one basket" of entrance exam scores, we may be simplifying the question too much.

The problem with asking simple questions is that we get simple answers, because that is all that we *can* get from a simple question. Again, there is nothing inherently wrong or bad about asking a simple question and getting a simple answer—*unless* we conclude that this simple answer tells us everything we need to know about our subject matter. In such a case, we would be guilty of what Sherlock Holmes criticized: "You see, but you do not observe" (Doyle, 1927, p. 162). Asking more complex questions may yield more complex answers, but those answers may give us a better idea of how the world actually works. Factorial designs give us the means to ask these more complex questions.

Choosing a Factorial Design

Three considerations are important when you choose a particular factorial design. At the heart of the choice are your experimental questions; factorial designs provide considerable flexibility when devising an experiment to answer your questions. Second, it will not surprise you that you should consider issues of control in your design choice because experimental design is primarily concerned with the notion of control. Third, due to the wide degree of experimental choices possible with factorial designs, considerations of a practical nature are also important.

Experimental Questions   The number of questions we can ask in a factorial experiment increases dramatically. Being able to ask additional questions is a great opportunity but it also puts a burden on us. When we ask additional questions, we must make certain that the questions coordinate with each other. Just as many people would not want to wear clothes with colors that clash, we do not want to ask questions that "clash." By clashing questions, we refer to questions that do not make sense when put together. No doubt you have sat in class and heard a student ask a question that seemed to have no relation to what was being covered in class. Experimental questions that have no relevance to each other may seem to clash when combined in the same experiment. For example, suppose you heard of a proposed experiment to find the effects of self-esteem and eye color on academic test performance. Does that planned experiment jar you somewhat? We hope it does. Does it make sense to combine self-esteem and eye color in an experiment? Does it make sense to examine the effects of eye color on test performance? This factor sounds like an IV that was thrown in simply because it could be. Could eye color be a logical IV? Perhaps it could in another situation. For example, eye color might well influence people's judgments of a target person's attractiveness or even of his or her intelligence. It seems unlikely, though, that eye color might affect one's test performance. We hope that "off-the-wall" combinations of IVs will be minimized by a review of the existing psychological literature. When you base your experimental questions on previous research and theory, the odds of using strange combinations of IVs are decreased.

Control Issues   We hope that by now you are able to anticipate the topic of discussion when you see the *Control Issues* heading. A glance at Figure 14-2 will remind you that we do need to consider independent versus correlated groups in factorial designs. A complicating factor for factorial designs is that we have to make this decision for each IV we include in an experiment.

Research psychologists typically assume that random assignment to groups will adequately equate the groups if you have approximately 10 participants per group. On the other hand, a correlated assignment scheme (matching or repeated measures) will provide you with greater assurance of the equality of the groups. We hope that by now you fully understand the reasoning behind these two approaches. If you need a review, look back to Chapters 10 and 12.

Practical Considerations   As IVs multiply in experimental designs, some of the practical issues involved become more complex. Often, when students find that they can ask more than one question in an experiment, they go wild, adding IVs left and right, throwing in everything but the proverbial kitchen sink. Although curiosity is a commendable virtue, it is necessary to keep your curiosity somewhat in check when designing an experiment. Remember the **principle of parsimony** that we encountered in Chapter 10: You are well advised to keep your experiment at the bare minimum necessary to answer the question(s) that most interest(s) you. We heard this principle cast in a slightly different light when a speaker was giving advice to graduate students about planning their theses and dissertations. This speaker advised students to follow the "KISS" principle: **K**eep **I**t **S**imple, **S**tupid. This piece of advice was not given as an insult or meant to be condescending. The speaker merely realized that there seems to be a natural tendency to want to answer too many questions in one brilliantly-conceived and wonderfully-designed experiment.

> **Principle of parsimony**
> The belief that explanations of phenomena and events should remain simple until the simple explanations are no longer valid.

With a two-group or multiple-group design, there is an obvious limitation on how many questions you can ask because of the single IV in those designs. However, with a factorial design, the sky seems to be the limit—you can use as many IVs with as many levels as you wish. However, you should always bear in mind that you are complicating matters when you add IVs and levels. Remember the two problems we mentioned earlier in the chapter: One complication occurs in actually conducting the experiment: More participants are required, more experimental sessions are necessary, you have more chances for things to go wrong, and so on. A second complication can occur in your data interpretation: Interactions between four, five, six, or more IVs become nearly impossible to interpret. It is probably this reason that explains why most factorial designs are limited to two or three IVs. Wise detectives limit their investigations to a few leads at a time rather than trying to simultaneously chase down every lead they get.

Variations on Factorial Designs

In Chapters 10 and 12 we saw two variations that have carried with us to this chapter, comparing different amounts of an IV and using measured IVs. For factorial designs, we add to this list the use of more than two IVs. Let's look at the two carryovers before looking at the new variation.

Comparing Different Amounts of an IV   We already mentioned this variation earlier in the chapter. When we created the hypothetical experiment diagrammed in Figure 14-10, we compared three different types (levels) of customers.

A caution is in order about adding levels to any IV in a factorial design. In the multiple-group design, when you used an additional level of your IV, you added only one group to your experiment. When you add a level to an IV in a factorial design, you add *several* groups to your experiment because each new level must be added under each level of your other independent variable(s). For example, expanding a 2×2 design to a 3×2 design requires 6 groups rather than 4. Enlarging a $2 \times 2 \times 2$ design to a $3 \times 2 \times 2$ design means using 12, rather than 8, groups. Adding levels in a factorial design increases groups in a multiplicative fashion.

Ex post facto research
A research approach in which the experimenter cannot directly manipulate the IV but can only classify, categorize, or measure the IV because it is predetermined in the participants (e.g., IV = sex).

Using Measured IVs   It will probably not surprise you to learn that we can use IVs that we do not manipulate in factorial designs also. It is important to remember that using a measured rather than a manipulated IV results in **ex post facto research**. Without the control that comes from directly causing an IV to vary, we must exercise extreme caution in drawing conclusions from such studies. Still, ex post facto studies give us our only means of studying IVs such as sex or personality traits.

Because factorial designs deal with more than one IV at a time, we can develop an experiment that uses one manipulated IV and one measured IV at the same time. Nicole Wolensky (2001), a student at Marquette University in Marquette, Wisconsin, conducted research that provides a good example of just such an experiment. She had elderly participants evaluate pictures of couples as a function of participant sex and age of couples in the photographs.

PSYCHOLOGICAL DETECTIVE   After reading this one-sentence description of Wolensky's experiment, can you tell which IV was manipulated and which was measured?

If you decided that participant sex was the measured IV and that age of couples in photos was the manipulated IV, you are correct. Of course, participant sex is always a measured variable—we cannot "cause" our participants to be male or female! Thus, the age of couples in the photographs *had* to be the manipulated variable. Wolensky showed half of her participants pictures of young couples and the other half of the participants saw pictures of elderly couples.

What are the implications for interpreting information from an experiment that uses both manipulated and measured IVs? We must still be cautious about interpreting information from the measured IV(s) because we did not cause the levels to vary. On the other hand, we are free to interpret information from manipulated IVs just as usual. Thus, Wolensky could be more certain about the results from viewing older or younger couples' photos than she could about why any effects due to participant sex occurred.

Dealing with More than Two IVs Designing an experiment with more than two IVs is probably the most important variation of the factorial design. In this section we will discuss the use of factorial designs with three IVs. Larger designs with more than three IVs follow the same basic strategies that we outline here. Again, we must caution you against adding IVs to an experiment without a good reason.

> **Three-way design** A factorial design that has three IVs.

Figure 14-11 depicts the simplest possible factorial design with three IVs (often referred to as a **three-way design**). As you can see, it is somewhat difficult to draw three-dimensional designs on a two-dimensional surface. This design has three IVs (A, B, and C), each with two levels. Thus, this design represents a $2 \times 2 \times 2$ experiment.

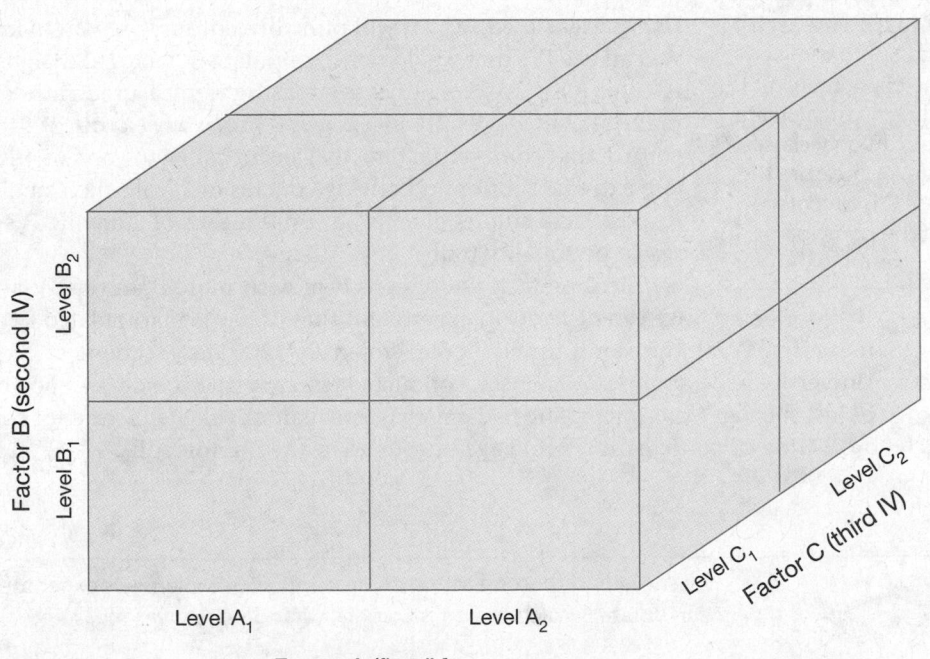

FIGURE 14-11 SIMPLEST POSSIBLE THREE-WAY FACTORIAL DESIGN ($2 \times 2 \times 2$).

FIGURE 14-12 SECOND EXPANSION OF MCCLELLAN AND WOODS'S (2001) HEARING DISABILITY STUDY.

We could expand this design by adding levels to any of the IVs, but remember that the number of treatment combinations increases in a multiplicative rather than additive fashion.

Let's look at a hypothetical example of a three-way design. If you look back at Figure 14-3, you will remember that we conceptualized an extension of McClellan and Woods's (2001) customer hearing study by adding a second IV: the sex of the sales-clerks. Imagine that we were also interested in testing for the effects of the customers' sex—in testing whether male and female customers receive help from salesclerks more quickly. This change would transform the design in Figure 14-3 to the design shown in Figure 14-12. We have "exploded" the design so that you can easily see each of the eight treatment combinations. Notice that there is a group of participants specified for each of those different treatment combinations.

 Figure 14-12 specifies eight different combinations of treatments (the three IVs). Would this design require eight different groups of clerks? Why or why not?

This design would require eight different groups of clerks if it is planned as a completely between-groups design. In that case, you would need to create eight different groups of clerks through random assignment. The design would also require eight different groups if you used matched sets of clerks. One possibility that would reduce the number of clerks needed would be the use of repeated measures. Could any of the three IVs be used with repeated measures? Clearly, sex of the salesclerks is out—a person cannot be both male and female. Customer hearing or sex have the possibility of being used as a repeated measure, depending on how you assign clerks to groups. Salesclerks could wait on both hearing and deaf customers. Likewise, clerks could wait on both male and female customers.

One more consideration is necessary before you could advocate the use of repeated measures—the DV. Can the DV be used more than once with the same salesclerks? If we continue to use response time as the DV, the answer would be "yes." There is nothing that would prevent us measuring a salesclerk's response time to more than one customer. On the other hand, some DVs cannot be used more than once. Again, remember the Burkeley et al. (2000) experiment in which participants solved anagrams. We cannot use the same anagrams in a repeated measures situation because the participants would have already solved them. Using repeated measures on anagram solving would require two different but equal sets of anagrams, which should be possible to design.

Thus, the not-so-short answer to the short question in the previous Psychological Detective section is "it depends." Although the design in Figure 14-12 specifies eight groups of salesclerks, it does not necessarily specify eight *different* groups of clerks. Our determination of the number of groups depends on whether we use independent groups or repeated measures.

One final point remains for us to cover about factorial designs that have more than two IVs. We have mentioned interaction effects several times in this chapter. As we add IVs, we also add more interaction effects to our design. If we have three IVs (*A*, *B*, and *C*) we would obtain information about four interactions—*AB*, *AC*, *BC*, and *ABC*. To make these interactions more specific, let's use Figure 14-12 as our example. Given that our experiment diagrammed in Figure 14-12 has customer hearing, salesclerk sex, and customer sex as IVs, our statistical tests will evaluate interactions for customer hearing and salesclerk sex, customer hearing and customer sex, salesclerk sex and customer sex, and for all three variables simultaneously (customer hearing, salesclerk sex, and customer sex). You will find as many interaction effects as there are unique combinations of the treatments.

PSYCHOLOGICAL DETECTIVE   Imagine that you had an experiment with four IVs—*A*, *B*, *C*, and *D*. List all the possible interactions.

Did you find that there are 11 possible interactions? Let's look at the possibilities:

Two-way (two IVs) interactions:	*AB, AC, AD, BC, BD, CD*
Three-way (three IVs) interactions:	*ABC, ABD, ACD, BCD*
Four-way (all four IVs) interactions:	*ABCD*

The idea of evaluating 11 different interactions, including one with a possibility of all four variables interacting at once, may be challenging enough for you to understand why we suggest that you limit your experiments to no more than three IVs.

REVIEW SUMMARY

1. Researchers create **factorial designs** by combining two-group or multiple-group designs.
2. We use factorial designs to test the effects of more than one IV on a particular DV at the same time. These designs allow us to test under conditions that are more like the real world than dealing with only one variable at a time.
3. When choosing a particular factorial design, you must consider your experimental questions, issues of control, and practical matters.
4. In a factorial design, we can deal with different types or amounts of an IV or with measured IVs, just as we can with a two-group or multiple-group design.
5. Factorial designs may consist of three or more IVs, although the statistical interpretation of such designs becomes more complicated because of an increasing number of interactions.

CHECK YOUR PROGRESS

1. Why are factorial designs merely combinations of what you learned about in Chapters 10 and 12? Drawing a picture may help you here.
2. Suppose a friend told you about her $2 \times 4 \times 3$ experimental design. Draw a diagram of this design. Explain its structure.
3. Describe (a) totally between groups, (b) totally within groups, and (c) mixed-groups designs. How are they similar? How are they different?
4. Why should your experimental questions be your first consideration in choosing a factorial design?
5. Suppose you wish to test children from two different racial groups. You would be dealing with a(n) _____ IV.
6. Your friend, who plans to take experimental psychology next term, tells you that she is very excited about taking the class because she already has her experiment planned. She wants to test the effects of parental divorce, socioeconomic status, geographical area of residence, parental education, type of preschool attended, and parents' political preference on the sex-role development of children. What advice would you offer this friend?
7. A 2×3 experiment has been conducted. How many interactions will be calculated?
    a. one   b. two   c. three   d. six

KEY TERMS

Factors, *312*	Factorial design, *313*
Independent variables, *312*	Main effect, *317*

LOOKING AHEAD

In this chapter we learned about the most sophisticated of all experimental designs—factorial designs that include multiple IVs. This material completes a three-chapter section on experimental design, data analysis, and interpretation. In the next chapter we will look at some alternative research approaches that you may, at some time, need to use.

15

Analyzing and Interpreting Experiments That Have Multiple Independent Variables

Before Your Statistical Analysis

We are certain that you remember this fact by now, but we will remind you that experimental design and statistical analysis go hand in hand. You must plan your experiment carefully, choosing the experimental design that best enables you to ask your questions of interest. Having selected your experimental design from the list of choices we are presenting guarantees that you will be able to analyze your data with a standard statistical test. Thus, you will be spared the experimental fate worse than death—collecting your data and finding no test with which to analyze the data.

Analyzing Factorial Designs

In Chapter 14, we examined designs that have more than one IV. We analyze factorial designs with the same type of statistical test that we used for analyzing multiple-group designs—analysis of variance (ANOVA). As we mentioned in Chapter 14, we need to be able to distinguish among the various ANOVA approaches so we often modify ANOVA with words that refer to the size of the design and the way we assign participants to groups. Labels you may hear that refer to the size of the design include *factorial ANOVA* as a general term or *two-way ANOVA* or *three-way ANOVA* for designs that have two or three IVs, respectively. Alternatively, researchers may indicate the size of the design as $X \times Y$, where X and Y represent the number of levels of the two factors, as we noted several times in Chapter 14. For example, labels that describe how researchers assign participants to groups might include *independent groups, completely randomized, completely between-subjects, completely between-groups, totally between-subjects*, or *totally between-groups* for designs that use random assignment for all IVs. Designs that use matching or repeated measures may be called *randomized block, completely within-subjects, completely within-groups, totally within-subjects*, or *totally within-groups*. Designs that use a mixture of "between" and "within" assignment procedures may be referred to as *mixed* or *split-plot factorial*. As you can see, the labels for factorial designs can get quite long. Again, if you understand the principles behind the designs, the names are usually not difficult to interpret. For example, you might hear about a *three-way totally between-groups* design or a *two-way mixed ANOVA*.

PSYCHOLOGICAL DETECTIVE Can you "decode" the two examples given in the previous sentence? What types of designs do these two cases indicate?

The design indicated by the "three-way totally between-groups" label would include three IVs ("three-way") and would use random assignment of participants in all conditions. "Two-way mixed ANOVA" refers to an experiment that has two IVs, one of which uses random assignment and one of which uses a correlated assignment technique (matching or repeated measures). Notice that these descriptions do not give us a full picture of the design because there is no numerical description that would allow us to know how many levels each IV has. To get the fullest amount of information, a label such as *a 2 × 3 × 2 completely between-groups design* is necessary. From this label, we know that there are three IVs that have two, three, and two levels, respectively. We also know that the experimenter assigned participants to each of the IVs in a random manner. Notice how much information about experimental design we can pack into a short, descriptive label.

Planning Your Experiment

In Chapter 13 we featured a hypothetical experiment to investigate the effects of dress on the time salesclerks took to wait on customers. That example used a multiple-group design because we compared three different styles of clothing to see how they affected clerks' responses. It should be clear to you that we must derive a new hypothetical experiment to use as an example because we are dealing with a new design.

 PSYCHOLOGICAL DETECTIVE How could we make a slight alteration in our clothing style experiment of Chapter 13 in order to make it appropriate for use as an example in this chapter? Give this question some careful thought—make the alteration as simple as possible. Draw a block diagram of your proposed experiment.

As is often the case when you are designing an experiment, there are many possible correct answers. The key feature that your altered experiment must contain is the *addition* of a second IV. Keeping the clothing difference as one IV and adding a second IV, your design should resemble Figure 15-1. Although you could have included more than two levels of either or both of your IVs, that would complicate the design. In

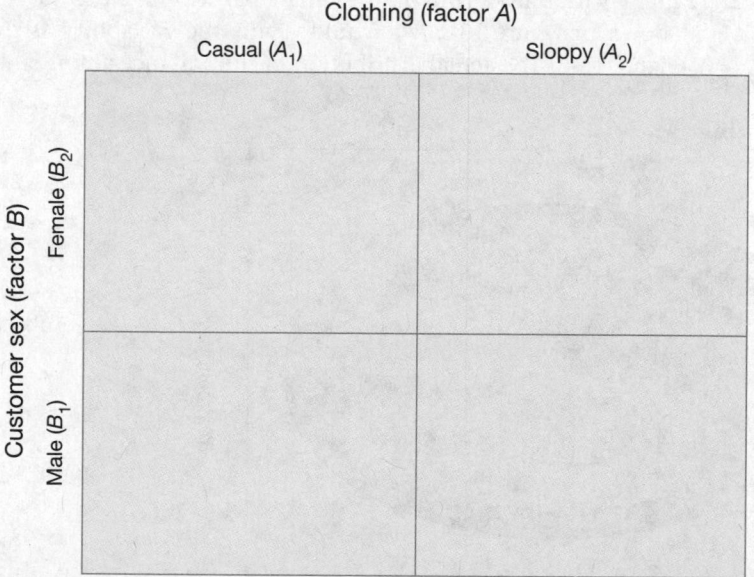

FIGURE 15-1 HYPOTHETICAL EXPERIMENT USING CLOTHING AND CUSTOMER SEX IVs.

asking you to keep your altered design simple, we also assumed you would not choose a three-IV design.

Our statistical example for this chapter will build on our example in Chapter 13. You will remember that we compared three different styles of clothing to determine whether the clothes made any difference in how quickly salespeople responded. Indeed, we found that clerks responded more quickly to customers in dressy or casual clothes than to customers in sloppy clothes. Suppose you are examining the data from the previous experiment and you think you detected an oddity in the data: It appears to you that salesclerks may have responded differently to female and male customers in addition to the different styles of dress. You decide to investigate this question in order to find out whether both customer sex and dress affect salesclerks' response times to customers. Because there was no difference between responses to customers in dressy and casual clothing (see Chapter 13), you decide to use only casual and sloppy clothes. Thus, you have designed a 2 × 2 experiment (see Figure 15-1) in which the two IVs are clothing style (casual and sloppy) and customer sex (male and female).

> **Factorial ANOVA**
> Analysis used to analyze data from designs that have two or more IVs.

> **Treatment variability**
> Variability in DV scores that is due to the effects of the IV (also known as *between-groups variability*).

> **Error variability**
> Variability in DV scores that is due to factors other than the IV such as individual differences, measurement error, and extraneous variation (also known as *within-groups variability*).

Rationale of Factorial ANOVA

The rationale behind **ANOVA for factorial designs** is basically the same as we saw in Chapter 12, with one major modification. We still use ANOVA to partition (divide) the variability into two sources—**treatment variability** and **error variability**. However, with factorial designs, the sources of treatment variability increase. Instead of having one IV as the sole source of treatment variability, factorial designs have multiple IVs and their interactions as sources of treatment variability. Thus, rather than partitioning the variability as shown in Figure 13-1, we would divide the variability as shown in Figure 15-2. The actual distribution of the variance among the factors

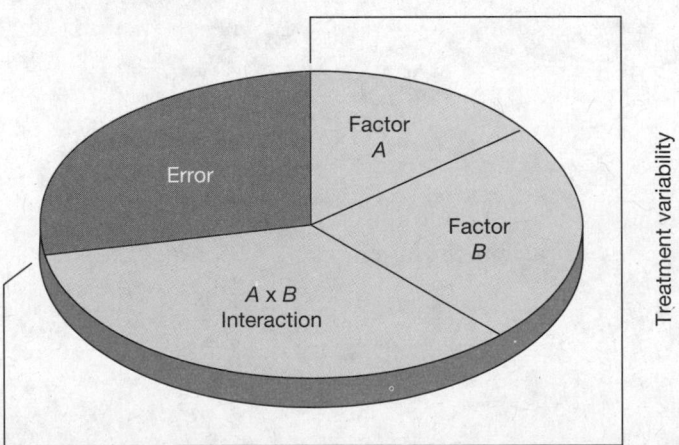

FIGURE 15-2 PARTITIONING THE VARIABILITY IN A FACTORIAL DESIGN THAT HAS TWO IVs.

would depend, of course, on which effects were significant. If you used a factorial design that had three IVs, the variability would be partitioned into even more components.

You might guess that we will add statistical formulas because we have added more components to the statistical analysis. You would be correct in this guess. You can turn back to Chapter 13 to review the general ANOVA equations for the one-IV situation. For a two-IV factorial design, we use the following equations:

$$F_A = \frac{\text{IV } A \text{ variability}}{\text{error variability}}$$

$$F_B = \frac{\text{IV } B \text{ variability}}{\text{error variability}}$$

$$F_{A \times B} = \frac{\text{interaction variability}}{\text{error variability}}$$

These equations allow us to separately evaluate the effects of each of the two IVs as well as their interaction. If we used a larger factorial design, we would end up with an F ratio for each of the IVs and each interaction.

Understanding Interactions

When two variables interact, their joint effect may not be obvious or predictable from examining their separate effects. Let us cite one of the most famous examples of an interaction effect. Many people find drinking a glass or two of wine to be a pleasurable experience. Many people find taking a drive to be relaxing. What happens if we combine these two activities—do we end up with an extremely pleasurable and relaxing experience? Of course not. We may end up with deadly consequences. Interaction effects often occur with different drugs. Hence, you often hear very strict guidelines and warnings about combining various drugs. Combinations of drugs, in particular, are likely to have synergistic effects so that a joint effect occurs that is not predictable from either drug alone. You may have seen interaction or **synergistic effects** when two particular children are together. Separately, the children are calm and well behaved. However, when they are put together, watch out! Detectives often face interaction effects in their work. A seemingly normal person, when confronted with a stressful day and an irritating situation, may react violently. Neither the stress nor the annoyance alone would have led to a violent crime, but their combination could turn deadly.

Synergistic effects
Dramatic consequences that occur when you combine two or more substances, conditions, or organisms. The effects are greater than what is individually possible.

Remember our earlier discussion of Figure 14-4 and the interaction pattern found there? In an experimental situation we are concerned with how different levels of different IVs interact with respect to the DV. A significant interaction means that the effects of the various IVs are not straightforward and simple. For this reason, we virtually ignore our IV main effects when we find a significant interaction. Sometimes interactions are difficult to interpret, particularly when we have more than two IVs or many levels of an IV. A strategy that often helps us make sense of an interaction is to graph it. By graphing your DV on the Y axis and one IV on the X axis, you can depict your other IV with lines on the graph (see Chapter 8). By studying such a graph, you can usually deduce what happened to cause a significant interaction. For example, by examining

Figure 14-4, you can see that the results for the customers' disability are not constant based on the sex of the salesclerks. The disability affected the behavior of male clerks to a much greater degree than it affected the behavior of female clerks. Thus, the effects of a customer's hearing disability were not straightforward; they depended on whether you were talking about female or male salesclerks. Remember that an interaction is present when the effect of one IV *depends on the specific level of the other IV*.

When you graph a significant interaction, you will often notice that the lines of the graph cross or converge. This pattern is a visual indication that the effects of one IV change as the second IV is varied. Nonsignificant interactions typically show lines that are close to parallel, as you saw in Figure 14-6. Gauthreaux (2000) found that reading an article relevant to a trial resulted in higher ratings of guilt than reading an irrelevant article. She also found that either hearing or not hearing an instruction to ignore the article made no difference in the guilt ratings. Further, there was no interaction between the two IVs (the lines on her graph were nearly parallel; see Figure 14-8, p. 321). As we cover our statistical examples in the next few pages, we will pay special attention to the interaction effects.

Two-Way ANOVA for Independent Groups

Our statistical analyses of factorial designs will provide us with more information than we got from two-group or multiple-group designs. The analyses will take longer to compute by hand, but they are not necessarily more complicated than those we saw in Chapters 11 and 13. They do provide more information because we have multiple IVs and interaction effects to analyze.

Calculating ANOVA by Hand

Let's begin with a quick review of our experimental design in Figure 15-1. We have four different groups of saleclerks waiting on either women dressed in sloppy clothes, women dressed casually, men dressed in sloppy clothes, or men dressed casually.

 Why does this experiment require a **two-way ANOVA for independent groups**?

Two-way ANOVA for independent groups Analysis technique for experiments that have two IVs that are both between-subjects factors.

First, the design is a two-way ANOVA because we have two IVs: customer clothing (casual or sloppy) and customer sex (male or female). The fact that we have four different groups of clerks, each waiting on one of our four groups, indicates that we have independent groups. The clerks are neither matched nor do they wait on more than one type of customer (repeated measures).

Just as with the one-way ANOVA, the computations require multiple formulas. Based on our generic formulas that we saw a few paragraphs ago, we need to find not only the between-groups and error variability, we also have to divide the between-groups variability into its sources.

What *are* the different sources for between-groups variability?

In a two-way ANOVA, we will break between-groups variability down into three components: the first IV, the second IV, and the interaction of the two IVs. If we add another IV, there are additional sources of variability: the third IV, the new two-way interactions, and the three-way interaction. Remember from Chapter 13 that we refer to the variability related to each effect as the **sum of squares**. Because we have more sources of variability, we have more sums of squares to compute than we did for a one-way ANOVA. Our calculations appear in Tables 15-1 and 15-2;

> **Sum of squares** The amount of variability in the DV attributable to each source.

TABLE 15-1 HYPOTHETICAL SALESCLERKS' RESPONSE TIMES (SECONDS) FOR COMPARING CLOTHING STYLES AND SEX OF CUSTOMERS

		CLOTHING			
		Casual		**Sloppy**	
		X	X^2	X	X^2
CUSTOMER SEX	**Female**	46	2,116	37	1,369	Female $M = 49.83$
		39	1,521	47	2,209	$\Sigma n = 12$
		50	2,500	44	1,936	
		52	2,704	62	3,844	
		48	2,304	49	2,401	
		54	2,916	70	4,900	
		$\Sigma = 289$	14,061	$\Sigma = 309$	16,659	$\Sigma X = 598$
		$M = 48.17$		$M = 51.50$		$\Sigma X^2 = 30,720$
	Male	38	1,444	47	2,209	Male $M = 57.17$
		50	2,500	69	4,761	$\Sigma n = 12$
		38	1,444	69	4,761	
		44	1,936	74	5,476	
		49	2,401	77	5,929	
		55	3,025	76	5,776	
		$\Sigma = 274$	12,750	$\Sigma = 412$	28,912	$\Sigma X = 686$
		$M = 45.67$		$M = 68.67$		$\Sigma X^2 = 41,662$

$\Sigma X = 563$ $\Sigma X = 721$ $\Sigma X = 1,284$
$\Sigma X^2 = 26,811$ $\Sigma X^2 = 45,571$ $\Sigma X^2 = 72,382$
$\Sigma n = 12$ $\Sigma n = 12$

Casual $M = 46.92$ Sloppy $M = 60.08$ Total Population $M = 53.50$ $\Sigma N = 24$

TABLE 15-2 **CALCULATIONS FOR TWO-WAY ANOVA FOR INDEPENDENT SAMPLES**

a. First, we find the total sum of squares. Note the similarity of the formula to that for finding a *SD*:

$$SS_{total} = 72,382 = \frac{(1,284)^2}{24} = 72,382 - 68,694 = 3,688$$

b. To find the clothing sum of squares, we use a similar formula but sum across the two types of clothing:

$$SS_{clo} = \frac{563^2}{12} + \frac{721^2}{12} - \frac{(1,284)^2}{24} = 26,414.083 + 43,320.083 - 68,694 = 1,040.17$$

To find the sum of squares for customer sex, we repeat the previous operation except that we sum across the customer sex variable:

$$SS_{csex} = \frac{598^2}{12} + \frac{686^2}{12} - \frac{(1,284)^2}{24} = 29,800.333 + 39,216.333 - 68,694 = 322.67$$

c. To find the interaction sum of squares, we work out an interesting formula for each of the four cells: We begin with the cell mean, subtract the two overall means for its column and row, and then add the overall mean. In each case we square the total, sum those four numbers, and then multiply by the number of participants per cell.

$$SS_{int} = 6[(48.17 - 46.92 - 49.83 + 53.5)^2 + (51.5 - 60.08 - 49.83 + 53.5)^2 + (45.67 - 46.92 - 57.17 + 53.5)^2 + (68.67 - 60.08 - 57.17 + 53.5)^2]$$
$$= 6[(4.92)^2 + (-4.91)^2 + (-4.92)^2 + (4.92)^2]$$
$$= 6[24.206 + 24.108 + 24.206 + 24.206]$$
$$= 6(96.726) = 580.36$$

Note: If you use the means to five decimal places as they show in the calculator, each sum = ±4.91667

$(\pm 4.91667)^2 = 24.173643(4) = 96.694572$
$6(96.694572) = 580.167 = 580.17$

d. To find the error sum of squares, we use the formula that we used for the total sum of squares and apply it to each of the four cells:

$$SS_{error} = \left(14,061 - \frac{289^2}{6}\right) + \left(16,659 - \frac{309^2}{6}\right) + \left(12,750 - \frac{274^2}{6}\right) + \left(28,912 - \frac{412^2}{6}\right)$$
$$= 140.833 + 745.5 + 237.333 + 621.333 = 1,744.999$$

e. Total $df = N - 1 = 24 - 1 = 23$
Customer sex df = # groups $- 1 = 2 - 1 = 1$
Clothing df = # groups $- 1 = 2 - 1 = 1$
Interaction df = (clothing df)(customer sex df) = (1)(1) = 1
Error $df = N -$ (# clothing groups)(# customer sex groups) = 24 - (2)(2) = 20

f. MS = SS/df
All values with 1 df have MS = SS
$MS_{error} = 1,745/20 = 87.25$

g. $F = SS_{treatment}/SS_{error}$
$F_{clothing} = 1,040.17/87.25 = 11.92$
$F_{customer\ sex} = 322.67/87.25 = 3.70$
$F_{interaction} = 580.17/87.25 = 6.65$

you will notice that they are quite similar to the calculations we used in Chapter 13. We begin by finding the sums of all groups' scores, squaring the scores, and summing the squared scores (see Table 15-1).

> **Total sum of squares** The total amount of variability in DV scores.

Total Sum of Squares   The formula for computing the **total sum of squares** appears in Table 15-2a; again, it is similar to the formula we used when we began calculating standard deviations. Notice that we are working with the total scores from all four groups and all their squared scores. After we have found the total sum of squares (3,688), we will partition (divide) it into its various components.

> **Treatment sum of squares** The amount of variability due to an IV.

Main Effect Sums of Squares   The main effect sums of squares are analogous to the **treatment sum of squares** from Chapter 13, which represented the variability due to the IV. However, remember that we have two IVs in this chapter so we must compute variability for each separately. You could compute the sum of squares for either IV first; the order is not important. We calculated the effect for clothing first because that IV has been our focus throughout the research project. Notice that the formula for computing the sum of squares for either main effect is the same—we simply sum the scores across the groups differently (see Figure 15-2b). We also hope that, by now, you have noticed how often you use the same subtraction term in your computations. So, although the formulas may look complicated they really are not. After our computations, we find that the sum of squares for clothing (1,040.17) is larger than the customer sex sum of squares (322.67).

> **Interaction sum of squares** The amount of variability due to an interaction.

Interaction Sum of Squares   In addition to variability from the main effects, there is also variability due to the interaction of the two IVs. The computations for the **interaction sum of squares** are more time consuming because we have to work with four means for each of the four cells. Still, *time consuming* does not mean difficult! After completing our calculations (see Figure 15-2c), we find that the sum of squares for the interaction of clothing and customer sex (580.17) falls between the sums of squares for the two IVs.

> **Error sum of squares** Variability in DV scores that is due to factors other than IVs and interactions; can include individual differences, measurement error, and extraneous variation.

Error Sum of Squares   As with the one-way ANOVA, the **error sum of squares** represents all the variability from sources other than the two IVs and their interaction (factors such as individual differences, errors in measurement, and extraneous variation). We hope to keep this source of variation relatively small through our efforts at control in designing and conducting the experiment (see Chapters 5 and 7). Again, the format of this formula should look somewhat familiar to you (see Figure 15-2d), because it has the basic approach of the *SD* formula. Notice that the error sum of squares is relatively large (1,745) compared to that of either IV or the interaction term.

As a check on your computational accuracy, the mean squares for the two IVs, their interaction, and the error term should (when added together) equal the total mean square. In our example, $1,040.17 + 322.67 + 580.17 + 1,745 = 3,688.01$, which equals what we computed for the total sum of squares (3,688). As you have probably noticed by now in statistical computations, answers may be "off" by .01 or .02 due to rounding. Larger differences, of course, may signal errors in your computations.

Mean square The "averaged" variability for each source; computed by dividing each source's sum of squares by its *df*.

Mean Squares   Remember from Chapter 13 that we must find the **mean square** for each source of variation in order to make them directly comparable. To find the mean square, we must first determine the **degrees of freedom (*df*)** for each source of variation. The total *df* are equal to $N - 1$, or 23 in this case. The two IVs both have 1 *df* because the *df* formula is the number of groups (levels of the IV) minus 1 ($2 - 1$ in these cases). The *df* for the interaction equals the *df* values for the two IVs multiplied together (1×1 in this case). The *df* for the error term is equal to the total N minus the number of groups for each IV multiplied together. In our example, $df_{error} = 24 - (2 \times 2) = 20$. Again, you can check your computations by adding all the *df* for the various effects to make certain that they are equal to the total *df*: $1 + 1 + 1 + 20 = 23$.

Degrees of freedom (*df*) The ability of a number in a specified set to assume any value.

To compute the mean squares, we must divide each sum of squares by its respective *df*. Because the *df* for the IVs and the interaction are all 1, the error term's mean square is the only one that differs from its sum of squares. In Table 15-2d, we see that the $MS_{error} = 1,745/20 = 87.25$.

F ratio The ratio calculated by dividing treatment or interaction mean squares by error mean square.

F Ratios   Referring back a few pages to the three **F ratio** formulas, you see that we compute *F*s by dividing the mean square for each source of variation by the error mean square. Remember that we will get *F* ratios for both IVs (clothing and customer sex) as well as their interaction. The *F* ratio for clothing is 11.92 (1,040.17/87.25), the *F* for customer sex is 3.70 (322.67/87.25), and the *F* ratio for the clothing × customer sex interaction is 6.65 (580.17/87.25). Remember that each *F* is a ratio of the variability due to its source compared to the variability due to various sources of error. Thus, if you think back to the "pie wedges" we drew in Chapter 13 (see Figure 13-1), each of these *F*s shows much more variability from the IV or interaction than from error.

Just as in Chapter 13, we have to use the *F* table from the appendix (Table A-4). All three *F* ratios we will examine have the same number of *df*: 1 for the numerator and 20 for the denominator. The table shows us that the critical *F* with 1 and 20 *df* is 4.35 at the .05 level and 8.10 at the .01 level. Thus, the main effect of clothing is significant at the .01 level because our calculated *F* (11.92) exceeds 8.10, and the interaction of clothing and customer sex is significant at the .05 level because its *F* ratio (6.65) is larger than 4.35. When our interaction is significant, it overrides any main effect that we find, so we pay no attention to the main effect. The reason that we ignore the main effect is that the main effect is contained within the interaction; if we interpreted the main effect in a straightforward fashion, we would be guilty of oversimplifying the effect of that IV. For example, looking at the means in Table 15-1, we would interpret the significant clothing effect as showing that customers in casual clothing received help more quickly (46.92 seconds) than customers in sloppy clothing (60.08 seconds). However, we have to remember that a significant interaction means that we must refer to *both* IVs to understand the findings.

PSYCHOLOGICAL DETECTIVE

From the means in Table 15-1, can you figure out why we have a significant interaction? Further, can you figure out what the findings show? It may be difficult for you to decipher the findings from the means alone. If you have difficulty discovering what happened by looking at the means, let us provide you with a hint: Was the pattern of clerks' responses to customers dressed in different clothing the same for customers of both sexes?

Usually, the simplest way to understand an interaction is to graph it. We have graphed the interaction in Figure 15-3. In examining the means, we find that clerks responded to casually dressed female customers in 48.17 seconds and to female customers wearing sloppy clothing in 51.50 seconds—a fairly small difference. On the other hand, male customers in casual clothing received help in 45.67 seconds whereas salesclerks waited on sloppily-dressed males in 68.67 seconds—quite a large difference. You should remember that we described interactions as occurring when the lines on a graph cross or converge and that parallel lines indicate no interaction. The crossing lines of Figure 15-3, in conjunction with the low probability of chance for the interaction term, denote a significant interaction. When we examine the figure, the point

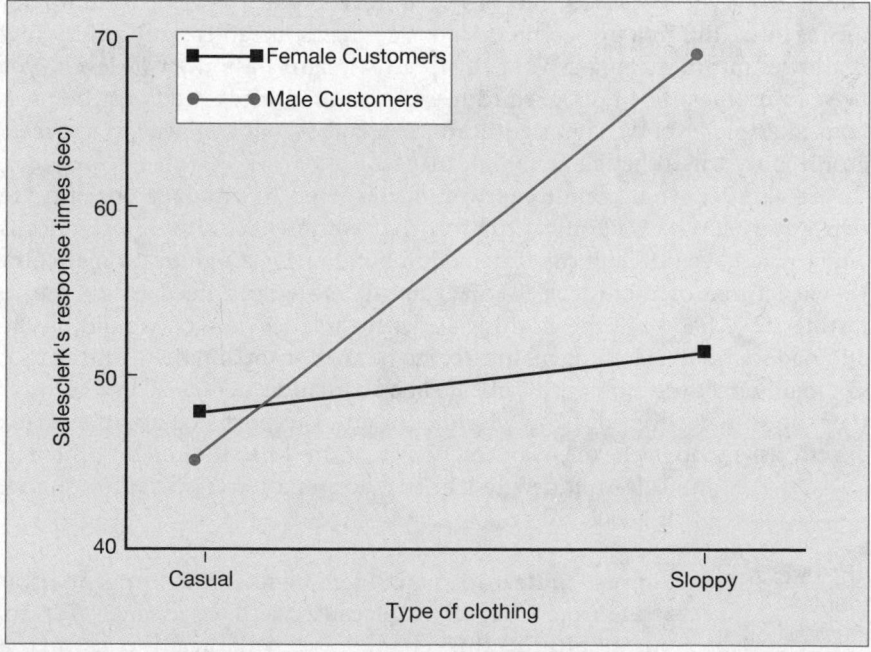

FIGURE 15-3 INTERACTION FOR CLOTHING AND CUSTOMER SEX EXPERIMENT.

that seems to differ most represents the clerks' response times to male customers in sloppy clothes. This mean is considerably higher than the others. Thus, we would conclude that clerks take longer to wait on men who are sloppily dressed than other customers. Notice that our explanation of an interaction effect *must* include a reference to both IVs in order to make sense—the previous sentence mentions the *male* customers in *sloppy* clothes. This explanation shows why we ignore the significant main effect: To simply say that clerks waited on customers in casual clothing more quickly than customers in sloppy clothing is misleading.

Post hoc tests
Statistical comparisons made between group means after finding a significant F ratio.

Post hoc Comparisons You will remember from Chapter 13 that post hoc tests are necessary with one-way ANOVA when we find a significant F ratio. We need to use **post hoc tests** in that situation because we would have a significant finding overall with a minimum of three means to compare. The significant F ratio in that situation simply means that the three means are significantly different somewhere. The post hoc tests allow us to determine which means are significantly different.

In a two-way ANOVA, however, post hoc tests may not be necessary for a variety of reasons. First, if your interaction is significant, remember that it supersedes the main effects. The purpose of post hoc tests is to test the various levels of a significant main effect. If the interaction renders the main effect moot, then there would be no need to use the post hoc tests. The second reason you might not need to conduct post hoc tests is that your experimental design makes them unnecessary. Suppose you conduct an experiment along the lines of this chapter (a 2×2) and find a significant main effect without a significant interaction. Thus, you will need to interpret the main effect. However, because it has only two levels, you will simply compare the two means as we did in a two-group design. The higher mean is significantly higher than the lower mean. As long as your IV (in any design) has only two levels, you do not need to use post hoc tests. A third reason you might not need post hoc tests is that your multiple-level IV is not significant. Remember that you need to test means for IV groups only when they show significance.

So—under what conditions would you need to conduct post hoc tests in a two-way ANOVA? The only situation that would necessitate post hocs is one in which you have no significant interaction but do have a significant main effect for an IV with three or more levels. For example, we would need to do the follow-up testing if we had used the clothing IV with three levels such we did in Chapter 13 and had found the clothing main effect to be significant and the clothing by customer sex main effect was not significant. If such a situation does arise in your research, we have good news for you. You would compute the post hoc analyses (Tukey HSD) exactly as you do in the one-way ANOVA situation (Kirk, 1968). Thus, there is no need to learn a new test or new formula for this chapter. Sometimes life is good!

Source table A table that contains the results of ANOVA. "Source" refers to the source of different types of variation.

Source Table You should remember the concept of a **source table** from Chapter 13. Because we have used ANOVA to analyze our results in this chapter, we will again construct a source table.

PSYCHOLOGICAL DETECTIVE Can you anticipate how a source table for a two-way ANOVA will differ from a source table for a one-way ANOVA?

Remember that the source table for a one-way ANOVA had only two sources of variability: between groups (IV) and within groups (error). However, a source table for a two-way ANOVA will have more sources listed; in addition to error variability, variability could come from the first IV (clothing), the second IV (customer sex), or their interaction.

PSYCHOLOGICAL DETECTIVE Can you anticipate how a source table for a two-way ANOVA will be similar to a source table for a one-way ANOVA?

The purpose of a source table does not change simply because we are showing results from a larger analysis. We will still report, for each source of variability, its sum of squares, df, mean square, F ratio, and probability of chance for each F ratio. Remember that our error term does not have an F ratio—we use it as the denominator in calculating the Fs for the various treatment effects. Table 15-3 shows the source table for our two-way ANOVA for independent samples. Notice that we have shown both the clothing main effect and interaction of clothing and customer sex as significant. Again, because the interaction is significant, we do not interpret the clothing effect.

> **Effect size** The magnitude or size of the experimental treatment (or interaction).

Effect Size   Remember that we previously told you about the importance of **effect size** so that we can determine how strong a significant effect is. In Chapter 13, we used η^2 as a measure of the proportion of variance accounted for by an effect. We will use the same measure here, partly because of its ease of computation and partly because it is simple to interpret. In Chapter 13 we told you that you could compute η^2 by using this formula: $\eta^2 = (F)(df_{\text{clo}})/(F)(df_{\text{clo}}) + df_{\text{error}}$. Fortunately,

TABLE 15-3   **HANDWRITTEN SOURCE TABLE FOR TWO-WAY ANOVA FOR INDEPENDENT SAMPLES**

Source	SS	df	MS	F	p
Clothes	1,040.17	1	1,040.17	11.92	<.01
Customer sex	322.67	1	322.67	3.70	<.10
Clothes × customer sex	580.17	1	580.17	6.65	<.05
W. Cell	1,745.00	20	87.25		
Total	3,688.00	23			

for a factorial design, we compute η^2 in the same manner. In this case we need to compute η^2 only for the interaction effect due to the fact that it overrides the main effects. Our computation of η^2 for the interaction effect shows:

$$\eta^2 = (F_{\text{interaction}})(df_{\text{interaction}})/(F_{\text{interaction}})(df_{\text{interaction}}) + df_{\text{error}}$$
$$= 6.65(1)/6.65(1) + 20$$
$$= 6.65/26.65 = .25$$

Thus, 25% of the variability in the data can be accounted for by the interaction of clothing and customer sex. This figure may seem low to you, but we must remember that the main effects do account for some variability in the data even though we do not interpret them due to the significant interaction.

Computer Analysis of Two-Way ANOVA for Independent Groups

It would be unusual for researchers to compute a two-way ANOVA by hand. Thus, we will show you generic computer output from a two-way ANOVA for independent groups. This output should be relatively similar to the output you will obtain from the computer package that you have available for analyzing complex ANOVA designs. The results appear in Table 15-4. A quick glance at the table reveals that the computer analysis has verified all of our hand calculations.

TABLE 15-4   COMPUTER OUTPUT FOR TWO-WAY ANOVA FOR INDEPENDENT SAMPLES

TABLE OF MEANS:

		CLOTHES		
		CASUAL	SLOPPY	ROW M
CUSTOMER	FEMALE	48.17	51.50	49.83
SEX	MALE	45.67	68.67	57.17
	COLUMN M	46.92	60.08	

POP. $M = 53.50$

SOURCE TABLE

SOURCE	SS	df	MS	F	p
CLOTHES	1040.17	1	1040.17	11.922	.0025
CUSTOMER SEX	322.67	1	322.67	3.698	.068
CLO × CUST SEX	580.17	1	580.17	6.649	.0179
W. CELL	1745.00	20	87.25		
TOTAL	3688.00	23			

Interpreting Computer Statistical Output   As in the past analyses, we examine the descriptive statistics at the top of Table 15-4. You can see that salesclerks took almost a minute, on average, to wait on the customers—the mean for the "total population" (all 24 clerks) was 53.50 seconds. The means for the clerks waiting on customers in casual and in shabby clothes were 46.92 and 60.08 seconds, respectively; for the female customers and the male customers, the means were 49.83 and 57.17 seconds, respectively. The descriptive statistics also show the combination of the two clothing styles and the two sexes. Clerks waiting on the casually dressed women averaged 48.17 seconds; those waiting on casually dressed men averaged 45.67. For the sloppy clothing, clerks waiting on women had a mean of 51.50 seconds whereas the clerks waiting on men took an average of 68.67 seconds. Because our hand and computer calculations agree, you have verified that you entered the data correctly.

The source table for the completely randomized factorial design appears at the bottom of Table 15-4. In the body of the source table we want to examine only the effects of the two IVs (clothing and customer sex) and their interaction. The remaining source (W. Cell) is the error term and is the term we use to test the IV effects. One important item to note is that different programs are likely to label the error term with a variety of different names (such as W. Cell in this case, "error," etc.). When we examine the main effects, we find that "Clothes" produced an F ratio of 11.92, with a probability of occurring by chance of .003. The effect of "Customer sex" shows an F ratio of 3.70, with a probability of .07. Remember that we get more exact probabilities from a computer than from the F table in the back of the book. In the F table you should find that the probability of "Clothes" falls below the .01 level. The "Customer Sex" IV shows **marginal significance**, which we usually attribute to probabilities of chance between 5% and 10%. Although marginal significance is not within the normal significance range, it is close enough that many experimenters discuss such results anyway. Keep in mind, when you deal with higher and higher probabilities of chance, that you are taking a greater risk of making a **Type I error** (see Chapter 9).

> **Marginal significance**
> Refers to statistical results with a probability of chance between 5% and 10%—in other words, almost significant but not quite. Researchers often talk about such results as if they reached the .05 level.

> **Type I error**   Accepting the experimental hypothesis when the null hypothesis is true.

Our next step is to examine the interaction between the two IVs. We have a two-way interaction because we have just the two IVs. The interaction between clothing and customer sex produced an F ratio of 6.65 and has $p = .02$, therefore denoting significance. Remember that a significant interaction renders the main effects moot because those main effects are qualified by the interaction and are not straightforward. Thus, to make sense out of these results, we must interpret the interaction. The first step in interpreting an interaction, as we saw, is to draw a graph of the results from the descriptive statistics. Figure 15-3 depicts this interaction.

Translating Statistics into Words   Remember that we are justified in drawing conclusions from our statistics *only if* we are certain that our experimental design and procedures had sufficient control to eliminate extraneous variables. Computers and statistical tests work only with the data you provide—they are not able to detect data from flawed experiments.

To interpret our statistics, let's return to the graph of significant interaction (Figure 15-3). When we examine the figure, the point that seems to differ most represents the clerks' response times to male customers in sloppy clothes. This mean is considerably higher than the others. Thus, we would conclude that clerks take longer to wait on men who are sloppily dressed than they do to wait on other customers. Notice that our explanation of an interaction effect *must* include a reference to both IVs in order to make sense—the previous sentence mentions the *male* customers in *sloppy* clothes.

PSYCHOLOGICAL DETECTIVE From looking at Figure 15-3, can you figure out why this interaction qualifies the significant and marginally significant main effects?

If we had drawn conclusions from the main effects, we would have decided that clerks waiting on customers in casual clothes were faster (46.92 seconds) than clerks waiting on those in sloppy clothes (60.08). Also, we would have concluded that clerks waiting on men took marginally longer (57.17) than those waiting on women (49.83). When you look at Figure 15-3, does it appear that clerks actually waited on sloppily dressed customers more slowly than those in casual clothes? No, only clerks waiting on *men* in sloppy clothes had longer response times. Does it seem that men received assistance more slowly than women? No, only the *men* in *sloppy clothes* had clerks who responded slowly. If you attempt to interpret the main effects in a straightforward fashion when you have a significant interaction you end up trying to make a gray situation into a black-and-white picture. In other words, you would be guilty of oversimplifying the results. Remember that an interaction occurs when the effect of one IV depends on the *specific* level of the other IV.

Our final step in interpreting the results is communicating our results to others. You will remember that we use a combination of statistical results and words to convey our findings in APA style. Here is one way you could present the results from this experiment:

> The effect of the clothing on clerks' response times was significant, $F(1, 20) = 11.92$, $p = .003$. The customer sex effect was marginally significant, $F(1, 20) = 3.70$, $p = .069$. However, the main effects were qualified by a significant interaction between clothing and customer sex, $F(1, 20) = 6.65$, $p = .018$, $\eta^2 = .25$. The results of the interaction appear in Figure 1 [*see Figure 15-3*]. Visual inspection of the graph shows that clerks' response times for the sloppily-dressed male customer condition were higher than the other conditions.

Once again, our goal is to communicate our results clearly with the words alone. Although the concept of interactions is somewhat complicated for readers who have no statistical background, we hope that any reader could understand our explanation of the results. However, we should note that, to fully understand the interaction, you should actually conduct further statistical tests. These tests are somewhat advanced—we suggest that you consult with your advisor if your research involves a significant interaction. (Be sure to remember this warning because you will see significant interactions again in this chapter.) Also, we remind you that η^2 is only one measure of effect size. Again, we included an effect size estimate only for the interaction because the significant interaction supersedes the main effects.

We want you to note two important points from this presentation of results. First, compared to the examples in Chapters 11 and 13, this written summary is longer. When you deal with factorial designs, you have more results to communicate, so your presentations will be longer. Second, although we presented the significance of the interaction and referred to a figure, we did not fully interpret the interaction. Results sections in experimental reports are only for presenting the results, not for full interpretation. As the APA *Publication Manual* (2001) notes in describing the results section, "discussing the implications of the results is not appropriate here" (p. 20).

REVIEW SUMMARY

1. When you use an experimental design that has two or more IVs and have only independent groups of participants, the proper statistical analysis is a factorial ANOVA for independent groups.
2. ANOVA partitions the variability in the DV into separate sources for all IVs and their interactions and for error. *F* ratios show the ratio of the variation for the experimental effects to the error variation.
3. A significant *F* ratio for a main effect indicates that the particular IV caused a significant difference in the DV scores.
4. A significant interaction *F* ratio indicates that the two (or more) IVs involved had an interrelated effect on the DV scores. To make sense of an interaction, you should graph the DV scores.
5. We use APA format to communicate our statistical results clearly and concisely. Proper format includes a written explanation of the findings documented with statistical results.

CHECK YOUR PROGRESS

1. You wish to compare the ACT or SAT scores of the freshman, sophomore, junior, and senior classes at your school as a function of sex. Draw a block diagram of this experiment. What design and statistical test would you use for this project?
2. What is an interaction effect? Why does a significant interaction render its associated main effects uninterpretable?
3. Suppose you are reading an experimental report. What would you know from the following sentence? *Reading speed was affected by both print size and age, with younger participants reading large print faster and older participants reading small print faster.*

    a. The interaction of print size and age was significant.

    b. The interaction of print size and age was not significant.

    c. The interaction of print size, age, and reading speed was significant.

    d. The main effects of print size and age were significant.

4. Suppose you have an *F* ratio of 3.25 with 2 and 20 *df*. Would this finding be significant? What is the probability level?

Two-Way ANOVA for Correlated Groups

Two-way ANOVA for correlated groups
Analysis technique for experiments that have two IVs that are both within-subjects factors (e.g., repeated measures).

The **two-way ANOVA for correlated groups** requires that we have two IVs (here, clothing and customer sex) with correlated groups for both IVs (see Figure 15-1). Most often, researchers would form these correlated groups by matching or by using repeated measures. In our example of the clothing–customer sex experiment, it is possible to use repeated measures on both IVs. We would merely get one sample of salesclerks and have them wait on customers of both sexes wearing each style of clothing.

PSYCHOLOGICAL DETECTIVE   Can you detect a flaw in the logic of having a single group of clerks waiting on all four types of customers?

There is no obvious flaw in using repeated measures in this experiment. Salesclerks are certainly accustomed to waiting on a variety of different customers in a short time span, so there should not be a problem in creating such a condition for this experiment. On the other hand, there are many experimental situations in which it would not be appropriate to use repeated measures. For example, imagine a classroom experiment that involved students reading chapters on the same topic from two different textbooks and then taking a quiz over each chapter. This hypothetical experiment would result in an advantage for the second quiz on each topic. Specifically, when students took the quiz, they would have read *two* chapters about the same topic. On the other hand, when they took their first quiz on each topic, they would have read only one chapter on the topic. Clearly, repeated measures on this textbook variable would not be appropriate. Thus, we would have to form correlated groups by forming matched groups of students. It is critical that you examine your experimental question and procedures for assigning participants to the groups in order to determine which specific experimental design to use.

Calculating ANOVA by Hand

Reviewing our experimental design, we have one group of salesclerks waiting on women dressed in sloppy clothes, women dressed casually, men in sloppy clothes, and men dressed casually.

PSYCHOLOGICAL DETECTIVE   Why does this design require a two-way ANOVA for correlated samples?

The design is a two-way ANOVA because of our two IVs (clothing and customer sex). The clerks each wait on all four types of groups (based on two types of clothing and two types of customer sex). Thus, the design is using repeated measures for both IVs.

Just as in our independent samples analysis earlier in this chapter, our task, when analyzing the data, is to divide the variability into its component parts so that we can determine which effects, if any, are significant. Thus, we need to divide the total sum of squares into the different sources of variability. Because we are using the same data, our calculations are highly similar to those for our two-way ANOVA for independent groups.

Calculating Sums of Squares   Think carefully about the logic of this analysis. The data are the same numbers that we used earlier in the chapter, so their total variability could not have changed. Thus, the total sum of squares for the correlated samples analysis will be identical to the figure in Table 15-2. Likewise, the variability due to the clothing, customer sex, and interaction could not have changed, so those figures remain the same also.

If the variability for the main effects, interaction, and overall data remain the same, how can the ANOVA for correlated groups show different results from the independent groups analysis?

This question requires careful thought and a good memory. If you have a good memory, you will remember that in Chapter 10 we told you correlated-groups designs reduce error variability. You may also remember that individual differences between our participants is one source of error variability. Using correlated-groups designs allows us to pull out the variability due to our participants from the error variability. If our error variability decreases, then the effects of the IVs and their interaction should be clearer to see.

Participant Sum of Squares   In Table 15-5 you will see how we calculate the variability due to our participants. Notice that we sum across our six participants rather than across groups—as we did to calculate the variability due to the main effects and interaction. Other than this difference, the formula is the same as the one we used for finding the sum of squares for either main effect. Notice how large the sum of squares for participants is (1,113) compared to the other sums of squares in Table 15-3. Because the variability between participants is often quite large, the fact that a correlated-groups analysis can isolate that variability enhances our chances of finding significance.

Can you figure out why would isolating the variability due to our participants increase our chance of finding significance?

TABLE ⬛ 15-5 ⬛ NEW CALCULATIONS NEEDED FOR TWO-WAY ANOVA
FOR CORRELATED SAMPLES

To calculate the variability for our participants, we need to get a sum of each salesclerks' total response times (remember that each salesclerk participates in all four conditions). Then we square that number and divide by the number of responses (four in this case).

CLERK #	RESPONSES	TOTAL	$\Sigma X^2 / N$
1	46 + 37 + 38 + 47	168	7,056
2	39 + 47 + 50 + 69	205	10,506.25
3	50 + 44 + 38 + 69	201	10,100.25
4	52 + 62 + 44 + 74	232	13,456
5	48 + 49 + 49 + 77	223	12,432.25
6	54 + 70 + 55 + 76	255	16,256.25
Total			69,807

Now we must subtract $(\Sigma X)^2 / N$

$69,807 - (1,284)^2/24 = 69,807 - 68,694 = 1,113$

This number is the sum of squares for the participants.

The benefit of isolating this variability is that we are able to remove it from our error term. We will explain further in the next section.

Error Sum of Squares We have two options for computing our error sum of squares at this point, but neither is totally, directly, from the data. It is a good idea to use both approaches and compare the results to make sure you have found the same value.

Both methods use subtraction so they are not very difficult. The first approach is simply to subtract all the sources of variation from the total sum of squares, with the error sum of squares being the remainder. In our example, we find:

$$SS_{Tot} - SS_{clo} - SS_{sex} - SS_{int} - SS_{part} = SS_{error}$$

$$3,688 - 1,040.17 - 322.67 - 580.17 - 1,113 = 632$$

The second approach involves calculating the error sum of squares as we did for the independent samples analysis. However, the result is *not* the error sum of squares for the correlated samples analysis because we have to remove the participant sum of squares from that earlier figure. In our example, we find:

$$1,745 - 1,113 = 632$$

Because our calculations agree, we are confident that our error sum of squares is correct.

At this point, compare our error sum of squares for the correlated analysis to the error sum of squares from the independent analysis in Table 15-3. Notice how much smaller our newly calculated error sum of squares is. This difference shows you the power of the correlated analysis to remove variation from the error term.

Mean Squares   As in Chapter 13, we must compute mean squares to make the variability estimates directly comparable. To calculate mean squares, we must have the df for each effect. We calculate the df for the total sum of squares, the main effects, and the interaction with the same equations we used for the between-groups analysis. However, there is again a change for the error term—we must take out the df for the participants effect. We calculate the df for participants from the formula $n - 1$ (n represents the number of participants in a group whereas N represents the total number of participants [or observations in this case] in the experiment). Thus, there are 5 df for the participants mean square. Those 5 df then "disappear" from the previous df for the error mean square, so that there are 15 for the correlated samples analysis.

Calculating mean squares proceeds exactly as we did in the independent samples analysis; simply divide each mean square by its respective df. As with the sums of squares, there is no difference between this analysis and our earlier computations. However, we do need to compute mean squares for the participants and error terms. For the participants effect, the MS is $1,113/5 = 222.6$. For the error term, MS = $632/15 = 42.13$. So, even though we lost df from the error term, the mean square is about half that from the independent samples analysis.

F Ratios   Because our MS_{error} term has changed, our F ratios from the first analysis will change also. Dividing the MS for each effect by the MS_{error} term yields F ratios of 24.69 for the IV of clothing, 7.66 for customer sex, and 13.77 for the interaction. Typically, researchers do not compute an F ratio for the participants effect.

Can you venture a guess as to why researchers do not test the participants effect?

If you test for a difference in participants, you will simply determine whether the participants differ from each other on the task. For example, testing the effect in this analysis would allow us to determine that different salesclerks took differing amounts of times to wait on customers. In other words, there would be variability in the data attributable to individual differences between salesclerks. Such a finding is not particularly profound—it would be akin to saying that students in a class tend to make different scores on an exam. Unless you are predicting that every participant will make exactly the same score on the variable you are measuring, this outcome is usually of little interest. However, if—for some reason—you wished to test for individual differences, you have the capability to do so. In our example, if you were so inclined, you would find that $F = 222.6/42.13 = 5.28$.

To determine the significance of our F ratios, we will use Table A-4 again. Our findings will be somewhat different than the earlier findings in this chapter because, for the two main effects and interaction, we will look under 1 and 15 *df* rather than 1 and 20. From the table, we find that the critical *F* ratios are 4.54 at the .05 level and 8.68 at the .01 level. Thus, the main effect of clothing and the interaction are significant at the .01 level, and the main effect of customer sex is significant at the .05 level. Although we noted that we are typically not interested in the difference among the participants, that effect is also significant at the .05 level.

 Given these results, how should we proceed to interpret them?

This question is basically a review question. If you answered that we should focus on the interaction, you are correct. The interaction overrides or qualifies the main effects so we must make sense of the interaction. Of course, we have previously interpreted the interaction in this chapter; that interpretation does not change because of the correlated samples. As a reminder, we found that salesclerks waited on the men dressed in sloppy clothes much more slowly than the three other groups of customers.

Post hoc Tests   As we saw earlier in the chapter, no post hoc tests are necessary for this analysis. Both our significant interaction and the fact that our IVs have only two levels tell us that we need no further analyses.

Source Table   Our source table will be quite similar to that of the independent groups analysis, with one important difference.

 Can you predict what that "one important difference" will be?

Because we have measured how much variability was due to our participants, we will need to include that factor in our source table—if we did not, there would appear to be missing variability because all the sources would not add up to the total variability. Table 15-6 shows our source table for this analysis. Notice that all of the effects are significant. We chose not to include an *F* ratio for the participants effect because, as we pointed out earlier, it is not very meaningful.

Effect Size   We will use the same method for computing η^2 that we used earlier in this chapter. Also, because of the significant interaction, we will compute η^2 for that treatment effect only.

$$\eta^2 = (F_{\text{interaction}})(df_{\text{interaction}})/(F_{\text{interaction}})(df_{\text{interaction}}) + df_{\text{error}}$$
$$= 13.77(1)/13.77(1) + 15$$
$$= 13.77/28.77 = .48$$

TABLE 15-6 HANDWRITTEN SOURCE TABLE FOR TWO-WAY ANOVA FOR CORRELATED SAMPLES

Source	SS	df	MS	F	p
Clothes	1,040.17	1	1,040.17	24.69	<.01
Customer sex	322.67	1	322.67	7.66	<.05
Clothes × customer sex	580.17	1	580.17	13.77	<.01
Participants	1,113.00	5	222.60		
Residual (error)	632.00	15	42.13		
Total	3,688.00	23			

Notice how much larger our effect size is for the correlated samples analysis than it was for the independent samples analysis (.25). This difference is striking evidence of the power of the correlated samples approach in experimentation.

Computer Analysis of Two-Way ANOVA for Correlated Samples

Again, it would be unusual for researchers to compute a two-way ANOVA by hand. We will present a computerized analysis that should be similar to the results that you would obtain from the statistical package that you might use.

Interpreting Computer Statistical Output The means for the factorial repeated measures analysis appear in Table 15-7. You will note that the group means are identical to those in Table 15-4 (the ANOVA for independent samples). This result is no surprise; we are analyzing the same numbers from Table 15-1. However, we used a different strategy for composing the groups in the analysis so our ANOVA results should be different.

The source table for the two-way ANOVA with correlated groups appears in the bottom portion of Table 15-7. The clothing effect is significant at the .001 level and the sex effect is significant at the .014 level. However, the significant clothing-by-sex interaction ($p = .001$) qualifies both of those effects. Notice that the computer provides us with more precise p values than we obtained from the F table. Remember that this interaction effect signifies that the results of the IVs are not consistent across each other. To make sense of the interaction, we must plot the means for the combinations of clothing and customer sex. You have seen this interaction plotted in Figure 15-3.

Translating Statistics into Words One important lesson to learn from these different analyses of the same data deals with the power of designing experiments in different ways. For example, take a minute to compare the source table for this analysis (Table 15-7) to the source table for the completely randomized analysis (Table 15-4). You will notice, in the correlated-samples design, that the F ratios are larger and the probabilities are smaller for both the IVs and their interaction. In previous chapters we told you that using correlated samples helps to reduce error variability by reducing some of the between-subjects variability. The result is typically a stronger, more powerful test of the treatment effects, as you see in this case.

TABLE `15-7` COMPUTER OUTPUT FOR TWO-WAY ANOVA
                FOR CORRELATED SAMPLES

TABLE OF MEANS:

		CLOTHES		
		CASUAL	SLOPPY	ROW M
CUSTOMER	FEMALE	48.17	51.50	49.83
SEX	MALE	45.67	68.67	57.17
	COLUMN M	46.92	60.08	

POP. $M = 53.50$

SOURCE TABLE

SOURCE	SS	df	MS	F	p
CLOTHES	1040.17	1	10.40.17	24.688	.001
CUSTOMER SEX	322.67	1	322.67	7.658	.014
CLO × CUST SEX	580.17	1	580.17	13.770	.001
RESIDUAL	632.00	15	42.13		
TOTAL	3688.00	23			

Of course, we must still communicate our results to other parties using APA style. We rely on our standard combination of words and numbers for the summary of the results—words to explain and numbers to document the findings. One possible way of summarizing these results follows:

> Both the main effects of clothing and customer sex were significant, $F(1, 15) = 24.69$, $p = .001$ and $F(1, 15) = 7.66$, $p = .014$, respectively. However, the interaction of clothing and customer sex was also significant, $F(1, 15) = 13.77$, $p = .001$, $\eta^2 = .48$. This interaction appears in Figure 1 [*see Figure 15-3*]. Salesclerks waiting on sloppily-attired male customers were considerably slower than salesclerks with any other combination of customer sex and clothing.

You would provide a fuller explanation and interpretation of this interaction in the discussion section of your experimental report.

Two-way ANOVA for mixed groups Analysis technique for experiments that have two IVs: one between-subjects factor and one within-subjects factor.

Two-Way ANOVA for Mixed Groups

The **two-way ANOVA for mixed groups** requires that we have two IVs (here, clothing and customer sex) with independent groups for one IV and correlated groups for the second IV. One possible way to create this design in our clothing-customer sex experiment would be to use a different randomly assigned group of salesclerks for each customer sex. Clerks waiting on each sex, however, would assist customers attired in both types of clothing. Thus, customer sex would be independent groups and constitute a between-subjects variable, whereas clothing would use repeated measures and be a within-subjects variable. Looking at Figure 15-1, note that different salesclerks would wait on men or women (looking down the diagram) and would wait on customers in both casual and sloppy clothes (across the top of the diagram). The DV scores (see Table 15-1) still represent response times of clerks to customers, but the same clerks produced the response times for each clothing type within the two customer sexes. This design is efficient because it requires fewer clerks to conduct the study and it minimizes the individual differences within the response times.

 Could you reverse the between- and within-subjects variables in this design?

This question basically asks whether you could have clerks wait on either men and women in casual clothing or men and women in sloppy clothing. In this case, the answer is yes—there is nothing magical about waiting on customers of the same sex or customers dressed in the same type of clothes. However, it is not always true that you can "reverse" a design as we can with this example. Remember that we alerted you earlier in the text that it is not possible to treat all IVs as within-subject variables.

Calculating ANOVA by Hand

Let's review our planned experimental design. We have one group of salesclerks waiting on men who are dressed in either casual or sloppy clothes, and we have a second group of clerks waiting on women who are dressed in either casual or sloppy clothes.

 What makes this design a mixed-groups design?

A mixed-groups design incorporates at least one between-subjects variable and at least one within-subjects variable. Different clerks wait on men and women, so customer sex is between subjects; the same clerks wait on customers in both types of clothing, so clothing is within subjects.

As we have done with the two earlier analyses in this chapter, we need to divide the total variability into its component portions so we can determine which effects, if any, are significant. We will show you how to divide the total sum of squares into the variability due to the main effects and the interaction. Once again, our computations will be quite similar to those we used for the two-way ANOVA for independent groups.

Calculating Sums of Squares   Again, it is the case that the basics have not changed from the first analysis of this chapter: We are dealing with the same data and, thus, the same variability from the clothing and customer sex variables, as well as their interaction.

If the variability from the main effects and their interaction remain the same, how can this analysis differ from the other two analyses of this chapter?

If your guess is that the answer to this question lies somewhere in the error term, you're doing well! However, what actually happens to the error term (compared to either of the other two analyses) is not predictable for students. Because we have a mixed design, we will divide some of the error variability into between-subjects variability and some into within-subjects variability. The trick, of course, is figuring out which is which!

Of our three sources of variability—clothing, customer sex, and their interaction—which do you think is between-subjects and which is within-subjects?

Part of this question is not too tough. You already know that customer sex is between-subjects because different clerks wait on men and on women and that clothing is within-subjects because the same clerks wait on customers in both types of clothing. The interaction is somewhat tricky, though, because it combines both within-subjects and between-subjects variables. The rule concerning such interactions is that statisticians consider them to be within-subject variables because they include a within-subject variable (in this case, clothing). Now that we know which of our sources of variability fall into which category, we need to partition our error variability into two error terms—one for customer sex (between-subjects) and one for clothing and the customer sex-clothing interaction.

Error Sums of Squares   In Table 15-8 you will see how we calculate the error sum of squares for the two error terms. In Table 15-8a you will notice that, in computing the error term for customer sex, we sum across the two clothing conditions for each clerk. We hope that this operation makes sense to you because we are interested in dealing only with the error variability for customer sex and thus want to ignore the other sources.

In Table 15-8b, you see the method for calculating the error term for clothing and the customer sex-by-clothing interaction. Notice that this set of computations entails working with the four different cell totals, each of which represents one of the combinations of customer sex and clothing. Again, given that we need an error term to assess the effect of the interaction, we hope this approach seems intuitively logical to you.

TABLE	15-8	NEW CALCULATIONS NEEDED FOR TWO-WAY ANOVA FOR MIXED SAMPLES

a. We can find our total error sum of squares by subtraction:

$$SS_{error} = SS_{total} - SS_A - SS_B - SS_{AB} = 3,688 - 322.67 - 1,040.17 - 580.17 = 1744.99$$

We have to obtain three different sums to work the formula for the error sum of squares for within-groups. All involve summing squared numbers and finding "averages" for those numbers

CUSTOMER SEX	CLERK	CASUAL RESPONSE	SLOPPY RESPONSE	Σ	$\Sigma X^2/n$
	1	46	37	83	3,444.5
	2	39	47	86	3,698
F	3	50	44	94	4,418
	4	52	62	114	6,498
	5	48	49	97	4,704.5
	6	54	70	124	7,688
	7	38	47	85	3,612.5
	8	50	69	119	7,080.5
M	9	38	69	107	5,724.5
	10	44	74	118	6,962
	11	49	77	126	7,938
	12	55	76	131	8,580.5
					Σ = 70,349

b.

	CASUAL	SLOPPY	Σ	$\Sigma X^2/n$ (# GROUPS) = $\Sigma X^2/12$
Female	289	309	598	29,800.333
Male	274	412	686	39,216.333
				Σ = 69,016.666

$$\Sigma (\Sigma X^2/n) = (289^2/6) + (309^2/6) + (274^2/6) + (412^2/6) = 70,637$$

Starting with the sum of all the squared scores (from Table 15-2), we then add or subtract our calculated "averages" as shown below:

$$SS_{error/within} = 72,382 - 70,637 - 70,349 + 69,016.667 = 412.67$$

Then we can subtract to find the error sum of squares for between-groups.

$$SS_{error/between} = 1,745 - 412.67 = 1,332.33$$

Mean Squares   We need to calculate mean squares in order to directly compare the amount of variability from all our sources. Of course, we first need *df* to calculate mean squares from our sums of squares. Because we have two error terms, we need to find *df* for each of them. The *df* for our between-subjects IV (customer sex) equals the number of groups for customer sex minus 1, multiplied by the number of clerks per group minus 1. In this case, the between-subjects error $df = (2 - 1)(6 - 1) = 10$. The *df* for the within-subjects effects (clothing and interaction) equals the number of groups for customer sex multiplied by the number of groups for clothing minus 1, multiplied by the number of clerks per group minus 1. In our example, the within-subjects $df = (2)(2 - 1)(6 - 1) = 10$.

 PSYCHOLOGICAL DETECTIVE   Would the *df* for the two error terms always be equal as in this case? If not, under what circumstances would they differ?

Actually, a 2×2 design is the *only* situation in which the error terms' *df* will be equal. We are sure that you have learned to be careful about making generalizations based on one example. This example, of course, is a perfect case in point.

To find our mean squares, we do as we have consistently done—divide the sum of squares by the associated *df*. The error mean square for the between-subjects IV is 1332.33 divided by its 10 *df*, which equals 133.23; the error mean square for the within-subjects effects is 412.67 divided by its 10 *df*, or 41.27.

F Ratios   Because we have new error mean squares, our *F* ratios will change from our previous analyses. For customer sex, we divide 322.67 by 133.23 for an *F* of 2.42. Following the same procedure, the *F* ratio for clothing is $1,040.17/41.27 = 25.20$; for the interaction, $F = 580.17/41.27 = 14.06$.

Once again, we use Table A-4 to determine whether our results are significant. With 1 and 10 *df*, our critical values are 4.96 at the .05 level and 10.04 at the .01 level. Using these values, we find significance for the clothing main effect at the .01 level and the customer sex-clothing interaction, also at the .01 level. We could ask you a Psychological Detective question about how to proceed at this point, but we are certain that you remember that the significant interaction renders the clothing main effect virtually meaningless. As we found earlier, clerks took longer amounts of time to wait on men who were dressed in sloppy clothing.

You may have noticed an interesting finding when comparing the results from the mixed analysis to the previous two analyses. The clothing effect was significant in the other two analyses, but not in this one. Any time you use a mixed design, the test of the between-subjects effect will be weaker than the tests of the within-subjects effects (Kirk, 1968). This difference is simply a property of this type of design. However, this information may be important to you when you plan an experiment and select your design. If the test of the between-subject effect is critical to you, a mixed design may not be the best choice.

TABLE 15-9 HANDWRITTEN SOURCE TABLE FOR TWO-WAY ANOVA FOR MIXED SAMPLES

Source	SS	df	MS	F	P
Between-subjects effects					
Customer sex	322.67	1	322.67	2.42	>.05
Error (cust. sex)	1,332.33	10	133.23		
Within-subjects effects					
Clothes	1,040.17	1	1,040.17	25.20	<.01
Clothes × customer sex	580.17	1	580.17	14.06	<.01
Error (within)	412.67	10	41.27		
Total	3,688.00	23			

Post Hoc Tests   As we have seen throughout this chapter, post hoc tests are not necessary for a 2 × 2 design. Consult Chapter 13 if you need to conduct post hoc analyses on an IV that has three or more levels.

Source Table   Our source table (see Table 15-9) differs from those we have seen previously in the chapter because of the division of error terms. Notice that the source table is divided into two parts, with the between-subject effect toward the top of the table and the within-subject effects near the bottom of the table. As we noted earlier, only the customer sex and interaction are significant.

Effect Size   Once again, we will compute η^2 as our measure of effect size. Because the interaction is significant, we will compute η^2 only for that interaction:

$$\eta^2 = (F_{\text{interaction}})(df_{\text{interaction}})/(F_{\text{interaction}})(df_{\text{interaction}}) + df_{\text{error}}$$
$$= (14.06)(1)/(14.06)(1) + 10$$
$$= .58$$

Once again, you will notice that the effect size has gotten larger, even from the ANOVA for correlated samples. The difference occurs because we have been able to reduce the error variability even more by partitioning it into two different types (between-groups and within-groups).

Computer Analysis of Two-Way ANOVA for Mixed Samples

We present the final computer output for the chapter. Although your statistics software package will likely show some deviation from this example, the two should be quite similar.

Interpreting Computer Statistical Output   The descriptive statistics appear at the top of Table 15-10. Once again, the descriptive statistics did not change from our first and second analysis—we are still analyzing the same data (see Table 15-1) for demonstration purposes.

TABLE 15-10 COMPUTER OUTPUT FOR TWO-WAY ANOVA FOR MIXED SAMPLES

TABLE OF MEANS:

		CLOTHES		
		CASUAL	SLOPPY	ROW *M*
CUSTOMER	FEMALE	48.17	51.50	49.83
SEX	MALE	45.67	68.67	57.17
	COLUMN *M*	46.92	60.08	

POP. *M* = 53.50

SOURCE TABLE

SOURCE	SS	df	MS	F	p
BETWEEN-SUBJECTS EFFECTS					
CUST. SEX	322.67	1	322.67	2.422	.151
ERROR (CUST. SEX)	1,332.33	10	133.23		
WITHIN-SUBJECTS EFFECTS					
CLOTHES	1,040.17	1	1,040.17	25.206	.001
CLO × CUST. SEX	580.17	1	580.17	14.059	.004
ERROR	412.67	10	41.27		
TOTAL	3688.00				

The source table appears at the bottom of Table 15-10. As you can see from the headings, the between-subjects effects (independent groups) and the within-subjects effects (repeated measures) are divided in the source table. This division is necessary because of the different error terms for the between-subjects and within-subjects effects. The interaction appears in the within-subjects portion of the table because it involves repeated measures across one of the variables involved.

PSYCHOLOGICAL DETECTIVE Which IV is the between-subjects variable, and why? Which IV is the within-subjects variable, and why?

No, that wasn't a trick question. It's just a simple review query to make sure you're paying attention. Customer sex is the between-subjects variable because different sales-clerks wait on men or women. The clothing is the within-subjects variable because each salesclerk waits on customers in both sloppy and casual clothes (repeated measures).

First, we notice that the computer has verified our earlier hand calculations. Turning to the specifics of the analysis, the information for the customer sex IV showed an *F* ratio of 2.42 and a probability of chance of .15. Therefore, the customers' sex made no significant difference in the salesclerks' response times. The clothing effect yielded an *F* ratio of 25.21 with a probability of .001, a significant finding. However, we also notice that the interaction of clothing and customer sex is signifi-cant (*p* = .004), with an *F* ratio of 14.06. Because of this significant interaction, we will not interpret the significant clothing result. Once again, we need to graph the interac-tion in order to make sense of it (see Figure 15-3).

This set of ANOVA results differs from either of the other two analyses in this chapter, again demonstrating the importance of experimental design in determining significance. It is important to remember that tests of between-subjects factors are rel-atively weaker than tests of within-subjects factors in a mixed design. The results of this analysis, when compared to the previous analysis, demonstrate that point.

Translating Statistics into Words   We have already completed some of our inter-pretation in our coverage of the statistical results. We know that the customer sex effect was not significant and that the clothing variable was significant. However, because the interaction between customer sex and clothing was significant, we ignore the clothing results and interpret the interaction.

Figure 15-3 shows that clerks who waited on casually-dressed women, casually-dressed men, and sloppily-dressed women responded more quickly than those who waited on sloppily-dressed men. How can we communicate these findings in APA for-mat? Here's one possibility:

Results from the mixed factorial ANOVA showed no effect of the customer sex, $F(1, 10) = 2.42$, $p = .15$. The clothing effect was significant, $F(1, 10) = 25.21$, $p = .001$. This main effect, however, was qualified by a significant customer sex by clothing interaction, $F(1, 10) = 14.06$, $p = .004$, $\eta^2 = .58$, which is shown in Figure 1 [*see Figure 15-3*]. This interaction shows that salesclerks who waited on sloppily-dressed male customers were slower in responding than clerks who waited on casually-dressed men or women dressed in either manner.

PSYCHOLOGICAL DETECTIVE   Note the similarity for the clothing and interaction effects in this mixed analysis and the completely within-groups analysis in the previous sec-tion. Why do you think the findings are similar in each case?

To answer this difficult question, you have to be able to see the similarities between these last two analyses. Although they may seem rather different, there is one important similarity between them. Both of these analyses, because of the underlying experimental designs, treat the clothing and interaction effects as within-groups effects. Thus, the two ANOVAs are essentially analyzing the same data in the same manner.

As a final word about the analyses in this chapter, please remember that you cannot analyze the same data using several different analyses in the real world of experimentation. We have used the same data for instructional purposes *and* to demonstrate how you could take one experimental idea and put it in the context of several possible experimental designs.

A Final Note

For simplicity's sake, all the analyses we have shown in this chapter have dealt with IVs that had only two levels. You remember from Chapter 13 that we often wish to test IVs that have more than two levels. In Figure 14-7 we showed you an example of a 3×3 design. That design had two IVs, that each have levels. Remember that significance for an IV that has three levels means that you would need to calculate a set of post hoc tests to determine exactly where the significance of that IV occurred.

The Continuing Research Problem

In Chapters 11 and 13 we began this section about our hypothetical continuing research problem. Our early interest was in determining whether customers in dressy or sloppy clothing received faster assistance from salesclerks. When we found that dressy clothes were associated with faster responses, we enlarged our research question to include three different types of clothing (Chapter 13). Evidence showed that customers dressed in either casual or dressy clothes were helped by salesclerks more quickly than customers dressed in sloppy clothing.

As you saw in Chapter 11, we began our research problem with a fairly simple question and we got a fairly simple answer. However, that research led to a slightly more complex question, and so on. You should expect your research problems to show a similar pattern. Although you may start with a simple question and expect one experiment to provide all the answers, that will rarely be the case. Keep your eyes open for new questions that arise after an experiment. Pursuing a line of **programmatic research** is challenging, invigorating, and interesting. Remember that pursuing such a line of research is how most famous psychologists have made names for themselves!

> **Programmatic research** A series of research experiments that deal with a related topic or question.

This chapter was more complex than either Chapter 11 or Chapter 13 because of the extra choice in experimental design. Let's review the steps we took in designing the experiments in this chapter. You may wish to refer to Figure 14-1 to follow each specific question.

Step 1 After our preliminary research in Chapters 11 and 13, we decided to use two IVs (clothing and customer sex) in these experiments. Each IV had two levels (clothing: casual, sloppy; customer sex: men, women). This design allows us to determine the effects of the clothing, the effects of the customer sex, and the interaction between clothing and customer sex.

Step 2   The DV was the time it took salesclerks to respond to customers.

Step 3a   With large numbers of salesclerks, we randomly formed four groups of salesclerks, with each waiting on one sex of customer in one type of clothing, resulting in a factorial between-groups design. We analyzed the response times using a factorial ANOVA for independent groups and found that clerks were slower to wait on male customers in sloppy clothing than all other customers (see Table 15-4 and Figure 15-3).

Step 3b   In a hypothetical situation with fewer clerks for the experiment, we used repeated measures on both IVs; that is, each salesclerk waited on both sexes of customers attired in both types of clothing, so that each clerk waited on four different customers. Thus, this experiment used a factorial within-groups design. We analyzed the data with a factorial ANOVA for correlated groups and found that clerks were slowest in waiting on sloppily dressed men (see Table 15-7 and Figure 15-3).

Step 3c   In a third hypothetical situation, we randomly assigned salesclerks to the two customer sex groups but used repeated measures on the clothing IV so that clerks waited either on men in both types of clothing or women in both types of clothing. This arrangement resulted in a factorial mixed-groups design (one IV using independent groups, one using correlated groups). We analyzed the response times with a factorial ANOVA for mixed groups and found the slowest response times for clerks to male customers in sloppy clothes (see Table 15-10 and Figure 15-3).

Step 4   We concluded that clothing and customer sex interacted to affect salesclerks' response times. Women received help quickly regardless of their attire, but men received help quickly only if they were not sloppily dressed. Men attired in sloppy clothes had to wait longer for help than the other three groups.

REVIEW SUMMARY

1. A factorial **ANOVA for correlated groups** is appropriate when your experimental design has two or more IVs and you used matched groups or repeated measures for all IVs.
2. A factorial **ANOVA for correlated groups** reduces error variability by partitioning out the variability due to individual differences in participants.
3. If you have a design that has two or more IVs and a mixture of independent and correlated groups for those IVs, you would use a factorial **ANOVA for mixed groups** to analyze your data.
4. Factorial ANOVA partitions the **error variability** into separate sources for between-subject and within-subject sources.
5. *F* ratios show the ratio of the variation for the experimental effects to the error variation. A significant *F* ratio for a main effect indicates that the particular IV caused a significant difference in the DV scores.

CHECK YOUR PROGRESS

1. You wonder whether test-taking practice and study courses can actually affect SAT or ACT scores. You recruit one group of students to help you. They take the test three times. Then you give them a study course for the test. They take an alternative form of the same test three times. Thus, each student has taken two different tests three times (to study practice effects) and each student has taken the study course (to assess its effects). Draw a block diagram of this design. What design and statistical test would you use for this project?

2. You are interested in the same question as in Problem 1, but you recruit two groups of students to help you. One group takes the SAT or ACT three times; the other group has a study course and then takes the SAT or ACT three times. Draw a block diagram of this design. What design and statistical test would you use for this project?

3. What is an interaction effect? How can you make sense of a significant interaction?

4. If you have a between-subjects effect that you need to test because it is critical to your experimental hypothesis, is a mixed ANOVA a good choice? Why or why not?

5. You wish to determine whether people's moods differ during the four seasons and by sex. What experimental design would you use for this research project? Why?

6. You choose to test people's preferences for fast-food hamburgers in three different restaurants (McDonald's, Burger King, and Wendy's) among three different age groups (children ages 4–12, college students, and senior citizens). What experimental design would you use for this project? Why?

EXERCISES

1. Suppose a friend approaches you and tells you that she wants to use age and sex as her independent variables and that she wants to use a factorial ANOVA to analyze her data. She wants to know if this experimental design is possible and how to set up her experiment. What do you say in response to her questions?

2. You have conducted an experiment in which you compared married, single, and divorced men's and women's reactions to different types of TV commercials. Which type of ANOVA should you use to analyze your data? Why?

3. You are curious as to whether dogs have a better sense of smell, vision, or feel. To ensure the groups' equality, you choose three dogs from each of 10 litters and test their ability to learn a maze with odor, visual, or tactile cues. You give the dogs three trials in each maze to see if their learning changes over time. Which type of ANOVA should you use to analyze your data? Why?

4. You have conducted an experiment in which you had male and female freshmen, sophomores, juniors, and seniors rate their attitude toward a course before and after they took it. Which type of ANOVA should you use to analyze your data? Why?

5. You are curious about whether male and female college students react differently on two types of quizzes. You randomly assign groups of men and women to either a fill-in-the-blank or multiple-choice quiz format. Analyze the quiz scores and draw a conclusion.

	Fill-in-the-Blank							**Multiple Choice**					
Men	16	18	21	16	15	17		21	19	22	23	21	20
Women	18	19	18	16	15	20		23	22	23	19	22	21

6. You are curious about whether male and female college students react differently on two types of quizzes. You randomly assign groups of men and women to either a fill-in-the-blank or multiple-choice quiz format. Analyze the quiz scores and draw a conclusion.

	Fill-in-the-Blank							**Multiple Choice**					
Men	16	18	21	16	15	17		21	19	22	23	21	20
Women	23	22	23	19	22	21		18	19	18	16	15	20

7. You are curious as to whether male and female college students perform differently on two chapters in a General Psychology course. You divide the class by gender and compare their performance on 25-point quizzes over the biology and developmental chapters. Each student takes both quizzes, and you match men and women on previous quiz scores. Analyze the quiz scores and draw a conclusion.

	Fill-in-the-Blank							**Multiple Choice**					
Men	16	18	21	16	14	17		18	19	18	16	16	20
Women	23	22	23	19	21	21		21	19	22	23	21	21

8. You are curious as to whether male and female college students perform differently on two chapters in a General Psychology course. You divide the class by gender and compare their performance on 25-point quizzes over the biology and developmental chapters. Each student takes both quizzes, and you match men and women on previous quiz scores. Analyze the quiz scores and draw a conclusion.

	Fill-in-the-Blank							**Multiple Choice**					
Men	16	18	21	16	14	17		23	22	23	19	21	21
Women	18	19	18	16	16	20		21	19	22	23	21	21

9. You are curious as to whether male and female college students perform differently on two chapters in a General Psychology course. You divide the class by gender and compare their performance on 25-point quizzes over the biology and developmental chapters. Each student takes both quizzes. Analyze the quiz scores and draw a conclusion.

	Fill-in-the-Blank							**Multiple Choice**					
Men	16	18	21	16	14	17		23	22	23	19	21	21
Women	21	19	22	23	21	21		22	20	23	24	22	22

10. You are curious as to whether male and female college students perform differently on two chapters in a General Psychology course. You divide the class by gender and compare their performance on 25-point quizzes over the biology and developmental chapters. Each student takes both quizzes. Analyze the quiz scores and draw a conclusion.

	Fill-in-the-Blank							**Multiple Choice**					
Men	16	18	21	16	14	17		17	18	20	17	13	16
Women	15	19	18	16	16	20		19	18	19	15	17	18

11. Write an APA-style conclusion for any of the results from Exercises 5–6.
12. Write an APA-style conclusion for any of the results from Exercises 7–8.
13. Write an APA-style conclusion for any of the results from Exercises 9–10.
14. Suppose you saw the set of means below. What results do you think you would find from ANOVA? Why?

	Time Spent Studying for Exam	
	Low	High
Men	69	71
Women	60	80

15. Suppose a friend brings you the data from a computer printout and asks for your help interpreting it. What can you tell your friend?

Source of Variation	SS	df	MS	F	p
Factor *A*	2,701.13	1	2,701.13	13.30	.001
Factor *B*	288.00	1	288.00	1.41	.25
Interaction	71.99	1	71.99	.35	.56
Error	5,682.76	28	202.95		
Total	8,743.88	31			

KEY TERMS

ANOVA for factorial designs, *340*

Treatment variability, *340*

Error variability, *340*

Synergistic effects, *341*

Two-way ANOVA for independent groups, *342*

Sum of squares, *343*

Total sum of squares, *345*

Treatment sum of squares, *345*

Interaction sum of squares, *345*

Error sum of squares, *345*

Mean square, *346*

Degrees of freedom (*df*), *346*

F ratio, *346*

Post hoc tests, *348*

Source table, *348*

Effect size, *349*

Marginal significance, *351*

Type I error, *351*

Two-way ANOVA for correlated groups, *354*

Two-way ANOVA for mixed groups, *360*

Programmatic research, *368*

LOOKING AHEAD

In this chapter we learned about the most sophisticated of all experimental designs—factorial designs that include multiple IVs. This material completes a six-chapter section on experimental design, data analysis, and interpretation. In the next chapter we will look at some alternative statistical tests you may need to use if your data do not meet some requirements for the tests we have examined thus far.

Alternative Research Designs

Although you may think that, by now, we have covered every conceivable type of research design that psychologists might use to gather data, you would be wrong. There are many other types of research designs. In this chapter we will consider some designs that researchers developed with specific purposes in mind. We will first look at research designs that help us to protect the internal validity of our experiments.

Protecting Internal Validity Revisited

Internal validity A type of evaluation of your experiment; it asks the question of whether your IV is the only possible explanation of the results shown for your DV.

In Chapter 5 we introduced the concept of **internal validity**. The issue of internal validity revolves around **confounding** and **extraneous variables**. When you have an internally valid experiment, you are reasonably certain that your IV is responsible for the changes you observed in your DV. You have established a **cause-and-effect relation**, knowing that the IV *caused* the change in the DV. For example, after many years of painstaking research, medical scientists know that cigarette smoking *causes* lung cancer. Although there are other variables that can also affect cancer, we know that smoking is a causative agent. Our goal as experimenters is to establish similar cause-and-effect relations in psychology. Experiments that are internally valid allow us to make statements such as "X causes Y to occur" with confidence.

Confounding Caused by an uncontrolled extraneous variable that varies systematically with the IV.

Extraneous variables Variables that may unintentionally operate to influence the dependent variable.

Examining Your Experiment from the Inside

In Chapter 5 we talked about the necessity for controlling extraneous variables in order to reach a clear-cut conclusion from our experiment. It is only when we have designed our experiment in such a way as to avoid the effects of potential extraneous variables that we can feel comfortable about making a cause-and-effect statement—that is, saying that variable X (our IV) *caused* the change we observed in variable Y (our DV). What we are trying to accomplish through our control techniques is to set up a buffer for our IV and DV so that they will not be affected by other variables. This reminds us of a cartoonlike toothpaste commercial we saw—perhaps you have seen it also. When the teeth brushed themselves with the particular brand of toothpaste being advertised, they developed a protective "invisible barrier" against tooth decay. In an analogous manner, our controls give our experiment a barrier against confounding (see Figure 16-1). Similarly, police detectives strive to make their case against a particular suspect airtight. If they have done their investigations well, the case against the accused should hold up well in court.

Cause-and-effect relation Occurs when we know that a particular IV (cause) leads to specific changes in a DV (effect).

Dealing with the internal validity of an experiment is an interesting process. We take many precautions aimed at increasing internal validity as we design and set up our experiment, and we usually evaluate our experiment with regard to internal validity after we have completed the research. If this approach seems a little strange to you, don't be alarmed—it does seem odd at first. Internal validity revolves around the question of whether your IV actually created any change that you observe in your DV. As you can see in Figure 16-1, if you learned your lessons from Chapter 5 well and used adequate

FIGURE 16-1 THE ROLE OF CONTROL PROCESSES IN PREVENTING EXPERIMENTAL CONFOUNDING.

control techniques, your experiment should be free from confounding and you can, indeed, conclude that your IV caused the change in your DV. Let's review briefly.

PSYCHOLOGICAL DETECTIVE   Imagine you have been given responsibility for conducting the famous Crest test—you are supposed to determine whether brushing with Crest actually does reduce cavities. Your boss wants you to use an experimental group (Crest) and a control group (Brand X) in the experiment. Write down at least *five* potential extraneous variables for this experiment before reading further.

Were you able to list five possible extraneous variables? The list could be quite long; you may have thought of some possibilities that we didn't come up with. (Although this exercise could easily have been an example dealing with confounding found in Chapter 5, it is also relevant to the issue of internal validity. If you fail to control an important extraneous variable, your experiment will not have internal validity.) Remember, any factor that systematically differs between the two groups (other than the type of toothpaste) could be an extraneous variable that would make it impossible to draw a definite conclusion about the effect of the toothpastes. Here's our (partial) list of possibilities:

number of times brushed per day

amount of time spent in brushing per day

how soon brushing occurs after meals

types of foods eaten

type of toothbrush used

dental genetics inherited from parents

degree of dental care received

different dentists' "operational definition" of what constitutes a cavity

whether the city's water is fluoridated

As we said, this list is not meant to be exhaustive—it merely gives you some ideas of factors that could be extraneous variables. To make certain you understand how an extraneous variable can undermine an experiment's internal validity, let's use an example from the previous list. In addition, we will discover why we take precautions aimed at internal validity *before* the experiment and assess the internal validity of an experiment *afterward*.

When you design the study, you want to make sure that people in the experimental and control groups brush their teeth an equivalent number of times per day. Thus, you would instruct the parents to have their children brush after each meal. Your goal is to have all children brush three times a day. Suppose that you conducted the experiment and gathered your data. When you analyzed the data, you found that the experimental group (Crest) had significantly fewer cavities than the control group (Brand X). Your conclusion seems straightforward at this point: Brushing with Crest reduces cavities compared to brushing with Brand X. However, as you dig deeper into your data, you look at the questionnaire that you had the parents complete and find that children in the experimental group averaged 2.72 brushings a day compared to 1.98 times per day for the control group. Now it is obvious that your two groups differ on two factors—the type of toothpaste used and the number of brushings per day. Which factor is responsible for the lower number of cavities in the experimental group? It is impossible to tell! There is no statistical test that can separate these two confounded factors. So, you attempted to control the brushing factor before the experiment to assure internal validity. You could not assess your control technique until after the experiment, when you found out that your experiment was not internally valid. A word to the wise should be sufficient: Good experimental control leads to internally valid experiments.

Remember that we listed nine threats to internal validity in Chapter 5. We also provided you with a variety of control strategies to deal with those threats. Now that you are familiar with research designs, we can explain how some research design strategies eliminate threats to internal validity. As you read about these strategies, you will see that some are a part of those designs from Chapters 10 through 15.

Protecting Internal Validity with Research Designs

There are two approaches you could take to fight the various threats to internal validity. In the first approach, you would attempt to come up with nine different answers, one for each threat. Although this approach would be effective in controlling the threats, it would be time consuming and, perhaps, difficult to institute that many different controls simultaneously. Perhaps the idea of controlling the threats through research design occurred to you, even if you could not come up with a specific recommendation. Detectives use standard police procedures to help them protect their cases; experimental design procedures can help us as psychological detectives.

In the six previous chapters we presented you with a variety of experimental designs, often noting various control aspects of those designs. However, we never mentioned the nine general threats to internal validity until this chapter. Can we apply experimental design to these problems? According to Campbell (1957) and Campbell and Stanley (1966), the answer is "yes." Let's take a look at their recommendations:

> **Random assignment** A control technique that ensures that each participant has an equal chance of being assigned to any group in an experiment.

Random Assignment   Although **random assignment** is not a specific experimental design, it is a technique that we can use within our experimental designs. Remember, with random assignment (see Chapter 9) we distribute the experimental participants into our various groups on a random (nonsystematic) basis. Thus, all participants have an equal chance of being assigned to *any* of our treatment groups. The purpose behind random assignment is to create different groups that are equal before beginning our experiment. According to Campbell and Stanley (1966), "the most adequate all-purpose assurance of lack of initial biases between groups is randomization" (p. 25). Thus, random assignment can be a powerful tool. The only drawback to random assignment is that we cannot *guarantee* equality through its use.

One caution is in order at this point. Because *random* is a frequently used term when dealing with experimental design issues, it sometimes has slightly different meanings. For example, in Chapters 10 through 15, we repeatedly referred to *independent groups* to describe groups of participants that were not correlated in any way (through matching, repeated measures, or natural pairs or sets). It is not unusual to see or hear such independent groups referred to as *random groups*. Although this label makes sense because the groups are unrelated, it is also somewhat misleading. Look back to Chapter 10, where we first talked about matching participants. At that point we stressed that, after making your matched pairs of participants, you *randomly assigned* one member of each pair to each group. The same is true of naturally occurring pairs (or sets) of participants. These randomly assigned groups would clearly *not* be independent. Because of the power of random assignment to equate our groups, we should use it at every opportunity. Campbell and Stanley (1966) noted that "within the limits of confidence stated by the tests of significance, randomization can suffice without the pretest" (p. 25). Thus, according to Campbell and Stanley, it may not even be necessary to use matched groups because random assignment can be used to equate the groups.

PSYCHOLOGICAL DETECTIVE   What is the major exception to Campbell and Stanley's argument that randomization will create equal groups?

Random selection
Choosing participants
from a population in such
a way that all possible
participants have an equal
opportunity to be chosen.

Selection A threat to
internal validity; if we
choose participants in
such a way that our
groups are not equal
before the experiment,
we cannot be certain that
our IV caused any differ-
ence we observe after the
experiment.

History A threat to internal validity; refers to
events that occur
between the DV measure-
ments in a repeated mea-
sures design.

Maturation An internal
validity threat; refers to
changes in participants
that occur over time dur-
ing an experiment; could
include actual physical
maturation or tiredness,
boredom, hunger, and
so on.

Testing A threat to internal validity that occurs
because measuring the DV
causes a change in the DV.

Statistical regression
A threat to internal validity that occurs when low
scorers improve or high
scorers fall on a second
administration of a test
due solely to statistical
reasons.

We hope that you remembered (from Chapters 10–15) that randomization is supposed to create equal groups *in the long run*.
Therefore, you need to be aware of randomization's *possible* short-
coming if you conduct an experiment with small numbers of participants. Although randomization may create equal groups with few
participants, we cannot be as confident about this possibility as
when we use large groups.

Finally, you should remember from Chapter 9 that random
assignment is *not* the same as **random selection**. Random assignment is related to the issue of internal validity, whereas the notion of
random selection is more involved with external validity, a topic we
will consider in the next chapter.

Experimental Design   Campbell and Stanley (1966) reviewed six
experimental designs and evaluated them in terms of controlling for
internal validity. They recommended three of the designs as being
able to control the threats to internal validity we listed in Chapter 5.
Let's examine their three recommended designs.

The Pretest-Posttest Control Group Design   The pretest-posttest control
group design appears in Figure 16-2. As you can see, this design consists of two randomly assigned groups of participants, both of which
are pretested, with one group receiving the IV.

The threats to internal validity that we summarized in Chapter 5
are controlled by one of two mechanisms in this design. The random
assignment of participants to groups allows us to assume that the
two groups are equated before the experiment, thus ruling out
selection as a problem. Using a pretest and a posttest for *both* groups
allows us to control the effects of **history, maturation**, and
testing because they should affect both groups equally. If the control group shows a change between the pretests and posttests, then
we know that some factor other than the IV is at work. **Statistical
regression** is controlled as long as we assign our experimental and

| R | O_1 | | O_2 | (control group) |
| R | O_3 | X | O_4 | (experimental group) |

KEY:
R = Random assignment
O = Pretest or posttest observation or measurement
X = Experimental variable or event
Each row represents a different group of participants.
Left-to-right dimension represents passage of time.
Any letters vertical to each other occur simultaneously.
(Note: This key also applies to Figures 16-3, 16-5, and 16-6)

FIGURE 16-2 THE PRETEST–POSTTEST CONTROL-GROUP DESIGN.

Interactions with selection Threats to internal validity that can occur if there are systematic differences between or among selected treatment groups based on maturation, history, or instrumentation.

Experimental mortality A threat to internal validity that can occur if experimental participants from different groups drop out of the experiment at different rates.

Instrumentation A threat to internal validity that occurs if the equipment or human measuring the DV changes its measuring criterion over time.

Diffusion or **imitation of treatment** A threat to internal validity that can occur if participants in one treatment group become familiar with the treatment of another group and copy that treatment.

control groups from the same extreme pool of participants. If any of the **interactions with selection** occur, they should affect both groups equally, thus equalizing those effects on internal validity.

The other threats to internal validity are not controlled, but the pretest–posttest control group design does give us the ability to determine whether or not they were problematic in a given experiment. We can check to see whether **experimental mortality** was a problem because we measure both groups on two occasions. **Instrumentation** is measured if we are dealing with responses to a test, for example, but it could still remain a problem if human interviewers or observers are used. There is simply no substitute for pretraining when you use humans to record or score data for you. Finally, **diffusion** or **imitation of treatments** could still remain a problem if participants from the control group (or different experimental groups) learn about the treatments for other groups. Again, though, you do have the control group as a "yardstick" to determine whether their scores increase or decrease in similar fashion to the experimental group's scores. If you see similar changes, you can suspect that internal validity controls may have failed.

The Solomon Four-Group Design   Figure 16-3 contains a diagram of the Solomon four-group design, first proposed by Solomon (1949). Notice that this design is identical to the pretest–posttest control-group design with the first two groups but adds an additional two groups—thus gaining the name *four-group design*. Because the Solomon four-group design has the same two groups as the pretest–posttest control-group design, it has the same protection against the threats to internal validity. As you will see in the next chapter, the main advantage gained by adding the two additional groups relates to external validity.

One problem with the Solomon design is statistical analysis of the data because there is no statistical test that can treat all six sets of data at the same time. Campbell and Stanley (1966) suggested treating the *posttest* scores as a factorial design, as shown in Figure 16-4. Unfortunately, this approach ignores all the pretest scores.

```
R   O_1       O_2
R   O_3   X   O_4
R             O_5
R         X   O_6
```

FIGURE 16-3 THE SOLOMON FOUR-GROUP DESIGN. This design is used to protect internal validity.

	No IV	Receives IV
Pretested	O_2	O_4
Unpretested	O_5	O_6

FIGURE 16-4 FACTORIAL TREATMENT OF SOLOMON FOUR-GROUP DESIGN POSTTEST SCORES.

The Posttest-Only Control-Group Design   Figure 16-5 shows the posttest-only control group design. As you can see by comparing Figure 16-5 to Figures 16-2 and 16-3, the posttest-only control-group design is a copy of the pretest–posttest control-group design but without the pretests included and is a copy of the two added groups in the Solomon four-group design. Does the lack of pretests render the posttest-only control-group design less desirable than the other two designs that included them? No, because we can count on the random assignment to groups to equate the two groups. Thus, using random assignment of participants to groups and withholding the IV from one group to make it a control group is a powerful experimental design that controls the threats to internal validity we covered in Chapter 5.

 PSYCHOLOGICAL DETECTIVE   After examining Figure 16-5, what type of design (from Chapters 10–15) does this appear to be?

We hope that you identified Figure 16-5 as the two-group design from Chapter 10. However, we must point out that it is *not* critical to have only two groups in this design. The posttest-only control-group design could be extended by adding

```
R        O₁
R    X   O₂
```

FIGURE 16-5 POSTTEST-ONLY CONTROL-GROUP DESIGN. This is a powerful design for protecting internal validity.

R		O_1
R	X_1	O_2
R	X_2	O_3
•	•	•
•	•	•
•	•	•
R	X_n	O_{n+1}

FIGURE 16-6 **AN EXTENSION OF THE POSTTEST-ONLY CONTROL-GROUP DESIGN.** This design allows for testing multiple treatment groups.

additional treatment groups, as shown in Figure 16-6. This extended design should remind you of the multiple-group design from Chapter 12. Finally, we could create a factorial design from the posttest-only control group by combining two of these designs simultaneously so that we ended up with a block diagram similar to those from Chapter 14.

PSYCHOLOGICAL **DETECTIVE** It should be clear that the posttest-only design is not defined by the number of groups. What is (are) the defining feature(s) of this design? Take a moment to study Figures 16-5 and 16-6 before answering.

The two features that are necessary to "make" a posttest-only control-group design are random assignment of participants to groups and the inclusion of a control (no-treatment) group. These features allow the design to derive cause-and-effect statements by equating the groups before the experiment and controlling the threats to internal validity.

We hope you can appreciate the amount of control that can be gained by the two simple principles of random assignment and experimental design. Although these principles are simple, they are quite elegant in the power they bring to the experimental situation. You would be wise not to underestimate their importance.

Conclusion

How important is internal validity? It is *the most important* property of any experiment. If you do not concern yourself with the internal validity of your experiment, you are wasting your time. Experiments are intended to produce cause-and-effect statements— to conclude that X causes Y to occur. If you merely wish to learn something about the association of two variables you can use one of the nonexperimental methods for acquiring data summarized in Chapter 19 or calculate a correlation coefficient. However, if you wish to investigate the cause(s) of a phenomenon, you must take care to control any extraneous variables that might affect your dependent variable. You cannot count on your statistical tests to provide the necessary control functions for you. Statistical tests merely analyze the numbers you bring to the test. They do not have the ability to remove confounding effects (or even to discern that confounding has occurred) in the data you bring.

REVIEW SUMMARY

1. One important control for internal validity is **random assignment** of participants to groups. This procedure assures us that the groups are equated before beginning the experiment.

2. **Random selection** refers to choosing our participants from a population so that all potential participants could be chosen. Random selection is important to external validity.

3. The **pretest–posttest control-group design** consists of two groups of participants that are randomly assigned to an experimental and control group, pretested and posttested, with the experimental group receiving the IV. This design controls for internal validity threats but has the problem of including a pretest.

4. The **Solomon four-group design** is a copy of the pretest-posttest control-group design except that it adds two groups that are not pretested. This design also controls for internal validity tests but there is no statistical test that can be used to analyze all six sets of data.

5. The **posttest-only control-group design** consists of two groups of participants, randomly assigned to an experimental and control group, with the experimental group receiving the IV treatment. Both groups are tested with a posttest. This design controls for internal validity threats and is free from other problems.

6. The posttest-only control-group design can be extended to include additional treatment groups or additional IVs.

7. It is essential for an experiment to be internally valid. Otherwise, no conclusion can be drawn from the experiment.

CHECK YOUR PROGRESS

1. The two general methods that we use to protect the internal validity of our experiment are _____ _____ and _____ _____.

2. Why is it essential to use random assignment of our participants to their groups?

3. Distinguish between *random assignment* and *random selection*.

4. What is the drawback of using the pretest–posttest control-group design to help with internal validity?

5. A friend tells you she was a participant in a psychology experiment and says, "It was crazy! We took a personality test, watched a film, and then took the same test again!" From this description, you could tell that she was in the _____.

   a. control group of a posttest-only control group design

   b. experimental group of a posttest-only control group design

c. control group of a pretest–posttest control group design

d. experimental group of a pretest–posttest control group design

6. What is the drawback of using the Solomon four-group design as a control for internal validity?

7. Diagram the posttest-only control-group design. Why is it a good choice for controlling internal validity?

Single-Case Experimental Designs

> **Single-case experimental design** An experiment that consists of one participant (also known as *N = 1 designs*).

> **Case-study approach** An observational technique in which we compile a record of observations about a single participant.

In the case of a **single-case experimental design** (also known as an *N* = 1 design), the name says it all. This term simply refers to an experimental design that has one participant. This approach, of course, is quite similar to the detective's strategy of pursuing a single suspect.

In Chapter 19 you will read about **case-study approach**, which may remind you of a single-case design. In a case study we conduct an intense observation of a single individual and compile a record of those observations. Case studies are often used in clinical settings. If you have taken an abnormal psychology course you probably remember reading case studies of people who have various disorders. The case study is an excellent descriptive technique— if you read about an individual who has a mental disorder, you get a vivid picture of what that disorder is like. However, a case study is *merely* a descriptive or observational approach; the researcher does not manipulate or control variables, but simply records observations. Thus, case studies do not allow us to draw cause-and-effect conclusions.

You will remember that we must institute control over the variables in an experiment in order to derive cause-and-effect statements. In a single-case design, we institute controls just as in a typical experiment—the only difference is that our experiment deals with only one participant. Also, just as in a typical experiment, we must take precautions dealing with the internal validity of a single-case design. We hope that the single-case design raises many questions for you. After all, it does go against the grain of some principles we have developed thus far. Let's take a quick look at this design's history and uses, which will help you understand its importance.

History of Single-Case Experimental Designs

The single-case experimental design has quite an illustrious past in experimental psychology (Hersen, 1982; Hersen & Barlow, 1976). In the 1860s Gustav Fechner explored sensory processes through the use of psychophysical methods. Fechner developed two concepts that you probably remember from your introductory psychology course: *sensory thresholds* and the *just noticeable difference* (*jnd*). Fechner conducted his work on an in-depth basis with a series of individuals. Wilhelm Wundt (founder of the first psychology laboratory) conducted his pioneering work on introspection with highly trained individual participants. Herman Ebbinghaus conducted perhaps the most

Reprinted with special permission of Tom Cheney.

"Sooner or later he'll learn that when he presses the bar, he'll receive a salary."

Much psychological knowledge has been gained from single-case designs.

famous examples of single-case designs in our discipline. Ebbinghaus was the pioneering researcher in the field of verbal learning and memory. His research was unique—not that he used the single-case design, but that he was the single participant in those designs. According to Dukes (1965), Ebbinghaus learned about 2,000 lists of nonsense syllables in his research over many years. Dukes provided several other examples of famous single-case designs with which you are probably familiar, such as Cannon's study of stomach contractions and hunger, Watson and Rayner's study of Little Albert's learned fears, and several researchers' work with language learning in individual apes.

Other than the ape-language studies that Dukes (1965) cited, all these single-case design examples date to the 1800s and early 1900s. Dukes found only 246 single-case examples in the literature between 1939 and 1963. Clearly, there are fewer examples of single-case designs than group designs in the literature.

Can you think of a reason why single-case designs may have been more popular in the past?

Hersen (1982) attributed the preference for group designs over single-case designs to statistical innovations made by Fisher. Sir Ronald A. Fisher was a pioneer of many statistical approaches and techniques. Most importantly for this discussion, in the 1920s, he developed ANOVA (Spatz, 2001), which we covered in some detail in Chapters 13 and 15. Combined with Gosset's early 1900s development of a test based on the *t* distribution (see Chapter 11), Fisher's work gave researchers a set of inferential statistical methods with which to analyze sets of data and draw conclusions. You may have taken these tests for granted and assumed that they had been around forever, but that is not the case. As these methods became popular and accessible to more researchers, the use of single-case designs declined. In today's research world, statistical analyses of incredibly complex designs can be completed in minutes (or even seconds) on computers that you can hold in your hand. The ease of these calculations has probably contributed to the popularity of group designs over single-case designs.

Uses of Single-Case Experimental Designs

> **Experimental analysis of behavior** A research approach popularized by B. F. Skinner, in which a single participant is studied.

There are still researchers who use single-case designs. Founded by B. F. Skinner, the **experimental analysis of behavior** approach continues to employ this technique. Skinner (1966) summarized his philosophy in this manner: "Instead of studying a thousand rats for one hour each, or a hundred rats for ten hours each, the investigator is likely to study one rat for a thousand hours" (p. 21). The Society for the Experimental Analysis of Behavior was formed and began publishing its own journals, the *Journal of the Experimental Analysis of Behavior* (in 1958) and the *Journal of Applied Behavior Analysis* (in 1968). Thus, single-case designs are still used today. However, the number of users is small in comparison to group designs, as you could guess with only a handful of journal titles devoted to this approach.

One question that might occur to you is "Why use a single-case design in the first place?" Sherlock Holmes knew that "the world is full of obvious things which nobody by any chance ever observes" (Doyle, 1927, p. 745). Dukes (1965) provided a number of convincing arguments for and situations that require single-case designs. Let's look at several: First, a sample of one is all you can manage if that sample exhausts the population. If you have access to a participant that is unique, you simply cannot find other participants. Of course, this example is perhaps closer to a case study than to an experiment because there would be no larger population to which you could generalize your findings. Second, if you can assume perfect generalizability, then a sample of one is appropriate. If there is only inconsequential variability among members of the population on a particular variable, then measuring one participant should be sufficient. Third, a single-case design would be most appropriate when a single *negative* instance would refute a theory or an assumed universal relation. If the scientific community believes that "reinforcement always increases responding," then finding one instance in which reinforcement does *not* increase responding invalidates the thesis. Fourth, you may simply have limitations on your opportunity to observe a particular behavior. Behaviors in the real world (i.e., nonlaboratory behaviors) may be so rare that you can locate only one participant who exhibits the behavior. Dukes used examples of people who feel no pain, who are totally color-blind, or who exhibit multiple personality disorder (again, close to a case study). You may remember reading about H.M.

when you studied memory in introductory psychology. Because of surgery for epilepsy that removed part of his brain, H.M. could no longer form new long-term memories. Researchers have studied H.M. for almost 50 years for clues about how the brain forms new memories (Corkin, 1984; Hilts, 1995). Fifth, when research is extremely time consuming and expensive, requires extensive training, or has difficulties with control, an investigator may choose to study only one participant. The studies in which researchers have attempted to teach apes to communicate through sign language, plastic symbols, or computers fall into this category. Thus, it is clear that there are instances in which a single-case design is totally appropriate.

General Procedures of Single-Case Experimental Designs

Hersen (1982) listed three procedures that are characteristic of single-case designs: repeated measures, baseline measurement, and changing one variable at a time. Let's see why each of these procedures is important.

Repeated Measures   When we deal with many participants, we often measure them only once and then average all our observations. However, when you are dealing with only one participant, it is important to make sure that the behavior you are measuring is consistent. Therefore, you would repeatedly measure the participant's behavior. Control during the measurement process is extremely important. Hersen and Barlow (1976) noted that the procedures for measurement "must be clearly specified, observable, public, and replicable in all respects" (p. 71). In addition, these repeated measurements "must be done under exacting and totally standardized conditions with respect to measurement devices used, personnel involved, time or times of day measurements are recorded, instructions to the subject, and the specific environmental conditions" (p. 71). Thus, conducting a single-case experiment and making repeated measurements do *not* remove the experimenter's need to control factors as carefully as possible.

> **Baseline** A measurement of a behavior that is made under normal conditions (i.e., no IV is present); a control condition.

Baseline Measurement   In most single-case designs, the initial experimental period is devoted to determining the **baseline** level of behavior. In essence, baseline measurement serves as the control condition against which to compare the behavior as affected by the IV. When you are collecting baseline data, you hope to find a stable pattern of behavior so that you can more easily see any change that occurs in the behavior after your intervention (IV). Barlow and Hersen (1973) recommended that you collect *at least* three observations during the baseline period in order to establish a trend in the data. Although you may not achieve a stable measurement, the more observations you have, the more confident you can be that you have determined the general trend of the observations. Figure 16-7 depicts a hypothetical stable baseline presented by Hersen and Barlow (1976). Notice that they increased their odds of finding a stable pattern by collecting data three times per day and averaging those data for the daily entry.

Changing One Variable at a Time   In a single-case design it is vital that, as the experimenter, you change only one variable at a time when you move from one phase of the experiment to the next.

FIGURE 16-7 A STABLE BASELINE. Hypothetical data for mean number of facial tics averaged over three daily 15-minute videotaped sessions.

Source: Figure 3-1 from *Single-Case Experimental Designs: Strategies for Studying Behavioral Change* (p. 77) by M. Hersen and D. H. Barlow, 1976, New York: Pergamon Press. Used with permission of the publisher.

PSYCHOLOGICAL DETECTIVE Why would it be important to change only one variable at a time in a single-case design?

We hope that the answer to this question came easily. Changing one variable at a time is a basic experimental control procedure that we have stressed many times. If you allow two variables to change simultaneously, then you have a confounded experiment and cannot tell which variable has caused the change in behavior that you observe. This situation is exactly the same in a single-case design. If you record your baseline measurement, change several aspects of the participant's environment, and then observe the behavior again, you have no way of knowing which changed aspect affected the behavior.

Statistics and Single-Case Experimental Designs

Traditionally, researchers have not computed statistical analyses of results from single-case designs. Not only has the development of statistical tests for such designs lagged behind multiple-case analyses, but there is also controversy about *whether* statistical analyses of single-case designs are even appropriate (Kazdin, 1976). Both Kazdin (1976) and Hersen (1982) summarized the arguments concerning statistical analyses. Let's take a quick look at this controversy.

The Case Against Statistical Analysis   As we mentioned, tradition and history say that statistical analyses are not necessary in single-case designs. The tradition has been to visually inspect ("eyeball") the data to determine whether or not change has taken place. Researchers who hold this position believe that treatments that do not produce visually apparent effects are either weak or ineffective. Skinner (1966) wrote that "rate of responding and changes in rate can be directly observed . . . [and] statistical methods are unnecessary" (p. 20).

Because many single-case studies involve clinical treatments, another argument against statistical analysis is that statistical significance is not always the same as clinical significance. A statistical demonstration of change may not be satisfying for practical application. "For example, an autistic child may hit himself in the head 100 times an hour. Treatment may reduce this to 50 times per hour. Even though change has been achieved, a much larger change is needed to eliminate behavior" (Kazdin, 1984, p. 89).

Finally, to the pro-statistics folks who argue that statistical analyses may help find effects that visual inspection would not (see next section), the anti-statistics camp makes the point that such subtle effects may not be replicable (Kazdin, 1976). As you will learn in the next chapter, if you cannot replicate a result it has no external validity.

The Case for Statistical Analysis   The argument for using statistical analyses of single-case designs revolves primarily around increased accuracy of conclusions. Jones, Vaught, and Weinrott (1977) have provided the most persuasive appeal for such analyses. They reviewed a number of studies published in the *Journal of Applied Behavior Analysis* that used visual inspection of data to draw conclusions. Jones et al. found that analyses of these data showed that sometimes conclusions drawn from visual inspections were correct and that sometimes the conclusions were incorrect. In the latter category, both Type I and Type II errors (see Chapter 9) occurred. In other words, some statistical analyses showed *no* effect when the researchers had said there was an effect and some analyses showed significant effects when the researchers had said there were none. Kazdin (1976) pointed out that statistical analyses are particularly likely to uncover findings that do not show up in visual inspection when a stable baseline is not established, new areas of research are being investigated, or testing is done in the real world, which tends to increase extraneous variation.

As you can tell, there is no clear-cut answer concerning the use of statistics with single-case designs. Most researchers probably make their decision in such a situation based on a combination of personal preference, the audience for the information, and potential journal editors. Covering the various tests used to analyze single-case designs is beyond the scope of this text. Adaptations of *t* tests and ANOVA have been used, but these approaches have suffered some problems. For further information about such tests, see Kazdin (1976).

A Refers to the baseline measurement in a single-case design.

B Refers to the outcome (treatment) measurement in a single-case design.

Representative Single-Case Experimental Designs

Researchers use standard notation for single-case designs, which makes the information easier to present and conceptualize. In this notation, **A** refers to the baseline measurement and **B** refers to the measurement during or after treatment. We read the notation for single-case designs from left to right to denote the passage of time.

A-B Design   In the **A-B design**, the simplest of the single-case designs, we make baseline measurements, apply a treatment, and then take a second set of measurements. We compare the B (treatment) measurements to the A (baseline) measurements in order to determine whether a change has occurred. This design should remind you of a pretest–posttest design except for the absence of a control group. In the A-B design, the participant's A measurements serve as the control for the B measurements.

A-B design   A single-case design in which you measure the baseline behavior, institute a treatment, and use a posttest.

For example, Hall et al. (1971) used this approach in a special-education setting. A 10-year-old boy (Johnny) continually talked out and disrupted the class, which led other children to imitate him. The researchers had the teacher measure Johnny's baseline talking-out behavior (A) for five 15-minute sessions under normal conditions. In implementing the treatment (B), the teacher ignored the talking out and paid more attention to Johnny's productive behavior (attention was *contingent* on the desired behavior), again for five 15-minute sessions. Johnny's talking out diminished noticeably.

Hersen (1982) rated the A-B design as one of the weakest for inferring causality and noted that it is often deemed correlational.

PSYCHOLOGICAL DETECTIVE   Why do you think the A-B design is weak concerning causality?

The A-B design is poor for determining causality because of many of the threats to internal validity that we saw in Chapter 5. It is possible that another factor could vary along with the treatment. This possibility is especially strong for extraneous variables that could be linked to time passage, such as history, maturation, and instrumentation. If such a factor varied across time with the treatment, then any change in B could be due to *either* the treatment or the extraneous factor. Because there is no control group, we cannot rule out the extraneous variable as a causative factor.

PSYCHOLOGICAL DETECTIVE   Can you think of a solution to the causality problem inherent in the A-B design? Remember that you cannot add a control group *or* participants because this is a single-case design. Therefore, any control must occur with the single participant.

The solution to this causality problem requires us to examine our next single-case design.

A-B-A Design   In the **A-B-A design**, the treatment phase is followed by a return to the baseline condition. If a change in behavior during B is actually due to the experimental

A-B-A design A single-case design consisting of a baseline measurement, a treatment, a posttest, and a return to the baseline condition. May not be recommended if the participant is left without a beneficial or necessary treatment in the second baseline.

treatment, the change should disappear when B is removed and you return to the baseline condition. If, on the other hand, a change in B was due to some extraneous variable, the change will not disappear when B is removed. Thus, the A-B-A design allows a causal relation to be drawn.

In Hall et al.'s (1971) experiment, the teacher did return to the baseline condition with Johnny. When the teacher began again to pay attention to Johnny's talking-out behavior, that behavior increased considerably. This return to the previous behavior strengthened the researchers' claim that the treatment had caused the original decrease in Johnny's talking out.

 There is one glaring drawback to the A-B-A design. Think about the implications of conducting a baseline-treatment-baseline experiment. Can you spot the drawback? How would you remedy this problem?

If you end your experiment on an A phase, this leaves the participant in a baseline condition. If the treatment is a beneficial one, the participant is "left hanging" without the treatment. The solution to this problem requires us to examine another single-case design.

A-B-A-B design
A single-case design consisting of a baseline, treatment, posttest, return to baseline, repeated treatment, and second posttest. This design gives the best chance of isolating causation.

A-B-A-B Design   As you can figure out by now, the **A-B-A-B design** begins with a baseline period followed by treatment, baseline, and treatment periods consecutively. This design adds a final treatment period to the A-B-A design, thereby completing the experimental cycle with the participant in a treatment phase. Hersen and Barlow (1976) pointed out that this design gives two transitions (B to A and A to B) that can demonstrate the effect of the treatment variable. Thus, our ability to draw a cause-and-effect conclusion is further strengthened.

Hall et al. (1971) actually used the A-B-A-B design in their experiment with Johnny. After measuring Johnny's baseline talking-out behavior (A) under normal conditions, the teacher implemented the treatment (B) by ignoring the talking out and paying attention only to Johnny's productive behavior. The teacher then repeated the A and B phases. Results from this study appear in Figure 16-8. This graph shows us several things. First, visual inspection of these results should be enough to convince us of the efficacy of the treatment—the difference between baseline and treatment conditions is dramatic. This graph is a good illustration of why many researchers who use single-case designs believe that statistics are unnecessary. Second, it is apparent that the treatment did work. When the teacher stopped attending to Johnny's talking-out behavior and paid attention to his productive behavior, the talking out decreased substantially. Third, we can determine that the increased productive behavior was caused by the contingent attention because of the rapid increase in talking out when the attention was removed (see Baseline$_2$ in Figure 16-8).

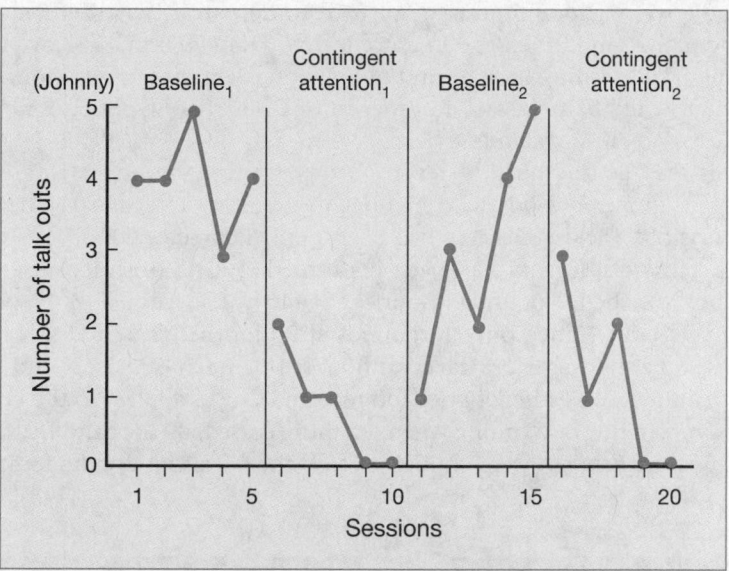

FIGURE 16-8 **TALKING-OUT BEHAVIOR IN A MENTALLY RETARDED STUDENT.** A record of talking-out behavior of an educable mentally retarded student. **Baseline_1**—before experimental conditions. **Contingent attention_1**—systematic ignoring of talking out and increased teacher attention to appropriate behavior. **Baseline_2**—reinstatement of teacher attention to talking-out behavior. **Contingent Attention_2**—return to systematic ignoring of talking out and increased attention to appropriate behavior.

Source: Figure 2 from "The Teacher as Observer and Experimenter in the Modification of Disrupting and Talking-out Behaviors" by R. V. Hall, R. Fox, D. Willard, L., Goldsmith, M. Emerson, M. Owen, F. Davis, and E. Porcia, 1971, *Journal of Applied Behavior Analysis, 4*, p. 143.

Design and the Real World From the preceding sections it should be clear that the A-B-A-B design is the preferred design for single-case research. However, we must ask whether typical practice actually follows the recommended path. Hersen and Barlow (1976) acknowledged that researchers often use the A-B design despite its shortcomings in terms of demonstrating causality. The main reason the A-B design is used concerns either the inability or undesirability to return to the baseline in the third stage. In the real world, perfect experimental design cannot always be used. We must simply accept that our ability to draw definitive conclusions in such instances is limited. Let's look at three common situations that preclude using a design other than the A-B design.

First, as is typical in many field experiments, it may be impractical to reverse a treatment. Campbell (1969, p. 410) urged politicians to conduct social reforms as experiments, proposing that they initiate a new policy on an experimental basis. If, after five years, there had been no significant improvement, he recommended that the politicians shift to a different policy. Political realities, of course, would not allow social change to be conducted experimentally. Campbell (1969) provided a good example of this problem. In 1955 Connecticut experienced a record number of traffic fatalities. The governor instituted a speeding crackdown in 1956, and traffic fatalities fell by more than 12%. Once this result occurred, it would have been politically stupid for the governor to announce, "We wish to determine whether the speeding crackdown actually caused the drop in auto deaths. Therefore, in 1957, we will relax our enforcement of speeding laws to find out whether fatalities increase once again." Yet this is what would be necessary in order to rule out rival hypotheses and draw a definitive cause-and-effect statement.

Second, it may be unethical to reverse a treatment. Lang and Melamed (1969) worked with a 9-month-old boy who had begun vomiting after meals when he was about 6 months old. Dietary changes had been implemented, medical tests had been conducted, exploratory surgery had been performed, but no organic cause could be found. The boy weighed 9 pounds, 4 ounces at birth, had gained to 17 pounds at 6 months of age, but weighed only 12 pounds at 9 months. The child was being fed through a nose tube and was in critical condition (see Figure 16-9A). Lang and Melamed instituted a treatment consisting of brief and repeated shocks applied to the boy's leg at the first signs of vomiting and ending when vomiting ceased. By the third treatment session, one or two brief shocks were enough to stop the vomiting. By the fourth day of

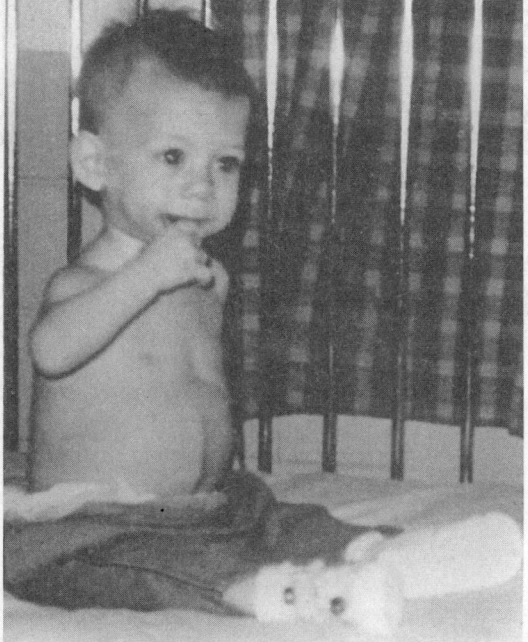

FIGURE 16-9 NINE-MONTH-OLD BOY HOSPITALIZED FOR FREQUENT VOMITING (A) BEFORE TREATMENT AND (B) AFTER TREATMENT (13 DAYS LATER). The photograph at the left was taken during the observation period just prior to treatment. (It clearly illustrates the patient's debilitated condition—the lack of body fat, skin hanging in loose folds. The tape around the face holds tubing for the nasogastric pump. The photograph at the right was taken on the day of discharge from the hospital, 13 days after the first photo. The 26% increase in body weight already attained is easily seen in the full, more infantlike face, the rounded arms, and more substantial trunk.)

Source: Figure 1 from "Avoidance Conditioning Therapy of an Infant with Chronic Ruminative Vomiting" by P. J. Lang and B. G. Melamed, 1969, *Journal of Abnormal Psychology, 74*, pp. 1–8.

treatment, vomiting stopped, so treatment was discontinued. Two days later, some vomiting occurred, so the procedure was reinstated for three sessions. Five days later, the child was dismissed from the hospital (see Figure 16-9B). A month later he weighed 21 pounds and 5 months later weighed over 26 pounds, with no recurrence of vomiting. Although this treatment bears some resemblance to an A-B-A-B design (because of the brief relapse), the additional session was not originally intended and was *not* conducted as an intentional removal of B to chart a new baseline—the researchers believed that the problem had been cured at the point treatment was discontinued. We are certain that you can see why ethical considerations would dictate an A-B design in this instance rather than the more experimentally rigorous A-B-A-B design.

Finally, it may be impossible, undesirable, or unethical to reverse a treatment if learning takes place during the treatment. Bobby Traffanstedt (1998), a student at the University of Central Arkansas in Conway, Arkansas, used an A-B design to modify a 10-year-old boy's TV watching and exercise behaviors. Traffanstedt wanted to teach the boy to spend less time watching TV and more time exercising. He used the operant procedures of shaping and reinforcement while working with the child for several weeks. The baseline (Week 1) and posttest (Weeks 2–9) behavior measures appear in Figure 16-10. As you can see, visual inspection of these data is convincing.

FIGURE 16-10 TEACHING A 10-YEAR-OLD BOY TO DECREASE TV VIEWING AND INCREASE EXERCISE.

Source: Adapted from "Weight Reduction using Behavior Modification" by B. Traffenstedt, 1998, *Journal of Psychological Inquiry, 3,* pp. 19–23.

Why did Traffanstedt (1998) *not* use the A-B-A-B design in this experiment?

Because Traffanstedt had successfully taught the child to spend less time watching TV and more time exercising, he did not want to "undo" this learning and return to the baseline condition. Traffanstedt had already attempted to gradually fade out the reinforcement over the course of Weeks 2 through 9, so going back to baseline was not really feasible. Having learned the new behaviors, it would make no sense to return the boy to the baseline condition.

The conclusion to this section is that you, as an experimenter, may find yourself caught in the middle. On the one hand, you have the knowledge of proper experimental design and what is necessary to yield cause-and-effect explanations. On the other hand, you have the realities of applied situations. The best rule of thumb for such situations is that you should use the most stringent experimental design you can, but you should not give up on an important project if you cannot use the absolute best design that exists. As a psychological detective, you have an edge on the real-life detective, who cannot apply a design even as rigorous as those we have presented in this section. The police detective must always work on a solution after the fact.

Additional Single-Case Designs   In presenting the A-B, A-B-A, and A-B-A-B designs, we have merely scratched the surface of single-case designs. We have covered the designs we think you might be likely to use in the near future. As our references show, entire books have been written about single-case designs. Hersen and Barlow (1976) covered many additional variations on single-case designs, including designs with multiple baselines, multiple schedules, and interactions. Thus, if you ever envision a single-case design that is more complicated than the ones we have presented in this text, we refer you to Hersen and Barlow (1976) or a similar book dealing with single-case designs.

REVIEW SUMMARY

1. **Single-case experimental designs** are experiments that deal with a single participant.
2. Single-case designs have several legitimate uses.
3. Single-case designs are characterized by repeated measures, **baseline** measurement, and changing one variable at a time.
4. There is controversy over the use of statistics with single-case designs. The traditional approach has been to draw conclusions by visually examining the data. Proponents of statistical analysis maintain that analysis yields more correct conclusions.

5. The **A-B-A-B** single-case design allows you the best chance to draw a cause-and-effect conclusion regarding a treatment. Realities of the real world often force the use of **A-B** designs, which are particularly prone to alternative explanations.

CHECK YOUR PROGRESS

1. Why were single-case designs quite popular in psychology's early years but less popular today?
2. How can a single-case design be used to disprove a theory?
3. To come up with a comparison in the single-case design, we first measure behavior before the treatment during the _____ period. To get a stable measurement, we should make at least _____ observations.
4. In essence, _____ serve(s) as the control condition in the single-case design.
    a. baseline measurements
    b. repeated measures
    c. changing one variable at a time
    d. experimental analysis of behavior
5. Summarize two arguments for and two arguments against statistical analysis of single-case designs.
6. Match the design with the appropriate characteristic:
    1. A-B   a. leaves the participant in a baseline phase
    2. A-B-A   b. best single-case design for determining cause-and-effect relations
    3. A-B-A-B   c. has many threats to internal validity
7. Why might you be forced to use an A-B single-case design in the real world? Give an original example of such a situation.

Quasi-Experimental Designs

Quasi-experimental design A research design used when you cannot randomly assign your experimental participants to the groups but do manipulate an IV and measure a DV.

In this section, we will deal with designs that are virtually identical to true experimental designs with the *exception* of random assignment of participants to groups. When we are able to manipulate an IV and measure a DV but *cannot* randomly assign our participants to groups, we must use a **quasi-experimental design**. Similarly, police detectives sometimes face situations in which they must build their case on circumstantial evidence rather than using direct evidence.

 PSYCHOLOGICAL DETECTIVE   What problem results when we cannot randomly assign research participants to groups?

Not being able to randomly assign our participants to their groups has the effect of violating an important assumption that allows us to draw cause-and-effect conclusions from our experiments—the assumption of equal groups before the experiment. Even if we can randomly select participants from a larger group, we cannot make cause-and-effect statements without random assignment. For example, you could randomly *select* students from an introductory psychology course but you could not randomly *assign* them to groups based on sex! As Campbell and Stanley (1966) pointed out, the assumption of random assignment has been an important part of statistics and experimental design since the time of Fisher. If we unknowingly began an experiment with unequal groups and our statistics showed a difference after the experiment, we would make a Type I error (see Chapter 9) by concluding that the IV caused the difference that was actually present from the outset. Clearly, this conclusion could be wrong.

In Chapter 19 we will cover ex post facto studies. Some writers categorize ex post facto and quasi-experimental designs together and some separate them. We will draw a small, but significant, distinction between the two. Ex post facto studies have an IV that has *already* occurred and that we cannot manipulate. Thus, if we wish to study sex differences on mathematics or English achievement, we are studying the IV of biological sex, which we cannot control or manipulate. Of course, because the IV is a pre-existing condition, we also cannot randomly assign our participants to groups.

On the other hand, in a quasi-experimental design, our participants belong to pre-existing groups that we cannot randomly assign, but we *do* have control over the IV—we can administer it when and to whom we wish. Thus, we could choose our participants on the basis of sex and *then* have some of them participate in a workshop designed to improve their math or English achievement. In this case, the workshop (or lack thereof) would serve as the IV for the preexisting groups of boys and girls, and the math or English achievement scores would be the DV. Obviously, random assignment is impossible in this case. Quasi-experimental designs are a step closer to true experimental designs than ex post facto studies because you, as the experimenter, are able to exert control over the IV and its administration. Being able to administer your own IV is preferable to having nature administer it for you, at least in terms of control.

The basic rationale for using quasi-experimental designs is the same as that for ex post facto studies—your inability to assign participants at random. According to Hedrick, Bickman, and Rog (1993), "A quasi-experimental design is not the method of choice, but rather a fallback strategy for situations in which random assignment is not possible" (p. 62). When dealing with selection variables that do not allow for random assignment, we have the choice of using a quasi-experimental design or simply ignoring an important or interesting experimental question. Instead of letting such questions go unasked, researchers resort to quasi-experimental research.

History of Quasi-Experimental Designs

It is difficult to trace the history of quasi-experimental designs. Although McGuigan (1960) did not include the term in the first edition of his classic experimental psychology text, Campbell and Stanley did use it in the title of their 1966 guide to experimental design. However, there is little doubt that researchers were tackling quasi-experimental design problems long before Campbell and Stanley's published work. Cook and Campbell (1979) noted that some researchers were writing about quasi-experiments in the 1950s, although the term did not originate until later. It is likely that Campbell and Stanley (1966) and Cook and Campbell (1979) are responsible for elevating quasi-experimental work to the respectable position it holds today.

Uses of Quasi-Experimental Designs

Hedrick et al. (1993) listed several specific situations that require quasi-experimental designs. Let's take a brief look at their list. First, there are many variables that simply make random assignment impossible. If we wish to study participants from certain groups (e.g., based on sex, age, previous life experiences, or personality characteristics), we must use quasi-experimental designs. Second, when you wish to evaluate an ongoing program or intervention (a retrospective study), you would need to use a quasi-experimental design. Because the program began before you decided to evaluate it, you would have been unable to use control procedures from the outset. Third, studies of social conditions demand quasi-experimental designs. You would not study the effects of poverty, race, unemployment, or other such social factors through random assignment. Fourth, it is sometimes the case that random assignment is not possible because of expense, time, or monitoring difficulties. For example, if you conducted a cross-cultural research project involving participants from several different countries, it would be nearly impossible to guarantee that the same random assignment procedures were used in each setting. Fifth, the ethics of an experimental situation, particularly with psychological research, may necessitate quasi-experimentation. For example, if you are conducting a research program to evaluate a certain treatment, you must worry about the ethics of withholding that treatment from people who could benefit from it. As you will see, quasi-experimentation provides a design that will work in such situations to remove this ethical dilemma.

Representative Quasi-Experimental Designs

Nonequivalent group design A design involving two or more groups that are not randomly assigned; a comparison group (no treatment) is compared to one or more treatment groups.

Unlike the single-case design, we do not include sections covering general procedures and statistics of quasi-experimental designs. It is difficult to derive general principles because the representative designs we are about to introduce are so varied in nature. Because quasi-experimental designs resemble true experiments, the use of statistics for quasi-experimental designs is not an issue; the traditional statistical tests used with true experiments are also appropriate for quasi-experiments.

Nonequivalent Group Design   The **nonequivalent group design** (Campbell & Stanley, 1966) appears in Figure 16-11 (see next page).

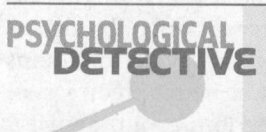
PSYCHOLOGICAL DETECTIVE   The nonequivalent group design should remind you of a design that we covered in the section on research designs that protect internal validity. Which design does it resemble? How is it different? What is the implication of this difference?

O_1 O_2 (comparison group)
O_1 X O_2 (treatment group)

KEY:
R = Random assignment
O = Pretest or posttest observation or measurement
X = Experimental variable or event
Each row represents a different group of participants.
Left-to-right dimension represents passage of time.
Any letters vertical to each other occur simultaneously.
Note: This key also applies to Figures 16-14, and 16-17.

FIGURE 16-11 THE NONEQUIVALENT GROUP DESIGN.

If you turn back to Figure 16-2 you will see that the nonequivalent group design bears a distinct resemblance to the pretest–posttest control-group design. However, the nonequivalent group design is missing the *R*s in front of the two groups; random assignment is *not* used to create the groups. The lack of random assignment means that our groups may differ before the experiment—thus the name *nonequivalent group* design.

You also will notice that the two groups are labeled as the *comparison group* (rather than control group) and the *treatment group* (rather than experimental group [from Hedrick et al., 1993]). The *treatment* to *experimental* change is not particularly important; those terms could be used interchangeably. However, changing the name from *control* to *comparison* group is important and meaningful. In the nonequivalent group design, this group serves as the comparison to the treatment group but cannot truly be called a control group because of the lack of random assignment.

It is possible to extend the nonequivalent group design to include more than one treatment group if you wish to contrast two or more treatment groups with your comparison group. The key to the nonequivalent group design is creating a good comparison group. As far as is possible, we attempt to create an equal group through our selection criteria rather than through random assignment.

> Examples of procedures for creating such a group include using members of a waiting list for a program/service; using people who did not volunteer for a program, but were eligible; using students in classes that will receive the curriculum (treatment) at a later date; and matching individual characteristics.
>
> (Hedrick et al., 1993, p. 59)

Geronimus (1991) provided a good example of creating a strong comparison group. She and her colleagues completed several studies of long-term outcomes for teen mothers. As you are probably aware, the stereotypical outcome for teen mothers is quite dismal—younger mothers are more likely to have negative experiences such as poverty, high dropout rates, and higher rates of infant mortality. However, Geronimus believed that family factors such as socioeconomic status might be better predictors of these negative outcomes than the actual teen pregnancy. Random assignment for research on this topic would be impossible—you could not randomly assign teenage girls to become pregnant or not. Thus, quasi-experimentation was necessary. In looking for a comparison group that would be as similar as possible, Geronimus decided to use the teenage mothers' sisters who did not become pregnant until later in life. Thus, although the assignment to groups was not random, the groups were presumably very near to equivalence, particularly with respect to family background factors. Interestingly enough, when family background was controlled in this manner, many of the negative outcomes associated with teen pregnancy disappeared. For example, there was no longer any difference in the dropout rates of the two groups. "For indicators of infant health and children's sociocognitive development, at times the trends reversed direction (i.e., controlling for family background, the teen birth group did better than the postponers)" (Geronimus, 1991, p. 465).

In Geronimus's research, the "pretest" (actually a matching variable in this case) consisted of finding two women from the same family, one who first became pregnant as a teenager and one who did not get pregnant until after age 20. In this case the groups may still have been nonequivalent, but they were highly equivalent on family background. Sometimes it is impossible to begin with equivalent groups, and the pretest serves much like a baseline measure for comparison with the posttest. In this type of situation, the label *nonequivalent groups* seems quite appropriate.

Janet Luehring, a student at Washburn University in Topeka, Kansas, and Joanne Altman, her faculty advisor, used a nonequivalent group design in their research project (Luehring & Altman, 2000). They measured students' performance on the Mental Rotation Task (MRT; Vandenberg & Kuse, 1978). For each item on the MRT, participants saw 5 three-dimensional shapes, with the first shape being the test stimulus. Two of the other four shapes were matches of the test stimulus when rotated; participants had to identify the two that were the same as the test stimulus. The MRT consists of 20 such items and normally has a 6-minute time limit. The preponderance of evidence from psychological research indicates that men tend to perform better on spatial tasks than women (Luehring & Altman, 2000). Luehring and Altman compared the performance of female students on the MRT to that of male students. Thus, the groups were not equal before the experiment began. The IV in Luehring and Altman's experiment consisted of performing the MRT under timed or untimed conditions. They found that women who performed the MRT under timed conditions made as few errors as men under timed or untimed conditions—only the women under untimed conditions made more errors than the other three groups. Because the two gender groups began the experiment as nonequivalent, the appropriate question after the experiment was not whether a difference existed, but whether the difference was the same as before the experiment (see Figure 16-12A) or whether the difference had changed in some way (see Figure 16-12B). In Luehring and Altman's experiment the difference between the two groups had grown smaller in the timed condition, thus supporting the hypothesis that the IV had an effect on performance on the MRT for women. Of course, there are several other possible outcomes that would also show some effect of the IV. More of Cook and Campbell's (1979) hypothetical outcomes appear in Figure 16-13. Can you interpret each set of findings pictured there?

Thus far, our discussion of this design has seemed similar to that of true experimental designs. What is different about quasi-experimental designs? The most important point to remember is that quasi-experimental designs are more plagued by threats to internal validity. Because you have not used random assignment, your interpretation

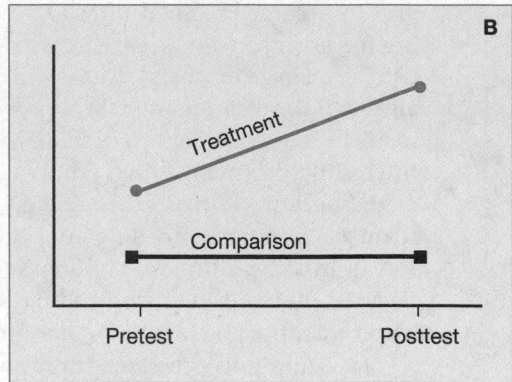

FIGURE 16-12 TWO POSSIBLE OUTCOMES IN A NONEQUIVALENT GROUP DESIGN.

Source: Thomas D. Cook and Donald T. Campbell, *Quasi-Experimentation: Design and Analysis.* Copyright © 1979 by Houghton-Mifflin Company. Reprinted by permission.

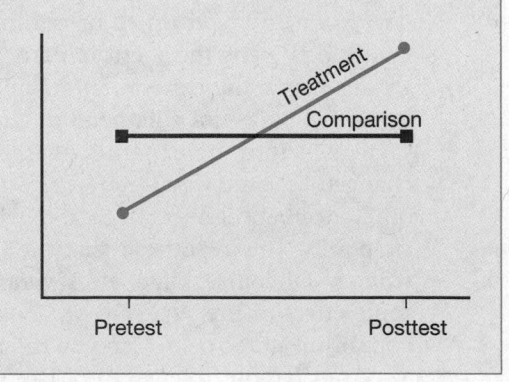

FIGURE 16-13 SEVERAL ADDITIONAL OUTCOMES IN A NONEQUIVALENT GROUP DESIGN.

Source: Thomas D. Cook and Donald T. Campbell, *Quasi-Experimentation: Design and Analysis.* Copyright © 1979 by Houghton-Mifflin Company. Reprinted by permission.

of the findings must be cautious. Cook and Campbell (1979) isolated four threats to internal validity that are not controlled in the nonequivalent group design. We will list these only briefly because they appeared in Chapter 5. First, *maturation* is a potential problem. Because the groups begin as unequal, there is a greater potential that results such as those shown in Figure 16-12B might be due to differential maturation of the groups rather than to the IV. Second, we must consider *instrumentation* in the nonequivalent group design. For example, if we demonstrate nonequivalence of our participants by using a scale during the pretest, we must worry about whether the scale is uniform—are the units of measurement equal throughout the scale? *Statistical regression* is the third internal validity threat present in the nonequivalent group design. Regression is particularly likely to be a problem if we select extreme scorers on the basis of our pretest. Finally, we must consider the threat to internal validity of an *interaction between selection and history*. If some local event differentially affected our treatment and comparison groups, we would have a problem.

In conclusion, the nonequivalent group design is a strong quasi-experimental design. Its strength lies in the fact that "it provides an approximation to the experimental design and that, with care, it can support causal inference" (Hedrick et al., 1993, p. 62). However, we must be aware that the threat of confounds is higher than for the true experimental designs. Hedrick et al. (1993) warned that "throughout both the planning and execution phases of an applied research project, researchers must keep their eyes open to identify potential rival explanations for their results" (p. 64). Often researchers who use quasi-experimental designs must address potential alternative hypotheses in their research reports.

> **Interrupted time-series design** A quasi-experimental design involving a single group of participants that includes repeated pre-treatment measures, an applied treatment, and repeated posttreatment measures.

Interrupted Time-Series Design   Another quasi-experimental design, the **interrupted time-series design**, involves measuring a group of participants repeatedly over time (the time series), introducing a treatment (the interruption), and measuring the participants repeatedly again (more of the time series). Look at Figure 16-14 to see a graphic portrayal of an interrupted time-series design. We should make an important point about Figure 16-14: There is nothing magical about using five observations before (O_1–O_5) and after (O_6–O_{10}) the treatment. Any number of observations large enough to establish a pattern can be used (Campbell & Stanley, 1966, showed four before and after; Cook & Campbell, 1979, showed five; Hedrick et al., 1993, showed six before and five after). As you can probably guess, the idea behind an interrupted time-series design is to look for changes in the trend of the data before and after the treatment is applied. Thus, the interrupted time-series design is similar to an A-B design. A change in trend could be shown by a change in the *level* of the behavior (see Figure 16-15A), a change in the *rate* (slope) of the pattern of behavior (see Figure 16-15B), or both (see Figure 16-15C).

| O_1 | O_2 | O_3 | O_4 | O_5 | X | O_6 | O_7 | O_8 | O_9 | O_{10} |

FIGURE 16-14 AN INTERRUPTED TIME-SERIES DESIGN.

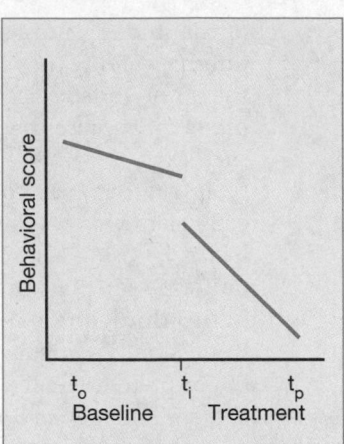

t_o = start of time series
t_i = an interruption point
t_p = end of time series

FIGURE 16-15 POTENTIAL CHANGES IN TREND IN A TIME-SERIES DESIGN. Change in level, no change in rate (part A). No change in level, change in rate (part B). Change in level, change in rate (part C).

Source: Portions of Figure 1 from "Time-Series Analysis in Operant Research" by R. R. Jones, R. S. Vaught, and M. Weinrott, 1977, *Journal of Applied Behavior Analysis, 10,* pp. 151–166.

Interrupted time-series designs have been used for quite some time. Campbell and Stanley (1966) referred to their use in much of the classical research of nineteenth-century biology and physical science. Cook and Campbell (1979) cited a representative 1924 study dealing with the effects of moving from a 10-hour to an 8-hour workday in London. Hedrick and Shipman (1988) used an interrupted time-series design to assess the impact of the 1981 Omnibus Budget Reconciliation Act, which tightened the eligibility requirements for Aid to Families with Dependent Children (AFDC) assistance. As shown in Figure 16-16, the immediate impact of this legislation was to lessen the number of cases handled by about 200,000. However, the number of cases after the change continued to climb at about the same slope it had before the change. Thus, the tightened eligibility requirements seemed to lower the *level* of the caseload but not its *rate*.

 Review the threats to internal validity summarized in Chapter 5. Which threat would seem to create the greatest potential problem for the interrupted time-series design?

According to Cook and Campbell (1979), the main threat to most interrupted time-series designs is *history*. One of the primary features of the interrupted time-series design is the passage of time to allow for many different measurements. This time passage raises the possibility that changes in behavior *could* be due to some important event other than the treatment. Because of the time taken by repeated measurements, another potential threat to internal validity is *maturation*. However, the repeated pretesting does allow for the assessment of any maturational trends; thus, if scores change at the same rate before and after the treatment, the change is due to maturation. *Instrumentation* could be a problem if record-keeping or scoring procedures change over the course of

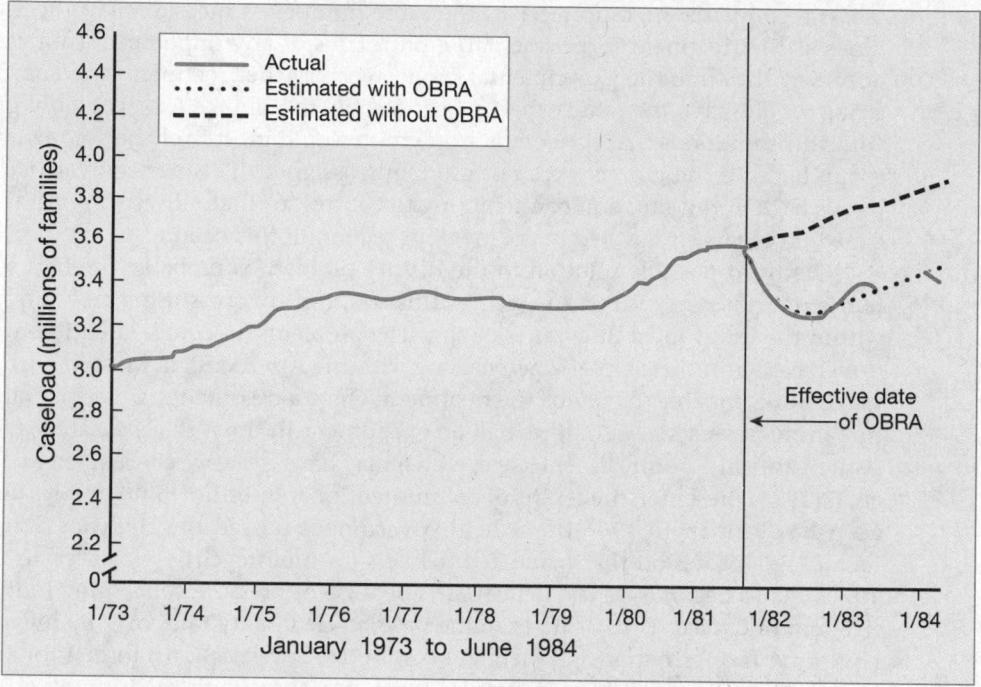

FIGURE 16-16 IMPACT OF TIGHTENED AFDC REQUIREMENTS ON CASELOAD.

Source: T. E. Hedrick and S. L. Shipman, "Multiple Questions Require Multiple Designs: An Evaluation of the 1981 Changes to the AFDC Program" *Evaluation Review, 12,* p. 438. Copyright © 1988 by Sage Publications, Inc. Reprinted by permission of Sage Publications, Inc.

time. Such a change, of course, would violate the principles of control in any experiment, not just an interrupted time-series design.

Although the interrupted time-series design can control for some of the internal validity threats, we still face the potential problem of history. This threat to internal validity is usually handled in one of three manners. First, Cook and Campbell (1979) advised frequent testing intervals. For example, if you test participants on a weekly rather than monthly, quarterly, or yearly basis, the probability of a major event occurring during the time period between the last pretest and the treatment is low. In addition, if you keep careful records of any possible effect-causing events during the quasi-experiment, it would be a simple matter to discern whether any occurred at the critical period when you administered the treatment. This first approach to controlling history is probably the most widely used because of its ease and the drawbacks of the other two solutions to be covered next.

A second solution to the history threat is to include a comparison (control) group that does not receive the treatment. Such a design appears in Figure 16-17. As you can

O_1	O_2	O_3	O_4	O_5	X	O_6	O_7	O_8	O_9	O_{10}
O_1	O_2	O_3	O_4	O_5		O_6	O_7	O_8	O_9	O_{10}

FIGURE 16-17 AN INTERRUPTED TIME-SERIES DESIGN WITH CONTROL GROUP.

see, the comparison group receives the same number of measurements at the same times as the treatment (experimental) group. Thus, if any important historical event occurs at the time the experimental group receives the treatment, the comparison group would have the same experience and show the same effect. The only problem with this solution is that the comparison group would most likely be a nonequivalent group because the groups were not randomly assigned. This nonequivalence would put us back in the situation of attempting to control for that difference, with the associated problems we covered in the previous section of this chapter.

The third possible solution to the history problem is probably the best solution but is not always possible. In essence, this solution involves using an A-B-A format within the interrupted time-series design. The problems, of course, are those we mentioned earlier in the chapter when dealing with the A-B-A design. Most importantly, it may not be possible to "undo" the treatment. Once a treatment has been applied, it is not always reversible. Also, if we halt an experiment in the A stage, we are leaving our participants in a nontreatment stage, which may have negative consequences. Hedrick et al. (1993) presented the results of an unintentional interrupted time-series design in an A-B-A format. In 1966 the federal government passed the Highway Safety Act, including a provision that mandated helmets for motorcyclists. However, in the late 1970s, states began to repeal helmet laws because of pressure concerning individuals' freedom of choice. Thus, if we examine motorcycle fatality rates over many years, we have an A (no restrictions), B (helmet laws), A (fewer restrictions) format for an interrupted time-series design. Figure 16-18 shows the graph Hedrick et al. (1993)

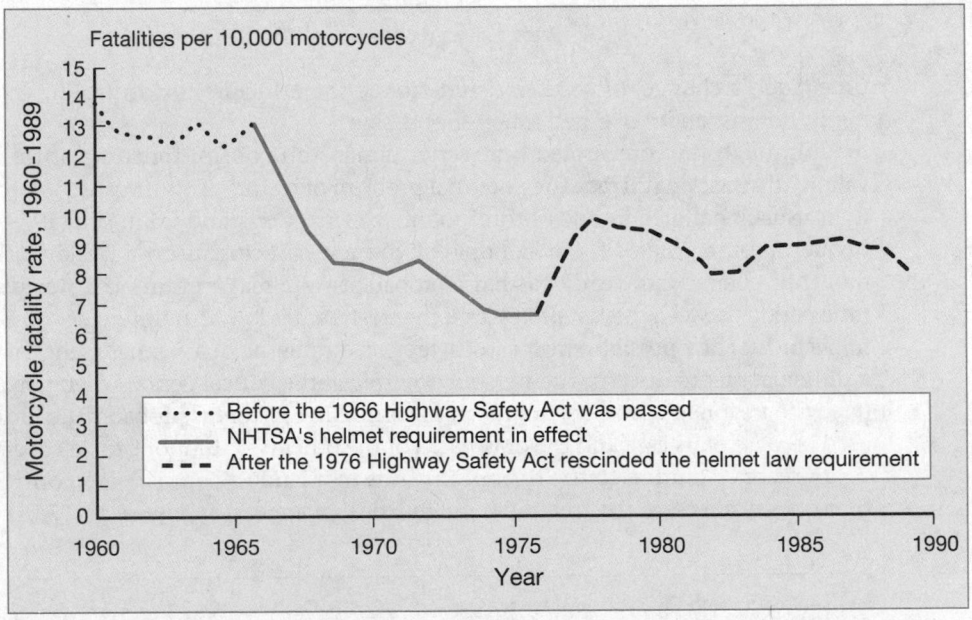

FIGURE 16-18 EFFECTS OF MANDATORY HELMET LAWS AND THEIR SUBSEQUENT REPEAL ON MOTORCYCLE FATALITIES.

Source: Motorcycle Helmet Laws Save Lives and Reduce Costs to Society (GAO/RCED-91–170, July), Washington, DC.

presented. Because of the drop in fatalities after the law was passed and the rise in fatalities after the repeal of the law in some states, it seems straightforward to derive a cause-and-effect relation from these data. Although this type of design allows for a convincing conclusion, again we must point out that the circumstances that created it are unusual and would be difficult, if not impossible, to recreate in many typical quasi-experimental situations.

In summary, the interrupted time-series design has the ability to uncover cause-and-effect relations. You must be especially careful of history effects when using this design; however, frequent testing helps reduce this threat. The interrupted time-series design is particularly helpful when dealing with applied types of problems such as therapeutic treatment or in educational settings.

REVIEW SUMMARY

1. **Quasi-experimental designs** are identical to true experimental designs except that participants are not randomly assigned to groups. Thus, our research groups may not be equal before the experiment, causing problems in drawing clear conclusions.
2. Unlike the case in **ex post facto designs**, we are able to control the IV in a quasi-experimental design.
3. There are many situations in which the impossibility of random assignment makes quasi-experimentation necessary.
4. The **nonequivalent group design** involves comparing two groups—one receiving the IV and one that does not receive the IV. The groups are nonequivalent because of the lack of random assignment.
5. In the nonequivalent group design, it is imperative to select a comparison group that is as similar as possible to the treatment group.
6. **Maturation, instrumentation, statistical regression**, and **selection history interactions** are all threats to internal validity in the nonequivalent group design.
7. An **interrupted time-series design** involves measuring participants several times, introducing an IV, and then measuring the participants several more times.
8. **History** is the main threat to internal validity in the interrupted time-series design. It can be controlled by testing frequently, including a comparison group, or removing the treatment after it has been applied (if possible).

CHECK YOUR PROGRESS

1. Differentiate between experimental designs, quasi-experimental designs, and ex post facto designs.
2. Give two reasons why you might choose to use a quasi-experimental design rather than an experimental design.

3. Match the design with the appropriate characteristics:
    1. Nonequivalent group design   A. typically has one group of participants
    2. Interrupted time-series design   B. has two groups of participants
                                          C. involves pretesting of participants
                                          D. does not involve pretesting participants
                                          E. is prone to the internal validity threat
                                             of history
                                          F. is prone to several internal validity
                                             threats

4. What was the key to Geronimus's (1991) research that allowed her to conclude that the effects of teenage pregnancy are not as negative as typically thought?

5. We summarized two interrupted time-series analyses in the text—one dealing with changing AFDC requirements (Figure 16-16) and one dealing with changing motorcycle helmet laws (Figure 16-18). Why are we more certain about our conclusion in the case of the helmet laws than with the AFDC requirements?

6. If Prohibition (the outlawing of alcoholic beverages in the 1920s) was treated as an experiment to determine its effects on alcohol consumption, what design would this represent?

    a. nonequivalent group

    b. single-case

    c. interrupted time-series with control group

    d. interrupted time-series

KEY TERMS

LOOKING AHEAD

At this point in the text you have learned how to complete the majority of the steps that are necessary to complete a psychological experiment. In this chapter you have learned about more specialized research designs used to protect your experiment's internal validity, when you have only one participant, or when you cannot assign participants to groups randomly. Before we move on to completing your experimental report, we will discuss the concept of external validity—how you can generalize your experimental results beyond your specific experiment.

External Validity and Critiquing Experimental Research

Internal validity A type of evaluation of your experiment; it asks the question of whether your IV is the only possible explanation of the results shown for your DV.

External validity
A type of evaluation of your experiment; do your experimental results apply to populations and situations that are different from those of your experiment?

Generalization Applying the results from an experiment to a different situation or population.

External Validity: Generalizing Your Experiment to the Outside

In Chapter 5, we covered the concept of **internal validity**, which is one way you must evaluate your experiment. As you will remember, internal validity concerns the question of whether your experiment is confounded—is your IV the only possible explanation for your finding? In this chapter we will cover another type of validity you should assess in your experiment.

The second type of evaluation that you must make of your experiment involves **external validity**. When you consider external validity, you are asking a question about **generalization**. The root word of *generalization* is *general*. Of course, *general* is essentially the opposite of *specific*. So, when we want to generalize our experimental results, we wish to move away from the specific to the more general. In essence, we would like to take our results beyond the narrow confines of our specific experiment. Imagine that you have conducted an experiment using 20 college students as your participants. Did your experimental question apply only to those 20 college students, or were you attempting to ask a general question that might be applicable to a larger group of students at your school, or to college students in general, or perhaps even to people in general? Few experimenters gather data that they intend to apply only to the participants they actually use in their experiments. Instead, they hope for general findings that will apply more broadly. When you examine different definitions of psychology, you find that many include a phrase about psychology being the "science of behavior." We don't think you've ever seen a definition that referred to the "science of blondes' behavior," or "the science of Californians' behavior," or "the science of children's behavior"—probably not even "the science of human behavior." Psychologists attempt to discover information that applies to everyone and everything. As Sherlock Holmes said, "One's ideas must be as broad as Nature if they are to interpret Nature" (Doyle, 1927, p. 37). When we discover principles that apply broadly, then we have found behavior that is lawful. Finding such principles is a tall order, especially for a single experiment, but we keep this goal in mind as we do our research. We are ever mindful of the need and desire to extend our findings beyond our specific experiment.

Let us share with you a dilemma that this chapter posed for us. The dilemma revolved around where to put this chapter in the text. By placing it where we have, near the end of the book, you may get the idea that you need to worry about evaluating your experiment for external validity only after you complete your experiment. Nothing could be farther from the truth. Rather, we hope that you constantly evaluate your experiment. Much of what we have written for this chapter is designed to help you evaluate your experiment from the day you begin planning your methodology. When designing their experiments, researchers take precautions that will allow them to increase the generalizability of their final results. So, our dilemma was whether to place this chapter near the beginning of the book or near the back. We chose to put it near the back because you do need to step back to take another look at your experiment after you have completed collecting, analyzing, and interpreting your data. It is here that you are about to write your experimental report (see Chapter 20). At this point you must decide how far you can legitimately generalize your results.

After you have satisfied yourself that your experiment (or an experiment that you are evaluating) is internally valid, then you can focus on its potential for external validity. As we mentioned, the question of external validity revolves around whether you can take the results of a particular experiment and generalize them beyond that original experiment. Generalization is an important aspect for any science—there are very few occasions when scientists wish to restrict their conclusions to only the relevant conditions of their original experiment. Although police detectives are usually interested in a specific culprit, they are also interested in developing criminal profiles that describe general traits of a specific type of offender (e.g., the profile of mass murderers or of child molesters).

Population generalization Applying the results from an experiment to a group of participants that is different and more encompassing than those used in the original experiment.

There are three customary types of generalization in which we are interested. In **population generalization**, we are concerned about applying our findings to organisms beyond our actual experimental participants. When our students conduct research with fellow students from Emporia State University or Kennesaw State University as participants, they are not interested in applying their results only to students at their respective colleges. We doubt that many of you who do experimental projects will try to answer a question about students only at your school. Likewise, psychologists are not typically concerned with trying to discover truths only about the humans or animals who actually compose the participants in their studies. Instead, in all cases we have just mentioned, the researchers (including you) are usually trying to discover general principles about behavior that are applicable to people or animals as a whole. Thus, we must concern ourselves with whether our results will apply to a larger group than our experimental participants.

Environmental generalization Applying the results from an experiment to a situation or environment that differs from that of the original experiment.

Environmental generalization refers to the question of whether our experimental results will apply to situations or environments that are different from those of our experiment. Again, it is doubtful that we are interested in finding results that are specific to the environment in which we tested our participants. Can we generalize our results from the college classroom or research lab in which we collected our data to other classrooms or labs or even the real-world environments in which behavior naturally occurs? For example, if students learn a list of words in a laboratory, does that behavior have any relevance to the real-world behavior of studying for an exam?

Temporal generalization Applying the results from an experiment to a time that is different from that when the original experiment was conducted.

Finally, **temporal generalization** describes our desire that our research findings apply at all times and not to only a certain time period. For example, the discovery of seasonal affective disorder (depression only during winter months) is an exception to generalized information about depressive disorders. Other examples of research findings that might be specific to a certain time are the many findings of gender differences from research in the 1960s. Today, after several decades of progress on women's rights, we should wonder whether the 1960s findings are still applicable. Such an issue raises thorny questions for the concept of temporal generalization.

We must ask questions about the external validity of our research results because of the very property that we mentioned in the first paragraph of this chapter—*internal validity*. To achieve a high degree of internal validity, researchers seek to exert control over a large number of factors. The best way to exert control over factors is to conduct your experiment in a lab (or similar setting) with participants who are highly similar.

Reread the last sentence. Explain why this statement is true. Can you figure out why exerting control, which helps us in terms of internal validity, ends up weakening our external validity?

When we conduct our research in a laboratory, we can control many factors that might function as extraneous variables in the real world. For example, you can control factors such as temperature, lighting, outside noise, and so forth. In addition, you control the time at which your participants come to the experimental situation as well as when and under what conditions they experience the IV. In short, the lab allows you to remove or hold constant the effects of many extraneous variables, which would be virtually impossible in the real world. In a similar fashion, using participants who are highly similar helps to reduce nuisance variation (see our discussion of nuisance variables in Chapter 5). For example, if you use only college students as participants, you will have an idea of their general reading ability if you have to compose a set of instructions for them to read. In the real world, potential participants would have a much wider range of reading abilities, thus adding nuisance variation to the experiment.

We hope that you can see that these advantages for internal validity become disadvantages for external validity. When we control so many factors so tightly, it is difficult to know if our results will apply to people or animals who are markedly different from our research participants and who encounter our research factors in the real world rather than in the artificial laboratory.

Threats to External Validity (Based on Methods)

Donald Campbell, who wrote extensively about internal validity, has also written widely about factors relating to external validity. We will summarize four factors affecting external validity from Campbell and Stanley (1966).

Interaction of Testing and Treatment   When Campbell and Stanley (1966) rated the three experimental designs for internal validity that we previously summarized (pretest–posttest control group, Solomon four-group, posttest-only control group) in Chapter 16, they also attempted to rate them concerning external validity (although that task is much more difficult). We will make several references back to Chapter 16, so you may wish to turn back for a quick review. The **interaction of testing and treatment** is the most obvious threat to external validity, and it occurs for the pretest–posttest control group design (see Figure 17-1) that we discussed in Chapter 16. External validity is threatened because both groups of participants are pretested and there is no control to determine whether the pretesting has an effect. As Solomon (1949) pointed out, "There is a great

> **Interaction of testing and treatment** A threat to external validity that occurs when a pretest sensitizes participants to the treatment yet to come.

```
R        O₁              O₂        (control group)
R        O₃      X       O₄        (experimental group)


KEY:
R = Random assignment
O = Pretest or posttest observation or measurement
X = Experimental variable or event

Each row represents a different group of participants.
Left-to-right dimension represents passage of time.
Any letters vertical to each other occur simultaneously.
```

FIGURE 17-1 THE PRETEST–POSTTEST CONTROL GROUP DESIGN.

possibility that merely taking a pre-test changes the subjects' attitudes toward the training procedures" (p. 141).

Imagine that you are working on an experiment dealing with prejudice toward people with mental disorders, specifically people with schizophrenia. You decide to test your participants by giving them a scale that measures their prejudice toward people with schizophrenia before showing them *A Beautiful Mind* (Grazer & Howard, 2001), a movie depicting John Nash's struggles with schizophrenia before he won a Nobel Prize for his work in mathematics. Does it seem likely that these people's responses to the movie will be different from those of a group of people who were not pretested? This question is the essence of an interaction between testing and treatment—because of a pretest, your participants' reaction to the treatment will be different. The pretest has a sensitizing effect on your participants; it is somewhat like giving a giant hint about the experiment's purpose before beginning the experiment. The pretesting effect is particularly troublesome for experiments that deal with attitudes and attitude change. This testing and treatment interaction is the reason that researchers developed nonpretesting designs such as the posttest-only control group design. Also, although the Solomon four-group design does incorporate pretests for two groups, it includes no pretesting of the remaining two groups, thus allowing for a measurement of any pretesting effect.

Interaction of Selection and Treatment   You will remember we covered "interactions with selection" as a threat to internal validity in Chapter 16. In those cases, selection potentially interacted with other threats to internal validity such as history, maturation, and instrumentation. In this instance, however, the threat to external validity consists of an interaction between selection and treatments.

An **interaction of selection and treatments** occurs when the effects that you demonstrate hold true only for the particular groups that you selected for your experiment. Campbell and Stanley (1966) noted that the threat of a selection–treatment interaction becomes greater as it becomes more difficult to find participants for your experiment. As it becomes harder to get participants, it becomes more likely that the participants you do locate will be unique and not representative of the general population.

Interaction of selection and treatment A threat to external validity that can occur when a treatment effect is found only for a specific sample of participants.

One of your authors ran into a selection and treatment interaction when he was attempting to complete his doctoral dissertation, in which he was testing a particular explanation of a common and easy-to-find phenomenon (better memory for material studied repeatedly at longer intervals rather than shorter intervals). Because of time pressures, he had to conduct his experiment during summer school. When he analyzed the data, the supposedly easy-to-find phenomenon was not evidenced by the statistics. Rather than concluding that the phenomenon did not exist (contrary to *much* published evidence), he decided that this finding was a result of a selection-treatment interaction. When he conducted his experiment a second time during the regular semester, the ubiquitous effect was found. It appears that for some reason, the summer school students were a unique population.

Reactive Arrangements   Reactive arrangements revolve around the artificial atmosphere of many psychological experiments. Because of our desire for control, we may create a highly contrived situation in a laboratory in which we attempt to measure a real-world behavior. There are some cases in which this type of arrangement is probably a dismal failure. As you saw in Chapter 7, experimental participants, particularly humans, seek clues about their environments. They may react to our experimental manipulations, but also to subtle cues that they find in the experimental situation. As Campbell and Stanley (1966) remarked, "The play-acting, outguessing, up-for-inspection, I'm-a-guinea-pig, or whatever attitudes so generated are unrepresentative of the school setting, and seem to be qualifiers of the effect of X, seriously hampering gen-

Reactive arrangements A threat to external validity caused by an experimental situation that alters participants' behavior, regardless of the IV involved.

eralization" (p. 20). Although their comment was directed at educational research, if we substitute "real world" for "school setting," the quotation remains valid. Thus, **reactive arrangements** refer to those conditions of an experimental setting (other than the IV) that alter our participants' behavior. We cannot be sure that the behaviors we observe in the experiment will generalize outside that setting because these artificial conditions do not exist in the real world.

The Hawthorne studies are often cited as classic examples of reactive arrangements (we will cover these studies in more detail in Chapter 19). Researchers studied productivity of a subset of plant workers over a period of time. This subset of workers tended to increase productivity regardless of the changes instituted in their environment. One of the representative experiments dealt with the level of illumination in a work area. A control group worked in a room with 10 foot-candles of light whereas the experimental group's illumination began at 10 foot-candles and was gradually decreased by 1 foot-candle at a time until it reached 3 foot-candles. At this point, "the operatives protested, saying that they were hardly able to see what they were doing, and the production rate

Demand characteristics Features from the experiment that inadvertently lead participants to respond in a particular manner.

decreased. The operatives could and did maintain their efficiency to this point in spite of the discomfort and handicap of insufficient illumination" (Roethlisberger & Dickson, 1939, p. 17).

In Chapter 7 we introduced the concept of **demand characteristics**. According to Orne (1962), demand characteristics can convey the experimental hypothesis to the participants and give them clues about how to behave. You (or your friends) may have experienced something similar to demand characteristics if you are a psychology major. When you tell people you are a psychology major, a common response is "Are you going to psychoanalyze me?" Rather than responding to you, people are responding to the demand characteristics of what they believe about psychology majors.

Orne said that it is impossible to design an experiment without demand characteristics. He also believed that demand characteristics make generalizations difficult because it is not clear from a set of research findings whether the participants are responding to an experiment's IV, its demand characteristics, or both. It seems that reactive arrangements tend to increase demand characteristics, thus creating further difficulties with generalization.

> **Multiple-treatment interference** A threat to external validity that occurs when a set of findings results only when participants experience multiple treatments in the same experiment.

Multiple-Treatment Interference As you can probably guess from the name of this threat to external validity, **multiple-treatment interference** can occur only in experiments that involve presenting more than one treatment to the same participants (repeated-measures designs). The potential problem that arises in repeated-measures designs is that the findings we obtain may be specific to situations in which the experimental participants experienced these multiple treatments. If they received only one treatment, then the experimental results may be different.

Campbell and Stanley (1966) cited Ebbinghaus's memory work as an example of multiple-treatment interference. Ebbinghaus was a pioneer in the field of verbal learning, conducting many experiments of learning lists of nonsense syllables by serving as his own experimental participant. He is responsible for giving us early versions of many common learning phenomena such as learning and forgetting curves. However, as it turns out, some of Ebbinghaus's findings are specific to people who have learned a large number of lists of nonsense syllables and do not apply to people learning a single list of nonsense syllables. Thus, Ebbinghaus's results show a clear failure to generalize, based on the concept of multiple-treatment interference.

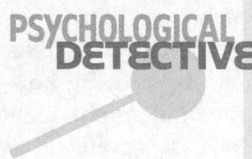
PSYCHOLOGICAL DETECTIVE

In Chapter 14 we discussed the multiple-group design. Under what condition is multiple-treatment interference a concern in the multiple-group design? When should you not worry about multiple-treatment interference in the multiple-group design?

By definition, multiple-treatment interference can occur only when participants experience more than one treatment. Experiencing more than one treatment occurs in the multiple-group design *if* you use repeated measures. However, the remaining variations on the multiple-group design would not allow for multiple-treatment interference. Independent groups, matched sets, or natural sets require using different participants in each group.

This ends the list of four threats to external validity summarized by Campbell and Stanley (1966). Let's take a brief look at five additional threats to external validity that are based on our experimental participants.

Threats to External Validity (Based on Our Participants)

We must always remember that our experimental participants are unique individuals just as the detective must remember that fact about each criminal. Certain unique traits may get in the way of our ability (or the detective's ability) to draw general conclusions.

> **Comparative psychology** The study of behavior in different species, including humans.

The Infamous White Rat   In 1950, Frank Beach sounded the alarm about a distressing tendency he saw in **comparative psychology**. By charting the publication trends in that field from 1911 to 1947, he found that more and more articles were being published but fewer species were being studied. The Norway rat became a popular research animal in the 1920s and began to dominate research in the 1930s. Beach examined 613 research articles and found that 50% of them dealt with the rat, despite the fact that the Norway rat represented only 0.001% of all living creatures that could be studied. In a follow-up study, Smith, Davis, and Burleson (1995) found that articles published between 1993 and 1995 showed attention to diversified species, but rats and pigeons accounted for over 75% of the studies published in *Journal of Experimental Psychology: Animal Behavior Processes* and *Animal Learning & Behavior* during those years.

First published in APA Monitor. Reprinted by permission of Warren A. Street.

"There's always an oddball subject that screws up your data."

Sometimes it's hard to tell which participants are more numerous in psychology experiments—lab rats or college students!

PSYCHOLOGICAL DETECTIVE   Why should Beach's data (and the follow-up study) give us reason for concern regarding external validity?

There are two obvious concerns with external validity that arise from these data. First, if you are interested in the behavior of subhumans, generalizing from rats (and pigeons) to all other animals may be a stretch. Second, if you are interested in generalizing from animal to human behavior, there are certainly closer approximations to humans than rats (and pigeons) in the animal kingdom.

The Ubiquitous College Student   We hope that you have conducted a literature search at this point in your course. If you have, you should have noticed that experimental articles contain a "subjects" or "participants" subsection within the methods section. (Remember that the label "participants" replaced "subjects" in the fourth edition of the APA *Publication Manual*, 1994).

If your literature search involved human participants, you probably noticed that college students very likely served as participants in the research you reviewed. There is a simple explanation for this fact. Psychology departments that support animal research typically have animal lab facilities—often colonies of rats, as we saw in the preceding section. Psychologists who want to conduct human research have no such labs filled with participants, of course, so they turn to a ready, convenient source of human participants—students in introductory psychology courses (a technique referred to as **convenience sampling**). Often students may be required to fulfill a certain number of hours of experimental participation in order to pass their introductory class. As well as providing a large supply of participants for psychology experiments, this requirement should be an educational experience for the students. Such requirements have generated heated debates, some of which have focused on ethics. You will note in the ethical principles covered in Chapter 3 that coercion is not acceptable in finding experimental participants.

> **Convenience sampling**
> A researcher's sampling of participants based on ease of locating the participants; often does not involve true random selection.

We are including this section not to focus on the ethics of using students as research participants but, rather, to focus on the implications of this reliance. Sears (1986) raised this very issue with regard to social psychology. He pointed out that early social psychologists studied a variety of types of participants, including populations as diverse as radio listeners, voters, soldiers, veterans, residents of housing projects, industrial workers, union members, and PTA members. However, by the 1960s psychology had become entrenched in using laboratory experiments with college students as participants.

Is it a problem to rely almost exclusively on college students? Clearly, such reliance is similar to the reliance on the white rat by animal researchers. Sears (1986) cited evidence concerning the differences between adolescents and adults and between college students and other late adolescents. He worried that several notable social psychology findings may be the product of using college students as participants rather than the larger population in general.

Reread the last sentence. Can you identify Sears's position as consistent with one of Campbell and Stanley's threats to external validity?

Sears's hypothesis that some social psychology findings may be specific to college students fits into Campbell and Stanley's selection–treatment interaction. If Sears is correct, then a specific treatment might "work" only for college students. In addition, a particular IV might have a stronger (or weaker) effect for college students than for the general population.

As an example, Sears mentioned that much of social psychology revolves around attitudes and attitude change: Research often shows that people's attitudes are easily changed. However, developmental research shows that the attitudes of late adolescents and young adults are less crystallized than those of older adults. Thus, we have to wonder whether people's attitudes really are easily changed or whether this finding is merely an artifact of the population that is most often studied—the college student.

Although Sears concentrated on social psychology findings, it does not take much thought to see how similar problems might exist in other traditional research areas of psychology. For example, because college students are both students and above average in intelligence, might their learning and memory processes be a poor representation of those processes in the general population? Motivational patterns in adolescents are certainly different in some ways from those processes in adults. The stresses affecting college students differ from those facing adults—might the coping processes be different also? We know that some mental illnesses are age related and therefore strike older or younger people more often. Overall, we should be careful in generalizing to the general population from results derived only from college students.

The "Opposite" or "Weaker" or "Inferior" or "Second" Sex   All four derogatory labels—*opposite*, *weaker*, *inferior*, and *second*—have been applied to women at various points in time. As you took your school's required history, literature, and humanities classes, you probably noticed that famous women were in short supply. For many years (some would argue still now), women have simply not had the same opportunities as men in many situations.

This supposed inferiority of women carried over into psychological theories. For example, Freud's theories are biased toward men—remember castration anxiety and the Oedipus complex? The "parallel" concepts for women of penis envy and the Electra complex seem almost to be afterthoughts. Feminists have repeatedly attacked the concept of penis envy, supposedly part of equating Freud's theory for women and men. Erik Erikson labeled his theory of psychosocial crises the "Eight Stages of Man." Not only did the name not acknowledge women, but neither did the stages. Many women have not identified with Erikson's stages to the extent that men have. As Carol Tavris (1992) eloquently pointed out about developmental theories, "Theorists writing on adult development assumed that adults were male. Healthy 'adults' follow a single line from childhood to old age, a steady path of school, career, marriage, advancement, a child or two, retirement, and wisdom—in that order" (p. 37).

Tavris's thesis is that "despite women's gains in many fields in the last twenty years, the fundamental belief in the normalcy of men, and the corresponding abnormality of women, has remained virtually untouched" (p. 17). Tavris's ideas make us face an interesting question: Are we developing a body of knowledge that pertains to all organisms, regardless of sex? One detail we will emphasize about APA style in Chapter 20 is its requirement of nonsexist language in writing. Words carry hidden meanings, and sexist writing may lead to generalizations that are unwarranted. As psychology students, you should definitely be attuned to this issue. Surveys of psychology undergraduates across the country find that almost three quarters of all psychology majors are women. You may even encounter difficulty finding male participants for your future experiments. Without adequate male representation, the generality of your findings could be questioned.

Again, a word of caution is in order. When we generalize our findings we typically generalize them to as large a segment of the population as we can. However, we should not generalize research conducted on only one sex to both sexes. Beware of drawing sexist conclusions from your research.

Even the Rats and Students Were White This section's heading is an adaptation of the title of Robert Guthrie's thought-provoking book *Even the Rat Was White* (1976). In the book, Guthrie chronicled many of the so-called "scientific" attempts to measure and categorize African Americans as inferior to Caucasians, such as anthropometric measurements (e.g., skull size and cranial capacity), mental testing, and the eugenics movement (improvement of heredity through genetic control).

Some psychology students may believe that there were no African-American pioneers in psychology; that assumption is far from the truth. Guthrie (1976) provided a list of the 32 African Americans who earned doctorates in psychology and educational psychology in American universities between 1920 and 1950. He provided brief background and career sketches for 20 of these individuals. Let us give you a glimpse of two of these persons. Guthrie devoted a chapter to Francis Cecil Sumner, whom he labeled the "Father of black American psychology" (p. 175). Sumner, born in Pine Bluff, Arkansas, was the first African American to earn a Ph.D. in psychology in the Western Hemisphere. He earned his degree from Clark University in June 1920. His chief instructor was G. Stanley Hall; he also took courses from E. G. Boring. Sumner's dissertation title was "Psychoanalysis of Freud and Adler," which was published in *Pedagogical Seminary* (later renamed the *Journal of Genetic Psychology*). Sumner went on to teaching positions at Wilberforce University and West Virginia Collegiate Institute. In 1928 he accepted a position at Howard University, becoming chair of the newly established department of psychology in 1930. Under Sumner's leadership, Howard became one of the major producers of African-American Ph.D.s in psychology. Sumner remained at Howard until his death in 1954.

Ruth Winifred Howard was the first African-American woman to earn a doctorate in psychology, from the University of Minnesota in 1934. (Inez Beverly Prosser had earned a Ph.D. in *educational psychology* from the University of Cincinnati one year earlier.) Howard's dissertation, "A Study of the Development of Triplets," was one of the first studies to deal with a sizable group of triplets. She completed a clinical internship at the Illinois Institute for Juvenile Research and spent her career in private practice in clinical psychology.

Just as history has failed to record the accomplishments of many women throughout time, it has largely ignored the accomplishments of African Americans and other minority groups. Jones (1994) pointed out the inherent duality of being an African American—that one is separately considered an African and an American. Other writers have made similar points about and pointed out problems for members of other minority groups—for example Marín (1994) for Hispanics, Lee and Hall (1994) for Asians, and Bennett (1994) for American Indians. According to Lonner and

Malpass (1994b), projections indicate that sometime in this century the United States will be 24% Hispanic, 15% African American, and 12% Asian. Thus, Caucasians will make up less than half the population for the first time in U.S. history. When we conduct research and make generalizations, we should be cautious that we do not exclude minority groups from our considerations.

Even the Rats, Students, Women, and Minorities Were American   Although experimental psychology's early roots are based in Europe, this aspect of the discipline quickly became Americanized, largely due to the influence of John B. Watson's behaviorism. For many years the study of human behavior was actually the study of *American* behavior. However, in the mid-1960s this imbalanced situation slowly began to change as psychologists started taking culture and ethnicity more seriously (Lonner & Malpass, 1994a). We mentioned this new emphasis on ethnicity in the previous section and wish to mention the notion of culture in this section.

> **Cross-cultural psychology** A branch of psychology whose goal is to determine the universality of research results.

The field of **cross-cultural psychology** has evolved from those changes that began in the 1960s. Today you can find textbooks and courses devoted to this topic. We introduced you to cross-cultural research in Chapter 7. Because cross-cultural psychology "tests possible limitations of our traditional knowledge by studying people of different cultures" (Matsumoto, 2000, p. 10), it is closely intertwined with external validity. In fact, cross-cultural psychology tests the very limits of external validity. It asks the question of how far a set of experimental findings can be extended to other cultures. If psychology is made up of findings that are applicable only to Americans, then we should not claim that we know everything there is to know about *human* behavior! Making an **ethnocentric** claim such as that is akin to American professional baseball claiming to play the *World* Series, which actually began as a series of games sponsored by the *World* newspaper. What about the professional teams in Japan and other countries? Similarly, we shouldn't study maternal behaviors in the United States and claim that we know everything there is to know about mothering. Again, a word to the wise: Let's be careful about making grandiose claims about external validity when we don't have all the data. With our shrinking world of today, it is becoming easier and easier to conduct true cross-cultural research. The books by Lonner and Malpass (1994b) and Matsumoto (2000) will give you some good ideas about behavioral differences that exist as a function of culture.

> **Ethnocentric** Other cultures are viewed as an extension of one's own culture.

The Devil's Advocate: Is External Validity Always Necessary?

Several years ago Douglas Mook (1983) published a thought-provoking article titled "In Defense of External Invalidity." In this article Mook attacked the idea that all experiments should be designed to generalize to the real world. He maintained that such generalization is not always intended or meaningful.

Mook cited as an example Harlow's work with baby rhesus monkeys and their wire-mesh and terrycloth surrogate mothers. As you probably remember, the baby monkeys received nourishment from the mesh mothers and warmth and contact from the cloth mothers. Later, when faced with a threatening situation, the baby monkeys ran to the cloth mothers for comfort. As virtually all introductory psychology students learn, Harlow's work has been used to support the importance of contact comfort for the development of attachment. Was Harlow's research strong in external validity? Hardly! Harlow's monkeys could scarcely be considered representative of the monkey population because they were born in the lab and orphaned. Was the experimental setting lifelike? Hardly! How many baby monkeys (or human infants) will ever be faced with a choice between a wire or cloth "mother"?

Did these shortcomings in external validity negate Harlow's findings? As Mook pointed out, that depends on the conclusion that Harlow wished to draw. What if Harlow's conclusion had been, "Wild monkeys in the jungle probably would choose terry-cloth over wire mothers, too, if offered the choice" (Mook, 1983, p. 381)? Clearly, this conclusion could not be supported from Harlow's research because of the external validity problems mentioned in the previous paragraph.

On the other hand, Harlow *could* conclude that his experiment supported a theory of contact comfort for mother-infant attachment over a nourishment-based (drive-reduction) theory. Is there a problem with this conclusion? No, because Harlow did not attempt a generalization—he merely drew a conclusion about a theory, based on a prediction from that theory. Mook argued that our concern with external validity is necessary only when we are trying to "predict real-life behavior in the real world" (p. 381). However, there are reasons to conduct research that do not involve trying to predict behavior in the real world. Mook pointed out four alternative goals of research that do not stress external validity. First, we may merely want to find out if something *can* happen (not whether it usually happens). Second, we may be predicting from the real world to the lab—seeing a phenomenon in the real world, we think it will operate in a certain manner in the lab. Third, if we can demonstrate that a phenomenon occurs in a lab's unnatural setting, the validity of the phenomenon may actually be strengthened. Finally, we may study phenomena in the lab that don't even have a real-world analogy.

We do not mean to undermine the importance of external validity by presenting Mook's arguments. However, it is important to know that not all psychologists worship at the shrine of external validity. Being concerned with real-world applications is certainly important, but (unlike internal validity) it is not an absolute necessity for every experiment. By the same token, the detective does not attempt to generate a generalized criminal profile for each crime that is committed.

PSYCHOLOGICAL DETECTIVE   Just as with internal validity, we have looked at nine different threats to external validity. We hope you have been considering these threats in light of your potential experiment. What can you do in an attempt to avoid external validity problems?

This is probably the most difficult Psychological Detective question of this chapter; there is a sense in which this question is a trick. It *may* be impossible to conduct a single experiment that has perfect external validity. If you attempted to devise an experiment that answered every threat to external validity that we listed, you might be old and gray before you completed the experiment. Imagine trying to find a pool of human experimental participants that would satisfy sex, race, ethnicity, and cultural generalizability. You would need to find large numbers of participants from around the world—clearly an impossible situation.

Does the dismal conclusion of the previous paragraph mean that we should merely throw up our hands and quit? Are we justified in ignoring the problem of external validity? Of course not! The important question becomes one of what steps we can take to maximize our chances of achieving external validity. First, we recommend that you pay particular attention to the first four external validity threats that we listed. To a large extent, you do have control over interactions of testing or selection and treatment, reactive arrangements, and multiple-treatment interference. Careful experimental planning can usually allow you to avoid problems with those factors.

If you can control the methodological threats to external validity, that leaves you with the participant-related threats. It is unrealistic to expect any one experiment to be able to include all the various participants we would need to generalize our results across the world's population. Campbell and Stanley (1966) wrote that "the problems of external validity are not logically solvable in any neat, conclusive way" (p. 17). What is the solution?

Replication An additional scientific study that is conducted in exactly the same manner as the original research project.

It seems logical that the solution must involve an approach we discussed in Chapter 1—**replication**. When we replicate an experimental finding, we are able to place more confidence in that result. As we begin to see the same result time after time, we become more comfortable with the idea that it is a predictable, regularly occurring result. However, it is shortsighted for us to continually test the same types of participants in every experiment we conduct, whether those participants are white rats or white American college students. Thus, we need to go beyond replication to experiments that involve replication with extension.

Replication with extension An experiment that seeks to confirm (replicate) a previous finding but does so in a different setting or with different participants or under different conditions.

In a **replication with extension** experiment, we retest for a particular experimental finding but we do so in a slightly (or even radically) different context. For example, if we think we know a great deal about how American college students learn lists of nonsense syllables, we should not try to generalize those results to all humans. Instead, we should broaden our participant population. Do the same rules apply when we test elderly people, children, and less-educated people? Do the same findings occur when we test Hispanic Americans, Asian Americans, and African Americans? Are the results similar in Japan, China, Peru, Australia, and so on? When we begin to collect data from experiments as indicated by the previous three sentences, then we truly start learning whether or not our findings are generally applicable.

There is another advantage to experiments that use replication with extension. Many times pure replication experiments are frowned on. Journals rarely, if ever, publish a straight replication study. Many undergraduates who complete required experimental projects are told that their projects must be original, that the project cannot be a replication study. Often, a replication with extension involves enough new work and produces enough new information that it will be acceptable either for a class requirement or for publication—or for both if you're extremely fortunate!

A 2001 research study by Carolyn Ann Licht, a student at Marymount Manhattan College in New York, and Linda Zener Solomon, her faculty advisor, illustrated a replication with extension experiment. Licht (2000) had previously compared stress levels of employees in two New York City organizations and found that stress levels were higher for employees of a nonprofit organization than for employees of a for-profit organization. Licht and Solomon extended the earlier study to include more organizations and more geographic areas. Their findings mirrored Licht's earlier findings, leading Licht and Solomon to conclude that the "results were consistent with previous findings and increased their external validity" (p. 14).

So what is the conclusion regarding external validity? We believe it is unrealistic to expect every (or any) experiment to be applicable to the entire world of animals or people. That type of external validity is probably a myth that exists only in fairy tales. However, we also believe that you should strive to make your experiment as externally valid as possible. That is, when you have choices, opt for the choices that will increase the external validity of your findings.

REVIEW SUMMARY

1. If your experiment is internally valid, then you can worry about **external validity**, which deals with applying your findings to new groups (**population generalization**), new situations (**environmental generalization**), and new times (**temporal generalization**).

2. There are many threats to external validity. The **interaction of testing and treatment** threat can occur if you pretest your participants and the pretest changes their reaction to the posttest.

3. The **interaction of selection and treatment** threat occurs if your findings apply only to the groups you selected for your experiment.

4. **Reactive arrangements** can threaten external validity if the experimental situation changes our participants' behavior.

5. **Multiple treatment interference** may threaten external validity if participants experience more than one treatment and this multiple participation causes a change in behavior.

6. Experimental psychology has been criticized for using only a narrow slice of possible types of participants in research. Animal research is particularly imbalanced by its overuse of white rats as participants.

7. Human research has tended to focus on white American college students as participants. Many theories seem to be aimed heavily or exclusively at men.

8. For reasons of external validity, there is currently a greater focus on research involving participants from the general population, women, ethnic minorities, and other cultures.

9. Mook has pointed out that there are occasional instances when the external validity question is not relevant to research.

10. It is nearly impossible to devise a single experiment that can answer all questions about external validity. Conducting experiments that involve replication with extension is a good way to simultaneously increase external validity and gather new information.

CHECK YOUR PROGRESS

1. What is external validity? Why is it important to psychology?

2. Generally speaking, as internal validity increases, external validity _____.

   a. increases

   b. decreases

   c. remains the same

   d. fluctuates unpredictably

3. Distinguish among population, environmental, and temporal generalization.

4. Why should we be concerned about trying to use different types of participants (such as minorities and people who are not college students) in psychology studies?

5. What is cross-cultural psychology? Why is it of particular relevance to this section of the chapter?

6. Match the external validity threat with the proper description.

1. testing-treatment interaction	A. An effect occurs only if participants experience all the experiment's treatment conditions.
2. selection-treatment interaction	B. Women, but not men, demonstrate an experimental effect.
3. reactive arrangements	C. Only participants who are pretested demonstrate an experimental effect.
4. multiple-treatment interference	D. Demand characteristics provide cues to the participants about how they should respond.

7. Why did Mook argue that external validity is not always necessary?

8. Why is the notion of external validity for a single experiment virtually impossible to achieve?

Critiquing Experimental Research

The information we are about to introduce is another reason we chose to place this chapter near the end of the text. Although we present this information to help you evaluate your own research, it is a certainty that, in the future, you will evaluate more studies conducted by other researchers than you will ever complete yourself. As you do a literature search for background information, you may look at hundreds of other articles. You will carefully scrutinize only a subset of those hundreds, but you will still read a good number of experimental articles. It is imperative that you are able to inspect those articles as closely as you would your own research project. You must be able to spot any flaws that might exist in these other studies because you will be basing your research on previous work of other researchers. If you base your study on research that has some flaw, your research may well end up being flawed. As an analogy, suppose you were a detective and needed to have fingerprints from a crime scene compared to one of your suspects. When you went to the lab, you accidentally picked up the fingerprint report from a different crime scene. How accurate would the lab analysis be for the original suspect? Not very accurate at all! The parallel to designing your experiment is fairly close. If you begin your experiment with an incorrect premise or assumption, your experiment is probably doomed from its beginning. So, again, it is important to be able to evaluate other researchers' experiments before you begin your own.

If you are like many students, the last sentence of the previous paragraph may cause you some worry. You may wonder, "Who am *I* to be critiquing research conducted and *published* by psychologists?" If you find yourself saying something like this, you are selling yourself short. One of the behaviors our educational system fosters (sometimes too well) is respect for authorities. In school we learned that when we didn't have the answer for something, we could consult an authority. We could look up the answer in our book or in an encyclopedia, or we could ask a teacher. There is certainly nothing wrong with that approach—it helps make life much simpler. But this constant reliance on consulting authorities sometimes blinds us to the importance of questioning the answers we get (see our discussion of ways to acquire knowledge in Chapter 1). Although we are not encouraging you to become a cynic about everything you hear, we do believe that it is important as well as valuable to carry a little healthy skepticism around with you. Thus, not only is it acceptable, but we even encourage you to read research reports with a critical eye. *Do* think critically about the methods, the results, and the conclusions. *Do* question assumptions that researchers seem to make. *Do* wonder if there are other ways of defining and measuring the variables the experimenters used. In other words, don't merely be a passive recipient of experimental information—carefully sift it, weigh it, and consider it before filing it away in your memory bank. Careful reading of and critical thinking about experimental reports has led many undergraduates (as well as graduate students and faculty members) to interesting and important research projects.

We present some guidelines to help you develop a critical eye when you read research reports (yours or those published by others) in Table 17-1. As you read these guidelines you will be struck by their similarity to many of the concepts and topics you have read about in this book. Critiquing a completed manuscript or published article is similar to reviewing your entire experimental psychology or research methods course. Our discussion of each guideline that follows is brief—to help you refresh your memory for the location of the relevant material, we have listed a chapter(s) for each guideline.

1. *Does the literature review adequately describe the research area? Is this material consistent with the specific research question?*

Typically, a student beginning the first research project is not sure where the research literature will lead. Similarly, the researcher has little idea of the methodology to be used at this point. Sometimes, as a research project evolves, the literature review and the actual experiment diverge somewhat over time. After you complete your project and work on the report, double-check to make certain that the actual project still shows a direct link with your research literature. It is possible that some additional library work will be necessary.

TABLE 17-1	GUIDELINES FOR CRITIQUING PSYCHOLOGICAL RESEARCH LITERATURE

1. Does the literature review adequately describe the research area? Is this material consistent with the specific research question? (Chapters 2, 20)

2. Is the research question stated clearly? Do you have a clear idea concerning the research to be reported? (Chapter 2)

3. In view of the research area and research question, are the hypotheses appropriate, clearly stated, and able to be stated in general implication form? (Chapter 2)

4. Are the key terms operationally defined? (Chapter 5)

5. Are the IVs and their levels appropriate? (Chapter 5)

6. Is the DV appropriate for this research? Should the researcher have included more than one DV if only one was recorded? (Chapter 5)

7. Are the controls sufficient and appropriate? Are there any uncontrolled variables that could affect the results of the experiment? (Chapter 5)

8. Did the author(s) use an appropriate research design to test the specific hypotheses and answer the general research question? (Chapters 10, 12, 14, 16, 19)

9. Assuming you had access to the appropriate equipment and materials, could you replicate the research after reading the method section? (Chapters 5, 20)

10. Did the researcher(s) use appropriate sampling procedures to select the participants and assign them to groups? (Chapters 5, 9)

11. What procedures were used to ensure group equivalence prior to the experiment? (Chapters 5, 7, 9, 10, 12, 14, 19)

12. Did the research use a sufficient number of participants? (Chapters 7, 9)

13. Were there any history, instrumentation, statistical regression, or mortality effects that might have influenced the results? (Chapters 5, 7)

14. Were the appropriate statistical tests used, and are they reported correctly? (Chapters 10, 11, 12, 13, 14, 15)

15. Did the author(s) report means, standard deviations, and a measure of effect size? (Chapters 11, 13, 15)

16. Are the tables and figures clearly and appropriately labeled and presented accurately? (Chapters 4, 20)

17. Does the author(s) correctly interpret the results? Does the discussion follow logically from the results? (Chapter 20)

18. Are the conclusions and generalizations valid and justified by the data? Did the author(s) consider other possible interpretations of the results? (Chapter 20)

19. Do all references cited in the text appear in the reference section, and vice versa? (Chapter 20)

20. Did the experimenter follow appropriate ethical procedures during all phases of the experiment? (Chapter 3)

Programmatic research A series of research experiments that deal with a related topic or question.

This problem is less likely to occur for experienced researchers. Because most researchers carry out **programmatic research**, their new research ideas are likely to build directly on their (and others') previous research. As you conduct more research studies, reviewing the *relevant* literature will become second nature for you.

Why is programmatic research important to psychology?

Programmatic research allows researchers to build on their previous findings in a narrow research area. Because they are specialists on a quite specific topic, they can often do research at a more penetrating depth than someone who does not know the area very well. Such a researcher would be akin to a detective who specializes in pursuing serial killers. Researchers who engage in programmatic research may advance our knowledge at a faster rate.

2. *Is the research question stated clearly? Do you have a clear idea concerning the research to be reported?*

There are a variety of ways researchers can give you some information about the question(s) asked in their report. The title and abstract should give you an indication of the research's topic, although they may not contain the specific question per se. You will find the author's review of relevant literature in the article's introduction. As you read further into the introduction, the literature should apply more specifically to the particular research question. You will often find the research question in the last paragraph of the introduction—sometimes it will appear as a question; sometimes you may have to infer the actual question from the context at that point (e.g., the variables mentioned and the relationship hypothesized among them). Regardless of whether you find a literal question, there should be no confusion about the intent of the research when you finish reading the introduction.

3. *In view of the research area and research question, are the hypotheses appropriate, clearly stated, and able to be stated in general implication form?*

The hypotheses, of course, are directly linked to the research question (as mentioned in the previous point). Thus, you should be clear about what the researcher's hypotheses are by the time you have read the introduction. Appropriate hypotheses are those that follow logically from the literature review. In other words, as you read the literature, you should be able to predict the hypotheses that are likely to follow. If you find a hypothesis that seems to come from nowhere and surprises you, it may be inappropriate—reread the introduction to make sure. A clearly stated hypothesis is one that you can easily understand without having to guess what the researcher is predicting. Remember that general implication form is the "if . . . then" format. *If* the researcher specifies a certain event (independent variable), *then* a certain outcome should occur (dependent variable). Although the researcher may not specifically use the general implication form, you should be able to restate the hypothesis using that form.

Why is the "if . . . then" approach of the general implication form important in phrasing a research hypothesis?

It is the "if . . . then" approach to research questions that allows us to draw cause-and-effect conclusions—assuming that the researcher has done a good job in designing the experiment. As long as the internal validity of the research is strong, the researcher should be able to conclude that the IV caused the change in the DV.

4. *Are the key terms operationally defined?*

The reader should not have to guess what a researcher means when he or she refers to a specific independent, dependent, or extraneous variable. Remember that operational definitions mean that you should define your variables in terms of the operations you use to manipulate, measure, or control them. For example, reading that rats ran a maze when they were hungry is too vague. The researcher should specify the number, type, and sex of the rats; provide a precise description (or a figure) of the maze; and describe "hunger" in terms of how it was manipulated (e.g., number of hours of food deprivation). Using operational definitions allows readers to compare and contrast different definitions of the same term by different researchers and to decide how they wish to manipulate, measure, or control similar variables in their experiments.

5. *Are the IVs and their levels appropriate?*

In dealing with beginning research students, we are surprised at how often students say that they wish to study a certain variable's effects (the IV), but then propose an experiment that doesn't directly deal with or manipulate that variable. Be sure that you pick a manipulation that is actually appropriate to the IV—don't choose something merely because it is easy or convenient to use. For example, imagine that a student wishes to use the IV of caffeine intake but takes the easy way out and simply asks students how many cups of coffee they drank that morning. It is likely that self-reported caffeine intake will not be as accurate as bringing participants into the lab and actually manipulating how much caffeine they ingest. If the manipulation is not clearly a good example of the IV, then it may not be appropriate.

Similarly, be sure to choose the levels of your IV appropriately. Many researchers choose to use proportional amounts of their IV: for example, using 5, 10, and 15 milligrams of a drug rather than 5, 9, and 12 milligrams. Many beginning researchers make the mistake of trying to include too many IV levels in one experiment. Remember that you cannot answer all possible questions in one experiment—choose levels of the IV to answer your experimental question, but do so economically (remember the principle of parsimony in Chapter 10). Apply these same guidelines to research that you read to determine whether the researcher's IV and levels are appropriate.

6. *Is the DV appropriate for this research? Should the researcher have included more than one DV if only one was recorded?*

The first question here is similar to the previous one. If a researcher wishes to study a particular outcome, the behavior chosen for measuring (the dependent variable) should be a good indicator of that outcome. In other words, the operational definition of the DV should be one that other researchers would judge to be valid. This caution is a particularly important one for many student researchers who may wish to measure some type of clinical outcome (e.g., clinical depression, schizophrenia) in their research. Often, measuring such a DV is not feasible for undergraduates, so they settle for a different DV. If you follow a similar process, make sure that the DV you do choose is appropriate to the literature you reviewed and the hypothesis you generated. In similar fashion, as you read research reports, decide whether you think the DV adequately measures the concept in question.

If you think that a different behavior would be a more valid DV, you may have generated a good idea for an experiment. For example, suppose other researchers have used GPA as a measure of academic achievement after teaching students a new study strategy. You might argue that GPA is too global a DV to measure the effects of study skills and therefore choose to use scores on a single test instead.

Sometimes a researcher's interest is so broad that a single DV will not adequately measure what the researcher wants. In such a case, the researcher should use multiple DVs to get a better sense of the concept she is measuring. Remember that we advised you to use multiple DVs *if* they added valuable information (see Chapter 5). This approach is economical—it is usually easier to give a smaller number of participants multiple measurements than to give a larger number of participants one measurement each. As you read research, look for DVs that you believe were measured in a "skimpy fashion." Again, enlarging the scope of the DV may give you a good experimental idea. Using the example from the previous paragraph, you might decide to measure the effects of the study skills on an entire semester's worth of tests rather than simply using one test.

7. *Are the controls sufficient and appropriate? Are there any uncontrolled variables that could affect the results of the experiment?*

This is one of the most critical questions you can ask of your experiment or those you read.

 Why is the question regarding control such an important question?

As we hope you remember, leaving variables uncontrolled can result in a confounded experiment, which leaves the researcher unable to draw a conclusion. As you scrutinize research (whether yours or other researchers'), be extremely vigilant for variables other than the IV that differed between groups. However, a caution is in order at this point. As you look for possible extraneous variables, you should concentrate on variables that have a legitimate or reasonable chance to actually make a difference. For example, unless you are testing for sex differences, having one group composed of women and another group composed of men is an invitation for extraneous variation. On the other hand, having one group in which most people complete a questionnaire in pen and another group where most of the people use a pencil is unlikely to create a difference on the questionnaire results. So, look for extraneous variation, but don't go overboard and find variation that most researchers would consider negligible.

8. *Did the author(s) use an appropriate research design to test the specific hypotheses and answer the general research question?*

This question relates to the caution that we gave at the beginning of the first research design chapter (Chapter 10). Remember that, with poor planning, it is possible to gather data for which there is no appropriate research design and, thus, no appropriate statistical test. Your task with this guideline is to make sure that research reports use designs that match the question they sought to answer. Therefore, you will need to look at the introduction to find the question and the method or results section to determine the design used. For example, if the researcher asked a question involving multiple IVs, the experiment should involve a factorial design. The flowchart that recurs at the beginning of Chapters 10, 12, and 14 will help you with this guideline.

9. *Assuming you had access to the appropriate equipment and materials, could you replicate the research after reading the method section?*

The method section (see Chapter 20) should contain enough detail about the variables and procedures of the experiment to enable a reader to replicate the experiment. The reader should not have to guess about any of the manipulations, measurements, or controls the researcher used. The reader must have all the vital details of the experiment in order to evaluate the operational definitions, the variables, and the procedures used in the experiment (see the previous five guidelines). Once again, knowing how other researchers conducted their experiments may help give you ideas about how you should plan your experiment.

10. *Did the researcher(s) use appropriate sampling procedures to select the participants and assign them to groups?*

Remember how often we have stressed the importance of random sampling and assignment in creating independent groups or the appropriate matching or repeated measures approach for correlated groups! This guideline is important for two different reasons—both internal and external validity. If a researcher uses sampling techniques that result in biased samples, the internal validity of the experiment is threatened because the groups are likely to be different before the experiment. Also, if poor sampling techniques are used, biased samples could threaten the external validity. If the samples are unique, then other samples may not show the same results.

PSYCHOLOGICAL DETECTIVE   Is there any difference between independent groups and correlated groups experiments in terms of internal or external validity?

As long as you use the proper techniques for creating independent or correlated groups, there should be no difference between the two approaches as far as internal or external validity are concerned. Remember—you create independent or correlated groups simply by the manner in which you assign participants to groups.

11. *What procedures were used to ensure group equivalence prior to the experiment?*

This guideline is related to the sampling guideline previously mentioned. Poor sampling techniques can result in biased samples. Biased samples are usually not equivalent before the experiment begins, so it would be impossible to draw valid conclusions about the effects of the IV. Thus, the internal validity of the experiment would be compromised. If you have reason to doubt the equivalence of your groups beforehand, you would be wise to use a pretest.

12. *Did the research use a sufficient number of participants?*

Many a student research project has been sabotaged by students who want to save a little time by running a small number of participants. In our view, this is a false economy. If you have spent weeks or months planning an experiment, the last thing you should do is try to save a few minutes by running fewer participants. With small numbers of data points, statistical tests are simply less powerful to detect differences—the differences between groups have to be *quite large* for the difference to turn out significant. However, with reasonably sized groups (at least 10 participants per group), the tests become powerful enough to detect smaller differences. Don't back yourself into a corner so that you use the age-old student lament after your experiment: "If I had run more participants, my differences might have been significant."

13. *Were there any history, instrumentation, statistical regression, or mortality effects that might have influenced the results?*

These factors that we discussed in Chapter 5 can undermine the internal validity of experiments. For history, be alert to outside events that occur that could affect the results; remember, for example, that political and social events that are not part of your research could affect participants' responses to attitude questionnaires. Be sure to check the operation of your equipment before each session to avoid instrumentation effects. Choosing extreme high- or low-scoring participants can result in lower or high scores, respectively, simply due to statistical regression. If many participants drop out of one condition in the experiment (i.e., mortality), the participants who are left in that condition may differ in some important way(s) from the participants in other conditions. Be vigilant about these problems both in your research and research that you read.

14. *Were the appropriate statistical tests used, and are they reported correctly?*

We have provided information in Chapters 10 through 15 that will help you evaluate this guideline for some experiments. However, remember that this text is not meant to give comprehensive coverage of all statistical tests that could be used in any experiment. You may need to consult an advanced statistics text or someone who teaches statistics to help you answer this question. On the other hand, this guideline points out the importance of becoming statistically knowledgeable so that you can evaluate this guideline on your own. Remember that statistics are merely a tool experimenters use to decipher the results they obtained—you should be well armed with the proper tools as you evaluate and conduct research.

15. *Did the author(s) report means, standard deviations, and a measure of effect size?*

Although researchers use inferential statistics to determine whether their data show statistical significance, inferential statistics tell only part of the story. Descriptive statistics give the reader a chance to further evaluate the researcher's findings. For example, group means may allow the reader to compare participants' performance against existing norms. Also, extremely large samples can produce statistically significant results with only small differences between groups—differences that may seem negligible when you see the actual means. Standard deviations may allow the reader to determine that nonsignificant findings are due to extreme variability between groups rather than small differences between means. Effect sizes give standard comparison units so that readers can compare significant differences from several different experiments. These examples are only a small sample of the information you can obtain by looking at descriptive statistics, so be sure to include them in your experimental report and look for them in published reports.

16. *Are the tables and figures clearly and appropriately labeled and presented accurately?*

Tables and figures exist to give a clearer and simpler presentation of data than is possible in writing. Thus, they usually present a large amount of data in a compact, concise mode. However, the data presentation will not be clear and simple if the author has done a poor job of composing the table or figure. Imagine trying to decipher a graph that had no legend—you would not know which line represented which group. Although you are unlikely to see tables or figures with such glaring problems, you may see ones that are poorly constructed or poorly labeled (see the discussion of graphing in Chapter 4). Just as paragraph after paragraph of statistical results can be confusing, a poorly constructed table or figure also can confuse the reader.

17. *Does the author(s) correctly interpret the results? Does the discussion follow logically from the results?*

The first question has two possible interpretations. First, did the researcher correctly interpret $p < .05$ as significant and $p > .05$ as nonsignificant? Although you would be quite unlikely to see this type of error in a published report, some students still get confused and make such errors in their rough drafts. Second, and more relevant, did the researcher give a correct interpretation of his or her results in light of previous research? Interpreting one's results is a matter that is open to some difference of opinion, as the term *interpret* implies. As you are no doubt aware, there are famous and noteworthy examples in psychology's history of researchers interpreting the same data in different manners. For example, behaviorists and cognitive psychologists look at language and argue whether it develops because of conditioning or an innate mechanism. Thus, as we have highlighted several times in these guidelines, a difference of opinion or in ideas could lead you to a potential experiment.

The second question of the guideline relates to whether the discussion "makes sense" given the data the researcher just presented. It seems obvious that the discussion should be related to the data that were just presented, but there are many exceptions. For example, some researchers seem bent on drawing conclusions that go far beyond the data they have presented. Although there is some room in the discussion for conjecture and opinion, authors should make it clear when conclusions follow from data and when they are engaging in speculation. We have noticed that many student researchers seem to quickly gloss over their results in a rush to make excuses for nonsignificant findings. If you are careful to tie your discussion directly to the results you found, you are much less likely to run into such problems.

18. *Are the conclusions and generalizations valid and justified by the data? Did the author(s) consider other possible interpretations of the results?*

This guideline grows out of the previous one. This difficulty often comes when researchers have a favorite theory that they espouse. Sometimes, this theoretical leaning is so strong that it seems to blind them to any alternative explanations. You may remember sitting in class, hearing a theoretical interpretation of a set of results, and thinking to yourself that an alternative theory could also satisfactorily explain the results. Once more, alternative explanations for findings may provide you with the impetus for a new experiment.

How can you help yourself to consider alternative explanations for experimental findings?

Considering alternative explanations, particularly for published findings, is often difficult for novice researchers. Typically, when you read a study you will find the author's explanation for the results convincing. We have found two approaches that may help you. First, you are probably familiar with the role of "devil's advocate." As you read a study, try to put yourself in that role—look for any aspect of the author's explanation (no matter how small) that you disagree with. Second, particularly in cases of your research, have another person who is unfamiliar with your project read your report. Often, an unbiased eye can find weaknesses in your arguments that you overlooked.

19. *Do all references cited in the text appear in the reference section, and vice versa?*

This guideline is one of the simplest to follow, yet is often a problem in unpublished reports (it is highly unlikely that you would find this problem in a published study). There should be a one-to-one correspondence of the citations in the text and the references at the end of the study. Unlike some term papers you may have written, the reference section of an APA-format report consists only of material that you have read and included in the report—it is not a bibliography of everything you read in generating your experimental idea.

20. *Did the experimenter follow appropriate ethical procedures during all phases of the experiment?*

To evaluate this guideline, you may need to refresh your memory of the ethical principles that psychologists follow in conducting research. You can find these principles in Chapter 3. Remember that there are ethical principles for both human and animal research, so you cannot avoid ethical responsibility through animal research. Because of the review process involved in published research, you should not find ethical violations in published research. However, some older research involves some procedures that have been hotly debated as far as their ethical nature is concerned—for example, we discussed the research by Milgram in Chapter 3 that involved considerable deception. Given the ethical principles in effect today, it is doubtful that such research studies would receive approval from institutional review boards.

REVIEW SUMMARY

1. You should read research reports with a critical eye, applying the guidelines for critiquing research.

2. When you read the introduction of a research report, you should scrutinize the literature review, the research question, the hypothesis or hypotheses, and the citations and references.

3. In the method section, you should focus your critique on the operational definitions, the independent and dependent variables, the control techniques, the research design, the experiment's replicability, the sampling procedures, group equivalence, the number of participants, and factors that could affect the internal validity of the research.

4. As you scrutinize the results section, pay particular attention to the descriptive and inferential statistics, as well as any visual data presentations.

5. When you read the discussion section, your critique should center on the interpretation of the results, the conclusions, and other potential explanations for the findings.

6. As you read the entire report, examine it carefully for ethical procedures.

CHECK YOUR PROGRESS

1. Why should students critically examine research reports, even those published by prominent psychologists?

2. How are the literature review and research question linked?

3. Why are control techniques necessary in experimentation?

4. Summarize three critique guidelines that deal with participants.

5. Describe how statistics are vital to research reports.

6. Researchers should present _____ in their research reports.

   a. only descriptive statistics

   b. only inferential statistics

   c. both descriptive and inferential statistics

   d. neither descriptive nor inferential statistics

7. How and why should the discussion be tied to the results in a research report?

KEY TERMS

Internal validity, *409*

External validity, *409*

Generalization, *409*

Population generalization, *410*

Environmental generalization, *410*

Temporal generalization, *410*

Interaction of testing and treatment, *411*

Interaction of selection and treatment, *412*

Reactive arrangements, *413*

Demand characteristics, *413*

Multiple-treatment interference, *414*

Comparative psychology, *415*

Convenience sampling, *416*

Cross-cultural psychology, *419*

Ethnocentric, *419*

Replication, *421*

Replication with extension, *421*

Programmatic research, *425*

LOOKING AHEAD

So far we have used inferential statistics to analyze the results of our research. In the next chapter we will examine several nonparametric tests of significance. These nonparametric tests are not inferential.

Data Transformations and Nonparametric Tests of Significance

As we have mentioned several times, the typical inferential statistical test of significance uses samples to make inferences about populations. In this chapter we examine a different kind of significance test: the nonparametric test of significance.

Assumptions of Inferential Statistical Tests and the F_{max} Test

> **Parametric tests**
> Inferential tests of significance that attempt to estimate population parameters.

Because inferential statistical tests of significance attempt to estimate population parameters, researchers also call them **parametric tests**. Inferential or parametric tests are based on assumptions that the researcher or statistician makes about the population. It is important that these assumptions are accurate; if they are violated, then the inferential statistical test may not be valid.

What are these assumptions that researchers make when they conduct parametric tests? There are two primary assumptions:

1. The populations from which you have drawn your samples are normally distributed (i.e., the populations have the shape of the normal curve).
2. The populations from which you have drawn your samples have equivalent variances. Most researchers refer to this assumption as **homogeneity of variance**.

> **Homogeneity of variance** An assumption of parametric tests of significance that the variances of the populations are equivalent.

How do you know if you have violated one or both of these assumptions? About the only way to test these assumptions is to examine your samples.

When you graph your sample data, if one or both of your samples are noticeably skewed (see Chapter 6), then it is likely that you have violated the assumption that the populations are normally distributed. If our samples are equal in size, we can use them to test the assumption that the population variances are equivalent. To make this test, an F_{max} **test** (see pp. 248–249), you simply divide the largest sample variance by the smallest sample variance. For example, assume that you conducted a multi-group experiment and obtained the following variances for your four groups ($n = 11$): Group 1 $s^2 = 22.14$, Group 2 $s^2 = 42.46$, Group 3 $s^2 = 34.82$, Group 4 $s^2 = 52.68$. We

> F_{max} **test** A test for the equality of variances in which the largest variance is divided by the smallest variance.

select the largest (52.68) and smallest (22.14) variances and plug them into the F_{max} formula as follows:

$$F_{max} = \frac{\text{largest sample variance}}{\text{smallest sample variance}} = \frac{52.68}{22.14} = 2.379$$

To evaluate the F_{max} statistic, use Table A-6. You enter this table at the $n - 1$ row and the k (number of samples in the study) column. For our example we use row 10 and column four. At the intersection of this row and column we find that 5.67 is the critical value for significance at the .05 level. Because our value of 2.38 is smaller than the critical value, we can conclude that our data do not violate the assumption of equality of variances.

What would you do if you had clearly violated either or both of the assumptions? One way to deal with this problem is to reduce your alpha level (i.e., go from .05 to .01). By making your alpha level more stringent you reduce the chances of making a Type I error. (Violating the assumptions increases the chances of making a Type I error.) Unfortunately, you do increase your chances of making a Type II error when you reduce your alpha level. A second way to deal with violation of the assumptions is to conduct a nonparametric test that is not based on these assumptions. We will discuss several of these tests shortly. A third procedure for dealing with violation of the assumptions is to use a data transformation.

Data Transformations

Data transformation
The application of an accepted mathematical procedure to all scores in a data set.

Data transformation is one technique that researchers use to deal with violations of the assumptions of inferential tests. Do not be misled by the title of this section; data transformation is a legitimate procedure. It is not some form of statistical cheating.

Data transformation involves the application of an accepted mathematical procedure to all scores in a data set. Some of the common data transformations include

- **Square root.** The researcher calculates the square root of each score.
- **Logarithmic.** The researcher calculates the logarithm of each score.
- **Reciprocal.** The researcher calculates the reciprocal (i.e., $1/X$) of each score.

What Data Transformations Do and Do Not Do

Data transformations change certain characteristics of distributions. For example, they can have the effect of normalizing distributions or equalizing variances between (among) distributions. Obviously, these changes might be very desirable if your research data violate one or both of the basic assumptions of the inferential statistical test you plan to use.

On the other hand, data transformations *do not* alter the relative position of the data in the sample. Thus, you can draw conclusions about between-group differences after you have used a data transformation.

Using Data Transformations and a Caveat

Once you have used a data transformation, then what? Assuming that your data transformation corrected the problem that prompted you to use it, you can proceed with your planned analysis. However, if you perform more than one type of analysis on your data, please remember to use the transformed data for *all* of your analyses. For example, you must use the transformed data for any post hoc tests you calculate following a significant ANOVA.

Also, you must be careful when you interpret the result of your statistical analyses and draw conclusions. Your interpretations and conclusions must be stated in terms of the transformed data, *not* in terms of the original data you gathered. This caution takes on more importance when you realize that after transforming data, you really can compare your results *only* with other research that has used the same data transformation. If all the researchers in your area are using the same data transformation, then everything is fine and you can compare your results with theirs. If you are the only researcher using a data transformation, then you will encounter some difficulties when you try to compare results.

Data transformation offers one alternative to deal with violations of the basic assumptions. Nonparametric tests of significance offer a second alternative.

Nonparametric Tests of Significance

Nonparametric test of significance A significance test that does not attempt to estimate population parameters such as means and variances.

As the title of this chapter indicates, another approach to conducting significance tests is to use a nonparametric test. A **nonparametric test of significance** is a significance test that does *not*, as the name implies, attempt to estimate population parameters such as means and variances.

Here is a psychological detective question for which you will have to don your thinking cap. Other than instances where the basic assumptions are violated, what other situations would lead us to use a nonparametric test?

If you thought, "you can't estimate population parameters with nominal or ordinal data because you can't calculate means and *SD*s," then give yourself an extra big pat on the back; researchers use nonparametric tests with nominal and ordinal data. Of course, as we indicated, if you have interval data and find that you have violated the assumptions of the inferential tests, then you might conduct a nonparametric test. In this situation, you will treat your interval data as if they were nominal or ordinal data.

Chi-Square Tests

Chi-square test A procedure that compares the fit or mismatch (similarity or dissimilarity) between two or more distributions.

You can conceptualize the **chi-square test** as a procedure that compares the fit or mismatch (similarity or dissimilarity) between two or more distributions. Because our data are frequencies, chi squares are nominal tests.

Chi-Square Test for Two Levels of a Single Nominal Variable

Expected frequency distribution The anticipated distribution of frequencies into categories.

When we have one nominal variable, there is an expected frequency distribution and an observed frequency distribution. The **expected frequency distribution** is the anticipated distribution

> **Observed frequency distribution** The actual distribution of frequencies into categories.

of frequencies into categories because of previous research results or a theoretical prediction. The **observed frequency distribution** is the actual distribution of frequencies that you obtain when you conduct your research.

The simplest chi-square test is one that compares the observed and expected frequencies for two levels or categories. For example, you read in the newspaper that the Democratic and Republican candidates in the current election are absolutely even in terms of voter preference; thus, the *expected frequency distribution* would be 50% Democratic and 50% Republican. In this example, voter preference is the single nominal variable and the two levels are Democratic and Republican. You conduct a voter preference survey of 100 people in your town and find that 64 people prefer the Democratic candidate, whereas 36 people prefer the Republican candidate. Your *observed frequency distribution* is 64–36. The *expected frequency distribution* would be 50 people who prefer the Democratic candidate (100 × 50%) and 50 people who prefer the Republican candidate (100 × 50%). These two distributions are shown below:

	Democratic Candidate	Republican Candidate
Expected Frequency Distribution for 100	50	50
Observed Frequency Distribution	64	36

Researchers use the chi-square procedure to determine if the mismatch between the expected and observed distributions is sufficiently large that it would occur rarely by chance.

Calculating the Chi-Square Statistic   Calculation of the chi-square statistic is based on the following formula:

$$\chi^2 = \Sigma \frac{(O - E)^2}{E}$$

Here is what you should do to calculate the chi-square statistic:

Step 1   Subtract the appropriate expected value from each corresponding observed value, square the difference, then divide this squared value by the expected value.

Step 2   Sum all the products you calculated in Step 1.

For our voter preference example,

$$\chi^2 = \Sigma \frac{(O - E)^2}{E} = \frac{(64 - 50)^2}{50} + \frac{(36 - 50)^2}{50} = \frac{(14)^2}{50} + \frac{(-14)^2}{50} = 3.92 + 3.92 = 7.84$$

Now we need to determine if our chi square is significant. You will need to consult Table A-7 to make this determination—yes, another table and more dfs to figure! In this case calculation of the df is very simple: Take the number of categories and subtract 1. In our example there are two categories (Democratic and Republican), so:

$$df = \text{categories} - 1 = 2 - 1 = 1$$

Looking at Table A-7 you can see that with $df = 1$ chi squares of 3.891 and 6.635 are required for significance at the .05 and .01 levels, respectively. Because our chi square of 7.84 is larger than either of these critical values, we can conclude that our result is significant at the .01 level. You would write this result in a research report as follows:

$$\chi^2(1, N = 100) = 7.84, \ p < .01$$

You should keep in mind that a significant nonparametric statistic does not convey the same meaning as a significant inferential statistic. With regard to chi square, remember that our initial question was whether the mismatch between the expected and observed frequency distributions was large enough to conclude that they were dissimilar. Our significant result indicates that the two distributions are not similar. With regard to our initial research problem, we can conclude that the distribution of voter preferences is different in our town than in the general population; our town appears to prefer the Democratic candidate. Even though we have two categories, which would be comparable to a two-groups experimental design (see Chapter 10), notice that we haven't indicated that "one group differs from the other." It's the expected and observed distributions that are either similar or dissimilar, not the groups. Now, let's calculate a chi square when we have more than two levels of a single nominal variable; this situation should remind you of the more than two groups research design (see Chapter 12).

Chi-Square Test for More Than Two Levels of a Single Nominal Variable

Here is a psychological detective question to start this section and let you check your understanding.

PSYCHOLOGICAL DETECTIVE The more than two levels of a single nominal variable chi-square test is similar to what experimental design that we have already covered?

If you answered, the one IV, multiple groups design (see Chapter 12), you are absolutely correct. Here is an example:

Diane Simonds, a student at the University of Alaska at Anchorage, Alaska, and her faculty supervisor, Brenda Rolfe-Maloney, studied the effects of relevant, irrelevant, or no visual stimuli on the memory of preschool children for a story that was read to them (Simonds & Rolfe-Maloney, 2002). While they listened to the story, one group of children viewed a relevant picture, another group viewed an irrelevant picture, whereas a third group did not view a picture during the reading of the story. After the preschoolers heard the story, the researchers asked them to view three pictures (the relevant picture, the irrelevant picture, and a third picture that had not been viewed) and to select the picture that best went with the story they had heard. The researchers counterbalanced the order for presenting the pictures (see Chapter 5).

The results were as follows:

	Viewed Relevant Picture During Story	Viewed Irrelevant Picture During Story	Did Not View Picture During Story
Percent who made the correct choice	45%	20%	35%

Obviously, viewing the relevant picture while hearing the story, compared to not seeing a picture, improved memory for the story. On the other hand, viewing an irrelevant picture while hearing the story hurt the memory for the story.

You decide to replicate this research with 90 preschoolers from a local day care center. You randomly assign the children to three equal groups: relevant picture, irrelevant picture, and no picture. The children hear the story under the respective conditions and then complete the memory test. You record the following data for your three groups:

	Relevant Picture	Irrelevant Picture	No Picture
Observed correct choices	15 of 30	8 of 30	11 of 30
		Total N observed $\times$ 34	

Now we need the expected frequencies in order to complete the chi-square analysis. How would you go about calculating them for this problem?

It's not at all difficult to find the expected frequencies for this problem; all you do is multiply the n for all categories (i.e., 34 for this problem) by the expected percentage for each category. Here are the calculations:

	Relevant Picture	Irrelevant Picture	No Picture
Expected frequencies	.45 $\times$ 34 = 15.30	.20 $\times$ 34 = 6.80	.35 $\times$ 34 = 11.90

Now it's a simple procedure to plug the expected and observed frequencies into the chi-square formula:

$$\chi^2 = \Sigma \frac{(O - E)^2}{E} = \frac{(15 - 15.30)^2}{15.30} + \frac{(8 - 6.80)^2}{6.80} + \frac{(11 - 11.90)^2}{11.90}$$

$$= \frac{(-.30)^2}{15.30} + \frac{(1.2)^2}{6.80} + \frac{(-.90)^2}{11.90} = .006 + .212 + .068 = .286$$

It is unlikely that a chi-square value that small is going to be significant; however, we need to check Table A-7 to make sure. How many *df* are there? If you remembered "number of categories minus one," and then said "three categories minus one," you are right. When we check Table A-7 for significance, we find that a value equal to or greater than 5.992 is required for significance at the .05 level. Because our value of .286 is far below the critical value, we can conclude that these distributions are not significantly dissimilar; our research results replicate the original data.

What if our chi square had been significant? When our nominal variable has three or more levels/categories, it is not readily apparent where the discrepancy between the observed and expected frequencies exists. This situation is analogous to having a significant ANOVA with more than two groups (see Chapters 12 and 13). In those situations you used post hoc tests to isolate the significant differences. Significant chi squares with more than two groups also require follow-up tests; however, we do not use specialized post hoc tests. Most researchers simply conduct a series of simpler, more focused chi-square tests. For example, had we obtained a significant chi square with our preschoolers' memory study, we could have performed three, two-group chi squares as follow-up tests: (a) irrelevant picture versus relevant picture, (b) irrelevant picture versus no picture, and (c) relevant picture versus no picture. The results of these three comparisons should help us understand the nature of our original, significant chi square.

Chi-Square Test for Two Nominal Variables

So far we have used chi-square tests to analyze data when we have one nominal variable with two or more categories. Now we turn to research where there are two nominal variables; this situation would be analogous to a multiple IV research design (see Chapter 14).

We will use research conducted by Brad Jurica and Kelly Alanis, students at Southwest Texas State University in San Marcos, Texas, and their faculty supervisor, Shirley Ogletree, to illustrate this type of chi-square test. These researchers (Jurica, Alanis, & Ogletree, 2002) were interested whether there were differences in video-game preference (nonviolent versus violent) between men and women.

PSYCHOLOGICAL DETECTIVE What are the two nominal variables in the Jurica et al. (2002) research?

If you answered *type of video game* (nonviolent versus violent) and *sex of game player* (men versus women) you are correct. Jurica et al. used naturalistic observation (see Chapter 19) to gather their data at a local video arcade. They found the following preferences (frequencies) for their participants.

| | Game Preference | | |
	Nonviolent	Violent	Total
Male	87 (Cell A)	65 (Cell B)	152
Female	24 (Cell C)	7 (Cell D)	31
Total	111	72	183

Obviously, these data are our *observed* frequencies. Now, we are faced with the task of obtaining the *expected* frequencies. Even though this task may appear daunting, it really is quite easy.

When you have two nominal variables, you will display your data in a contingency table like the one just presented. A **contingency table** shows the distribution of frequencies and totals for two nominal variables. To find the expected frequency for any of the cells of your contingency table, you should use the following formula:

Contingency table
A table that shows the distribution of frequencies and totals for two nominal variables.

$$\text{Expected frequency} = (\text{Row total} \times \text{Column total})/\text{Total}$$

For example, for Cell A:

$$\text{Expected A} = (\text{row total} \times \text{column total})/\text{grand total}$$
$$= (152 \times 111)/183 = 16{,}872/183 = 92.20$$

For a 2 × 2 contingency table, once you have found the expected frequency for one cell you can find the remainder by using the row and column total and subtracting:

$$\text{Expected B} = 152 - 92.20 = 59.80$$
$$\text{Expected C} = 111 - 92.20 = 18.80$$
$$\text{Expected D} = 72 - 59.80 = 12.20$$

Here are the observed and (expected) frequencies:

| | Game Preference | | |
	Nonviolent	Violent	Total
Male	87 (92.20)	65 (59.80)	152
Female	24 (18.80)	7 (12.20)	31
Total	111	72	183

When you have a 2×3 or larger contingency table, you will have to use the formula to find a few more expected frequencies before you can use subtraction to find the remainder.

Now let's calculate chi square for the video game example. You will be happy to know that the formula does not change; therefore:

$$\chi^2 = \Sigma \frac{(O - E)^2}{E}$$

We simply need to take the observed and expected frequencies for the four cells and plug them into the formula:

$$\chi^2 = \frac{(87 - 92.20)^2}{92.20} + \frac{(65 - 59.80)^2}{59.80} + \frac{(24 - 18.80)^2}{18.80} + \frac{(7 - 12.20)^2}{12.20}$$

$$= \frac{27.04}{92.20} + \frac{27.04}{59.80} + \frac{27.04}{18.80} + \frac{27.04}{12.20}$$

$$= .293 + .452 + 1.438 + 2.216$$

$$= 4.399$$

Is this chi-square value significant? We hope you said, "We'll need to know the *df* before we can tell." Calculating the *df* for a contingency table is a bit different than when you have only one nominal variable; however, it's just as easy. For the contingency table, the *df* formula is:

$$df = (\text{number of rows} - 1)(\text{number of columns} - 1)$$

For our video game example:

$$df = (2 - 1)(2 - 1) = (1)(1) = 1$$

A quick check of the chi-square table (Table A-7) indicates that the critical value for significance at the .05 level with $df = 1$ is 3.841. So, our calculated value of 4.399 is significant.

What does this significant result mean? The interpretation of chi square for a contingency table is a bit different than our interpretation of chi square for one nominal variable. For the contingency table we have two or more observed distributions. For the video-game example we have two distributions: the distribution of nonviolent and violent frequencies (a) for the men and (b) for the women. The chi square for a contingency table tests to determine if the distributions in the table have similar or different patterns. If the chi square is *not* significant, then the distributions are similar; in such cases researchers say that the distributions are *independent*. If the distributions are *independent*, then the pattern for one category is essentially the same as the pattern for the other level(s). If chi square is significant, then the distributions are dissimilar, and researchers say that they are *dependent*. If the distributions are *dependent*, then the pattern for one category (e.g., men in our example) is not the same as the pattern for the other level(s) (e.g., women); in other words, the nature of the pattern on one nominal variable depends on the specific category or level of the other nominal variable.

> **Chi-square test for independence**
> Chi-square tests for contingency tables.

Because of the independent–dependent distinction, statisticians often refer to chi-square tests for contingency tables as **chi-square tests for independence**. Here's how Jurica et al. (2002) described the dependent nature of their data. "Even though the participants played more nonviolent games overall, the men were more likely than the women to play violent arcade games" (Jurica et al., 2002, p. 147).

Let's see how our formulas and considerations apply to a larger contingency table. Assume that the local sports complex has hired your industrial psychology firm to determine if fans have similar or different food preferences at different kinds of sporting events. You obtain the following sales figures for the final basketball, football, and baseball games of the season:

		Food Preferences (Frequencies)			
		Hot Dogs	Hamburgers	Nachos	Total
	Basketball	37 (Cell A)	150 (Cell B)	211 (Cell C)	398
Sport	Football	24 (Cell D)	137 (Cell E)	201 (Cell F)	362
	Baseball	53 (Cell G)	172 (Cell H)	236 (Cell I)	461
	Total	114	459	648	1221

Now, do you remember how to calculate the expected frequencies? We'll do a couple to help you get started:

$$\text{Expected A} = (\text{row total} \times \text{column total})/\text{grand total}$$
$$= \frac{398 \times 114}{1221} = \frac{45,372}{1221} = 37.159$$
$$\text{Expected B} = (\text{row total} \times \text{column total})/\text{grand total}$$
$$= \frac{398 \times 459}{1221} = \frac{182,682}{1221} = 149.616$$
$$\text{Expected D} = (\text{row total} \times \text{column total})/\text{grand total}$$
$$= \frac{362 \times 114}{1221} = \frac{41,268}{1221} = 33.798$$

Now it's your turn to work on the remaining expected frequencies.

PSYCHOLOGICAL DETECTIVE Given that we have already calculated the expected frequencies for three cells, how many more will you have to calculate before you can fill in the table by using subtraction from the row and column totals?

If you decided that you would have to actually calculate only one more expected frequency, then you are correct. Go ahead and calculate the expected frequency for Cell E; your answer should be 136.083.

Now, let's calculate the remaining frequencies by subtraction:

Step 1   To find expected C: subtract (expected A) + (expected B) from the row total.

$$= 398 - (37.159 + 149.616)$$
$$= 211.225$$

Step 2   To find expected F: subtract (expected D) + (expected E) from the row total.

$$= 362 - (33.798 + 136.083)$$
$$= 192.119$$

Step 3   To find expected G: subtract (expected A) + (expected D) from the column total.

$$= 114 - (37.159 + 33.798)$$
$$= 43.043$$

Step 4   To find expected H: subtract (expected B) + (expected E) from the column total.

$$= 459 - (149.616 + 136.083)$$
$$= 173.301$$

Step 5   To find expected I: subtract (expected C) + (expected F) from the column total.

$$= 648 - (211.225 + 192.119)$$
$$= 244.656$$

Now that we have all the expected frequencies, we can calculate chi square:

$$\chi^2 = \Sigma \frac{(O - E)^2}{E} = \frac{(37 - 37.159)^2}{37.159} + \frac{(150 - 149.616)^2}{149.616} + \frac{(211 - 211.225)^2}{211.225}$$

$$+ \frac{(24 - 33.798)^2}{33.798} + \frac{(137 - 136.083)^2}{136.083} + \frac{(201 - 192.119)^2}{192.119} + \frac{(53 - 43.043)^2}{43.043}$$

$$+ \frac{(172 - 173.301)^2}{173.301} + \frac{(236 - 244.656)^2}{244.656}$$

$$= .007 + .001 + .0002 + 2.8404 + .0062 + .4105 + 2.3033 + .0098 + .3063$$

$$= 5.8847$$

How many df are there? Remember:

$$df = (\text{number of rows} - 1)(\text{number of columns} - 1)$$
$$= (3 - 1)(3 - 1) = 4$$

A quick check of Table A-7 indicates that 9.488 (with $df = 4$) is the critical value for significance at the .05 level. Because our value of 5.8779 is far below the critical value, we can conclude that the three distributions of food preferences are similar. They are *independent* of the type of sport. Practically speaking, your industrial psychology consulting firm can tell the sports complex that their order does not depend on the type of sport.

 What would you do if your chi square had been significant?

Obviously there are more than two groups (categories) involved in the analysis of 2×3 and larger contingency tables. When we had one nominal variable and more than two groups, our approach, following a significant chi square, was to conduct a series of simpler, more focused chi-square tests; this approach also will work in the situation where we have two nominal variables and three or more levels (categories) on one of the variables.

For example, *had* the chi-square been significant for our food-preference and sport example, we could have done follow-up tests that analyzed matrices such as those shown in Figure 18-1 (see p. 447). As Figure 18-1 indicates, the general procedure is to move from more complex analyses to simpler contingency tables. Thus, our analyses would move from our original 3×3 contingency table to 2×3 tables, and then, if needed, to 2×2 tables. Finally, we need to add that, at least to the best of our knowledge, there is no way to calculate an effect size for the chi-square procedure.

Clearly, researchers have numerous analyses they can perform when they have gathered nominal data. In the next section we examine several of the statistical procedures that researchers use when they have ordinal data.

REVIEW SUMMARY

1. Because inferential significance tests attempt to estimate population parameters, researchers also call them **parametric tests**.

2. Inferential tests are based on assumptions such as normality of population distributions and equivalence of population variances (**homogeneity of variance**).

3. The F_{max} **test** evaluates the assumption of equivalence of variances by comparing the largest and smallest variances.

4. **Data transformation** involves the application of an accepted mathematical procedure, such as the square root procedure, to *all* scores in a data set. Data transformations may normalize distributions and equalize variances.

5. A **nonparametric test of significance** does not estimate population parameters.

6. The **chi-square test** is a nominal data procedure that compares frequency distributions.

7. Researchers use chi-square tests with one nominal variable that has two or more levels/categories and two nominal variables that each have two or more levels.

8. A **contingency table** displays the obtained frequencies for two nominal variables.

9. A **chi-square test for independence** is appropriate when there are two nominal variables.

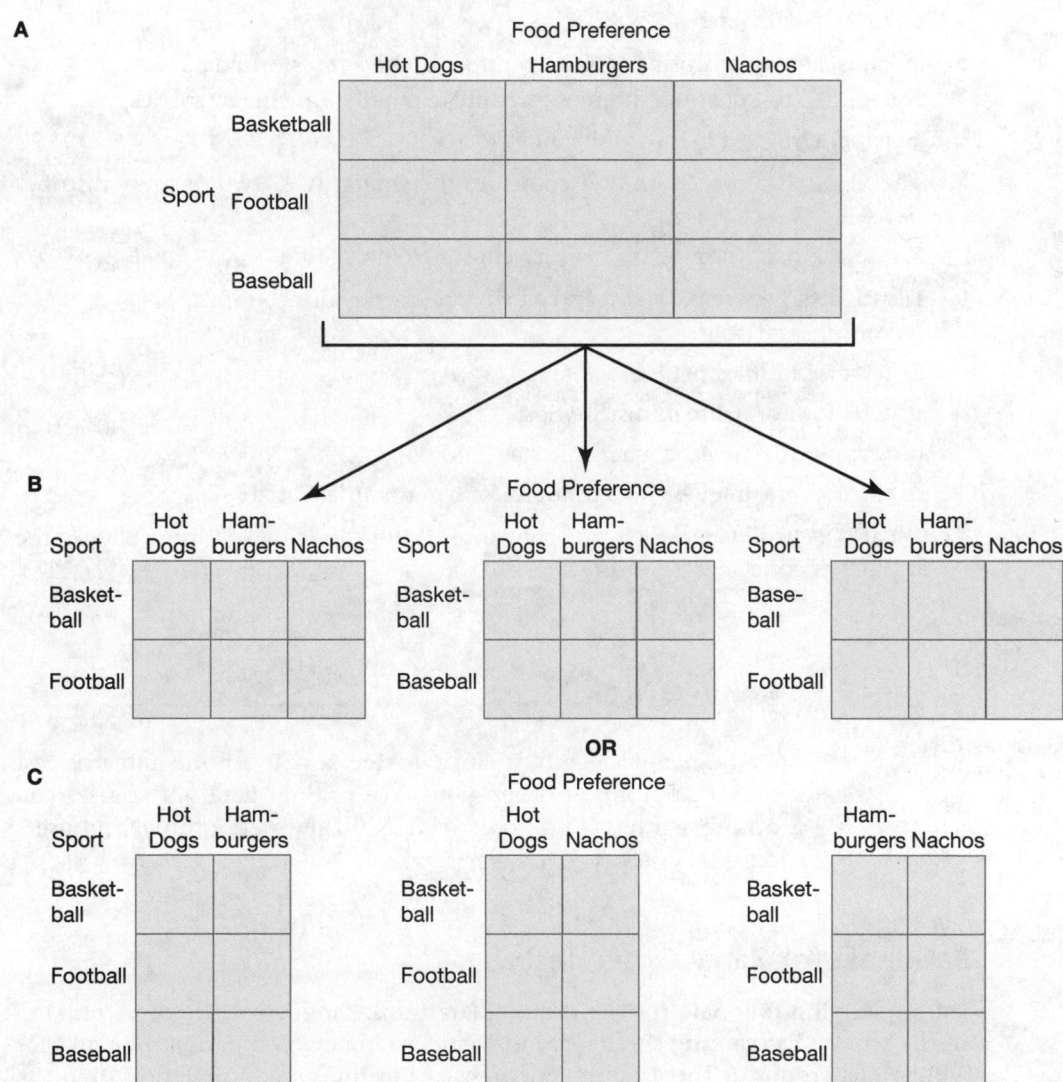

FIGURE 18-1 A SIGNIFICANT, COMPLEX CHI SQUARE TEST (PART A) CAN LEAD TO FURTHER, SIMPLIFIED CHI-SQUARE TESTS (PARTS B OR C).

CHECK YOUR PROGRESS

1. Explain what might happen if the assumptions of an inferential statistical test are violated.

2. The F_{max} test is best associated with _____.

   a. homogeneity of variance

   b. a skewed distribution

   c. nominal data tests

   d. ordinal data tests

3. What is a data transformation? Why do researchers transform data?

4. A(n) _____ test does not attempt to estimate population characteristics.

   a. parametric   b. nonparametric   c. *t*   d. *F*

5. The _____ is a procedure that compares the similarity of two or more distributions.

   a. *t* test   b. *F* test   c. chi-square procedure   d. F_{max}

6. Distinguish between *expected* and *observed* frequency distributions.

7. A contingency table _____.

   a. tests for homogeneity of variance

   b. tests for normality of distribution

   c. is appropriately used when you have ordinal data

   d. displays the frequencies and totals for two nominal variables

8. What is a chi-square test for independence? If this test is significant, what can the researcher conclude?

Rank–Order Tests

Rank–order test A non-parametric test that is appropriate when you have ordinal data.

As the name suggests, a **rank–order test** is a nonparametric test that is appropriate when you have ordinal data. Of course, you can treat interval and ratio data as if they were ordinal and use a rank–order test.

Rationale for Rank–Order Tests

The underlying rationale for the ordinal-data (rank–order) tests involves ranking all the scores, disregarding specific group membership, and comparing the ranks for the various groups. If the groups were drawn from the same population then the ranks should not differ appreciably between (among) the groups. If the IV was effective then the ranks will not be evenly distributed between (among) the groups; smaller ranks will be associated with one group and larger ranks will be associated with another group(s). Let's consider a rank–order test and see how this principle works.

Mann–Whitney U Test
A rank–order test for use with two independent groups that are relatively small.

Mann–Whitney U Test

Researchers use the **Mann–Whitney U Test** with two independent groups that are relatively small ($n = 20$ or less). Here's an example.

You have developed a new method for teaching spelling to second graders. You conduct an experiment to determine if your new method is superior to the method being used. You randomly assign 12 second-graders to two equal groups ($n_1 = n_2 = 6$). You teach spelling to Group 1 in the traditional manner, whereas Group 2 learns to spell with your new method. After two months, both groups complete the same 30-word spelling test. Table 18-1 shows the number of correctly spelled words and the rank for each student's performance. Because neither group is normally distributed, the assumption of normal distribution appears to have been violated; hence, the nonparametric Mann–Whitney U Test is appropriate. The steps for conducting this test follow.

Step 1 Rank all scores in your data set (disregarding group membership); the one lowest score is assigned the rank of 1 (see Table 18-1).

Step 2 Sum the ranks for each group (see Table 18-1).

Step 3 Compute a U value for *each* group according to the following formulas: (Where: ΣR_1 = sum of ranks in Group 1 and ΣR_2 = sum of ranks in Group 2.)

$$U_1 = (n_1)(n_2) + \frac{n_1(n_1 + 1)}{2} - \Sigma R_1$$

$$= (6)(6) + \frac{(6)(6 + 1)}{2} - 23$$

$$= 36 + 21 - 23$$

$$= 34$$

$$U_2 = (n_1)(n_2) + \frac{n_2(n_2 + 1)}{2} - \Sigma R_2$$

$$= (6)(6) + \frac{(6)(6 + 1)}{2} - 55$$

$$= 36 + 21 - 55$$

$$= 2$$

TABLE 18-1 SPELLING METHODS DATA (NUMBER OF CORRECT WORDS) USED IN CALCULATING THE MANN–WHITNEY U TEST

TRADITIONAL METHOD		NEW METHOD	
X	Rank	X	Rank
2	1	15	6
4	2	18	7
5	3	22	9
12	4	24	10
13	5	25	11
19	8	27	12
Σ ranks = 23		Σ ranks = 55	

Step 4   Determine which U value (U_1 or U_2) to use to test for significance. For a *two-tailed test*, you will use the smaller U. For a *one-tailed test*, you will use the U for the group you predict will have the larger sum of ranks.

For our example, we predicted that the children who used our new spelling method would have higher scores on the spelling test and, therefore, have higher ranks. Hence we use U_2 when we test for significance.

Step 5   Obtain the critical U value from Table A-8. For our example, we will use the values for the one-tailed test (pp. 554–557). You enter the table by finding the column for n_1 and the row for n_2. Go to the intersection of the specific row and column. (In our example, $n_1 = n_2 = 6$, so we find the intersection of column 6 and row 6. However, you should note that group size does not need to be equal.) At the intersection of row 6 and column 6, you will see that the critical value at the .05 level is 7, whereas the critical value at the .01 level is 3.

Step 6   Compare your calculated U value to the critical value from Table A-8. To be significant, your calculated U value must be equal to or *less than* the table value. Yes, that's right, the value you calculate needs to be *smaller than* the table value to be significant; this is a big change from the significance tests we've considered previously. Keep this difference in mind; we will encounter it again. Hence, our result is significant at the .01 level (our calculated U value of 2 is less than the critical value of 3.) Because the ranks of the children who used the new spelling method were significantly higher than the ranks of the children who used the traditional method, we can conclude that the new method is superior.

Step 7   To calculate an effect size for the Mann–Whitney U test, simply disregard the rule about N and reanalyze your data using the rank sums test (see the next section). By following the rank sums procedures, you will be able to calculate an η^2 to determine effect size.

Rank Sums Test

> **Rank sums test** A rank–order test for use with two independent groups and one or both of the groups has 20 or more participants.

If your research used two independent groups *and* the n in one or both groups is greater than 20, then the **rank sums test** is the appropriate ordinal data statistic. Even though the rank sums test is best suited for larger groups, we will reuse the spelling-method data (see Table 18-1) to illustrate its calculation and interpretation. Here are the steps for calculating the rank sums test. After completing the Mann–Whitney U Test, we are sure that some of them will be familiar.

Step 1   Rank order *all* the scores in your data set (disregarding group membership). The lowest score is assigned the rank of 1. (See Table 18-1.)

Step 2   Select one group and sum the ranks (ΣR). We selected the traditional method group; the $\Sigma R = 23$.

Step 3   Use the following formula to calculate the expected sum of ranks (ΣR_{exp})

$$\Sigma R_{exp} = \frac{n(N+1)}{2}$$
$$= \frac{6(12+1)}{2}$$
$$= 78/2$$
$$= 39$$

Step 4   Use the ΣR and ΣR_{exp} for the selected group to calculate the rank sums z statistic according to the following formula:

$$z_{\text{rank sums}} = \frac{\Sigma R - \Sigma R_{exp}}{\sqrt{\dfrac{(n_1)(n_2)(N+1)}{12}}}$$
$$= \frac{23-39}{\sqrt{\dfrac{(6)(6)(12+1)}{12}}} = \frac{-16}{\sqrt{\dfrac{(36)(13)}{12}}} = \frac{-16}{\sqrt{39}}$$
$$= \frac{-16}{6.245}$$
$$= -2.562$$

Step 5   Use Table A-2 to determine the critical z value for the .05 level. If you have a directional hypothesis (one-tailed test), you will find the z that occurs 45% from the mean. For a nondirectional (two-tailed test), you will find the z that occurs 47.50% from the mean. (Remember that you split the alpha level equally for a two-tailed test. Hence, for the .05 level you will test at the .025 level in both tails.) These values are 1.645 (45%) and 1.96 (47.50%), respectively.

PSYCHOLOGICAL DETECTIVE   Should we use the one- or two-tailed value for our spelling-method example? Why?

Because we predicted that our new method would produce better spelling performance, we would use a one-tailed test.

Step 6   Disregard the sign of your calculated z statistic (i.e., use the absolute value) and compare it to with the critical value. Because our calculated rank sums z (2.562) is larger than the critical value (1.645), our two groups differ significantly and we can conclude that our new spelling method was successful in improving spelling performance when compared to the traditional method.

Step 7 Calculate an effect size. You can use the following formula to calculate η^2.

$$\eta^2 = \frac{(z_{\text{rank scores}})^2}{12-1}$$

For our example:

$$\eta^2 = \frac{(-2.562)^2}{12-1}$$
$$= .597$$

This η^2 value indicates that the spelling method accounted for 59.70% of the variability. This effect size is large.

Wilcoxon T Test

> **Wilcoxon T Test** A rank–order test for use with two related or dependent groups.

When you have two related groups and ordinal data, the **Wilcoxon T Test** (or *Wilcoxon matched-pairs signed-ranks test*) is your statistic of choice. Here is a research example to illustrate the calculation and use of this statistic.

A researcher believes that viewing a video showing the benefits of recycling will result in more positive recycling attitudes and behaviors. Ten volunteers complete a recycling questionnaire (higher scores = more positive attitudes) before and after viewing the video. Table 18-2 shows the pre- and post-video recycling scores. Here are the steps for calculating the Wilcoxon T test:

Step 1 Find the difference between the scores for each pair. It doesn't matter which score is subtracted, just be consistent throughout all the pairs (see Table 18-2, column 4).

Step 2 Assign ranks to all *nonzero* differences. Disregard the sign of the difference. The smallest difference = rank 1. Tied differences receive the average of the ranks they are tied for (see Table 18-2, column 5).

Step 3 Determine the ranks that are based on positive differences (see Table 18-2, column 6) and the ranks that are based on negative differences (see Table 18-2, column 7).

Step 4 Sum the positive and negative ranks. These sums are the T values you will use to determine significance.

Step 5 If you have a nondirectional hypothesis (two-tailed test) you will use the smaller of the two sums of ranks. If you have a directional hypothesis you will have to determine which sum of ranks your hypothesis predicts will be smaller. For your recycling video example, if the video is effective in improving recycling attitudes, we would predict an increase in post-video scores. Therefore, there should be a large number of negative ranks; hence, we predict that that the sum of the positive ranks will be small. Consequently, the Wilcoxon T for our example is the sum of the positive ranks (27).

Step 6 N for the Wilcoxon T Test equals the number of *nonzero* differences. For our video example $N = 9$.

Step 7   Table A-9 lists the critical values for the Wilcoxon T Test. To be significant the calculated value must be equal to or *less* than the table value. For $N = 9$ a value of 5 or less is required for significance. Because our calculated value of 27 is far above the critical value, we can conclude that the video did not improve recycling attitudes.

Step 8   We are not aware of any procedure to calculate an effect size for the Wilcoxon T Test.

TABLE 18-2   PRE- AND POST-VIDEO RECYCLING ATTITUDE SCORES USED TO CALCULATE THE WILCOXON T TEST

PAIR	PRE-VIDEO RECYCLE SCORE	POST-VIDEO RECYCLE SCORE	DIFFERENCE SCORE	RANK	+RANKS	−RANKS
1	17	21	−4	3		3
2	21	32	−11	7		7
3	33	28	5	4.5	4.5	
4	38	10	28	9	9	
5	12	12	0			
6	13	8	5	4.5	4.5	
7	21	19	2	1.5	1.5	
8	17	15	2	1.5	1.5	
9	12	24	−12	8		8
10	18	10	8	6	6	
					$\Sigma = 27$	$\Sigma = 18$

Where $N = 9$ (number of nonzero differences)

Kruskal–Wallis H Test

Kruskal–Wallis H Test
A rank-order test for use with three or more independent groups.

So far we've considered ordinal tests for two groups. Because researchers use the **Kruskal–Wallis H Test** when they have more than two groups and ordinal data, it is analogous to a one-way between subjects ANOVA (see Chapter 13).

Here's an example of a research situation where the Kruskal–Wallis H Test would be the appropriate analysis. A sport psychologist compared three methods of teaching putting to beginning golfers. The methods were visual imagery, repetitive practice, and the combination of visual imagery and repetitive practice. The researcher randomly assigned 21 equally inexperienced golfers to three equal groups. Following equivalent amounts of training, each golfer attempted to sink 25 putts from

| TABLE | 18-3 | GOLF PUTTING SCORES (RANKS) USED TO CALCULATE THE KRUSKAL–WALLIS H STATISTIC |

VISUAL IMAGERY	REPETITIVE PRACTICE	VISUAL IMAGERY + REPETITIVE PRACTICE
6	3	12
10	1	18
14	4	19
7	8	11
13	9	15
16	2	20
17	5	21
$\Sigma R_1 = 83$	$\Sigma R_2 = 32$	$\Sigma R_3 = 116$
$(\Sigma R_1)^2 = 6899$	$(\Sigma R_2)^2 = 1024$	$(\Sigma R_3)^2 = 13{,}456$
$n_1 = 7$	$n_2 = 7$	$n_3 = 7$
$N = 21$		

the same locations on the putting green. The researcher rank-ordered (smaller rank = lower score) *all* the final performances. Table 18-3 shows the results. Here are the steps needed to calculate the H statistic:

Step 1 Rank *all* scores (1 = lowest score, see Table 18-3).

Step 2 Sum the ranks for each group/condition (see Table 18-3).

Step 3 Square the sum of ranks for each group/condition (see Table 18-3).

Step 4 Using the following formula, calculate the sum of squares between groups:

$$SS_{\text{bet gr}} = \frac{(\Sigma R_1)^2}{n_1} + \frac{(\Sigma R_2)^2}{n_2} + \cdots + \frac{(\Sigma R_k)^2}{n_k}$$

$$= \frac{6889}{7} + \frac{1024}{7} + \frac{13{,}456}{7}$$

$$= 984.143 + 146.286 + 1922.286 = 3052.715$$

Step 5 Using the following, formula calculate H:

$$H = \left(\frac{12}{N[N+1]}\right)(SS_{\text{bet gr}}) - 3(N+1)$$

$$= \left(\frac{12}{12[21+1]}\right)(3052.715) - 3(21+1)$$

$$= (.026)(3052.715) - 66$$

$$= 13.3706$$

Step 6 Use the chi-square table (Table A-7) to find the critical value for H. The *df* for the H test = $k - 1$ where k is the number of groups/conditions. For our golf example, $df = k - 1 = 3 - 1 = 2$. Thus, the critical value that our calculated H must *exceed* to be significant at the .05 level is 5.991. Because our calculated H = 13.3706 is greater than the table value, it is significant. In fact, it is significant at $p < .01$. Thus, we can conclude that the different types of practice produced at least one significant difference between two of the groups (see Step 8 below).

Step 7 Calculate an effect size. You can calculate η^2 by using this formula:

$$\eta^2 = \frac{H}{N-1}$$

For our golf example:

$$\eta^2 = \frac{13.3706}{21-1} = .6685$$

This η^2 value indicates that the type of practice IV accounted for 66.85% of the variability. A large effect size, indeed.

Step 8 If appropriate, conduct post hoc tests. The procedure for conducting such tests is similar to conducting follow-up tests when you have nominal data. In short, you devise simpler follow-up analyses. For the example we just completed, you could use Mann–Whitney U Tests to make the following comparisons: (a) visual imagery versus repetitive practice, (b) visual imagery versus visual imagery + repetitive practice, and (c) repetitive practice versus visual imagery + repetitive practice.

Researchers also use several additional ordinal data tests of significance. We have presented the ones you are most likely to need in your own research and that you will encounter when you read research-based journal articles.

REVIEW SUMMARY

1. **Rank–order tests** are nonparametric tests that researchers use with ordinal data. They test for unequal distribution of ranks between (among) groups.
2. The **Mann–Whitney U Test** is an ordinal data test that researchers use when they have two relatively small, independent groups.
3. Researchers use the **rank sums test** to analyze ordinal data when they have two independent groups and one or both of the groups has more than 20 participants.
4. Researchers use the **Wilcoxon T Test** (Wilcoxon matched-pairs signed-ranks test) to analyze ordinal data when they have two related groups.
5. The **Kruskal–Wallis H Test** is an ordinal test that is appropriate with more than two groups. It is analogous to a one-way, between subjects ANOVA.

CHECK YOUR PROGRESS

1. Explain the rationale involved in conducting rank–order significance tests.
2. Researchers use the _____ with two, relatively small, independent samples.

   a. Wilcoxon T Test
   b. Mann–Whitney U Test
   c. Kruskal–Wallis H Test
   d. rank sums test

3. Researchers use the _____ with two related samples.

   a. Wilcoxon T Test
   b. Mann–Whitney U Test
   c. Kruskal–Wallis H Test
   d. rank sums test

4. The _____ is analogous to a one-way, independent samples ANOVA.

   a. Wilcoxon T Test
   b. Mann–Whitney U Test
   c. Kruskal–Wallis H Test
   d. rank sums test

5. Researchers use the _____ with two independent samples when one or both of the samples are large.

   a. Wilcoxon T Test
   b. Mann–Whitney U Test
   c. Kruskal–Wallis H Test
   d. rank sums test

EXERCISES

1. You are in charge of the school cafeteria and you want to stock the most preferred items. Unfortunately, you can only stock one frozen dessert; hence, you must choose between Red Crunchers and Green Zingers. Lacking any reason to expect that one dessert will be preferred over the other, you obtain a random sample of 75 school children who try the two desserts and pick their favorite. Thirty children prefer Red Crunchers, whereas 45 children prefer Green Zingers. What is your decision? Why (be thorough)?

2. Calculate a chi-square test for the following data. Use the .05 level to test for significance. Indicate what followup tests, if any, should be conducted.

Category	Expected	Observed
1	10%	4
2	20%	7
3	40%	24
4	20%	8
5	10%	7

3. Carry out a chi-square test for independence (use .05) for the following contingency table:

		Variable 2			
		Level 1	Level 2	Level 3	Level 4
Variable 1	Level 1	7	8	19	34
	Level 2	12	18	22	71

4. The following are data for two sets of athletes:

   Group 1—54, 59, 77, 93, 136, 154, 159, 216, 227
   Group 2—12, 32, 39, 40, 51, 56, 59, 155

   Use the Mann–Whitney U Test to determine if the groups differ significantly (use .05).

5. Use the rank–sums test to determine if these two groups differ significantly (use .05):

   Group 1—7, 11, 19, 14, 26, 18, 8, 22, 16, 12, 17, 29, 12, 15, 24, 19, 17, 9, 18, 13, 18
   Group 2—25, 31, 27, 36, 19, 38, 42, 36, 29, 41, 33, 37, 30, 28

6. Sixteen rat pups from the *same* litter are randomly assigned to two groups and then tested under control and experimental conditions. Their data are as follow:

   Control—19, 22, 24, 30, 53, 80, 44, 53
   Experimental—16, 7, 21, 24, 80, 107, 40, 28

   Use the appropriate ordinal data test to determine if the groups differ significantly (use .05).

7. A researcher tests three groups of participants on a psychomotor test under three levels of illumination (dim, average, bright). The results are:

   Dim illumination—24, 6, 15, 25, 32, 24, 29
   Average illumination—16, 15, 18, 19, 8, 13, 18
   Bright illumination—25, 19, 16, 17, 45

   Use the Kruskal–Wallis H Test to determine if the groups differ significantly (use .05). Perform any followup tests that might be warranted.

8. Complete a chi-square test for the following data (use .05):

Category	Expected	Observed
A	10%	15
B	15%	10
C	20%	15
D	20%	15
E	20%	25
F	15%	20

9. Calculate a chi-square test for each of the following contingency tables. Test for significance at the .05 level.

5	8
8	5

5	8	8
8	5	5

10. A researcher matches two groups of high school students on age, gender, and grade point average. The researcher then randomly assigns the groups to treatments; one group receives a newly designed driver education course whereas the second group receives the traditional driver education course. Their scores on the written portion of the driver's license examination are:

    Group 1 (new method)—61, 84, 73, 88, 94, 67, 76, 83, 78
    Group 2 (traditional method)—62, 64, 66, 72, 63, 74, 77, 63, 64

    Use the appropriate ordinal data test to determine significance (use .05). Interpret your results.

11. Use the Mann–Whitney U Test to determine if these two groups differ significantly (use .05).

    Group 1—1, 6, 8, 9, 11, 14, 16, 18, 21, 23
    Group 2—15, 17, 19, 20, 22, 26, 28, 31, 34, 37

12. Two groups have the following ordinal scores:

    Group 1—63, 50, 48, 57, 73, 66, 82, 58, 66, 77, 68, 80, 55, 86, 78, 74, 65, 83, 79, 84
    Group 2—42, 37, 49, 36, 46, 53, 31, 37, 41, 44, 33, 35, 45, 47, 55, 30, 29, 38, 38, 40

    Use the rank–sums test to determine if these groups differ significantly (use .05).

13. A researcher is interested whether athletes, members of Greek organizations, and nonGreeks/nonathletes differ in terms of their self-esteem. The researcher obtains the following scores:

    Athletes—46, 37, 53, 31, 49, 34, 43, 58, 55
    Greek organization members—62, 51, 46, 38, 54, 56, 49, 64, 66
    NonGreeks/nonathletes—42, 59, 57, 48, 58, 44, 45, 52

    Use the Kruskal–Wallis H Test to determine if these groups differ significantly (use .05). Perform any appropriate followup tests. Interpret your results.

14. A researcher conducts a field study to determine whether men or women are better at obeying traffic regulations. The researcher records the number of male and female drivers who do and do not come to a complete stop at a designated intersection. The results are as follows:

	Stopped completely	Did not stop completely
Men	63	97
Women	82	54

    Perform the appropriate statistical analysis (use .05) and interpret your results.

15. Apply the Kruskal–Wallis H Test to the following data (use .05). Perform any appropriate followup tests.

    Group 1—16, 7, 19, 24, 31
    Group 2—24, 6, 15, 25, 32, 24, 29
    Group 3—16, 15, 18, 19, 6, 13, 18
    Group 4—25, 19, 16, 17, 42, 45

KEY TERMS

Parametric tests, *435*	Observed frequency distribution, *438*
Homogeneity of variance, *435*	Contingency table, *442*
F_{max} test, *435*	Chi-square test for independence, *444*
Data transformation, *436*	Rank–order test, *448*
Nonparametric test of significance, *437*	Mann–Whitney U Test, *449*
	Rank sums test, *450*
Chi-square test, *437*	Wilcoxon T Test, *452*
Expected frequency distribution, *437*	Kruskal–Wallis H Test, *453*

LOOKING AHEAD

Up to this point we have dealt with experimental research methods almost exclusively. In the next chapter you will learn about nonexperimental research methods. The descriptive and observational techniques provide ways to gather data in situations where it may not be possible or desirable to conduct a scientific experiment. Likewise, researchers can gather valuable data in situations where they are not able to control the relevant variables. Finally, researchers have used surveys, questionnaires, tests, and inventories for decades to gather significant data.

19

Nonexperimental Methods

Not all research projects use the experimental method. In fact, researchers have developed a large number of nonexperimental strategies. Just because they are classified as nonexperimental does not mean that these methods produce inferior results. As you will see, the choice of a nonexperimental research strategy depends on the type of problem being investigated, where it is being investigated, and the nature of the data the researcher gathers.

> **Descriptive research methods** Research methods that do not involve the manipulation of an IV.

Descriptive Methods

Because several of these methods do not involve the manipulation of an IV, they are called **descriptive research methods**. When we use descriptive methods, we can only speculate about causation.

Archival and Previously Recorded Sources of Data

In some instances researchers may not gather their own data; they may answer their research question by using data recorded by other individuals. For example, an investigator may analyze public health and census data years after they were collected to answer questions about socioeconomic status, religion, or political party affiliation. In some instances the records and data you need to consult are stored in a central location. The Archives of the History of American Psychology were established at the University of Akron in 1974 for conducting research on the history of psychology. Although the letters, documents, and photographs contained in this collection were originally produced for numerous reasons, researchers now use them to answer questions about the history of our discipline.

You also can access several archival sources online. For example, the National Opinion Research Center has conducted the General Social Survey (GSS) almost annually since 1972. The responses of more than 35,000 respondents to a wide range of socially relevant questions are available at http://www.icpsr.umich.edu/gss/home.htm. The number of research questions that can be addressed with this huge body of information seems endless. There is no charge for accessing this site; we encourage you to peruse it.

Not all sources of previously recorded data are stored in an archive or library or are available online for our use. There are numerous real-life sources. For example, if you are interested in differences in sexual preoccupation between men and women, you might choose to examine graffiti on the walls of public restrooms.

PSYCHOLOGICAL DETECTIVE

The use of archival and previously recorded data is certainly in line with being a psychological detective. You are putting together bits and pieces of data to answer research questions. Unfortunately, there are several problems associated with this approach to gathering information. Consider conducting this type of research and see what problems you can discover.

Potential Problems   There are several potential problems associated with using archival and previously recorded sources of data. First, unless you are dealing with the papers and documents of a few clearly identified individuals, you will not know exactly who left the data you are investigating. Not knowing the participants who comprise your sample will make it difficult to understand and generalize your results. Consider the graffiti example. You may choose to record graffiti from restrooms on your campus. Who created this graffiti? Did a representative sample of students create it? Although common sense may tell you that the sample of graffiti writers is not representative of students on your campus, let alone college students in general, you do not know. Your ability to make statements other than those that merely describe your data is severely limited.

Second, the participants may have been selective in *what* they chose to write. Clearly, this consideration may be important in our graffiti example where we are evaluating the presence of sexual comments. What others chose to record may drastically influence our conclusions in other instances. For example, until recently, what we knew about Wilhelm Wundt—founder of scientific psychology—was provided by E. B. Titchener, who originally translated Wundt's books and papers from German into English. Unfortunately, Titchener chose to misrepresent Wundt on several occasions; hence, our impression of Wundt may be severely distorted (Goodwin, 1999). Fortunately, Wundt's original writings are still available for retranslation and examination. Even if his works are retranslated, we will still face the possible problem that Wundt may have omitted things from his own writings that he did not want to share with others. Whenever researchers use archival or previously recorded sources they cannot avoid this problem of *selective deposit*.

A third problem with this type of data concerns the survival of such records. In our study of graffiti, it will be important to know something about the cleaning schedule for the restroom(s) we are observing. Are they scrubbed clean each day or is the graffiti allowed to accumulate? In this example, the data in which you are interested will probably not have a very high survival rate. Printed materials may not fare much better. During the 1920s John Watson and his call to behaviorism made psychology immensely popular in the United States; the number of journal articles and books written during this period attest to its popularity. It was only recently, however, that researchers discovered a very popular magazine, *Psychology: Health, Happiness, and Success*, which was published from 1923 to 1938 (Benjamin, 1992). Why the mystery surrounding this once-popular magazine? The problem had to do with the type of paper on which the magazine was printed. The high acid content of the paper led to rapid disintegration of these magazines; hence, only a precious few have survived.

Comparisons with the Experimental Method   Certainly, researchers can gain valuable information from archival and prerecorded sources. However, we must be aware of the problems of a nonrepresentative sample, data that are purposely not recorded, and data that have been lost. A comparison of using this technique with conducting an experiment reveals other weaknesses in addition to these limitations. Because we examined data and documents produced at another time, under potentially unknown circumstances, we are not able to exercise any control with regard to gathering these data. Hence, we are unable to make any type of cause-and-effect statement; the best we can do is speculate about what might have occurred.

These concerns notwithstanding, this type of research can yield interesting and valuable results. For example, much of what you read in a history of psychology text is the product of archival research. In the next section we examine methods that we use to observe the phenomenon of interest firsthand.

Observational Techniques

Even though the techniques described in this section involve the direct observation of the phenomenon or behavior of interest, they do not involve the direct manipulation of any variables by the experimenter. Being able to specify which responses we will observe is as close to control as we come with these methods. Among the most common observational techniques are case studies, naturalistic observation, and the use of surveys or questionnaires.

Case study Intensively observing and recording the behavior of a single participant

Case Studies   When we conduct **case studies** we intensively observe and record the behavior of a single (possibly two) participant(s) over an extended period of time. Because there are no guidelines for conducting a case study, the procedures employed, behaviors observed, and reports produced may vary substantially.

Frequently, scientists use case studies in clinical settings to help formulate hypotheses and ideas for further research. For example, the French physician Paul Broca (1824–1880) reported the case study of a patient nicknamed "Tan" because he said nothing except the word "tan" and an occasional obscenity when he was frustrated or annoyed (Howard, 1997). Based on his observations, Broca hypothesized that the center controlling the production of speech was located in the frontal lobe of the left hemisphere of the brain and that this area was damaged in the patient's brain. An autopsy indicated that Broca's hypothesis was correct. This case study provided the inspiration for numerous subsequent studies that provided considerable information concerning the neurological system that is responsible for the comprehension and production of speech. Other examples of case studies might involve the observation of a rare animal in the wild or at a zoological park, a specific type of mental patient in a hospital, or a gifted child at school.

Although case studies often provide interesting data, their results may be applicable only to the individual participant who was observed. In other words, the researcher should not generalize beyond the studied participant when using the case study method. Additionally, because the researcher manipulates no variables, use of the case study method precludes establishing cause-and-effect relations. On the other hand, if your research goal is to understand the behavior of one individual (such as Broca's study of Tan), then the case study may be the perfect research procedure. Your understanding of the behavior of one individual may lead to more general predictions.

Naturalistic observation Seeking answers to research questions by observing behavior in the real world.

Naturalistic Observation   **Naturalistic observation** involves seeking answers to research questions by observing behavior in the real world. For example, each spring animal psychologists interested in the behavior of migrating sandhill cranes conceal themselves in camouflage blinds to observe the roosting behavior of these birds on the Platte River in central Nebraska. For another example, a researcher who is interested in the behavior of preschool children might go to a day-care center to observe the children.

The possibilities for conducting studies using naturalistic observation are limited only by our insight into a potential area of research. Regardless of the situation we choose, we have two goals in using naturalistic observation. The first goal should be obvious from the name of the technique: to describe behavior as it occurs in the natural setting without the artificiality of the laboratory. If the goal of research is to understand behavior in the real world, what better place to gather research data than in a natural setting? The second goal of naturalistic observation is to describe the variables that are present and the relations among them. Returning to our sandhill crane example, naturalistic observation may provide clues concerning why the birds migrate at particular times of the year and those factors that seem to determine the length of stay in a certain area.

In a naturalistic observation study, it is important that the researcher not interfere with or intervene in the behavior being studied. For example, in our study of preschoolers, the observer should be as inconspicuous as possible. For this reason, the use of one-way mirrors that allow researchers to observe without being observed is popular.

 PSYCHOLOGICAL DETECTIVE   Why should the researcher be concealed or unobtrusive in a study using naturalistic observation?

The main reason the researcher must be unobtrusive in studies using naturalistic observation is to avoid influencing or changing the behavior of the participants being observed. The presence of an observer is not part of the natural setting for sandhill cranes or preschoolers; they may well behave differently in the presence of observers.

> **Reactance** or **reactivity effect** The finding that participants respond differently when they know they are being observed.

The **reactance** or **reactivity effect** refers to the biasing of the participants' responses because they know they are being observed. Perhaps the most famous example of a reactivity effect occurred in a study conducted at the Western Electric Company's Hawthorne plant located on the boundary between Chicago and Cicero, Illinois, in the late 1930s (Roethlisberger & Dickson, 1939). The purpose of the research was to determine the effects of factors such as working hours and lighting on productivity. When researchers compared productivity of the test participants to that of the general plant, an unusual finding emerged. The test participants produced at a higher rate, often under test conditions that were inferior to those normally experienced. For example, even though the room lighting was well below normal levels, productivity increased. What caused these individuals to produce at such a high rate? The answer was simple: Because these workers knew they were research participants and that they were being observed, their productivity increased. Thus, the knowledge that one is participating in an experiment and is being observed may result in dramatic changes in behavior. Because of the location of the original study, this reactivity phenomenon is often referred to as the **Hawthorne effect**.

> **Hawthorne effect** Another name for reactance or reactivity effect.

Having considered the general nature of naturalistic observation, we will examine a specific observational project more closely.

Anastasia Gibson and Kristie Smith, students at the University of Alabama in Huntsville, Alabama, and their supervisor, Aurora Torres, conducted an interesting study that used naturalistic observation. They were interested in examining the relation between glancing behavior of people using an ATM and the proximity of other customers (Gibson, Smith, & Torres, 2000). Based on previous studies of social distance and personal space, they predicted that other potential customers would not invade the personal space of the person using the ATM and that glancing behavior would decrease as other customers approached the 4-ft. radius that defined the personal-space boundary. The researchers were "in inconspicuous locations where we could view the ATM" (Gibson et al., 2000, p. 150). Contrary to their predictions, the results indicated that glancing behavior *increased* as proximity between the person using the ATM and other potential customers *decreased*.

As you may have surmised by now, the main drawback with the use of naturalistic observation is, once again, the inability to make cause-and-effect statements. Because we do not manipulate any variables when we use this technique, such conclusions are not possible.

Why use naturalistic observation if it does not allow us to make cause-and-effect statements? The first reason is quite straightforward: Naturalistic observation may be our only choice of research techniques to study a particular type of behavior. Psychologists who are interested in reactions to natural disasters—such as earthquakes, tornadoes, and fires—cannot ethically create such life-threatening situations just to study behavior; they must make their observations under naturally occurring conditions. Conducting an experiment in which researchers manipulate variables is only one of many legitimate techniques researchers use to gather data.

A second reason for using naturalistic observation is as an adjunct to the experimental method. For example, we might use naturalistic observation before conducting an experiment to give us an indication of the relevant variables involved in the situation. Once you have an idea about which variables are (and are not) important, then you can conduct systematic, controlled studies of these variables in the laboratory setting. Once you have conducted laboratory experiments you may want to return to the natural setting to see whether the insights gained in the laboratory are indeed mirrored in real life. Hence, psychologists may use naturalistic observation before and after an experimental research project to acquire further information concerning relevant variables.

Participant observation A type of naturalistic observation where the observer becomes part of the group being studied.

Participant Observation   When using naturalistic observation, researchers attempt to be as unobtrusive as possible. However, with **participant observation**, the researcher abandons his concealment and becomes part of the group being studied. Yes, the participant observer is just like the detective who goes undercover to acquire information.

Researchers often use this research technique when the goal of the research project is to learn something about a specific culture or socioeconomic group. The investigator assumes the role of a member of the group and makes observations from this vantage point.

Participant observation is not limited to the study of human behavior; it can also be implemented in animal studies. The study of chimpanzees in the Ghombe Stream Reserve in Africa by Jane Goodall is a good example of the use of this technique with nonhumans. Goodall spent enough time observing the chimpanzees each day that they finally treated her more as a member of the chimpanzee group than as an outside observer. Such acceptance facilitated her observations.

When the researcher is interested in observing an entire culture, as opposed to certain specific behaviors, Glesne (1999) indicated we are using **ethnography**, a research technique based on the anthropological tradition of research. In the ethnographic approach, you would spend a long time becoming immersed in the "culture" of the population being studied. We enclosed the word culture in quotation marks in the previous sentence because we do not refer to culture only in the cross-cultural sense of the word (e.g., different tribes, countries, continents). For example, you might wish to study an inner-city ghetto or a teenage gang using this approach. As a researcher, you become immersed in this culture for a long period of time and you gather data through participant observation and interviewing.

> **Ethnography** A descriptive research approach that involves becoming a part of the culture you study.

Glesne (1999) differentiated between two types of participant observation depending on the degree of participation. The "observer as participant" refers to a researcher who primarily observes a situation but who interacts with the others involved in the study. She used the example of Peshkin's semester-long study of a fundamentalist Christian school in which the researchers predominantly sat in the back of the classroom, took notes, and had little interaction. On the other hand, the "participant as observer" refers to the researcher who becomes a part of the culture by working and interacting extensively with the others. Glesne spent a year in St. Vincent, where she socialized, assisted in farm work, and even became an intermediary with governmental agricultural agencies. There is a cost-benefit relation with these two approaches: The more immersed in a culture you become, the more you stand to learn about it. However, you stand to lose your objectivity about a culture as you become more immersed in it. To be a good participant observer, you likely would have to fit Dr. Watson's description of Sherlock Holmes: "Your really are an automaton—a calculating machine. There is something positively inhuman in you at times" (Doyle, 1927, p. 96). You can probably understand why strict experimentalists, by placing a premium on objectivity and control, shy away from ethnographic research.

PSYCHOLOGICAL DETECTIVE The participant observer technique has considerable appeal as a research procedure; the researcher is actually a part of the situation under study. What better way to acquire the desired information! Despite such appeal, this procedure has its drawbacks and weaknesses. What are they?

There are two drawbacks to the use of participant observation: First, an extended period of time may be necessary before the participant observer is accepted as a member of the group that is under study. Has such an extended period been budgeted into the overall design of the project in terms of both cost and time? Moreover, just being part of the situation does not guarantee that the observer will be accepted. If such acceptance is not granted, the amount of information that can be acquired is severely limited. If the observer is accepted and becomes part of the group, then a loss of objectivity may result. Thus, time, finances, acceptance, and objectivity may pose severe problems for participant observer research.

As with the other observation techniques, the ability to make cause-and-effect statements is the second problem with participant observer research. Even though the participant observer may be close to the source of relevant information, no attempts are made to manipulate IVs or control extraneous variables.

Clinical perspective
A descriptive research approach aimed at understanding and correcting a particular behavioral problem.

Clinical Perspective Although some people categorize the **clinical perspective** or model as a subcategory of participant observation, Schein (1987) argued convincingly that it should be considered separately. There are several key differences between the two approaches:

- A client typically chooses the clinician, whereas the participant observer chooses the others to be studied.
- Unlike participant observers, clinicians cannot be unobtrusive because they have been asked to participate in the situation.
- Although the participant observer can remain passive, clinicians must intervene in the situation.
- The participant observer's goal is understanding, whereas the clinician's goal is helping.

Thus, the participant observer is content to be inside a system enough to develop a full understanding of the dynamics and interaction patterns. On the other hand, the clinician wishes not only to develop this understanding but also to change the dynamics and interaction patterns. Often the clinician deals with only a narrow slice of the whole, wanting to get an in-depth understanding of the problem area. The participant observer, however, wants to develop a broad picture of the entire behavioral and interpersonal spectrum. The clinical approach is related to the detective who attempts to generate a psychological profile of a particular suspect.

An important question, of course, relating to both participant observation and the clinical perspective is how researchers scientifically validate what they have found. According to Schein (1987), the key for participant observers is replication—if another participant observer studies the same culture, will the conclusions be the same? On the other hand, for clinicians the key to validity is being able to predict the results of a given intervention—will this particular type of therapy help this patient?

In this section we examined four observational research strategies: case studies, naturalistic observation, participant observation, and the clinical perspective. Once you have decided which type of observational research you will conduct, then you will have to decide which behaviors to observe and how to record your observations.

Choosing Behaviors and Recording Techniques   It is one thing to say you are going to conduct an observational study, but it is another task to actually complete such a project. Just because the researcher does not manipulate the variables does not mean that a great deal of planning has not taken place. As is true with *any* research project, you must make several important decisions before beginning the project. Let's examine several of these decisions.

It seems simple enough to indicate that all behaviors will be observed; hence, everything of interest will be captured. Saying may be quite different from (and much easier than) doing, however. For example, observing and recording all behaviors may necessitate using video equipment, which may, in turn, make the observer identifiable. A participant observer with a video camera would probably not be especially effective. Likewise, had Anastasia Gibson and her colleagues (2000) used video equipment in their naturalistic study of glancing behavior at the ATM, their obvious presence could have influenced the behavior of their participants. Hence, they remained as inconspicuous as possible when they observed the customers.

Because they did not observe at exactly the same time each afternoon, Gibson et al. (2000) used a procedure known as time sampling. **Time sampling** involves making observations at different time periods in order to obtain a more representative sampling of the behavior of interest. The selection of time periods may be determined randomly or in a more systematic manner. Moreover, the use of time sampling may apply to the same or different participants. If you are observing a group of preschoolers, using the time-sampling technique will allow you to describe the behavior of interest over a wide range of times in the same children. However, using time sampling may purposely result in the observation of different participants and increase the generality of our observations. On the other hand, Gibson et al. did not make any nighttime observations; hence, their results may not apply to *all* times of day. In fact, they indicated that "It would be interesting to see whether or not proximity or glancing behavior are influenced by the amount of sunlight at hand" (Gibson et al., 2000, p. 151).

> **Time sampling** Making observations at different time periods.

It also is important to note that Gibson et al. (2000) observed customers at four different ATMs: two machines were located outside ("one outside a mall and one in an urban shopping area," p. 150) whereas "two indoor ATMs were inside discount department stores" (p. 150). Why did they make observations in these different locations? Had they limited their observations to one ATM in one location, they would not be able to generalize their results beyond that one machine to other ATMs. By observing four different ATMs, they used a technique known as situation sampling. **Situation sampling** involves observing the same behavior in several different situations. This technique offers the researcher two advantages: First, by sampling behavior in several different situations, you are able to determine whether the behavior in question changes as a function of the context in which you observed it. For example, a researcher might use situation sampling to determine if the amount of personal space we prefer differs from one culture to another or from one geographic area of a country to another.

> **Situation sampling** Observing the same behavior in different situations.

The second advantage of the situation sampling technique involves the fact that you are likely to observe different participants in the different situations. Because different individuals are observed, our ability to generalize any behavioral consistencies we notice across the various situations is increased. Because Gibson et al. (2000) made observations at four different ATMs and obtained the same results at each one, they could not attribute their findings to the customers at one specific machine.

Even if you have decided to time sample or situation sample, there is still another major decision you must make before you actually conduct your research project. You need to decide if you plan to present the results of your research project in a *qualitative* or *quantitative* manner. If you choose the *qualitative approach*, then your report will consist of a description of the behavior in question (a narrative record) and the conclusions prompted by this description. Such narrative records can be in the form of written or tape-recorded notes that you make during or after observing the behavior. Video recordings also are frequently made. If you write or tape-record notes after the behavior has occurred, you should record them as soon as possible. In all instances the language and terms used should be as clear and precise as possible; the observer should avoid making speculative comments.

Using More than One Observer: Interobserver Reliability   Another consideration we must deal with in the case of observational research is whether we will use one or more observers. As the good detective knows, there are two main reasons for using more than one observer: First, one observer may miss or overlook a bit of behavior, and second, there may be some disagreement concerning exactly what was seen and how it should be rated or categorized. More than one observer may be needed even when videotape is used to preserve the complete behavioral sequence; someone has to watch the videotape and rate or categorize the behavior contained there.

Interobserver reliability The extent to which observers agree.

When two individuals observe the same behavior, it is possible to see how well their observations agree. The extent to which the observers agree is called **interobserver reliability**. Low interobserver reliability indicates that the observers disagree about the behavior(s) they observed; high interobserver reliability indicates agreement. Such factors as fatigue, boredom, emotional and physical state, and experience can influence interobserver reliability. If both observers are well rested, interested in their task, and in good physical and emotional health, then high interobserver reliability should be obtained. An observer's physical, emotional, and attitudinal state can be detected and dealt with easily. Additionally, the need for training observers should be considered. The importance of thorough training, especially when observing complex and subtle behaviors, cannot be stressed too much. Such training should include clear, precise definitions of the behavior(s) to be observed. The trainer should provide concrete examples of positive and negative instances of the behavior in question—if at all possible.

Even if you follow all of these guidelines, it may be difficult to obtain high interobserver reliability. In some instances the problem may reside in the type of behavior being observed and how the observers code the behaviors. For example, think of how difficult it is for two observers to agree on (a) instances of "empathy," "shame," and "self-consciousness" in two-year-old children, (b) the difference between aggression and teasing in 10-year-olds, and (c) whether a 6-week-old infant has smiled. These examples point to the difficulty in obtaining and the importance of having interobserver reliability.

How can you measure interobserver reliability? A simple technique involves determining the number of agreements between the two observers and the number of opportunities the observers had to agree. Once these numbers have been determined, they are used in the following formula:

$$\frac{\text{No. of times observers agree}}{\text{No. of opportunities to agree}} \times 100 = \text{Percent of agreement}$$

The final calculation indicates the percentage of agreement.

What is a good measure of interobserver reliability? Although there are no rules to follow, a review of articles published in the two most recent issues of several journals indicated that all articles reporting interobserver reliability had at least 85% agreement.

Qualitative Research

Qualitative research
Research conducted in a natural setting that seeks to understand a complex human behavior by developing a complete narrative description of that behavior.

Almost since its inception, the nature of research has evolved and changed; it continues this evolution today. One of the newer forms of research is **qualitative research**. According to Creswell (1994), qualitative research "is defined as an inquiry process of understanding a social or human problem, based on building a complex, holistic picture, formed with words, reporting detailed views of informants, and conducted in a natural setting" (p. 2). The qualitative research style is much less formal and impersonal, and the reader of a qualitative research report can expect to find such additions as "definitions that evolved during a study" (Creswell, 1994, p. 7).

The observation that definitions might evolve or develop during a study suggests that the vocabulary of the qualitative researcher may be quite different from the vocabulary of the traditional experimental researcher. It is. In fact, qualitative researchers have developed a whole new language (Gubrium & Holstein, 1997). Most qualitative descriptions feature substantially less scientific jargon and the reader is likely to encounter more personal, even emotional, words. The qualitative researcher believes that a full description of human behavior includes people's *feelings* in addition to what they are doing and how they are doing it. If the participant is the final judge of what constitutes an accurate account or description of a situation, then personal terms will be the order of the day.

As Creswell's definition suggests, the qualitative researcher is committed to studying *particular* people in *specific* settings. This commitment favors the reporting of details as opposed to generalities and promotes a concern for the quality of life by the qualitative researcher. The definition also indicates that qualitative researchers place a premium on naturalism. If the researcher wants to answer the *what* and *how* questions about the behavior and interactions of people in their typical environment, then what better place to study people than in their natural environment?

The type of reasoning and logic used by qualitative researchers differs significantly from the reasoning and logic used by the typical experimental researcher. For years the accepted mode of reasoning has involved *deductive logic*, where hypotheses and theories spawn specific experiments designed to evaluate them. (However, as we noted in Chapters 1 and 2, Proctor and Capaldi, 2001, noted that a growing number of professionals do not believe that theory-driven research is the best option open to researchers.) Qualitative researchers prefer to use *inductive logic* where the data (information) provided by the participants is assimilated, and a pattern or theory to explain the phenomenon of interest emerges from this growing body of information.

The nature of the problem studied by qualitative research differs significantly from the typical experimental investigation. Unlike the experimental research problem, which likely will be associated with a significant amount of previously reported research, qualitative research deals with problems for which little or no information exists. It is the researcher's task to ferret out and delineate the relevant variables and determine how these variables are related to each other.

Unlike traditional hypothesis-testing research where the researcher develops a specific, rather narrowly focused experimental hypothesis, qualitative research begins with a more global question: These more global issues are frequently called *guiding hypotheses* (Marshall & Rossman, 1989). These guiding hypotheses are often followed by several subquestions that reflect specific, more narrowed aspects of the research project. It is important that none of these research questions, whether they are global or subquestions, constrain the researcher.

Data analytic procedures also differ greatly between traditional quantitative approaches and the newer qualitative research strategies. As we saw in Chapter 1, the time-honored procedure followed by generations of experimental researchers is to conduct the experiment (gather the research data), analyze the data, and then prepare a written report based on the results of the data analysis. To the contrary, qualitative researchers typically analyze their data "*simultaneously* with data collection, data interpretation, and narrative reporting writing" (Creswell, 1994, p. 153). This logic makes sense in view of the ever-developing nature of the qualitative research project: The categories of responses are forever emerging and changing and the nature of the explanation is forever being modified.

Correlational Studies

Correlational study
Determination of the relation between two variables.

In its basic form, a **correlational study** involves the measurement and determination of the relationship between two variables (hence the term *correlation*). In terms of control, empirical measurement, and statistical analysis, a correlational study is likely to be more rigorous.

Let's examine an example of correlational research. Scott Weaver, a student at the State University of New York—College at Plattsburg, and his faculty supervisor, Katherine Dunham, were interested in determining what factors correlated with (*predicted*) different types of youth violence. They administered several questionnaires, including a survey that measured the participant's history of violence, to a sample of 131 male and female college students. Once they gathered the data, they correlated such factors as parenting style, affective empathy, academic performance, and father presence during childhood and adolescence with the scores on the history of violence questionnaire. Their data revealed several interesting correlations. For example, participants whose fathers were present during adolescence reported fewer violent acts (a *negative* correlation). Such "predictors have the potential to contribute to the design of violence prevention and intervention programs" (Weaver & Dunham, 2002, p. 3).

Researchers use correlational studies when data on two variables are available but we can only measure, rather than manipulate, either variable. Although we can determine the degree of relation that exists between these two variables, we are not able to offer a cause-and-effect statement concerning these two variables.

Review Summary

1. **Descriptive research methods** are nonexperimental procedures for acquiring information. They do not involve the manipulation of variables.

2. Some researchers make use of archival and previously recorded sources of data. Although the use of such data avoids biasing participants' responses, this approach suffers from lack of generalizability, selective deposit, and selective survival.

3. Although observational techniques do not involve the direct manipulation of variables, they do allow the researcher to directly observe the behavior(s) of interest.

4. Case studies involve the intensive observation of a single participant over an extended period of time. They are often used in clinical settings.

5. **Naturalistic observation** involves directly observing behaviors in the natural environment. In these studies the observer should remain unobtrusive in order to avoid a **reactance** or **reactivity effect** on the part of the participants.

6. When the **participant observation** approach is used, the observer actually becomes a member of the group that is under study. An extensive time commitment may be required to conduct this type of study.

7. Because the observer may not be able to observe all behaviors at all times, decisions concerning which behaviors to observe, as well as when and where to observe them, must be made.

8. **Time sampling** involves making observations at different time periods, whereas **situation sampling** involves observing the same behavior(s) in several different situations.

9. The use of more than one observer may be desirable to avoid missing important observations and to help resolve disagreements concerning what was or was not observed. **Interobserver reliability** refers to the degree to which the observers agree.

10. **Qualitative research** is conducted in a natural setting. It seeks to understand a complex human behavior by developing a complete narrative description of that behavior.

11. A **correlational study** involves the measurement and determination of the relation between two variables.

CHECK YOUR PROGRESS

1. What is the reactance effect? How is it avoided by the use of archival sources of data?

2. "Selective deposit" is a problem associated with

   a. case studies

   b. naturalistic observation

   c. cause-and-effect research

   d. archival research

3. Matching

1. case study	A. behavior is observed in the real world
2. naturalistic observation	B. establishes a set of rules to assign symbols to events
3. Hawthorne effect	C. behavior of a single individual is observed over a lengthy period of time
4. participant observation	D. observing participants influences their behavior
5. measurement	E. experimenter joins the group being studied

4. Why are time sampling and situation sampling employed?

5. What is interobserver reliability? How is it calculated?

6. You decide to learn about a Pacific island culture by going to live there for a year. What approach does this exemplify?

   a. clinical perspective   b. ethnography

   c. grounded theory   d. ecological psychology

Ex Post Facto Studies

Can we conduct experimental research on variables that we cannot control or manipulate? Yes, we can conduct research on such variables but we must be cautious when drawing conclusions. When we work with IVs that we cannot or do not manipulate, we are conducting an **ex post facto study**. *Ex post facto* is a Latin phrase meaning "after the fact." When we conduct an ex post facto study, we are using an IV "after the fact"—it has already varied before we arrived on the scene. A great deal of detective work would seem to fall into this category. Because the experimenter has no control over administering the IV, let alone determining who receives this variable and under what conditions it is administered, the ex post facto study clearly qualifies as a descriptive research technique. However, it does have some properties in common with experimental methods.

> **Ex post facto study**
> The variable(s) to be studied are selected after they have occurred.

Let's look at an example of student research using an ex post facto approach. Carolyn Licht (2000), of Marymount Manhattan College in New York City, evaluated occupational stress as a function of sex of participant and whether the participants worked for a nonprofit or for profit organization. Her results showed "that employees perceive more occupational stress in nonprofit than in for-profit organizations," and that "men report more stress than women in most situations" (Licht, 2000, p. 46).

 What causes Licht's research to fall into the ex post facto category?

Because Licht had no control over sex of the participants and type of organization the participants worked for, these variables put this project in the ex post facto category. In the next section we will consider research employing surveys, questionnaires, tests, and inventories. Such research is quite popular.

Surveys, Questionnaires, Tests, and Inventories

Whether they are used in experimental or nonexperimental research, investigators frequently use surveys, questionnaires, tests, and inventories to assess attitudes, thoughts, and emotions or feelings. One reason surveys and questionnaires are popular is that they appear to be quite simple to conduct; when you want to know how a group of individuals feel about a particular issue, all you have to do is ask them or give them a test. As we will see, appearances can be quite deceptive; it is not as easy to use this technique as it appears. What type of instrument is best suited for our particular project? There are numerous choices available to us. We first consider surveys and questionnaires, then we turn our attention to tests and inventories.

Surveys and Questionnaires

Surveys typically request our opinion on some topic or issue that is of interest to the researcher. There are two basic types of surveys: descriptive and analytic. Although we will discuss these types separately, you should keep in mind that some surveys are designed to serve both purposes.

Types of Surveys The purpose of your research project will determine the type of survey you choose to administer. If you seek to determine what percentage of the population has a certain characteristic, holds a certain opinion, or engages in a particular behavior, then you will use a **descriptive survey**. The Gallup Polls, which evaluate voter preferences, and the Nielsen television ratings are examples of descriptive surveys. When a researcher uses this type of survey, there is no attempt to determine what the relevant variables are and how they may relate to the behavior in question. The end product is the description of a particular characteristic or behavior of a sample with the hope that this finding is representative of the population from which the sample was drawn.

Descriptive survey
Seeks to determine the percentage of the population that has a certain characteristic, holds a particular opinion, or engages in a particular behavior.

Analytic survey Seeks to determine the relevant variables and how they are related.

An **analytic survey** seeks to determine what the relevant variables are and how they might be related. For example, Amanda Gray, a student at Agnes Scott College in Decatur, Georgia, and her faculty supervisor, Jennifer Lucas, used the Subjective Impedence Scale (Novaco, Stokols, & Milanesi, 1990) to determine "automobile commuters' subjective perceptions of travel impedence and their driver stress" (Gray & Lucas, 2001, p. 79). They found that one of the key determinants of commuters' stress level is the *perception* of impedence, regardless of whether it actually occurred.

What about conducting research in areas where there are no readily available surveys? To address the issues you are interested in, you may have to construct your own survey. We *strongly* encourage you to exhaust every possibility before you attempt to construct your own survey. They look like they are easy to construct, but nothing could be farther from the truth.

If you have decided that the only option is to construct a survey, you will have to choose the questions for your analytic survey *very carefully* before the survey is administered. In fact, it will probably be necessary to do some pilot testing of the analytic survey before you use it in a full-scale investigation.

Pilot testing
Preliminary, exploratory testing that is done prior to the complete research project.

Pilot testing refers to any testing and evaluating that is done in advance of the complete research project. During this preliminary stage, a small number of participants are tested and the researcher may even use in-depth interviews to help determine the type of questions that should appear on the final survey instrument.

Developing a Good Survey or Questionnaire   A good survey or questionnaire, one that measures the attitudes and opinions of interest in an unbiased manner, cannot be developed overnight; considerable time and effort typically go into its construction.

TABLE	19-1	STEPS IN DEVELOPING A GOOD SURVEY OR QUESTIONNAIRE
Step 1		Decide what type of instrument to use. How will the information be gathered?
Step 2		Identify the types of questions to use.
Step 3		Write the items: They should be clear, short, and specific.
Step 4		Pilot-test and seek opinions from knowledgeable others.
Step 5		Determine the relevant demographic data to be collected.
Step 6		Determine administration procedures and develop instructions.

Once you have decided exactly what information your research project seeks to ascertain, there are several steps that you should follow in order to develop a good survey or questionnaire. These steps appear in Table 19-1.

The first step is to determine how the information you seek is to be obtained. Will you use a mail survey? Will your project involve the use of a questionnaire that is administered during a regular class session at your college or university? Will trained interviewers administer your questionnaire in person, or will a telephone interview be conducted? Decisions such as these will have a major impact on the type of survey or questionnaire you will develop.

Once you have made a decision concerning the type of instrument to be developed, you can give attention to the *nature* of the questions that you will use and the types of responses the participants will make to these questions. Among the types of questions that are frequently used in surveys and questionnaires are the following:

1. **Yes–No Questions.** The respondent answers "yes" or "no" to the items.
   EXAMPLE:
   The thought of death seldom enters my mind.
   (Source: Templer's Death Anxiety Scale; Templer, 1970.)

2. **Forced Alternative Questions.** The respondent has to select between two alternative responses.
   EXAMPLE:
   A. There are institutions in our society that have considerable control over me.
   B. Little in this world controls me. I usually do what I decide to do.
   (Source: Reid–Ware Three-Factor Locus of Control Scale; Reid & Ware, 1973.)

3. **Multiple-Choice Questions.** The respondent must select the most suitable response from among several alternatives.
   EXAMPLE:
   Compared to the average student:
   A. I give much more effort.
   B. I give an average amount of effort.
   C. I give less effort.
   (Source: Modified Jenkins Activity Scale; Krantz, Glass, & Snyder, 1974.)

4. **Likert-type Scales.** The individual answers a question by selecting a response alternative from a designated scale. A typical scale might be the following: (5) *strongly agree*, (4) *agree*, (3) *undecided*, (2) *disagree*, or (1) *strongly disagree*.

   EXAMPLE:

   I enjoy social gatherings just to be with people.

   A. not at all characteristic of me   B. not very characteristic of me
   C. slightly characteristic of me   D. fairly characteristic of me
   E. very much characteristic of me

   (Source: Texas Social Behavior Inventory; Helmreich & Stapp, 1974.)

5. **Open Ended Questions.** The respondent must construct her own answer to a question.

   EXAMPLE:

   How would you summarize your chief problems in your own words?

   (Source: Mooney Problem Check List; Mooney, 1950.)

Clearly, the questions you choose to use on your survey or questionnaire will directly influence the type of data you will gather and be able to analyze when your project is completed. If you choose the yes–no format, you will be able to calculate the frequency or percentage of such responses for each question. The use of a Likert-type scale allows you to calculate an average or mean response to each question. Should you choose to use open-ended questions, you will either have to decide how to code or quantify the responses or you will have to establish a procedure for preparing a summary description of each participant's answers.

The third step is to actually write the items for your survey or questionnaire. As a general rule, these questions should be clear, short, and specific; use familiar vocabulary; and be at the reading level of the individuals you intend to test. When preparing your items, you should avoid questions that might constrain the respondents' answers. For example, you might ask your participants to rate the effectiveness of the President of the United States in dealing with "crises." Assuming that the president has dealt with several crises, it may not be clear whether the question is referring to one particular type of crisis or another. Hence, the respondents will have to interpret the item as best they can; their interpretation may not coincide with your intended meaning. Also, researchers should avoid using questions that might bias the respondents' answers. A negatively worded question may result in a preponderance of negative answers, whereas a positively worded question may result in a preponderance of positive answers.

 Consider this yes–no question: "Do you agree that wealthy professional athletes are overpaid?" What is wrong with this question and how could you improve it?

By indicating that professional athletes are wealthy, you have created a mental set that suggests that they may be overpaid. Thus, your respondents may be biased to answer "yes." Also, using the word "agree" in the question may encourage yes answers.

If the researcher rewrites the question as follows, it is less likely to bias the respondents' answers: "Are professional athletes overpaid?"

The next step is to pilot test your survey or questionnaire. It is important to ask others, especially professionals who have expertise in your area of research interest, to review your items. They may be able to detect biases and unintended wordings that you had not considered. It will also be helpful, at this preliminary stage to administer your questionnaire to several individuals and then discuss the questions with them. Often there is nothing comparable to the insights of a participant who has actually completed a testing instrument. Such insights can be invaluable as you revise your questions. In fact, you may find it necessary to pretest and revise your survey in this manner several times before developing a final draft.

The fifth step involves a consideration of the other relevant information that you want your participants to provide. Frequently such information falls under the heading of **demographic data**, which may include such items as age, sex, annual income, size of community, academic major, and academic classification. For example, recall the research on sex differences in spatial task performance by Robyn Scali (Scali & Brownlow, 2001) that we considered in Chapter 1. "Because training and prior experience may have an effect on spatial ability, we assessed experience with art, math, sports, and similar tasks" (Scali & Brownlow, 2001, p. 6). Clearly, Scali and Brownlow were attentive to demographic needs.

> **Demographic data**
> Information about participants' characteristics such as age, sex, income, and academic major.

Although the need for this step may seem obvious, it is important to review these items carefully to ensure that you have not forgotten to request a vital bit of information. We cannot begin to tell you how many survey projects designed to evaluate male–female differences were less than successful because they failed to include an item that requested the participant's sex.

The final step is to clearly specify the procedures that will be followed when the survey or questionnaire is administered. If the survey is self-administering, what constitutes the printed instructions? Are they clear, concise, and easy to follow? Who will distribute and collect the informed consent forms and deal with questions that may arise? If your survey or questionnaire is not self-administering, then you must prepare an instruction script. The wording of this set of instructions must be clear and easily understood. Whether you present these instructions in a face-to-face interview, over the telephone, or in front of a large class of students, you (or the person giving them) must thoroughly practice and rehearse them. The researcher in charge of the project must be sure that all interviewers present the instructions in the same manner on all occasions. Likewise, questions raised by the participants must also be dealt with in a consistent manner.

As we saw, the final step in creating a good survey involves a determination of the administration procedures. Because these choices are crucial to the success of this type of research, we will examine the three basic options—mail surveys, personal interviews, and telephone interviews—in more detail.

Mail Surveys   Most likely, you have been asked to complete a survey you received in the mail. This popular technique is used to gather data on issues that range from our opinions on environmental problems to the type of food we purchase.

One advantage of sending surveys through the mail is that the researcher does not have to be present while the survey is being completed. Thus, surveys can be sent to a much larger number of participants than a single researcher could ever hope to contact in person.

Although it is possible to put a survey in the hands of a large number of respondents, there are several disadvantages associated with this research strategy: First, the researcher cannot be sure who actually completes the survey. Perhaps the intended respondent was too busy to complete the survey and asked a family member or friend to finish it. Hence, the time and trouble that was spent in creating a random sample from the population of interest may be severely jeopardized.

Even if the intended respondent completes the survey, there is no guarantee that the respondent answered the questions in the same order in which they appeared on the survey. If the order of answering questions is relevant to the project, then this drawback may be a major obstacle to the use of mail surveys.

The low return rate associated with the use of mail surveys highlights another problem. In addition to disappointment and frustration, low return rates suggest a potential bias in the researcher's sample. What type of individuals returned the surveys? How did they differ from those individuals who did not return the surveys? Were they the least (most) busy? Were they the least (most) opinionated? We really do not know, and as the response rate drops lower, the possibility of having a biased sample increases. What constitutes a good response rate to a mail survey? Because it is not uncommon to have a response rate of 25% to 30% for a mail survey, response rates of 50% and higher are considered to be quite acceptable.

Assume that you are planning to conduct a mail survey project. You are concerned about the possibility of having a low response rate and want to do everything to ensure the return of your surveys. What can you do to increase your response rate?

Researchers have developed several strategies designed to increase the response rates of mail surveys. Some of these techniques are:

1. The initial mailing should include a letter that clearly summarizes the nature and importance of the research project, how the respondents were selected, and the fact that all responses are confidential. You should include a prepaid envelope for the return of the completed survey.

2. It may be necessary to send an additional mailing(s) to your respondents. Because the original survey may have been misplaced or lost, it is important to include a replacement. One extra mailing may not be sufficient; you may find it necessary to send two or three requests before you achieve an acceptable response rate. These extra mailings are typically sent at two- to three-week intervals.

Not all researchers endorse the use of mail surveys. Low response rates, incomplete surveys, and unclear answers are among the reasons that cause some researchers to use direct interviews to obtain data. These interviews may be done in person or over the telephone.

Personal Interviews   When a trained interviewer administers a survey in a respondent's home, the response rate climbs dramatically. It is not uncommon to have a 90% completion rate under these circumstances. In addition to simply increasing the response rate, the trained interviewer is able to cut down on the number of unusable surveys by clarifying ambiguous questions, making sure that all questions are answered in the proper sequence, and generally assisting with any problems that the respondents may experience.

Although this technique offers some advantages when compared to the mail survey, there are drawbacks. First, the potential for considerable expenditure of time and money exists. Time has to be devoted to the training of the interviewers. Once trained, they will have to be paid for their time on the job. Second, the fact that an individual is administering the survey introduces the possibility of interviewer bias. Some interviewers may present some questions in a more positive (or negative) manner than do other interviewers. Only careful and extensive training of all interviewers to present all items in a consistent, neutral manner can overcome this potential difficulty. Finally, the prospect of administering surveys in the home is becoming less appealing and feasible. In many instances no one is at home during the day, and an increasing number of people are not willing to sacrifice their leisure evening hours to complete a survey. Additionally, the high crime rates in many urban areas have served to discourage face-to-face interviewing. In its place many investigators have turned to telephone interviewing.

Telephone Interviews   In addition to overcoming several of the problems associated with personal interviews and mail surveys, telephone interviewing offers several other advantages. For example, the development of random-digit dialing allows researchers to establish a random sample with ease: The desired number of calls is specified and the computer does the rest. It is noteworthy that a random sample generated in this manner will contain both listed and unlisted telephone numbers because the digits in each number are selected randomly. With over 95% of all households in the United States currently having telephones, previous concerns about creating a biased sample consisting of only households having telephones seem largely unfounded.

Computer technology has increased the desirability of conducting telephone interviews in other ways. For example, it is now possible to enter the participant's responses directly as they are being made. Hence, the data are stored directly in the computer and are ready for analysis at any time.

Despite these apparent advantages, telephone interviews do have potential drawbacks. Even though technology has assisted telephone researchers, it also has provided an obstacle. Many households are now equipped with answering machines or caller ID that allow incoming calls to be screened. Hence, potential respondents may be lost because they refused to answer the phone. Even if the call is answered, it is easier to say "no" to an unseen interviewer on the telephone than to a person at your front door. These two situations lower the response rate and raise the possibility of a biased sample.

The use of the telephone also prohibits the use of visual aids that might serve to clarify certain questions. Because the telephone interviewer cannot see the respondent, it is not possible to evaluate nonverbal cues such as facial expressions, gestures, and posture. Such cues might suggest that a certain question was not completely understood or that an answer is in need of clarification.

Not being in face-to-face contact with the respondent also makes it more difficult to establish rapport. Hence, telephone respondents may not be as willing to participate in the survey. This potential lack of willingness has led to the use of shorter survey instruments.

Although surveys and questionnaires are popular research tools with many investigators, there are other ways to gather data. Since the late 1800s, when Sir Francis Galton (1822–1911) attempted to evaluate people's ability or intelligence by measuring physical attributes such as reaction time or visual acuity, psychologists have developed a large number of tests and inventories for a wide variety of purposes.

Tests and Inventories

Unlike surveys and questionnaires, which are designed to evaluate opinions on some topic or issue, tests and inventories are designed to assess a specific attribute, ability, or characteristic possessed by the individual being tested. In this section we look at the characteristics of good tests and inventories and then discuss three general types of tests and inventories: achievement, aptitude, and personality.

Characteristics of Good Tests and Inventories   Unlike surveys and questionnaires, the researcher is less likely to be directly involved with the development of a test or inventory. Because their development and pilot testing has already taken place, you will need to scrutinize the reports concerning the development of each test or inventory you are considering. A good test or inventory should possess two characteristics: It should be valid and it should be reliable.

Validity The extent to which a test or inventory measures what it is supposed to measure.

Validity   A test or inventory has **validity** when it actually measures what it is supposed to measure. If your research calls for a test that measures spelling achievement, you want the instrument you select to measure that ability, not another accomplishment such as mathematical proficiency.

Content validity The extent to which test items actually represent the type of material they are supposed to.

There are several ways to establish the validity of a test or inventory. **Content validity** indicates that the test items actually represent the type of material they are supposed to. A panel of expert judges is often used to assess the content validity of test items. Although the more subjective evaluation of such judges may not lend itself to a great deal of quantification, their degree of agreement, known as **interrater reliability**, can be calculated. Interrater reliability is similar to interobserver reliability. The main difference is that interrater reliability measures agreement between judgments concerning a test item, whereas interobserver reliability measures agreement between observations of behavior.

Interrater reliability Degree of agreement among judges concerning the content validity of test or inventory items.

Concurrent validity Degree to which the score on a test or inventory corresponds with another measure of the designated trait.

We can establish **concurrent validity** when we already have another measure of the desired trait or outcome and can compare the score on the test or inventory under consideration with this other measure. For example, the scores made by a group of patients on a test designed to measure aggression might be compared with a diagnosis of their aggressive tendencies made by a clinical psychologist. If the test and the clinical psychologist rate the aggressiveness of the patients in a similar manner, then concurrent validity for the test has been established. Often our second measure may not be immediately accessible. When the test score is to be compared with an outcome that will occur in the future, the researcher is attempting to establish the **criterion validity** of the test. Thus, criterion validity refers to the ability of the test or inventory to predict the outcome or criterion. For example, it is the desired outcome that the SAT and ACT predict first-semester performance in college. To the extent that these tests are successful at predicting first-semester GPAs, their criterion validity has been established.

Criterion validity Is established by comparing the score on a test or inventory with a future score on another test or inventory.

Reliability   Once we have determined that a particular test is valid, we also want to make sure that it is reliable. **Reliability** refers to the extent that the test or inventory is consistent in its evaluation of the same individuals over repeated administrations. For example, if we have developed a test to measure aptitude for social work, we would want individuals who score high (or low) on our test on its first administration to make essentially the same score when they take the test again. The greater the similarity between scores produced by the same individuals on repeated administrations, the greater the reliability of the test or inventory.

Reliability Extent to which a test or inventory is consistent in its evaluation of the same individuals.

Reliability is typically assessed through the test-retest or split-half procedures. When the **test–retest procedure** is used, the test is simply given a second time and the scores from the two tests are compared; the greater the similarity, the higher the reliability.

Test–retest procedure Determination of reliability by repeatedly administering a test to the same participants.

On the surface, the test–retest procedure appears to be quite straightforward and reasonable. However, there may be a problem with establishing reliability in this manner. What is it?

The main problem with the test-retest procedure concerns the fact that the participants are repeatedly administered the same test or inventory. Having already taken the test or inventory may result in the individuals remembering the questions and answers the next time the instrument is administered. Therefore, their answers may be biased by the previous administration. If a lengthy time period elapses between administrations, the participants might forget the questions and answers and this familiarity problem might be overcome. However, this lengthy time period may influence reliability in yet another manner. An extended time period allows the participants to have numerous experiences and learning opportunities between administrations. These experiences, called *history effects* (see Chapter 5) may influence their scores when the test or inventory is given again. Hence, the reliability measure may become influenced by the experiences that intervened between the two testing sessions.

Split-half technique
Determination of reliability by dividing the test or inventory into two subtests and then comparing the scores made on the two halves.

It is possible to overcome the problems of test familiarity and lengthy time periods separating administrations by using the split-half approach. The **split-half technique** of establishing reliability involves dividing a test or inventory into two halves or subtests and then administering them to the same individuals on different occasions or by administering the entire test and then splitting it into two halves. Because the questions that comprise the two subtests were drawn from the same test, it is assumed that they are highly related to each other if the test is reliable. Typically, the questions that comprise these two subtests are selected randomly or in some predetermined manner, such as odd–even. The higher the degree of correspondence between scores on the two subtests, the greater the reliability of the overall test from which they were selected.

Having determined that a test or inventory should be valid and reliable, we now examine several types of these instruments that are currently used for research and predictive purposes.

Achievement test
Designed to evaluate an individual's level of mastery or competence.

Types of Tests and Inventories   **Achievement** tests are given when an evaluation of an individual's level of mastery or competence is desired. For example, doctors must pass a series of state medical board examinations before they are allowed to practice medicine and lawyers must pass the state bar examination before they are allowed to practice law. The score that distinguishes passing from failing determines the minimum level of achievement that must be attained. You can probably think of many achievement tests you have taken during your life.

Aptitude test Designed to assess an individual's potential ability or skill in a particular job.

At many colleges and universities, the counseling center or career development office offers students the opportunity to take an aptitude test to assist them in selecting a major or making a career choice. An **aptitude test** is used to assess an individual's ability or skill in a particular situation or job. For example, the Purdue Pegboard Test is often administered to determine one's aptitude for jobs that require manual dexterity. According to Anastasi (1988), "This test provides a measure of two types of activity, one requiring gross movements of hands, fingers, and arms, and the other involving tip-of-the-finger dexterity needed in small assembly work" (p. 461). Similarly, if you are planning to attend graduate school, you will probably be required to take the GRE. For most graduate schools, the two most important scores on the GRE are those of the verbal and quantitative subtests. These scores are used as measures of your aptitude to successfully complete verbal and quantitative courses on the graduate level.

Personality test or **inventory** Measures a specific aspect of the individual's motivational state, interpersonal capability, or personality.

The **personality test** or **inventory** measures a specific aspect of an individual's motivational state, interpersonal capability, or personality (Anastasi & Urbina, 1997). The use of a personality inventory in research is exemplified by a project reported by Dana Bodner and C. D. Cochran, students at Stetson University in DeLand, Florida, and their faculty advisor, Toni Blum (Bodner, Cochran, & Blum, 2000). The purpose of this study was to validate a scale, the General Unique Invulnerability Scale (GUI), which measures general optimism about unique invulnerability (the belief that you will not experience negative events or misfortunes). These researchers administered the GUI to a sample of 40 skydivers and a sample of 40 college students and found that skydivers had higher GUI scores than did the college students. It is not surprising that skydivers would have stronger belief in unique invulnerability than the typical college student who does not engage in this risky behavior.

REVIEW SUMMARY

1. In an **ex post facto** study the variables have been experienced before they are examined by the researcher; thus, control and manipulation of variables cannot be accomplished.

2. Surveys, questionnaires, tests, and inventories are used to assess attitudes, thoughts, and emotions or feelings.

3. **Descriptive surveys** seek to determine the percentage of a population that has a certain characteristic, holds a certain opinion, or engages in a particular behavior. **Analytic surveys** seek to determine the variables that are relevant in a situation and their relation.

4. The steps to be completed in developing a good survey or questionnaire include considering the types of instrument to be developed, determining the types of questions to be used, writing the items, pilot testing, determining the relevant demographic data to be collected, and deciding on administration procedures.

5. **Demographic data** include relevant information, such as gender, age, income, and educational level, about the participants.

6. Mail surveys can be sent to a large number of potential respondents. However, the researcher cannot be sure who actually completed the survey or in what order they completed the questions. Low response rates for mail surveys can be dealt with by stressing the importance of the project and by sending additional mailings.

7. Personal interviews yield a higher rate of completed surveys but are costly in terms of time and money. The increase in the number of working families and the escalating crime rate in urban areas have made the use of personal interviews less desirable.

8. Telephone interviews allow the researcher to reach a large number of respondents more efficiently than personal interviews and mail surveys. However, answering machines and the inability to see nonverbal cues are drawbacks to this approach.

9. Tests and inventories should be **valid** (measure what they are supposed to measure) and **reliable** (consistent in their evaluation).

10. Validity may be established by the **content, concurrent**, and **criterion** methods.

11. The **test–retest** and **split-half** procedures are used to establish reliability.

12. **Achievement tests** evaluate level of mastery or competence. **Aptitude tests** assess an individual's ability or skill in a particular situation or job. A **personality test** or **inventory** measures a specific aspect of the individual's motivational state, interpersonal capability, or personality.

CHECK YOUR PROGRESS

1. Matching

   1. descriptive survey   A. affects ability to predict the outcome
   2. analytic survey   B. may include age, sex, and annual income
   3. pilot testing   C. indicates the percentage having a certain characteristic
   4. demographic data   D. compares scores on two separate measures
   5. concurrent validity   E. tries to determine what the relevant variables are
   6. criterion validity   F. does testing or evaluating in advance of the complete research project

2. Describe the steps involved in creating a good survey.
3. How can the low return rate of mail surveys be improved?
4. Why is the use of personal interviews declining?
5. Distinguish between achievement and aptitude tests.

KEY TERMS

Descriptive research methods, *461*

Case study, *463*

Naturalistic observation, *463*

Reactance or reactivity effect, *464*

Hawthorne effect, *464*

Participant observation, *465*

Ethnography, *466*

Clinical perspective, *467*

Time sampling, *468*

Situation sampling, *468*

Interobserver reliability, *469*

Qualitative research, *470*

Correlational study, *471*

Ex post facto study, *473*

Descriptive survey, *474*

Analytic survey, *475*

Pilot testing, *475*

Demographic data, *478*

Validity, *481*

Content validity, *481*

Interrater reliability, *481*

Concurrent validity, *481*

Criterion validity, *482*

Reliability, *482*

Test–retest procedure, *482*

Split-half technique, *483*

Achievement test, *483*

Aptitude test, *483*

Personality test or inventory, *483*

LOOKING AHEAD

At this point, you may have finished planning, conducting, and analyzing your own research project. Still one task lies ahead—writing the research report, which is the culmination of your research effort. In the next chapter, we will cover how researchers write their reports in APA style. We will also learn from a student author, who has published two articles, what the publication process is like.

Writing, Assembling, and Publishing an APA-Format Research Report

The final step in the scientific process is communicating your results to other people who are interested in your research topic. As you have seen in numerous police shows, detectives also have to spend time writing their reports. Their purpose is no different from ours—communicating to a particular audience what has happened. Sherlock Holmes knew the importance of communicating clearly when he said to Watson, "Never trust to general impressions, my boy, but concentrate yourself upon details" (Doyle, 1927, p. 197). We have hinted at writing and organizing various parts of a manuscript in APA format throughout several chapters of this book. In this chapter we will cover all the aspects of writing a research report in APA format. We will use a student research project as our example, tracing it from the research through the manuscript preparation to publication. In this chapter, we will carefully examine Allison Dickson, James Morris, and Keri Cass's (2001) research project concerning the effects of race of performer and type of music on ratings of a musical performer. Dickson, Morris, and Cass were students at Southwestern University, Georgetown, Texas, and Traci Giuliano was their supervising professor. We include this research as an example not to intimidate you, but to show you what is possible at the undergraduate level to complete a research project and then publish its results.

What Is APA Format?

Although several styles exist for the preparation of reports in various academic disciplines, psychologists developed their own format to meet their specific needs. Because the APA originally developed this style, it is often referred to as **APA format**. In Chapter 1 we saw that in the 1920s, University of Wisconsin psychologist Joseph Jastrow found a need to bring uniformity to the publication of research articles in our field. The lack of a set model or pattern had resulted in published research reports that were nearly impossible to compare. In addition to the fact that there was no prescribed order for the presentation of information, there also was no consistent manner for describing one's methodology, procedure, or data analysis. In short, the order and manner of presentation varied from one article to the next. The development of the APA format for preparing papers was an attempt to bring order to this state of chaos.

> **APA format** Accepted APA form for preparing reports of psychological research.

The particular form for preparing APA format papers is found in the fifth edition of the *Publication Manual of the American Psychological Association* (American Psychological Association, 2001). The APA *Publication Manual* (*PM*) has changed and evolved since it was first published in 1952. Many of the changes that have occurred over the years, as well as much of the actual format itself, were implemented to assist printers—after all, APA format was adopted to help make the publication of journal articles more uniform. Although many earlier APA format topics had the printer in mind, the latest edition of the *PM* clearly shows the influence and importance of the computer. For example, the earlier requirement of large $1\frac{1}{2}$-inch margins has been replaced by more computer-friendly 1-inch margins. Likewise, the reference section has reverted back to hanging indentations (the first line begins at the margin and subsequent lines are indented) from the third edition because computers and word processing programs can easily deal with hanging indents. In addition to being computer friendly, the general layout and

Headings Titles for various sections of a psychology paper designed to help the reader understand the outline and importance of parts of the paper.

design of the APA format paper are reader friendly. For example, using separate, specifically designated sections allows the reader to know exactly which part of the project is being dealt with. Authors use **headings** to divide the APA format paper into sections and to help the reader understand the paper's organization.

However, before we get started, we need to make an important point: This chapter is not meant to substitute for the *PM*. There is simply no way for us to condense a 439-page book into a single chapter for this text. You should buy a *PM* and think of it as an investment in your future. As well as using it in this class, you will use it when you write term papers in other psychology classes and for any writing you will do if you go to graduate school in psychology. In addition, other academic disciplines are beginning to adopt APA style for their writing assignments. One of your authors has had colleagues in education, political science, and communication disorders borrow his *PM* for pointers on formatting and style.

Sections of the APA Format Paper

The major components of an APA format paper are, in order:

1. Title page
2. Abstract
3. Introduction
4. Method section
5. Results section
6. Discussion section
7. References
8. Appendixes (if any)
9. Author note
10. Tables (if any)
11. Figures (if any)

As we look at the various sections of the APA format paper, we will refer to the Dickson, Giuliano, Morris, and Cass manuscript as an example (Figures 20-1 through 20-16; *M* indicates manuscript and the number after *M* represents page order). In addition, you can refer to the published article (Dickson, Giuliano, Morris, & Cass, 2001) displayed in Figures 20-17 through 20-21 (*JA* indicates journal article) to see how a submitted manuscript is formatted as a journal article. (After our initial citation, the correct format for citing this manuscript is Dickson et al., 2001; we will refer to it using only Dickson's name in order to conserve space.)

Title page The first page of an APA format paper. It includes the manuscript page header, the running head, the manuscript's title, and the name(s) of the author(s) and their affiliation(s).

Manuscript page header The first two or three words of the report's title. Appears with the page number on each page of the research report.

Title Page

The **title page** of Dickson's manuscript appears in Figure 20-1. The *PM* contains information about the title page on pages 10–12 and 296–298. The important features are the manuscript page header, page number, running head, author(s), and affiliation(s). The **manuscript page header** consists of the first two or three words

Eminem Versus Charley   1

Running head: RACE, STEREOTYPES, AND PERCEPTIONS OF PERFORMERS

Eminem Versus Charley Pride: Race, Stereotypes, and

Perceptions of Rap and Country Music Performers

Allison J. Dickson, Traci A. Giuliano, James C. Morris, and Keri L. Cass

Southwestern University

FIGURE 20-1 (M1). TITLE PAGE.

of the title and is used to identify pages of a particular manuscript should they become separated. It appears in the upper right-hand portion of each page, two lines above the 1-inch margin. The page header appears either five spaces to the left of the page number or two lines above the page number. Neither the page number nor the page header should extend beyond the margin on the right side of the page. The manuscript page header and page number appear on *all* pages of the paper, *except* the figures.

Two lines below the manuscript page header, flush against the left margin, we find the **running head**. The running head is a condensed title that will be printed at the top of alternate pages when your paper is published in a journal. When you type the running head on the title page, it is in all-capital letters. Also, note that the *h* in running head is not capitalized. The running head "should be a maximum of 50 characters, including letters, punctuation, and spaces between words" (APA *Publication Manual*, 2001, p. 12). As you can see in Figure 20-1, Dickson used different phrases for her manuscript page header and the running head. Although the same phrase might be a logical choice for both elements, APA style does not specify that they should be identical. The manuscript page header may not make sense, but the running head should communicate information about the contents of your manuscript because it would actually be printed with a published article (see Figure 20-18).

Running head
A condensed title that is printed at the top of alternate pages of a published article.

The title of the paper, which is centered, may begin six or eight lines below the page number. Capitalize the first word and all major words of the title. Your title should summarize clearly and simply the nature of the research you are reporting, but it should not be overly long. APA's recommended length for the title is 10 to 12 words. If your title is too long to fit on one line then you can type it on two lines. You should be especially careful when you choose a title for your paper. Although it is often tempting to compose a title that is cute or catchy, such titles are often failures at communicating anything about the article's content. Keep in mind that many people will read your title and will use it to decide whether to read the entire paper. Dickson's title is slightly longer than APA's guideline; the subtitle fully communicates that the paper deals with the variables of race, stereotypes, and perceptions of musical performers. Her title is slightly longer than the recommended length because of the four-word "main" title—although it does not communicate much about the content of the article it is certainly attention-getting. Your instructor (or journal editor) may give you some leeway with the 10 to 12 word recommendation, as in this case.

The name of the author is double-spaced below the title. The author's institutional affiliation is double-spaced below the author's name. If there is more than one author, the authors' names appear in order of importance of their contributions to the research project. If authors are from the same institution, all the names are on one line, if they will fit. Dickson's final manuscript included an additional author. The project was a group effort by Dickson, Morris, and Cass for their research methods course, so they were the original authors. Giuliano was the professor of the class and helped them develop their ideas, supervised the research project, assisted in the statistical analysis and interpretation, and participated with Dickson in cowriting the manuscript for submission after the class was finished. Morris and Cass did not participate in rewriting the manuscript after the class. Thus, although the research originated as a student group project, by the time it was published it had become a team effort among three students and a faculty member. Sometimes it is difficult to decide whether an individual merits being listed as an author on a publication. According to the *PM*, "Authorship encompasses not only those who do the actual writing but also those who have made substantial scientific contributions to a study" (APA, 2001, p. 6). This guideline is somewhat vague and results in people having to make "judgment calls" about authorship.

Abstract

> **Level 1 heading** A centered section title in which the first letters of major words are capitalized. Occupies a line by itself.

Figure 20-2 shows the abstract page. Note, once again, the placement of the manuscript page header and page number. The word "Abstract" is centered and appears two lines below the page number. (A centered section title in which the first letters of major words are capitalized is designated as a **Level 1 heading**. Remember that headings help to demarcate sections of the APA format paper. A full section explaining different levels of headings appears on p. 519.)

Imagine that you have just picked up a journal issue and are skimming through the journal to see if you might be interested in reading this or that article. What feature of the article will you use as a guide when deciding whether to read a particular article in its entirety? What information would you use when making this decision?

Of course, the title of this section answers the first question: You will use the abstract as a guide to determine whether you want to read the complete article. The

Eminem Versus Charley   2

Abstract

The present study explored the effects of stereotype deviation in the music industry on people's perceptions of performers. One hundred college students (48 men, 52 women) examined a profile of a fictitious performer containing a picture, a brief biography, and a lyric sample. As part of a 2-way between-subjects design, participants made judgments about either a Black or a White musician who performed either rap or country music. The results showed that a Black rap performer was rated more favorably than a Black country performer, and a White country performer was rated more favorably than a White rap performer. Consistent with predictions, people who violate societal expectations are judged more harshly than are people who conform to societal expectations, particularly in cases involving strong preexisting racial stereotypes.

FIGURE 20-2 (M2). ABSTRACT.

> **Abstract** A brief description of the research that is presented in an APA format paper.

abstract of an experimental report consists of a brief (up to 120 words), one-paragraph description of the research presented in your paper. In order to help you make an educated decision about pursuing an article in depth, the paragraph that comprises the abstract should include a description of the intent and conduct (including participants and method) of your project, the results you obtained, and the project's implications or applications. Also, it is important to note that the abstract is typed in block form; there is no indentation on the first line.

The *PM* states that an abstract for an experimental study should contain information about the problem, participants, experimental method, findings, and conclusions.

Can you find information about each of the five topics (problem, participants, method, findings, conclusion) in the Abstract in Figure 20-2?

Here's where we found the relevant information:

Problem—line 1

Participants—line 2

Experimental Method—lines 2–5

Findings—lines 5–6

Conclusions—lines 6–8

Did you find all the necessary information? Writing a good abstract is challenging because of the large amount of information that must be covered in so little space. You can find more information about abstracts on pages 12–15 and 298 of the *PM*.

Introduction

Introduction The first major section of the APA format paper. Contains the thesis statement, review of relevant literature, and experimental hypothesis.

Your **introduction** section begins on page 3 of your report. Notice that the word "Introduction" does not appear as the Level 1 heading that begins this section. Rather, you repeat the title from page 1. Be sure that the title is *exactly* the same in both places. Figure 20-3 shows the first page of Dickson's introduction section. Figure 20-4 shows the second page of the introduction. The concluding page of the introduction section appears in Figure 20-5.

We like to use the analogy of a funnel to describe a good introduction section. Like the introduction, a funnel starts off broad, then narrows to a specific focus. At the end the focus is very specific and, in the case of the introduction section, leads to a logical experimental question: Your experiment. In Dickson's example, the first paragraph is broad, establishing the race and genre of musicians as the variables of interest. The second and third paragraphs provide basic background information about racial stereotypes. The fourth and fifth paragraphs begin to narrow the funnel. Here, you read about some specific effects of stereotypes and race associated with music, as well as the effects of stereotype inconsistencies. Finally, the last paragraph lays out the specific experimental hypothesis of this research.

 PSYCHOLOGICAL DETECTIVE   Can you identify the thesis statement in Dickson's introduction?

Thesis statement A statement of the general research topic of interest and the perceived relation of the relevant variables in that area.

The first sentence on page 5 (Figure 20-5) forms the thesis statement for Dickson's manuscript. The **thesis statement** should indicate the general topic in which you are interested and your general view of the relation of the relevant variables in that area. Beginning with "we expected that," you see the specific predictions made for the performance of participants rating musical artists under stereotype-consistent conditions compared to stereotype-inconsistent conditions. Some writers prefer to present the thesis statement in the opening paragraph of the introduction. The exact location is not important, as long as you include your thesis statement somewhere in the introduction. The *PM* provides more information concerning introductions on pages 15–17.

Other than presenting the thesis statement, the introduction serves to report the results of previous research that support or refute your thesis statement. This material represents the outcome of your literature review. Give careful thought to its presentation; good organization and a logical flow of ideas are important ingredients. The introduction is similar to telling a story to someone who may not be familiar with what you are talking about; you must be clear and not make unwarranted assumptions.

Eminem Versus Charley Pride: Race, Stereotypes, and

Perceptions of Rap and Country Music Performers

What do Eminem and Charley Pride have in common? Perhaps the connection these two performers share is subtle, but they are in fact quite similar in at least one aspect of their careers. Both Charley Pride, a Black country music performer, and Eminem, a White rap performer, deviate from social expectations that are a part of the music industry. Specifically, these two musicians defy cultural stereotypes by performing types of music that are not typically associated with their race.

Racial stereotypes exist in most individuals, and they can influence subsequent judgments made by a perceiver (Devine, 1989; Dovidio, Evans, & Tyler, 1986; Gaertner & McLaughlin, 1983). For example, Gaertner and McLaughlin (1983) studied the effect of racial stereotypes on perceptions and found that White students responded faster to positive stereotyped words (e.g., *smart*) when the words followed the race *White* rather than *Black*. In addition, Sagar and Schofield (1980) examined the perceptions made by sixth-grade boys about ambiguous behavior. They found that both Black and White boys construed ambiguously aggressive behaviors (such as one child bumping into another) as being more threatening if the actions were performed by a Black boy rather than a White boy. Most people today would not be likely to openly express racist beliefs, but the results of the above studies support the aversive racism perspective, which suggests that subtle and indirect forms of racism persist in society today (Dovidio & Gaertner, 1991; Gaertner & Dovidio, 1986). That is, although current cultural values emphasize fairness and racial equality, White individuals have a historic tradition of having negative beliefs concerning Blacks and other minority groups (Dovidio, Brigham, Johnson, & Gaertner, 1996). Consequently, racial stereotypes continue to exist and to influence interactions among individuals in society, but perhaps in more subtle ways.

Because stereotypes can influence the judgments and behaviors of perceivers, deviations from a stereotype should have similar effects. In general, the expectations of the perceiver and the extent to which these expectations are confirmed or disconfirmed can influence judgments. When behavior only slightly varies from expectations, the difference might not be noticed, but perceivers often magnify the discrepancy when actions differ significantly from expectations. This phenomenon is known as the contrast effect (Brehm, Kassin, & Fein, 1999). In fact, a person who displays behavior inconsistent with societal expectations is often evaluated more extremely than is a person who

FIGURE 20-3 (M3). FIRST PAGE OF INTRODUCTION.

behaves consistently with expectations (Knight, Giuliano, & Sanchez-Ross, 2001). Jackson, Sullivan, and Hodge (1993) examined the effects of describing stereotype-consistent or stereotype-inconsistent behavior of Black out-group targets and White in-group targets on social evaluations made by participants who assessed a college application. They found that people who deviate from a norm are judged more extremely than if they behave as the norm dictates. Specifically, stereotype-inconsistent Black applicants with strong credentials were evaluated more favorably than were strong White applicants, and stereotype-inconsistent White applicants with weak credentials were evaluated less favorably than were weak Black applicants.

Both stereotypes and stereotype-inconsistent behavior affect the evaluations individuals make about other people in a variety of social interactions. Fried (1996, 1999) studied biased reactions involving the music industry and found that individuals had very different reactions to music labeled as *rap* or *country* despite the fact that the song lyrics were exactly the same. In two studies, she found that people generally considered rap music to be more violent and more offensive than country music. Furthermore, a folk song that was presented as being performed by a Black artist was judged more negatively than the very same song when it was presented as being performed by a White artist (Fried, 1996). Fried (1999) attributed her results to stereotypes in that rap is usually associated with Black culture whereas country music is often thought of as being a part of White culture. By priming a Black stereotype with the use of the label *rap*, it is possible that individuals apply negative stereotypes that have been shown to be associated with African Americans (Brigham, 1971). Therefore, racial stereotypes can impact evaluations of music performers (Fried, 1996, 1999).

According to Fiske and Taylor (1991), long-held stereotypes are not easily altered, but modification of stereotypes may begin with a divergence by stereotyped individuals or groups. Previous research has examined the effects of stereotypes and stereotype deviation on people's evaluations of other individuals (Jackson et al., 1993; Knight et al., 2001). The present study attempted to integrate and expand on these concepts in relation to the music industry. Specifically, whereas Fried (1996, 1999) examined the effect of either the race of the performer or the -labeled genre of music of a song on evaluations about the music itself, the design of the present experiment explored the interactive effects of the race of the performer and the genre of music on participants' evaluations of the performer. In doing so, we explored the difference between perceptions of persons who adhere to social expectations versus persons who deviate from the stereotype.

FIGURE 20-4 (M4). SECOND PAGE OF INTRODUCTION.

Eminem Versus Charley   5

Consistent with previous research (Jackson et al., 1993; Knight et al., 2001), we expected that participants would judge performers who behave consistently with social norms (i.e., Black rap artists and White country performers) more favorably than performers who deviate from societal expectations (i.e., White rap artists and Black country performers). That is, because country music is associated with White culture, a Black country performer does not exhibit behavior consistent with this stereotype and, as a result, this performer should elicit negative judgments. The same reaction should occur with a White rap artist because his or her behavior is inconsistent with the stereotype that rap is predominantly a part of Black culture.

Method

Participants

Data were collected from 100 undergraduates (48 men, 52 women) at Southwestern University, a small liberal arts college in the Southwest. Demographically, the university is composed primarily of White, middle- to upper middle-class students; as such, the current sample (which was representative of the campus at large) consisted almost exclusively of White students. Participant volunteers ranged in age from 18 to 26 years ($M = 19.77$ years). Data from four participants were excluded from the analysis because these participants either failed to follow instructions or they did not pass the manipulation check. Specifically, these participants were unable to identify the race of the performer and genre of his music that was presented in the their survey packet.

Design and Procedure

The present study used a 2 (race of performer: Black or White) x 2 (genre of music: rap or country) between-subjects design to explore the effect of the race of a performer and the genre of music on perceptions of the performer. We recruited participants from various locations on campus and asked them to contribute to an investigation exploring "people's perceptions of music." Once they agreed, participants viewed a picture of a male performer, read a brief biography about him, and read a lyric sample of his music. Next, they completed a survey in which they made judgments about the performer and his music, and they responded to filler questions concerning their taste in music in general to corroborate the cover story. Each participant was randomly assigned to one of four experimental conditions and read a profile of either a Black rap artist, a White rap artist, a Black country performer, or a White country performer. Measures of the primary dependent variable (i.e., how favorably participants rated the performers) were embedded among filler questions in the survey. Following completion of the survey and a brief

FIGURE 20-5 (M5). LAST PAGE OF INTRODUCTION; FIRST TWO METHOD SUBSECTIONS.

Citation A notation in text that a particular reference was used. The citation provides the name(s) of the author(s) and date of the work's publication.

Reference A full bibliographic record of any work cited in the text of a psychological paper.

Reference section A complete listing of all the references cited in a psychological paper.

First you establish the big picture. Then you begin to fill in the details. Your ultimate goal is to lead the reader to a description of what you plan to do in your experiment. This description usually appears at the end of the introduction section. It is here that you will state your experimental hypothesis.

Although we cannot teach you *how* to write in the limited space available, we can give you a few pointers that will assist you as you prepare your introduction section. Note that every fact-based statement is supported by a **citation** to a **reference**. If you wish to locate one of the references cited, you can find the necessary information in the **reference section** (also known as the reference list) at the end of the paper (see Figures 20-14 and 20-15). As you can see from Dickson's introduction, when citing references in the text of an APA format paper, you use the last name of the author(s) and the year of publication. Such citations can take one of two forms. In the first form, the authors are either the subject or the object in a sentence in the text. In such cases only the date of the publication appears in parentheses. An example of this type of citation takes the following form:

Jackson, Sullivan, and Hodge (1993) examined the effects . . .

In the second form of citation, you may wish to cite a reference only as support for a statement you have made. In this instance you would include the author(s) *and* the year of publication *inside* the parentheses. An example of this type of citation takes the following form:

This phenomenon is known as the contrast effect (Brehm, Kassin, & Fein, 1999).

There are two additional considerations for this type of citation. When there are multiple authors, the name of the last author is preceded by the ampersand (&) sign, *not* the word "and." When you cite more than one study within parentheses, you should arrange the references alphabetically by the first author's last name.

What if you are citing two papers published in the same year by exactly the same authors? How can you distinguish between these papers when you cite them in your research report?

To report papers published in the same year, simply place a lowercase *a* or *b* after the date of each reference in question. Thus, if you had two 2000 references by Smith and Jones, you would cite them as follows:

Smith and Jones (2000a, 2000b)
or
(Smith & Jones, 2000a, 2000b)

The *a* and *b* designations will also appear as part of the complete citation of the article in the reference section (see section on *References* later in this chapter).

When a citation includes three to five authors, include each author's last name in the first citation, with subsequent citations using only the first author's name, followed by et al. (Latin for "and others") and the date. As shown in paragraphs 3 and 5 of Dickson's introduction, this rule creates the following citations:

Jackson, Sullivan, and Hodge (1993) (*first citation* [*paragraph 3*])
(Jackson et al., 1993) (*second citation* [*paragraph 5*])

If a citation includes six or more authors, *all* citations (including the first) consist of the first author's last name followed by et al. and the date. However, in the reference section, you would include all names. The *PM* provides more information about reference citations in text on pages 207–214.

A second pointer on writing in APA style is that the use of unbiased language is imperative. **Unbiased language** is language that does not state or imply a prejudice toward any individual or group. According to the *PM*:

> **Unbiased language**
> Language that does not display prejudice toward an individual or group.

APA is committed both to science and to the fair treatment of individuals and groups, and policy requires authors of APA publications to avoid perpetuating demeaning attitudes and biased assumptions about people in their writing. Constructions that might imply bias against persons on the basis of gender, sexual orientation, racial or ethnic group, disability, or age should be avoided. Scientific writing should be free of implied or irrelevant evaluation of the group or groups being studied.

Long-standing cultural practice can exert a powerful influence over even the most conscientious author. Just as you have learned to check what you write for spelling, grammar, and wordiness, practice reading over your work for bias. You can test your writing for implied evaluation by reading it while (a) substituting your own group for the group or groups you are discussing or (b) imagining you are a member of the group you are discussing.

(Maggio, 1991, pp. 61–62)

Once you have presented your thesis statement, reviewed the relevant literature, and stated your experimental hypothesis, you are ready to tell the readers how you conducted your research. We turn to this topic next.

Method

> **Method section** The second major section of the APA format paper. Contains information about the participants, the apparatus, materials, and testing instrument(s), and the procedures used in the experiment.

The objective of the **method section** is to provide sufficient detail about your experiment to enable readers to evaluate its appropriateness or replicate your study, should they desire. The method section is typically made up of three subsections: *participants, apparatus* (also designated *materials* or *testing instruments*), and *procedure*. Note that "Method" is a Level 1 section head. You do not begin the method section on a new page if there is room on the previous page. There is no break between the introduction, method, results, and discussion sections of an APA format paper. You begin on a new sheet of paper only if a heading falls on the last line of a page; if it does, move it to the next page and begin the section there.

Participants subsection The first subsection of the method section. Provides full information about the participants in the study.

Participants (Subjects) The **participants subsection** enumerates and describes the experimental participants. Figure 20-5 shows the first subsection of Dickson's method section; the *PM* (p. 19) indicates that "subjects" is a permissible label if an experimenter uses animals in the experiment. (Note that "Participants" is a **Level 3 heading**.)

The subsection on participants answers three questions: Who participated in the study? How many participants were there? How were the participants selected? As you can see in Figure 20-5, Dickson gathered data from 100 students at Southwestern University. The students were almost evenly divided by sex; we see their age range, average age, and racial composition. She provided details about four participants who were excluded from the research for various reasons. Notice that she described the participants (and their important characteristics) in sufficient detail to allow a replication of the study. The only missing information is any inducement the participants received for being in the study; Dickson labeled them "volunteers," but we do not know if they received extra credit in a class, monetary payment, or anything else. See pages 18–19 of the *PM* for more information about this subsection.

Level 3 heading A section title that is left-margin justified, underlined, and has the first letter of each major word capitalized. Occupies a line by itself.

If you use animal subjects, your description needs to be detailed enough to allow another investigator to replicate your samples. In addition to providing sample selection information, you need to indicate any special arrangements such as housing conditions, dietary conditions, and so on. The following description of animal subjects, from a paper on evaluating rats' behavior in a startle paradigm by Megan Kazlauskas (a student at Saint Anslem College in Manchester, New Hampshire) and Mark Kelland, her faculty advisor, is a good example of the type of information to include:

In this study we examined stargazer rats (homozygous stg/stg; stg group) and unaffected littermates (heterozygous stg/+; LM group) provided by Dr. Charles R. Ashby, Jr., of the Brookhaven National Laboratory (Upton, NY). Rat pups were bred in the vivarium and phenotyped at 14 days of age as stargazers or littermates, based upon the demonstration of stargazing behavior. After weaning, the rats were housed in pairs (stargazer with littermate), in rooms maintained at 25°C, 40% humidity, a 12-hr light/dark cycle (light, 0700–1900 hrs), with food and water available ad libitum. After being shipped to Saint Anselm College the rats were allowed to accommodate for 7 days, being maintained on a 12-hr light/dark cycle (light, 0800–2000 hrs), with food and water ad lib. All behavior measurements were performed during the light cycle, from 0800 to 1200 hrs.

(Kazlauskas & Kelland, 1997, p. 92)

Materials subsection The second subsection of the method section. When appropriate, contains information about materials other than equipment used in the experiment.

Apparatus, Materials, or Testing Instruments Figure 20-6 shows the **materials subsection** of the method section. This subsection can have various names depending on what you use in your particular experiment; you should choose the term that best describes the elements you used in conducting your experiment. Dickson chose "Materials" because she created written information for her research. If you use items such as slides, pictures, videotapes, or paper-and-pencil tests that are not standardized, you would probably want to

Eminem Versus Charley   6

manipulation check that focused on the performer's race and the genre of music, we explained the purpose of the

present study to the participants and asked them not to discuss it with anyone.

Materials

A three-page experimental packet, which ostensibly contained a survey about people's perceptions of

music, was distributed along with an envelope. The first page contained a "performer profile" and included a color

picture of a Black or White male performer, a brief biography about him indicating that he was either a rap or

country performer, and a lyric sample from one of his songs. The subsequent pages contained the survey, which was

used to measure participants' reactions to what they had seen and read on the previous page.

Each performer profile contained a biography that included the name of the performer (i.e., D.J. Jones), his

hometown (Atlanta, Georgia), and a brief summary of his musical career (e.g., "D.J. has been singing since he was

14, and recently signed a record deal with a major country label. He will soon be on an international tour opening for

a popular country artist"). To create the sample song lyrics, we slightly altered and combined two rock songs (May,

1973; May & Staffell, 1973). With the exception of the two manipulations, we used the same biography and song

lyrics in each of the four experimental conditions. The first manipulation altered the genre of music (i.e., rap or

country) that the artist performed. Specifically, the name of the performer and the type of music he performed was

labeled beneath his picture, and this label coincided with the genre of music described in the biography. Next, a

photograph manipulated the race of the performer so that each biography was accompanied by a picture of either a

Black or a White man. To ensure that the only attribute differing between the Black and White performers was in

fact race, we conducted a pilot test in a Research Methods class to match the Black and White performers on

attractiveness and age. The participants in the pilot test were all White, which is representative of the ethnic

composition of the participants in the present study. From a pool of 20 color photographs of nonfamous Black and

White men selected from magazines, the two stimuli selected for the present study were most similar in perceived -

attractiveness and age.

Following the performer profile were the questions that assessed perceptions of the performer and his

music, as well as the musical tastes of the participants. Embedded among demographic questions (e.g., sex and age)

and other filler questions (e.g., "On average, how many CDs and/or tapes do you buy a month?") were the items that

examined participants' perceptions of the performer. Specifically, participants rated on 7-point scales with endpoints

FIGURE 20-6 (M6). MATERIALS SUBSECTION OF METHOD SECTION.

label this section Materials. For example, in a study of identifying facial expressions, Sagles, Coley, Espiritu, Zahregian, and Velayo (faculty advisor) students at Pace University (New York, New York), indicated in this subsection that "The 35-mm photos of the target individuals, taken from the base of the chin to the top of the forehead, excluded their attire and body type" (2002, p. 33).

> **Apparatus subsection**
> The second subsection of the method section. When appropriate, contains information about the equipment used in the experiment.

If you use equipment in the experiment, you should label this subsection **Apparatus**. You should briefly describe the equipment used in the experiment and its function(s) in this subsection. If your equipment was commercially produced, mention the name of the manufacturer and the model number of the equipment. For example, Ball, Kargl, Kimpel, and Siewert (2001), students at Wheaton College in Wheaton, Illinois, used one piece of standard laboratory equipment labeled in this manner in their study of the effects of mood on reaction time: "Lafayette Instrument Multi-Choice Reaction Timers (Lafayette Instrument Co., Model #63014) measured participants' reactions times" (p. 23). If your equipment was custom made, provide a more detailed description. In the case of complex equipment, you may want to include a diagram. If you report any physical measurements, such as height, weight, or distance, you must report them in metric units. The *PM* contains extensive sections describing the use of metric measurements and their correct abbreviations (see pp. 130–136).

> **Testing instrument(s) subsection** The second subsection of the method section. When appropriate, contains information about standardized tests used in the experiment.

If your "equipment" consists of standardized psychological testing materials, then the label of **Testing Instruments** (or **Measures**) would be appropriate. For example, Bruderick and Ernst (2000), a student and faculty member from Hillsdale College in Hillsdale, Michigan, described the instruments they used in a study of college student drinking in the following manner:

> Positive and negative alcohol expectancies were measured using the CEAO questionnaire (Comprehensive Effects of Alcohol; Fromme, Stroot, & Kaplan, 1993). . . . We used Cahalan's Quantity-Frequency Index (CQFI; Cahalan, Cisin, & Crossley, 1969) to determine level of drinking.
>
> (p. 63)

If your experiment entailed the use of more than one category, then you should combine the relevant names when labeling this subsection. The *PM* contains a short section concerning this subsection on pages 19–20.

> **Procedure subsection**
> The third subsection of the method section. Provides a step-by-step account of what the participants and experimenter did during the experiment.

Procedure   The **procedure subsection** (see Figures 20-5, 20-6) summarizes how you conducted the experiment. In addition to describing the steps that you followed, you need to include a description of the experimental manipulations and controls (see Chapter 6), such as randomization, balancing, constancy, or counterbalancing, that you employed. Summarize any instructions you used unless they are unusual or complex. In the latter instance, you may want to present the instructions word for word.

If the experiment is involved and has several stages or phases, the procedure section can become lengthy. Dickson's procedure section is intermediate in length. In contrast, the procedure involved in the administration of a questionnaire may be straightforward and brief. For example, in their study of collegiate alcohol use, Bruderick and Ernst (2000, p. 64) indicated:

> We tested the participants as a group in a classroom. The questionnaire packets were administered so that half of the participants completed the CEOA first and the CQFI second (Packet A); the remaining participants completed the CQFI first and the CEOA second (Packet B). The abstainer sheet and the demographic sheet followed the CEOA and CQFI in each packet. Before the experimenter instructed the participants to begin, she read the instructions as the participants followed along in their questionnaire packet. The instructions assured the participants of their anonymity.
>
> (p. 64)

Your primary goal in the procedure subsection is to describe how you conducted your experiment. You should give enough information to allow a replication of your method, but do not include unnecessary details (e.g., note that you recorded times with a stopwatch—the brand and model number would be overkill).

PSYCHOLOGICAL DETECTIVE What critical methodological details do you find in Dickson's procedure subsection?

Critical details are pertinent points that another experimenter would need to copy in a replication study. We believe that the following details are critical:

2×2 design

between-subjects design

recruited participants from various locations on campus

order of presentation of materials

random assignment

DV questions embedded among filler questions

debriefing after participation

four experimental conditions (type of artists: Black rap, White rap; Black country; White country)

Did we include any details that you left out? If so, reread the procedure subsection to see why we thought that detail is absolutely necessary. For example, did you ignore the method of participant recruitment? We believe that this detail clarifies our earlier question about whether participants received any inducement to take part in the experiment—it appears unlikely from this statement.

The procedure subsection is typically the longest of the three components of the method section. Its length will vary depending on the complexity of your experiment. Dickson's procedure section is shorter than the materials section but her procedure was rather simple and she needed to include more detail about the materials she used. To read more about the procedure subsection, check page 20 of the *PM*.

Finally, you should not be surprised to find variations in researchers' method sections. Sections with combined names (e.g., *Design and Procedure* in Dickson's case) or with subsections in different orders are not unusual (Dickson's *Materials* section came after the *Procedure*). The key point is that experimenters should provide you with the information you need to understand what they did in their experiment and how they did it.

Results

> **Results section** The third major section of the APA format paper. Contains information about the statistical findings from the experiment.

We introduced the format for the **results section** in Chapter 10 and reinforced those ideas in Chapters 12 and 14 when we discussed the notion of translating statistics into words. We do not use the word *translating* lightly—to some people, statistics resembles a foreign language. It is your job in the results section to decode the meaning of your numbers into words for the reader. At the same time you must provide the factual, numerical basis to back your decoding. The *PM* covers the presentation of statistical results on pages 20–26 and 136–147. Figure 20-7 contains Dickson's results section. As you conduct your library research, you may notice that sometimes authors combine the results and discussion sections into one section in a published journal article. This combination is common for certain journals or for shorter experimental articles. It is likely that your instructor will want you to keep your sections separate.

Inferential Statistics   As you write the results section, you should assume that your reader has a good understanding of statistics. Therefore, you do not review basic concepts such as how to reject the null hypothesis and so on. The most important information to report is the specific findings from your inferential statistics. In Dickson's paper you see an example of how to report results from factorial ANOVAs (*F* tests; see Chapter 15 for review) and post hoc *t* tests.

 Why did Dickson use a factorial ANOVA to analyze her data? What was or were her IV(s)? What was or were her DV(s)?

First, you should remember from Chapters 14 and 15 that a factorial ANOVA is appropriate when you have more than one IV—thus, you should look for more than one IV in Dickson's experiment. One focus of the experiment was race of the performer, so one IV was race (Black versus White). The other IV was the genre of music of the performer (rap versus country).

In the procedure and materials subsections, you found out that Dickson had participants rate the performers on four scales and then averaged the scores on the four scales. Therefore, the experiment had one DV: the overall index rating of the performers.

In presenting inferential statistical results, you must present the test that was used, the *df* for the test, the test statistics, the probability level, and a measure of effect labeled at 1 (*not at all*) and 7 (*very much*): (a) "Overall, how much do you like this performer?"; (b) "How talented do you think this performer is?"; (c) "How legitimate is this performer?"; and finally (d) "How successful do you predict this performer will be in the music industry?" Because these items were highly correlated, they were combined into an overall index reflecting participants' favorability of the performer (Cronbach's α = .80). The scores on the four items were averaged together, and consistent with the scales on the individual items, the overall index is on a 7-point scale with higher numbers representing a more favorable perception of the performer and lower numbers indicating an unfavorable perception.

Results

A 2 (race of performer: Black or White) x 2 (genre of music: rap or country) between-subjects analysis of variance (ANOVA) was performed on the index assessing the favorability of the performer (i.e., likability, perceived talent, perceived legitimacy, and predicted success). Data analysis revealed a significant main effect of race such that Black performers (M = 4.32, SD = .91) were rated more positively than were White performers (M = 3.76, SD = 1.00), $F(1, 92)$ = 10.42, p = .002, η^2 = .10. However, this main effect was qualified by the significant two-way interaction between race of performer and genre of music, which was consistent with predictions, $F(1, 92)$ = 26.72, p = .0001, η^2 = .23. An inspection of the means in Figure 1 shows that participants rated a Black rap artist (M = 4.79, SD = .68) more favorably than a Black country artist (M = 3.85, SD = .87), $t(46)$ = 4.17, p = .0001; however, they judged a White country artist (M = 4.19, SD = .92) more favorably than a White rap artist (M = 3.33, SD = .91), $t(46)$ = 3.24, p = .0001. There was no main effect of genre of music, $F < 1$, *ns*: Participants reported similar ratings for rap performers (M = 4.06, SD = 1.09) and country performers (M = 4.02, SD = .90).

Discussion

The present study integrated and expanded on two lines of research. First, it extended previous research (Fried, 1996, 1999) on stereotyping involving the music industry. Whereas Fried (1996, 1999) examined reactions to music lyrics based on either the genre label or the performer's race, our study considered the interactive effect of both the race of the performer and the genre of music on people's evaluations of performers. The current study also differs from previous research conducted by Fried (1996, 1999) in that the lyrics in our study did not attempt to convey negative images such as violence or aggression. That is, Fried (1996, 1999) asked participants specifically

FIGURE 20-7 (M7). RESULTS SECTION; PORTION OF DISCUSSION SECTION.

size. In looking at Dickson's results, the second sentence provides us with a good example:

> Data analysis revealed a significant main effect of race such that Black performers ($M = 4.32$, $SD = .91$) were rated more positively than were White performers ($M = 3.76$, $SD = 1.00$), $F(1, 92) = 10.42$, $p = .002$, $\eta^2 = .10$.

Notice that the statistical findings at the end of the sentence give us all five pieces of information: an F test (analysis of variance) was used, there were 1 and 92 degrees of freedom, the calculated test value was 10.42, the probability of these data occurring if the null hypothesis is true was two in a thousand, and the effect size was small (.10). You should present the same type of information for findings relevant to the experimental hypothesis even if you do not find statistical significance. Although information from different test statistics may appear in a slightly different fashion, these five basic pieces of information are always necessary. We presented a set of t test results in Chapter 11 to which you can refer. You can find examples of how to present other statistical test results on pages 138–139 of the *PM*.

Descriptive Statistics   In order to give a full picture of the data, it is customary to present descriptive statistics in addition to the inferential statistics. Means and standard deviations typically allow readers to get a good feel for the data. With a small number of groups, you can present the descriptive statistics in the text (as Dickson did), as we showed you in Chapter 11. On the other hand, with many groups it may be more efficient and clearer to present the descriptive statistics in either a table or a figure, which we will discuss next.

Complementary Information   When presenting your results, you must first decide how best to give the reader the necessary information. If your statistical information is relatively simple, merely reporting your findings in words and numbers is usually adequate. For more complex analyses or results, you may wish to include tables or figures to further explicate your words and numbers.

> **Figure** A pictorial representation of a set of results.

Figures   Because Dickson's DV showed a significant interaction, she used a **figure** to clarify the presentation of results. The figure appears in Figure 20-8. Figures can take the form of graphs (line, bar, circle, pie, scatter, or pictorial graphs), charts, dot maps, drawings, or photographs.

The *PM* presents information regarding figures on pages 176–201. As you can guess from the number of pages devoted to figures, they can be complex to deal with. However, the vast majority of the *PM* information about figures involves preparing figures for publication. Because you will probably be submitting your research paper as a class requirement, your instructor may not be a stickler for enforcing every APA requirement on figures you submit with your paper. For example, you can see from Figure 20-9 that figure caption(s) appear on a separate page in a manuscript prepared for publication. Your instructor may choose to have you put your caption on the page with each figure.

It is likely that the majority of figures you use will be line graphs or bar graphs (see Chapter 4) that depict findings similar to Dickson's. Graphs are particularly good for showing interaction patterns. Because we showed interaction patterns in Chapters 14

Eminem Versus Charley   14

FIGURE 20-8 (M14). DICKSON ET AL.'S FIGURE.

and 15 with line graphs, we have reformatted Dickson's figure as a line graph in Figure 20-10. It may be easier for you to see the interaction from the line graph than from the bar graph. Regardless of what type of figure you decide to use, you probably have access to a number of good software programs for graphing. For your class project, ask your instructor about his or her preference as to how you should produce a figure. Regardless of how you create your figures, one rule is constant: Be certain that

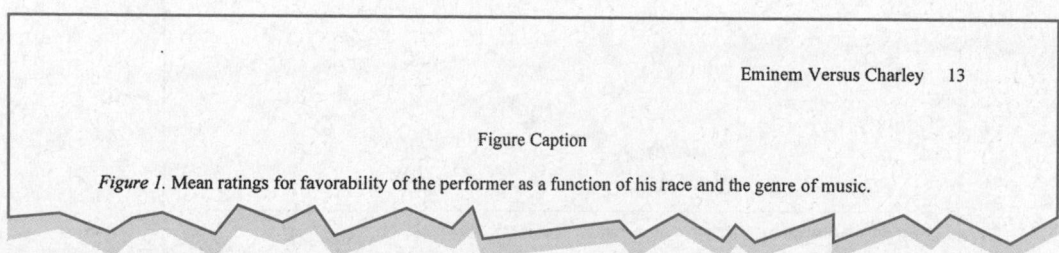

Eminem Versus Charley   13

Figure Caption

Figure 1. Mean ratings for favorability of the performer as a function of his race and the genre of music.

FIGURE 20-9 (M13). CAPTION FOR DICKSON ET AL'S FIGURE.

FIGURE 20-10 ADAPTION OF DICKSON'S RESULTS TO LINE GRAPH.

you refer to your figures in the text at an appropriate place. This reference will cue the reader to look at the figure in order to process its meaning.

> **Table** A chart containing an array of descriptive statistics.

Tables   A **table** consists of a display of data, usually in numerical form. A table is an alternative to presenting data in pictorial form as a figure. To use a table, your data display should be large enough that it would be difficult or confusing to present it in the text.

You often have to decide between using a table or a figure to present your data. Notice that Dickson presented her data only with a figure rather than a table. We have adapted the data from her Figure 1 into the format that you see in Figure 20-11 (Dickson would have included a manuscript page header and page number if this page were actually in her manuscript.) The advantage of the table over the figure is that standard deviations can be included in the table. The advantage of the figure over the table is accessibility—the data, particularly the significant interaction, seem easier to

Table 1
Perceived Favorability of Performance Based on Performer's Race and Music Genre

	Performer's Race	
Music Genre	Black	White
Rap		
M	3.85	4.19
SD	.87	.92
Country		
M	4.79	3.33
SD	.68	.91

Note: Favorability ratings made on a scale from 1 *(negative)* to 7 *(positive)*.

FIGURE 20-11 ADAPTION OF DICKSON'S RESULTS TO TABLE.

understand and conceptualize in the pictorial presentation. Based on these advantages, the figure seemed a better choice in this situation. For your experimental report, your decision may be different. APA presents many guidelines for developing tables (see pages 147–176 of the *PM*). You should check with your instructor to find out which guidelines you must follow in your paper. Because you will typically generate a table directly in your word-processing program (or on your typewriter), you may find a table easier to produce than a figure. However, you should make your choice of a table versus a figure on the quality of information provided to the reader rather than on ease of production. Again, if you use a table in your paper, be sure to refer to it at the appropriate point.

PSYCHOLOGICAL DETECTIVE   Can you think of a specific situation in which you would prefer a table over a figure?

The most obvious answer to this question is a situation in which you have a large number of means to present but for which there is not a significant interaction. We hope that a comparison of Figures 20-8 and Figure 20-11 convinced you of the benefit of a figure for portraying interactions.

> **Discussion section**
> The fourth major section of the APA format paper. Contains a summary of the experiment's results, a comparison of those results to previous research, and the conclusion(s) from the experiment.

Discussion

You can find Dickson's **discussion section** in Figures 20-7, 20-12, and 20-13. According to the *PM* (pp. 26–27), you can address issues such as problem choice, levels of analysis, and application and synthesis in the discussion section. We like the somewhat simpler and clearer guidelines laid out in the previous edition of the *PM* (APA, 1994, p. 19), which recommended that you be guided by three questions in the discussion section:

- *What have I contributed here?*
- *How has my study helped to resolve the original problem?*
- *What conclusions and theoretical implications can I draw from my study?*

Typically, authors answer these three questions by (a) briefly restating their findings, (b) comparing and contrasting their findings to previous research cited in the introduction, and (c) giving their interpretation of their findings. The most recent edition of the *PM* covers writing the discussion section in pages 26–27.

Restating Results   Your first task in the discussion section is to recap your results as briefly as possible. Typically, you will summarize only your significant findings, unless a null finding is particularly meaningful. If you conducted a large study that had many outcomes, you may wish to feature only the most important findings at this point—usually those findings that have some bearing on your experimental hypothesis. This summary ensures that the reader can extract the most important information from your results section.

about their negative impressions of the song lyrics (e.g., its offensiveness, its threat to society, its need for warning labels), whereas the current study emphasized overall impressions of the performer. Rap may be more often associated with negative topics, but these topics can be found in both rap and country music. We chose to use neutral lyrics in the present study because we were not focusing on the relation between negative themes and music genre. Instead, the current study was based on findings that rap is associated with a Black culture that has both positive and negative attributes (Brigham, 1971). We examined the connection between music genre and the stereotype-consistent or stereotype-inconsistent race of the performer. In our study, participants judged Black rap artists more favorably than Black country music performers, whereas they judged White country music performers more favorably than White rap artists. These results support the hypothesis that individuals who deviate from societal expectations are judged more negatively than are individuals who adhere to social norms (Jackson et al., 1993; Knight et al., 2001). Manis, Nelson, and Shedler (1988) found that extreme stereotypes yielded contrast effects when behavior was discrepant from the established stereotype. In the present study, Black country music performers and White rap artists contrast from fairly ingrained societal expectations and thus received more negative judgments than the performers who adhere to societal norms.

The present study could be extended in a number of ways. For example, like Fried's (1996, 1999) research, the current study also presented the lyric sample to participants on paper. It would be interesting to explore whether an audio-recorded lyric sample would affect participants' evaluations of performers or the music. Perhaps auditory processing and visual processing of stereotype-consistent and stereotype-inconsistent information differ. In addition, the present study could broaden its scope by including a more varied sample of participants. That is, future studies could incorporate participants of different races and ages. The data in the current study were collected primarily from White undergraduate students at a liberal arts university, and the results from such a homogenous sample may not necessarily generalize to alternative populations or settings. Furthermore, exploring alternate stereotype violations could support the findings of the present study, and one area of interest could be the world of sports. For instance, Black hockey players violate societal expectations similar to the apparent violation made by Black country music performers and White rap performers. According to our findings, Black hockey players would receive more negative evaluations than would White hockey players because their behavior is inconsistent with societal expectations.

FIGURE 20-12 (M8). SECOND PAGE OF DISCUSSION.

Eminem Versus Charley   9

Because the population of other minority groups (e.g., Latinos) is approaching that of the Black population in America, future research concerning racial stereotypes in the music industry could examine the impact of the increasing popularity of Latin music (Gonzales, 1990). Garcia and Zapatel (2000) recently examined how the labels *Black rap*, *Latino rap*, and *alternative music* influence perceptions made by both Anglo and Hispanic participants and found that participants' perceptions of music differed depending on their own race. Specifically, Hispanic participants judged music labeled *Latino rap* more positively than music labeled *alternative*, whereas Anglo participants rated music labeled *alternative* more favorably than music labeled *Latino rap*. Similar to previous findings (Jackson et al., 1993), out-group categories (i.e., *Latino rap* for Anglo participants and *alternative* music for Hispanic participants) were judged more negatively than were categories that corresponded to the participants' ethnicity. Extended to a more diverse sample, the present study could offer support for the idea that out-group categories are judged more negatively than in-group categories by examining the relation between participants' ethnicities and their evaluations of rap and country music. Thus, regardless of the race of the performer, Black participants would be expected to rate country music more negatively than rap music, whereas White participants would be expected to judge rap music more negatively than country music. Furthermore, it would be interesting to determine whether or not performers of Latin music will remain primarily Latin and to examine perceptions of stereotype-consistent and stereotype-inconsistent performers in this genre. If future performers do deviate from racial stereotypes, the present study suggests that non-Latino performers of Latin music would be perceived less favorably than would Latino performers.

In closing, Eminem and Charley Pride share a connection in that their actions deviate from widespread stereotypes that specific races are associated with certain types of music. Although people may recognize these two performers because of their musical talent, it is more likely that they are recognized because they were bold enough to defy stereotypes in the music industry. By being a White rap artist and a Black country music performer, Eminem and Charley Pride became forerunners for performers who do not adhere to social norms, and they may have possibly influenced numerous music fans to expect the unexpected.

FIGURE 20-13 (M9). FINAL PAGE OF DISCUSSION.

If you examine Dickson's discussion section, you will find that she used the three techniques listed just before this section. In the first paragraph she summarized the information from the results section in one sentence: "In our study, participants judged Black rap artists more favorably than Black country music performers, whereas they judged White country music performers more favorably than White rap artists" (Dickson et al.,

2001, p. 178). The sentence describes the significant interaction that Dickson found rather than the main effect of race because the interaction qualified the race effect.

Comparing Results to Previous Research   It is important for you to evaluate how your results "stack up" against previous findings in your area of research you summarized in your introduction. The previous research studies will be related to, but not the same as, your experiment. Typically, you will have made a prediction before the experiment about your expected findings based on your survey of previous research. You should tell the reader how accurate your predictions were. This information will help the reader to draw conclusions. For example, if you correctly predicted your results from previous research, the previous research and your study are both validated. On the other hand, if your prediction is not borne out, some doubt is cast—either your research or the previous research may be flawed in some way.

Looking at the first paragraph of Dickson's discussion section, you will see the comparison to previous research findings. In this case, the previous research studies were related to Dickson's study because they dealt with stereotyping and music. On the other hand, these studies were different because they did not specifically combine performer's race and genre of music. Dickson's study demonstrated an interaction between those two variables, which was an important finding.

Interpreting the Results   This portion of the discussion section gives you more of a free hand to engage in conjecture and speculation than any other portion of the experimental writeup. It is here that you draw the "bottom line" to your study: What is your overall conclusion? What are the implications of your results for any psychological theories? How can your results be applied in various settings—the laboratory, the real world, our body of psychological knowledge? What new research should grow out of this study? As you can see, there are a variety of questions you can address in your discussion section. Not all these questions are appropriate for every study—pick the ones that are most important for your particular experiment.

The interpretation of Dickson's results appears in the last three sentences of the discussion section's first paragraph. The results of this study supported the notion that people who deviate from societal expectations are judged more harshly than people who conform to stereotypes.

The second and third paragraphs of Dickson's manuscript include possible directions for future research.

 How many ideas for further research can you find in these two paragraphs?

We see four possible experiments mentioned:

1. Using audio-recorded lyrics rather than printed lyrics
2. Using participants from populations other than White students
3. Exploring racial stereotype expectations in sports settings
4. Extending the music genre to include Latin music

You may wish to mentally file this example away for future reference. As you read discussion sections of published articles, you might find ideas for your own research projects.

References

There are two important reasons why it is your responsibility to provide a complete list of accurate references to any published works that you cite in your research report. First, you must give credit to the original author(s) for any ideas and information that you got from reading other works. If you take exact wordings, paraphrases, or even ideas from an author without giving credit for that source, you are guilty of **plagiarism** (see Chapter 3). Second, you are providing a historical account of the sources you used in the event that a reader wishes to read them in their entirety. Have you ever worked on a term paper and "lost" a good source that you had read because you didn't write down all the necessary bibliographic information and couldn't find it again? Most of us have had this experience, and it is quite frustrating. You can prevent that frustrating experience by providing your reader with a complete and accurate reference list. The *PM* describes the reference list on page 28 and provides general pointers about the list as well as examples of APA format for 95 different types of sources on pages 240–281. Reference formatting is so important that the *PM* now has a separate chapter (Chapter 4, pp. 215–281) devoted to this topic.

> **Plagiarism** Using someone else's work without giving credit to the original source.

Before going further, we need to distinguish between a reference list and a bibliography, which you might have learned about in English classes. The reference list is *not* a list of every source that you read when you were writing your introduction and planning your experiment. The only references that you list are those from which you actually obtained information and cited somewhere in your paper. If you do not cite a particular source, you should not reference it.

The list of references begins on a new page after the end of your discussion section. You will find Dickson's references in Figures 20-14 and 20-15.

PSYCHOLOGICAL DETECTIVE   Look at Figures 20-14 and 20-15. How many different types of reference formats can you find? Can you identify each type?

There are five different types of references represented in Dickson's list:

1. Book: Brehm, Kassin, & Fein; Fiske & Taylor; Gonzales
2. Journal article: Brigham; Devine; Dovidio, Evans, & Tyler; Fried (both); Gaertner & McLaughlin; Jackson, Sullivan, & Hodge; Knight, Giuliano, & Sanchez-Ross; Manis, Nelson, & Shedler; Sagar & Schofield
3. Chapter in edited book: Dovidio, Brigham, Johnson, & Gaertner; Dovidio & Gaertner; Gaertner & Dovidio
4. Conference presentation: Garcia & Zapatel
5. Music recording: May; May & Staffell

References

Brehm, S. S., Kassin, S. M., & Fein, S. (1999). *Social psychology* (4th ed.). Boston: Houghton Mifflin.

Brigham, J. C. (1971). Ethnic stereotypes. *Psychological Bulletin, 76,* 15-38.

Devine, P. G. (1989). Stereotypes and prejudice: Their automatic and controlled components. *Journal of Personality and Social Psychology, 56,* 5-18.

Dovidio, J. F., Brigham, J. C., Johnson, B. T., & Gaertner, S. L. (1996). Stereotyping, prejudice, and discrimination: Another look. In N. C. Macrae, C. Stangor, & M. Hewstone (Eds.), *Stereotypes & stereotyping* (pp. 276-322). New York: Guilford Press.

Dovidio, J. F., Evans, N., & Tyler, R. B. (1986). Racial stereotypes: The contents of their cognitive representations. *Journal of Experimental Social Psychology, 22,* 22-37.

Dovidio, J. F., & Gaertner, S. L. (1991). Changes in the expression and assessment of racial prejudice. In H. R. Knopke, R. J. Norrell, & R. W. Rogers (Eds.), *Opening doors: Perspectives on race relations in contemporary America* (pp. 119-148). Tuscaloosa: University of Alabama Press.

Fiske, S. T., & Taylor, S. E. (1991). *Social cognition* (2nd ed.). New York: McGraw-Hill.

Fried, C. B. (1996). Bad rap for rap: Bias in reactions to music lyrics. *Journal of Applied Social Psychology, 26,* 2135-2146.

Fried, C. B. (1999). Who's afraid of rap: Differential reactions to music lyrics. *Journal of Applied Social Psychology, 29,* 705-721.

Gaertner, S. L., & Dovidio, J. F. (1986). The aversive form of racism. In J. F. Dovidio & S. L. Gaertner (Eds.), *Prejudice, discrimination, and racism: Theory and research* (pp. 61-89). Orlando, FL: Academic Press.

Gaertner, S. L., & McLaughlin, J. P. (1983). Racial stereotypes: Associations and ascriptions of positive and negative characteristics. *Social Psychology Quarterly, 46,* 23-30.

Garcia, S. D., & Zapatel, J. P. (2000, January). *Perceptions of lyrics as a function of ethnicity and music genre.* Paper presented at the annual meeting of the Social Psychologists in Texas, San Antonio.

Gonzales, J. L., Jr. (1990). *Racial and ethnic groups in America: A collection of readings.* Dubuque, IA: Kendall/Hunt.

FIGURE 20-14 (M10). FIRST PAGE OF REFERENCE LIST.

Eminem Versus Charley   11

Jackson, L. A., Sullivan, L. A., & Hodge, C. N. (1993). Stereotype effects on attributions, predictions, and

evaluations: No two social judgments are quite alike. *Journal of Personality and Social Psychology, 65,* 69-

84.

Knight, J. L., Giuliano, T. A., & Sanchez-Ross, M. G. (2001). Famous or infamous? The influence of celebrity

status and race on perceptions of responsibility for rape. *Basic and Applied Social Psychology, 23,* 183-190.

Manis, M., Nelson, T. E., & Shedler, J. (1988). Stereotypes and social judgment: Extremity, assimilation, and

contrast. *Journal of Personality and Social Psychology, 55,* 28-36.

May, B. (1973). The night comes down. [Recorded by Queen]. On *Queen* [Record]. London: EMI Records.

May, B., & Staffell, T. (1973). Doing all right. [Recorded by Queen]. On *Queen* [Record]. London: EMI Records.

Sagar, H. A., & Schofield, J. W. (1980). Racial and behavioral cues in Black and White children's perceptions of

ambiguously aggressive acts. *Journal of Personality & Social Psychology, 39,* 590-598.

FIGURE 20-15 (M11). LAST PAGE OF REFERENCE LIST.

As you look at a reference, you will find that the information about author(s) and date is listed first. This location makes it easy for the reader to see an author and date citation in your text and then to find the corresponding reference in your reference list. The reference list is alphabetized by the surname of the first author. If you have more than one article by the same first author, you alphabetize by the name of the second author. If the author information for two or more articles is identical, you should arrange the references by date, with the earliest article listed first. If the author information and dates are identical, alphabetize by the first main word of the title, and add lowercase letters (a, b, etc.) to the date to differentiate the articles, as we previously mentioned.

The title of the scholarly work is the next piece of information, followed by supplementary information that helps a reader locate that work. As you can see, the supplementary information differs depending on the particular type of reference you are using. Let's take a look at the general format for the three different types of references you are most likely to use in your papers.

Periodical Articles   The *PM* shows examples of 22 different types of references to periodicals on pages 240–247. Your most typical use of periodicals will probably be to reference articles in journals. The general format for periodicals is as follows (example adapted from APA, 2001, p. 239):

Author, A. A., Author, B. B., & Author, C. C. (date). Title of article. *Title of Periodical, vol,* ppp–ppp.

For examples you can examine the 10 references in Figures 20-14 and 20-15 that we listed as the answer to the last *Psychological Detective* question. The last names and initials of *all* authors appear in the same order as in the journal article. You will remember we mentioned using et al. for multiple-author works earlier in this chapter. You typically *do not* use et al. in the reference list—list all authors (APA has made an exception to this rule when there are more than six authors—you list the first six in typical reference format and add et al. after the sixth name). The date refers to the year in which the particular journal issue containing the article was published. Be careful here—you may need to look at the front of the journal to get this information.

Type the title of the article with *only* the first word capitalized and *not* italicized. If the article title includes a colon, capitalize the first word after the colon also. In addition, you should capitalize any words that are normally capitalized (e.g., names, states, organizations, or test names).

On the other hand, type the journal title with all primary words capitalized (APA's definition is any word of four letters or more). Words such as *a, and*, and *the* are not capitalized unless they are the first word or follow a colon. The journal title *is* italicized, as is the volume number of the journal (and its following comma), which immediately follows the journal title. Type only the volume number—do not precede it by "Vol." or "V." It is often the case that volumes of journals also have issue numbers. For example, volume 59 represents the 2004 issues of *American Psychologist*; each month's issue is represented by its own number. Thus, the January 2004 issue would be Volume 59, Number 1, and so on. Most journals use continuous pagination throughout a volume. That is, the first issue of a new volume begins on page 1 and the pages run continuously until the next volume, which begins with page 1. In this case, the issue number is not needed to find the referenced article and does not appear in the reference. A few journals, however, begin *each issue* with page 1. If this is the case, then the issue number is necessary to find the article and is included in the reference. This reference format follows (example adapted from APA, 2001, p. 240):

Author, A. A., Author, B. B., & Author, C. C. (date). Title of article. *Title of Periodical, vol*(n), ppp–ppp.

Notice that the issue number (n) appears within parentheses (no space after the volume number) and is *not* italicized. Finally, give the inclusive page numbers of the article—numbers only, no "p." or "pp." preceding.

Books   The *PM* provides 11 examples of references to books on pages 248–251. This category consists of references to entire books rather than to chapters in edited books. The general format for book references is (example adapted from APA, 2001, p. 248):

Author, A. A. (date). *Title of work*. Location: Publisher.

We have used a one-author example here, but don't be misled by it. You should include all authors' names and initials (see Brehm, Kassin, & Fein in Dickson's reference list), just as in the journal examples given previously. Use the date of the original publication of the book, which usually appears at the front of the book facing the title page.

The book title's format is a combination of the styles seen earlier for article titles and journal titles. It follows the style for an article title in terms of capitalization—you should capitalize only the first word (and first word after a colon or normally capitalized words). However, like a journal title, the book's title is italicized.

The location and the name of the publisher appear in the last portion of the reference. If the city, such as New York, is well known for publishing (see p. 217 of the *PM* for a complete list), you type it alone. Otherwise, you must give the city and state (two-letter postal abbreviation) or country. Many publishers now have offices in several locations—typically the first location listed would be the one referenced. The name of the publisher is given in a brief form, omitting "superfluous terms, such as *Publishers, Co.*, or *Inc.*, which are not required to identify the publisher" (APA, 2001, p. 230). Many times you will find that a corporate author and publisher are the same, as with the *PM*. In such a case, rather than repeat the author information for the publisher, you simply type "Author" after the location (e.g., see the reference to the *PM* in the reference list for this book). Dickson's manuscript has three examples of references to books.

Chapters from Edited Books   Most edited books contain chapters written by different authors. The type of reference we are about to present allows you to cite information from a single chapter within such a book. The *PM* gives seven examples of such references on pages 252–255. The general format of such a reference is (example adapted from APA, 2001, p. 252):

Author, A. A., & Author, B. B. (date). Title of chapter. In C. C. Editor, D. D. Editor, &
    E. E. Editor (Eds.), *Title of book* (pp. nnn–nnn). Location: Publisher.

As you can see, this type of reference is much like a journal article reference combined with a book reference. This example includes two authors and three editors, but any number of either is possible. You would provide the information concerning author(s) and date as we have previously discussed. The title of the chapter refers to the specific smaller work within the larger book. Capitalize the chapter title in the same manner as a journal article title—capitalize only the first word, first word after a colon, and words that are normally capitalized.

List all the editors' names. Notice that you do not reverse the initials and surnames. After a comma, you list the book's title (italicized), with capitalization in the same fashion as mentioned previously for a book title. The inclusive pages of the chapter appear parenthetically after the book's title to make it easier for the reader to locate the specific chapter in the book. Finally, include the location and publisher information as for any book. Dickson's manuscript includes three examples of chapters in edited books, as listed previously.

World Wide Web Sources   Providing references for information that you obtain from the World Wide Web is just as important as providing references for written material—in fact, it may be even more important. Unlike journal articles or books, material on the Web can change quite rapidly. Authors can modify Web information from day to day, which can create a problem with keeping current. The *PM* has an extensive section dealing with electronic media references, which includes 25 examples of Internet and Web references, on pages 268–281. Because there are so many different types of electronic media sources, it is impossible to cover them all. We will provide an example of a citation to information on a Web site; if you have a different type of source, be sure to consult the *PM*.

American Psychological Association. (2003). *APA Style.org: Electronic references*. Retrieved December 9, 2003 from: http://www.apastyle.org/elecref.html

Note that this reference style is similar to a book reference. However, you include the actual retrieval site and date. This additional information allows a reader to find the site and to determine whether the information still exists (or perhaps has been updated) at that site. Providing an exact date of retrieval is extremely important for these reasons.

The relevant text citation for this reference would be the same for a book; in this case, it would be (American Psychological Association, 2003). If you wish to cite an entire Web site (rather than a specific document on the Web site), you can simply list the site in the text—no reference is necessary (e.g., http://www.apa.org for the APA site).

Other References   Although we expect that most of your references will be to periodicals, books, and chapters in edited books, the *PM* has 30 examples of other types of references you might use. These other references include technical and research reports, proceedings of meetings and symposia, doctoral dissertations and master's theses, unpublished works and publications of limited circulation, reviews, and audiovisual media. No matter what type of material you wish to reference, the *PM* will have a format for you.

A Disclaimer   The fourth edition of the *PM* (APA, 1994) used a different reference format. Although all the information included was the same, the appearance of the references was different. In the older format, the initial line of each reference was indented and subsequent lines begin at the left margin. However, when references were printed in journal articles, this margin situation was reversed—the first line began at the left margin and subsequent lines were indented (referred to as a "hanging indent"). With this type of formatting, the first authors' names stand out and are easier to locate. Under the new *PM* (2001) guidelines, manuscript references are formatted exactly as they are in publication.

We give you this explanation to alert you to the possibility that you might see an older student's paper with references formatted in the old manner. It is not unusual for students to find previous copies of research papers to use as examples. If you copy that style of reference format, you will be in error. As you have examined the manuscript pages of Dickson's paper and the published product, you may have noted other differences.

PSYCHOLOGICAL DETECTIVE   Can you figure out why an APA formatted manuscript and a published article (or final copy) might differ in appearance?

APA format is intended to help authors and journal editors produce a product more easily. On the other hand, in a published article or final copy, the appearance of the document is the more important goal. Instructors have a difficult dilemma deciding whether to require strict APA format or to require a more aesthetically appealing product.

Appendix

Most published articles do not contain an appendix because of space limitations, but they are more common in student papers (*PM*, 2001, p. 324). Typically you include information that might help readers understand some detail(s) of your study but that would be distracting in the body of the paper. The *PM* gives examples such as a new computer program, an unpublished test that you used, a mathematical proof, a list of stimuli used, and the description of a complex piece of equipment (p. 28).

Dickson included an appendix in her article that contained the lyrics to the music used in the experiment. We have not included the appendix in the text because of space limitations (but the reference to the appendix appears in the Materials subsection in Figure 20-19).

Author Note

> **Author note** A note at the end of an experimental report that contains information about the author or paper for readers' use.

Your manuscript may or may not have an **author note**, depending on your instructor's preferences. If you do use an author note, begin it on a new page. As you can see from Dickson's author note in Figure 20-16, she acknowledged several people who helped on the project and provided a name and address for readers to contact for information or copies of the paper. Other information that might be included would be an acknowledgment of an earlier presentation of the paper (e.g., at a conference) or sources of financial support that made the study possible. The *PM* provides information about the author note on pages 29, 203–205, and 300.

Eminem Versus Charley   12

Author Note

We would like to thank Jennifer Knight for her advice and input on this study, Marie Helweg-Larsen for

her helpful comments on an earlier draft of this manuscript, Alan Swinkels for his assistance with graphic

illustrations, and Johnnie Dickson for her proofreading skills and patience.

Correspondence concerning this study should be addressed to Traci Giuliano at Southwestern University,

Georgetown, TX 78626-6144. Electronic mail may be sent to giuliant@southwestern.edu.

FIGURE 20-16 (M12). AUTHOR NOTE PAGE.

Headings

To recapitulate, APA format papers use a different type of heading for each section of the report. The major sections of the report, such as the introduction, method, results, and discussion, are introduced by a Level 1 heading. Subsections within these main sections are introduced by lower-level headings. For example, the participants, apparatus, and procedure subsections of the method section are generally introduced by a Level 3 heading.

Level 3 headings are left-margin justified, are italicized, have the first letter of each major word capitalized, and occupy a line by themselves. Should you need to further subdivide these subsections, use a **Level 4 heading**. Level 4 headings are indented five spaces, italicized, have only the first letter of the first word capitalized, and end with a period. You begin typing on the same line following the period that concludes a Level 4 heading.

> **Level 4 heading** A section title that is indented five spaces, underlined, has only the first word capitalized, and ends with a period; it does not occupy a separate line.

Table 20-1 summarizes the five types of section heads used in APA format articles. Level 1 and Level 3 headings are the ones most frequently used in preparing a research report that describes a single experiment (as in Dickson's example). As we have seen, however, the description of a single experiment may require the use of Level 4 headings when the participants, apparatus, and procedure subsections are further subdivided (see Table 20-1). Likewise, when you are presenting more than one experiment, you will use Level 1, 2, 3, and 4 headings as shown in Table 20-1.

REVIEW SUMMARY

1. Psychologists have developed their own format, **APA style**, for the preparation of scientific reports.
2. The major sections of an APA paper include the title page, abstract, introduction, method, results, discussion, references, author note, tables, and figures.
3. The **title page** of a manuscript includes a manuscript page header and page number, the running head, the title, and author information.
4. The **abstract** provides a brief (100–120 words) summary of the contents of the paper.
5. The **introduction section** includes a thesis statement, literature review, and statement of the experimental hypothesis.
6. The **method section** contains a thorough description of the participants (**participants subsection**), the objects used in the experiment (**apparatus, materials**, or **testing instruments subsection**), and what took place during the study (**procedure subsection**).
7. The **results section** presents inferential and descriptive statistics to describe the experimental outcomes. **Figures** or **tables** may aid in presenting the statistical information.
8. In the **discussion section**, the researcher draws conclusions from the experiment by summarizing the results, comparing the results to previous research, and interpreting the results.
9. The **reference list** provides bibliographic information for any works cited in the paper. APA format includes different reference formats for periodical articles, books, chapters from edited books, and a host of other sources.

TABLE 20-1 LEVELS AND LOCATIONS OF HEADINGS USED IN AN
APA-FORMAT PAPER SELECTING THE LEVELS OF HEADING

Find the section of your paper that breaks into the finest level of subordinate categories. Then use the guidelines that follow to determine the level, position, and arrangement of headings. Few articles require all levels of heading. Note that each subheading must have at least one counterpart at the same level within a section; for brevity, the examples that follow do not include counterparts.

One level. For a short article, one level of heading may be sufficient. In such cases, use only centered uppercase and lowercase headings (Level 1).

Two levels. For many articles in APA journals, two levels of headings meet the requirements. Use Level 1 and Level 3 headings:

Procedure ◀──(Level 3)

If the material subordinate to the Level 1 headings is short or if many Level 3 headings are necessary, indented, italicized lowercase paragraph headings (Level 4) may be more appropriate than Level 3 headings. (A Level 4 heading should apply to all text between it and the next heading, regardless of the heading level of the next heading.)

Three levels. For many articles, three levels of headings are needed. Use Level 1, Level 3, and Level 4 headings.

In a single-experiment study, these three levels of headings may look like this:

In a *multiexperiment study*, these three levels of headings may look like this:

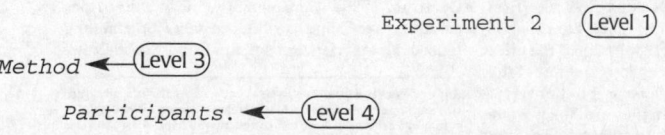

Four levels. For some articles, particularly multiexperiment studies, monographs, and lengthy literature reviews, four levels of headings are needed. Use heading Levels 1 through 4:

Five levels. Occasionally, an article requires five levels of headings. In such cases, subordinate all four levels above by introducing a Level 5 heading—A CENTERED UPPERCASE HEADING above the other four.

Source: This material has been reproduced from the *Publication Manual of the American Psychological Association*, fifth edition, pp. 114–115. Copyright © 2001 by the American Psychological Association. Reprinted with permission. Neither the original nor this reproduction can be reproduced or distributed in any form or by any means, or stored in a database or retrieval system, without prior written permission of the American Psychological Association.

Eminem Versus Charley Pride: Race, Stereotypes, and Perceptions of Rap and Country Music Performers

Allison J. Dickson

Traci A. Giuliano*

James C. Morris

Keri L. Cass

Southwestern University

The present study explored the effects of stereotype deviation in the music industry on people's perceptions of performers. One hundred college students (48 men, 52 women) examined a profile of a fictitious performer containing a picture, a brief biography, and a lyric sample. As part of a 2-way between-subjects design, participants made judgments about either a Black or a White musician who performed either rap or country music. The results showed that a Black rap performer was rated more favorably than a Black country performer, and a White country performer was rated more favorably than a White rap performer. Consistent with predictions, people who violate societal expectations are judged more harshly than are people who conform to societal expectations, particularly in cases involving strong preexisting racial stereotypes.

W HAT DO EMINEM AND CHARLEY PRIDE HAVE in common? Perhaps the connection these two performers share is subtle, but they are in fact quite similar in at least one aspect of their careers. Both Charley Pride, a Black country music performer, and Eminem, a White rap performer, deviate from social expectations that are a part of the music industry. Specifically, these two musicians defy cultural stereotypes by performing types of music that are not typically associated with their race.

Racial stereotypes exist in most individuals, and they can influence subsequent judgments made by a perceiver (Devine, 1989; Dovidio, Evans, & Tyler, 1986; Gaertner & McLaughlin, 1983). For example, Gaertner and McLaughlin (1983) studied the effect of racial stereotypes on perceptions and found that White students responded faster to positive stereotyped words (e.g., *smart*) when the words followed the race *White* rather than *Black*. In addition, Sagar and Schofield (1980) examined the perceptions made by sixth-grade boys about ambiguous behavior. They found that both Black and White boys construed ambiguously aggressive behaviors (such as one child bumping into another) as being more threatening if the actions were performed by a Black boy rather than a White boy. Most people today would not be likely to openly express racist beliefs, but the results of the above studies support the aversive racism perspective, which suggests that subtle and indirect forms of racism persist in society today (Dovidio & Gaertner, 1991; Gaertner & Dovidio, 1986). That is, although current cultural values emphasize fairness and racial equality, White individuals have a historic tradition of having negative beliefs concerning Blacks and other minority groups (Dovidio, Brigham, Johnson, & Gaertner, 1996). Consequently, racial stereotypes continue to exist and to influence interactions among individuals in society, but perhaps in more subtle ways.

Author note. We would like to thank Jennifer Knight for her advice and input on this study, Marie Helweg-Larsen for her helpful comments on an earlier draft of this manuscript, Alan Swinkels for his assistance with graphic illustrations, and Johnnie Dickson for her proofreading skills and patience.

Correspondence concerning this study should be addressed to Traci Giuliano at Southwestern University, Georgetown, TX 78626-6144. Electronic mail may be sent to giuliant@southwestern. edu.

FIGURE 20-17 (JA1).

Source: From "Eminem Versus Charley Pride: Race, Stereotypes, and Perceptions of Rap and Country Music Performers" by A. J. Dickson, T. A. Giuliano, J. C. Morris, and K. L. Cass, 2001, *Psi Chi Journal of Undergraduate Research, 6,* pp. 175–180. Used with permission of the publisher.

RACE, STEREOTYPES, AND PERCEPTIONS OF PERFORMERS □ *Dickson, Giuliano, Morris, and Cass*

Because stereotypes can influence the judgments and behaviors of perceivers, deviations from a stereotype should have similar effects. In general, the expectations of the perceiver and the extent to which these expectations are confirmed or disconfirmed can influence judgments. When behavior only slightly varies from expectations, the difference might not be noticed, but perceivers often magnify the discrepancy when actions differ significantly from expectations. This phenomenon is known as the contrast effect (Brehm, Kassin, & Fein, 1999). In fact, a person who displays behavior inconsistent with societal expectations is often evaluated more extremely than is a person who behaves consistently with expectations (Knight, Giuliano, & Sanchez-Ross, 2001). Jackson, Sullivan, and Hodge (1993) examined the effects of describing stereotype-consistent or stereotype-inconsistent behavior of Black out-group targets and White in-group targets on social evaluations made by participants who assessed a college application. They found that people who deviate from a norm are judged more extremely than if they behave as the norm dictates. Specifically, stereotype-inconsistent Black applicants with strong credentials were evaluated more favorably than were strong White applicants, and stereotype-inconsistent White applicants with weak credentials were evaluated less favorably than were weak Black applicants.

Both stereotypes and stereotype-inconsistent behavior affect the evaluations individuals make about other people in a variety of social interactions. Fried (1996, 1999) studied biased reactions involving the music industry and found that individuals had very different reactions to music labeled as *rap* or *country* despite the fact that the song lyrics were exactly the same. In two studies, she found that people generally considered rap music to be more violent and more offensive than country music. Furthermore, a folk song that was presented as being performed by a Black artist was judged more negatively than the very same song when it was presented as being performed by a White artist (Fried, 1996). Fried (1999) attributed her results to stereotypes in that rap is usually associated with Black culture whereas country music is often thought of as being a part of White culture. By priming a Black stereotype with the use of the label rap, it is possible that individuals apply negative stereotypes that have been shown to be associated with African Americans (Brigham, 1971). Therefore, racial stereotypes can impact evaluations of music performers (Fried, 1996, 1999).

According to Fiske and Taylor (1991), long-held stereotypes are not easily altered, but modification of stereotypes may begin with a divergence by stereo-typed individuals or groups. Previous research has examined the effects of stereotypes and stereotype deviation on people's evaluations of other individuals (Jackson et al., 1993; Knight et al., 2001). The present study attempted to integrate and expand on these concepts in relation to the music industry. Specifically, whereas Fried (1996, 1999) examined the effect of either the race of the performer or the labeled genre of music of a song on evaluations about the music itself, the design of the present experiment explored the interactive effects of the race of the performer and the genre of music on participants' evaluations of the performer. In doing so, we explored the difference between perceptions of persons who adhere to social expectations versus persons who deviate from the stereotype.

Consistent with previous research (Jackson et al., 1993; Knight et al., 2001), we expected that participants would judge performers who behave consistently with social norms (i.e., Black rap artists and White country performers) more favorably than performers who deviate from societal expectations (i.e., White rap artists and Black country performers). That is, because country music is associated with White culture, a Black country performer does not exhibit behavior consistent with this stereotype and, as a result, this performer should elicit negative judgments. The same reaction should occur with a White rap artist because his or her behavior is inconsistent with the stereotype that rap is predominantly a part of Black culture.

Method

Participants

Data were collected from 100 undergraduates (48 men, 52 women) at Southwestern University, a small liberal arts college in the Southwest. Demographically, the university is composed primarily of White, middle- to upper middle-class students; as such, the current sample (which was representative of the campus at large) consisted almost exclusively of White students. Participant volunteers ranged in age from 18 to 26 years ($M = 19.77$ years). Data from four participants were excluded from the analysis because these participants either failed to follow instructions or they did not pass the manipulation check. Specifically, these participants were unable to identify the race of the performer and genre of his music that was presented in the their survey packet.

Design and Procedure

The present study used a 2 (race of performer: Black or White) × 2 (genre of music: rap or country) between-subjects design to explore the effect of the

FIGURE 20-18 (JA2).

RACE, STEREOTYPES, AND PERCEPTIONS OF PERFORMERS □ *Dickson, Giuliano, Morris, and Cass*

race of a performer and the genre of music on perceptions of the performer. We recruited participants from various locations on campus and asked them to contribute to an investigation exploring "people's perceptions of music." Once they agreed, participants viewed a picture of a male performer, read a brief biography about him, and read a lyric sample of his music. Next, they completed a survey in which they made judgments about the performer and his music, and they responded to filler questions concerning their taste in music in general to corroborate the cover story. Each participant was randomly assigned to one of four experimental conditions and read a profile of either a Black rap artist, a White rap artist, a Black country performer, or a White country performer. Measures of the primary dependent variable (i.e., how favorably participants rated the performers) were embedded among filler questions in the survey. Following completion of the survey and a brief manipulation check that focused on the performer's race and the genre of music, we explained the purpose of the present study to the participants and asked them not to discuss it with anyone.

Materials

A three-page experimental packet, which ostensibly contained a survey about people's perceptions of music, was distributed along with an envelope. The first page contained a "performer profile" and included a color picture of a Black or White male performer, a brief biography about him indicating that he was either a rap or country performer, and a lyric sample from one of his songs. The subsequent pages contained the survey, which was used to measure participants' reactions to what they had seen and read on the previous page.

Each performer profile contained a biography that included the name of the performer (i.e., D.J. Jones), his hometown (Atlanta, Georgia), and a brief summary of his musical career (e.g., "D.J. has been singing since he was 14, and recently signed a record deal with a major country label. He will soon be on an international tour opening for a popular country artist"). To create the sample song lyrics, we slightly altered and combined two rock songs (May, 1973; May & Staffell, 1973; see Appendix A). With the exception of the two manipulations, we used the same biography and song lyrics in each of the four experimental conditions. The first manipulation altered the genre of music (i.e., rap or country) that the artist performed. Specifically, the name of the performer and the type of music he performed was labeled beneath his picture, and this label coincided with the genre of music described in the biography. Next, a

photograph manipulated the race of the performer so that each biography was accompanied by a picture of either a Black or a White man. To ensure that the only attribute differing between the Black and White performers was in fact race, we conducted a pilot test in a Research Methods class to match the Black and White performers on attractiveness and age. The participants in the pilot test were all White, which is representative of the ethnic composition of the participants in the present study. From a pool of 20 color photographs of nonfamous Black and White men selected from magazines, the two stimuli selected for the present study were most similar in perceived attractiveness and age.

Following the performer profile were the questions that assessed perceptions of the performer and his music, as well as the musical tastes of the participants. Embedded among demographic questions (e.g., sex and age) and other filler questions (e.g., "On average, how many CDs and/or tapes do you buy a month?") were the items that examined participants' perceptions of the performer. Specifically, participants rated on 7-point scales with endpoints labeled at 1 *(not at all)* and 7 *(very much):* (a) "Overall, how much do you like this performer?"; (b) "How talented do you think this performer is?"; (c) "How legitimate is this performer?"; and finally (d) "How successful do you predict this performer will be in the music industry?" Because these items were highly correlated, they were combined into an overall index reflecting participants' favorability of the performer (Cronbach's $\alpha = .80$). The scores on the four items were averaged together, and consistent with the scales on the individual items, the overall index is on a 7-point scale with higher numbers representing a more favorable perception of the performer and lower numbers indicating an unfavorable perception.

Results

A 2 (race of performer: Black or White) × 2 (genre of music: rap or country) between-subjects analysis of variance (ANOVA) was performed on the index assessing the favorability of the performer (i.e., likability, perceived talent, perceived legitimacy, and predicted success). Data analysis revealed a significant main effect of race such that Black performers ($M = 4.32$, $SD = .91$) were rated more positively than were White performers ($M = 3.76$, $SD = 1.00$), $F(1, 92) = 10.42$, $p = .002$, $\eta^2 = .10$. However, this main effect was qualified by the significant two-way interaction between race of performer and genre of music, which was consistent with predictions, $F(1, 92) = 26.72$, $p = .0001$, $\eta^2 = .23$. An inspection of the means in Figure 1 shows that participants rated a Black rap artist ($M =$

FIGURE 20-19 (JA3).

RACE, STEREOTYPES, AND PERCEPTIONS OF PERFORMERS □ *Dickson, Giuliano, Morris, and Cass*

FIGURE 1

Mean ratings for favorability of the performer as a function of his race and the genre of music.

4.79, $SD = .68$) more favorably than a Black country artist ($M = 3.85$, $SD = .87$), $t(46) = 4.17$, $p = .0001$; however, they judged a White country artist ($M = 4.19$, $SD = .92$) more favorably than a White rap artist ($M = 3.33$, $SD = .91$), $t(46) = 3.24$, $p = .0001$. There was no main effect of genre of music, $F < 1$, ns. Participants reported similar ratings for rap performers ($M = 4.06$, $SD = 1.09$) and country performers ($M = 4.02$, $SD = .90$).

Discussion

The present study integrated and expanded on two lines of research. First, it extended previous research (Fried, 1996, 1999) on stereotyping involving the music industry. Whereas Fried (1996, 1999) examined reactions to music lyrics based on either the genre label or the performer's race, our study considered the interactive effect of both the race of the performer and the genre of music on people's evaluations of performers. The current study also differs from previous research conducted by Fried (1996, 1999) in that the lyrics in our study did not attempt to convey negative images such as violence or aggression. That is, Fried (1996, 1999) asked participants specifically about their negative impressions of the song lyrics (e.g., its offensiveness, its threat to society, its need for warning labels), whereas the current study emphasized overall impressions of the performer. Rap may be more often associated with negative topics, but these topics can be found in both rap and country music. We chose to use neutral lyrics in the present study because we were not focusing on the relation between negative themes and music genre. Instead, the current study was based on find-

ings that rap is associated with a Black culture that has both positive and negative attributes (Brigham, 1971). We examined the connection between music genre and the stereotype-consistent or stereotype-inconsistent race of the performer. In our study, participants judged Black rap artists more favorably than Black country music performers, whereas they judged White country music performers more favorably than White rap artists. These results support the hypothesis that individuals who deviate from societal expectations are judged more negatively than are individuals who adhere to social norms (Jackson et al., 1993; Knight et al., 2001). Manis, Nelson, and Shedler (1988) found that extreme stereotypes yielded contrast effects when behavior was discrepant from the established stereotype. In the present study, Black country music performers and White rap artists contrast from fairly ingrained societal expectations and thus received more negative judgments than the performers who adhere to societal norms.

The present study could be extended in a number of ways. For example, like Fried's (1996, 1999) research, the current study also presented the lyric sample to participants on paper. It would be interesting to explore whether an audio-recorded lyric sample would affect participants' evaluations of performers or the music. Perhaps auditory processing and visual processing of stereotype-consistent and stereotype-inconsistent information differ. In addition, the present study could broaden its scope by including a more varied sample of participants. That is, future studies could incorporate participants of different races and ages. The data in the current study were collected primarily from White undergraduate students at a liberal arts university, and the results from such a homogenous sample may not necessarily generalize to alternative populations or settings. Furthermore, exploring alternate stereotype violations could support the findings of the present study, and one area of interest could be the world of sports. For instance, Black hockey players violate societal expectations similar to the apparent violation made by Black country music performers and White rap performers. According to our findings, Black hockey players would receive more negative evaluations than would White hockey players because their behavior is inconsistent with societal expectations.

Because the population of other minority groups (e.g., Latinos) is approaching that of the Black population in America, future research concerning racial stereotypes in the music industry could examine the impact of the increasing popularity of Latin music (Gonzales, 1990). Garcia and Zapatel (2000) recently examined how the labels *Black rap, Latino rap*, and

FIGURE 20-20 (JA4).

RACE, STEREOTYPES, AND PERCEPTIONS OF PERFORMERS □ *Dickson, Giuliano, Morris, and Cass*

alternative music influence perceptions made by both Anglo and Hispanic participants and found that participants' perceptions of music differed depending on their own race. Specifically, Hispanic participants judged music labeled *Latino rap* more positively than music labeled *alternative*, whereas Anglo participants rated music labeled *alternative* more favorably than music labeled *Latino rap*. Similar to previous findings (Jackson et al., 1993), out-group categories (i.e., *Latino rap* for Anglo participants and *alternative* music for Hispanic participants) were judged more negatively than were categories that corresponded to the participants' ethnicity. Extended to a more diverse sample, the present study could offer support for the idea that out-group categories are judged more negatively than in-group categories by examining the relation between participants' ethnicities and their evaluations of rap and country music. Thus, regardless of the race of the performer, Black participants would be expected to rate country music more negatively than rap music, whereas White participants would be expected to judge rap music more negatively than country music. Furthermore, it would be interesting to determine whether or not performers of Latin music will remain primarily Latin and to examine perceptions of stereotype-consistent and stereotype-inconsistent performers in this genre. If future performers do deviate from racial stereotypes, the present study suggests that non-Latino performers of Latin music would be perceived less favorably than would Latino performers.

In closing, Eminem and Charley Pride share a connection in that their actions deviate from widespread stereotypes that specific races are associated with certain types of music. Although people may recognize these two performers because of their musical talent, it is more likely that they are recognized because they were bold enough to defy stereotypes in the music industry. By being a White rap artist and a Black country music performer, Eminem and Charley Pride became forerunners for performers who do not adhere to social norms, and they may have possibly influenced numerous music fans to expect the unexpected.

References

Brehm, S. S., Kassin, S. M., & Fein, S. (1999). *Social psychology* (4th ed.). Boston: Houghton Mifflin.

Brigham, J. C. (1971). Ethnic stereotypes. *Psychological Bulletin, 76,* 15–38.

Devine, P. G. (1989). Stereotypes and prejudice: Their automatic and controlled components. *Journal of Personality and Social Psychology, 56,* 5–18.

Dovidio, J. F., Brigham, J. C., Johnson, B. T., & Gaertner, S. L. (1996). Stereotyping, prejudice, and discrimination: Another look. In N. C. Macrae, C. Stangor, & M. Hewstone (Eds.), *Stereotypes & stereotyping* (pp. 276–322). New York: Guilford Press.

Dovidio, J. F., Evans, N., & Tyler, R. B. (1986). Racial stereotypes: The contents of their cognitive representations. *Journal of Experimental Social Psychology, 22,* 22–37.

Dovidio, J. F., & Gaertner, S. L. (1991). Changes in the expression and assessment of racial prejudice. In H. R. Knopke, R. J. Norrell, & R. W. Rogers (Eds.), *Opening doors: Perspectives on race relations in contemporary America* (pp. 119–148). Tuscaloosa: University of Alabama Press.

Fiske, S. T., & Taylor, S. E. (1991). *Social cognition* (2nd ed.). New York: McGraw-Hill.

Fried, C. B. (1996). Bad rap for rap: Bias in reactions to music lyrics. *Journal of Applied Social Psychology, 26,* 2135–2146.

Fried, C. B. (1999). Who's afraid of rap: Differential reactions to music lyrics. *Journal of Applied Social Psychology, 29,* 705–721.

Gaertner, S. L., & Dovidio, J. F. (1986). The aversive form of racism. In J. F. Dovidio & S. L. Gaertner (Eds.), *Prejudice, discrimination, and racism: Theory and research* (pp. 61–89). Orlando, FL: Academic Press.

Gaertner, S. L., & McLaughlin, J. P. (1983). Racial stereotypes: Associations and ascriptions of positive and negative characteristics. *Social Psychology Quarterly, 46,* 23–30.

Garcia, S. D., & Zapatel, J. P. (2000, January). *Perceptions of lyrics as a function of ethnicity and music genre.* Paper presented at the annual meeting of the Social Psychologists in Texas, San Antonio.

Gonzales, J. L., Jr. (1990). *Racial and ethnic groups in America: A collection of readings.* Dubuque, IA: Kendall/Hunt.

Jackson, L. A., Sullivan, L. A., & Hodge, C. N. (1993). Stereotype effects on attributions, predictions, and evaluations: No two social judgments are quite alike. *Journal of Personality and Social Psychology, 65,* 69–84.

Knight, J. L., Giuliano, T. A., & Sanchez-Ross, M. G. (2001). Famous or infamous? The influence of celebrity status and race on perceptions of responsibility for rape. *Basic and Applied Social Psychology, 23,* 183–190.

Manis, M., Nelson, T. E., & Shedler, J. (1988). Stereotypes and social judgment: Extremity, assimilation, and contrast. *Journal of Personality and Social Psychology, 55,* 28–36.

May, B. (1973). The night comes down. [Recorded by Queen]. On *Queen* [Record]. London: EMI Records.

May, B., & Staffell, T. (1973). Doing all right. [Recorded by Queen]. On *Queen* [Record]. London: EMI Records.

Sagar, H. A., & Schofield, J. W. (1980). Racial and behavioral cues in Black and White children's perceptions of ambiguously aggressive acts. *Journal of Personality & Social Psychology, 39,* 590–598.

FIGURE 20-21 (JA5).

10. The **author note** allows the author to thank people for their help, cite a previous presentation of the findings, and designate a contact person for information about the experiment.

11. The specific sections of the APA format paper are designated by various headings. **Level 1** and **Level 3 headings** are most commonly used with experimental reports. For more complex papers, **Level 4 headings** may need to be added.

CHECK YOUR PROGRESS

1. What is meant by the term *APA format*? Why was it developed?

2. Matching

   1. manuscript page header
   2. running head
   3. Level 1 heading
   4. Level 3 heading

   5. Level 4 heading

   6. thesis statement

   A. indicates the general topic you are interested in
   B. centered, upper- and lowercase letters
   C. first two or three words of the title
   D. left margin, underlined, upper- and lowercase letters
   E. condensed title
   F. indented five spaces, underlined, only first word is capitalized, ends with period

3. Why is the abstract the most widely read section of most research reports?

4. How is the introduction section similar to what is found in a typical term paper? How is it different?

5. A citation includes three authors. The third citation of this study in the text should

   a. list all three authors

   b. list just the first author

   c. list the first author followed by et al.

   d. none of the above

6. List three different purposes of the method section. Which do you think is most important? Why?

7. We draw conclusions with _____ statistics and create a picture of our data with _____ statistics.

8. Could you use figures or tables as your sole information in a results section? Why or why not?

9. Matching

   1. Title Page
   2. Abstract
   3. Introduction
   4. Method
   5. Results
   6. Discussion
   7. References
   8. Author Note

   A. presents statistical findings
   B. a short summary of the article
   C. includes full address of author
   D. reports the "bottom line" of the experiment
   E. includes manuscript page header and running head
   F. bibliographic information
   G. reviews previous research
   H. tells how the experiment was conducted

10. Some people believe that the discussion section is the most important section of an experiment report. Do you agree? Why or why not?

11. Why is the reference for a chapter from an edited book more complex than the reference for either a journal article or a book?

Writing in APA Style

We hope that you were a good student in your English composition classes because good writing is quite important when writing your research report. As we noted earlier, we do not want to attempt to teach writing, but we do want to provide some pointers you may find helpful. The topic of Chapter 2 in the *PM* is "Expressing Ideas." You should read that chapter carefully. In the next sections we will give you some general and specific guidelines that will assist you in writing your research report. As you will see, there are some differences between APA style and the way you learned to write in English classes. Scientific writing style is different in many ways from creative writing.

General Guidelines

The main objective of scientific writing is clear communication. It is your job to communicate your ideas as clearly as possible to the reader. The *PM* provides you with several hints about how to accomplish this goal. Be sure to read pages 31–40 in the *PM* to supplement the following information.

Orderly Presentation of Ideas   The key idea here is continuity. From the beginning of your research report to the end, you are writing a continuous idea or thought in which you tell the reader about your experiment. Do you remember sitting in class and getting lost in a lecture because you couldn't tell where the teacher was going (or where the teacher had been)? Those little side excursions in a lecture ("chasing rabbits") may be a delightful diversion in class, but they do tend to make you lose track of where you're going. Don't detour as you write your manuscript. Get on track and stay there with singlemindedness of purpose.

Smoothness of Expression   Writing in a continuous fashion will greatly aid your smoothness of expression. Creative writing is often not smooth because it uses literary devices to create tension or to conceal plot lines or to hide a surprise for later. Remember that scientific writing's goal is communication rather than escape and entertainment. One of the best things you can do to make your writing smooth is to work on transition sentences when you shift from one topic to another. Try to avoid abrupt shifts that make readers feel they have run into a wall.

Economy of Expression   Again, with your primary goal being communication, it is important to be direct and to the point in your writing. When journal editors work on submitted manuscripts they have only a limited number of pages available for the printed journal; thus, it is to their advantage to have manuscripts that are short and communicative rather than long and unclear. Some people are surprised to find out that you can often shorten your writing and make it clearer at the same time. The *PM*

"IN THE SOCIAL SCIENCES WE HARDLY USE NUMBERS, BUT WE CAN WRITE LONG, COMPLICATED SENTENCES."

Courtesy of Sidney Harris.

We hope you recognize that both statements in this cartoon are incorrect. In psychology, we do use numbers and we work hard at communicating clearly.

specifically advises you to avoid jargon, wordiness, and redundancy. Also, you should not repeat yourself. (Yes, that second sentence was there on purpose—did you catch the unnecessary repetition?)

Precision and Clarity   We encourage you to work on becoming a wordsmith rather than a wordmonger. As you probably know, a smith is someone who works with a particular material (e.g., a tinsmith, a goldsmith). A wordsmith works carefully with words, whereas a wordmonger uses words carelessly. Make sure the words you use fit the exact purpose and meaning that you have in mind. One of the major problems many of us have with writing is that we write in the same manner that we speak. Ambiguities may occur in speech, but we often clarify matters because we can interact directly with the speaker. Interaction is not possible when reading a text passage. Therefore, choose your words carefully so that you truly do say what you mean. Such clarity rarely occurs on a first attempt at writing—be sure that you reread and edit everything you write.

Strategies to Improve Writing Style   The *PM* (APA, 2001, p. 40) suggests three approaches to becoming a more effective writer.

1. **Write from an outline.** If you have a "road map" for your writing, you are more likely to arrive at your destination in a timely fashion.
2. **Write your first draft, put it away, and read it after a delay.** If you attempt to cram your writing into a short time period, you will have difficulty editing your writing because you are likely to have the same thoughts you had a few minutes earlier. By giving yourself a time break, you are more likely to see the things you missed the first time—and it will be easier to think of ways to correct the problems.

3. **Ask someone to evaluate your writing.** It is usually quite helpful to have at least one other person read your papers before you submit them. It is easier for someone who is unfamiliar with the work to spot inconsistencies, weaknesses, ambiguities, and other flaws in your writing. Of course, you are asking *only* for a critique of your writing style, not the substance of your paper. Having someone help you with substance is unethical unless that person is a co-author. Some instructors offer to critique rough drafts of your work—you should always take advantage of such an offer. Ask classmates to critique your writing and offer to do the same for them. You may learn a great deal both from their critique and from reading and critiquing someone else's writing.

Grammatical Guidelines

The *PM* covers a variety of guidelines about grammar on pages 40–61. Most of these guidelines are standard conventions of grammar that you learned in grammar classes. We urge you to review these pages. Rather than turning this book into a grammar handbook at this point, we will cover only those conventions that are specific to APA style or with which students seem to have difficulty.

Passive Voice   According to the *PM*, you should use active voice rather than passive voice when writing your research report. In passive voice, the true object of the verb becomes the subject of the sentence and the true subject becomes the object (Bellquist, 1993). Passive voice often appears in methods sections because writers use the passivity to avoid personalizing that section. Let us give an example to clarify:

> After viewing the slides, a recall test was given to participants.

This sentence is not direct and active; rather, it is indirect and passive. The test should be the object of the sentence, not the subject. Who did the acting? Presumably the experimenter did, but the experimenter is not even present in this sentence.

Reread the passive voice sentence. Can you recast it in active voice?

Actually, there are several ways you could change this sentence to make it active, depending on whether you want to include the experimenter. You could write:

> I gave the participants a recall test after they viewed the slides.

If you have coauthors for your experiment, the sentence could become this:

> We gave the participants a recall test after they viewed the slides.

Although many experimenters seem to be uncomfortable using first person (I, we), the *PM* specifically permits it. In fact, the *PM* specifically says to avoid third person references to yourself (e.g., "the experimenter," pp. 37–38). If you still wish to avoid first person, you could write:

> The participants completed a recall test after viewing the slides.

In each of these sample sentences, you now have actors acting (active voice) rather than having something done to them (passive voice).

That* versus *Which   Clauses beginning with *that* are termed restrictive clauses and should be essential to the meaning of the sentence. On the other hand, clauses beginning with *which* can be either restrictive or nonrestrictive (simply adding additional information). In APA style, you should confine yourself to using *which* for nonrestrictive clauses only. Thus, *that* and *which* should not be used interchangeably. Using *which* is similar to making an "oh, by the way" addition to your sentence. To further help you distinguish the difference, remember that nonrestrictive clauses should be set off with commas. Let's look at some examples:

> The stimulus items *that* the participants did not recall were the more difficult items.

The phrase "that the participants did not recall" is essential to the sentence's meaning. Imagine the sentence without that phrase—it would make no sense.

> The stimulus items, *which* were nouns, appeared on a computer monitor.

The phrase "which were nouns" is not essential to the meaning of this sentence. If we delete this phrase, the sentence retains its original meaning. The phrase does add some additional information about the stimulus items, but this information could be included elsewhere.

Words that have Temporal Meaning   The words *since* and *while* can cause difficulty in scientific writing because they have more than one meaning in everyday usage. Writers often use *since* interchangeably with *because* and use *while* to substitute for *although*. Some grammar stylebooks allow these multiple uses. APA style, however, does not. You should use *since* and *while* only for temporal purposes—in other words, to make time comparisons. Thus, use *while* to denote events that occur at the same time and *since* to denote that time has passed. Again, here are some examples:

> Many different IQ tests have evolved *since* Binet's original version.

Note that here *since* refers to time that has occurred after Binet's test; this sentence is acceptable.

> *Since* the XYZ group scored higher, we concluded that they learned the material better.

This use of *since* is incorrect—you should substitute *because* in its place.

> *While* the participants were studying the verbal items, they heard music.

Note that *while* in this sentence tells you that studying and music playing occurred simultaneously; this sentence is acceptable.

While some psychologists believe in Skinner's ideas, many others have rejected his beliefs.

This use of *while* is incorrect—nothing is occurring at the same time. Instead, a contrast is being drawn. You should substitute *although* in this sentence.

Bias in Language   Remember that we stressed the use of unbiased language earlier in this chapter. We believe that this type of writing is important in helping maintain a neutral (unbiased) approach to science. Thus, we wish to remind you of the need for removing biased terms from your writing. The *PM* (APA, 2001, pp. 61–76) gives three guidelines that may be helpful in reducing bias in writing.

- **Describe at the appropriate level of specificity.** In other words, you should describe persons as specifically as you can. When we use broad terms to describe people, we are more likely to include people who should not be included. For example, "Japanese Americans" is more specific than "Asian Americans."
- **Be sensitive to labels.** When we use stereotyped labels, we are likely using terms that contain bias. Basically, we should refer to groups as they wish to be referred to rather than imposing our labels on them. When at all possible, it is better to avoid labels. As the *PM* points out, "people diagnosed with schizophrenia" is both more accurate and more preferred than "schizophrenics" (APA, 2001, p. 64).
- **Acknowledge participation.** This guideline is generally aimed at experiments that use human participants, although it would not hurt us to keep it in mind for animal studies also. The general idea of this guideline is to make sure you remember that the participants in your experiment are individuals. This idea formed the rationale for changing the label *subjects* to the label *participants*. Using active rather than passive voice also helps to personalize your participants.

A Disclaimer   Please remember that we could not possibly squeeze all the grammar guidelines from the *PM* into this section. Again, we chose to highlight the few that we did because they may differ from what you learned in English classes or because we know that students (and professors) tend to have trouble with these points of grammar and usage. We did not leave out the others because they are unimportant or even less important. We urge you to read pages 40–61 in the *PM* to review your knowledge of grammar.

APA Editorial Style

Chapter 3 of the *PM* addresses APA editorial style on pages 77–214—virtually a third of the book. This chapter gives writers a style guide to follow that will help create uniformity in writings by different authors in different publications. We have already covered the most important aspects of APA editorial style in this chapter—levels of headings, metrication, statistical copy in text, tables, figures, reference citations in text, and reference lists.

In addition to the important aspects of APA editorial style we have covered to this point, you should be aware that the *PM* gives you guidance on issues such as punctuation, spelling, capitalization, italics, abbreviations, seriation, quotations, numbers, footnotes, and appendixes. Again, we do not have the space it would take to address every possible concern in this chapter. When you have questions about any of these matters, consult Chapter 3 in the *PM*.

Preparing Your Manuscript

Chapter 5 of the *PM* (pp. 283–320) provides the guidelines you need in order to actually type your experimental paper. This chapter is probably one of the most-used chapters in the *PM* because it includes three examples of sample papers (pp. 306–320). These sample papers include notations of specific *PM* sections for each important component of the paper. We hope that the combination of the sample manuscript in this chapter and the sample papers in the *PM* make typing your paper a relatively simple matter.

Chapter 5 of the *PM* is primarily a reference chapter, much like Chapters 3 and 4. You should consult it whenever you have a question about typing a specific portion of your manuscript. Let us provide you with a short list of the highlights of the typing instructions:

- **Line Spacing.** Double-space everything everywhere.
- **Margins.** Use at least 1-inch margins on all sides. Keep in mind that for the top margin, this margin refers to the point at which the text begins rather than the manuscript page header and number. Thus, you can set the top margin in your word processor to less than 1 inch so that the text begins at least 1 inch down from the top of the paper.
- **Lines.** Set your word processor to left justification. Your paper should have a ragged right edge throughout (i.e., the right margin should *not* line up down the page like it does in this book). Do not divide or hyphenate words between lines.
- **Pages.** Number all pages (including the title page; excepting figures) consecutively. The following sections should begin on new pages: title page, abstract, introduction (remember not to label it *Introduction*), references, appendixes, author note, footnotes, tables (a separate page for each), figure captions (all on one sheet), figures (each on a separate page).
- **Word Spacing.** Space once after all punctuation, including plus and minus signs in equations. There is no spacing before or after hyphens (-) or dashes (– or —). Type a hyphen to denote a negative value; in this case, use a space before the hyphen but not after.
- **Quotations.** Enclose quotations that are shorter than 40 words in double quotation marks (") and write them as part of the text. You should block (indent) longer quotations from the left margin—be sure to double-space them.

Consult Table 20-2 for a more comprehensive checklist of guidelines regarding APA formatting of your manuscript. If you have questions about other matters as you type your manuscript, consult Chapter 5 of the *PM*.

TABLE 20-2 CHECKLIST FOR CORRECT APA FORMATTING

GENERAL FORMATTING AND TYPING

	PUBLICATION MANUAL SECTION
• There are 1-in. (2.54-cm) margins on all four sides of each page of the manuscript.	5.04
• The typeface is the correct size (12 points on a word processor) and the correct style (serif typefaces such as Courier or Times Roman).	5.02
• The manuscript is double-spaced throughout, including title page, references, tables, figure captions, author notes, and appendixes.	5.03
• The page header is the first two or three words of the title.	5.06
• The page number appears (a) on the same line with the page header and is five spaces to the right or (b) below the page header.	5.06
• The page header and page number are typed at the top of each page of the manuscript (except pages containing figures).	5.06
• The page header and figure number are handwritten on the back of figures (or on the front, outside the image area of the figure).	5.22
• There is only one space after these punctuation marks: commas, colons, semicolons, punctuation at the end of sentences, periods in citations, and all periods in the references section.	5.11
• Lowercase letters in parentheses have been used to indicate a series of events or items within a paragraph.	5.12
• Words are not broken (hyphenated) at the end of a line.	5.04
• All units of measurements have correct abbreviations.	3.25, 3.51

• Arabic numbers have been used correctly to express
    all numbers in the abstract
    numbers that are 10 or larger
    numbers that immediately precede a unit of measurement
    numbers that represent fractions and percentages
    number that represent times, dates, ages, participants, samples, populations, scores, or points on a scale
    numbers less than 10 *only when* those numbers are compared to a number greater than 10 (e.g., "Participants included 15 humanities and 3 natural science majors.")
	3.42

Words have been correctly used to express
    numbers less than 10
    numbers at the beginning of a title, sentence, or heading
	3.43

TITLE PAGE

The running head is aligned with the left margin and is equal to or less than 50 characters and spaces long.	5.15, 1.06
The author note *does not* appear on the title page; instead, the author note appears on a separate page after tables, figures, and appendixes (if included).	3.89, 5.20

(continued)

TABLE 20-2 (CONTINUED)

ABSTRACT

The word Abstract is typed at the top of the page.	5.16
The first line of the abstract is even with the left margin.	5.16
The abstract is not more than 120 words.	1.07, 5.16

BODY OF THE MANUSCRIPT

There are *no* one-sentence paragraphs.	2.03
Gender-inclusive language is used through plural pronouns (e.g., *they, their*), by using nouns (e.g., *one, an individual, participant's*), sparse use of *he or she* or *she or he*, or by sparse use of alternating between gendered pronouns (e.g., *he . . . ; she . . .*).	2.13
The words *male* and *female* are used *only* as adjectives (e.g., *female* quail), whereas the words *men, women, boys*, and *girls* are used as nouns.	Table 2.1
Quotations are word-for-word accurate and page numbers are provided.	3.35, 3.39
The word *while* is used *only* to indicate events that take place simultaneously (alternatives: *although, whereas, and, but*).	2.10
The word *since* is used *only* to indicate the passage of time (alternative: *because*).	2.10
Terms that are abbreviated are written out completely the first time they are used, then always abbreviated thereafter.	3.21
Latin abbreviations are used sparingly and *only* in parenthetical material.	3.24
The word *and* is used in citations outside of parentheses.	3.95
The ampersand (&) is used in citations within parentheses.	3.07, 3.95
When two or more citations are in parentheses, the citations are typed in the same order in which they appear in the references section.	3.99
Each and every citation used in the manuscript is correctly typed in the references section.	4.01, 4.02
The phrase *et al.* is used with each citation that lists six or more authors, and with each citation that lists three to five authors *after* the first instance of that citation.	3.95
In the method section the word *participants* is consistently used (use *subjects* only with animals).	1.09, 2.12
In the results section all test statistics (e.g., *F, t, p*) are italicized.	3.19, 3.58

REFERENCES SECTION

All entries are typed in alphabetical order.	4.04
Each and every entry occurs in the body of the manuscript.	4.01
Authors' names are separated by commas.	4.08
The volume numbers of journals are italicized.	4.11
Each entry is typed in a "hanging indent" format, meaning that the first line of each reference is flush with the left margin and subsequent lines are indented.	4.07, 5.18
The names of journals, book chapters, and books are correctly capitalized.	4.11

Source: Adapted from J. Dunn, K. Ford, K. L. Rewey, J. A. Juve, A. Weiser, and S. F. Davis, 2001, "A Modified Presubmission Checklist," *Psi Chi Journal of Undergraduate Research, 6*, 142–144.

A Student's View of the Publication Process

Yes, preparing an APA-format paper does involve a reasonable amount of effort. However, the rewards for this effort are genuine and substantial. You will have mastered a valuable skill, writing in an accepted scientific format, and you will have a completed paper that you can submit for publication. Throughout this book we have "gently encouraged" you to take advantage of professional development opportunities such as presenting your research at a convention and publishing your research. Let's conclude with a more in-depth look at the publication process. It's not as daunting as you might think.

Your faculty advisor can assist you in deciding where to submit your paper (we made some suggestions in Chapter 1). Once you have made that decision, you need to consult a recent issue of the journal you have selected to determine exactly how many copies to send, as well as any other special requirements the journal may have. Follow these instructions *very* carefully. When your submission is received, the editor, most likely, will send your paper to several (usually three) reviewers who will read, critique, and evaluate your work. Once the reviewers have finished reading and critiquing your paper, each one will make a publication recommendation (such as accept, accept pending minor revisions, accept pending major revisions, reject but encourage revision, or reject) to the editor. The editor will evaluate the reviewers' recommendations and comments and then make a final publication decision concerning your paper. The editor's letter describing her publication decision, as well as the reviewers' comments and critiques (often including the copies of your paper that they have marked and returned to the editor), are then returned to you. This process can take two or more months, so be patient.

It is likely that you will have to revise your paper one or more times before the editor and reviewers determine that it is suitable for publication. Don't give up! If you are interested in understanding the publishing process from the editor's point of view, we recommend that you read Smith's (1998) article. Consult with your faculty advisor at each step of the process. Having a publication is well worth the time and effort you will expend.

Very briefly, those are our views on the publication process. In Chapter 19 you read about Carolyn Licht's research on occupational stress (Licht, 2000; Licht & Solomon, 2001). Here are Carolyn's own views on the publication process.

The Dance of the Researcher

The publication process is both a frustrating and exhilarating experience. It takes commitment, perseverance, and discipline to make it to the culminating moment in which you see your work in print. When that moment happens, all the time and effort expended is forgotten and all you feel like doing is getting up and dancing a jig.

I had my first opportunity to discover the exhilaration associated with conceptualizing, analyzing, and preparing my research for presentation and publication as a sophomore in college. I had never done any formal research of any kind before, having been a ballet dancer for the previous decade of my life, and was a bit overwhelmed when my first assignment for my experimental psychology class was to create and execute a project from scratch. I decided to pick a subject that was something I and others could easily relate to—occupational stress. If I had known how consuming the research would become over the next few years, I probably would have picked a less "stressful" topic. This school assignment opened my eyes to the limitations, obstacles, and rewards faced by researchers trying to develop a workable hypothesis, gather and analyze data, and present results.

What I found to be the most interesting aspect about the research and publication process, ironically, was how closely it paralleled the work I did in my previous career as a professional ballet dancer. The ultimate goal and satisfaction of both endeavors is the sharing of your labor with others outside of your immediate circle. The journey that must be taken to get to this point is full of frustrations, obstacles, criticisms, and excitement; the cliché "No pain, No gain" seems apropos to characterize the overall process. The "dance" begins with an idea that takes form as the dancer/researcher collects the data (choreography and music/literature review and survey results), begins the rehearsal process, and analyzes all the components to see how they come together. The frustration of realizing that the pieces are not flowing together as smoothly as predicted, such as when you send out 500 surveys and receive only 100 completed ones back, is reminiscent of discovering that you have run out of choreography before the music is over. Ultimately you must return to the drawing board and either collect more data or reconceptualize the original premise of the piece. Eventually, however, a moment arrives in which what once was only an idea in your mind becomes a reality; although the form it takes may be far from what you had originally conceived.

The pride you feel when you have completed the research and submitted it to a journal for publication is similar to the joy you feel when you perform your dance for the first time on stage. You learn quickly, however, as you receive your first critiques from the journal reviewers, that you are still in dress rehearsal and are far from being ready for the final performance. I remember vividly the crushing feeling I got when I opened the large manila envelope containing the four drafts of my "perfect" paper, only to discover the massive number of red marks and comments concerning everything that was wrong and needed to be addressed before my work would even be considered for publication. The fact that many of the various suggestions from the reviewers were contradictory (one loved a section of the paper while another said it should be deleted all together) only added to my feelings of despair. Gratefully in the midst of all the criticism was also the glimmer of hope, the encouragement I needed to "rehearse" a bit longer, which consisted of a simple checked box on the comment sheets from the reviewers; the box marked was "accepted pending revisions" as opposed to the one next to it that said "rejection." With less work than I had anticipated, the next box to be checked would be the one marked "accepted for publication"; all the effort and energy exerted no longer seemed at all troublesome as the excitement of the pending publication became the focus of my attention.

When I saw my name in print, the feeling of pride and the boost to my self-esteem was incredible, but as I read my article in the journal, I realized that this was just the first step in what was going to be a lifelong journey in the field of psychology. I looked at my paper and understood that although my results were fascinating, they were limited because of the nature of the question and the research design. I wanted—no, I needed to discover if my findings were true on a larger scope, with a diverse population, in different settings. I knew at that moment what so many researchers before me have learned, that research questions are never definitively answered, rather they simply raise more questions that stimulate the researcher to continue the journey exploring the path ahead.

Ultimately, this college experimental research assignment resulted in two publications in the *Psi Chi Journal of Undergraduate Research* (Licht, 2000; Licht & Solomon, 2001), a poster presentation at the Eastern Psychological Association's National

Convention in Baltimore, an oral presentation at the Honors Colloquium at my college, citations in two textbooks, and, most importantly, it was a substantial contributing factor to my decision to pursue and eventual acceptance into a doctoral program in clinical psychology. In addition, I discovered, through my numerous interactions with the editor of the journal, that the publication process is a way to connect with others in the field, and to develop professional relationships and true friendships that become the true rewards of taking this particular journey.

Carolyn Licht

We hope that you, too, will have the opportunity to have the experience of publishing your manuscript as Carolyn did. Although there is hard work involved, the payoff is worth it all. We will remind you of the publication opportunities we mentioned in Chapter 1. As we have stressed throughout this book, publishing is not something that is beyond your capabilities. If you never give it a try, you certainly can't succeed. Good luck!

REVIEW SUMMARY

1. The primary goal of scientific writing is clear communication.
2. Goals that aid in clear communication are orderly presentation of ideas, smoothness of expression, economy of expression, and a striving for precision and clarity.
3. To improve your writing style you should write from an outline, put away your first draft before editing it, and have someone evaluate your writing.
4. You should use active voice whenever possible when writing your research report.
5. *That* should be used only with restrictive clauses, which include information that is essential to the meaning of a sentence. *Which* should be used in nonrestrictive clauses, which add information but are not essential to a sentence's meaning.
6. *Since* should not be used to substitute for *because*, nor should *while* substitute for *although*. Both *since* and *while* should be used only for temporal (time-related) meaning.
7. Psychologists strive to use unbiased language in their writing.
8. APA style includes guidelines on diverse matters such as punctuation, capitalization, quotations, numbers, appendixes, typing guidelines, and so on.
9. The *Publication Manual of the American Psychological Association* (APA, 2001) is the stylebook for psychological writing. It contains a wealth of information about the writing process.

CHECK YOUR PROGRESS

1. What would be wrong with writing your research paper in the style of Twain, Hemingway, or Faulkner? Be as specific as possible in your answer.
2. What are the three strategies to improve your writing style? As you list each strategy, also tell what you would have to change about your writing style to incorporate the strategy.

3. Which of the following illustrates passive voice?
    a. The experimenter gave the memory test to the participants.
    b. The participants took the personality test after a rest period.
    c. The endurance test was given by the experimenter's assistant.
    d. All of the above
    e. None of the above
4. Change each of the following sentences in passive voice to active voice.
    An experiment was conducted by Jones (1995).
    The participants were seated in desks around the room.
    The stimulus items were projected from the rear of the cubicle.
    A significant interaction was found.
5. Choose the correct sentence from each pair below. Add punctuation if necessary. Justify your answers:
    a. The experimenter tested the animals which were older first.
       The experimenter tested the animals that were older first.
    b. A room which was a classroom was the testing environment.
       A room that was a classroom was the testing environment.
6. Decide whether each sentence below is correct or incorrect. If it is incorrect, correct it.
    Since you are the oldest, you should go first.
    Since I began that class I have learned much about statistics.
    While we are watching TV, we can also study.
    While you are older than me, I should still go first.
7. Use unbiased language to express each phrase:
    Orientals   elderly
    mankind   girls and men
    mothering   chairman
    homosexuals   depressives
8. Correct the following incorrect expressions:
    a+b=c   trial - by - trial
    – 1   Enter: Your name

KEY TERMS

APA format, *487*
Headings, *488*
Title page, *488*
Manuscript page header, *488*

Running head, *489*
Level 1 heading, *490*
Abstract, *491*
Introduction, *492*

LOOKING AHEAD

At this point we have reached the end of this text—there is no Chapter 21 to look ahead to. We do, however, look ahead to your research career. Perhaps your research career will be nonexistent; you may not be required to design, plan, and conduct an experiment as part of this course or another course. In this case, we hope you have learned something about research that will make you a critical consumer of research information in the future. Perhaps your research career will entail only one study—the one you conduct for this course. We believe this book will prove helpful for you in that endeavor. Finally, perhaps some of you now envision an ongoing research career for yourselves. We hope this book has opened your eyes to the powerful possibilities of experimental research in psychology and that you are eager to follow that path in the future.

Regardless of what your future plans regarding research are, we hope we have made you think, challenged you to work, helped you contemplate conducting research, and perhaps entertained and amused you a little along the way. All of you will be faced with research in some fashion in your futures. We wish you luck as you begin your journey.

appendix A

Statistical Tables

TABLE **A-1** NORMAL CURVE AREAS: PERCENTAGE OF THE NORMAL CURVE BETWEEN THE MEAN AND THE *z* SCORES SHOWN

z	% Mean to z	z	% Mean to z	z	% Mean to z
.00	.00	.27	10.64	.54	20.54
.01	.40	.28	11.03	.55	20.88
.02	.80	.29	11.41	.56	21.23
.03	1.20	.30	11.79	.57	21.57
.04	1.60	.31	12.17	.58	21.90
.05	1.99	.32	12.55	.59	22.24
.06	2.39	.33	12.93	.60	22.57
.07	2.79	.34	13.31	.61	22.91
.08	3.19	.35	13.68	.62	23.24
.09	3.59	.36	14.06	.63	23.57
.10	3.98	.37	14.43	.64	23.89
.11	4.38	.38	14.80	.65	24.22
.12	4.78	.39	15.17	.66	24.54
.13	5.17	.40	15.54	.67	24.86
.14	5.57	.41	15.91	.68	25.17
.15	5.96	.42	16.28	.69	25.49
.16	6.36	.43	16.64	.70	25.80
.17	6.75	.44	17.00	.71	26.11
.18	7.14	.45	17.36	.72	26.42
.19	7.53	.46	17.72	.73	26.73
.20	7.93	.47	18.08	.74	27.04
.21	8.32	.48	18.44	.75	27.34
.22	8.71	.49	18.79	.76	27.64
.23	9.10	.50	19.15	.77	27.94
.24	9.48	.51	19.50	.78	28.23
.25	9.87	.52	19.85	.79	28.52
.26	10.26	.53	20.19	.80	28.81

TABLE A-1 (CONTINUED)

z	% Mean to z	z	% Mean to z	z	% Mean to z
.81	29.10	1.14	37.29	1.47	42.92
.82	29.39	1.15	37.49	1.48	43.06
.83	29.67	1.16	37.70	1.49	43.19
.84	29.95	1.17	37.90	1.50	43.32
.85	30.23	1.18	38.10	1.51	43.45
.86	30.51	1.19	38.30	1.52	43.57
.87	30.78	1.20	38.49	1.53	43.70
.88	31.06	1.21	38.69	1.54	43.82
.89	31.33	1.22	38.88	1.55	43.94
.90	31.59	1.23	39.07	1.56	44.06
.91	31.86	1.24	39.25	1.57	44.18
.92	32.12	1.25	39.44	1.58	44.29
.93	32.38	1.26	39.62	1.59	44.41
.94	32.64	1.27	39.80	1.60	44.52
.95	32.89	1.28	39.97	1.61	44.63
.96	33.15	1.29	40.15	1.62	44.74
.97	33.40	1.30	40.32	1.63	44.84
.98	33.65	1.31	40.49	1.64	44.95
.99	33.89	1.32	40.66	1.65	45.05
1.00	34.13	1.33	40.82	1.66	45.15
1.01	34.38	1.34	40.99	1.67	45.25
1.02	34.61	1.35	41.15	1.68	45.35
1.03	34.85	1.36	41.31	1.69	45.45
1.04	35.08	1.37	41.47	1.70	45.54
1.05	35.31	1.38	41.62	1.71	45.64
1.06	35.54	1.39	41.77	1.72	45.73
1.07	35.77	1.40	41.92	1.73	45.82
1.08	35.99	1.41	42.07	1.74	45.91
1.09	36.21	1.42	42.22	1.75	45.99
1.10	36.43	1.43	42.36	1.76	46.08
1.11	36.65	1.44	42.51	1.77	46.16
1.12	36.86	1.45	42.65	1.78	46.25
1.13	37.08	1.46	42.79	1.79	46.33

TABLE A-1 (CONTINUED)

z	% Mean to z	z	% Mean to z	z	% Mean to z
1.80	46.41	2.13	48.34	2.46	49.31
1.81	46.49	2.14	48.38	2.47	49.32
1.82	46.56	2.15	48.42	2.48	49.34
1.83	46.64	2.16	48.46	2.49	49.36
1.84	46.71	2.17	48.50	2.50	49.38
1.85	46.78	2.18	48.54	2.51	49.40
1.86	46.86	2.19	48.57	2.52	49.41
1.87	46.93	2.20	48.61	2.53	49.43
1.88	46.99	2.21	48.64	2.54	49.45
1.89	47.06	2.22	48.68	2.55	49.46
1.90	47.13	2.23	48.71	2.56	49.48
1.91	47.19	2.24	48.75	2.57	49.49
1.92	47.26	2.25	48.78	2.58	49.51
1.93	47.32	2.26	48.81	2.59	49.52
1.94	47.38	2.27	48.84	2.60	49.53
1.95	47.44	2.28	48.87	2.61	49.55
1.96	47.50	2.29	48.90	2.62	49.56
1.97	47.56	2.30	48.93	2.63	49.57
1.98	47.61	2.31	48.96	2.64	49.59
1.99	47.67	2.32	48.98	2.65	49.60
2.00	47.72	2.33	49.01	2.66	49.61
2.01	47.78	2.34	49.04	2.67	49.62
2.02	47.83	2.35	49.06	2.68	49.63
2.03	47.88	2.36	49.09	2.69	49.64
2.04	47.93	2.37	49.11	2.70	49.65
2.05	47.98	2.38	49.13	2.71	49.66
2.06	48.03	2.39	49.16	2.72	49.67
2.07	48.08	2.40	49.18	2.73	49.68
2.08	48.12	2.41	49.20	2.74	49.69
2.09	48.17	2.42	49.22	2.75	49.70
2.10	48.21	2.43	49.25	2.76	49.71
2.11	48.26	2.44	49.27	2.77	49.72
2.12	48.30	2.45	49.29	2.78	49.73

TABLE **A-1** (CONTINUED)

z	% Mean to z	z	% Mean to z	z	% Mean to z
2.79	49.74	2.88	49.80	2.97	49.85
2.80	49.74	2.89	49.81	2.98	49.86
2.81	49.75	2.90	49.81	2.99	49.86
2.82	49.76	2.91	49.82	3.00	49.87
2.83	49.77	2.92	49.82	3.50	49.98
2.84	49.77	2.93	49.83	4.00	50.00
2.85	49.78	2.94	49.84	4.50	50.00
2.86	49.79	2.95	49.84		
2.87	49.79	2.96	49.85		

TABLE **A-2** CRITICAL VALUES FOR PEARSON PRODUCT-MOMENT CORRELATION COEFFICIENTS, r. TO BE SIGNIFICANT, THE OBTAINED r MUST BE EQUAL TO OR LARGER THAN THE TABLE VALUE

	α Levels (Two-tailed test)				
df	.1	.05	.02	.01	.001
	α Levels (One-tailed test)				
(*df* = N − 2)	.05	.025	.01	.005	.0005
1	.98769	.99692	.999507	.999877	.9999988
2	.90000	.95000	.98000	.990000	.99900
3	.8054	.8783	.93433	.95873	.99116
4	.7293	.8114	.8822	.91720	.97406
5	.6694	.7545	.8329	.8745	.95074
6	.6215	.7067	.7887	.8343	.92493
7	.5822	.6664	.7498	.7977	.8982
8	.5494	.6319	.7155	.7646	.8721
9	.5214	.6021	.6851	.7348	.8371
10	.4973	.5760	.6581	.7079	.8233
11	.4762	.5529	.6339	.6835	.8010
12	.4575	.5324	.6120	.6614	.7800
13	.4409	.5139	.5923	.6411	.7603
14	.4259	.4973	.5742	.6226	.7420
15	.4124	.4821	.5577	.6055	.7246
16	.4000	.4683	.5425	.5897	.7084

17	.3887	.4555	.5285	.5751	.6932
18	.3783	.4438	.5155	.5614	.6787
19	.3687	.4329	.5034	.5487	.6652
20	.3598	.4227	.4921	.5368	.6524
25	.3233	.3809	.4451	.4869	.5974
30	.2960	.3494	.4093	.4487	.5541
35	.2746	.3246	.3810	.4182	.5189
40	.2573	.3044	.3578	.3932	.4896
45	.2428	.2875	.3384	.3721	.4648
50	.2306	.2732	.3218	.3541	.4433
60	.2108	.2500	.2948	.3248	.4078
70	.1954	.2319	.2737	.3017	.3799
80	.1829	.2172	.2565	.2830	.3568
90	.1726	.2050	.2422	.2673	.3375
100	.1638	.1946	.2301	.2540	.3211

Source: Table VII of Fisher and Yates (1963), *Statistical Tables for Biological, Agricultural and Medical Research,* published by Longman Group, Ltd., London.

TABLE A-3   THE *t* DISTRIBUTION*

	α Levels for two-tailed test					
df	**.20**	**.10**	**.05**	**.02**	**.01**	**.001**
	α Levels for one-tailed test					
	.10	**.05**	**.025**	**.01**	**.005**	**.0005**
1	3.078	6.314	12.706	31.821	63.657	636.619
2	1.886	2.920	4.303	6.965	9.925	31.598
3	1.638	2.353	3.182	4.541	5.841	12.924
4	1.533	2.132	2.776	3.747	4.604	8.610
5	1.476	2.015	2.571	3.365	4.032	6.869
6	1.440	1.943	2.447	3.143	3.707	5.959
7	1.415	1.895	2.365	2.998	3.499	5.408
8	1.397	1.860	2.306	2.896	3.355	5.041
9	1.383	1.833	2.262	2.821	3.250	4.781
10	1.372	1.812	2.228	2.764	3.169	4.587
11	1.363	1.796	2.201	2.718	3.106	4.437
12	1.356	1.782	2.179	2.681	3.055	4.318

TABLE A-3 (CONTINUED)

	α Levels for two-tailed test					
df	.20	.10	.05	.02	.01	.001
	α Levels for one-tailed test					
	.10	.05	.025	.01	.005	.0005
13	1.350	1.771	2.160	2.650	3.012	4.221
14	1.345	1.761	2.145	2.624	2.977	4.140
15	1.341	1.753	2.131	2.602	2.947	4.073
16	1.337	1.746	2.120	2.583	2.921	4.015
17	1.333	1.740	2.110	2.567	2.898	3.965
18	1.330	1.734	2.101	2.552	2.878	3.922
19	1.328	1.729	2.093	2.539	2.861	3.883
20	1.325	1.725	2.086	2.528	2.845	3.850
21	1.323	1.721	2.080	2.518	2.831	3.819
22	1.321	1.717	2.074	2.508	2.819	3.792
23	1.319	1.714	2.069	2.500	2.807	3.767
24	1.318	1.711	2.064	2.492	2.797	3.745
25	1.316	1.708	2.060	2.485	2.787	3.725
26	1.315	1.706	2.056	2.479	2.779	3.707
27	1.314	1.703	2.052	2.473	2.771	3.690
28	1.313	1.701	2.048	2.467	2.763	3.674
29	1.311	1.699	2.045	2.462	2.756	3.659
30	1.310	1.697	2.042	2.457	2.750	3.646
40	1.303	1.684	2.021	2.423	2.704	3.551
60	1.296	1.671	2.000	2.390	2.660	3.460
120	1.289	1.658	1.980	2.358	2.617	3.373
∞	1.282	1.645	1.960	2.326	2.576	3.291

*To be significant the t obtained from the data must be equal to or larger than the value shown in the table.

Source: Table A-3 is taken from Table III of Fisher and Yates, *Statistical Tables for Biological, Agricultural and Medical Research*. Published by Longman Group UK Ltd., 1974. We are grateful to the Longman Group UK Ltd., on behalf of the literary Executor of the late Sir Ronald A. Fisher, F.R.S. and Dr. Frank Yates F.R.S. for permission to reproduce Table III from *Statistical Tables for Biological, Agricultural and Medical Research* 61E (1974).

TABLE A-4 THE F DISTRIBUTION*

.05 (Roman) and .01 (Boldface) α Levels for the distribution of F

Degrees of freedom (For the numerator)

Each cell: .05 level (Roman) / **.01 level (Boldface)**

df (denom.)	1	2	3	4	5	6	7	8	9	10	11	12	14	16	20	24	30	40	50	75	100	200	500	∞
1	161 / **4,052**	200 / **4,999**	216 / **5,403**	225 / **5,625**	230 / **5,764**	234 / **5,859**	237 / **5,928**	239 / **5,981**	241 / **6,022**	242 / **6,056**	243 / **6,082**	244 / **6,106**	245 / **6,142**	246 / **6,169**	248 / **6,208**	249 / **6,234**	250 / **6,258**	251 / **6,286**	252 / **6,302**	253 / **6,323**	253 / **6,334**	254 / **6,352**	254 / **6,361**	254 / **6,366**
2	18.51 / **98.49**	19.00 / **99.00**	19.16 / **99.17**	19.25 / **99.25**	19.30 / **99.30**	19.33 / **99.33**	19.36 / **99.34**	19.37 / **99.36**	19.38 / **99.38**	19.39 / **99.40**	19.40 / **99.41**	19.41 / **99.42**	19.42 / **99.43**	19.43 / **99.44**	19.44 / **99.45**	19.45 / **99.46**	19.46 / **99.47**	19.47 / **99.48**	19.47 / **99.48**	19.48 / **99.49**	19.49 / **99.49**	19.49 / **99.49**	19.50 / **99.50**	19.50 / **99.50**
3	10.13 / **34.12**	9.55 / **30.82**	9.28 / **29.46**	9.12 / **28.71**	9.01 / **28.24**	8.94 / **27.91**	8.88 / **27.67**	8.84 / **.27.49**	8.81 / **27.34**	8.78 / **27.23**	8.76 / **27.13**	8.74 / **27.05**	8.71 / **26.92**	8.69 / **26.83**	8.66 / **26.69**	8.64 / **26.60**	8.62 / **26.50**	8.60 / **26.41**	8.58 / **26.35**	8.57 / **26.27**	8.56 / **26.23**	8.54 / **26.18**	8.54 / **26.14**	8.53 / **26.12**
4	7.71 / **21.20**	6.94 / **18.00**	6.59 / **16.69**	6.39 / **15.98**	6.26 / **15.52**	6.16 / **15.21**	6.09 / **14.98**	6.04 / **14.80**	6.00 / **14.66**	5.96 / **14.54**	5.93 / **14.45**	5.91 / **14.37**	5.87 / **14.24**	5.84 / **14.15**	5.80 / **14.02**	5.77 / **13.93**	5.74 / **13.83**	5.71 / **13.74**	5.70 / **13.69**	5.68 / **13.61**	5.66 / **13.57**	5.65 / **13.52**	5.64 / **13.48**	5.63 / **13.46**
5	6.61 / **16.26**	5.79 / **13.27**	5.41 / **12.06**	5.19 / **11.39**	5.05 / **10.97**	4.95 / **10.67**	4.88 / **10.45**	4.82 / **10.27**	4.78 / **10.15**	4.74 / **10.05**	4.70 / **9.96**	4.68 / **9.89**	4.64 / **9.77**	4.60 / **9.68**	4.56 / **9.55**	4.53 / **9.47**	4.50 / **9.38**	4.46 / **9.29**	4.44 / **9.24**	4.42 / **9.17**	4.40 / **9.13**	4.38 / **9.07**	4.37 / **9.04**	4.36 / **9.02**
6	5.99 / **13.74**	5.14 / **10.92**	4.76 / **9.78**	4.53 / **9.15**	4.39 / **8.75**	4.28 / **8.47**	4.21 / **8.26**	4.15 / **8.10**	4.10 / **7.98**	4.06 / **7.87**	4.03 / **7.79**	4.00 / **7.72**	3.96 / **7.60**	3.92 / **7.52**	3.87 / **7.39**	3.84 / **7.31**	3.81 / **7.23**	3.77 / **7.14**	3.75 / **7.09**	3.72 / **7.02**	3.71 / **6.99**	3.69 / **6.94**	3.68 / **6.90**	3.67 / **6.88**
7	5.59 / **12.25**	4.74 / **9.55**	4.35 / **8.45**	4.12 / **7.85**	3.97 / **7.46**	3.87 / **7.19**	3.79 / **7.00**	3.73 / **6.84**	3.68 / **6.71**	3.63 / **6.62**	3.60 / **6.54**	3.57 / **6.47**	3.52 / **6.35**	3.49 / **6.27**	3.44 / **6.15**	3.41 / **6.07**	3.38 / **5.98**	3.34 / **5.90**	3.32 / **5.85**	3.29 / **5.78**	3.28 / **5.75**	3.25 / **5.70**	3.24 / **5.67**	3.23 / **5.65**
8	5.32 / **11.26**	4.46 / **8.65**	4.07 / **7.59**	3.84 / **7.01**	3.69 / **6.63**	3.58 / **6.37**	3.50 / **6.19**	3.44 / **6.03**	3.39 / **5.91**	3.34 / **5.82**	3.31 / **5.74**	3.28 / **5.67**	3.23 / **5.56**	3.20 / **5.48**	3.15 / **5.36**	3.12 / **5.28**	3.08 / **5.20**	3.05 / **5.11**	3.03 / **5.06**	3.00 / **5.00**	2.98 / **4.96**	2.96 / **4.91**	2.94 / **4.88**	2.93 / **4.86**
9	5.12 / **10.56**	4.26 / **8.02**	3.86 / **6.99**	3.63 / **6.42**	3.48 / **6.06**	3.37 / **5.80**	3.29 / **5.62**	3.23 / **5.47**	3.18 / **5.35**	3.13 / **5.26**	3.10 / **5.18**	3.07 / **5.11**	3.02 / **5.00**	2.98 / **4.92**	2.93 / **4.80**	2.90 / **4.73**	2.86 / **4.64**	2.82 / **4.56**	2.80 / **4.51**	2.77 / **4.45**	2.76 / **4.41**	2.73 / **4.36**	2.72 / **4.33**	2.71 / **4.31**
10	4.96 / **10.04**	4.10 / **7.56**	3.71 / **6.55**	3.48 / **5.99**	3.33 / **5.64**	3.22 / **5.39**	3.14 / **5.21**	3.07 / **5.06**	3.02 / **4.95**	2.97 / **4.85**	2.94 / **4.78**	2.91 / **4.71**	2.86 / **4.60**	2.82 / **4.52**	2.77 / **4.41**	2.74 / **4.33**	2.70 / **4.25**	2.67 / **4.17**	2.64 / **4.12**	2.61 / **4.05**	2.59 / **4.01**	2.56 / **3.96**	2.55 / **3.93**	2.54 / **3.91**
11	4.84 / **9.65**	3.98 / **7.20**	3.59 / **6.22**	3.36 / **5.67**	3.20 / **5.32**	3.09 / **5.07**	3.01 / **4.88**	2.95 / **4.74**	2.90 / **4.63**	2.86 / **4.54**	2.82 / **4.46**	2.79 / **4.40**	2.74 / **4.29**	2.70 / **4.21**	2.65 / **4.10**	2.61 / **4.02**	2.57 / **3.94**	2.53 / **3.86**	2.50 / **3.80**	2.47 / **3.74**	2.45 / **3.70**	2.42 / **3.66**	2.41 / **3.62**	2.40 / **3.60**
12	4.75 / **9.33**	3.88 / **6.93**	3.49 / **5.95**	3.26 / **5.41**	3.11 / **5.06**	3.00 / **4.82**	2.92 / **4.65**	2.85 / **4.50**	2.80 / **4.39**	2.76 / **4.30**	2.72 / **4.22**	2.69 / **4.16**	2.64 / **4.05**	2.60 / **3.98**	2.54 / **3.86**	2.50 / **3.78**	2.46 / **3.70**	2.42 / **3.61**	2.40 / **3.56**	2.36 / **3.49**	2.35 / **3.46**	2.32 / **3.41**	2.31 / **3.38**	2.30 / **3.36**

Degrees of freedom (for the denominator)

TABLE A-4 (CONTINUED)

.05 (Roman) and .01 (Boldface) α Levels for the distribution of F

Each cell shows the .05 value (Roman) over the .01 value (Boldface), given as .05 / **.01**.

Degrees of freedom (For the numerator)

df (denom.)	1	2	3	4	5	6	7	8	9	10	11	12	14	16	20	24	30	40	50	75	100	200	500	∞
13	4.67 / **9.07**	3.80 / **6.70**	3.41 / **5.74**	3.18 / **5.20**	3.02 / **4.86**	2.92 / **4.62**	2.84 / **4.44**	2.77 / **4.30**	2.72 / **4.19**	2.67 / **4.10**	2.63 / **4.02**	2.60 / **3.96**	2.55 / **3.85**	2.51 / **3.78**	2.46 / **3.67**	2.42 / **3.59**	2.38 / **3.51**	2.34 / **3.42**	2.32 / **3.37**	2.28 / **3.30**	2.26 / **3.27**	2.24 / **3.21**	2.22 / **3.18**	2.21 / **3.16**
14	4.60 / **8.86**	3.74 / **6.51**	3.34 / **5.56**	3.11 / **5.03**	2.96 / **4.69**	2.85 / **4.46**	2.77 / **4.28**	2.70 / **4.14**	2.65 / **4.03**	2.60 / **3.94**	2.56 / **3.86**	2.53 / **3.80**	2.48 / **3.70**	2.44 / **3.62**	2.39 / **3.51**	2.35 / **3.43**	2.31 / **3.34**	2.27 / **3.26**	2.24 / **3.21**	2.21 / **3.14**	2.19 / **3.11**	2.16 / **3.06**	2.14 / **3.02**	2.13 / **3.00**
15	4.54 / **8.68**	3.68 / **6.36**	3.29 / **5.42**	3.06 / **4.89**	2.90 / **4.56**	2.79 / **4.32**	2.70 / **4.14**	2.64 / **4.00**	2.59 / **3.89**	2.55 / **3.80**	2.51 / **3.73**	2.48 / **3.67**	2.43 / **3.56**	2.39 / **3.48**	2.33 / **3.36**	2.29 / **3.29**	2.25 / **3.20**	2.21 / **3.12**	2.18 / **3.07**	2.15 / **3.00**	2.12 / **2.97**	2.10 / **2.92**	2.08 / **2.89**	2.07 / **2.87**
16	4.49 / **8.53**	3.63 / **6.23**	3.24 / **5.29**	3.01 / **4.77**	2.85 / **4.44**	2.74 / **4.20**	2.66 / **4.03**	2.59 / **3.89**	2.54 / **3.78**	2.49 / **3.69**	2.45 / **3.61**	2.42 / **3.55**	2.37 / **3.45**	2.33 / **3.37**	2.28 / **3.25**	2.24 / **3.18**	2.20 / **3.10**	2.16 / **3.01**	2.13 / **2.96**	2.09 / **2.89**	2.07 / **2.86**	2.04 / **2.80**	2.02 / **2.77**	2.01 / **2.75**
17	4.45 / **8.40**	3.59 / **6.11**	3.20 / **5.18**	2.96 / **4.67**	2.81 / **4.34**	2.70 / **4.10**	2.62 / **3.93**	2.55 / **3.79**	2.50 / **3.68**	2.45 / **3.59**	2.41 / **3.52**	2.38 / **3.45**	2.33 / **3.35**	2.29 / **3.27**	2.23 / **3.16**	2.19 / **3.08**	2.15 / **3.00**	2.11 / **2.92**	2.08 / **2.86**	2.04 / **2.79**	2.02 / **2.76**	1.99 / **2.70**	1.97 / **2.67**	1.96 / **2.65**
18	4.41 / **8.28**	3.55 / **6.01**	3.16 / **5.09**	2.93 / **4.58**	2.77 / **4.25**	2.66 / **4.01**	2.58 / **3.85**	2.51 / **3.71**	2.46 / **3.60**	2.41 / **3.51**	2.37 / **3.44**	2.34 / **3.37**	2.29 / **3.27**	2.25 / **3.19**	2.19 / **3.07**	2.15 / **3.00**	2.11 / **2.91**	2.07 / **2.83**	2.04 / **2.78**	2.00 / **2.71**	1.98 / **2.68**	1.95 / **2.62**	1.93 / **2.59**	1.92 / **2.57**
19	4.38 / **8.18**	3.52 / **5.93**	3.13 / **5.01**	2.90 / **4.50**	2.74 / **4.17**	2.63 / **3.94**	2.55 / **3.77**	2.48 / **3.63**	2.43 / **3.52**	2.38 / **3.43**	2.34 / **3.36**	2.31 / **3.30**	2.26 / **3.19**	2.21 / **3.12**	2.15 / **3.00**	2.11 / **2.92**	2.07 / **2.84**	2.02 / **2.76**	2.00 / **2.70**	1.96 / **2.63**	1.94 / **2.60**	1.91 / **2.54**	1.90 / **2.51**	1.88 / **2.49**
20	4.35 / **8.10**	3.49 / **5.85**	3.10 / **4.94**	2.87 / **4.43**	2.71 / **4.10**	2.60 / **3.87**	2.52 / **3.71**	2.45 / **3.56**	2.40 / **3.45**	2.35 / **3.37**	2.31 / **3.30**	2.28 / **3.23**	2.23 / **3.13**	2.18 / **3.05**	2.12 / **2.94**	2.08 / **2.86**	2.04 / **2.77**	1.99 / **2.69**	1.96 / **2.63**	1.92 / **2.56**	1.90 / **2.53**	1.87 / **2.47**	1.85 / **2.44**	1.84 / **2.42**
21	4.32 / **8.02**	3.47 / **5.78**	3.07 / **4.87**	2.84 / **4.37**	2.68 / **4.04**	2.57 / **3.81**	2.49 / **3.65**	2.42 / **3.51**	2.37 / **3.40**	2.32 / **3.31**	2.28 / **3.24**	2.25 / **3.17**	2.20 / **3.07**	2.15 / **2.99**	2.09 / **2.88**	2.05 / **2.80**	2.00 / **2.72**	1.96 / **2.63**	1.93 / **2.58**	1.89 / **2.51**	1.87 / **2.47**	1.84 / **2.42**	1.82 / **2.38**	1.81 / **2.36**
22	4.30 / **7.94**	3.44 / **5.72**	3.05 / **4.82**	2.82 / **4.31**	2.66 / **3.99**	2.55 / **3.76**	2.47 / **3.59**	2.40 / **3.45**	2.35 / **3.35**	2.30 / **3.26**	2.26 / **3.18**	2.23 / **3.12**	2.18 / **3.02**	2.13 / **2.94**	2.07 / **2.83**	2.03 / **2.75**	1.98 / **2.67**	1.93 / **2.58**	1.91 / **2.53**	1.87 / **2.46**	1.84 / **2.42**	1.81 / **2.37**	1.80 / **2.33**	1.78 / **2.31**
23	4.28 / **7.88**	3.42 / **5.66**	3.03 / **4.76**	2.80 / **4.26**	2.64 / **3.94**	2.53 / **3.71**	2.45 / **3.54**	2.38 / **3.41**	2.32 / **3.30**	2.28 / **3.21**	2.24 / **3.14**	2.20 / **3.07**	2.14 / **2.97**	2.10 / **2.89**	2.04 / **2.78**	2.00 / **2.70**	1.96 / **2.62**	1.91 / **2.53**	1.89 / **2.48**	1.84 / **2.41**	1.82 / **2.37**	1.79 / **2.32**	1.77 / **2.28**	1.76 / **2.26**
24	4.26 / **7.82**	3.40 / **5.61**	3.01 / **4.72**	2.78 / **4.22**	2.62 / **3.90**	2.51 / **3.67**	2.43 / **3.50**	2.36 / **3.36**	2.30 / **3.25**	2.26 / **3.17**	2.22 / **3.09**	2.18 / **3.03**	2.13 / **2.93**	2.09 / **2.85**	2.02 / **2.74**	1.98 / **2.66**	1.94 / **2.58**	1.89 / **2.49**	1.86 / **2.44**	1.82 / **2.36**	1.80 / **2.33**	1.76 / **2.27**	1.74 / **2.23**	1.73 / **2.21**
25	4.24 / **7.77**	3.38 / **5.57**	2.99 / **4.68**	2.76 / **4.18**	2.60 / **3.86**	2.49 / **3.63**	2.41 / **3.46**	2.34 / **3.32**	2.28 / **3.21**	2.24 / **3.13**	2.20 / **3.05**	2.16 / **2.99**	2.11 / **2.89**	2.06 / **2.81**	2.00 / **2.70**	1.96 / **2.62**	1.92 / **2.54**	1.87 / **2.45**	1.84 / **2.40**	1.80 / **2.32**	1.77 / **2.29**	1.74 / **2.23**	1.72 / **2.19**	1.71 / **2.17**

Degrees of freedom (for the denominator)

df																									
26	4.22 / 7.72	3.37 / 5.53	2.98 / 4.64	2.74 / 4.14	2.59 / 3.82	2.47 / 3.59	2.39 / 3.42	2.32 / 3.29	2.27 / 3.17	2.22 / 3.09	2.18 / 3.02	2.15 / 2.96	2.10 / 2.86	2.05 / 2.77	1.99 / 2.66	1.95 / 2.58	1.90 / 2.50	1.85 / 2.41	1.82 / 2.36	1.78 / 2.28	1.76 / 2.25	1.72 / 2.19	1.70 / 2.15	1.69 / 2.13	26
27	4.21 / 7.68	3.35 / 5.49	2.96 / 4.60	2.73 / 4.11	2.57 / 3.79	2.46 / 3.56	2.37 / 3.39	2.30 / 3.26	2.25 / 3.14	2.20 / 3.06	2.16 / 2.98	2.13 / 2.93	2.08 / 2.83	2.03 / 2.74	1.97 / 2.63	1.93 / 2.55	1.88 / 2.47	1.84 / 2.38	1.80 / 2.33	1.76 / 2.25	1.74 / 2.21	1.71 / 2.16	1.68 / 2.12	1.67 / 2.10	27
28	4.20 / 7.64	3.34 / 5.45	2.95 / 4.57	2.71 / 4.07	2.56 / 3.76	2.44 / 3.53	2.36 / 3.36	2.29 / 3.23	2.24 / 3.11	2.19 / 3.03	2.15 / 2.95	2.12 / 2.90	2.06 / 2.80	2.02 / 2.71	1.96 / 2.60	1.91 / 2.52	1.87 / 2.44	1.78 / 2.35	1.75 / 2.30	1.75 / 2.22	1.72 / 2.18	1.69 / 2.13	1.68 / 2.09	1.65 / 2.06	28
29	4.18 / 7.60	3.33 / 5.42	2.93 / 4.54	2.70 / 4.04	2.54 / 3.73	2.43 / 3.50	2.35 / 3.33	2.28 / 3.20	2.22 / 3.08	2.18 / 3.00	2.14 / 2.92	2.10 / 2.87	2.05 / 2.77	2.00 / 2.68	1.94 / 2.57	1.90 / 2.49	1.85 / 2.41	1.80 / 2.32	1.77 / 2.27	1.73 / 2.19	1.71 / 2.15	1.68 / 2.10	1.65 / 2.06	1.64 / 2.03	29
30	4.17 / 7.56	3.32 / 5.39	2.92 / 4.51	2.69 / 4.02	2.53 / 3.70	2.42 / 3.47	2.34 / 3.30	2.27 / 3.17	2.21 / 3.06	2.16 / 2.98	2.12 / 2.90	2.09 / 2.84	2.04 / 2.74	1.99 / 2.66	1.93 / 2.55	1.89 / 2.47	1.84 / 2.38	1.79 / 2.29	1.76 / 2.24	1.72 / 2.16	1.69 / 2.13	1.66 / 2.07	1.64 / 2.03	1.62 / 2.01	14
32	4.15 / 7.50	3.30 / 5.34	2.90 / 4.46	2.67 / 3.97	2.51 / 3.66	2.40 / 3.42	2.32 / 3.25	2.25 / 3.12	2.19 / 3.01	2.14 / 2.94	2.10 / 2.86	2.07 / 2.80	2.02 / 2.70	1.97 / 2.62	1.91 / 2.51	1.86 / 2.42	1.82 / 2.34	1.76 / 2.25	1.74 / 2.20	1.69 / 2.12	1.67 / 2.08	1.64 / 2.02	1.61 / 1.98	1.59 / 1.96	15
34	4.13 / 7.44	3.28 / 5.29	2.88 / 4.42	2.65 / 3.93	2.49 / 3.61	2.38 / 3.38	2.30 / 3.21	2.23 / 3.08	2.17 / 2.97	2.12 / 2.89	2.08 / 2.82	2.05 / 2.76	2.00 / 2.66	1.95 / 2.58	1.89 / 2.47	1.84 / 2.38	1.80 / 2.30	1.74 / 2.21	1.71 / 2.15	1.67 / 2.08	1.64 / 2.04	1.61 / 1.98	1.59 / 1.94	1.57 / 1.91	16
36	4.11 / 7.39	3.26 / 5.25	2.86 / 4.38	2.63 / 3.89	2.48 / 3.58	2.36 / 3.35	2.28 / 3.18	2.21 / 3.04	2.15 / 2.94	2.10 / 2.86	2.06 / 2.78	2.03 / 2.72	1.98 / 2.62	1.93 / 2.54	1.87 / 2.43	1.82 / 2.35	1.78 / 2.26	1.72 / 2.17	1.69 / 2.12	1.65 / 2.04	1.62 / 2.00	1.59 / 1.94	1.56 / 1.90	1.55 / 1.87	17
38	4.10 / 7.35	3.25 / 5.21	2.85 / 4.34	2.62 / 3.86	2.46 / 3.54	2.35 / 3.32	2.26 / 3.15	2.19 / 3.02	2.14 / 2.91	2.09 / 2.82	2.05 / 2.75	2.02 / 2.69	1.96 / 2.59	1.92 / 2.51	1.85 / 2.40	1.80 / 2.32	1.76 / 2.22	1.71 / 2.14	1.67 / 2.08	1.63 / 2.00	1.60 / 1.97	1.57 / 1.90	1.54 / 1.86	1.53 / 1.84	18
40	4.08 / 7.31	3.23 / 5.18	2.84 / 4.31	2.61 / 3.83	2.45 / 3.51	2.34 / 3.29	2.25 / 3.12	2.18 / 2.99	2.12 / 2.88	2.07 / 2.80	2.04 / 2.73	2.00 / 2.66	1.95 / 2.56	1.90 / 2.49	1.84 / 2.37	1.79 / 2.29	1.74 / 2.20	1.69 / 2.11	1.66 / 2.05	1.61 / 1.97	1.59 / 1.94	1.55 / 1.88	1.53 / 1.84	1.51 / 1.81	19
42	4.07 / 7.27	3.22 / 5.15	2.83 / 4.29	2.59 / 3.80	2.44 / 3.49	2.32 / 3.26	2.24 / 3.10	2.17 / 2.96	2.11 / 2.86	2.06 / 2.77	2.02 / 2.70	1.99 / 2.64	1.94 / 2.54	1.89 / 2.46	1.82 / 2.35	1.78 / 2.26	1.73 / 2.17	1.68 / 2.08	1.64 / 2.02	1.60 / 1.94	1.57 / 1.91	1.54 / 1.85	1.51 / 1.80	1.49 / 1.78	20
44	4.06 / 7.24	3.21 / 5.12	2.82 / 4.26	2.58 / 3.78	2.43 / 3.46	2.31 / 3.24	2.23 / 3.07	2.16 / 2.94	2.10 / 2.84	2.05 / 2.75	2.01 / 2.68	1.98 / 2.62	1.92 / 2.52	1.88 / 2.44	1.81 / 2.32	1.76 / 2.24	1.72 / 2.15	1.66 / 2.06	1.63 / 2.00	1.58 / 1.92	1.56 / 1.88	1.52 / 1.82	1.50 / 1.78	1.48 / 1.75	21
46	4.05 / 7.21	3.20 / 5.10	2.81 / 4.24	2.57 / 3.76	2.42 / 3.44	2.30 / 3.22	2.22 / 3.05	2.14 / 2.92	2.09 / 2.82	2.04 / 2.73	2.00 / 2.66	1.97 / 2.60	1.91 / 2.50	1.87 / 2.42	1.80 / 2.30	1.75 / 2.22	1.71 / 2.13	1.65 / 2.04	1.62 / 1.98	1.57 / 1.90	1.54 / 1.86	1.51 / 1.80	1.48 / 1.76	1.46 / 1.72	22
48	4.04 / 7.19	3.19 / 5.08	2.80 / 4.22	2.56 / 3.74	2.41 / 3.42	2.30 / 3.20	2.21 / 3.04	2.14 / 2.90	2.08 / 2.80	2.03 / 2.71	1.99 / 2.64	1.96 / 2.58	1.90 / 2.48	1.86 / 2.40	1.79 / 2.28	1.74 / 2.20	1.70 / 2.11	1.64 / 2.02	1.61 / 1.96	1.56 / 1.88	1.53 / 1.84	1.50 / 1.78	1.47 / 1.73	1.45 / 1.70	23
50	4.03 / 7.17	3.18 / 5.06	2.79 / 4.20	2.56 / 3.72	2.40 / 3.41	2.29 / 3.18	2.20 / 3.02	2.13 / 2.88	2.07 / 2.78	2.02 / 2.70	1.98 / 2.62	1.95 / 2.56	1.90 / 2.46	1.85 / 2.39	1.78 / 2.26	1.74 / 2.18	1.69 / 2.10	1.63 / 2.00	1.60 / 1.94	1.55 / 1.86	1.52 / 1.82	1.48 / 1.76	1.46 / 1.71	1.44 / 1.68	24
55	4.02 / 7.12	3.17 / 5.01	2.78 / 4.16	2.54 / 3.68	2.38 / 3.37	2.27 / 3.15	2.18 / 2.98	2.11 / 2.85	2.05 / 2.75	2.00 / 2.66	1.97 / 2.59	1.93 / 2.53	1.88 / 2.43	1.83 / 2.35	1.76 / 2.23	1.72 / 2.15	1.67 / 2.06	1.61 / 1.96	1.58 / 1.90	1.52 / 1.82	1.50 / 1.78	1.46 / 1.71	1.43 / 1.66	1.41 / 1.64	25

Degrees of freedom (for the denominator)

.05 (Roman) and .01 (Boldface) α Levels for the distribution of F

Degrees of freedom (For the numerator)

(denom.)	1	2	3	4	5	6	7	8	9	10	11	12	14	16	20	24	30	40	50	75	100	200	500	∞	
60	4.00 **7.08**	3.15 **4.98**	2.76 **4.13**	2.52 **3.65**	2.37 **3.34**	2.25 **3.12**	2.17 **2.95**	2.10 **2.82**	2.04 **2.72**	1.99 **2.63**	1.95 **2.56**	1.92 **2.50**	1.86 **2.40**	1.81 **2.32**	1.75 **2.20**	1.70 **2.12**	1.65 **2.03**	1.59 **1.93**	1.56 **1.87**	1.50 **1.79**	1.48 **1.74**	1.44 **1.68**	1.41 **1.63**	1.39 **1.60**	26
65	3.99 **7.04**	3.14 **4.95**	2.75 **4.10**	2.51 **3.62**	2.36 **3.31**	2.24 **3.09**	2.15 **2.93**	2.08 **2.79**	2.02 **2.70**	1.98 **2.61**	1.94 **2.54**	1.90 **2.47**	1.85 **2.37**	1.80 **2.30**	1.73 **2.18**	1.68 **2.09**	1.63 **2.00**	1.57 **1.90**	1.54 **1.84**	1.49 **1.76**	1.46 **1.71**	1.42 **1.64**	1.39 **1.60**	1.37 **1.56**	27
70	3.98 **7.01**	3.13 **4.92**	2.74 **4.08**	2.50 **3.60**	2.35 **3.29**	2.23 **3.07**	2.14 **2.91**	2.07 **2.77**	2.01 **2.67**	1.97 **2.59**	1.93 **2.51**	1.89 **2.45**	1.84 **2.35**	1.79 **2.28**	1.72 **2.15**	1.67 **2.07**	1.62 **1.98**	1.56 **1.88**	1.53 **1.82**	1.47 **1.74**	1.45 **1.69**	1.40 **1.62**	1.37 **1.56**	1.35 **1.53**	28
80	3.96 **6.96**	3.11 **4.88**	2.72 **4.04**	2.48 **3.56**	2.33 **3.25**	2.21 **3.04**	2.12 **2.87**	2.05 **2.74**	1.99 **2.64**	1.95 **2.55**	1.91 **2.48**	1.88 **2.41**	1.82 **2.32**	1.77 **2.24**	1.70 **2.11**	1.65 **2.03**	1.60 **1.94**	1.54 **1.84**	1.51 **1.78**	1.45 **1.70**	1.42 **1.65**	1.38 **1.57**	1.35 **1.52**	1.32 **1.49**	29
100	3.94 **6.90**	3.09 **4.82**	2.70 **3.98**	2.46 **3.51**	2.30 **3.20**	2.19 **2.99**	2.10 **2.82**	2.03 **2.69**	1.97 **2.59**	1.92 **2.51**	1.88 **2.43**	1.85 **2.36**	1.79 **2.26**	1.75 **2.19**	1.68 **2.06**	1.63 **1.98**	1.57 **1.89**	1.51 **1.79**	1.48 **1.73**	1.42 **1.64**	1.39 **1.59**	1.34 **1.51**	1.30 **1.46**	1.28 **1.43**	100
125	3.92 **6.84**	3.07 **4.78**	2.68 **3.94**	2.44 **3.47**	2.29 **3.17**	2.17 **2.95**	2.08 **2.79**	2.01 **2.65**	1.95 **2.56**	1.90 **2.47**	1.86 **2.40**	1.83 **2.33**	1.77 **2.23**	1.72 **2.15**	1.65 **2.03**	1.60 **1.94**	1.55 **1.85**	1.49 **1.75**	1.45 **1.68**	1.39 **1.59**	1.36 **1.54**	1.31 **1.46**	1.27 **1.40**	1.25 **1.37**	125
150	3.91 **6.81**	3.06 **4.75**	2.67 **3.91**	2.43 **3.44**	2.27 **3.14**	2.16 **2.92**	2.07 **2.76**	2.00 **2.62**	1.94 **2.53**	1.89 **2.44**	1.85 **2.37**	1.82 **2.30**	1.76 **2.20**	1.71 **2.12**	1.64 **2.00**	1.59 **1.91**	1.54 **1.83**	1.47 **1.72**	1.44 **1.66**	1.37 **1.56**	1.34 **1.51**	1.29 **1.43**	1.25 **1.37**	1.22 **1.33**	150
200	3.89 **6.76**	3.04 **4.71**	2.65 **3.88**	2.41 **3.41**	2.26 **3.11**	2.14 **2.90**	2.05 **2.73**	1.98 **2.60**	1.92 **2.50**	1.87 **2.41**	1.83 **2.34**	1.80 **2.28**	1.74 **2.17**	1.69 **2.09**	1.62 **1.97**	1.57 **1.88**	1.52 **1.79**	1.45 **1.69**	1.42 **1.62**	1.35 **1.53**	1.32 **1.48**	1.26 **1.39**	1.22 **1.33**	1.19 **1.28**	200
400	3.86 **6.70**	3.02 **4.66**	2.62 **3.83**	2.39 **3.36**	2.23 **3.06**	2.12 **2.85**	2.03 **2.69**	1.96 **2.55**	1.90 **2.46**	1.85 **2.37**	1.81 **2.29**	1.78 **2.23**	1.72 **2.12**	1.67 **2.04**	1.60 **1.92**	1.54 **1.84**	1.49 **1.74**	1.42 **1.64**	1.38 **1.57**	1.32 **1.47**	1.28 **1.42**	1.22 **1.32**	1.16 **1.24**	1.13 **1.19**	400
1000	3.85 **6.66**	3.00 **4.62**	2.61 **3.80**	2.38 **3.34**	2.22 **3.04**	2.10 **2.82**	2.02 **2.66**	1.95 **2.53**	1.89 **2.43**	1.84 **2.34**	1.80 **2.26**	1.76 **2.20**	1.70 **2.09**	1.65 **2.01**	1.58 **1.89**	1.53 **1.81**	1.47 **1.71**	1.41 **1.61**	1.36 **1.54**	1.30 **1.44**	1.26 **1.38**	1.19 **1.28**	1.13 **1.19**	1.08 **1.11**	1000
∞	3.84 **6.64**	2.99 **4.60**	2.60 **3.78**	2.37 **3.32**	2.21 **3.02**	2.09 **2.80**	2.01 **2.64**	1.94 **2.51**	1.88 **2.41**	1.83 **2.32**	1.79 **2.24**	1.75 **2.18**	1.69 **2.07**	1.64 **1.99**	1.57 **1.87**	1.52 **1.79**	1.46 **1.69**	1.40 **1.59**	1.35 **1.52**	1.28 **1.41**	1.24 **1.36**	1.17 **1.25**	1.11 **1.15**	1.00 **1.00**	∞

Degrees of freedom (for the denominator)

*To be significant the F obtained from the data must be equal to or larger than the value shown in the table.

Source: *Statistical Methods* (6th ed.) by G. W. Snedecor and W. G. Cochran, 1967, Ames, Iowa: Iowa State University Press. Used by permission of the Iowa State University Press.

TABLE A-5   VALUES OF STUDENTIZED RANGE STATISTIC, q_k

For a one-way ANOVA, or a comparison of the means from a main effect, the value of k is the number of means in the factor.

To compare the means from an interaction, find the appropriate design (or number of cell means) in the table below and obtain the adjusted value of k. Then, use adjusted k as k to find the value of q_k.

VALUES OF ADJUSTED k

Design of study	Number of cell means in study	Adjusted value of k
2×2	4	3
2×3	6	5
2×4	8	6
3×3	9	7
3×4	12	8
4×4	16	10
4×5	20	12

Values of q_k for $\alpha = .05$ are **dark numbers** and for $\alpha = .01$ are light numbers.

Degrees of freedom within groups (degrees of freedom in denominator of F ratio)	α	2	3	4	5	6	7	8	9	10	11	12
1	.05	**18.00**	**27.00**	**32.80**	**37.10**	**40.40**	**43.10**	**45.40**	**47.40**	**49.10**	**50.60**	**52.00**
	.01	90.00	135.00	164.00	186.00	202.00	216.00	227.00	237.00	246.00	253.00	260.00
2	.05	**6.09**	**8.30**	**9.80**	**10.90**	**11.70**	**12.40**	**13.00**	**13.50**	**14.00**	**14.40**	**14.70**
	.01	14.00	19.00	22.30	24.70	26.60	28.20	29.50	30.70	31.70	32.60	33.40
3	.05	**4.50**	**5.91**	**6.82**	**7.50**	**8.04**	**8.48**	**8.85**	**9.18**	**9.46**	**9.72**	**9.95**
	.01	8.26	10.60	12.20	13.30	14.20	15.00	15.60	16.20	16.70	17.10	17.50
4	.05	**3.93**	**5.04**	**5.76**	**6.29**	**6.71**	**7.05**	**7.35**	**7.60**	**7.83**	**8.03**	**8.21**
	.01	6.51	8.12	9.17	9.96	10.60	11.10	11.50	11.90	12.30	12.60	12.80
5	.05	**3.64**	**4.60**	**5.22**	**5.67**	**6.03**	**6.33**	**6.58**	**6.80**	**6.99**	**7.17**	**7.32**
	.01	5.70	6.97	7.80	8.42	8.91	9.32	9.67	9.97	10.20	10.50	10.70
6	.05	**3.46**	**4.34**	**4.90**	**5.31**	**5.63**	**5.89**	**6.12**	**6.32**	**6.49**	**6.65**	**6.79**
	.01	5.24	6.33	7.03	7.56	7.97	8.32	8.61	8.87	9.10	9.30	9.49
7	.05	**3.34**	**4.16**	**4.69**	**5.06**	**5.36**	**5.61**	**5.82**	**6.00**	**6.16**	**6.30**	**6.43**
	.01	4.95	5.92	6.54	7.01	7.37	7.68	7.94	8.17	8.37	8.55	8.71
8	.05	**3.26**	**4.04**	**4.53**	**4.89**	**5.17**	**5.40**	**5.60**	**5.77**	**5.92**	**6.05**	**6.18**
	.01	4.74	5.63	6.20	6.63	6.96	7.24	7.47	7.68	7.87	8.03	8.18
9	.05	**3.20**	**3.95**	**4.42**	**4.76**	**5.02**	**5.24**	**5.43**	**5.60**	**5.74**	**5.87**	**5.98**
	.01	4.60	5.43	5.96	6.35	6.66	6.91	7.13	7.32	7.49	7.65	7.78
10	.05	**3.15**	**3.88**	**4.33**	**4.65**	**4.91**	**5.12**	**5.30**	**5.46**	**5.60**	**5.72**	**5.83**
	.01	4.48	5.27	5.77	6.14	6.43	6.67	6.87	7.05	7.21	7.36	7.48

TABLE A-5 (CONTINUED)

Degrees of freedom within groups (degrees of freedom in denominator of F ratio)	α	2	3	4	5	6	7	8	9	10	11	12
							k = number of means being compared					
11	.05	3.11	3.82	4.26	4.57	4.82	5.03	5.20	5.35	5.49	5.61	5.71
	.01	4.39	5.14	5.62	5.97	6.25	6.48	6.67	6.84	6.99	7.13	7.26
12	.05	3.08	3.77	4.20	4.51	4.75	4.95	5.12	5.27	5.40	5.51	5.62
	.01	4.32	5.04	5.50	5.84	6.10	6.32	6.51	6.67	6.81	6.94	7.06
13	.05	3.06	3.73	4.15	4.45	4.69	4.88	5.05	5.19	5.32	5.43	5.53
	.01	4.26	4.96	5.40	5.73	5.98	6.19	6.37	6.53	6.67	6.79	6.90
14	.05	3.03	3.70	4.11	4.41	4.64	4.83	4.99	5.13	5.25	5.36	5.46
	.01	4.21	4.89	5.32	5.63	5.88	6.08	6.26	6.41	6.54	6.66	6.77
16	.05	3.00	3.65	4.05	4.33	4.56	4.74	4.90	5.03	5.15	5.26	5.35
	.01	4.13	4.78	5.19	5.49	5.72	5.92	6.08	6.22	6.35	6.46	6.56
18	.05	2.97	3.61	4.00	4.28	4.49	4.67	4.82	4.96	5.07	5.17	5.27
	.01	4.07	4.70	5.09	5.38	5.60	5.79	5.94	6.08	6.20	6.31	6.41
20	.05	2.95	3.58	3.96	4.23	4.45	4.62	4.77	4.90	5.01	5.11	5.20
	.01	4.02	4.64	5.02	5.29	5.51	5.69	5.84	5.97	6.09	6.19	6.29
24	.05	2.92	3.53	3.90	4.17	4.37	4.54	4.68	4.81	4.92	5.01	5.10
	.01	3.96	4.54	4.91	5.17	5.37	5.54	5.69	5.81	5.92	6.02	6.11
30	.05	2.89	3.49	3.84	4.10	4.30	4.46	4.60	4.72	4.83	4.92	5.00
	.01	3.89	4.45	4.80	5.05	5.24	5.40	5.54	5.56	5.76	5.85	5.93
40	.05	2.86	3.44	3.79	4.04	4.23	4.39	4.52	4.63	4.74	4.82	4.91
	.01	3.82	4.37	4.70	4.93	5.11	5.27	5.39	5.50	5.60	5.69	5.77
60	.05	2.83	3.40	3.74	3.98	4.16	4.31	4.44	4.55	4.65	4.73	4.81
	.01	3.76	4.28	4.60	4.82	4.99	5.13	5.25	5.36	5.45	5.53	5.60
120	.05	2.80	3.36	3.69	3.92	4.10	4.24	4.36	4.48	4.56	4.64	4.72
	.01	3.70	4.20	4.50	4.71	4.87	5.01	5.12	5.21	5.30	5.38	5.44
∞	.05	2.77	3.31	3.63	3.86	4.03	4.17	4.29	4.39	4.47	4.55	4.62
	.01	3.64	4.12	4.40	4.60	4.76	4.88	4.99	5.08	5.16	5.23	5.29

From B. J. Winer, *Statistical Principles in Experimental Design*, McGraw-Hill, 1962; abridged from H. L Harter, D. S. Clemm, and E. H. Guthrie, The probability integrals of the range and of the studentized range, WADC Tech. Rep. 58–484, Vol. 2, 1959, Wright Air Development Center, Table II.2, pp. 243–281. Reproduced with permission of The McGraw-Hill Companies, Inc.

TABLE A-6 CRITICAL VALUES OF THE F_{max} TEST

Critical values for $\alpha = .05$ are **dark numbers** and for $\alpha = .01$ are light numbers.

k = number of samples in the study

$n - 1$	α	2	3	4	5	6	7	8	9	10	11	12
4	.05	**9.60**	**15.50**	**20.60**	**25.20**	**29.50**	**33.60**	**37.50**	**41.40**	**44.60**	**48.00**	**51.40**
	.01	23.20	37.00	49.00	59.00	69.00	79.00	89.00	97.00	106.00	113.00	120.00
5	.05	**7.15**	**10.80**	**13.70**	**16.30**	**18.70**	**20.80**	**22.90**	**24.70**	**26.50**	**28.20**	**29.90**
	.01	14.90	22.00	28.00	33.00	38.00	42.00	46.00	50.00	54.00	57.00	60.00
6	.05	**5.82**	**8.38**	**10.40**	**12.10**	**13.70**	**15.00**	**16.30**	**17.50**	**18.60**	**19.70**	**20.70**
	.01	11.10	15.50	19.10	22.00	25.00	27.00	30.00	32.00	34.00	36.00	37.00
7	.05	**4.99**	**6.94**	**8.44**	**9.70**	**10.80**	**11.80**	**12.70**	**13.50**	**14.30**	**15.10**	**15.80**
	.01	8.89	12.10	14.50	16.50	18.40	20.00	22.00	23.00	24.00	26.00	27.00
8	.05	**4.43**	**6.00**	**7.18**	**8.12**	**9.03**	**9.78**	**10.50**	**11.10**	**11.70**	**12.20**	**12.70**
	.01	7.50	9.90	11.70	13.20	14.50	15.80	16.90	17.90	18.90	19.80	21.00
9	.05	**4.03**	**5.34**	**6.31**	**7.11**	**7.80**	**8.41**	**8.95**	**9.45**	**9.91**	**10.30**	**10.70**
	.01	6.54	8.50	9.90	11.10	12.10	13.10	13.90	14.70	15.30	16.00	16.60
10	.05	**3.72**	**4.85**	**5.67**	**6.34**	**6.92**	**7.42**	**7.87**	**8.28**	**8.66**	**9.01**	**9.34**
	.01	5.85	7.40	8.60	9.60	10.40	11.10	11.80	12.40	12.90	13.40	13.90
12	.05	**3.28**	**4.16**	**4.79**	**5.30**	**5.72**	**6.09**	**6.42**	**6.72**	**7.00**	**7.25**	**7.48**
	.01	4.91	6.10	6.90	7.60	8.20	8.70	9.10	9.50	9.90	10.20	10.60
15	.05	**2.86**	**3.54**	**4.01**	**4.37**	**4.68**	**4.95**	**5.19**	**5.40**	**5.59**	**5.77**	**5.93**
	.01	4.07	4.90	5.50	6.00	6.40	6.70	7.10	7.30	7.50	7.80	8.00
20	.05	**2.46**	**2.95**	**3.29**	**3.54**	**3.76**	**3.94**	**4.10**	**4.24**	**4.37**	**4.49**	**4.59**
	.01	3.32	3.80	4.30	4.60	4.90	5.10	5.30	5.50	5.60	5.80	5.90
30	.05	**2.07**	**2.40**	**2.61**	**2.78**	**2.91**	**3.02**	**3.12**	**3.21**	**3.29**	**3.36**	**3.39**
	.01	2.63	3.00	3.30	3.40	3.60	3.70	3.80	3.90	4.00	4.10	4.20
60	.05	**1.67**	**1.85**	**1.96**	**2.04**	**2.11**	**2.17**	**2.22**	**2.26**	**2.30**	**2.33**	**2.36**
	.01	1.96	2.20	2.30	2.40	2.40	2.50	2.50	2.60	2.60	2.70	2.70

(*Note: n* = number of scores in each condition or cell.)

From Table 31 of E. Pearson and H. Hartley, *Biometrika Tables for Statisticians*, Vol. 1, 3rd ed. Cambridge: Cambridge University Press, 1966. Reprinted with permission of the Biometrika Trustees.

TABLE A-7 CRITICAL VALUES OF CHI SQUARE: THE χ^2-TABLES

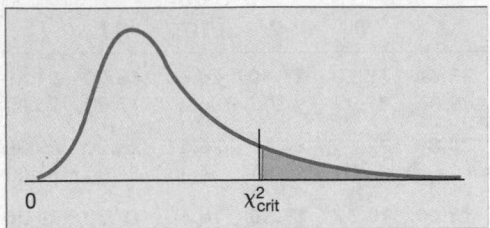

Level of significance

df	$\alpha = .05$	$\alpha = .01$
1	3.84	6.64
2	5.99	9.21
3	7.81	11.34
4	9.49	13.28
5	11.07	15.09
6	12.59	16.81
7	14.07	18.48
8	15.51	20.09
9	16.92	21.67
10	18.31	23.21
11	19.68	24.72
12	21.03	26.22
13	22.36	27.69
14	23.68	29.14
15	25.00	30.58
16	26.30	32.00
17	27.59	33.41
18	28.87	34.80
19	30.14	36.19
20	31.41	37.57
21	32.67	38.93
22	33.92	40.29
23	35.17	41.64

TABLE A-7 (CONTINUED)

df	Level of significance	
	$\alpha = .05$	$\alpha = .01$
24	36.42	42.98
25	37.65	44.31
26	38.88	45.64
27	40.11	46.96
28	41.34	48.28
29	42.56	49.59
30	43.77	50.89
40	55.76	63.69
50	67.50	76.15
60	79.08	88.38
70	90.53	100.42

From Table IV of R. A. Fisher and F. Yates, *Statistical Tables for Biological, Agricultural, and Medical Research*, 6th ed. London: Longman Group Ltd., 1974. Reprinted by permission of Addison-Wesley Longman, Ltd.

TABLE A-8 CRITICAL VALUES OF THE MANN-WHITNEY *U*

To be significant, the U_{obt} must be equal to or be *less than* the critical value. (Dashes in the table indicate that no decision is possible.) Critical values for $\alpha = .05$ are **dark numbers** and for $\alpha = .01$ are light numbers.

Two-tailed test

n_2 (no. of scores in Group 2)	α	n_1 (no. of scores in Group 1)								
		1	2	3	4	5	6	7	8	9
1	.05	—	—	—	—	—	—	—	—	—
	.01	—	—	—	—	—	—	—	—	—
2	.05	—	—	—	—	—	—	—	0	0
	.01	—	—	—	—	—	—	—	—	—
3	.05	—	—	—	—	0	1	1	2	2
	.01	—	—	—	—	—	—	—	—	0
4	.05	—	—	—	0	1	2	3	4	4
	.01	—	—	—	—	—	0	0	1	1
5	.05	—	—	0	1	2	3	5	6	7
	.01	—	—	—	—	0	1	1	2	3
6	.05	—	—	1	2	3	5	6	8	10
	.01	—	—	—	0	1	2	3	4	5
7	.05	—	—	1	3	5	6	8	10	12
	.01	—	—	—	0	1	3	4	6	7
8	.05	—	0	2	4	6	8	10	13	15
	.01	—	—	—	1	2	4	6	7	9
9	.05	—	0	2	4	7	10	12	15	17
	.01	—	—	0	1	3	5	7	9	11
10	.05	—	0	3	5	8	11	14	17	20
	.01	—	—	0	2	4	6	9	11	13
11	.05	—	0	3	6	9	13	16	19	23
	.01	—	—	0	2	5	7	10	13	16
12	.05	—	1	4	7	11	14	18	22	26
	.01	—	—	1	3	6	9	12	15	18
13	.05	—	1	4	8	12	16	20	24	28
	.01	—	—	1	3	7	10	13	17	20
14	.05	—	1	5	9	13	17	22	26	31
	.01	—	—	1	4	7	11	15	18	22
15	.05	—	1	5	10	14	19	24	29	34
	.01	—	—	2	5	8	12	16	20	24
16	.05	—	1	6	11	15	21	26	31	37
	.01	—	—	2	5	9	13	18	22	27
17	.05	—	2	6	11	17	22	28	34	39
	.01	—	—	2	6	10	15	19	24	29
18	.05	—	2	7	12	18	24	30	36	42
	.01	—	—	2	6	11	16	21	26	31
19	.05	—	2	7	13	19	25	32	38	45
	.01	—	0	3	7	12	17	22	28	33
20	.05	—	2	8	13	20	27	34	41	48
	.01	—	0	3	8	13	18	24	30	36

TABLE A-8 (CONTINUED)

n_1 (no. of scores in Group 1)										
10	11	12	13	14	15	16	17	18	19	20
—	—	—	—	—	—	—	—	—	—	—
—	—	—	—	—	—	—	—	—	—	—
0	0	1	1	1	1	1	2	2	2	2
—	—	—	—	—	—	—	—	—	0	0
3	3	4	4	5	5	6	6	7	7	8
0	0	1	1	1	2	2	2	2	3	3
5	6	7	8	9	10	11	11	12	13	13
2	2	3	3	4	5	5	6	6	7	8
8	9	11	12	13	14	15	17	18	19	20
4	5	6	7	7	8	9	10	11	12	13
11	13	14	16	17	19	21	22	24	25	27
6	7	9	10	11	12	13	15	16	17	18
14	16	18	20	22	24	26	28	30	32	34
9	10	12	13	15	16	18	19	21	22	24
17	19	22	24	26	29	31	34	36	38	41
11	13	15	17	18	20	22	24	26	28	30
20	23	26	28	31	34	37	39	42	45	48
13	16	18	20	22	24	27	29	31	33	36
23	26	29	33	36	39	42	45	48	52	55
16	18	21	24	26	29	31	34	37	39	42
26	30	33	37	40	44	47	51	55	58	62
18	21	24	27	30	33	36	39	42	45	48
29	33	37	41	45	49	53	57	61	65	69
21	24	27	31	34	37	41	44	47	51	54
33	37	41	45	50	54	59	63	67	72	76
24	27	31	34	38	42	45	49	53	56	60
36	40	45	50	55	59	64	67	74	78	83
26	30	34	38	42	46	50	54	58	63	67
39	44	49	54	59	64	70	75	80	85	90
29	33	37	42	46	51	55	60	64	69	73
42	47	53	59	64	70	75	81	86	92	98
31	36	41	45	50	55	60	65	70	74	79
45	51	57	63	67	75	81	87	93	99	105
34	39	44	49	54	60	65	70	75	81	86
48	55	61	67	74	80	86	93	99	106	112
37	42	47	53	58	64	70	75	81	87	92
52	58	65	72	78	85	92	99	106	113	119
39	45	51	56	63	69	74	81	87	93	99
55	62	69	76	83	90	98	105	112	119	127
42	48	54	60	67	73	79	86	92	99	105

TABLE A-8 (CONTINUED)

One-tailed test

n_2 (no. of scores in Group 2)	α	\multicolumn{9}{c}{n_1 (no. of scores in Group 1)}
		1	2	3	4	5	6	7	8	9
1	.05	—	—	—	—	—	—	—	—	—
	.01	—	—	—	—	—	—	—	—	—
2	.05	—	—	—	—	0	0	0	1	1
	.01	—	—	—	—	—	—	—	—	—
3	.05	—	—	0	0	1	2	2	3	3
	.01	—	—	—	—	—	—	0	0	1
4	.05	—	—	0	1	2	3	4	5	6
	.01	—	—	—	—	0	1	1	2	3
5	.05	—	0	1	2	4	5	6	8	9
	.01	—	—	—	0	1	2	3	4	5
6	.05	—	0	2	3	5	7	8	10	12
	.01	—	—	—	1	2	3	4	6	7
7	.05	—	0	2	4	6	8	11	13	15
	.01	—	—	0	1	3	4	6	7	9
8	.05	—	1	3	5	8	10	13	15	18
	.01	—	—	0	2	4	6	7	9	11
9	.05	—	1	3	6	9	12	15	18	21
	.01	—	—	1	3	5	7	9	11	14
10	.05	—	1	4	7	11	14	17	20	24
	.01	—	—	1	3	6	8	11	13	16
11	.05	—	1	5	8	12	16	19	23	27
	.01	—	—	1	4	7	9	12	15	18
12	.05	—	2	5	9	13	17	21	26	30
	.01	—	—	2	5	8	11	14	17	21
13	.05	—	2	6	10	15	19	24	28	33
	.01	—	0	2	5	9	12	16	20	23
14	.05	—	2	7	11	16	21	26	31	36
	.01	—	0	2	6	10	13	17	22	26
15	.05	—	3	7	12	18	23	28	33	39
	.01	—	0	3	7	11	15	19	24	28
16	.05	—	3	8	14	19	25	30	36	42
	.01	—	0	3	7	12	16	21	26	31
17	.05	—	3	9	15	20	26	33	39	45
	.01	—	0	4	8	13	18	23	28	33
18	.05	—	4	9	16	22	28	35	41	48
	.01	—	0	4	9	14	19	24	30	36
19	.05	0	4	10	17	23	30	37	44	51
	.01	—	1	4	9	15	20	26	32	38
20	.05	0	4	11	18	25	32	39	47	54
	.01	—	1	5	10	16	22	28	34	40

TABLE A-8 (CONTINUED)

n_1 (no. of scores in Group 1)

10	11	12	13	14	15	16	17	18	19	20
—	—	—	—	—	—	—	—	—	**0**	**0**
—	—	—	—	—	—	—	—	—	—	—
1	**1**	**2**	**2**	**2**	**3**	**3**	**3**	**4**	**4**	**4**
—	—	—	0	0	0	0	0	0	1	1
4	**5**	**5**	**6**	**7**	**7**	**8**	**9**	**9**	**10**	**11**
1	1	2	2	2	3	3	4	4	4	5
7	**8**	**9**	**10**	**11**	**12**	**14**	**15**	**16**	**17**	**18**
3	4	5	5	6	7	7	8	9	9	10
11	**12**	**13**	**15**	**16**	**18**	**19**	**20**	**22**	**23**	**25**
6	7	8	9	10	11	12	13	14	15	16
14	**16**	**17**	**19**	**21**	**23**	**25**	**26**	**28**	**30**	**32**
8	9	11	12	13	15	16	18	19	20	22
17	**19**	**21**	**24**	**26**	**28**	**30**	**33**	**35**	**37**	**39**
11	12	14	16	17	19	21	23	24	26	28
20	**23**	**26**	**28**	**31**	**33**	**36**	**39**	**41**	**44**	**47**
13	15	17	20	22	24	26	28	30	32	34
24	**27**	**30**	**33**	**36**	**39**	**42**	**45**	**48**	**51**	**54**
16	18	21	23	26	28	31	33	36	38	40
27	**31**	**34**	**37**	**41**	**44**	**48**	**51**	**55**	**58**	**62**
19	22	24	27	30	33	36	38	41	44	47
31	**34**	**38**	**42**	**46**	**50**	**54**	**57**	**61**	**65**	**69**
22	25	28	31	34	37	41	44	47	50	53
34	**38**	**42**	**47**	**51**	**55**	**60**	**64**	**68**	**72**	**77**
24	28	31	35	38	42	46	49	53	56	60
37	**42**	**47**	**51**	**56**	**61**	**65**	**70**	**75**	**80**	**84**
27	31	35	39	43	47	51	55	59	63	67
41	**46**	**51**	**56**	**61**	**66**	**71**	**77**	**82**	**87**	**92**
30	34	38	43	47	51	56	60	65	69	73
44	**50**	**55**	**61**	**66**	**72**	**77**	**83**	**88**	**94**	**100**
33	37	42	47	51	56	61	66	70	75	80
48	**54**	**60**	**65**	**71**	**77**	**83**	**89**	**95**	**101**	**107**
36	41	46	51	56	61	66	71	76	82	87
51	**57**	**64**	**70**	**77**	**83**	**89**	**96**	**102**	**109**	**115**
38	44	49	55	60	66	71	77	82	88	93
55	**61**	**68**	**75**	**82**	**88**	**95**	**102**	**109**	**116**	**123**
41	47	53	59	65	70	76	82	88	94	100
58	**65**	**72**	**80**	**87**	**94**	**101**	**109**	**116**	**123**	**130**
44	50	56	63	69	75	82	88	94	101	107
62	**69**	**77**	**84**	**92**	**100**	**107**	**115**	**123**	**130**	**138**
47	53	60	67	73	80	87	93	100	107	114

From the *Bulletin of the Institute of Educational Research*, 1, No. 2, Indiana University, with permission of the publishers.

TABLE A-9 CRITICAL VALUES OF THE WILCOXON T

To be significant, the T_{obt} must be equal to or *less than* the critical value. (Dashes in the table indicate that no decision is possible.) In the table, N is the number of nonzero differences that occurred when T_{obt} was calculated.

Two-tailed test

N	$\alpha = .05$	$\alpha = .01$	N	$\alpha = .05$	$\alpha = .01$
5	—	—	28	116	91
6	0	—	29	126	100
7	2	—	30	137	109
8	3	0	31	147	118
9	5	1	32	159	128
10	8	3	33	170	138
11	10	5	34	182	148
12	13	7	35	195	159
13	17	9	36	208	171
14	21	12	37	221	182
15	25	15	38	235	194
16	29	19	39	249	207
17	34	23	40	264	220
18	40	27	41	279	233
19	46	32	42	294	247
20	52	37	43	310	261
21	58	42	44	327	276
22	65	48	45	343	291
23	73	54	46	361	307
24	81	61	47	378	322
25	89	68	48	396	339
26	98	75	49	415	355
27	107	83	50	434	373

TABLE A-9 (CONTINUED)

One-tailed test

N	α = .05	α = .01	N	α = .05	α = .01
5	0	—	28	130	101
6	2	—	29	140	110
7	3	0	30	151	120
8	5	1	31	163	130
9	8	3	32	175	140
10	10	5	33	187	151
11	13	7	34	200	162
12	17	9	35	213	173
13	21	12	36	227	185
14	25	15	37	241	198
15	30	19	38	256	211
16	35	23	39	271	224
17	41	27	40	286	238
18	47	32	41	302	252
19	53	37	42	319	266
20	60	43	43	336	281
21	67	49	44	353	296
22	75	55	45	371	312
23	83	62	46	389	328
24	91	69	47	407	345
25	100	76	48	426	362
26	110	84	49	446	379
27	119	92	50	466	397

From F. Wilcoxon and R. A. Wilcox, *Some Rapid Approximate Statistical Procedures, Revised Edition* (Pearl River, NY: Lederle Laboratories, 1964).

appendix B

Check Your Progress Answers

Chapter 1

Check Your Progress page 12

1. tenacity
2. a
3. Your perception that the world may be altered and your knowledge base would not be accurate.
4. 1-C; 2-D; 3-A; 4-B; 5-E
5. The "self-correcting nature of science" refers to the fact that because scientific findings are open to public scrutiny, they can be replicated. Replications will reveal any errors and faulty logic.
6. b
7. The experimenter attempts to establish a cause-and-effect relation between the IV that is manipulated and the DV that is recorded.
8. b

Check Your Progress page 21

1. The steps involved in the research process include the following:
   Problem. You detect a gap in the knowledge base.
   Literature Review. Consulting previous reports determines what has been found in the research area of interest.
   Theoretical Considerations. The literature review highlights theories that point to relevant research projects.
   Hypothesis. The literature review also highlights hypotheses (statements of the relationship between variables in more restricted domains of the research area). Such hypotheses will assist in the development of the experimental hypothesis—the predicted outcome of your research project.
   Experimental Design. You develop the general plan for conducting the research project.
   Conduct the Experiment. You conduct the research project according to the experimental design.
   Data Analysis and Statistical Decisions. Based upon the statistical analysis, you decide whether the independent variable exerted a significant effect upon the dependent variable.
   Decisions in Terms of Past Research and Theory. The statistical results guide decisions concerning the relationship of the present research project to past research and theoretical considerations.
   Preparation of the Research Report. You prepare a research report describing the rationale, conduct, and results of the experiment according to accepted American Psychological Association (APA) format.
   Sharing Your Results: Presentation and Publication. You share your research report with professional colleagues at a professional society meeting and/or by publication in a professional journal.
   Finding a New Problem. Your research results highlight another gap in our knowledge base and the research process begins again.
2. d
3. d
4. d

5. The reasons for taking a research methods or experimental psychology course include that they
    a. assist you in other psychology courses
    b. enable you to conduct a research project after graduation
    c. assist you in getting into graduate school
    d. help you to become a knowledgeable consumer of psychological research

Chapter 2

Check Your Progress page 44

1. 1-C; 2-A; 3-B; 4-F; 5-E; 6-D
2. testable; likelihood of success
3. Nonsystematic sources of research ideas include those instances or occurrences that make us believe that the research idea was unplanned. These types of research ideas are shown through "inspiration," "serendipity," and "everyday occurrences." Systematic sources of research ideas are carefully organized and logically thought out. This source of research ideas may be found in "past research," "theory," and "classroom lectures."
4. c
5. d
6. Synthetic statements are used in the experimental hypothesis because they can be either true or false.
7. General implication form presents the experimental hypothesis as an "if . . . then" statement where the if portion of the statement refers to the IV manipulation and the then portion of the statement refers to the predicted changes in the DV.
8. d
9. inductive, deductive
10. b

Chapter 3

Check Your Progress page 64

1. The atrocities of World War II where prisoners of war were unwillingly subjected to experiments using drugs, viruses, and toxic agents. The Tuskegee syphilis study examined the course of untreated syphilis in a group of men who did not realize they were being studied. Doctors in the Willowbrook experiment purposely infected patients with hepatitis and did not give them treatment in order to study the development of the disease. Milgram's research on obedience studied the reaction to demands from an authority in participants who were being deceived.
2. The Nuremberg Code stressed the need to
    a. obtain participants' consent to participate in research
    b. inform participants about the nature of the research project
    c. avoid risks where possible
    d. protect participants against risks
    e. conduct research using qualified personnel
3. Deception may be needed if the results of a research project would be biased or contaminated by the participants knowing the nature of the experiment. A more general statement on the informed consent document in conjunction with a clear indication that the participants may terminate the project at any time might be used. Complete debriefing should follow the experiment.
4. a
5. d

6. The guidelines for the ethical use of animals in research involve attention to each of the following:

I. *Justification of Research.* The research should have a clear scientific purpose.

II. *Personnel.* Only trained personnel who are familiar with the animal care guidelines should be involved with the research. All procedures must conform to appropriate federal guidelines.

III. *Care and Housing of Animals.* Animal housing areas must comply with current regulations.

IV. *Acquisition of Animals.* If animals are not bred in the laboratory, they must be acquired in a lawful, humane manner.

V. *Experimental Procedures.* "Humane consideration for the well-being of the animal should be incorporated into the design and conduct of all procedures involving animals, while keeping in mind the primary goal of experimental procedures—the acquisition of sound, replicable data."

VI. *Field Research.* Field research must be approved by the appropriate review board. Investigators should take special precautions to disturb their research population(s) and the environment as little as possible.

VII. *Educational Use of Animals.* The educational use of animals must be approved by the appropriate review board. Instruction in the ethics of animal research is encouraged.

7. The IRB is the Institutional Review Board. The typical IRB at a college or university is composed of faculty members from a variety of disciplines, members from the community, and a veterinarian if animal proposals are considered. The IRB examines proposed procedures, questionnaires, the informed consent document, debriefing plans, the use of pain in animals, and proposed procedures for animal disposal.

8. The experimenter is responsible for the ethical conduct of the research project and the ethical presentation of the research results.

9. Plagiarism refers to the use of someone else's work without giving credit to the original author. Fabrication of data involves the creation of fictitious research data. Pressures for job security (tenure), salary increases, and ego involvement in the research are factors that might lead to such unethical behaviors.

Chapter 4

Check Your Progress page 73

1. d
2. c
3. c
4. b
5. d
6. c
7. d

Check Your Progress page 86

1. a
2. d
3. The ordinate is the vertical axis; it should be approximately two-thirds the size of the abscissa (horizontal axis). The DV is plotted on the ordinate, whereas the IV is plotted on the abscissa.
4. b
5. a
6. d
7. c

Chapter 5

Check Your Progress page 103

1. variable
2. 1-E; 2-C; 3-A; 4-F; 5-B; 6-D
3. c
4. c
5. You should record more than one DV if the additional DV(s) add meaningful information.
6. c

Check Your Progress page 115

1. 1-C; 2-A; 3-B; 4-E; 5-D
2. a
3. a
4. When within-subject counterbalancing is used, each participant experiences more than one sequence of IV presentations. When within-group counterbalancing is used, each participant experiences a different sequence of IV presentations.
5. n! refers to factoring or breaking a number into its component parts and then multiplying these component parts. n! can be used to determine the number of sequences required for complete counterbalancing: $4! = 4 \times 3 \times 2 \times 1 = 24$.
6. b
7. The incomplete counterbalancing procedure refers to the use of some, but not all, of the possible sequences of treatment administration.

Check Your Progress page 125

1. a
2. b
3. It is important to evaluate your experiment for internal validity because you cannot place any confidence in your results if your experiment does not have internal validity. Cause-and-effect statements cannot be made without internal validity.
4. 1-B; 2-C; 3-D; 4-A
5. 1-D; 2-A; 3-B; 4-C
6. In this experiment the internal validity threat of selection is likely. Because we selected participants who are senior citizens, it is possible that they will have less formal education than college students of today. Obtaining a college education was not as common for today's senior citizens when they were young.
7. a

Chapter 6

Check Your Progress page 137

1. Because it takes into account only the highest and lowest scores and disregards the distribution of scores in between, the range does not convey much information.
2. a
3. Because the percentage of scores occurring between the mean and any standard deviation (e.g., $+1$, $+2$, -1, -2) away from the mean is constant, standard deviation scores from one distribution can be compared with standard deviation scores from other distributions.
4. a
5. c

Check Your Progress page 145

1. c
2. The standard error of the mean is useful because it tells you how much variability you can expect to find in the population from which you drew the sample(s) in your research.
3. d
4. b
5. a
6. c
7. c
8. b

Chapter 7

Check Your Progress page 155

1. Once a precedent or established pattern for using a particular type of research participant is begun, it is likely that that type of participant will be used in experiments in the research area in question.
2. White rats and college students are the favorite participants in psychological research because of precedent and availability. An established pattern of research with these two populations has been established, and they are easy to obtain.
3. a
4. c
5. a
6. The experimenter must be careful not to become a slave to elaborate pieces of equipment. If this situation occurs, then it is likely that the equipment may begin dictating the type of research that is conducted and/or the type of DV that is recorded.

Check Your Progress page 164

1. The experimenter's physiological characteristics, psychological characteristics, and personal expectancies for the outcome of the experiment can operate as extraneous variables and influence the responses of the participants.
2. 1-C; 2-A; 3-B; 4-E; 5-D
3. a
4. Automated equipment and instruments to present instructions and record data are frequently used to control for experimenter expectancies because they help minimize experimenter contact with the participants. By minimizing contact with the participants, the experimenter is less likely to influence the outcome of the experiment.
5. b
6. c

Check Your Progress page 170

1. a
2. c
3. The goal of cross-cultural psychology is incompatible with ethnocentrism because ethnocentrism views other cultures as an extension of that culture. Hence, according to an ethnocentric view, there is no need for cross-cultural research.
4. Culture can influence the choice of the research problem, the nature of the experimental hypothesis, selection of the IV(s), selection of the DV(s), selection of participants, sampling procedures, and the type of questionnaire that is used.
5. b

Chapter 8

Check Your Progress page 183

1. d
2. A positive correlation indicates that as one variable increases, the other variable under consideration also increases, whereas a perfect positive correlation indicates that for every unit of increase in one variable there is a corresponding increase of one unit in the other variable.
3. a
4. b

Check Your Progress page 190

1. c
2. Effect size refers to the magnitude or size of the experimental treatment or the size or magnitude of a correlation.
3. Generally speaking, as the sample size increases the critical value required to achieve significance becomes smaller. Because smaller inferential statistics and correlation coefficients are associated with smaller effect sizes, a result may be significant yet have a small effect size.
4. d
5. a
6. The regression equation is the statistical basis of prediction. It states that the predicted value on the criterion variable is equal to a (the point at which the regression line intersects the Y axis) + (b [the regression coefficient] $\times X$ (the predictor variable]).
7. c

Chapter 9

Check Your Progress page 209

1. Because we draw samples rather than testing an entire population, we can never be 100% certain about our conclusions.
2. Null hypothesis: Caffeine has no effect on performance
Nondirectional alternative hypothesis: People who have ingested caffeine will perform differently on a task from people who have not ingested caffeine
Directional alternative hypothesis: People who have ingested caffeine will perform a task more quickly than people who have not ingested caffeine
3. No, you could not analyze the data in question #2 with a one-sample t test if you tested two groups (one with caffeine and one without). You *could* analyze the data from #2 with a one-sample t test *if* you had pre-existing data from a population.
4. "Level of significance" refers to the point at which the experimenter feels that a result occurs rarely by chance. If an experimental result occurs rarely by chance, we conclude that it is significant. Although the experimenter arbitrarily sets the level of significance, tradition has established the .05 level as an accepted level of significance.
5. Because researchers don't always know how a research project is going to turn out, it is safer to state a nondirectional hypothesis and use a two-tailed test. If a directional hypothesis is stated and the results turn out differently, then the experimenter is forced to reject the experimental hypothesis even though differences may exist between the groups.
6. a
7. a
8. c

Check Your Progress page 214

1. population; sample
2. Random sampling occurs when every member of the population has an equal chance of being selected. Random sampling with replacement occurs when the chosen items are returned to the population and can be selected on future occasions. When random sampling without replacement is used, the chosen item is not returned to the population.
3. Random sampling is important so that we can assume that our groups are representative of the population and so that we assume our groups are equal.
4. Stratified random sampling involves randomly selecting participants from a single layer or strata in the population (e.g., a limited age range). When stratified random sampling is used, group homogeneity is increased. The more homogeneous the sample, the less chances there are for nuisance variables to operate. The less the chance for nuisance variables to operate, the smaller the within-group variability.
5. The single-strata research approach attempts to secure research data from a single, specified segment of the population of interest. The cross-sectional research approach involves the comparison of two or more groups of participants during the same, rather limited, time span. The longitudinal research approach involves gathering information from a group of participants over an extended period of time.

Chapter 10

Check Your Progress page 229

1. We cannot conduct a valid experiment with only one group because we have to have a second group for comparison purposes. We cannot tell whether our IV has any effect if we cannot compare the experimental group to a control group.
2. levels
3. Independent groups consist of participants who are totally unrelated to each other. Correlated groups are composed of pairs of participants who have some relationship to each other because (a) they have some natural relationship (natural pairs), (b) are matched with each other (matched pairs), or (c) are the same participants (repeated measures). This difference is important to experimental designs because it is one of the three questions we ask to choose an appropriate design for an experiment.
4. 1-D; 2-A; 3-B; 4-C
5. We must be cautious about the use of random assignment when we have small numbers of participants because the groups may end up being unequal before the experiment.
6. If your experiment could use either independent or correlated groups, you would most likely base your decision on the number of participants available to you. We often use correlated groups when we have a small number of participants so that we can be more confident about the equality of our groups. If you have many potential participants, independent groups will typically be equal.
7. b

Check Your Progress page 236

1. It is important for our groups to be equal before the experiment so that any difference we detect in our DV can be attributed to the IV.
2. between-groups variability; error variability
3. b
4. Correlated groups have the advantages of ensuring equality of the participants before the experiment and of reducing error variability. Independent groups are advantageous in that they are simpler than correlated groups and that they can be used in experimental situations that preclude correlated groups.
5. Many different answers are possible to the question about comparing differing amounts of an IV. Some representative examples include amount of study time or amount of reinforcement in a learning experiment, amount of pay or bonus on job performance,

and length of therapy to treat a particular problem. As long as you chose a single IV and varied its amount (rather than presence versus absence), your answer should be correct.

6. Again, many different answers are possible. Some possible answers include different types of life experiences, different majors, different musical preferences, and different hometowns. As long as you chose two levels of an IV that cannot be manipulated, your answer is correct.

Chapter 11

Check Your Progress page 251

1. 1-B; 2-D; 3-C; 4-F; 5-E; 6-A
2. "Level of significance" refers to the point at which the experimenter feels that a result occurs rarely by chance. If an experimental result occurs rarely by chance, we conclude that it is significant. Although the experimenter arbitrarily sets the level of significance, tradition has established the .05 level as an accepted level of significance.
3. We would conduct an independent-groups t test when we have one IV with two groups; the groups are independent of each other (no relationship such as matching, repeated measures, or natural pairs).
4. We usually look for descriptive statistics first on a computer printout because this information helps us understand how the groups performed on the DV.
5. homogeneity of variance; heterogeneity of variance
6. words; numbers (statistical information)
7. Group A, with a mean of 75, scored significantly higher than Group B, which had a mean of 70.

Check Your Progress page 261

1. To compare the stereotyping of a group of male executives before and after the ERA, you would use a t test for correlated samples because this represents repeated measures.
2. a
3. a
4. a
5. c
6. Research is a cyclical, ongoing process because each experiment typically raises new questions. A multitude of examples of cyclical research could be given. For example, you might test a new antihyperactivity drug against a control group. If the drug is helpful, then you would need additional research to determine the most effective dosage. In the future, you would want to test this drug against new drugs that arrive on the market.

Chapter 12

Check Your Progress page 273

1. The two-group design is the building block for the multiple-group design because the multiple-group design essentially takes a two-group design and adds more groups to it. Thus, the multiple-group design is similar to changing a two-group design into a three-group design (or larger).
2. one, three
3. A multiple-group design allows you to ask and answer more questions than does a two-group design. You may be able to run only one experiment instead of two or three. Therefore, the multiple-group design is more efficient than the two-group design—you can save time, effort, participants, and so on.
4. There are many correct answers to this question. If you chose an IV that has more than two levels, your answer should be correct. For example, if you wished to test attendance in college students as a function of classification, you would use a multiple-group design with four groups (freshmen, sophomores, juniors, seniors).

5. Matched sets, repeated measures, and natural sets are all considered correlated groups because participants in such groups are related in some way.

Check Your Progress page 278

1. There is no real limit on the number of groups in a multiple-group design. Practically speaking, it is rare to see more than four or five groups for a particular IV.
2. How many groups are required to adequately test your experimental hypothesis? Will you learn something important if you include more levels of your IV?
3. provide more control than independent groups designs
4. Practical considerations are more demanding in multiple correlated groups designs because there are simply more "equated" participants with which to deal. In repeated measures, participants must take part in more experimental sessions. Matched sets must include three (or more) matched participants. Natural sets require larger sets of participants.
5. To compare personality traits of firstborn, lastborn, and only children, we would use a multiple independent groups design (unless you matched participants on some variable). Repeated measures and natural sets are impossible (can you figure out why?). This would represent an ex post facto study because you cannot manipulate an individual's birth order.

Chapter 13

Check Your Progress page 296

1. This experiment would require a multiple independent groups design with four groups. The necessary statistical test would be a one-way ANOVA for independent groups (students could not be in more than one classification simultaneously).

CLASSIFICATION

Freshman	Sophomore	Junior	Senior

2. Because we have more than two groups, it is necessary to compute post hoc tests to tell which groups are significantly different from the others.
3. between groups; within groups
4. Given the statistical information shown, we can conclude that students perform differently on their three attempts at taking the ACT or SAT (i.e., there is a statistically significant difference).
5. To draw a full and complete conclusion from Question 4, you would need the results from post hoc tests comparing the three means. With this information you could conclude whether students improve over time in taking the entrance exam.
6. It depends. Do you want to measure four different groups of people in the four seasons (multiple independent groups) or the same people's moods across the four seasons? Either approach is possible, but at this point in the chapter, you only have learned about independent groups. Using this approach, you should measure a large number of participants.
7. You will need to have different people to eat at all four restaurants (multiple independent groups).

Check Your Progress page 307

1. This question requires a multiple correlated groups design with three groups. The proper statistical test would be a one-way ANOVA for correlated groups because each student takes the test three times (repeated measures).

ACT/SAT ATTEMPTS

1st Attempt	2nd Attempt	3rd Attempt

2. The three sources of variability in a correlated-groups design are the IV, the participants, and error

3. Based on the statistics, you can conclude that there is a difference in the ACT or SAT scores for students who took the test three times. However, you do not know which scores are higher or lower.

4. To draw a full and complete conclusion from Question 3, you would need the results from post hoc tests comparing the three means. With this information you could conclude whether students improve over time in taking the entrance exam.

5. It was important to have the information from Chapter 11's continuing research problem so that we could begin a follow-up experiment with the knowledge that customers' clothing affects clerks' response times. The follow-up experiment, then, compared clerks' response times to three different clothing styles.

6. To test mood changes by seasons, you would need to measure the same people's moods across the four seasons (multiple correlated groups design).

7. You would need to have the same people to eat at all four restaurants (multiple correlated groups).

Chapter 14

Check Your Progress page 326

1. The two-group design is related to the factorial design because it forms the underlying basis of a factorial design. For example, a 2 × 2 factorial design is simply two two-group designs combined (see the shaded section below).

2. There is a practical limit to the number of IVs you can use in an experiment so that you will be able to interpret the results easily. Interactions involving many variables can be quite difficult to understand.

3. d

4. 1-C; 2-A; 3-B

5. two; four

6. Numerous correct answers are possible. Your answer should consist of an experiment with two IVs. One IV should be a between-subjects variable (no relationship between participants); one should be a within-subjects variable (repeated measures, matching, or natural groups). For example, you might assign students to either a group that takes an ACT or SAT preparation course or does not take such a course (between subjects). Each group would take the ACT or SAT twice (repeated measures).

Check Your Progress page 335

1. Factorial designs are combinations of the designs in Chapters 10 and 12 because a factorial design results from adding two (or more) simple designs (one IV each) together into a single design with two (or more) IVs; (e.g., see Figure 14-8).

2. A 2 × 4 × 3 experimental design consists of three IVs; one has two levels, one has four levels, and one has three levels:

3. Totally between-groups designs use independent groups of participants for each IV. Totally within-groups designs use correlated groups of participants for all IVs. Mixed-groups designs have at least one IV that uses independent groups of participants and one that uses correlated groups. These designs are similar in that they are all factorial designs. They differ, of course, in the way that the experimenter assigns participants to groups.

4. Your experimental questions should be your first consideration in choosing a factorial design because the number of questions you ask will determine how many IVs your experiment will have.

5. measured

6. Your friend has listed six IVs that she wishes to include in her experiment. This is too ambitious for a beginning project, and the results could be incredibly difficult to interpret because of the many potential interactions.

7. a

Chapter 15

Check Your Progress page 353

1. Your experimental design has two IVs: classification and sex. Both are between-subject variables because a participant cannot be in more than one group. You would use the factorial between-group design and test the data with a factorial ANOVA for independent groups. Your block diagram would look like the following:

Male	Female

2. An interaction effect is the simultaneous effect of two IVs in such a way that the effects of one IV depend on the particular level of the second IV. A significant interaction overrides any main effects because the interaction changes the meaning of the significant main effect.

3. a

4. The critical F values with 2 and 20 df are 3.49 (.05 level) and 5.85 (.01 level). The F value given (3.25) is less than either critical F value, so the finding is not significant, $p > .05$.

Check Your Progress page 370

1. This experimental design has two IVs: test-taking practice and study course. Both are within-subject variables because each participant takes the tests repeatedly and takes the study course. You would use the factorial within-group design and use a factorial ANOVA for correlated groups to analyze the data. Your block diagram would be the following:

	1st Try	2nd Try	3rd Try
No study course			
With study course			

2. Again, you still have two IVs: the practice and the course. However, the study course is now a between-subject variable because some participants take it and some do not. Test-taking practice is a within-subject variable because each participant takes the test three times (repeated measures). Thus, you have factorial mixed-group design and would use

a factorial ANOVA for mixed groups. Your block diagram would be the same as the one shown for Question 1—only the assignment of participants to groups differs.

3. An interaction effect is the simultaneous effect of two IVs in such a way that the effects of one IV depend on the particular level of the second IV. A significant interaction overrides any main effects because the interaction changes the meaning of the significant main effect. The easiest way to make sense of a significant interaction is to draw a figure depicting the interaction—how the groups scored on the DV as a function of both IVs.

4. A mixed ANOVA is not a particularly good way to test a critical between-subjects effect because the power of the test is lowest for the between-subjects effect.

5. This experiment has two IVs—the seasons and sex. Sex is always a between-subject variable, so you must choose between the factorial between-group design and the factorial mixed-groups design. Your decision rests upon how you wish to treat the participants relative to the seasons. If you use different participants for each season, both IVs would be between subjects and you would use the factorial between-group design. If you wish to use the same participants for each season, you would use the factorial mixed-groups design. Your selection of a particular design would probably depend on how many participants you can find—with large numbers, using a between-subject manipulation is acceptable.

6. This experiment has two IVs—restaurant and age. Age must be between subjects; restaurant could be either between or within subjects based on whether the same or different people eat at each restaurant. Thus, your choices are the same as for Question 5.

Chapter 16

Check Your Progress page 382

1. random assignment; experimental design
2. It is essential to randomly assign participants to groups to help assure that the groups are equal before the experiment.
3. Random selection refers to choosing participants from a population in a nonsystematic manner. Random assignment refers to allocating those randomly selected participants to different groups in a nonsystematic manner.
4. It is problematic to use the pretest–posttest control group design to help with internal validity because this design cannot control all internal validity threats.
5. d
6. The drawback of using the Solomon four-group design to control for internal validity is that there is no statistical test to analyze all the data from this design.
7. The posttest-only control group design is a good choice for controlling internal validity because it seems to control the internal validity threats covered in Chapter 6.
   Drawing a general diagram of the posttest-only control group design is not possible because the design can vary depending on the number of treatment groups in the experiment (e.g., see Figures 12-5 and 12-6).

Check Your Progress page 395

1. The use of single-case designs has decreased recently because of statistical innovations—an increase in both statistical tests and computerized analysis programs.
2. A single-case design can be used to disprove a theory because it takes only a single negative instance to invalidate a theory's general applicability.
3. baseline; three
4. a
5. *For:* Visual inspections of data may lead to incorrect conclusions. Statistical analysis gives increased accuracy.
   Against: Treatments should produce effects that are visually apparent. Clinical significance is more important than statistical significance.
6. 1-C; 2-A; 3-B

7. You might be forced to use an A-B single-case design in the real world because it can be impractical or unethical to reverse a treatment. Many examples are possible. Suppose you work with an individual who suffers from anorexia or bulimia. You institute a treatment and the individual shows marked improvement. However, you fear that removing the treatment could result in a recurrence of the problem.

Check Your Progress page 405

1. Experimental designs involve manipulation of IVs, control of extraneous variables, and measurement of DVs so that cause-and-effect relationships can be determined. Ex post facto designs involve IVs that have already occurred or that are predetermined, such as sex. Quasi-experimental designs involve manipulating IVs with groups of participants that are predetermined, such as causing something to vary between men and women.

2. You might choose to use a quasi-experimental design rather than an experimental design in a situation when random assignment is impossible or if you wish to evaluate an ongoing program.

3. 1-B, C F, 2-A, D*, E

4. The key element in Geronimus's research that allowed a more positive conclusion about teen pregnancy was the realization that finding a true control group would be impossible; hence the need for a strong comparison group.

5. We are more certain about our conclusion in the helmet law case because it simulated an A-B-A design, whereas the AFDC study was only an A-B design. If we can return to the baseline condition, we usually get a better reading of our results.

6. d

Chapter 17

Check Your Progress page 423

1. External validity is the ability to take your experimental findings and apply them beyond the experimental participants to the larger population. It is important to psychology so that we can develop general findings that apply to large groups of organisms.

2. b

3. Population generalization involves applying results from participants to the larger group. Environmental generalization involves applying your results to different settings than the original experiment. Temporal generalization involves applying experimental results to different times than in the experiment.

4. Using different types of participants helps increase the external validity of our findings.

5. Cross-cultural psychology involves testing psychological principles in different cultures to determine the generality of those principles. It is relevant to this chapter because it deals with external validity.

6. 1-C; 2-B; 3-D; 4-A

7. Mook thinks that external validity is necessary only when we are attempting to predict behavior in the real world. Much research in psychology is not aimed at such prediction, and Mook believes that external validity is not necessary in such situations.

8. It is almost impossible to achieve external validity in a single experiment because of the large number of threats to external validity. Usually an experiment can answer only one such threat at a time.

*Figure 16-14 gives the impression that the interrupted time-series design includes pretesting—in some cases, it may actually be pretesting. In many situations that use this design, however, the observations before the treatment are not true pretests because they were not made with an experiment in mind; rather, they may often simply represent data that were already available (e.g., sales records). This is a fine distinction, and it could easily be argued that both designs actually include pretesting.

Check Your Progress page 433

1. Students should critically examine any research report for errors or faulty thinking. It is possible for anyone to make a mistake.
2. The literature review should lead directly to the research question. After reading the literature review, the research question is the next logical question to ask.
3. Control techniques are necessary in experimentation to prevent extraneous variables from affecting experimental results; these techniques allow for cause-and-effect explanations.
4. Three critique guidelines that deal with participants:
   a. Participants should be randomly selected from a population and randomly assigned to groups.
   b. Participant groups should be equal before the experiment.
   c. The research should use an adequate number of participants.
5. Statistics are vital to research reports because they provide the numerical evidence to support the author's claims.
6. c
7. The discussion should be tied to the results of a research report so that the researcher does not go beyond the data in drawing conclusions.

Chapter 18

Check Your Progress page 448

1. If the statistical assumptions of an inferential statistical test are violated, the statistical test might not be valid.
2. a
3. Data transformation is the application of an accepted mathematical procedure, such as the square root, logarithmic, and reciprocal functions, to all scores in a data set. Researchers use data transformations because they change certain characteristics of distributions. Because a data transformation may normalize sample distributions and equalize variances between (among) sample distributions, it can help avoid violation of the statistical assumptions that are the basis of inferential statistical tests.
4. b
5. c
6. The expected frequency distribution is the anticipated distribution of frequencies based on the results of previous research or theoretical predictions. The observed frequency distribution is the distribution of frequencies you obtain when the research is conducted.
7. d
8. A chi-square test for independence is the chi-square procedure that is applied to data in contingency tables (i.e., when there are two variables that each have at least two levels). If the chi square is significant, then the distributions are dissimilar and the researcher can conclude that the nature of the pattern on one nominal variable depends on the specific category or level of the other nominal variable.

Check Your Progress page 456

1. If the IV you administered had a significant effect, then the ranks will not be distributed evenly between (among) the groups; smaller ranks will be associated with one group and larger ranks will be associated with another group(s).
2. b
3. a
4. c
5. d

Chapter 19

Check Your Progress page 473

1. The reactance or reactivity effect refers to the biasing or influencing of the participants' scores or responses because they know they are being observed. Archival research avoids the reactance effect because the researcher does not observe the participants and the data of interest are recorded before they are used in the research project.
2. d
3. 1-C; 2-A; 3-D; 4-E; 5-B
4. Situation sampling and time sampling are used to provide greater generality for the research project.
5. The extent to which two observers agree is called interobserver reliability. It is calculated by dividing the number of times the observers agree by the number of opportunities for agreement and multiplying by 100. These calculations result in the percent agreement.
6. b

Check Your Progress page 485

1. 1-C; 2-E; 3-F; 4-B; 5-A; 6-D
2. The steps involved in developing a good survey include (a) determining how the information you seek is to be obtained and what type of instrument will you use, (b) determining the nature of the questions that will be used, (c) writing the items for your survey, (d) pilot testing your survey or questionnaire, (e) considering what demographic data are desired, and (f) specifying the procedures that will be followed in administering the survey or questionnaire.
3. The low return rate of mail surveys can be increased by (a) including a letter that clearly summarizes the nature and importance with the initial mailing (a self-addressed, prepaid return envelope should be included with the initial mailing) and (b) sending additional mailings at two- to three-week intervals.
4. The use of personal interviews is declining because (a) the expense involved in conducting them has increased greatly, (b) the fact that an individual administers the surveys increases the possibility for bias, and (c) the appeal of going from door to door is decreasing because of unavailability of respondents and high crime rates in large metropolitan areas.
5. Achievement tests are used to assess an individual's level of mastery or competence. Aptitude tests are used to assess an individual's skills or abilities.

Chapter 20

Check Your Progress page 525

1. "APA format" refers to the accepted, standard form for preparing the results of psychological research that has been adopted by the American Psychological Association. APA format was developed in order to bring standardization and uniformity to the publication of research in the field of psychology.
2. 1-C; 2-E; 3-B; 4-D; 5-F; 6-A
3. The abstract is the most widely read section of most research reports because it is published in *Psychological Abstracts* and computerized indices such as PsycLIT.
4. The introduction is similar to a typical term paper because it summarizes a body of knowledge about a relatively narrow topic. It is different from a term paper because it provides a rationale and lead-in to a particular experiment.
5. c
6. The method section is designed to describe (a) the research participants, (b) the equipment or materials used in the research, and (c) the manner in which the experiment was conducted. Although all this information is important, the procedures are probably the

most important because they allow other researchers to replicate the study. If different participants or equipment (materials) are used, external validity would simply be increased.

7. inferential; descriptive
8. No, you could not use figures or tables as your sole information in a results section. Figures and tables are meant to supplement descriptive and inferential statistics, not to replace them.
9. 1-E; 2-B; 3-G; 4-H; 5-A; 6-D; 7-F; 8-C
10. Although this answer involves opinion, you can make a strong argument that the discussion section is the most important section because it summarizes the experiment's evidence, ties that evidence into previous findings, and draws an overall conclusion.
11. The reference for a chapter from an edited book is more complex than a journal article or book reference because such a reference must include information about both the chapter and the book.

Check Your Progress page 536

1. You should not write your research paper in the style of a famous writer because your primary goal is communication rather than entertainment.
2. Three strategies used to improve writing style are (a) write from an outline, (b) write a draft and put it away for some time before rereading it, and (c) have another person read and evaluate your writing. You will have to answer for yourself what you need to change about your writing in order to incorporate these suggestions.
3. c
4. a. Jones (1995) conducted an experiment.
   b. The participants sat in desks around the room.
   c. I (or "The experimenter") projected the stimulus items from the rear of the cubicle.
   d. I found a significant interaction. *or* The data showed a significant interaction.
5. a. The experimenter tested the animals that were older first. (It is important to distinguish the older participants from the younger.)
   b. The room, which was a classroom, was used for testing. (The notation that the room is a classroom is probably merely a side comment that is not vital in describing the room.)
6. a. Because you are the oldest, you should go first. "Since" was incorrect because a justification was implied rather than a time reference.
   b. "Since" I began that class I have learned much about statistics. Correct because since denotes something has happened after beginning the class.
   c. "While" we are watching TV, we can also study. Correct because while denoted that watching TV and studying will occur at the same time.
   d. Although you are older than me, I should still go first. "While" was incorrect because a contrast was implied rather than a time reference.
7. Orientals—Asians
elderly—elderly people (or use specific age range)
mankind—humankind or humans
girls and men—women and men
mothering—parenting
chairman—chair
homosexuals—lesbian, gay
depressives—depressed patients
8. $a + b = c$
trial-by-trial
-1
Enter: Your name

appendix C

Answers to Exercises

Chapter 4

1. Frequency distribution

Score	Tally	Frequency	Percentage
1	III	3	7.50
2	II	2	5.00
3	II	2	5.00
4	NJ I	6	15.00
5	NJ	5	12.50
6	NJ	5	12.50
7	NJ II	7	17.50
8	NJ	5	12.50
9	III	3	7.50
10	II	2	5.00

2. Grouped frequency distribution

Altruism Score Interval	Frequency	Percentage
1–2	5	12.50
3–4	8	20.00
5–6	10	25.00
7–8	12	30.00
9–10	5	12.50

3. Pie chart

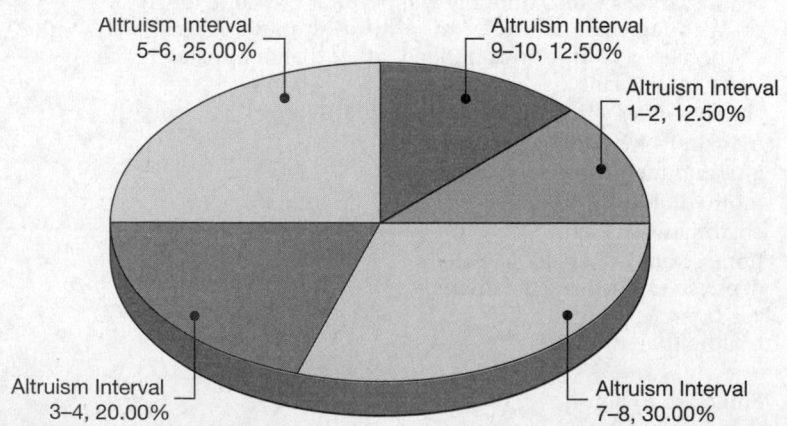

Altruism Interval 5–6, 25.00%
Altruism Interval 9–10, 12.50%
Altruism Interval 1–2, 12.50%
Altruism Interval 3–4, 20.00%
Altruism Interval 7–8, 30.00%

4. Histogram

5. Frequency polygon

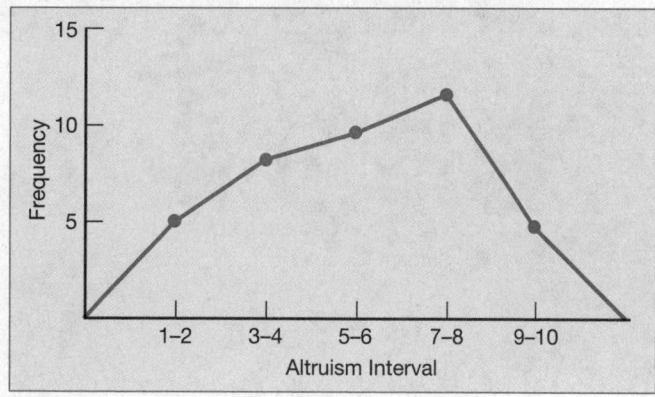

6. Mode—actually there are two modes: 12 and 27
Median = 19
Mean = 388/15 = 25.866
Because a few high scores have inflated the mean, the median would be the most representative measure of central tendency.

7. a. Distribution where the mean is greater than the mode
1, 1, 1, 4, 7, 8   Mode = 1   Mean = 3.666
b. Distribution where the median and the mean are equal
3, 4, 5, 6, 7,   Median = 5   Mean = 5
c. Distribution where the median is greater than the mode
3, 4, 4, 5, 6, 7, 8   Median = 5   Mode = 4

8. The mean number of false memories was .25.

9. Frequency distribution

Complaint	Tally	Frequency	Percentage
ED	ℕ III	8	24.2424
AD	ℕ IIII	9	27.2727
DE	ℕ III	8	24.2424
SD	ℕ III	8	24.2424
		N = 33	

10. Bar graph

11. Line graph

12.

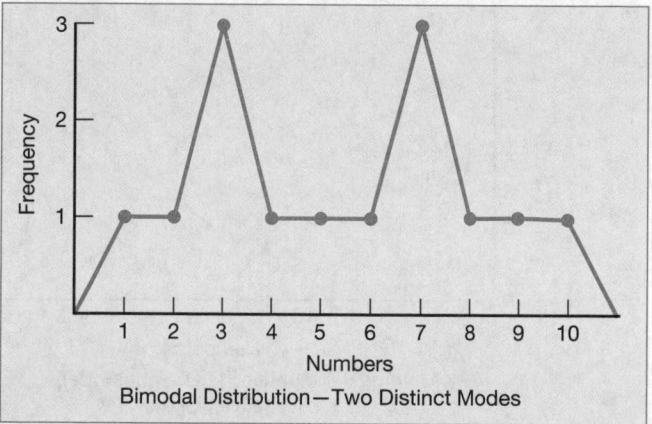

Bimodal Distribution—Two Distinct Modes

13.

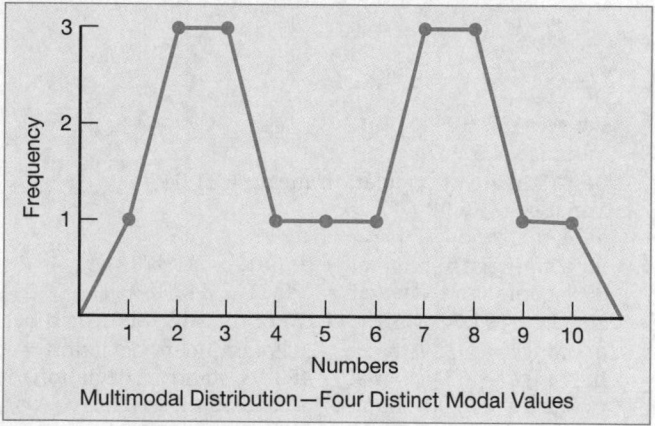

Multimodal Distribution—Four Distinct Modal Values

14. 51 appears at the 50th percentile

15.

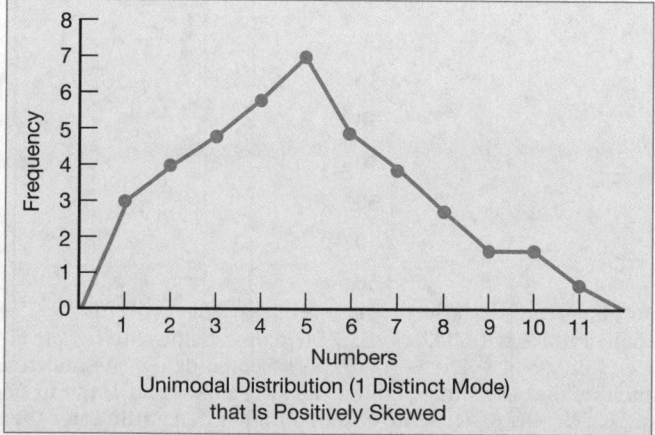

Unimodal Distribution (1 Distinct Mode)
that Is Positively Skewed

16.

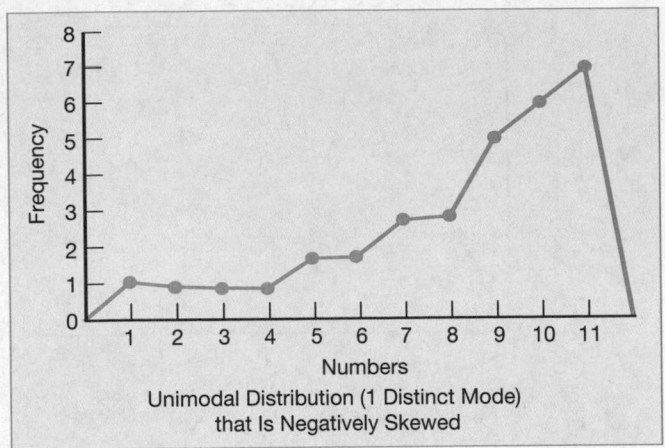

Unimodal Distribution (1 Distinct Mode)
that Is Negatively Skewed

Chapter 6

1. Range $= 82 - 8 = 74$
2. Variance $= 329.78$
3. Best estimate of population mean $= 21.04$
   Variance $= 26.92$
   SEM $= 5.2953$
4. 95% confidence interval $= 10.6613 - 31.4187$
   99% confidence interval $= 7.4311 - 34.6489$
5. $z = 2.00$ 97.72% (50 + 47.72) of the students scored below this score
6. a. range $= .67$, variance $= .0494$, standard deviation $= .2222$
   b. range $= .67$, variance $= 493.55$, standard deviation $= 22.216$
   c. range $= 670$, variance $= 49355.55$, $SD = 222.16$
7. a. $z = .70$ b. $z = -.80$ c. $z = 1.80$ d. $z = 2.10$

8.

Score	Deviation score
1	-3.50
2	-2.50
3	-1.50
4	$-.50$
5	$.50$
6	1.50
7	2.50
8	3.50

   Sum of squared deviation score $= 42$ Variance $= 42/8 = 5.25$ $SD = 2.2913$
9. Female child $z = 1.6842$ 95.35% scored below the female child
   Male child $z = 1.4625$ 92.79% scored below the male child
   Conclude that the female child is making a better adjustment because she had a higher
   z score. Therefore, her score was in a higher percentile than the male child's score.

10.

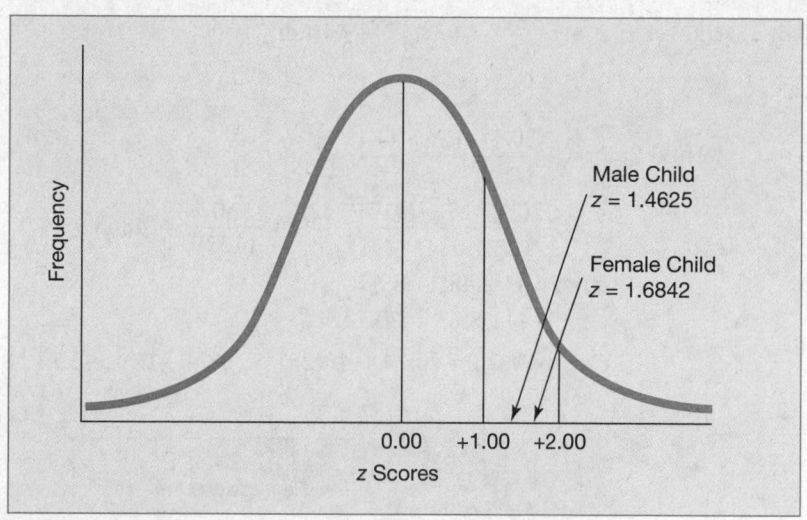

11. Median = 2.8   Mean = 2.78   Variance = .826   *SD* = .9088
12. Person 1 = 60   Person 2 = 57.50   Person 3 = 65   Person 4 = 56.30
Person 5 = 40.70
13. a.   SEM = 7.50   b.   SEM = 5.00   c.   SEM = 3.75
14. Set 1—95% confidence interval −17.0644–53.0644
        99% confidence interval −27.9773–63.9773
Set 2—95% confidence interval −89–303
        99% confidence interval −150 − 364
Set 3—95% confidence interval−41.1628–125.1628
        99% confidence interval −67.0457–151.0457
15. a.   40.2648   b.   126.6966   c.   5.6534   d.   85.7569

Chapter 8

1. $r = .933$ $p < .01$
predictor variable = hours studied
criterion variable = grade
2. $r^2 = .870$ 87% of the variance is accounted for by this correlation
3.

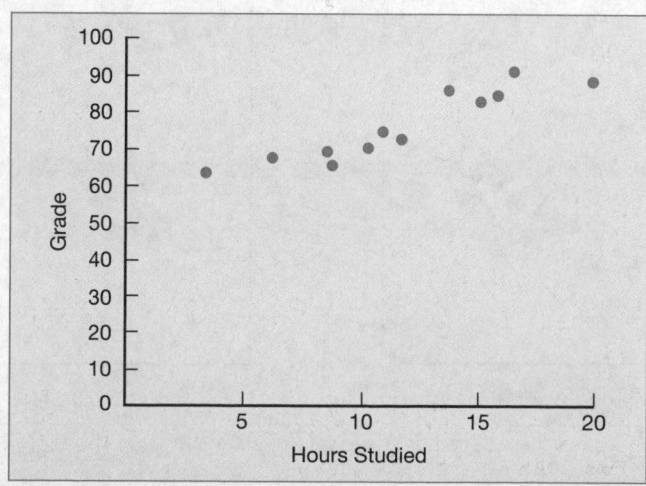

4.   Method 1: $b = r\dfrac{SD_y}{SD_x} = .933\dfrac{4.5976}{8.9438} = .48$

Method 2: $b = \dfrac{N\Sigma XY - (\Sigma X)(\Sigma Y)}{N\Sigma X^2 - (\Sigma X)^2}$

$= \dfrac{12(11,318) - (917)(142)}{12(71,034) - (917)^2} = \dfrac{5602}{11519} = .4863$

$a = 76.41 - .48(11.83)$

$= 76.41 - 5.67 = 70.74$

$\hat{Y} = a + b(X) = 70.74 + .48(25) = 70.74 + 12 = 82.74$

5.

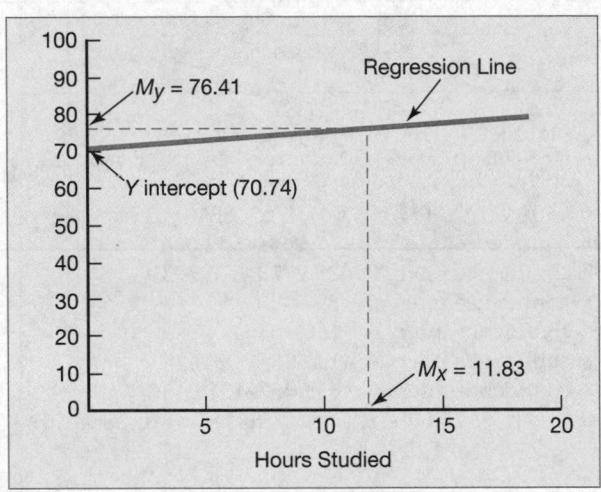

6.

A. Perfect Positive Correlation

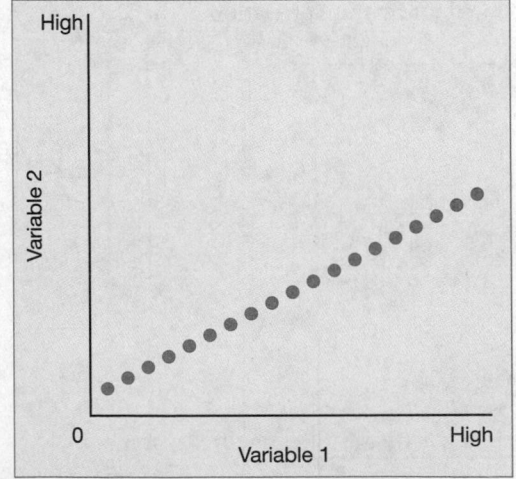

B. Positive, but not Perfect, Correlation

C. Near Zero Correlation

D. Perfect Negative Correlation

E. Negative, but not Perfect, Correlation

7. $r = -.467$ a negative, but not perfect, correlation $p = .35$ not significant
8. $r = .165$ a weak, positive correlation $p = .724$ not significant
9. Exercise 7: $r^2 = .2180$ 21.80% of the variance accounted for by this correlation
Exercise 8: $r^2 = .0272$ 2.72% of the variance accounted for by this correlation

10. Participant 7's predicted score on Measure 2 = 14.8348

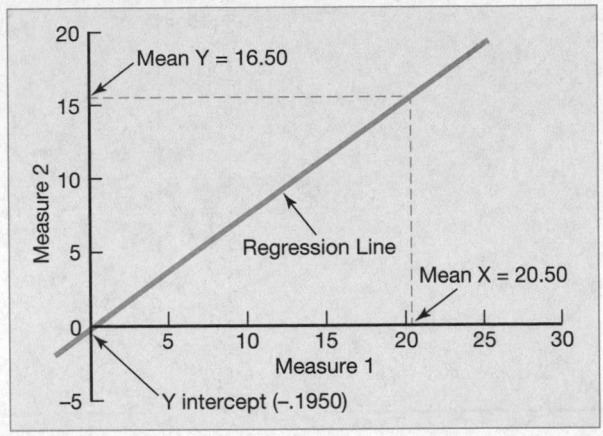

11. Set 1: $r = .906$, $p = .002$ (significant at .01 level)
Set 2: $r = -.809$, $p = .015$ (not significant at .01 level)
Set 3: $r = -.234$, $p = .577$ (not significant at .01 level)

12. Set 1: $r^2 = .8208$ 82.08% of the variance accounted for by this correlation
Set 2: $r^2 = .6544$ 65.44% of the variance accounted for by this correlation
Set 3: $r^2 = .0547$ 5.47% of the variance accounted for by this correlation
Set 1 shows the strongest effect because a greater percentage of the variance is accounted for by this correlation.

13. Set 1: Participant 9's predicted Test 2 score = 79.63
Set 2: Participant 9's predicted Test 2 score = 74.3892
Set 3: Participant 9's predicted Test 2 score = 59.9135

14. Set 1: Participant 9's predicted Test 1 score = 82.79
Set 2: Participant 9's predicted Test 1 score = 74.05
Set 3: Participant 9's predicted Test 1 score = 74.09

15. Worker 1: Predicted job satisfaction score = 48.16
Worker 2: Predicted job satisfaction score = 24.85
Worker 3: Predicted job satisfaction score = 52.57
Worker 4: Predicted job satisfaction score = 44.38
Worker 5: Predicted job satisfaction score = 36.19

Chapter 9

1. probability of rolling a 1 = 1/6 or 16.67% or .1667
The probability of rolling a 1 is *not* different than the probability of rolling any other single number from 2 to 6.

2. H_0: $\mu = 100$
H_1: $\mu \neq 100$ (two-tailed)
H_1: $\mu > 100$ (one-tailed)

3. The probability of a z score of 2.68 is .0037.
Yes, you should conclude that the children are above average because the probability of the z score is so low.

4. The probability of a z score of 1.04 is .1492.
It seems unlikely that the children are above average because the probability of the z score is relatively high (.1492).

5. The probability of a z score of 1.38 is .0838.
   The children could be above average—we are uncertain because the probability of the z score is somewhat low (.0838), but not as low as we would like to draw a conclusion (.05).

6. $df = N - 1 = 20 - 1 = 19$
   Critical value of t for a one-tailed test with 19 df = 1.729

7. $df = N - 1 = 10 - 1 = 9$
   Critical value of t for a one-tailed test with 9 df = 1.833
   The critical t value is different than for #6 because of fewer df. Thus, the critical t must increase.

8. $t(9) = 2.11$, $.10 < p < .05$, marginally significant
   It is not clear whether the course achieved its goal—the score of 1038 is marginally higher than 1000.

9. If you used a one-tailed test for Problem 8, $t(9) = 2.11$, $p < .05$, so it would be significant.
   The potential problem created by using a one-tailed test is that you would have been unable to detect whether the course actually had a detrimental effect and lowered GRE scores.

10. $t(19) = 2.98$, $p < .01$
    This difference is significant; yes, the course improved the scores.

11. $t(99) = 1.40$, $p < .20$
    This difference is not significant; no, the course had no effect.

12. $M = 41.53$; $t(14) = .15$, $p > .20$
    There is no difference between means; the seniors are no different from previous students.

13. $M = 43.2$; $t(14) = 1.94$, $p < .10$
    This year's seniors scored marginally higher than previous students.

14. $M = 38.2$; $t(14) = 4.29$, $p < .001$
    This year's seniors scored significantly lower than previous students

15. You would be most likely to make a Type I error for #13, if you concluded that the difference was significant—because the probability of the result occurring by chance is fairly high (>.05).

Chapter 11

1. It is possible to use age as an IV and test the data with a t test, but she can have only two groups. She would have to decide whether she wanted to test participants of two specific ages, or young versus old, or some other comparison involving only two groups.

2. You should use the t test for correlated samples because you measured attitudes of the groups before and after the movie, which indicates repeated measures.

3. You should use the t test for independent samples because you have compared differences between men and women, which are independent groups (no mention of matching).

4. You should use the t test for correlated samples because you chose 2 dogs from each litter, which indicates natural pairs.

5. You should use the t test for correlated samples because you matched students on their GPAs (matched pairs).

6. Independent t test because of random assignment
   M(help) = 8.4, M(no help) = 7.4
   $t = 2.30$ $df = 18$ $p = .033$ (two-tailed)
   Parental help on homework resulted in higher quiz scores.

7. Independent *t* test because of random assignment
   M(help) = 8.4, *M*(no help) = 8.1
   t = .57   *df* = 18   *p* = .58 (two-tailed)
   Parental help on homework made no difference in quiz scores.
8. Independent *t* test because of random assignment
   M(help) = 8.4, *M*(no help) = 7.5
   t = 1.87   *df* = 18   *p* = .078 (two-tailed)
   Parental help on homework resulted in marginally higher quiz scores.
9. Correlated *t* test because of repeated measures (quiz over both units)
   M(help) = 8.4, *M*(no help) = 7.6
   t = 2.75   *df* = 9   *p* = .022 (two-tailed)
   Parental help on homework resulted in higher quiz scores.
10. Correlated *t* test because of repeated measures (quiz over both units)
    M(help) = 8.4, *M*(no help) = 7.9
    t = 1.86   *df* = 9   *p* = .096 (two-tailed)
    Parental help on homework resulted in marginally higher quiz scores
11. Correlated *t* test because of repeated measures (quiz over both units)
    M(help) = 8.4, *M*(no help) = 7.9
    t = 1.63   *df* = 9   *p* = .138 (two-tailed)
    Parental help on homework did not affect quiz scores.
12. #6: $t(18)$ = 2.30, *p* = .033, parental help on homework resulted in higher quiz scores
    #7: $t(18)$ = .57, *p* = .58, parental help on homework had no effect on quiz scores
    #8: $t(18)$ = 1.87, *p* = .078, parental help on homework resulted in marginally higher quiz scores
13. #9: $t(9)$ = 2.75, *p* = .022, parental help on homework resulted in higher quiz scores
    #10: $t(9)$ = 1.86, *p* = .096, parental help on homework marginally higher quiz scores
    #11: $t(9)$ = 1.63, *p* = .138, parental help on homework had no effect on quiz scores
14. Group 1 scored significantly higher than Group 2 (*p* = .002)
15. There was no difference in the scores of Group 1 and Group 2 (*p* = .19).
    or
    The difference in the scores of Group 1 and Group 2 was likely due to chance (*p* = .19).

Chapter 13

1. It is possible to use age as an IV and test the data with a one-way ANOVA; she must have at least three groups. For example, she could test participants of three or four specific ages, or young versus middle age versus old, or some other comparison involving three (or more) groups.
2. No, your friend cannot use age and sex as IVs and test the data with a one-way ANOVA. One-way ANOVAs test the data from only 1 IV. Your friend must simplify the design or wait until Chapter 15 to use this design.
3. You should use a one-way ANOVA for correlated groups because you used repeated measures (students gave ratings before and after a course).
4. You should use a one-way ANOVA for independent groups because you used three different groups (marital status) with no mention of matching.
5. You should use a one-way ANOVA for correlated groups because you used natural groups (3 dogs from each litter).
6. You should use a one-way ANOVA for correlated groups because you matched students on GPA (matched groups).

7. One-way ANOVA for independent groups because of random assignment
   Means: Group 1 = 6.6   Group 2 = 6.7   Group 2 = 6.8
   $F = .04$ $df = 2 \& 27$ $p = .96$
   There was no significant difference among study techniques.
8. One-way ANOVA for independent groups because of random assignment
   Means: Group 1 = 6.2   Group 2 = 6.3   Group 2 = 7.3
   $F = 2.79$ $df = 2 \& 27$ $p = .079$
   Marginal difference among study techniques; Group 3 may have performed better than Groups 1 and 2.
9. One-way ANOVA for independent groups because of random assignment
   Means: Group 1 = 6.2   Group 2 = 6.3   Group 2 = 7.6
   $F = 4.32$ $df = 2 \& 27$ $p = .024$
   There was a significant difference among study techniques; Group 3 performed better than Groups 1 and 2.
10. One-way ANOVA for correlated groups because of matching
    Means: Group 1 = 6.6   Group 2 = 6.7   Group 2 = 6.8
    $F = .06$ $df = 2 \& 18$ $p = .94$
    There was no significant difference among study techniques
11. One-way ANOVA for correlated groups because of matching
    Means: Group 1 = 6.2   Group 2 = 6.3   Group 2 = 7.3
    $F = 4.18$ $df = 2 \& 18$ $p = .032$
    There was a significant difference among study techniques; Group 3 performed better than Groups 1 and 2.
12. One-way ANOVA for correlated groups because of matching
    Means: Group 1 = 6.2   Group 2 = 6.3   Group 2 = 7.1
    $F = 3.03$ $df = 2 \& 18$ $p = .074$
    There was a marginal difference among study techniques; Group 3 may have performed better than Groups 1 and 2.
13. #7: $F(2, 27) = .04$, $p = .96$, no significant difference among study techniques
    #8: $F(2, 27) = 2.79$, $p = .079$, marginal difference among study techniques
    #9: $F(2, 27) = 4.32$, $p = .024$, a significant difference among study techniques
14. #10: $F(2, 18) = .06$, $p = .94$, no significant difference among study techniques
    #11: $F(2, 18) = 4.18$, $p = .032$, a significant difference among study techniques
    #12: $F(2, 18) = 3.03$, $p = .074$, a marginal difference among study techniques
15. There is a significant difference among the means for the three groups ($p = .009$). Because the means for Groups 1 and 2 are virtually identical, Group 3's mean is higher than the other two.

Chapter 15

1. Yes, your friend could use a factorial ANOVA to analyze data from an experiment using age and sex as IVs—factorial ANOVA is used for research designs with more than 1 IV. She could use independent groups for both IVs or matched groups for either or both IVs.
2. You should use a factorial ANOVA for independent groups for this experiment because you have two IVs (3 marital statuses and 2 genders); there is no indication of matching or repeated measures for either IV.
3. You should use a factorial ANOVA for correlated groups for this experiment because you have two IVs (type of cues and trials), both of which are correlated in nature. You have formed natural groups for the cues variable because you chose 3 dogs from each litter. The trials variable is repeated measures (3 trials in each maze).

4. You should use a factorial ANOVA for mixed groups for this experiment because you have two IVs (classification and rating time), with one (classification) being independent groups and the other (rating time) being correlated groups. Classification is independent because there are different students in each classification and there is no mention of natural groups or matching. Rating time is correlated because each student rates the course before and after.

5. Factorial ANOVA for independent groups because of random assignment to quiz formats and gender.

MEANS:

	Fill-in-the-blank	Multiple choice	
Men	17.17	21.00	19.08
Women	16.67	21.67	19.67
	17.42	21.33	

SOURCE TABLE:

Source of variation	SS	df	MS	F	p
Sex	2.04	1	2.04	0.66	0.42
Quiz format	92.04	1	92.04	29.93	0.000024
Interaction	0.04	1	0.04	0.014	0.91
Error	61.5	20	3.08		
Total	155.62	23			

Students performed better on multiple-choice quizzes than fill-in-the-blank ($p < .001$). No gender difference ($p = .42$), no interaction ($p = .91$)

6. Factorial ANOVA for independent groups because of random assignment to quiz formats and gender.

MEANS:

	Fill-in-the-blank	Multiple choice	
Men	17.50	21.00	19.25
Women	21.50	16.67	19.58
	19.50	19.33	

SOURCE TABLE:

Source of variation	SS	df	MS	F	p
Sex	0.67	1	0.67	0.23	0.64
Quiz format	0.17	1	0.17	0.06	0.81
Interaction	80.67	1	80.67	27.66	0.000038
Error	58.33	20	2.92		
Total	139.84	23			

No difference due to quiz format ($p = .81$) or gender ($p = .81$). Significant interaction ($p < .001$) shows that men performed better on multiple-choice quizzes whereas women performed better on fill-in-the-blank quizzes.

7. Factorial ANOVA for correlated groups because gender groups are matched and quiz format uses repeated measures.

MEANS:

	Fill-in-the-blank	Multiple choice	
Men	17.00	17.83	17.42
Women	21.50	21.17	21.34
	19.25	19.50	

SOURCE TABLE:

Source of variation	SS	df	MS	F	p
Sex	92.04	1	92.04	35.13	.00004
Quiz format	.38	1	.38	.15	.70
Interaction	2.05	1	2.05	.91	.36
(Participants)	21.86	5			
Error	39.30	15	2.62		
Total	155.63	23			

Women performed better on quizzes than men ($p < .001$). No quiz format difference ($p = .70$), no interaction ($p = .36$)

8. Factorial ANOVA for correlated groups because gender groups are matched and quiz format uses repeated measures

MEANS:

	Fill-in-the-blank	Multiple choice	
Men	17.00	21.50	19.25
Women	17.83	21.17	19.50
	17.42	21.34	

SOURCE TABLE:

Source of variation	SS	df	MS	F	p
Sex	.38	1	.38	.15	.70
Quiz format	92.04	1	92.04	35.13	.00004
Interaction	2.05	1	2.05	.91	.36
(Participants)	21.86	5			
Error	39.30	15	2.62		
Total	155.63	23			

Students performed better on multiple-choice quizzes than fill-in-the-blank ($p < .001$). No gender difference ($p = .70$), no interaction ($p = .36$)

9. Factorial ANOVA for mixed groups (repeated measures on quizzes)

MEANS:

	Fill-in-the-blank	Multiple choice	
Men	17.00	21.50	19.25
Women	21.17	22.17	21.67
	19.09	21.84	

SOURCE TABLE:

Source of variation	SS	df	MS	F	p
Sex	12.04	1	12.04	2.91	.12
Error (between)	41.42	10	4.14		
Quiz format	18.38	1	18.38	13.36	.004
Interaction	45.38	1	45.38	33.00	.0002
Error (within)	13.75	10	1.38		
Total	130.97	23			

No gender difference ($p = .12$). Students performed better on multiple-choice quizzes ($p = .004$). This main effect is superceded by a significant interaction ($p < .001$; men performed better on multiple-choice quizzes compared to fill-in-the-blank; women performed equally on both quiz formats).

10. Factorial ANOVA for mixed groups (repeated measures on quizzes)

MEANS:

	Fill-in-the-blank	Multiple choice	
Men	17.00	16.83	16.92
Women	17.33	17.67	17.50
	17.17	17.25	

SOURCE TABLE:

Source of variation	SS	df	MS	F	p
Sex	2.04	1	2.04	.29	.61
Error (between)	71.42	10	7.14		
Quiz format	.04	1	.04	.03	.87
Interaction	.38	1	.38	.27	.62
Error (within)	14.08	10	1.41		
Total	87.96	23			

No quiz format difference ($p = .87$), no gender difference ($p = .61$), no interaction ($p = .62$)

11. #5: There was no effect on quiz scores due to gender, $F(1, 20) = .66$, $p = .42$. Students performed better on multiple-choice quizzes ($M = 21.33$) than fill-in-the-blank quizzes ($M = 17.42$), $F(1, 20) = 29.93$, $p < .001$. The interaction of gender and quiz format was not significant, $F(1, 20) = .01$, $p = .91$.

#6: There was no effect on quiz scores due to gender, $F(1, 20) = .23$, $p = .64$, nor due to quiz format, $F(1, 20) = .06$, $p = .81$. The interaction of gender and quiz format was significant, $F(1, 20) = 27.66$, $p < .001$. Men performed better on multiple-choice quizzes ($M = 21.00$) than fill-in-the-blank quizzes ($M = 17.50$), whereas women performed better on fill-in-the-blank quizzes ($M = 21.50$) than multiple-choice quizzes ($M = 16.67$).

12. #7: The effect of gender on quiz scores was significant, $F(1, 15) = 35.13$, $p < .001$, with women ($M = 21.34$) scoring higher than men ($M = 17.42$). There was no effect of quiz format, $F(1, 15) = .15$, $p = .70$. The interaction of gender and quiz format was not significant, $F(1, 15) = .91$, $p = .36$.

#8: There was no effect on quiz scores due to gender, $F(1, 15) = .15$, $p = .70$. Students performed better on multiple-choice quizzes ($M = 21.34$) than fill-in-the-blank quizzes ($M = 17.42$), $F(1, 15) = 35.13$, $p < .001$. The interaction of gender and quiz format was not significant, $F(1, 15) = .91$, $p = .36$.

13. #9: There was no effect on quiz scores due to gender, $F(1, 10) = 2.91$, $p = .12$. Students performed better on multiple-choice quizzes ($M = 21.84$) than fill-in-the-blank quizzes ($M = 19.09$), $F(1, 10) = 13.36$, $p = .004$. The interaction of gender and quiz format was significant, $F(1, 10) = 33.00$, $p < .001$. Men performed better on multiple-choice quizzes ($M = 21.50$) than fill-in-the-blank quizzes ($M = 17.00$), whereas women performed about the same on fill-in-the-blank quizzes ($M = 21.17$) and multiple-choice quizzes ($M = 22.17$).

#10: There was no effect on quiz scores due to gender, $F(1, 10) = .29$, $p = .61$, nor due to quiz format, $F(1, 10) = .03$, $p = .87$. Also, the interaction of gender and quiz format was not significant, $F(1, 10) = .27$, $p = .62$.

14. There would be no difference between men and women, as both means would be 70. The effect of time spent studying would probably be significant, as the low-time group had a mean score of 64.5 and the high-time group had a mean of 75.5. The interaction would probably be significant—women benefited from the extra study time, but men did not.

15. Factor A had a significant effect ($p = .001$). The two groups within Factor A would have significantly different means (there would be two groups within A because there is only 1 df for that factor). Factor B ($p = .25$) and the interaction of A and B ($p = .56$) were not significant.

Chapter 18

1. $\chi^2(2) = 3.852$ $p < .05$
Stock green zingers because the observed distribution was significantly different from the expected distribution. More children preferred green zingers.
2. $\chi^2(4) = 3.10$ $p > .10$ Not significant, no further tests necessary
3. $\chi^2(3) = 2.806$ $p > .10$ Not significant.
4. $U_1 = 8.5$ $p < .01$ (Two-tailed test)
5. Rank Sums $z = -5.61$ $p < .01$ The two groups differ significantly.
6. T negative ranks = 15 $N = 8$ Not significant.
7. H = 7.1078 $df = 2$ $p < .05$
Subsequent Mann-Whitney U tests indicate that a marginally significant difference (smallest U = 7) exists between the Moderate- and Bright-Illumination groups. The other pair-wise comparisons are not significant.
8. $\chi^2(5) = 9.57$ $p > .05$ Not significant.
9. a. $\chi^2(1) = 1.3844$ $p > .05$ Not significant.
   b. $\chi^2(2) = 1.8568$ $p > .05$ Not significant.
10. T = 6.50 $N = 9$ Not significant.
The new method did not improve significantly the scores on the written portion of the driver's license exam.
11. $U_2 = 12$ $n_1 = n_2 = 10$ $p < .01$
12. Rank sums $z = 5.27$ $p < .01$ The groups differ significantly.
13. H = 3.2474 $df = 2$ Not significant.
14. $\chi^2(1) = 12.8591$ $p < .01$
Significantly different proportions of men and women stopped/did not stop at the stop sign. A higher percentage of men did not stop completely.
15. H = 5.2726 $df = 3$ $p > .05$ Not significant.

glossary

A Refers to the baseline measurement in a single-case design.

A-B design A single-case design in which you measure the baseline behavior, institute a treatment, and use a posttest.

A-B-A design A single-case design consisting of a baseline treatment, a posttest, and a return to the baseline condition. May not be recommended if the participant is left without a beneficial or necessary treatment in the second baseline.

A-B-A-B design A single-case design consisting of a baseline, treatment, posttest, return to baseline, repeated treatment, and second posttest. This design gives the best chance of isolating causation.

Abscissa The horizontal or X axis of a graph.

Abstract A brief description of the research that is presented in an APA format paper.

Achievement test Designed to evaluate an individual's level of mastery or competence.

Alternative (or experimental) hypothesis A hypothesis that says that all differences between groups are not due to chance (i.e., the effect of the IV).

Analytic statement Statements that are always true.

Analytic survey Seeks to determine the relevant variables and how they are related.

APA format Accepted APA form for preparing reports of psychological research. Also known as APA style.

Apparatus subsection The second subsection of the method section. When appropriate, contains information about the equipment used in the experiment.

Aptitude test Designed to assess an individual's potential ability or skill in a particular job.

Asymptotic Refers to tails of distributions that approach the baseline but never touch the baseline.

Author note A note at the end of an experimental report that contains information about the author or paper for the reader's use.

B Refers to the outcome (treatment) measurement in a single-case design.

Balancing A control procedure that achieves group equality by distributing extraneous variables equally to all groups.

Bar graph A graph in which the frequency for each category of a qualitative variable is represented as a vertical column or bar. The columns of a bar graph do not touch.

Baseline A measurement of a behavior that is made under normal conditions (i.e., no IV is present); a control condition.

Between-groups variability Variability in DV scores that is due to the effects of the IV.

Between-subjects comparison Refers to a contrast between groups of participants who were randomly assigned to groups.

Biomodal distribution A frequency distribution that has two high points or prominent categories.

Carryover effect The effects of one treatment persist or carry over and influence responses to the next treatment.

Case study Intensively observing and recording the behavior of a single participant.

Case-study approach An observational technique in which we compile a record of observations about a single participant.

Cause-and-effect relation Occurs when we know that a particular IV (cause) leads to specific changes in a DV (effect).

Chi-square test A procedure that compares the fit or mismatch (similarity or dissimilarity) between two or more distributions.

Chi-square test for independence Chi-square tests for contingency tables.

Citation A notation in text that a particular reference was used. The citation provides the name(s) of the author(s) and the date of the work's publication.

Clinical perspective A descriptive research approach aimed at understanding and correcting a particular behavioral problem.

Coefficient of determination The squared Pearson product moment correlation coefficient (r^2). When multiplied by 100, the coefficient of determination indicates the percentage of variance accounted for.

Cohort A group of individuals born during the same time period.

Comparative psychology The study of behavior in different species, including humans.

Complete counterbalancing All possible treatment sequences are presented.

Concurrent validity Degree to which the score on a test or inventory corresponds with another measure of the designated trait.

Confidence interval An interval that has a specific percentage associated with it.

Confounded experiment An experiment in which an extraneous variable varies systematically with the IV; makes drawing a cause-and-effect relationship impossible.

Confounding A situation in which the results of an experiment can be attributed to either the operation of an IV or an extraneous variable; caused by an uncontrolled variable that varies systematically with the IV.

Constancy A control technique by which an extraneous variable is reduced to a single value that is experienced by all participants.

Content validity The extent to which test items actually represent the type of material they are supposed to.

Contingency table A table that shows the distribution of frequencies and totals for two nominal variables.

Contradictory statement Statements that are always false.

Control Two meanings: directly manipulating (1) a factor of interest in a research study to determine its effects or (2) other, unwanted variables that could influence the results of a research project.

Control group In a two-group design, the group of participants that does not receive the IV.

Control procedure One of several steps experimenters take to ensure that potential extraneous variables are controlled. Examples include random assignment, matching, and so on.

Convenience sampling A researcher's sampling of participants based on ease of locating the participants; often does not involve true random selection.

Correlated assignment A method of assigning research participants to groups so that there is a relationship between small numbers of participants; these small groups are then randomly assigned to treatment conditions (also known as *paired* or *matched assignment*).

Correlated groups Groups of research participants that are related some way—through matching, repeated measures, or natural sets.

Correlation The extent or degree to which two variables are related.

Correlation coefficient A single number that represents the degree of relation (i.e., "co-relation") between two variables.

Correlational study Determination of the relation between two variables.

Counterbalancing A procedure for controlling order effects by presenting different treatment sequences.

Criterion validity Is established by comparing the score on a test or inventory with a future score on another test or inventory.

Criterion variable The variable that is being predicted.

Critical region The region in a distribution that signifies research significance; usually the extreme .05 of a distribution.

Cross-cultural psychology A branch of psychology whose goal is to determine the universality of research results.

Cross-sectional research Comparison of two or more groups during the same, rather limited, time period.

Cultural response set Tendency of a particular culture to respond in a certain matter.

Culture Lasting values, attitudes, and behaviors that are shared by a group and transmitted to subsequent generations.

Data transformation The application of an accepted mathematical procedure to all scores in a data set.

Debriefing session The nature and purpose of an experiment are explained at its conclusion.

Deductive logic Reasoning that proceeds from general theories to specific cases.

Degrees of freedom (*df*) The ability of a number in a specified set to assume any value.

Demand characteristics Features of the experiment that inadvertently lead participants to respond in a particular manner.

Demographic data Information about participants' characteristics such as age, sex, income, and academic major.

Dependent variable (DV) A response or behavior that is measured. It is desired that changes in the DV are directly related to manipulation of the IV.

Descriptive research methods Research methods that do not involve the manipulation of an IV.

Descriptive statistics Procedures used to summarize a set of data.

Descriptive study Seeks to determine the percentage of the population that has a certain characteristic, holds a particular opinion, or engages in a particular behavior.

Deviation scores The difference between any single score and the mean of the distribution $(X - M)$.

Differential carryover The response to one treatment depends on which treatment was administered previously.

Diffusion or imitation of treatment A threat to internal validity that can occur if participants in one treatment group become familiar with the treatment of another group and copy that treatment.

Directional research hypothesis Prediction of the specific outcome of an experiment.

Discussion section The fourth major section of the APA format paper. Contains a summary of the experiment's results, a comparison of those results to previous research, and the conclusion(s) from the experiment.

Distribution of means A distribution in which the separate scores are sample means.

Double-blind experiment An experiment in which both the experimenter and the participants are unaware of which treatment the participants are receiving.

Effect size The size or magnitude of the effect caused by an IV or the size or magnitude of a correlation; the magnitude or size of the experimental treatment (or interaction).

Elimination A control technique whereby extraneous variables are completely removed from an experiment.

Emic A culture-specific finding.

Empirical Objectively quantifiable observations.

Environmental generalization Applying the results from an experiment to a situation or environment that differs from that of the original experiment.

Error sum of squares Variability in DV scores that is due to factors other than IVs and interactions; can include individual differences, measurement error, and extraneous variation.

Error variability Variability in DV scores due to factors other than the IV, such as individual differences, measurement error, and extraneous variation (also known as *within-groups variability*).

Ethnocentric Other cultures are viewed as an extension of one's own culture.

Ethnography A descriptive research approach that involves becoming a part of the culture you study.

Etic A finding that is the same in different cultures.

Ex post facto research A research approach in which the experimenter cannot directly manipulate the IV but can only classify, categorize, or measure the IV because it is predetermined in the participants (e.g., IV = sex).

Ex post facto study The variable(s) to be studied are selected after they have occurred.

Expected frequency distribution The anticipated distribution of frequencies into categories.

Experience IV Manipulation of the amount of training or learning.

Experiment An attempt to determine the cause-and-effect relations that exist in nature. Involves the manipulation of an independent variable (IV), recording of changes in a dependent variable (DV), and control of extraneous variables.

Experimental analysis of behavior A research approach popularized by B. F. Skinner, in which a single participant is studied.

Experimental design The general plan for selecting participants, assigning participants to experimental conditions, controlling extraneous variables, and gathering data.

Experimental group In a two-group design, the group of participants that receives the IV.

Experimental mortality A threat to internal validity that can occur if experimental participants from different groups drop out of the experiment at different rates.

External validity A type of evaluation of your experiment; do your experimental results apply to populations and situations that are different from those of your experiment?

Extraneous variable Undesired variables that may operate to influence the DV and, thus, invalidate an experiment; uncontrolled variables that can cause unintended changes between groups.

F ratio The ratio calculated by dividing treatment or interaction mean squares by error mean square.

Fabrication of data Those instances where the experimenter either deliberately alters or creates research data.

Factorial ANOVA Analysis used to analyze data from designs that have two or more IVs.

Factorial design An experimental design that has more than one IV.

Factors Synonymous with IVs.

Figure A pictorial representation of a set of results.

F_{max} Test A test for the equality of variances in which the largest variance is divided by the smallest variance.

Frequency distribution A table showing how often each score occurred.

Frequency polygon A graph that is constructed by placing a dot in the center of each bar of a histogram and then connecting the dots.

General implication form Statement of the research hypothesis in an "if . . . then" form.

Generalization Applying the results from an experiment to a different situation or population.

Good participant effect The tendency of participants to behave as they perceive the experimenter wants them to behave.

Grouped frequency distribution A table showing how often scores occurred in larger (combined) categories or intervals.

Hawthorne effect Another name for reactance or reactivity effect.

Headings Titles for various sections of a psychology paper designed to help the reader understand the outline and importance of parts of the paper.

Heterogeneity of variance Occurs when we do not have homogeneity of variance; this means that our two (or more) groups' variances are not equivalent.

Histogram A graph in which the frequency for each category of a quantitative variable is represented as a vertical column that touches the adjacent column.

History A threat to internal validity; refers to events that occur between the DV measurements in a repeated measures design.

Homogeneity of variance An assumption of parametric tests of significance that the variances of the populations are equivalent; the assumption that the variances are equal for two (or more) groups you plan to compare statistically.

Hypothesis An attempt to organize certain data and specific IV–DV relation within a specific portion of a larger, more comprehensive theory.

Incomplete counterbalancing Only a portion of all possible sequences are presented.

Independent groups Groups of participants that are formed by random assignment.

Independent variable (IV) A stimulus or aspect of the environment that the experimenter directly manipulates to determine its influence on behavior.

Inductive logic Reasoning that proceeds from specific cases to general conclusions or theories.

Inferential statistics Procedures used to analyze data after an experiment is completed; used to determine whether the IV has a significant effect.

Institutional Review Board (IRB) The university committee that is responsible for determining whether a proposed research project conforms to accepted ethical standards.

Instrumentation A threat to internal validity that occurs if the equipment or human measuring the DV changes its measuring criterion over time.

Interaction The joint, simultaneous effect on the DV of more than one IV.

Interaction of selection and treatment A threat to external validity that can occur when a treatment effect is found only for a specific sample of participants.

Interaction of testing and treatment A threat to external validity that occurs when a pretest sensitizes participants to the treatment yet to come.

Interaction sum of squares The amount of variability due to an interaction.

Interactions with selection Threats to internal validity that can occur if there are systematic differences between or among selected treatment groups based on maturation, history, or instrumentation.

Internal validity A type of evaluation of your experiment; asks whether your IV is the only possible explanation of the results shown for your DV.

Interobserver reliability The extent to which observers agree.

Interrater reliability Degree of agreement among judges concerning the content validity of test or inventory items.

Interrupted time-series design A quasi-experimental design involving a single group of participants that includes repeated pretreatment measures, and applied treatment, and repeated posttreatment measures.

Interval estimate   An estimated range that is likely to include the population parameter of interest.

Interval-level data   Measurement that permits rank ordering of events with the assumption of equal intervals between adjacent events.

Interval scale   A scale of measurement that permits rank ordering of events with the assumption of equal intervals between adjacent events.

Introduction   The first major section of the APA format paper. Contains the thesis statement, review of relevant literature, and experimental hypothesis.

Kruskal–Wallis H Test   A rank–order test for use with three or more independent groups.

Kurtosis   Term pertaining to the shape (how peaked or flat) of a distribution.

Leptokurtic   A tall, peaked distribution.

Level 1 heading   A centered section title in which the first letters of major words are capitalized. Occupies a line by itself.

Level 3 heading   A section title that is left-margin justified, underlined, and has the first letter of each major word capitalized. Occupies a line by itself.

Level 4 heading   A section title that is indented five spaces, underlined, has only the first word capitalized, and ends with a period; it does not occupy a separate line.

Levels   Different amounts or types of an IV used in an experiment (also known as *treatment conditions*).

Line graph   A graph that is frequently used to depict the results of an experiment.

Logical syllogism   A scheme of formal logic or argument consisting of a major premise, a minor premise, and a conclusion.

Longitudinal research project   Obtaining research data from the same group of participants over an extended period of time.

Main effect   Refers to the sole effect of one IV in a factorial design.

Mann–Whitney U Test   A rank–order test for use with two independent groups that are relatively small.

Manuscript page header   The first two or three words of the report's title. Appears with the page number on each page of the research report.

Marginal significance   Refers to statistical results with a probability of chance between 5% and 10%—in other words, almost significant but not quite. Researchers often talk about such results as if they reached the .05 level.

Matched pairs   Research participants in a two-group design who are measured and equated on some variable before the experiment.

Matching variable   A potential extraneous variable on which we measure our research participants and from which we form sets of participants who are equal on the variable.

Materials subsection   The second subsection of the method section. When appropriate, contains information about materials other than equipment used in the experiment.

Maturation   An internal validity threat; refers to changes in participants that occur over time during an experiment; could include actual physical maturation or tiredness, boredom, hunger, and so on.

Mean   The arithmetic average of a set of numbers. Found by adding all the scores in a set and then dividing by the number of scores.

Mean square   The "averaged" variability for each source; computed by dividing each source's sum of squares by its *df*.

Measurement   The assignment of symbols to events according to a set of rules.

Median   The number that divides a distribution in half.

Mesokurtic   A middle-shaped distribution as compared to a leptokurtic and a platykurtic distribution.

Method section   The second major section of the APA format paper. Contains information about the participants, the apparatus, materials, and testing instrument(s), and the procedures used in the experiment.

Mixed assignment   A factorial design that has a mixture of independent groups for one IV and correlated groups for another IV. In larger factorial designs, at least one IV has independent groups and at least one has correlated groups (also known as *mixed groups*).

Mode   The score in a distribution that occurs most often.

Mortality   A threat to internal validity that can occur if experimental participants from different groups drop out of the experiment at different rates.

Multimodal distribution   A frequency distribution having several high points or prominent categories. (Technically, a bimodal distribution is a multimodal distribution.)

Multiple-treatment interference   A threat to external validity that occurs when a set of findings results only when participants experience multiple treatments in the same experiment.

Natural pairs   Research participants in a two-group design who are naturally related in some way (e.g., a biological or social relationship).

Naturalistic observation   Seeking answers to research questions by observing behavior in the real world.

Nay-sayers   Participants who tend to answer "no" to all questions.

Negative correlation   As scores on one variable increase, scores on the second variable decrease.

Negatively skewed distribution   A nonsymmetrical distribution where there is a cluster of higher scores.

Nominal scale   A scale of measurement in which events are assigned to categories.

Nondirectional research hypothesis   A specific prediction concerning the outcome of an experiment is not made.

Nonequivalent group design   A design involving two or more groups that are not randomly assigned; a comparison group (no treatment) is compared to one or more treatment groups.

Nonparametric test of significance   A significance test that does not attempt to estimate population parameters such as means and variances.

Nonreactive measures   DV measurements that do not influence the DV being measured.

Nonsystematic sources   Sources for research ideas that present themselves in an unpredictable manner; a concerted attempt to locate researchable ideas has not been made.

Normal distribution   A symmetrical, unimodal, bell-shaped distribution that has half of the scores above the mean and half of the scores below the mean.

Nuisance variable Unwanted variables that can cause the variability of scores within groups to increase.

Null hypothesis A hypothesis that says that all differences between groups are due to chance (i.e., not the operation of the IV).

Observed frequency distribution The actual distribution of frequencies into categories.

One-sample *t* test An inferential test to compare a sample mean to a population mean.

One-tailed test A directional test of significance.

One-way ANOVA A statistical test used to analyze data from an experimental design with one independent variable that has three or more groups (levels).

One-way ANOVA for correlated groups A one-way ANOVA that uses correlated groups of participants (also known as *repeated-measures ANOVA*).

One-way ANOVA for independent groups A one-way ANOVA that uses independent groups of participants (also known as *completely randomized ANOVA*).

Operational definition Defining the independent, dependent, and extraneous variables in terms of the operations needed to produce them.

Ordinal scale A scale of measurement that permits events to be rank ordered.

Ordinate The vertical or Y axis of a graph.

Parameter A statistical value for an entire population; characteristic of a population.

Parametric tests Inferential tests of significance that attempt to estimate population parameters.

Participant characteristics Aspects of the participant, such as age, sex, or personality traits, that are treated as if they are IVs.

Participant observation A type of naturalistic observation where the observer becomes part of the group being studied.

Participant sum of squares In an ANOVA for correlated groups, the variability that is due to individual differences among the participants.

Participants at minimal risk Participation in an experiment does not place the participants under physical or emotional risk.

Participants at risk By participating in an experiment, the participants are placed under some type of physical or emotional risk.

Participants subsection The first subsection of the method section. Provides the fill information about the participants in the study.

Pearson product–moment correlation coefficient The correlation coefficient researchers calculate when both variables are interval or ratio scale measurements. Symbolized by *r*.

Percentage A standard method of designating a portion of a total; ranges from 0% (none of the total) to 100% (all of the total).

Perfect negative correlation Exists when an increase of one unit in one variable is always accompanied by the same proportional decrease in the other variable.

Perfect positive correlation Exists when an increase of one unit in one variable is always accompanied by the same proportional increase in the other variable.

Personality test or inventory Measures a specific aspect of the individual's motivational state, interpersonal capability, or personality.

Physiological IV A physiological state of the participant that the experimenter manipulates.

Pie chart Graphical representation of the percentage allocated to each alternative as a slice of a circular pie.

Pilot testing Preliminary, exploratory testing that is done prior to the complete research project.

Placebo effect An experimental effect that is due to expectation or suggestion rather than the IV.

Plagiarism Using someone else's work without giving credit to the original source.

Platykurtic A broad, flat distribution.

Population The complete set of individuals or events.

Population generalization Applying the results from an experiment to a group of participants that is different and more encompassing than those used in the original experiment.

Positive correlation As scores on one variable increase, scores on the second variable also increase.

Positively skewed distribution A nonsymmetrical distribution where there is a cluster of lower scores.

Post hoc tests Statistical comparisons made between group means after finding a significant *F* ratio.

Power The probability that a statistical test will be significant (i.e., the experimental hypothesis will be accepted when it is true).

Practice effect A beneficial effect on a DV measurement caused by previous experience with the DV.

Precedent An established pattern.

Predictor variable The variable that is being predicted from.

Principle of falsifiability Results not in accord with the research hypothesis are taken as evidence that this hypothesis is false.

Principle of parsimony The belief that explanations of phenomena and events should remain simple until the simple explanations are no longer valid.

Probability Determination of the likelihood that a given event will occur.

Procedure subsection The third subsection in the method section. Provides a step-by-step account of what the participants and experimenter did during the experiment.

Programmatic research A series of research experiments that deal with a related topic or question.

Proportion A standard method of designating a portion of the total; ranges from .00 (none of the total) to 1.00 (all of the total); particularly used in statistics rather than percentages.

Qualitative research Research conducted in a natural setting that seeks to understand a complex human behavior by developing a complete narrative description of that behavior.

Quasi-experimental design A research design used when you cannot randomly assign your experimental participants to the groups but do manipulate an IV and measure a DV.

Random assignment A control technique that ensures that each participant has an equal chance of being assigned to any group in the experiment.

Random sample A sample in which every member of the population has an equal likelihood of being included.

Random sampling with replacement Once chosen, a score, event, or participant can be returned to the population to be selected again.

Random sampling without replacement Once chosen, a score, event, or participant cannot be returned to the population to be selected again.

Random selection A control technique that ensures that each member of the population has an equal chance of being chosen for an experiment.

Randomization A control technique that ensures that each participant has an equal chance of being assigned to any group in an experiment.

Range A measure of variability that is computed by subtracting the smallest score from the largest score.

Rank–order test A nonparametric test that is appropriate when you have ordinal data.

Rank sums test A rank–order test for use with two independent groups and one or both of the groups has 20 or more participants.

Ratio-level data Measurement that permits rank ordering of events with the assumptions of equal intervals between adjacent events and a true zero point.

Ratio scale A scale of measurement that permits rank ordering of events with the assumption of equal intervals between adjacent events and a true zero point.

Reactance or reactivity effect The finding that participants respond differently when they know they are being observed.

Reactive arrangements A threat to external validity caused by an experimental situation that alters participants' behavior, regardless of the IV involved.

Reactive measures DV measurements that actually change the DV being measured.

Rectangular distribution A frequency distribution in which each category contains the same number of scores.

Reference A full bibliographic record of any work cited in the text of a psychological paper.

Reference section A complete listing of all the references cited in a psychological paper.

Regression The prediction of one variable from knowledge of another variable.

Regression equation The basic statistical equation that is the basis for prediction.

Regression line Graphical display of the relation between values on the predictor variable and predicted values on the criterion variable.

Reliability Extent to which a test or inventory is consistent in its evaluation of the same individuals.

Reliable Producing consistent measurements.

Repeated measures An experimental procedure in which research participants are tested or measured more than once.

Replication An additional scientific study that is conducted in exactly the same manner as the original research project.

Replication with extension An experiment that seeks to confirm (replicate) a previous finding but does so in a different setting or with different participants or under different conditions.

Research design The general plan for selecting participants, assigning participants to experimental conditions, controlling extraneous variables, and gathering data.

Research idea Identification of a gap in the knowledge base or an unanswered question in an area of interest.

Research or experimental hypothesis The experimenter's predicted outcome of a research project.

Response set The experimental context or testing situation influences the participants' responses.

Results section The third major section of the APA format paper. Contains information about the statistical findings from the experiment.

Robust Refers to a statistical test that can tolerate violations of its assumptions (e.g., homogeneity of variance) and still yield results that are valid.

Rosenthal effect The experimenter's preconceived idea of appropriate responding influences the treatment of participants and their behavior.

Running head A condensed title that is printed at the top of alternate pages of a published article.

Sample A group that is selected to represent the population.

Scale of measurement A set of measurement rules.

Scatterplot A graphical depiction of a correlation.

Selection A threat to internal validity; if we choose participants in such a way that our groups are not equal before the experiment, we cannot be certain that our IV caused any difference we observe after the experiment.

Sequence or order effects The position of a treatment in a series determines, in part, the participants' response.

Serendipity Situations in which we look for one phenomenon but find something else.

Significant A statistical result that is not likely to have occurred by chance ($p < .05$).

Single-blind experiment An experiment in which the experimenter (or participants) is unaware of the treatment the participants are receiving.

Single-case experimental design An experiment that consists of one participant (also known as $N = 1$ *designs*).

Single-strata approach Gathering data from a single stratum of the population of interest.

Situation sampling Observing the same behavior in different situations.

Skewed distribution A nonsymmetrical distribution.

Slope The steepness of the regression line.

Source table A table that contains the results of ANOVA. "Source" refers to the source of different types of variation.

Split-half technique Determination of reliability by dividing the test or inventory into two subtests and then comparing the scores made on the two halves.

Standard deviation (*SD*) A measure of variability equal to the square root of the variance; has important relations to the normal curve.

Standard error (SE) The standard deviation of a sampling distribution.

Standard error of the mean (SEM) The square root of the variance of a distribution of means.

Statistical regression A threat to internal validity that occurs when low scorers improve or high scorers fall on a second administration of a test due solely to statistical reasons.

Statistically significant A research result that occurred rarely by chance.

Statistics Branch of mathematics that involves the collection, analysis, and interpretation of data.

Stimulus or environmental IV An aspect of the environment that the experimenter manipulates.

Stratified random sampling Random samples are drawn from specific subpopulations or strata of the general population.

Subjective probability Your estimate of the probability of a given event's likelihood.

Sum of squares The amount of variability in the DV attributable to each source.

Synergistic effects Dramatic consequences that occur when you combine two or more substances, conditions, or organisms. The effects are greater than what is individually possible.

Synthetic statement Statements that can be either true or false.

Systematic sources Thoroughly examined, carefully thought-out sources for research topics.

_t_ distribution A distribution used in place of the normal distribution for small samples; it resembles a normal distribution but is less peaked.

_t_ test An inferential statistical test used to evaluate the difference between two means.

Table A chart containing an array of descriptive statistics.

Temporal generalization Applying the results from an experiment to a time that is different from that when the original experiment was conducted.

Tenacity Acceptance of knowledge or information simply because it has been presented repeatedly.

Testing A threat to internal validity that occurs because measuring the DV causes a change in the DV.

Testing instrument(s) subsection The second subsection of the method section. When appropriate, contains information about standardized tests used in the experiment.

Test–retest procedure Determination of reliability by repeatedly administering a test to the same participants.

Theory A formal statement of the relations among the IVs and DVs in a given area of research.

Thesis statement A statement of the general research topic of interest and the perceived relation of the relevant variables in that area.

Three-way design A factorial design that has three IVs.

Time sampling Making observations at different time periods.

Title page The first page of an APA format paper. It includes the manuscript page header, the running head, the manuscript's title, and the name(s) of the author(s) and their affiliation(s).

Total sum of squares The total amount of variability in the data from an experiment.

Treatment groups Groups of participants that receive the IV.

Treatment sum of squares The amount of variability in the data due to the IV.

Treatment variability Variability in the DV scores that is due to the effects of the IV (also known as *between-groups variability*).

True experiment An experiment in which the experimenter directly manipulates the IV.

Two-tailed test A nondirectional test of significance.

Two-way ANOVA for correlated groups Analysis technique for experiments that have two IVs that are both within-subjects factors (e.g., repeated measures).

Two-way ANOVA for independent groups Analysis technique for experiments that have two IVs that are both between-subjects factors.

Two-way ANOVA for mixed groups Analysis technique for experiments that have two IVs that are both between-subjects factors.

Type I error Accepting the alternative (experimental) hypothesis when the null hypothesis is true.

Type II error Accepting the null hypothesis when the alternative (experimental) hypothesis is true.

Unbiased language Language that does not display prejudice toward an individual or group.

Unimodal distribution A frequency distribution that has one high point or prominent category.

Valid Measuring what is supposed to be measured.

Validity The degree to which a knowledge claim is accurate; the extent to which a test or inventory measures what it is supposed to measure.

Variability The extent to which scores spread out around the mean.

Variable An event or behavior that can assume two or more values.

Variance A single number that represents the total amount of variation in a distribution; also, the square of the standard deviation; σ^2.

Wilcoxon T Test A rank–order test for use with two related or dependent groups.

Within-group counterbalancing Presentation of different treatment sequences to different participants.

Within-groups variability Same as error variability.

Within-subject counterbalancing Presentation of different treatment sequences to the same participant.

Within-subjects comparison Refers to a contrast between groups of participants who were assigned to groups through matched pairs, natural pairs, or repeated measures.

Y intercept The point at which the regression line crosses the vertical (Y) axis.

Yea-sayers Participants who tend to answer "yes" to all questions.

_z_ score A measure, in standard deviations, of the distance of a raw score above or below the mean. They typically range from $+3$ to -3.

Zero correlation Two variables under consideration are not related.

references

American Psychological Association. (1982). *Ethical principles in the conduct of research with human participants*. Washington, DC: Author.

American Psychological Association. (1985). *Guidelines for ethical conduct in the care and use of animals*. Washington, DC: Author.

American Psychological Association. (1992). *Guidelines for ethical conduct in the care and use of animals*. Washington, DC: Author.

American Psychological Association. (1994). *Publication manual of the American Psychological Association* (4th ed.). Washington, DC: Author.

American Psychological Association (2001). *Publication manual of the American Psychological Association* (5th ed.). Washington, DC: Author.

American Psychological Association. (2001). *Thesaurus of psychological index terms* (9th ed.). Washington, DC: Author.

American Psychological Association. (2002). Ethical principles of psychologists and code of conduct. *American Psychologist, 57*, 1060–1073.

American Psychological Association. (2003). *Electronic references*. Retrieved August 20, 2004 from http://www.apastyle.org/elecref.html.

Anastasi, A. (1988). *Psychological testing* (6th ed.). New York: Macmillan.

Anastasi, A., & Urbina, S. (1997). *Psychological testing* (7th ed.). Upper Saddle River, NJ: Prentice Hall.

Aron, A., & Aron, E. N. (2003). *Statistics for psychology* (3rd ed.). Upper Saddle River, NJ: Prentice Hall.

Aronson, E., & Carlsmith, J. M. (1968). Experimentation in social psychology. In G. Lindzey and E. Aronson (Eds.), *The handbook of social psychology* (2nd ed., pp. 1–79). Reading, MA: Addison-Wesley.

Ball, R. M., Kargl, E. S., Kimpel, J. D., & Siewert, S. L. (2001). Effect of sad and suspenseful mood induction on reaction time. *Psi Chi Journal of Undergraduate Research, 6*, 21–27.

Barlow, D. H., & Hersen, M. (1973). Single-case experimental designs. *Archives of General Psychiatry, 29*, 319–325.

Baumrind, D. (1964). Some thoughts on the ethics of research: After reading Milgram's "Behavioral Study of Obedience." *American Psychologist, 19*, 421–423.

Beach, F. A. (1950). The snark was a boojum. *American Psychologist, 5*, 115–124.

Beauchamp, T. L., & Childress, J. F. (1979). *Principles of biomedical ethics*. New York: Oxford University Press.

Bellquist, J. E. (1993). *A guide to grammar and usage for psychology and related field*. Hillsdale, NJ: Erlbaum.

Benjamin, L. T., Jr. (1992, April). *Health, Happiness, and Success: The popular psychology magazine of the 1920s*. Paper presented at the annual meeting of the Eastern Psychological Association, Boston, MA.

Bennett, S. K. (1994). The American Indian: A psychological overview. In W. J. Lonner & R. Malpass (Eds.), *Psychology and culture* (pp. 35–39). Boston: Allyn and Bacon.

Blumenthal, A. L. (1991). The intrepid Joseph Jastrow. In G. A. Kimble, M. Wertheimer, & C. L. White (Eds.), *Portraits of pioneers in psychology* (pp. 75–87). Washington, DC: American Psychological Association.

Bodner, D., Cochran, C. D., & Blum, T. L. (2000). Unique invulnerability measurement in skydivers: Scale validation. *Psi Chi Journal of Undergraduate Research, 5*, 104–108.

Boice, M. L., & Gargano, G. J. (2001). Part-set cuing is due to strong, not weak, list cues. *Psi Chi Journal of Undergraduate Research, 6*, 118–122.

Bonds-Raacke, J. M., Wright, K. L., Lewin, J. M., & Nelson, E. M. (2001). The sleeper effect on students' attitudes toward animal cognition. *Psi Chi Journal of Undergraduate Research, 6*, 32–36.

Boring, E. G. (1950). *A history of modern psychology* (2nd ed.). New York: Appleton-Century-Crofts.

Bridgman, P. W. (1927). *The logic of modern physics*. New York: Macmillan.

Broad, W. J. (1980). Imbroglio at Yale (I): Emergence of a fraud. *Science, 210*, 38–41.

Bruderick, J. & Ernst, D. (2000). The relation between positive and negative alcohol expectancies and alcohol use in college students. *Psi Chi Journal of Undergraduate Research, 5*, 60–67.

Burkley, E., III, McFarland, S., Walker, W., & Young, J. (2000). Informed consent: A methodological confound? *Psi Chi Journal of Undergraduate Research, 5*, 43–45.

Campbell, D. T. (1957). Factors relevant to the validity of experiments in social settings. *Psychological Bulletin, 54*, 297–312.

Campbell, D. T. (1969). Reforms as experiments. *American Psychologist, 24*, 409–429.

Campbell, D. T., & Stanley, J. C. (1966). *Experimental and quasi-experimental designs for research*. Boston: Houghton Mifflin.

Claus, M. K. (2000). Gendered toy preferences and assertiveness in preschoolers. *Journal of Psychological Inquiry, 5*, 15–18.

Cohen, J. (1977). *Statistical power analysis for the behavioral sciences* (rev. ed.). New York: Academic Press.

Cook, T. D., & Campbell, D. T. (1979). *Quasi-experimentation: Design & analysis issues for field settings*. Boston: Houghton Mifflin.

Corkin, S. (1984). Lasting consequences of bilateral medial temporal lobectomy: Clinical course and experimental findings in H.M. *Seminars in Neurology, 4*, 249–259.

Creswell, J. W. (1994). *Research design: Qualitative and quantitative approaches*. Thousand Oaks, CA: Sage.

Darley, J. M., & Latané, D. (1968). Bystander intervention in emergencies: Diffusion of responsibility. *Journal of Personality and Social Psychology, 8*, 377–383.

Davis, S. F., Armstrong, S. L. W., & Huss, M. T. (1993). Shock-elicited aggression is influenced by lead and/or alcohol exposure. *Bulletin of the Psychonomic Society, 31*, 451–453.

Davis, S. F., Grover, C. A., & Erickson, C. A. (1987). A comparison of the aversiveness of denatonium saccharide and quinine in humans. *Bulletin of the Psychonomic Society, 25,* 462–463.

Davis, S. F., Grover, C. A., Erickson, C. A., Miller, L. A., & Bowman, J. A. (1987). Analyzing the aversiveness of denatonium saccharide. *Perceptual and Motor Skills, 64,* 1215–1222.

Department of Psychology, Bishop's University. *Plagiarism pamphlet.* Supplied December 23, 1994.

Dickson, A. J., Giuliano, T. A., Morris, J. C., & Cass, K. L. (2001). Eminem versus Charley Pride: Race, stereotypes, and perceptions of rap and country music performers. *Psi Chi Journal of Undergraduate Research, 6,* 175–180.

Dion, K. K., Berscheid, E., & Walster, E. (1972). What is beautiful is good. *Journal of Personality and Social Psychology, 24,* 285–290.

Doyle, A. C. (1927). *The complete Sherlock Holmes.* Garden City, NY: Doubleday.

Driggers, K. J., & Helms, T. (2000). The effects of salary on willingness to date. *Psi Chi Journal of Undergraduate Research, 5,* 76–80.

Dukes, W. F. (1965) *N* = 1. *Psychological Bulletin, 64,* 74–79.

Dunn, J., Ford, K., Rewey, K. L., Juve, J. A., Weiser, A., & Davis, S. F. (2001). A modified presubmission checklist. *Psi Chi Journal of Undergraduate Research, 6,* 142–144.

Festinger, L. (1957). *A theory of cognitive dissonance.* Stanford, CA: Stanford University Press.

Freeman, N. J., & Punzo, D. L. D. (2001). Effects of DNA and eyewitness evidence on juror decisions. *Psi Chi Journal of Undergraduate Research, 6,* 109–117.

Friedman, M., & Rosenman, R. H. (1974). *Type A behavior and your heart.* New York: Knopf.

Gauthreaux, V. M. (2000). Relating pretrial publicity, judicial instruction, and thought suppression with guilt ratings. *Psi Chi Journal of Undergraduate Research, 5,* 21–28.

Geronimus, A. T. (1991). Teenage childbearing and social and reproductive disadvantage: The evolution of complex questions and the demise of simple answers. *Family Relations, 40,* 463–471.

Gibson, A. R., Smith, K., & Torres, A. (2000). Glancing behavior of participants using automated teller machines while bystanders approach. *Psi Chi Journal of Undergraduate Research, 5,* 148–151.

Gilbert, D. T., & Malone, P. S. (1995). The correspondence bias. *Psychological Bulletin, 117,* 21–38.

Glesne, C. (1999). *Becoming qualitative researchers: An introduction* (2nd ed.). New York: Longman.

Gonzales, J., Castillo, M., & Swinkels, A. (2002). Perceptions of contagious emotions. *Psi Chi Journal of Undergraduate Research, 7,* 185–191.

Goodwin, C. J. (1999). *A history of modern psychology.* New York: Wiley.

Gray, A. D., & Lucas, J. L. (2001). Commuters' subjective perceptions of travel impedance and their stress levels. *Psi Chi Journal of Undergraduate Research, 6,* 79–83.

Grazer, B. (Producer), & Howard, R. (Producer/ Director). 2001. *A beautiful mind* [Motion picture]. United States: Universal Studios.

Gubrium, J. F., & Holstein, J. A. (1997). *The new language of qualitative method.* New York: Oxford University Press.

Guerin, B. (1986). Mere presence effects in humans: A review. *Journal of Personality and Social Psychology, 22,* 38–77.

Guthrie, R. V. (1976). *Even the rat was white: A historical view of psychology.* New York: Harper & Row.

Hall, R. V., Fox, R. Willard, D. Goldsmith, L., Emerson, M., Owen, M., Davis, F., & Porcia, E. (1971). The teacher as observer and experimenter in the modification of disputing and talking-out behaviors. *Journal of Applied Behavior Analysis, 4,* 141–149.

Hayes, K. M., Miller, H. R., & Davis, S. F. (1993). *Examining the relationships between interpersonal flexibility, self-esteem, and death anxiety.* Paper presented at the annual meeting of the Southwestern Psychological Association, Corpus Christi, TX.

Hedrick, T. E., Bickman, L., & Rog, D. J. (1993). *Applied research design: A practical guide.* Newbury Park, CA: Sage.

Hedrick, T. E., & Shipman, S. L. (1988). Multiple questions require multiple designs: An evaluation of the 1981 changes to the AFDC program. *Evaluation Review, 12,* 427–448.

Helmreich, R., & Stapp, J. (1974). Short form of the Texas Social Behavior Inventory (TSBI), an objective measure of self-esteem. *Bulletin of the Psychonomic Society, 4,* 473–475.

Hersen, M. (1982). Single-case experimental designs. In A. S. Bellack, M. Hersen, & A. E. Kazdin (Eds.), *International handbook of behavior modification and therapy* (pp. 167–203). New York: Plenum Press.

Hersen, M., & Barlow, D. H. (1976). *Single-case experimental designs: Strategies for studying behavioral change.* New York: Pergamon Press.

Hilts, P. J. (1995). *Memory's ghost: The strange tale of Mr. M and the nature of memory.* New York: Simon & Schuster.

Horvat, J., & Davis, S. F. (1998). *Doing psychological research.* Upper Saddle River, NJ: Prentice Hall.

Howard, D. (1997). Language in the human brain. In M. D. Rugg (Ed.), *Cognitive neuroscience* (pp. 277–304). Cambridge: MA: MIT Press.

Huff, D. (1954). *How to lie with statistics.* New York: Norton.

Jones, J. H. (1981). *Bad blood: The Tuskegee syphilis experiment.* New York: Free Press.

Jones, J. M. (1994). The African American: A duality dilemma? In W. J. Lonner & R. Malpass (Eds.), *Psychology and culture* (pp. 17–21). Boston: Allyn and Bacon.

Jones, M. D. (2001). The effects of noise and sex on children's performance on recall and spatial tasks. *Psi Chi Journal of Undergraduate Research, 6,* 63–67.

Jones, R. R., Vaught, R. S., & Weinrott, M. (1977). Time-series analysis in operant research. *Journal of Applied Behavior Analysis, 10,* 151–166.

Jurica, B., Alanis, K., & Ogletree, S. (2002). Sex differences related to video arcade game behavior. *Psi Chi Journal of Undergraduate Research, 7,* 145–148.

Kalat, J. (2001). *Biological psychology* (7th ed.). Belmont, CA: Wadsworth.

Kazlauskas, M. A., & Kelland, M. D. (1997). Behavioral evaluation of the stargazer mutant rat in a tactile startle paradigm. *Psi Chi Journal of Undergraduate Research, 2,* 90–98.

Kazdin, A. E. (1976). Statistical analyses for single-case experimental designs. In M. Hersen & D. H. Barlow (Eds.), *Single-case experimental designs: Strategies for studying behavioral change* (pp. 265–316). New York: Pergamon Press.

Kazdin, A. E. (1984). *Behavior modification in applied settings* (3rd ed.). Homewood, IL: Dorsey Press.

Keith-Spiegel, P. (1991). *The complete guide to graduate school admission: Psychology and related fields.* Hillsdale, NJ: Erlbaum.

Keith-Spiegel, P., & Wiederman, M. W. (2000). *The complete guide to graduate school admission: Psychology, counseling, and related professions* (2nd ed.). Mahwah, NJ: Erlbaum.

Keppel, G., Saufley, W. H., Jr., & Tokunaga, H. (1992). *Introduction to design & analysis: A student's handbook* (2nd ed.). New York: W. H. Freeman.

Kiker, K. (2001). Developmental changes in children's measurement errors. *Psi Chi Journal of Undergraduate Research, 6,* 68–74.

Kimmel, A. J. (1988). *Ethics and values in applied social research.* Beverly Hills, CA: Sage.

Kirk, R. E. (1968). *Experimental design: Procedures for the behavioral sciences.* Belmont, CA: Brooks/Cole.

Kirk, R. E. (1996, April). *Practical significance: A concept whose time has come.* Southwestern Psychological Association presidential address. Houston, TX.

Kirk, R. E. (2003). The importance of effect magnitude. In S. F. Davis (Ed.), *Handbook of research methods in experimental psychology* (pp. 83–105). Oxford, UK: Blackwell.

Koestler, A. (1964). *The act of creation.* New York: Macmillan.

Korn, J. H. (1988). Students' roles, rights, and responsibilities as research participants. *Teaching of Psychology, 15,* 74–78.

Krantz, D. S., Glass, D. C., & Snyder, M. L. (1974). Helplessness, stress level, and the coronary-prone behavior pattern. *Journal of Experimental Social Psychology, 10,* 284–300.

Landrum, R. F., & Davis, S. F. (2004). *The psychology major: Career options and strategies for success* (2nd ed.). Upper Saddle River, NJ: Prentice Hall.

Lang, P. J., & Melamed, B. G. (1969). Avoidance conditioning therapy of an infant with chronic ruminative vomiting. *Journal of Abnormal Psychology, 74,* 1–8.

Langley, W. M., Theis, J., Davis, S. F., Richard, M. M., & Grover, C. A. (1987). Effects of denatonium saccharide on the drinking behavior of the grasshopper mouse (Onychomys leucogaster). *Bulletin of the Psychonomic Society, 25,* 17–19.

Larey, A. (2001). Effect of massage and informal touch on body-dissatisfaction, anxiety, and obsessive-compulsiveness. *Journal of Psychological Inquiry, 6,* 78–83.

Lawson, T. J. (1995). An advisor update: Gaining admission into graduate programs in psychology. *Teaching of Psychology, 22,* 225–227.

Lee, D. J., & Hall, C. C. I. (1994). Being Asian in North America. In W. J. Lonner & R. Malpass (Eds.), *Psychology and culture* (pp. 29–33). Boston: Allyn and Bacon.

Lehmann, E. L. (1993). The Fisher, Neyman-Pearson theories of testing hypotheses: One theory or two? *Journal of the American Statistical Association, 88,* 1242–1248.

Licht, C. A. (2000). Occupational stress as a function of type of organization and sex of employee. *Psi Chi Journal of Undergraduate Research, 5,* 46–55.

Licht, C. A. (2001). Occupational stress as a function of type of organization and sex of employee: A reassessment. *Psi Chi Journal of Undergraduate Research, 6,* 14–20.

Loftus, E. F. (1979). *Eyewitness testimony.* Cambridge, MA: Harvard University Press.

Lonner, W. J., & Malpass, R. (1994a). Preface. In W. J. Lonner & R. Malpass (Eds.), *Psychology and culture* (pp. ix–xiii). Boston: Allyn and Bacon.

Lonner, W. J., & Malpass, R. (1994b). When psychology and culture meet: An introduction to cross-cultural psychology. In W. J. Lonner & R. Malpass (Eds.), *Psychology and culture* (pp. 1–12). Boston: Allyn and Bacon.

Losch, M. E., & Cacioppo, J. T. (1990). Cognitive dissonance may enhance sympathetic tonus, but attitudes are changed to reduce negative affect rather than arousal. *Journal of Experimental Social Psychology, 26,* 289–304.

Luehring, J., & Altman, J. D. (2000). Factors contributing to sex differences on the mental rotation task. *Psi Chi Journal of Undergraduate Research, 5,* 29–35.

Mack, D., & Rainey, D. (1990). Female applicants' grooming and personnel selection. *Journal of Social Behavior and Personality, 5,* 399–407.

Mahoney, M. J. (1987). Scientific publication and knowledge politics. *Journal of Social Behavior and Personality, 2,* 165–176.

Marin, G. (1994). The experience of being a Hispanic in the United States. In W. J. Lonner & R. Malpass (Eds.), *Psychology and culture* (pp. 23–27). Boston: Allyn and Bacon.

Marshall, C., & Rossman, G. B. (1989). *Designing qualitative research.* Newbury Park, CA: Sage.

Martin, K. Farruggia, S., & Yeske, K. (1993, May). *The effects of stress on reported state and trait anxiety.* Psi Chi paper presented at the annual meeting of the Midwestern Psychological Association, Chicago, IL.

Matsumoto, D. (1997). *Culture and modern life.* Pacific Grove, CA: Brooks/Cole.

Matsumoto, D. (2000). *Culture and psychology: People around the world* (2nd ed.). Belmont, CA: Wadsworth.

McClellan, K. S., & Woods, E. B. (2001). Disability and society: Appearance stigma results in discrimination toward deaf persons. *Psi Chi Journal of Undergraduate Research, 6,* 57–62.

McGuigan, F. J. (1960). *Experimental psychology.* Englewood Cliffs, NJ: Prentice Hall.

McInerny, R. M. (1970). *A history of Western philosophy.* Notre Dame, IN: University of Notre Dame Press.

McKibban, A. R., & Nelson, S. (2001). Subjective well-being: Are you busy enough to be happy? *Psi Chi Journal of Undergraduate Research, 6,* 51–56.

Medewar, P. B. (1979). *Advice to a young scientist.* New York: Harper & Row.

Milgram, S. (1963). Behavioral study of obedience. *Journal of Abnormal and Social Psychology, 67,* 371–378.

Milgram, S. (1964). Issues in the study of obedience: A reply to Baumrind. *American Psychologist, 19,* 848–852.

Milgram, S. (1974). *Obedience to authority: An experimental view.* New York: Harper & Row.

Miller, H. B., & Williams, W. H. (1983). *Ethics and animals.* Clifton, NJ: Humana Press.

Miller, J. G. (1984). Culture and the development of everyday social explanation. *Journal of Personality and Social Psychology, 46,* 961–978.

Miller, N. E. (1985). The value of behavioral research on animals. *American Psychologist, 40,* 423–440.

Montgomery, M. D., & Donovan, K. M. (2002, April). *The "Mozart effect" on cognitive and spatial task performance, revisited.* Poster presented at the annual meeting of the Southwestern Psychological Association, Corpus Christi, TX.

Mook, D. G. (1983). In defense of external invalidity. *American Psychologist, 38*, 379–387.

Mooney, R. L. (1950). *Mooney problem check list.* New York: The Psychological Corporation.

Myers, D. G. (2002). *Social psychology* (7th ed.). Boston: McGraw-Hill.

Nash, S. M. (1983). *The relationship between early ethanol exposure and adult taste preference.* Paper presented in J. P. Guilford/Psi Chi undergraduate research competition.

Novaco, R. W., Stokols, D., & Milanesi, L. (1990). Objective and subjective dimensions of travel impedance as determinants of commuting stress. *American Journal of Community Psychology, 18*, 231–257.

Orne, M. T. (1962). On the social psychology of the psychological experiment: With particular reference to demand characteristics and their implications. *American Psychologist, 17*, 776–783.

Pepperberg, I. M. (1994). Numerical competence in an African gray parrot (*Psittacus erithacus*). *Journal of Comparative Psychology, 108*, 36–44.

Proctor, R. W., & Capaldi, E. J. (2001). Improving the science education of psychology students: Better teaching of methodology. *Teaching of Psychology, 28*, 173–181.

Purdy, J. E., Reinehr, R. C., & Swartz, J. D. (1989). Graduate admissions criteria of leading psychology departments. *American Psychologist, 44*, 960–961.

Reagan, T. (1983). *The case for animal rights.* Berkeley: University of California Press.

Reid, D. W., & Ware, E. E. (1973). Multidimensionality of internal-external control: Implications for past and future research. *Canadian Journal of Behavioural Research, 5*, 264–271.

Roethlisberger, F. J., & Dickson, W. J. (1939). *Management and the worker.* Cambridge, MA: Harvard University Press.

Rosenthal, R. (1966). *Experimenter effects in behavioral research.* New York: Appleton-Century-Crofts.

Rosenthal, R. (1976). *Experimenter effects in behavioral research* (enlarged ed.). New York: Irvington Press.

Rosenthal, R. (1977). Biasing effects of experimenters. *ETC: A Review of General Semantics, 34*, 253–264.

Rosenthal, R. (1985). From unconscious experimenter bias to teacher expectancy effects. In J. B. Dusek, V. C. Hall, & W. J. Meyer (Eds.), *Teacher expectancies* (pp. 37–65). Hillsdale, NJ: Lawrence Erlbaum Associates.

Rosenthal, R., & Fode, K. L. (1963). The effect of experimenter bias on the performance of the albino rat. *Behavioral Science, 8*, 183–189.

Rosenthal, R., & Jacobson, L. (1968). *Psychodynamics in the classroom.* New York: Holt.

Rosenthal, R., & Rosnow, R. L. (1984). *Essentials of behavioral research.* New York: McGraw-Hill.

Rosenthal, R., & Rosnow, R. (1991) *Essentials of behavioral research* (2nd ed.). New York: McGraw-Hill.

Ross, L. (1977). The intuitive psychologist and his shortcomings: Distortions in the attribution process. In L. Berkowitz (Ed.), *Advances in experimental social psychology* (Vol. 10, pp. 173–220). New York: Academic Press.

Sagles, S. E., Coley, S., Espiritu, G., Zahregian, P., & Velayo, R. (2002). Effects of racial background and sex on identifying facial expressions and person perception. *Psi Chi Journal of Undergraduate Research, 7*, 31–37.

Sasson, R., & Nelson, T. M. (1969). The human experimental subject in context. *Canadian Psychologist, 10*, 409–437.

Scali, R. M., & Brownlow, S. (2001). Impact of instructional manipulation and stereotype activation on sex differences in spatial task performance. *The Psi Chi Journal of Undergraduate Research, 6*, 3–13.

Schein, E. H. (1987). *The clinical perspective in fieldwork.* Newbury Park, CA: Sage.

Schroeppel, N., & Carlo, G. (2001). Sympathy and perspective taking as mediators of gender differences in altruism. *Journal of Psychological Inquiry, 6*, 7–11.

Sears, D. O. (1986). College sophomores in the laboratory: Influences of a narrow data base on social psychology's view of human nature. *Journal of Personality and Social Psychology, 51*, 515–530.

Selvidge, P. R. (2000). Effects of recall requirements on strategy selection in a visual-spatial span task. *Psi Chi Journal of Undergraduate Research, 5*, 68–72.

Shuter, R. (1977). A field study of nonverbal communication in Germany, Italy, and the United States. *Communication Monographs, 44*, 298–305.

Simonds, D. C., & Rolfe-Maloney, B. (2002). Effect of visual stimuli on preschoolers' memory for verbal material. *Psi Chi Journal of Undergraduate Research, 7*, 116–121.

Singer, P. (1975). *Animal liberation.* New York: Random House.

Skinner, B. F. (1961). *Cumulative record* (Expanded edition). New York: Appleton-Century-Crofts.

Skinner, B. F. (1966). Operant behavior. In W. K. Honig (Ed.), *Operant behavior: Areas of research and application* (pp. 12–32). New York: Appleton-Century-Crofts.

Small, W. S. (1901). An experimental study of the mental processes of the rat. *American Journal of Psychology, 11*, 133–165.

Smith, R. A. (1985). Advising beginning psychology majors for graduate school. *Teaching of Psychology, 12*, 194–198.

Smith, R. A. Another perspective on publishing: Keeping the editor happy. *Psi Chi Journal of Undergraduate Research, 3*, 51–55.

Smith, R. A., Davis, S. F., & Burleson, J. (1996). *Snark hunting revisited: The status of comparative psychology in the 1990s.* Paper presented at the meeting of the Southwestern Comparative Psychology Association, Houston, TX.

Solomon, R. L. (1949). An extension of control group design. *Psychological Bulletin, 46*, 137–150.

Sou, E. K., & Irving, L. M. (2002). Students' attitudes toward mental illness: A Macao-U.S. cross-cultural comparison. *Psi Chi Journal of Undergraduate Research, 7*, 13–22.

Spatz, C. (2001). *Basic statistics: Tales of distributions* (7th ed.). Belmont, CA: Wadsworth.

Steele, C. M., Southwick, L. L., & Critchlow, B. (1981). Dissonance and alcohol: Drinking your troubles away. *Journal of Personality and Social Psychology, 41*, 831–846.

Strauss, A., & Corbin, J. (1990). *Basics of qualitative research: Grounded theory procedures and techniques.* Newbury Park, CA: Sage.

Tavris, C. (1992). *The mismeasure of woman.* New York: Touchstone.

Templer, D. I. (1970). The construction and validation of a death anxiety scale. *Journal of General Psychology, 82*, 165–177.

Thomas, J., Rewey, K. L., & Davis, S. F. (2002). Professional development benefits of publishing in the *Psi Chi Journal of Undergraduate Research*. *Eye on Psi Chi, 6*(2), 30–35.

Traffanstedt, B. (1998). Weight reduction using behavior modification: Modifying sedentary behavior. *Journal of Psychological Inquiry, 3*, 19–23.

Vandenberg, S. G., & Kuse, A. R. (1978). Mental rotations, a group test of three-dimensional spatial visualization. *Perceptual and Motor Skills, 47*, 599–604.

Vaughn, E. J. (2002, April). *Matching hypothesis and physical attractiveness*. Paper presented at the Arkansas Symposium for Psychology Students, Arkadelphia.

Walker, K. A., Arruda, J. E., & Greenier, K. D. (1999). Assessment of perceptual biases extracted from the Visual Analogue Scale. *Psi Chi Journal of Undergraduate Research, 4*, 57–63.

Walter, K. D., Brownlow, S., Ervin, S. L., & Williamson, N. (1998). Something in the way she moves: The influence of shoe-altered gait on motion and trait impressions of women. *Psi Chi Journal of Undergraduate Research, 3*, 163–169.

Watson, L. (1998). The effects of noise volume on performance of a cognitive task. *Psi Chi Journal of Undergraduate Research, 3*, 99–104.

Weaver, S. R., & Dunham, K. (2001). Predictors of a new typology of youth violence. *Psi Chi Journal of Undergraduate Research, 7*, 3–12.

Weinberg, R. A. (1989). Intelligence and IQ: Landmark issues and great debates. *American Psychologist, 44*, 98–104.

Weintraub, D., Higgins, M., Beishline, M., Matchinsky, D., & Pierce, M. (1994, November). *Do impostors really hold irrational beliefs?* Paper presented at the annual meeting of the Association for Psychological and Educational Research in Kansas, Lawrence, KS.

Weiss, J., Gilbert, K., Giordano, P., & Davis, S. F. (1993). Academic dishonesty, Type A behavior, and classroom orientation. *Bulletin of the Psychonomic Society, 31*, 101–102.

Wells, R. (2001). Susceptibility to illness: The impact of cardiovascular reactivity and the reducer-augmenter construct. *Journal of Psychological Inquiry, 6*, 12–16.

Wolensky, N. H. (2001). The effects of society standards of physical attractiveness on body esteem in the elderly. *Psi Chi Journal of Undergraduate Research, 6*, 153–160.

Yang, K. S. (1983). Causal attributions of academic success and failure and their affective consequences. *Chinese Journal of Psychology, 24*, 65–83.

Zajonc, R. B. (1965). Social facilitation. *Science, 149*, 269–274.

index

Name Index

Subject Index